THE
SEIZURE
OF POWER

Fascism in Italy 1919–1929

Adrian Lyttelton was born in 1937, son
of the late Viscount Chandos. Educated at
Eton, he read Modern History at Magdalen
College, Oxford and in 1960 was elected to a
Fellowship of All Souls College. Since
1968 he has been a Fellow of St Antony's
College, Oxford.

THE
SEIZURE
OF POWER

Fascism in Italy
1919-1929

Adrian Lyttelton

Charles Scribner's Sons

New York

1 3 5 7 9 11 13 15 17 19 I/C 20 18 16 14 12 10 8 6 4 2

Printed in Great Britain
Library of Congress Catalog Card Number 73-3005

SBN 684-13402-0

CONTENTS

CONTENTS

PREFACE

This book is the product of a number of years' research in Italy. I was impelled to undertake the study by curiosity about how Fascism could have first arisen and succeeded in Italy and about the nature and extent of its influence on Italian society. It seemed to me that the period from 1922–9 had been less well studied than the preceding period and that, for comprehensible moral reasons, the study of the opposition to Fascism had progressed further than the study of Fascism itself. In the last few years this situation has changed, and there is now a great volume of work in Italian, of which I have tried to take account. Nevertheless, this book, except for the introductory section, is largely based on original research in the State archives, in newspaper files and in contemporary writings.

This work has been made possible by the assistance of a number of institutions and persons, whose help I gratefully acknowledge. My greatest debt is to the Warden and Fellows of both All Souls and St Antony's College, Oxford, who supported me during the research and writing of this book. In addition, I am especially indebted to the former Warden of St Antony's, Mr F. W. Deakin, for his expert knowledge and suggestions. The friendship, advice and criticism of Dr Roberto Vivarelli has been of inestimable value to me during the whole period of my research. My thanks are due to the Italian institutions which have aided my researches. First and foremost, I must thank Dr Costanzo Casucci and the other archivists of the Archivio Centrale dello Stato for their knowledge, patience and good will, which alone made my researches possible. My thanks are also due to the staff of the Biblioteca Nazionale in Florence; to the Istituto per la Storia della Resistenza in Toscana; the Archivio di Stato of Bologna; the Istituto Gramsci of Rome, and the Library of the Chamber of Deputies.

In addition my warmest thanks are due to the following individuals: Professor Alberto Aquarone, Professor Gaetano Arfe, Senator Eugenio Artom, Professor Giampiero Carocci, Professor Renzo De Felice, Professor Piero Melograni, Dr Gian Giacomo Migone, Dr Renato Mieli, Dr Claudio Pavone, Signorina Nina Ruffini, Dr Salvatore Sechi and Professor Paolo

Ungari, the late On. Alberto Carocci, Senator Paratore and Cesare Rossi. I have profited from discussion with my friends and colleagues Denis Mack Smith, Tim Mason, Joaquin Romero Maura, Stuart Woolf and Paul Corner. Dr P. G. Edwards and Professor Michaelis also enlightened me on specific points. I have had a number of fruitful arguments with Mr Guido Di Meo.

Finally, my thanks are due to Mr Peter Coxson and the typists of his agency for their patience and hard work in deciphering and preparing my manuscript.

I

INTRODUCTION

This is a study not of the origins of Fascism but of 'the seizure of power', a description which demands a further word of explanation. In Italy, in spite of the drama of the March on Rome, the subversion of the liberal order by Fascism was a piecemeal process, starting in 1921 and not concluded until 1928–9. So this is a study not just of the mechanics of a *coup d'état*, but of the impact of a new type of political movement on Italian government and society. It is intended not only to show the reasons for the success of Fascism in conquering political power, but also how that power, even at its greatest, was limited. Fascism had aspirations to be 'totalitarian'; Mussolini virtually invented the term. But, leaving on one side the question of how far the totalitarian nightmare can ever be fully realized, it is clear that Mussolini's grip on Italian society was not as firm, his influence so pervasive, as that of a Hitler or a Stalin. Fascism left huge areas of Italian life practically untouched. Nonetheless it would, in my opinion, be mistaken to believe that Fascism did not mark a sharp break in Italy's development. Many men and even institutions from the liberal regime survived, but they had to fit into a new framework. In a modernizing society, a far-reaching change in the methods by which political power was exercised could not fail to have repercussions on economic and social and intellectual life.

I hope that this book will also be read as a modest contribution towards the general study of Fascism. Although my purpose is to relate the peculiar historical circumstances which made possible and conditioned the success of *Italian* Fascism, the reader should be warned that the movement cannot be viewed in correct perspective if the European dimension of Fascism is not kept in mind. Fascism was, after all, more characteristic of an age than of any one nation or people. National character and national history may certainly provide explanations for the differences between the Fascists, the Nazis and the Iron Guard; but it would be rash to say that they had no features in common. The Fascists themselves, heirs to romantic nationalism, were fond of asserting the absolute individuality of race or nation, and therefore of their own movements, but one should not take these assertions as gospel, any more than the student of 'international Communism' should overlook the influence of national traditions.

Fascism and Italian History

The Italian historian Gaetano Salvemini was among the first to fight against the conception of Fascism as a peculiar product of the Italian national character. It must be admitted that this view has always been popular in England. While our *amour propre* is certainly flattered by foreign imitation of our models of government, we have generally viewed defections from democracy with an odd complacency. They confirmed, after all, the peculiar virtues of our own institutions and character. Even a distinguished historian like G. M. Trevelyan did not altogether help to correct the popular view of Italian politics as a kind of synthesis of the national addictions to *bel canto* and the stiletto. Trevelyan saw 'the historical causes of the present state of affairs in Italy' as residing in the unbroken millennial continuity of the politics of the piazza : 'Italy never had a Hampden', and without our 'obscure hereditary instinct' for parliamentary government, it was natural that the Italian constitutional experiment should have failed. Similar explanations, although they may often contain incidental *aperçus*, will not really do: the victory of National Socialism and the sporadic successes enjoyed by movements of the radical right even in the advanced democracies should have made it clear that Fascism was not just a part of Italian folklore.[1]

But it would be unfair to Trevelyan not to recognize that the tendency to see Fascism as the inevitable outcome of a long process of national decline was widespread also among Italian writers. The great publicist of Southern Italy, Giustino Fortunato, described Fascism as a revelation of the ancient vices and defects of Italy,[2] and this line of interpretation has since usually been known as the 'revelation thesis'. This pessimistic view of Italian history has been chiefly concerned to explain the failure of the mass of the Italian people to resist Fascism, rather than their active participation. Moralists saw the success of Fascism as dependent upon the attitudes of passive resignation, conformity and subservience to power prevalent among the majority ; they traced these attitudes above all to two causes, poverty and Catholicism. For Piero Gobetti, the brilliant young theorist of the 'liberal revolution', it was the failure to develop an idea of individual moral responsibility, due to the lack of a Reformation, which made the Italians unfitted for self-government.[3] Other writers, like G. A. Borgese, put the accent on the unrealistic yearning after Roman glories. Borgese described 'the Italian disease' as a combination of cultural megalomania with a political and military inferiority complex. 'Too stubbornly, for too long have the Italians entertained the queerest and most distorted ideas about themselves and others. They have thought themselves a nation of geniuses in a universe of dunces, and a mass of cowards in a world of the brave.'[4]

There is a danger in this type of interpretation, revealing though it may sometimes be. If one sees Fascism as the inevitable result of Italy's backwardness, or of the Italian *volksgeist*, one is in fact conceding the case made by the regime's apologists, who argued that democracy was a foreign import which had proved unrealistic and unsuitable in Italy.[5] Modern Italian history is not an unbroken record of failure or stagnation; on the contrary, social change and the aspiration towards a more effective democracy were, paradoxically, necessary preconditions for the emergence of Fascism. The problem is, in fact, as Salvemini stated, why 'the Italians felt the need to get rid of their free institutions exactly at the moment in which they should have been proud of the results achieved through them. One would rather have expected a step forward towards more advanced forms of democracy. How was it that at such a moment the Italians opened their doors to dictatorship ?'[6]

One part of the explanation must be in the general European upheaval of the First World War. The interpretation of Fascism as the result of the First World War was carried furthest by Benedetto Croce when he described it as a 'parenthesis' in the history of Italy. Fascism-as-parenthesis and Fascism-as-revelation have been the two opposite poles of historical discourse about Fascism.[7] The former substitutes *Zeitgeist* for *Volksgeist* as the covering explanation. There is some advantage in this: it has helped to distinguish Fascism from other types of dictatorship as a novel phenomenon. Croce's own examination of the intellectual humus out of which Fascism grew showed that many of the ingredients of the Fascist mentality were not peculiar to Italy. No great nation altogether escaped the irrationalist *trahison des clercs* or the infatuations of imperialism. However the interpretation of Fascism as a 'parenthesis', or even, as Croce put it elsewhere, as a 'moral malady'[8] to which all Europe was subject, still leaves unexplained why it was in Italy that the movement first took root and won power.

The entry of Italy into the war was a meditated decision, and there is no doubt that in the minds of the statesmen responsible for intervention internal political motives were present. The governing class (or a part of it) was not just surprised by an external catastrophe but chose to go to meet it. Even the peculiar international position of Italy, a partner in 1914 of an alliance with her hereditary enemy, cannot simply be taken as a fact of nature.

Above all, the moral and even economic effects of the war cannot be divorced from the way in which Italy entered the contest in May 1915. In a real sense, Fascism itself was born in 1914–15; and the split between interventionists and neutralists produced a violent laceration of the political fabric, a bitterness of feeling, more characteristic of a civil than of a 'national' war. The divisions in the country and their consequences cannot be understood except in the light of the relationship, or lack of it, between the State and the mass of the Italian people.

3

This leads one back inevitably to the Risorgimento. Real historical controversy about the connection of Fascism with the Italian past, conducted at a level above that of the denunciation and the brilliant but unsupported intuition, has not gone further. Like all great political movements, the Risorgimento aroused more aspirations than it could fulfil. The Post-Risorgimento pessimism about Italy's development which became so marked after 1880 has been well described by an American historian, J. A. Thayer.[9] It is tempting to conclude that this cultural pessimism, resulting from *anomie*, was the real evil which give birth to Fascism. However though this is persuasive as an account of the origins of the Fascist mentality, it obviously leaves some of the most important questions unanswered. The cultural discontents of a handful of intellectuals and publicists (which were not unique to Italy) would not by themselves have overturned Italian democracy, and the permanent structural weaknesses which made the Italian polity vulnerable to Fascism cannot be ignored. The Post-Risorgimento critics were concerned with real as well as imagined deficiencies.

It may be unjust to speak of the Risorgimento as a 'failed revolution',[10] since in one way or another it was bound to fall short of the extravagant and conflicting ambitions which were inseparably bound up with romantic nationalism. However it is still necessary to ask: what were the 'failures' and what were their consequences?

The earliest and most familiar form of the 'failed revolution' thesis goes back to the frustrations of the left, and in particular to the dramatic renunciation made by Garibaldi in favour of Victor Emmanuel II, and its aftermath. National unity was not achieved by a great popular movement, ending in a republic, but was instead imposed from above by 'royal conquest'.[11] This democratic complaint was sometimes combined with the more nationalistic regret that Italian unity had owed so much to diplomacy and foreign help.

Secondly, the Risorgimento failed to satisfy hopes of religious and moral reform. These were not simply a peculiar aberration of Mazzini, with his 'religion of humanity'; they were shared, although in a more sober and less pronounced form, by several of the statesmen of the Right. Underlying their concern was an objective problem of the utmost importance: the hostility of the Catholic Church to the new Italian state, and the hold which it had on popular feeling.

Thirdly, the Risorgimento was not a social revolution. There was no general redistribution of landed property, except between nobility and bourgeoisie. There was consequently also no mobilization of the masses (especially the peasants) in the service of the nation, and they did not identify their interests with the new State. Later writers emphasized the incompleteness of the Risorgimento even as a 'bourgeois revolution'. The backwardness of Italian industrial and commercial development and the persistence of archaic semi-feudal relationships in the South were the proofs of the failure or immaturity of the Italian bourgeoisie.[12] The lack of a well-developed modern class of entrepreneurs allowed the cultural and political predominance of a backward-looking, economically parasitic, humanistic tradition to remain unchallenged.[13]

The result of all these separate failures, it could be held, was one great deficiency : the continued lack of a widely diffused 'civic culture'. Wavering between a superstitious conformity to religious authority and an anarchic individualism which expressed itself in violence and a disrespect for law, the average Italian had an inadequate conception both of his rights as citizen and his duties as subject. In so far as he had genuine political concerns, these tended to be local and factional in character. As I have already suggested, this is a one-sided and exaggerated picture : it would not hold good without qualification for 1870, let alone 1914. For a more balanced summary, one can turn to the historian Luigi Salvatorelli : 'Whoever had drawn up a balance of Italian political development on the eve of the European War would have found that it marked a culminating point. Italy was in the process of creating a national, liberal and social democracy. There was, however, a general factor of weakness present in the still limited diffusion of political education, and in the consequent narrowness of the base of the ruling class.'[14] A very brief look at the conditions of unification from this point of view will serve to set subsequent developments in perspective.

The liberals of the Risorgimento made it possible to govern a united Italy by means of parliamentary institutions. In a sense, this achievement owed a good deal not only to the skill of Cavour and his devotion to the liberal ideal, but to the relative weakness of the Piedmontese monarchy. The terms of the 1848 Statute, which conceded constitutional government to Piedmont, allowed the King freedom to choose and dismiss his ministers, while conceding control of finance to Parliament. This particular division of powers invited conflict and was unlikely to be a permanent solution. A similar situation existed in Prussia, and there, in the constitutional crisis of the early 1860s, it was parliamentary control of finance that was effectively sacrificed to the independence of the monarchy. In Italy the reverse was true : the 1852 Cavour ministry was virtually imposed by Parliament, and it succeeded in reorganizing the bureaucracy so that it answered to the ministers rather than the Crown.[15] Two years later, the crisis provoked by the Government's proposal to dissolve the monasteries seemed to give the King an excellent opportunity to recover the initiative. But he failed : and this turn of events was critical. It determined the liberal direction which Italian political development was to take, in contrast to that of Germany, even though the latter was by far the more socially homogeneous and developed society. The Piedmontese monarchy of the nineteenth century could not match the military glories of Prussia, or even Austria, and this was probably the decisive reason why various attempts to re-establish the Crown's independence met with failure.[16] However, this weakness also made the monarchy less effective as a symbol of national unity after 1860 : and this could only have been compensated for by really strong popular feeling. But this was lacking; Mazzini's ideal of democratic nationhood was not realized.

Mazzini and many other democrats had not seen the Risorgimento as an isolated national movement, but as 'the Italian prelude to a vast European movement of freedom and justice'.[17] European, rather than just Italian, developments put an end to this dream: the failure of the 1848 revolutions, the dictatorship of Louis Napoleon and the Bismarckian solution to the unification of Germany made a narrowing of outlook inevitable. The sense of 'mission' remained, divorced from its original European context, and for the disciples of Mazzini there was a strong temptation to view it in exclusively nationalist terms.

In Italy itself, the decisive failure of the democrats was in 1848 rather than 1860. During the intervening period the Piedmontese and monarchist solution had steadily gained in prestige. But the democratic movement retained enough strength to make the moderates, who controlled the process of unification, uneasy: Garibaldi's expedition, if it made unity possible, was also a threat. The moderates' fears led to a hardening of their attitude to the problems of the organization of the new state. An 'unconditional unitarianism' took the place of an earlier willingness to consider regional claims and differences.[18] This was indeed only part of a wider tendency to stress the ideals of order and authority at the expense of liberty: the balance of Italian liberalism shifted to the right. It is true that this involution was the subject of vigorous and open criticism, which was not denied political expression and contributed to the eventual victory of the left in 1876. However the important fact is that the early years of the new state created a pattern of institutions and practices which were hard to change, and which often acted as a brake on further development. Analogies have been drawn between the unification of Italy and that of Germany: in both cases the union was formally carried out by dynastic rather than democratic methods. But the differences are more important than the similarities. The victory of Prussia meant the triumph of the authoritarian east over the more democratic south and west of Germany; Italy, on the other hand, was unified by the most progressive state in the peninsula. Piedmont had had a constitution since 1848, and it was one of the most prosperous regions in Italy, with easily the highest literacy rates. The progress of Piedmontese society gave a firm basis to the development of liberal political institutions and political thought which was elsewhere lacking.[19] In particular, the political thought of Southern liberalism put stronger emphasis on the action of the State as a power above society and less on civil liberties.[20]

The effects of the encounter with the Southern political tradition were paralleled by the effects of the discovery of the real South, in its misery and ignorance. Cavour and the moderates had always been admirers of the English pattern of local self-government, and had endorsed French liberal criticisms of the centralized Napoleonic state. They had initially therefore favoured the concession of some kind of regional autonomy. But these ideas were abandoned under the influence of the fear and disillusionment provoked by contact with the South. The local governing class appeared both corrupt and weak: and it seemed likely that if given autonomy the Neapolitan provinces would either follow Garibaldi or a Bourbon revival. Above all, the uncontrollable violence of peasant discontent threatened to erupt into a general *jacquerie* : and the outbreak of brigandage in some measure gave substance to these fears. The campaign to repress the brigands, in fact, led to the suspension of normal legal guarantees and a regime of martial law.[21]

The leaders of the right were not moved by conservatism pure and simple in their conversion to centralized government. They genuinely believed, and with good reason, that the South could only make progress as a result of the action of the State directed by an enlightened minority. But in practice this aim was obscured by the need to gain the political support of influential local factions : the State ended by underwriting the power of the Southern notables and lending them the support of its forces of repression and its resources of patronage.[22] The victory of bureaucratic centralization thus disillusioned the federalists without really satisfying the advocates of strong purposeful government : it contributed to the general feeling of resentment against the new state's restrictiveness and denial of genuine political participation. Garibaldi (thanks to the shabby treatment of his volunteers) became a symbol of the forces of popular enthusiasm which had been denied expression.

In fairness to the moderates, however, one has to admit that to organize the political participation of any large quotient of the Italian people in a stable form would have been very hard : in 1861, 74 per cent of the population of Italy was illiterate, while the percentage in the southern regions reached levels of between 85 and 90 per cent.[23] Illiteracy, moreover, cannot be considered as an isolated fact : it was associated with bad communications, the absence of a national market, and desperate poverty ; all obstacles in their own right to effective political mobilization. The restriction of the suffrage was given a certain justification by the existence of these objective hindrances to the exercise of popular sovereignty.

These structural weaknesses in Italian society do much to explain the deficiences of the political system during the next forty years. The limitation on the numbers of those willing and able to engage in political activity favoured the development of interest groups and clienteles rather than parties with general programmes or ideologies.

Parliamentary Government in Italy

Before the First World War Italy was governed by a regime which can best be described as a limited and artificial democracy. By this, I mean a form of representative government which can only work so long as the majority of the population is not politically mobilized. 'Demobilization' may result from : (1) a formal limitation of the electorate (this was true in Italy up till the introduction of universal manhood suffrage in 1912); (2) the apathy of a large part of the electorate, who do not vote; (3) methods of corruption, government pressure and intimidation which severely limit the freedom of voting. The second and third factors are usually found together, and are interdependent. They encourage the persistence of the phenomenon known as 'clientelism' or '*caciquismo*', which is characterized by the strength of political interests based on local personal influence and their systematic interference in administration. However within the system of limited or artificial democracy, clientelism need not be universal; areas of clientelistic politics may and generally do coexist with areas in which organized political parties are dominant.

The postwar crisis out of which Fascism arose signified that the system of artificial democracy had become obsolete. The succession was open: and the choice lay between an advance to a fuller form of democracy, social revolution, or dictatorship.

Before the war the parliamentary deputies were elected by single-member constituencies, as in England, although the existence of a second ballot gave greater scope for tactical alliances between individuals or parties. The system of proportional representation, introduced in 1919, became the focus of controversy between the supporters of the old and the new order of things. In part, its opponents used proportional representation as an excuse for their failure to come to terms with the consequences of universal suffrage and the war. But there were also substantial reasons for their hostility. The single-member constituency had been a premise of the pre-war political order. This order, linked with the name of Giolitti, has been variously described as a 'parliamentary dictatorship' and as a 'prefectocracy'.[24] Under the old electoral system deputies could rely on the strength of their local influence and connections. They could thus be free from party ties. On the other hand they were highly dependent on the Government, the source of the patronage without which their clienteles would disintegrate. The Prefects, who negotiated this patronage, also controlled the police and had the right to interfere in local government. The Minister of the Interior controlled the Prefects, who therefore naturally used their powers to punish his enemies and reward his friends.[25] The existence of a mass of deputies whose only loyalty was to the Government made the formation of parliamentary majorities an easier matter than it was to be under proportional representation. However already in the 1913 elections, the first to be held under universal suffrage, the methods of the administration provoked a strong reaction, and in 1919 the Prime Minister Nitti announced his intention of foregoing the use of government influence.[26]

The Minister of the Interior, rather than the Cabinet as a whole, directed the machine of government pressure and patronage, and although other ministries could grant many favours, they remained in a subordinate position. Even the Prime Minister, if he did not also control the Interior Ministry, was regarded as little more than a titular chief, enjoying the shadow rather than

8

the substance of power. Consequently there was great scope for the creation of an essentially personal dominance over Parliament. Giolitti's principal right-wing critic, the editor of the *Corriere Della Sera* Luigi Albertini, explained the aberrant character of this form of rule when contrasted with the orthodox model of Parliamentary government:

When a homogeneous majority, formed, by the physical law, as it were, of the attraction of similar ideas . . . raises to the Government the man whose energy and personal authority make him best able to effect the programme entrusted to him . . . it is not a personal government, but a government of the majority. When instead it is the statesman who forms the majority, which he unites around him . . . by means of the most discordant agreements . . . then the statesman may do good as well as harm . . . but the corruption of the parliamentary regime becomes deeper and deeper and may prepare the way for future disasters. What force of attraction can public life exercise when the representative of the nation is transformed into an automaton which must go where the Government wants . . . ?[27]

The crucial weakness of this system of government was that it limited and diminished the effective responsibility of the executive to the legislature, and therefore to the electorate. This was, in turn, largely a consequence of the way in which the electorate conceived of the deputies' responsibility to them. In 1878 one of the leaders of the left, Zanardelli, had complained that 'the deputies . . . must make themselves rather than the representatives of the nation, the agents of the electors', and that as a result of this perversion of their representative function they became more concerned with 'the ante-chambers of the ministries' than with the Chamber of Deputies.[28] The growth of literacy and the enlargement of the suffrage which this made possible certainly had a great effect in modifying the conditions of the political contest; even before 1913 many deputies, perhaps the majority, had to reckon with a genuine public opinion rather than with a handful of 'grand electors'. But the dualism of Italian society and economic life was reflected in politics. South of Rome widespread illiteracy and political apathy still allowed the clientele to flourish, and government influence still determined the majority of elections in the Mezzogiorno.

The introduction of proportional representation and the end of the Giolittian system also affected the position of the monarchy. Before the war, the fluidity of party lines made it necessary for the King to exercise his discretion in deciding when and how a change of government was necessary. The advantage which the government in office enjoyed in 'making' the elections made the royal faculty of granting or refusing a dissolution of the chamber potentially important. Although Victor Emmanuel III used his prerogatives with caution, the King enjoyed a degree of liberty in choosing Prime Ministers and influencing the choice of subordinates that he did not possess under postwar conditions, when laborious and detailed bargaining between groups became the rule.

The delays and difficulties in forming and maintaining coalitions during

9

the postwar period gave an edge to the criticism, voiced by the right, that the parliamentary groups had encroached upon the royal prerogative. This criticism was the latest manifestation of the recurrent attempts by the right to justify a 'return to the Statute' by exposing the deficiencies of parliamentary government.

From Trasformismo to Giolitti

The flowering of anti-parliamentary literature in Italy dates from the decade of the 1880s. Although the resentment of the right at its fall from power in 1876 certainly stimulated the growth of anti-parliamentary feeling in conservative circles, this explanation does not account either for the breadth or the persistence of the criticism. There is little doubt that by the middle of the 1880s disillusionment with the working of the system was general and profound.[29]

Criticism centred on two features: the illegitimate mutual interference of Parliament and administration, and the 'absence of real parties'.[30] There had never been in reality a golden age in which these two features were absent. Even in Piedmont between 1848 and 1860 the tendency for government power to emancipate itself from parliamentary control was already acutely felt.[31] Equally, the hopes of those who believed in the English model of a contest between two great and clearly defined parties, alternating in power, were quickly disappointed by the famous *connubio*, when Cavour freed himself from dependence on the right wing of the moderates and allied with Rattazzi and a part of the left. This was the first of those surprising 'transformations, of parties which later gave rise to the term '*trasformismo*', a concept which with time became increasingly complex and charged with hostile meaning. In its original usage, the term *trasformismo* described the alliance in 1882 between the leaders of the two historic parties, Depretis and Minghetti, which marked the end of the old distinction between left and right. This original meaning should be distinguished from the wider and less precise use of the term to describe a whole characteristic complex of bargaining between groups and individuals.[32] Giustino Fortunato, the great *meridionalista*, accepted the end of the old parties as right and inevitable; but he equally firmly repudiated the actual configuration of the Parliament elected in 1876 and still more that of its successors. 'The old parties became factions, rather than giving birth to defined and distinct parties, and the factions were subdivided into groups which were increasingly incapable of doing good, because increasingly alien to the modern concept of a democratic state – that is to say a state in which the participation of the citizens . . . is broad and effective'.[33]

Between 1861 and 1876 the left had come to assume the function of representing the injured interests of the South. Southern grievances were, of course, of the greatest seriousness and importance: however, given the restriction of the suffrage and the dominance of landed property, it is not surprising that their political interpretation should have been narrow and partial. The demand that the South should get a larger share of public works, while legitimate, sanctioned and encouraged the purchase of individual deputies by the government of the day through piecemeal concessions, which usually benefited only a small circle of 'grand electors'. The accession of the left to power in 1876 therefore promoted the increasing concern of politics with the adjustment of local interests too restricted even to be called regional. The politics of Depretis were built on this subsoil of corrupt bargaining, and it is this which explains the moral aversion attached to *trasformismo*.

It can be argued that the governments of the left, if their political morality was questionable, at least performed an important historical function in liberating the forces making for industrial growth. The increase in corruption which struck observers during the 1880s may be attributed in part to the efforts of industrial capitalism to break out of its agrarian shell; the formation of industry in a society still largely governed by traditional values is likely to be a rather devious process. However this raises the more general question of the direction taken by Italy's industrial development and its political and social effects.

There has been much controversy over the significance of the 'spurt' of industrial growth between 1879 and 1887. On balance it seems fair to say that although this brief period of expansion cannot be called a 'take-off into self-sustained growth', since it failed to ride out the ensuing depression, it was an important and necessary prelude to the industrial revolution of the Giolittian period after 1900. The governments of the left, by introducing protective tariffs and by a more favourable attitude to business, did help to create a climate more favourable for investment and the modernization of industry. At least, no other convincing explanation has yet been found for the sudden upswing of those years.[34] However this does not mean to say that government policy was well designed to promote long-term industrial development. The new tariffs introduced in 1887 probably did a great deal more harm than good. The high protection accorded to the iron and steel industry damaged the more hopeful prospects of the engineering industries: the high price of home-produced iron and steel made them uncompetitive in the world market and limited them to the satisfaction of home demand.

At the same time a high tariff on wheat was introduced, as a compensation to the landowners for industrial protection. The political effects of the 1887 tariffs were extremely serious. The decision to create a national steel industry was defended by invoking the needs of national defence, and the new iron, steel and shipbuilding interests were heavily dependent on a lavish programme of battleship construction. The link between an uncompetitive heavy industry dependent on state contracts and the pursuit of an imperialist power policy, first forged between 1882 and 1887, was ominous for the future. The alliance between Northern industrial interests and Southern *latifondisti* brought into being by the tariff was a powerful obstacle to democratic development.[35] The wheat duty, high taxation, and the tariff war with France which greatly accentuated the crisis in agricultural exports all had disastrous effects on the standard of living of the majority.[36] They helped to produce a decade of revolt and reaction.

The 1880s can be seen as a critical period in which Italy 'missed the bus', both economically and politically. Industrial expansion and democratic development were both interrupted after 1887 by a period of crisis and regression, in part explained by the missed opportunities of the preceding years.

The advent of the left to power and even the extension of the suffrage in 1881 had not made the political class notably more representative of the needs of a wider section of the community. The ideal of liberalism as an exchange of power between enlightened elites, able to express some of the demands of those outside the circle of active political participation, was discredited.

Between 1880 and 1900 popular protest against the narrowly based Risorgimento state began to take on an organized form. Socialism won many converts not only among the urban workers but among the landless labourers of the Po Valley. After Leo XIII's famous encyclical *Rerum Novarum*, the Catholic social movement also spread rapidly. The advisers of the monarchy and most of the ruling class could conceive of no answers to this development except repression. Parliamentary government was menaced first by the nationalistic authoritarianism of Crispi and then by the conservative demand for a return to the Statute, i.e., to the free choice of ministers by the Crown, independent of Parliament. Both Crispi and the conservative leader Sonnino were in different ways strongly influenced by their admiration for Germany.

At the turn of the century, however, Italian society embarked on a new and more hopeful course. The disaster of Adowa in 1896 meant the temporary abandonment of imperialist ambitions : in the last years of the century the end of the long world depression brought about an economic revival : and after the reactionary experiment of General Pelloux in 1898–9, the 'policy of coercion' against labour and the free press was dropped. Democratic socialism, Giolitti's liberal attitude towards the regulation of labour conflicts, and the reform of the banking system all helped to prevent a repetition of earlier catastrophes. The new king, Victor Emmanuel III, who succeeded after his father Umberto had been assassinated, put his trust in liberal and parliamentary methods.

During the period from 1896 to 1914 Italy had her industrial revolution. Industrial production almost doubled, the national income grew by approximately 50 per cent, and industrial investment trebled. The 'industrial triangle' of Genoa, Turin and Milan was firmly established.[37] Even at the end of this period, however, Italy was still far more an agricultural than an industrial nation : the numbers employed in agriculture were still about double those in industry. The growth of modern large-scale industry had as yet done little to resolve the problems of chronic unemployment or under-employment. The South, with 40 per cent of the population, participated in industrial progress only to a very small degree. The disparities in social development between north and south consequently became much more pronounced than at the time of unification; by 1911 the illiteracy rate was only 11 per cent in Piedmont and 15 per cent in Lombardy, but in the Southern regions it varied between 50 and 70 per cent.[38] The prosperity of the Giolittian years favoured political stability in the short term; however economic growth in the end produced a different type of society, in which Giolitti's politics began to seem old-fashioned.

Not even the intelligent flexibility of Giolitti could overcome the division of Italian politics into three great and exclusive camps, the Liberal, the Catholic and the Socialist. He restored the Liberal state, which had seemed in danger of foundering, but much ground had been lost. Both the Socialists and the clericals had built up formidable organizations, in spite of the frequent attempts at repression. Neither officially accepted the legitimacy of the Italian state. On their side the Liberals, representing the mass of the bourgeoisie and especially the professional classes, would not admit that the control of the levers of power by other forces was fully legitimate. The monarchy became the symbol and the justification for this attitude towards the State; it was *their* State, and all other forces were suspected of trying to disintegrate it. Giolitti saw the danger of this, and tried hard to break down the dividing walls between the Liberals and the other camps; but the monarchy, to which Giolitti was loyal both by conviction and from necessity, stood as an obstacle in the way of this attempt. Neither the Socialists nor the Catholics would altogether renounce their rejection of a sovereignty which for different reasons they regarded as illegitimate.

From Giolitti's point of view, the combination of this fundamental distrust with a practical readiness to compromise was an excellent thing in the short run. It enabled him to keep his allies in a subordinate role; the Catholics, in particular, were greatly restricted in their force and autonomy by the reservations of Pius x towards any organization which admitted the democratic principle. In the long run, however, there was a serious moral weakness in this form of co-operation. Giolitti's policy had the opposite purpose to that of Depretis; yet it is no accident that the accusation of *trasformismo* was revived against Giolitti's attempts to entice both the Socialists and the clericals within the constitutional fold. The upholders of principle in each 'bloc' revolted against what seemed to be an agreement exclusively between interests. For some time revisionism was apparently triumphant. Giolitti could boast that the Socialists had 'put Marx in the attic'.[39] This was a rash claim. The case of the Catholics is less obvious. There was a strong tendency among their leaders, both ecclesiastical and lay, to enter into a conservative compromise with the Liberals in order to contain Socialism. But this tendency was in conflict with the rising forces of Christian Democracy. The conservative preoccupations of Pius x delayed the emergence of the problem of relations between the governing class and a popular political Catholicism. The political inflexibility and inexperience of the Popular party were a consequence of this delay; the elder statesmen of the party, such as Filippo Meda, were too moderate and pro-Liberal to be sure of commanding the support of their followers, yet no one else possessed the authority of long parliamentary practice. The problem of reconciling the Liberal-democratic state with the Catholic political ideology, was to pose itself with unexpected abruptness in the difficult conditions of the postwar period.

2

THE CRISIS OF THE LIBERAL STATE

Nationalism and the Revolt against Giolitti

The men of the Risorgimento had seen the revival of Italy as part of a general European movement towards liberty and self-government. Mazzini's belief in the nation was inseparable from his conception of the progress of humanity. But for both left and right the aftermath of the Risorgimento had brought disillusionment. Patriots and liberals came to feel that the ideals for which they had fought had roused no echoes among the mass of the people. The religious problem had not been solved either along the lines of a reconciliation with the Church, as Gioberti had suggested, or through the spread of the new religion of humanity in which Mazzini had put his faith; as a result the governing and intellectual classes found themselves isolated, and uncomfortably conscious that the state had only shallow roots in popular sentiment. The old dreams of 'primacy' and 'mission', unfulfilled, continued nonetheless to haunt their imagination.

Meanwhile the real primacy in Europe had passed into the hands of the other new nation, Germany, whose successes in war, foreign policy and industry contrasted so vividly with Italy's failures and with a backwardness whose full extent had been first revealed by the investigations of *meridionalisti* and social reformers. The result was a growing admiration for German methods and German ideals. First among these was the strong authoritarian state in which the abstract ideals of liberalism were sacrificed to the needs of a *Realpolitik* based on 'positive science, production and force'.[1] The changing idea of the nation mirrored this development. For Mazzini, the nation could owe its reality only to the will and consciousness of its members; but for Crispi the nation became an *a priori* fact, determined by natural causes (geography, law, language and race) and independent of the wishes of the citizens who inhabited its territory. The national destiny, or mission, now conceived as an end in itself and not as a step towards the realization of the

15

ideals of humanity, came at the same time to be viewed as a force of nature or a religious truth, which the individual had no choice but to accept.[2]

It was a lonely and unsuccessful writer from the republican Romagna, Alfredo Oriani, who translated the Mazzinian concept of 'mission' into the language of imperialism. 'All our millennial struggles to found the nation, the blood of our heroism and the tragedies of our genius aimed but at this day, on which Italy has re-entered history as an immortal actress after her long confinement, and once more sails the seas, the bearer of a new civilization :[3] this was how Oriani greeted Italy's first modest colonial enterprises.

Imperialist sentiment in Italy developed out of the need to compensate for failure rather than to celebrate success. First of all, the old sense of shame that Italy had not 'made herself' but had had to rely on foreign help was revived in a more acute form by the defeats of Custozza and Lissa in 1866. Then in 1881 France's occupation of Tunis sparked off an explosive emotional reaction which led Italy into her first colonial ventures. Finally the defeat by the Abyssinians at Adowa (1896), if it disillusioned public opinion in general, was nonetheless the critical event which set the founders of the new Nationalist movement on their path. These young publicists, whom one might call the generation of 1896, argued that the cowardice of the bourgeoisie had permitted the humiliation of the nation and the victory of socialism.[4] At first they made little impact, but after Austria's annexation of Bosnia-Herzegovina in 1908, which signified not only the worsening of general European tensions but another moral defeat for Italy, the strident voices of Italian nationalism began to reach a wider audience.

The frenetic rhetoric of the 1880s, aptly christened 'megalomania',[5] had anticipated some of the themes of later nationalism. Rocco de'Zerbi called for 'a bath of blood' to cure the Italian people of their sentimental weakness; the image was revived by Giovanni Papini in 1913.[6] This repellent slogan may have been too extreme for most tastes, but rhetoric, as the anti-imperialist conservative Stefano Jacini remarked, was undoubtedly a national vice. Italian patriotism was a 'form of mind pervaded by literature';[7] poets and historians had led the way in the creation of a national consciousness. For the 'cultured classes', the sense of nationhood and the literary language were associated values of which they were the exclusive guardians; the masses, clerical or subversive, spoke dialect. The romantic image of the poet as the legislator and prophet of the race was one aspect of this state of mind. It was natural that poets should seek to respond to the expectations of their public and should exploit the patriotic theme.

After his first successes Gabriele D'Annunzio declared that 'I am not, and do not wish to be, a *mere* poet' and turned his attention to 'national' subjects.[8] Another leading poet, Pascoli, in spite of the intimate character of his best verse, was similarly convinced that he had a civil mission to perform. The image of Italy as the suffering 'proletarian' among the nations was his invention,[9] later to be taken up and elaborated into a theory by Enrico Corradini.

Both D'Annunzio and Pascoli sought to take their place in the apostolic succession of inspired national bards, from Alfieri to Foscolo through Manzoni to Carducci.

The contribution made by D'Annunzio to nationalism was, of course, richer, more varied and infinitely more important than that of Pascoli. He embellished the indigenous patriotic tradition with the sophistication of the European decadence, and married refinement and sensuality to the national cause.

From Nietzsche he borrowed the figure of the Superman; at first depicted in the form of the aesthete, the great lover and the connoisseur of spiritual sensations, the Superman was later identified with the masterful man of action, capable of controlling multitudes and shaping events by the strength of his will.[10] To his admiring public, D'Annunzio seemed in his own career to have embodied all these various aspects of the Superman. In the First World War the aesthete became a hero. But the aesthete in D'Annunzio always had the upper hand, even when he turned to war and politics; he judged actions and programmes according to the strength of the sensations which they could evoke. This attitude explains both his brilliance as a propagandist and his ultimate inadequacy as a political leader.[11]

In terms of content, D'Annunzio performed an important service for nationalism by imposing the themes of naval expansion and the Adriatic on public attention. There is no doubt that his cult of Venice, presented as the true heir of the Roman spirit, was deliberately designed for this purpose; it was not for nothing that the Naval League sent him a message of congratulation after the performance of *la Nave*, that extraordinary (and now ridiculous) blend of patriotic rhetoric, phoney mysticism and sado-masochistic sex.[12] But it was the general psychological effect produced by his writings, in conjunction with his personal myth, that was really important. It has been brilliantly described by the Italian historian, Nino Valeri:

. . . that literature was, in fact, militant politics, fascinating propaganda, psychologically the most suitable to win for the national and imperial idea broad strata of dissatisfied Italians, especially the so-called *petit-bourgeois*, who felt the sting of mediocrity most keenly.

Many youths . . . tired of Giolittian good sense, flat, grey, everyday, accommodating, . . . and dissatisfied with a banal existence bureaucratically regulated by a meagre stipend, in which nothing ever happened, attributed political substance to this literary barbarism. . . .[13]

D'Annunzio offered an outlet for the instinctual revolt against bureaucratic regularity and cultural deprivation. The range of his influence was not restricted to those who actually read him; one should not forget that the pioneers of the film epic drew on his work, and that best-selling novelists like Guido da Verona diffused a vulgarized version of his ethos among a wider public than the poet himself could command.[14] The cultural revolt against 'Giolittianism', however, cannot simply be identified with petty-bourgeois frustrations. There was also an intellectual revolt: the younger generation of the intelligentsia in the majority shared in a profound dissatisfaction with the existing order. The problem, in their eyes, remained that of the 'incomplete Risorgimento . . . a movement made by politics, diplomacy and even literature, and terribly poor, in collective effort, popular sacrifice, in short in blood shed'.[15] But the Risorgimento was still favourably compared with the succeeding period. It became a commonplace to contrast the corruption of parliamentary government under *trasformismo* with 'the heroic Italian period of the Risorgimento when the state had been created by the labours of restricted minorities'.[16] If the tradition of the right exalted the rule of the wise and cultured few which had been overthrown in 1876, the tradition of the left too glorified the 'heroic imposition' of the nation by a minority on the uncomprehending mass of the people.[17] What was needed, therefore, was a new ruling class which would rescue Italy from Giolittian stagnation, and would succeed in integrating the masses in the state where earlier elites had failed.

Some of these intellectuals found their inspiration in Pareto's theory of elites. It is true that Pareto always insisted that his theory was purely scientific: but this is hardly convincing. At times, he might seem to draw the conclusion that the triumph of socialism was inevitable; but his predictions were really prophecies. That is to say, they had the function of shaking bourgeois complacency and making possible a restoration of the honest values of combat.[18]

The truth which Pareto was concerned to bring home was above all that of the harsh destiny reserved for those who allowed themselves to be taken in by high-sounding ethical appeals. Humanitarianism and reluctance to use force were the sure signs of an elite in decline, and only war could arrest the progress of socialism.[19] It is not surprising that this theory should have appealed to the nationalists. Giuseppe Prezzolini, in the first of the nationalist periodicals, *Il Regno*, wrote to Pareto, 'You see in the theory of aristocracies a scientific theory: I see in it instead a scientific justification of my present political needs'.[20]

On the other side of the barricades Pareto had an ally and friend in Georges Sorel, with whom he was in regular correspondence. They found much common ground in their detestation of Parliament and middle-class cowardice embodied in reformist socialism and its democratic allies, and in their conviction that political ideologies cannot be measured by criteria of objective truth but only by their greater or lesser effectiveness in moving men to action.[21] There was a cross-fertilization of ideas: Sorel influenced Enrico Corradini and the Nationalists, while Pareto was read by Mussolini in his Socialist days.[22]

After 1910 nationalism began to crystallize into a definite shape. The ideologues of the Nationalist Association, Enrico Corradini and Alfredo

Rocco, developed a reactionary political doctrine of some consistency at the cost of alienating many of the movement's earlier sympathizers, who had believed in a democratic or liberal form of nationalism.[23] Their most notable ideological achievement was to transfer the concept of class struggle to the international plane. The idea of the 'proletarian nation', which Corradini borrowed from Pascoli, was a memorable formula which expressed the sense of grievance felt at the exclusion of the late-comer Italy from the imperial table. They pointed to Italy's demographic expansion as the proof that she was a 'young nation', physiologically akin not to decadent France but to virile Germany: Italian imperialism was therefore justified by over-population and would provide a national home for all those unfortunates at present forced to emigrate and thus lost to the national community.[24] Emigration was at its height in the years before the war, reaching an all-time peak of 873,000 in 1913,[25] so that the Nationalist argument appeared relevant. It was sufficiently ambiguous to appeal both to employers who disliked the effect of emigration in raising wages and to poor Southern peasants, potential or actual emigrants, who really believed that there would be land for all in Libya.[26]

The Nationalists drew on the 'organic' conceptions of society elaborated by conservative thinkers, and particularly on the ideas of Charles Maurras and the *Action Française*. However Alfredo Rocco explained that the ideology of the *Action Française* needed revision, since it was the doctrine of a nation whose days of glory and expansiveness lay in the past whereas Italy's lay in the future: and whatever one may think of this claim, there was a real difference between Italian and French nationalism. The former was distinguished by its positive attitude to the process of industrial growth.[27] Rocco gave a new and contemporary significance to the idea of the corporative order, no longer seen as a medieval utopia interested only in agriculture and the artisan, but as a modern organization of the forces of production. The Nationalists became the spokesmen of protectionist heavy industry.[28]

This was an issue which as yet still divided the nationalists from the revolutionary syndicalists. Sorel had incorporated the orthodox economists' critique of protectionism into his revolutionary condemnation of the tacit alliance between industrialists and reformist socialism. Social peace, he argued, was not only morally undesirable, because it allowed a free rein to modern tendencies towards decadence and egoism, but also economically retrograde, because it was dependent on the maldistribution of resources made inevitable by protectionism.[29] These arguments found a particular response among Southern intellectuals in revolt against the Socialist party's neglect of the Mezzogiorno and its exclusive attention to the 'working-class oligarchies' of the industrial north.[30] But if *liberismo* divided the syndicalists from the nationalists, they were united in a common hatred of democracy and admiration of violence. By 1910–11 voices on both sides acknowledged their spiritual kinship.[31] More and more, at a time when the pace of international

events was quickening, the hopes, discontents and frustrations of the intellectuals came to be centred upon war. Even Liberals like Giovanni Amendola,
who rejected the Nationalist obsession with territorial expansion and the
idea of 'war for war's sake', nevertheless believed that only a great war could
prove the unity of the nation, restore the virtues of sacrifice and courage and
end the dominion of egoistic hedonism.[32] The new popularity of the hitherto
neglected writings of Oriani find an explanation in this state of mind. 'The
revolt of the ideal': the title was a banner for the moral and intellectual
rejection of the existing order. It would be a serious distortion to view this
revolt as leading necessarily to Fascist conclusions. The ideals of militant
anti-Fascism, in fact, can often be traced back to this same source. However
the fascination exercised by the myth of war as moral revolution and collective
passion leading to redemption was nevertheless the essential, though not
sufficient, condition for the formation of the Fascist mentality.

1911–15 : From the Libyan War to the Great War

By 1911 Italy was a more powerful and more confident nation than she had
been in 1900. However from 1908 onwards the pace of industrial expansion
slackened considerably. The recession, combined with the effect of the counter-
organization of the employers, reacted unfavourably on the working-class
movement. The percentage of successful strikes declined, and so did membership in the unions. Employers whose profit margins were under pressure were
less disposed to be conciliatory, while the worsening of the economic situation
encouraged working-class radicalism. Consequently Giolitti found it harder
than before to play the part of mediator and peace-maker between capital
and labour. At the same time, the recession stimulated the growth of the free-
trade campaign, which was often coupled with criticism of the union movement for its tacit connivance with industrial protectionism.[33]

The reformists in the Socialist party, on whose co-operation Giolitti
relied, had triumphed over their opponents in the 1908 Florence Congress.
Unfortunately, however, it was easier to talk about reforms than to get them
carried out. Salvemini was the most effective critic of the reformists' hesitations and lack of concrete initiatives. He urged the party without success to
throw itself into an all-out campaign for free trade, electoral liberty in the
South, universal suffrage and tax reform. Opposition to Giolitti as the cor-
rupter of the South was a *sine qua non* for Salvemini. On the other hand, the
right of the reformists, led by Bissolati and Bonomi, argued that the only way
to circumvent conservative resistance to reform was through participation in
the government. They were extremely critical of the party organization and
saw the future in a labour party on the English model, controlled and financed
by the unions.[34]

In 1911 Giolitti returned to power with a programme which included
universal suffrage and the nationalization of life insurance. This had a

powerful attraction for the reformist Socialists, and Bissolati, though he still declined office, defied the party taboos by accepting the King's invitation to take part in the consultations for the formation of the new government. Turati regarded Bissolati's visit to the Palace as premature and compromising ; a split began to open in the ranks of the reformists, although they agreed to vote in favour of Giolitti's ministry.[35]

It seemed as if Giolitti was now on the point of realizing his grand design for a reforming ministry with Socialist support. But at this critical moment he overreached himself : his balancing act became too ambitious. It was the Agadir crisis rather than internal politics which explains the timing of Giolitti's decision to invade Libya. However the war also fitted into the normal pattern of his political strategy. He was concerned with the growth of right-wing opposition to his policies and knew that failure to take Libya would provoke a storm of criticism.[36] He hoped at the same time that he could placate the Socialists by assuring them that there would be no change in internal policy and that he had no intention of surrendering to Nationalist hysteria. Bissolati and Bonomi refused to vote against the ministry ; this much was in accordance with his calculations. But the war revived all the latent distrust of the monarchy and militarism which continued to smoulder beneath the surface of the working-class movement. Giolitti and Turati had, after all, first come together in opposition to Crispi's 'megalomania' and pursuit of colonial triumphs ; so it is not surprising that Turati denounced the Libyan expedition as 'the betrayal of democracy' and concluded that 'the destiny of Italy has been decided, probably for the period of an entire generation'.[37] The reformists were divided and discredited, and the majority of the Socialist party, swept along by the passionate rhetoric of the new man from the anarchistic, anti-clerical, republican Romagna, Mussolini, repudiated their optimistic and parliamentarian strategy. The Libyan war brought anti-militarism once again into the forefront of Socialist politics ; and Mussolini reactivated the issue of the republic.[38] Socialist hostility severely reduced the advantages which Giolitti had hoped to gain by the introduction of universal suffrage. Universal suffrage also made the Liberals more dependent upon Catholic support : the revelation after the elections of the 'Gentiloni Pact', whereby 330 candidates had individually agreed to sign a 7-point policy pledge drawn up by the Catholic electoral union, in return for the support of the lay organizations and the clergy, made this clear.[39] There was a sharp reaction on the left, and the anti-clerical Radical party passed to the opposition ; this finally convinced Giolitti that the time had come for one of his characteristic withdrawals to await better times.[40]

The revival of ideological intransigence and the coming of universal suffrage were reflected in a change in the nature of the parties. Far from withering away, as both Croce and Salvemini had predicted,[41] they became more vigorous and more determined to enforce discipline : in all the left-wing parties the executives made a determined effort to reduce the autonomy of the parliamentary groups. A new generation, who were deeply influenced by the free traders and *meridionalisti*, and especially by Salvemini, challenged the leadership of the authoritative and experienced parliamentarians such as Turati, Barzilai (Republican) or Marcora and Sacchi (Radical), guilty of connivance with 'Giolittianism'.[42]

Giolitti's successor was Antonio Salandra. He stood for a real alternative: the formation of a strong, united Conservative-Liberal party in alliance with the Catholics and the Nationalists. The appeal of this decided conservatism was strengthened by the revival of Socialist intransigence.[43] The parties of order now faced a really deliberate and aggressive strategy of subversion, as Mussolini sought to galvanize the 'static' mass of the working-class movement with the aid of those 'dynamic minorities', such as the syndicalists, whom he saw as the true motive force of revolution.[44] For the first but not the last time Mussolini succeeded in mobilizing new masses of the previously disorganized and inarticulate, and in establishing a personal relationship with them which enabled him radically to threaten the stability of the existing political structures.[45] The politics of intoxication were beginning to drive out the politics of reason, and from the start Mussolini's part in this process was central.

The new style of subversive politics reached a climax in the 'red week' of June 1914. This was an outburst of violent rioting, which in the Romagna attained the proportions of a serious insurrection. The epicentre of the movement lay in the regions (Romagna and Ancona) where anarchist and republican traditions were strong as well as socialism. The outcome, however, revealed the shortcomings of Mussolini's strategy. His methods came under severe criticism not only from the reformists but from other members of the Socialist left-wing. Serrati, later to become the leader of the Socialist party, criticized him for appealing to 'the amorphous mass' of the 'unorganized', and pointed out the futility of trusting to improvization to bring about revolution.[46] Red week, however, had not disillusioned the masses of new Socialist supporters. Far from strengthening the reformists, it had confirmed the victory of the intransigents. The occasion which had triggered off the movement had been an anti-militarist demonstration; the coming of the war therefore 'found the nation divided irreparably in two on the very theme that now, unexpectedly, became fundamental'.[47]

During the few days when it seemed possible that Italy might enter the war on the side of her allies Germany and Austria-Hungary, the left momentarily recovered its unity. A broad opposition front, stretching from the revolutionary syndicalists through the Socialists to the radicals, joined in the demonstrations for neutrality. It is a disputed question how far this opposition was really decisive. For the Foreign Secretary San Giuliano at least, the strictly diplomatic reasons against intervention on the side of the Central Powers were enough: but Sonnino, a powerful influence on Salandra, opposed neutrality and without doubt the strength of the opposition and the fear of provoking a democratic revolution helped to make the decision against war with the Entente irreversible.[48]

But the unity of the left shattered when the issue instead became that of intervention on the side of the Entente. The effect of the new situation was most dramatically felt by those 'dynamic minorities' exalted by Mussolini. For them, France stood for the Revolution, the Commune and the barricades; Germany for pedestrian respectability and the suffocating power of the bureaucratic party machine: in addition, the cause of war attracted them because it was intrinsically more 'dynamic' than the defence of neutrality.[49] The effect of the intervention crisis was therefore that the Socialists lost many of those elements and leaders, to begin with Mussolini, who had been the spearhead of active subversion, while remaining committed to a long-term policy of revolution. This does much to explain the character of *massimalismo*, as the policy pursued by the intransigent and neutralist majority of the Socialists came to be known.

The Socialist attitude to the war both exemplified and helped to confirm this passivity. The leaders of the party early agreed that there was no prospect of success for a revolutionary general strike against the entry of Italy into the war. The only effective political alternative would have been an attempt to end the isolation of the Socialist party and conclude an alliance with Giolitti in favour of neutrality. This policy, however, though favoured by some of the reformists, was rejected. It is, in fact, very doubtful that it was ever a real alternative. Giolitti's 'neutralism' was only conditional; he believed that Italy could gain satisfactory territorial concessions from Austria-Hungary as the price of neutrality, and he knew that an alliance with the Socialists would weaken his bargaining position.[50] There is no doubt that opposition to the war was deeply rooted in the pacifism of most urban workers and peasants, at least in the north and centre of Italy: but on the streets the Socialists were unable to defeat or even match the impressive interventionist demonstrations. Perhaps because they felt that they were fighting a battle lost from the outset, they lost control of the *piazza*. This inferiority had political consequences of the utmost gravity, over and beyond the immediate issue of Italy's entry into the war. The 'dynamic minorities' who had failed to win a victory *with* socialism had now triumphed *against* it: in the 'radiant days of May' a new version of the activist myth was born.

It was not just socialism which was defeated by the interventionist demonstrations of May 1915. Turati found the weak point in the arguments of the democratic interventionists when, in his speech to Parliament, he remarked that 'the war which is to reinforce the democratic institutions of Latin Europe seems to have produced this first effect, even before it has broken out: that of having destroyed the vigour and dignity of our parliamentary institutions.'[51]

In spite of the signs that social change and universal suffrage had made the preservation of the old equilibrium more difficult, it would be rash to conclude that the predominance of Giolitti had come to an end even before the outbreak of war. His resignation in March 1914 followed a normal rhythm : he liked to retire from office early in the lifetime of a parliament and return after a year or so. The majority was still faithful to him, and Salandra had to proceed with great caution.

At the outset the question of war strengthened the cohesion of the Liberal governing class. The decided stand taken by the parties of the democratic left in favour of intervention was an obstacle to a new alliance between them and Giolitti : but they were also viewed with suspicion by Salandra. The 'parties of order' were united by the conviction that it was up to the Government, and not public opinion, to dictate the course of foreign policy. There was at first no very clear difference between the ideas of Giolitti and those of Salandra and Sonnino on foreign policy : even if the former did advise the Government strongly against entering the war in autumn 1914, he believed, as we have seen, that neutrality must be purchased by Austrian territorial concessions, and this was an alternative which the Government was also willing to consider.[52] But one of Salandra's paramount aims was to keep Giolitti out of power and if possible to supplant him as the leader of the Liberal majority. This explains why he deliberately kept him in the dark about negotiations with the Entente. This secrecy put both Salandra and Giolitti and their supporters in a false position. In May 1915, when Giolitti found out what had been going on, the majority of Parliament deserted the Government. Three hundred deputies left their visiting cards on Giolitti when he arrived in Rome.

Salandra acknowledged his own defeat and gave in the resignation of his cabinet. But Giolitti was unwilling to form a government. He recognized that his known opposition to war would weaken his bargaining position in negotiations with Austria and he believed that failure to obtain substantial territorial concessions would be fatal for the prestige of the monarchy and its defenders. His refusal rendered the parliamentary majority impotent ; they had put their trust in a man rather than a policy. No one would accept responsibility and this ensured the victory of the interventionists.

Giolitti was better at avoiding crises than at facing them, and his supporters, for the most part passively dependent upon his judgement, had little strength of their own.

It is probable that Salandra's decision in favour of war had been much influenced by considerations of internal policy. Especially after Giolitti had made public his preference for Italian neutrality, war came in Salandra's eyes to be identified with the aim of destroying the Giolittian system in all its manifestations. War, Salandra believed, while making it possible to repress revolutionary demonstrations and limit criticism, would restore the prestige of the monarchy, the army and conservative liberalism.[53] Opposition to Giolitti was a powerful element also in the interventionism of the intellectuals and other opinion leaders, such as Luigi Albertini and the

24

Corriere, or the free-trade group ; and the agrarians of the Po Valley saw the war as a chance to overthrow his policy of toleration towards the Socialist leagues in the countryside.[54]

The Nationalists were obviously delighted to deal a blow to democratic liberalism and the chances of social reform. They joined with the revolutionary interventionists of the *fasci di azione rivoluzonaria* in denouncing Giolitti's 'treachery'. Giolitti's contacts with the German ambassador Bülow were eagerly exploited as proof that they had been united in a conspiracy together with the German directors of the Banca Commerciale to sell Italy's birthright.[55] D'Annunzio, summoned back from his French exile by Albertini, the editor of the *Corriere Della Sera*, took the lead in exciting the interventionist mobs: '. . . in your Rome they are trying to strangle the nation with a Prussian noose handled by that old, thick-lipped executioner whose fugitive heels know the way to Berlin.'[56] Albertini, like the sorcerer's apprentice, had raised forces which he could not control. When in 1918–19 it was his turn to defend a reasonable foreign policy against nationalist hysteria, he was to find that 1915 had set a fatal precedent.

The May 1915 crisis was not an unequivocal victory for Salandra either. It divided the Liberals whom he had hoped to unite and brought him back to power with the aid of the 'piazza' and of democratic opinion, which he had always tried to reject.[57] The moral leadership of the Liberal party was fatally compromised from the outset ; Salandra's attempt at restoration had hastened the collapse of the old order.

The War, 1915–18

Italy entered the war divided and unprepared. Salandra and his cabinet showed a tragic inability to grasp the nature of the war. They believed in the possibility of a short war with limited, egoistic directives ; it was to be Italy's private war, and help from her allies was to be viewed with suspicion. The Cabinet soon lost confidence in the military genius of their Commander-in-Chief, Cadorna : but, overawed by the impressive public image of his infallibility created by the press and unable to think of a successor, they did nothing to replace him. The result was a regime of divided responsibility, with strategy and foreign policy determined independently and without much reference to each other.[58]

It would be unfair, however, to blame Salandra and his colleagues for all the deficiencies in the political direction of the war. The sheer momentum of the military and economic effort strained the fragile administrative social structures of Italy, as Giolitti had predicted. A vast new military bureaucracy was improvised, with the almost inevitable concomitants of waste, corruption and Parkinsonian multiplication ; the civilian bureaucracy also grew in quantity but not in quality, and the war industries, in their necessarily disordered expansion, profited fully from the weakness of parliamentary and administrative controls. The result was the birth of a new military-bureaucratic-industrial complex, accustomed to bypassing Parliament: the great armaments firms bought up or subsidized a number of important newspapers, through which they could exercise increased political pressure.[59]

Salandra, however, was weakened in his dealings with Cadorna by his deliberate neglect of Parliament and public opinion. His attitude was typical of the failings of Italian liberalism. The battle for intervention had given a new vitality to the democratic left. Republicans, social-reformists and radicals had been the first to take up the cause of intervention. But Salandra, still pursuing his *idée fixe* that the war was a heaven-sent opportunity for the regeneration of the Liberal party, refused to let others share the glory.[60] He cold-shouldered the Democrats, and they reacted to his indifference by attacking his 'isolation', his lack of energy and his authoritarian insensitivity towards Parliament. In June 1916, after the initial success of the Austrian counter-offensive in the Trentino, they brought him down.

Against Salandra, the Democratic interventionists had stood out for the rights of Parliament and public opinion. Nonetheless, as Turati had predicted, Democratic supporters of the war found themselves in an awkward dilemma. They could not forget that the majority of deputies had been willing to follow Giolitti into neutrality,[61] nor could they close their eyes to the widespread popular opposition to the war. Inevitably, they tended to blame this mass hostility on Socialist or clerical agitation.

The official Socialist attitude to the war was summarized in a formula invented by C. Lazzari: 'neither support nor sabotage'. This policy of inaction was followed fairly strictly during the first eighteen months of the war: both in Parliament and in the chief communal councils, in fact, the reformists continued in practice to guide the conduct of the party. But by the critical year of 1917 Lazzari's formula was no longer able to conceal the divisions within the party. In 1917, not only the Russian revolution but mutinies in the French army and riots in Germany showed that in all the belligerent countries, the hard crust of patriotism was beginning to crack under the strain; in Italy, divided from the outset and the weakest of the major nations both militarily and economically, an explosion of popular hostility was almost inevitable. In this heightened tension, the extreme left of the party saw their opportunity, and an organized splinter group of active revolutionaries began to form, with the Neapolitan Amadeo Bordiga as their chief spokesman. This 'new left', the nucleus of the future Communist party, soon had a powerful following in most of the major cities – Rome, Naples, Florence, Turin and even the reformist stronghold of Milan.[62] It was in Turin, a centre of the armaments industry, that the propaganda of the revolutionaries worked most effectively. The riots of August 1917, set off by a bread shortage, soon became revolutionary in intention: but the hoped-for fraternization between workers and soldiers did not take place, and by the third day even the local extremist organizer, Barberis, agreed that it was hopeless to continue.[63] The Turin riots marked the highest point reached by revolutionary agitation during the war.

As the war moved into its most critical stage, many of the Democrats were driven by their fears of Socialist subversion or Giolittian intrigue for a compromise peace, to demand a harsher and more intolerant policy on the home front. Political debate tended to polarize around the life and death issues of the conduct of the war and the possibilities of peace; as during the intervention crisis, the Democrats were forced to form a common front with the Nationalists and their allies, whose war aims were dictated entirely by power politics. For the interventionist left, lacking the support of a majority in Parliament or a decisive role in government, there was a great temptation to assume a 'Jacobin' role as the self-appointed guardians of the nation with a mandate to suppress subversion and combat apathy by all available means. However the threat of 'defeatism' was a real one, and even the more level-headed interventionists were inclined to think the Government's policy too liberal. The leniency of the Minister of the Interior, Orlando, was particularly suspect as he was a follower of Giolitti. Bissolati, the leader of the interventionist left, though he condemned the hysteria of Mussolini and the lunatic fringe, was convinced that more stringent measures were needed to combat Socialist and clerical propaganda.[64] The Democratic left was increasingly contaminated by anti-parliamentary and imperialist tendencies.

The apostles of 'revolutionary war', Mussolini and the patriotic syndicalists, were especially active in organizing 'committees of internal resistance', which naturally enjoyed Nationalist approval: they even tried, it seems, to persuade Cadorna to stage a *coup d'état* in the spring of 1917. This plot came to nothing, probably because Cadorna retained soldierly scruples about interference in politics: however as the situation on the home front deteriorated, he became more and more susceptible to the constant stream of insinuations and provocation which came from the 'resistance committees', and also from the great armaments manufacturers Pio and Mario Perrone of the Ansaldo combine.[65] In a series of notes of extraordinary ferocity, he charged the Government with allowing the subversive atmosphere of the home front to poison the morale of the troops while they went on leave: he hinted ominously that he would not much longer consent to regard internal politics as outside his sphere of competence.

Only three weeks after the Turin riots came the disaster of Caporetto. The Italian army lost 300,000 prisoners and most of the Veneto was occupied by the Austrians. Caporetto brought about the fall of Cadorna: but the long polemic over Government leniency towards subversion which had preceded the disaster lent plausibility to the Commander-in-Chief's claim that it had not been a defeat so much as a 'military strike'. Even Bissolati at first believed Cadorna's version of events.[66] The collapse, largely caused

27

by military error, harsh discipline and neglect of the soldier's welfare, was thus seen by most of the interventionists and the patriotic public as the result of deliberate treachery. An Italian 'stab-in-the-back' legend was born.

The blame for the disaster did not fall only on the Socialists. The neutralist clergy and the Vatican came equally under suspicion; Mussolini distinguished himself particularly in 'exposing' clerical treachery. In the eyes of the interventionists, Benedict xv's peace note of 1 August 1917 shared with Socialist propaganda the responsibility for the subversion of morale among the troops. His reference to the 'useless slaughter' was coupled in interventionist denunciations with the exclamation of the reformist Socialist Claudio Treves: 'Next winter, no one in the trenches !'[67]

The interventionists also feared that Giolitti was preparing to make a come-back as the leader of all those who wanted peace at any price. This was unjust, but some Giolittians certainly hoped that their leader would return to negotiate the end of hostilities. The suspicions of the interventionists increased when the Giolittian deputies organized themselves into a single group, the *Unione parlamentare*. They reacted by founding their own group, the *Fascio parlamentare di difesa nazionale*. The original inspiration and leadership of this group clearly came from the right; the publicist Giovanni Preziosi, a defrocked priest and anti-semite, and his friend the great economist Maffeo Pantaleoni, who was by this time nationalist to the point of paranoia, were its principal promoters.[68] However its membership was not confined to reactionaries; the *Fascio* succeeded in uniting all the different sections of the interventionists, from Mussolini through Bissolati to Salandra, irrespective of their pre-war beliefs. The alliance, based on the understanding that political differences must be subordinated to the patriotic imperative, in fact confirmed the nationalistic hegemony over the whole of the interventionist forces.[69]

However the political results of Caporetto were not one-sided. In some respects the defeat brought about a more democratic conduct of the war. The Government, now headed by Orlando, was largely successful in reasserting political control over the army. Diaz, Cadorna's successor, was a less stubborn character, and a close friend of the Minister of the Treasury, Nitti. Under the stress of necessity, the direction of the war effort became more intelligent. The Orlando government was the first to take seriously the problem of propaganda, whether at home, or aimed at the enemy, or at Italy's allies. The policy of Orlando was marked by an increased concern for the material problems of the soldiers and their families, and by an intensified effort to persuade them that the war was worth fighting, through the promise of a just peace and a reformed society. However Orlando's 'new course' was not free from danger. The new emphasis on propaganda led to an increased involvement of the army in politics. The Propaganda Services ('Servizi P'), operating with considerable independence, helped to form the cadres of politicized young officers who were to be the backbone of the Fascist movement.[70]

In foreign policy also, there was an apparent change of approach. The effects of Wilson's new diplomacy made themselves felt, and the importance of the 'principle of nationality' as a propaganda weapon for subverting the Austro-Hungarian army was at last recognized even by the generals. The Democratic, anti-annexationist school, which wanted Italy to cultivate the friendship of the Slavs, made itself heard after having been almost silent during the first years of the war.[71]

But clarity in foreign policy aims was prevented by the need for national concord. Although Orlando recognized the advantage of encouraging the Slav independence movements to weaken Austria, he lacked the confidence to replace his Foreign Secretary, Sonnino, who wished to have nothing to do with them. Sonnino had become an almost irreplaceable symbol of intervention, and his resignation would have meant a general political crisis. Determined, obstinate and wedded to a conservative view of the aims of the war, Sonnino continued to go his own way. The Treaty of London, which he had negotiated with England, France and Russia in 1915, gave central Dalmatia, with its overwhelmingly Slav population, to Italy, and the defence of this acquisition was the keystone of his foreign policy; he hoped for the preservation of the Habsburg Empire and saw the new national movements patronized by Wilson and, in Italy, Bissolati, as the most dangerous threat to the settlement which he desired.

The 'Congress of the Subject Nations', held in April 1918, drew up the 'Pact of Rome' which announced the acceptance by Italy of the aspirations of the Yugoslavs and Czechs to national independence: however even the Nationalists accepted the Pact, and although it was without doubt a propaganda success for the democratic interests, it did not really commit the Government to revising the terms of the Treaty of London. When peace was concluded, the ambiguity of Orlando's policy was still unresolved.

Orlando was successful in overcoming the earlier interventionist suspicions of his conciliatory approach. However he had to pay the price of a partial retreat from his earlier tolerance of the Socialists.

His government was persuaded by interventionist clamour to take severe measures against the Socialist leaders. Both the editor of *Avanti!*, Serrati, and the party secretary, Lazzari, were given prison sentences and as a result the angry seclusion of the party became even more complete. Turati tried in his parliamentary speeches to efface the image of Socialist defeatism: he declared that with the Austrians on the River Piave, the defence of national independence was a duty even for Socialists. However his attitude to the war was repudiated by the party, and with it his attempts to provide a platform for the postwar reconciliation and co-operation of Socialists and Democrats. The change in the character of Socialist aims in the last years of the war can be shown by a comparison between the programme of 8 May

1917 'for the peace and for the postwar period', which still envisaged a democratic and republican revolution with a strong reformist accent on immediate and concrete social claims, and that adopted by the party *direzione* in December 1918. This programme, whose character was basically determined by the decisions of the Rome party congress (September 1918), accepted no solution short of the dictatorship of the proletariat; the proposal to call a constituent assembly was written off as 'a bourgeois demand'. With this decision, the Socialists closed the door on the possibility of a *rapprochement* with the democrats.[72]

The Postwar Crisis

Victory and peace did not put an end to the permanent state of crisis in Italian government and society. On the contrary, the divisions which had been partially suppressed during the war now made themselves felt with full force. Existing leaders and institutions had to cope with a crisis of legitimacy, with the general breakdown of old loyalties and identification with the Liberal regime,[73] and with a widespread refusal of law and the rules indispensable for the survival of a political community. Some kind of dramatic change was inevitable; the conflicting and confused aspirations of the masses of workers, peasants and ex-combatants, of ex-officers and intellectuals, were at one in their demand for some kind of new order. Even official spokesmen promised sweeping changes.[74]

The sense of pride which many Italians undoubtedly felt at the result of the war soon turned sour. The rebuff to Italy's claims at the Peace Conference were magnified by Nationalist propaganda into the myth of the 'mutilated victory':[75] Italy acquired the psychology of a defeated nation. The main responsibility for this lay with Orlando and Sonnino, who, deaf to the warnings of Bissolati, failed to take account of the well-advertised determination of Wilson to defend the rights of nationality. They replied to Wilson's ill-judged attempt to appeal over their heads to Italian public opinion by walking out of the Versailles conference.[76] This gesture was not only futile on the international level, but whipped up excitement inside Italy to a new pitch, and in consequence greatly increased the final disillusionment with the peace. The bitter resentment in Italy against the attitude of her richer and more powerful allies was admittedly understandable and far from wholly unjustified. Their support for national rights in the Adriatic region was at variance with the high-handed way in which German minorities were treated.

This inconsistency gave new plausibility to the interpretation, shared by the Nationalists on the right and the admirers of Lenin on the left, which saw the war as a struggle between rival imperialisms, and the slogans of national self-determination and the defence of democracy as mere camouflage. Public opinion turned against the Liberal ruling class, pilloried by the left as warmongers and by the right as silly humanitarians, too inhibited and indecisive to secure their share in the spoils; but the greatest sufferers of all were the democratic interventionists. The Nationalists and their allies, including a great part of the Press, had been quick to insinuate that Bissolati, Salvemini and their friends were endangering the fruits of victory by their remissive attitude : they were blamed for the diplomatic reverses which they alone had foreseen. Branded as '*Rinunciatari*', only second to the treacherous 'Bolsheviks' in their responsibility for the mutilated victory, the leaders of the Democratic interventionists were deserted by most of their followers, and found themselves generals without an army. For the majority of the Socialists, this only confirmed the validity of their own intransigence ; they viewed the defeat of Bissolati and his friends with a certain *Schadenfreude*.

The Adriatic question served as a rallying point not only for the Nationalists, but for the new 'patriotic' groups of which Mussolini and the *fasci* were the most conspicuous. Here was an issue on which the protests of the 'dynamic minorities', accustomed to action in the piazza, would meet with the sympathy of most of bourgeois public opinion ; even the democrats were moved by the fate of Fiume, with its Italian majority. Orlando was succeeded in June 1919 by Francesco Nitti. At home, Nitti stood for the revival of effective parliamentary government and a return to peacetime conditions ; consistently with this he aimed at a reconciliation with the Giolittians and the burial of wartime feuds. His foreign policy, unfortunately, did not altogether make it easier for him to achieve these sensible objectives. Nitti feared that if Italy continued to refuse agreement on the Adriatic question, America and England would withdraw their financial aid and cut off coal supplies, thus causing a total economic collapse which would probably lead to revolution. To avert this terrible danger he was prepared to play down Italy's claims. Nitti went too far in his reaction against the emotional superficiality of Orlando. He appeared to admit defeat too easily ; and the 'realistic' economic arguments by which he tried to justify his policies only acted as an irritant which further inflamed patriotic sentiment.[77] This made him more vulnerable to the attacks of the Nationalists, Mussolini and other enemies of democracy.

The Italian army had no record of active intervention in politics. But the war had brought great changes in its composition, and still more in its prestige and importance. The increasingly active involvement of the Army in politics after Caporetto has already been mentioned. After the armistice, the Army commands and their propaganda services continued to pursue a policy of their own in the newly occupied territories of Dalmatia, Fiume and Venezia Giulia. Their initiatives, however, had been encouraged and sanctioned by Orlando and Sonnino. On 3 December 1918 the Prime Minister and the Foreign Secretary, with the Commander-in-Chief, Diaz, had approved a memorandum drawn up by General Badoglio which called for the subversion and destruction of the new Yugoslav state by 'all possible means'. This was a charter for the activity of the Army and Navy in 'creating' public opinion in Dalmatia, 'suggesting' the organization of pro-Italian rallies, and suppressing Slav demonstrations.[78]

The higher ranks of the services had a strong material interest in creating a state of tension on the borders which would justify the maintenance of a swollen military establishment. At the end of the war there were 1246 generals, compared with 142 at the outset, and the generals' fear of redundancy powerfully reinforced their nationalism.[79] The Orlando government appeased the military by keeping the Army practically on a wartime footing : in June 1919 there were still a million and a half men under arms. Nitti was known to favour rapid demobilization and a drastic reduction in military expenditure. A number of generals, among them the King's cousin, the Duke of Aosta, seem to have been actively involved in planning some kind of a *pronunciamento* designed to prevent his succession to Orlando.[80] Although these plots came to nothing, it remained true that neither the Army nor the Navy could be relied upon to obey orders. The trouble was not confined to the high commands : the junior officers were perhaps even more susceptible to right-wing subversion.

The reduction of the Italian garrison in Fiume was the spark which set off the train of powder carefully laid by the Nationalists. The Man of Providence was at hand in the shape of Gabriele D'Annunzio, now a war hero as well as poet. On 12 September 1919 he entered Fiume at the head of two thousand mutinous troops. Nitti, who had counted on the Army to stop him, received a rude shock. However the occupation of Fiume did not lead to the results hoped for by D'Annunzio and his backers ; it failed to bring about a general military sedition, or even the fall of Nitti. During 1920 the astute policy of Giolitti and Sforza, who used the enterprise as a lever to extract concessions from Yugoslavia, was successful in destroying D'Annunzio's political platform. But the Fiume adventure nonetheless had very serious results. It undermined the authority of the State, which was forced to tolerate and bargain with rebellious officers and adventurers on equal terms.[81] The mythology of the Nationalist right was powerfully reinforced ; to many young Italians, D'Annunzio's enterprise seemed to revive the glories of Garibaldi and the 'volunteer tradition'.

No less serious, in creating the impression of the impotence of parliamentary government and the unworkability of democracy, was the advance of *massimalismo*. The largely unco-ordinated spread of popular disorder and violence during 1919 was in large part a result of the rapid inflation, and of the problems of demobilization, aggravated by the absolutely inadequate economic policy of the Orlando ministry. It aroused fears that the revolution invoked so confidently might really be at hand. In these circumstances, the Government and the public authorities were grateful to receive the help of the *fasci*, and of other groups who organized themselves for direct action against the Socialists.[82]

In the face of these threats from right and left, all attempts to create a new order in society and state which would satisfy the aspirations and appease the discontents aroused by the war were doomed to failure. Nitti failed both in his dramatic appeal to the 'workers and peasants' to support him against D'Annunzio and militarism, and in his endeavours to re-create the old Giolittian working relationship with the reformist parliamentary leaders. His experience showed the difficulty of pursuing even a moderately progressive policy in the face of Socialist hostility, which deprived the Government of mass support. The only part of the 'democratic revolution' which he carried through was electoral reform; but the introduction of proportional representation and the abstention of the Government from interference in the elections, although they marked the acceptance of the need for a more sincere approach, had some unfortunate consequences. In the elections of November 1919 the Socialists (156) and the Popolari (100) between them won half the seats in Parliament. The disappearance of the old methods and mechanisms for forming a Government majority made necessary the formal negotiation of coalitions : but in a period of stress and crisis, the new mentality needed to make this system of government workable was lacking, and Parliament reflected all too faithfully the divisions and uncertainties of the nation. Nitti did not seem to foresee the results of his innovations, or to realize what was required in the new situation. He extended his doctrine of non-interference to the point of passivity; his programme was too timid to make an impact, and in his relationship with the PPI he showed himself slow to appreciate the changed and more binding nature of political alliances.[83] Nitti, with his wide knowledge of Europe and America, his financial and economic expertise, and his genuine democratic sympathies, apparently had the best claims of any politician to be considered the 'new man' needed to restore confidence in the Liberal ruling class; but he revealed himself too much a prisoner of their traditional limitations and assumptions. For all his modernity he was nonetheless a man of the South, 'formed in a backward social environment, totally deprived of organized parties or . . . an advanced working-class' :[84] consequently he still practised a style of politics which was based on personalities, not parties, and which did not succeed in establishing a direct relationship with the nation. His attitude to the postwar crisis was rather like that of certain Enlightenment philosophers faced by the French Revolution; his reasonable economist's vision was not one to excite enthusiasm, nor did it permit him a real understanding of the magnitude of the upheaval. His autobiographical *Revelations*, written in later life, are full of exclamations at the 'follies' and 'absurdity' of the postwar political scene; Nitti never quite ceased to expect that other men would be as matter-of-fact, logical and moderate as himself.[85]

Gaetano Salvemini and other Democrats had hoped that the war would produce a new, reformed governing class. They now experienced bitter disillusionment at the return of Giolitti. The truth was, however, that the old man was the only authoritative politician to put forward a political and economic programme which really held out some hope of appeasing popular unrest.

Giolitti was aware, unlike Nitti, of the need to take the initiative; he saw that in the postwar crisis Liberal government had to be active to survive,[86] and in spite of his reputation of waiting on events, he showed that he was capable of energy and decision. However Giolitti found it easier to revise his objectives than his art of government. It was inevitable that the 'old magician', for all his capacity to understand some aspects of the new situation, should in other ways have remained firmly attached to the tried methods of the period of his greatest success. Giolitti was still less able than Nitti to reconcile himself to the new regime of proportional representation, the mass parties and the parliamentary groups. Without doubt much of Giolitti's criticism of the workings of the new parliamentary system, and of the conduct of the two mass parties, was valid : but, since he was no longer strong enough to confine the political struggle within its old boundaries, since he could not change the rules, his suspicion and dislike of these decisive innovations in the political structure only added one more element of rigidity to the situation. The old and the new politics clashed most decisively and disastrously in the persons of Giolitti and the Sicilian priest Don Sturzo, the secretary of the PPI. To the former, it was already an absurdity for a party secretary who was not a Member of Parliament to dictate its policy;[87] that the secretary was also a priest was, to a man of Giolitti's generation, an outright monstrosity. Sturzo on his side cordially returned the hostility ; as a Sicilian, he had seen the workings of the pre-war system at their most corrupt, and the chief obstacle to his efforts to create a strong Democratic Catholic party was represented by the clerico-moderate tradition which Giolitti had favoured and exploited.

The dilemma of Sturzo was a cruel one ; to prevent the fragmentation of his party into a multitude of local ecclesiastical pressure groups, and to hold together conflicting political and social tendencies, he was driven to put his trust in centralized organization and in a notable degree of intransigence in negotiation.[88] Since Turati and the reformist leaders resisted Giolitti's overtures, as they had Nitti's, and until it was too late refused to break the unity of the Socialist party, all coalitions until the March on Rome needed the participation of the PPI in order to survive. The party was inexperienced and consequently hesitant to accept responsibility, as was shown by the refusal of Meda to try to form a government after the fall of Nitti, and again in 1922.[89]

Unwilling to govern, the Popolari were reluctant to follow. Their co-operation with the various postwar ministries was hedged around by so many conditions and reservations that they helped to bring about the paralysis of parliamentary government. However the old 'government parties' which accused the Popolari of bringing politics to a standstill were themselves not free from responsibility.

The constitutional parties (which together still controlled just under half the seats in Parliament) were divided by old rancours and new rivalries, often of crippling intensity. The war had, of course, created the deepest rift, that between neutralists and interventionists; it had converted the long-standing disagreement between Giolitti and Salandra into active hatred. However the bitter quarrel between Giolitti and Nitti was largely of postwar origin. Whereas the first of these feuds at least corresponded to a profound difference in political outlook, the latter was the product of personal and financial rivalries, which exploded after Giolitti's return to the Government in June 1920.[90] It was thus far more serious in its effects, since it divided the most progressive and democratic of the constitutionalist forces. Proportional representation tended to crystallize and prolong these antagonisms, and to create artificial and superfluous groupings in Parliament; the old clienteles of the South did not lose their importance, but became more independent of the Government and therefore more troublesome.[91]

The instability of governments and the delays in legislation allowed the bureaucracy to hold on to the new power which it had acquired during the war; the habit of passing important legislation by decree, which could be excused in wartime as a temporary expedient, now appeared as a proof of the impotence of parliamentary government, and a surrender to the allied forces of officialdom and the great pressure groups.[92] The return of Giolitti had seemed to many like a promise of the restoration of pre-war standards of security and order, but this restoration proved to be a mirage which receded as he advanced. The conviction grew that the failings of the political system could only be remedied by a period of authoritarian government; the inconclusiveness, as well as the violence, of the political struggle created the foundations for the acceptance of dictatorship.

The crisis in the state machine and in Parliament was accompanied by a crisis in law and order and by the growth of private political violence. On the left, this took the traditional forms of intimidation, connected with strikes, of riots and protests in the piazza. But as early as May 1919, the burning of the *Avanti!* offices showed that the small groups of ex-officers and shock troops had a decisive advantage over the Socialists in the politics of violence.

However during 1919 the activities of Fascist or Nationalist squads remained sporadic and usually marginal in their immediate political effects. It was D'Annunzio in the Fiume adventure who first succeeded in creating a new technique for the evocation of irrational hatreds and loyalties. 'The occupation of Fiume . . . will furnish Fascism with the model for its militia and its uniforms, the names for its squads, its war-cry and its liturgy. Mussolini will copy from D'Annunzio the whole of his stage scenery, including the dialogues with the crowd . . . D'Annunzio will be the victim of the greatest piece of plagiarism ever seen.'[93]

If Mussolini was able to copy D'Annunzio successfully, this was not only

35

due to his exceptional ability to assimilate all ideas and techniques, but also because in his formative period, as a Socialist, he had already come under the fascination of Nietzsche, of Sorel and of the individualist anarchist, Max Stirner. Culture reinforced temperament; the personality of Mussolini was decisive for the course and fortunes of the Fascist movement. Even before the war, he had shown a formidable ability to make his own way. The son of a blacksmith and a schoolmistress, from the revolutionary Romagna, by the age of thirty he had become the editor of *Avanti!*, one of the leading positions in the Socialist party. Mussolini had found his vocation with some difficulty. As a child, he seems to have been difficult, lonely and aggressive. His schoolteacher mother sent him to a strongly Catholic school when he was nine; he was expelled for violence to another pupil. It is not unreasonable to suppose that his life-long contempt for morality and religion, his individualism and dislike of being tied down, owe something to this traumatic experience. He identified from boyhood on with his father's populist, anarchic, Socialism: the paternal image sanctioned his extraordinary insufferance of all forms of discipline, his jealous preservation of a rebel's autonomy against all attempts to socialize or tame. Outside politics, no opening offered itself to him except the career of an elementary schoolteacher: he knew all the desperation of the fitfully employed intellectual, with aspirations and talents apparently too great for his opportunities, unused to manual labour but only precariously able to avoid it. Politics, more specifically political journalism, solved all this and gave him for the first time a sure sense of his own identity. After adventurous experiences in Switzerland and the Trentino, he had the fortune to get his first good job, as editor of the Forlì newspaper *Lotta di Classe*, at a moment when the social situation of the Romagna was becoming particularly explosive, and on the eve of the political crisis caused by the Libyan war. He exploited this opportunity with Machiavellian *virtù* to become the leader of revolutionary socialism.[94]

Even before the war small groups of syndicalist intellectuals had found common ground with the Nationalists, and had attempted to elaborate a form of 'national socialism': but such attempts only acquired political significance during the intervention crisis, when Mussolini, with his personal entourage of revolutionaries, joined syndicalists like Michele Bianchi, Corridoni and De Ambris in the *fasci di azione rivoluzionaria*. His conversion to the war owed something to the realization that revolutionary socialism had reached an impasse, and something to his sympathy for France. With the aid of funds gathered from a variety of sources, Italian and foreign, he founded a newspaper, the *Popolo d'Italia*, which was both the centre of 'revolutionary interventionism' and his own personal instrument of propaganda. At the end of the war, it was the newspaper which gave him the platform he needed for his political recovery.[95]

The occupation of the factories in September 1920 was the watershed between the revolutionary and the reactionary phases of the postwar crisis.[96] The failure to make the movement into a revolution demonstrated the inadequacies of *massimalismo* : the arguments of Bordiga and Gramsci for the acceptance of the decisions of the Third International, and for a small, homogeneous party on the Bolshevik model, acquired a new cogency. The task and *raison d'être* of the new Communist party was to be the organization of revolution ; but during the period of its gestation the terms of the political and class conflict were profoundly altered. The international conjuncture, first of all, was unfavourable : September 1920 marked the end of the revolutionary wave not only in Italy but in Europe, with the defeat of the Red Army before Warsaw.[97] In Italy, the occupation of the factories ended in a technical victory, but for the Socialists it was a psychological defeat. The onset of depression and severe unemployment reinforced the decline of revolutionary enthusiasm. In these circumstances, the rigid Communist programme could attract the support of only a minority of the party and a very small fraction of the Socialist electorate. In the unions, the Communists were at first even weaker. Consequently their secession at the Congress of Livorno in January 1921 in the short term only contributed to the demoralization of the working-class movement.

The Fascists did not, as they later claimed, destroy the menace of revolution in Italy. During the occupation of the factories Mussolini, so far from heading resistance, tried to offer his services as a mediator.[98] Once the menace was past, however, the Fascists were able to profit from the fear and indignation of bourgeois opinion. The industrialists blamed the Government's weakness for destroying business confidence, but the decisive impulse to reaction came from the agrarians.

In the agricultural provinces of Emilia and the Po Valley even before the war the spokesmen of the *agrari* had denounced the existence of a 'State within the State', constituted by the Socialist leagues. The latter owed their strength to the mass of under-employed day labourers, but they had succeeded in extending their influence also over many of the *mezzadri* (share-croppers) and small tenants. In 1919–20, a wave of agricultural strikes swept through not only the Po Valley, but the previously quieter hill regions of the Veneto, Umbria and Tuscany, where *mezzadria* or leasehold tenancies were more common than wage labour. The Catholic trade unions as well as the Socialists took a leading part in this movement.[99] The agrarians complained vociferously about the lack of Government protection. They started to talk openly of organizing their own defence, and it was natural that they should turn for help to the *fasci*, as the most aggressive of the anti-Socialist groups. In the autumn of 1920, after the occupation of the factories, new local elections were held. In several big cities, like Florence and Turin, anti-Socialist coalitions were successful (a fact which showed a decline in support for the Socialists since 1919) ; but the Socialists won many new victories in provincial capitals and smaller communes. Both the 'capitals of Fascism',

Bologna and Milan, had been governed by Socialist administrations since 1914, and local government in several provinces had passed entirely into their hands. Local Socialist power united the discontents of the middle-class and the interests of the rich. In the provincial cities, the old professional classes who had provided their governing elite saw their defeat as the submersion of the civilized, 'historic' city by the only recently and imperfectly urbanized suburbs; the town councils possessed important powers of taxation, and often controlled savings and agricultural credit banks. The flourishing co-operative movement, and the practice of municipal ownership and purchase, were an obvious target for the hostility of small shopkeepers and traders.[100]

The winter and spring of 1920-1 was the decisive period of Fascist expansion. The Fascist *squadristi* conducted a systematic campaign of terror against the Socialists and their local institutions (communal councils, party branches, trade unions, co-operatives and even cultural circles). The reaction spread through the whole of the Po Valley, and with even greater ferocity throughout most of Tuscany, Umbria and Apulia.

The Fascist movement was welcomed by the great majority of the Liberal press as a sign of the revival of the bourgeoisie. It was not, at this time, a 'party', and it welcomed members from other organizations – Republican, Liberal or Catholic – without forcing them to abandon formally their old allegiances. This composite character, together with its elementary and brutal tactics and ideological confusion, encouraged the belief that the movement was a temporary phenomenon, and that it could be absorbed by the old order. The tactical ability of Mussolini enabled him to exploit this belief, and to profit fully from the mistakes of the Socialists. Giolitti, by conceding workers' participation in the control of factory management, had hoped to provide a platform for the collaboration of Turati, the reformists and the unions with his government. In the immediate aftermath of the occupation of the factories, when even conservatives like Albertini were so shaken in their confidence that they believed that surrendering power to the CGL might be the only alternative to revolution,[101] collaboration could have been achieved on the best possible terms for the reformist Socialists : but fears of the inevitable accusations of betrayal, and of having to bear the responsibility for the unpopular measures of economic reconstruction which could be seen to be necessary, held them back. The Socialists ought to have seen the dangers inherent in the bourgeoisie's recovery of confidence at the end of 1920, but they allowed their power to ebb without taking any positive action.

The Congress of Livorno, which split the party 'to the left', with the formation of the PCI, but kept *massimalisti* and reformists united, did not fulfil Giolitti's hopes. The economic and financial situation was very important in adding to Giolitti's resentment against the unco-operative attitude of the Socialists. In order to check inflation, Giolitti had to end the bread subsidy (the issue had already brought down Nitti's government), and the Socialists used obstructive tactics in Parliament in an unsuccessful attempt to block its abolition. The failure of Giolitti's 'opening to the left' determined him to take the fatal step of calling new elections; he hoped to be able to control and use Fascism, and with its help to bring the Socialists to reason.[102]

The Fascist movement could not have won such rapid victories without help from both the Army and the civil authorities. The growth of the *fasci* in 1920–1 was powerfully assisted and sometimes even initiated by the regular Army. The mutiny at Ancona in June 1920 must have awakened doubts about the reliability of the troops if they were used to suppress internal disorders; the occupation of the factories in September greatly intensified the fear of revolution. This helps to explain why at this time the General Staff issued a circular recommending support of the *fasci*; although the War Minister, Bonomi, officially discouraged this initiative, his action was much too half-hearted to be really effective.[103] The higher ranks of the Army continued to view the Fascist movement with 'cautious benevolence'; at the least, they left a free rein to the 'active sympathy and co-operation' afforded by the great majority of the regimental officers.[104] The younger officers had been encouraged by the attitude of many of their superiors to consider the ties of discipline as no longer binding when they conflicted with the cause of patriotism. The anti-militarist propaganda of the Socialists, the frequent incidents in which working-class groups attacked officers on leave, and the report of the commission of inquiry on Caporetto, seen as an attempt by the parliamentary class to appease the neutralists and conceal its own failings at the expense of the Army's reputation, all inflamed their grievances. The majority of the younger officers were reservists, soon to be demobilized, who could not be expected to take the detached view of civilian politics formerly typical of the career soldier: this was especially true in the case of those who had been set free to complete their university education, while remaining technically in active service.[105]

Some of the military leaders, it is true, at first viewed this collaboration and the spectacular progress of Fascism with mixed feelings: although sympathetic to Fascist aims, they were anxious that the reputation of the Army for political neutrality should be restored.[106]

However the failure of parliamentary government to restore order, to create conditions in which the Army could once more safely attend to the business of external defence without worrying about internal politics, and the vacillation of successive governments over the question of military reorganization, helped to destroy these uncertainties. By the summer of 1922, the military elite, like other elites, no longer concealed its sympathies for Fascism. The main responsibility for this, even when the self-interest and the Nationalist preconceptions of the soldiers have been recognized, must rest with the political class. They were neither able to re-impose a strict discipline, nor to evolve a policy which would successfully conciliate both the material interests and the sentiments of the officers. They thus encouraged the Army, as a leading military commentator put it, to 'fend for itself'; and to regard the democratic parliamentary order as irrevocably hostile to its aspirations and even to its existence.[107]

The Fascist movement received vital assistance not only from the Army, but from civilian authorities as well. The question of collusion is here more complex. It seems clear that, as in the Army, it was at the lower levels of the hierarchy that the strongest impulse towards collaboration was felt. The ordinary policeman or *carabiniere* (in this, similar to the officer but different from the conscript recruit) could hardly fail to sympathize with the Fascists after he had been exposed for two years to the constant harassment, insults and often violence, of the extreme left. In these circumstances even the Prefects were often virtually powerless to prevent the forces nominally under their control from acting with gross partiality.[108] However in considering the attitude of the Government and the Prefects, a distinction has to be made. It is true that even during the elections of 1921 the Government repeatedly ordered the Prefects to repress Fascist violence: however it was a part of Italian official tradition to allow a pretty free hand to the friends of the ministry, and by calling elections and allowing the Fascists to join national blocs under Government patronage Giolitti robbed his own instructions of credibility.[109] The prefectoral system, as already described, since it required the Prefects to act on their discretion, and politically, rather than taking purely administrative decisions according to precedent and regulation, could not easily be 'neutral' and was extremely sensitive to changes in the political climate. Thus, ironically, it was possible both for *agrari* and industrialists in the summer of 1920 to see in the systematic appeasement of the Socialists by the Prefects, at the expense of property rights, the main reason which necessitated 'self-defence' through the financing of the *fasci*, and for some of the same Prefects to be justly accused of conniving at the violence of the *squadristi* in 1921–2. The character of the system also made the lack of stable government after the fall of Giolitti peculiarly disastrous. Increasingly the Prefects were made to feel that in obeying Government instructions to act against the Fascists they were endangering their own careers, since it was very likely that under pressure the Government would modify or revoke its own measures. The same factors affected the attitude of the magistrates; but here, perhaps, given the relatively greater degree of independence from the Government, the role of spontaneous class prejudice was more important than in the case of the Prefects. The law, applied with rigid severity against left-wing offenders, was usually benevolent and dilatory in dealing with Fascist crimes.[110]

This attitude of the organs of government and justice, compounded equally of partiality and fear, allowed the Fascists to bring about the piecemeal disintegration of the Liberal State. By perpetuating the climate of civil war, they themselves helped to heighten the yearning for authority, order and an end to perpetual crisis, which was to allow Mussolini to present himself as the saviour of the nation.

3

THE RISE OF THE FASCIST MOVEMENT

The Anti-Party

Unlike 'conservatism', 'communism' or even 'national-socialism', the word 'Fascism' offers no immediate statement of aims or principles.[1] It was a commonplace of Fascist writing that the movement precedes the doctrine, and not vice versa.[2] In a real sense, this was true. The *fasci di combattimento* were in origin an attempt to preserve the political heritage of the *fasci di azione rivoluzionaria*,[3] who had themselves been a loose grouping of men coming from different parties brought together by their advocacy of Italy's entry into the war.[4] It was, therefore, to an event – the war – and the reaction to it – interventionism – that Fascism traced its pedigree, not to any previously formed body of doctrine, social philosophy or economic interest.

The members of the interventionist *fasci*, as their name indicated, thought of themselves as revolutionaries. The revolutionary syndicalists were the original nucleus of the movement, who set the ideological tone. The salient characteristic of the 1915 *fasci*, other than interventionism, was the belief that they, the elite, the 'dynamic minority', were the true revolutionaries, distinguished by their idealism and activism from the mass of voters or followers. When this concept of revolution was cut loose from its Marxist context, from an intellectual belief in a generally predetermined course of history and a moral belief in the egalitarian ends of socialism, it could become the creed of a group devoted essentially to the pure aim of seizing power by violence.[5]

The possibility of such a development was already latent in Mussolini's socialism. The tendency to speak of an absolute dichotomy between ideals and interests, the challenging assertion that socialism was not a 'theorem' but a 'faith', that 'Illusion is perhaps the only reality in life', showed an extreme subjectivism which clearly distinguishes his concept of the revolutionary advance-guard from Lenin's, with which it has sometimes been compared.[6] There is some continuity between the revolutionary's contempt for the average trade unionist as 'a petty-bourgeois who only obeys the voice of interest, deaf to the call of the ideal', and the Fascist's contrast between the spirit of sacrifice shown in the trenches and the egoistic materialism of the factory workers.[7] The link between the two was in the concept of the revolutionary war, in which the true 'people' showed their worth against both the false proletariat of the Socialists and the cowardly bourgeoisie. This concept suffered a metamorphosis between 1915 and 1919; from the idea of revolution *through* war, it changed into the idea of revolution *as* war.

The revolutionary interventionists had seen one truth with clarity; that war was more likely than peace to create the conditions for a revolution. The war, they saw, would create such an upheaval in society as to be itself revolutionary. It would 'force the radical revision of all parties and philosophies, breaking down all established habits of mind'.[8] It was true, too, that the participation of the masses in the war would make them more effective as combatants in the social revolution. However someone who actively supported entry into the war could hardly stand back and, like Lenin, reap the profit from its effects by a policy of 'revolutionary defeatism'. The interventionists' war had to have a moral as well as a theoretical justification. This could be found, as for the Democrats, in the belief that the victory of Germany and Austria would mean the triumph of the reaction in Europe. There remained, however, the contradiction that if the war was to be won, there must be a truce in the battle against the State, which must instead be strengthened and made more efficient, if only temporarily. To face this dilemma openly required an unusual degree of patience and moral courage; it was tempting to evade it. Originally, for most of the revolutionary interventionists, patriotism and socialism had been distinct principles, united only in a contingent and temporary alliance; the intervention was not intended as a substitute for revolution. But in the heat of battle, and under the pressure of Socialist hostility, the two principles became confused. The myth that the action of a resolute minority had imposed entry into the war on a reluctant and in part treacherous governing class, could be used to justify the claim that the events of May 1915 already constituted the first stage in a kind of 'permanent revolution'.[9] For the revolutionary interventionists of 1919, the famous saying of Clausewitz, 'war is a continuation of politics by other means', needed to be reversed. The 'revolution' was to be a continuation of the war. This posture was ambivalent. It could mean support for the social aspirations which the war had, genuinely, quickened among the ex-combatants as among the industrial workers; it could also mean the prolongation into peace of the atmosphere of the 'home front', and the use of violence against the 'reactionary' forces of neutralism. The isolation of the revolutionary interventionists, the failure of their ideas of a 'national socialism' to make much impression on the working-class and peasantry, and the menacing advance of Bolshevism all made for an increasing emphasis on the latter alternative.

The *fasci di combattimento* at the time of their foundation lacked both ideological cohesion and numbers. Mussolini, by his conception and presentation of the movement, converted both these weaknesses into essential elements of his propaganda. At the end of the war he had immediately perceived how he could turn his own uncertainty and isolation to profit, by elevating them into a conscious theory of opportunism. 'I sought the pulse of the crowd and I understood how, in the midst of the general disorientation, there was a public for me.'[10] As De Ambris and the early interventionists had predicted, the war had indeed brought a breakdown in many established 'habits of mind' and principles, and it was to those who had been ideologically disorientated or socially uprooted by war that Mussolini made his primary appeal, through the slogan of the 'anti-party' which would be hostile to all 'credos' and 'dogmas'.[11] This was designed both to preserve the tradition of the first interventionist *fasci* and to capture the mood of postwar discontent and undirected revolt. It was to be the vehicle for the protest of the new forces thrown up by the war against the constraint of rules, organizations and bureaucracies ; it was to express an impatience with formed systems of doctrine and principles, all condemned as equally obsolete. A flexible structure would allow the maximum liberty to the individual members : 'Statutes, regulations, etc., all that is party stuff.'[12] The 'anti-party' could be reconciled both with elitist disdain for the 'numbered flock' of the mass parties, and with the attempt to play on democratic resentments against the entrenched power of the party oligarchies. Socialism was subtly identified with established religion ; the Fascists were the 'heretics'. In this way the iconoclastic, anti-clerical and rebellious heritage of the historic Risorgimento left, as well as the new nihilism, could be mobilized against the peril of 'red clericalism'.[13] The contrast between 'movement' and 'party' also served to justify an attitude of extreme flexibility which allowed Mussolini to make whatever tactical adjustments he felt necessary, and it had the important practical advantage of assisting the assimilation of new members. The opposition was stated with the greatest clarity in Mussolini's famous speech of March 1921 : 'Fascism is not a Church. It is more like a training ground. It is not a party. It is a movement. . . . We are the heretics of all the Churches. We can permit ourselves the luxury of being both aristocrats and democrats'.[14] It was not until the middle of 1921, when the movement had swelled to vast proportions, that the disadvantages revealed themselves and the old concept had to be modified to allow the constitution of a 'party'.

It was a corollary of the spirit in which the *fasci* had been conceived that their *programme* should be treated as provisional and not binding. All politicians have to depart from their programmes to meet the necessities of the moment ; but not all recognize with conscious foresight that it is their intention to do so. Hannah Arendt observes that, in this sense, 'The first to consider programmes and platforms as needless scraps of paper and embarrassing promises, inconsistent with the style and impetus of a movement, was Mussolini. . . .'[15] The founding rally of the *fasci* on 23 March 1919 in Piazza S. Sepolcro did not formally adopt a programme; the so-called 'programme' of Piazza S. Sepolcro was not in fact formulated until June 1919. At the rally Mussolini announced his adoption of the programme of another organization, the interventionists' Unione Italiana del Lavoro, but this adoption was phrased in very generic terms, and did not really commit him or the *fasci* to approval of its specific points.[16]

In 1919 Mussolini still partially disguised the true nature of his 'practical relativism'; there was an attempt to present the *fasci* as a movement which stood for the pragmatic pursuit of immediate reforms, without reference to abstract ideological goals.[17] This was in keeping with the overtures which Mussolini was making to the 'realists' on the right of the Socialist party and the trade unionists, with the aim of an electoral alliance including the Republicans and the Social Reformists. But this was a temporary phase which little suited Mussolini's temperament or the aggressive, 'combatant' nature of his following, orientated to action rather than discussion, lacking the technical skills or the mass support necessary to impose a serious programme of reforms. The first Fascist programme contained radical demands: the financial proposals called for a progressive tax on capital, the confiscation of all property belonging to the religious congregations, and of 85 per cent of war profits. But at the Florence Congress in October, Michele Bianchi hinted broadly at the true nature of Fascist 'problemism' : 'The modern part of the Italian bourgeoisie . . . can adopt even this part [social and financial] of the programme of the *fasci*; all the more when the reflection is made that as the *fasci* are an organization without ready-made doctrines, problems are faced by them not in series but according to whether the moment is ripe.'[18]

The electoral defeat suffered by the *fasci* in November 1919 brought with it the danger of the total dissolution of the movement. Organization and morale were both at a low ebb. The imperative need for funds, which in this situation could alone ensure survival, increased the dependence of Mussolini on his financial backers. The electoral failure in itself suggested the lesson that it was from the right that the movement could, for the time being, most easily acquire an enlarged public. Important, too, was the general change of mood in the country; in 1919 the hopes and the promises of war were still so dominant that even the Nationalists and some industrialists were prepared to give verbal support to claims which they would later dismiss as demagogy. The mood of 1920 on the right and among the industrialists was already more resistant. The rightward swing of Fascism must be seen in relation to all these factors. It was accompanied by the exodus of the 'left', and was reflected in modifications of the original programme. Between February and August 1920, the changes were above all evident on the points which

45

regarded industry and labour relations. The references to social legislation remained, but with a studied vagueness : the concrete references to the minimum wage and the eight-hour day disappeared. Workers' representation, previously admitted for the 'technical functioning of industry', was now explicitly to be limited to 'personnel questions'.[19] The Fascist programme and much of their ideology had an instrumental character. They were tools for winning support. Fascist ideology, which can be easily written off as a tissue of inconsistencies if one analyses it for formal doctrinal content, reveals its meaning if one looks at it in terms of the various social groups to whom it appealed. It was marked by an 'eclectic functionalism'.[20] At the same time, one should not assume that all the leaders and propagandists of the movement were simply cynical manipulators of opinion. Very often they shared the passions and preconceptions of their publics.

One must start, therefore, by an analysis of the restricted groups which formed the movement during 1919–20. These were mostly made up of 'marginal men', adventurers and ex-revolutionaries. Just as the disorientated became 'heretics', so the isolated became an 'elite'. In both cases, propaganda transformed a weakness into a source of psychological satisfaction and high morale. The very insignificance of the early Fascist movement in terms of numbers and social backing fostered an elite consciousness. The small 'elites' of 1919–20 were the detonator which set off the mass movement of 1921.

The 'Fascists of the first Hour'

The revolutionary syndicalists, together with the Socialists who had left the party with Mussolini, formed the hard professional core of the new movement of 1919. They were the only group with real political experience, and their knowledge of revolutionary techniques of agitation and organization was invaluable. Amid the changes and upheavals of the movement between 1919–22, three men preserved a certain continuity in the central leadership of the *fasci* : Cesare Rossi, Giovanni Marinelli and Michele Bianchi. Rossi and Marinelli were Mussolini's two most faithful henchmen, and Marinelli also controlled the movement's funds. Michele Bianchi, secretary of the party from 1921–2, had a more independent position. It was Bianchi who, in 1919, stood out most strongly for an 'anti-demagogic' policy and for alliance with the right as well as the left of the interventionist and patriotic forces.[21] The two political secretaries of the movement who preceded Bianchi, Longoni and Pasella, were also syndicalists ; the last was the chief organizer during the critical period of 1920–1. The syndicalists were the 'professionals' of Fascism, and such structure as the movement ever possessed was largely their work. A study of the *Sansepolcristi* (as the men who attended the rally of 23 March were called) reveals the presence of an important group of working-class syndicalists. They can be characterized as an upwardly mobile 'elite', seeking social promotion through the trade unions and the Socialist party, and also through self-help, artisan enterprise and war service. The characteristics of 'national syndicalism', with its stress on quality versus quantity, and on the 'necessary hierarchies' of the working class, reflect the experience of this group. In military terms they represented the NCO type, and were often active *squadristi*; contrary to what one might think, these working-class recruits did not tend to fade out during the later history of the movement. However they were almost entirely confined to Milan and one or two other industrial centres, in Liguria, Piombino, etc.[22]

All attempts to expand the working-class base of the movement during 1919–20 were fruitless. The elections of November 1919 made this failure evident, and Cesare Rossi at the Second Fascist Congress drew the conclusions with brutal clarity. Results had shown that the proletariat and socialism were 'an inseparable whole': therefore it was useless to talk of opposing the one but not the other. It followed, also, from the extremist attitude of the masses that the idea of action for a republic must be given up, as the movement would not stop with democracy but lead to communism, and that the *fasci* must therefore defend the present regime. This clarity did not please all sections of the movement.[23]

Mussolini on 1 August 1918 had changed the sub-title of the *Popolo d'Italia* from 'a Socialist Newspaper' to 'the newspaper of the combatants and producers'. It was above all on the hopes and resentments of the returning ex-servicemen that Mussolini sought to build the movement of the *fasci*. The movement capitalized on the failure of the Government to have a coherent demobilization policy by taking up the cause of the veterans, by demanding that they should enjoy preference in employment, better pensions, a combatant's insurance policy, etc. The importance of these modest practical activities for Fascist recruiting must have been considerable,[24] although probably only a part of the recruits gained in this way stayed in the movement for long.

Mussolini proclaimed the need to give an 'internal social content to the war';[25] the demands for the nationalization of war industries and the punitive taxation of war profits sought to meet the indignation directed against the '*imboscati*' who had made fortunes while others did the fighting; support for the principle of the 'armed nation' and the founding of a short-term national militia was in line with the thinking of the more modern-minded younger officers, and the lowering of the voting age to eighteen showed a special concern with the age-group of the most recent recruits. On the other hand, the propaganda of the Fascist movement sought to prolong rather than to heal the division between the front-line combatants and the rest of the country, and to delay the 'demobilization of spirits'. Observers who had at the outset been sympathetic to Mussolini and to the new *fasci*, and had even participated in the movement, saw this perpetuation of wartime categories and enmities as the cardinal error of the movement. Thus Pietro Nenni, then an interventionist Republican, and one of the founding members of the Bologna *Fascio*, wrote at the time of the first Fascist Congress that 'the sooner we get away from the war and free ourselves from mental battledress, the more the political order will find its basis in the old parties . . . these movements . . . seem to show, sometimes unintentionally, more seeds of civil war than of reconstruction.'[26]

Fascism failed in 1919 to win over the mass of the rank and file of the ex-servicemen. Even the minority of convinced supporters of the war who were not absorbed by the Socialists or the Popolari did not identify themselves with Fascism. The official ex-combatant movement, an important and radical force in the South, where the old parties were inadequate, remained firmly democratic, opposed to the extreme bellicose and nationalist tendency of the *fasci*, and suspicious of their dubious alliances with members of the old bourgeois parties.[27]

The appeal of Fascism was, instead, to the elite among the ex-servicemen, to the *arditi* (shock troops) above all, to the volunteers, and to the officers in general. Mussolini's famous article on 1 August 1918 (see above) had announced that 'the combatants . . . go from Diaz down to the last infantry-man' and it was on the officers, rather than the rank and file, that the original Fascism made its greatest impact. In all countries at the end of the war the reserve officers, economically and psychologically unable to return to peace-time conditions, constituted a special category, definable in terms of experience rather than class, without which the success of Fascism cannot be explained.[28] This military element was perhaps the most important of all the components of Fascism; the young officers found an outlet for their talents and experience in the organization of a movement which, by their work, became increasingly militarized. Negatively their lack of political experience left an equal mark in a vague, ill-defined, purely psychological radicalism which could be easily manipulated. It is nonetheless true that it was among the ex-officers, rather than the syndicalists (the amateurs in politics rather than the professionals), that impatience with the tactical manoeuvres of Mussolini was most serious. The Fascist movement, especially after D'Annunzio's march on Fiume had made him into the hero of all the ardent military and student youth, was only part of the national-revolutionary front. The demand for radical action to instal a new regime which would sweep away Parliament, conceived of as the obstacle to the reconciliation of labour and the nation, eventually led to a sharp split between the left wing of D'Annunzio's legionaries, guided by De Ambris and Mussolini.[29]

When Mussolini betrayed D'Annunzio at the end of 1920, the Fascist movement itself was split. Primarily the division, it is important to understand, was not one between different social programmes or conceptions, but one between the pragmatism of Mussolini, wishing to use Parliament and make alliances with the old parties, and the pursuit of integral intransigence.[30] The D'Annunzian, syndicalist, national-revolutionary labels could cover different social attitudes; on the one hand there were legionaries such as Eno Mecheri, who resigned from the *fasci* in early 1920 over the question of their hostility to strikes in the public services;[31] on the other hand there were Pietro Marsich, another 'D'Annunzian' and a theorist of 'bourgeois resistance', and Grandi, the two most articulate opponents of the Pact of Pacification with the Socialists in 1921. Marsich wanted the re-organization of the State on syndicalist lines, with legislation entrusted to technical councils; but his revolution was to be elitist and 'anti-demagogic'.[32]

A third element in early Fascism, overlapping considerably with that of the ex-officers, was the 'intellectual proletariat' or *bohème*. The Futurists were the spearhead and most articulate representatives of this group, Marinetti's speech to the First Congress was entitled 'the proletariat of genius': 'When Italy is freed from the burden of Monarchy, Senate and Papacy, the proletariat of Italian genius will finally give the greatest results.'[33]

The Futurists sympathized with national-revolutionary criticisms of the conservative pragmatism of Mussolini and the Fascist leadership; they were the most vocal critics of the involution of the movement between November 1919 and May 1920. Marinetti and his supporters were above all angered by the abandonment of republicanism and anti-clericalism, although they also agreed with the left wing of the syndicalists that strikes of an economic as opposed to political nature ought not to be opposed.[34] The Futurists certainly embodied a kind of radicalism; their desire for the destruction of the symbols of the past was genuine. But this radicalism was aesthetic and psychological rather than social in character; it was rooted in a pseudo-heroic individualist rejection of society and tradition. Marinetti's speech at the S. Sepolcro rally is revealing; he declared his opposition to the 'levelling tendencies' which were current in the postwar situation, and announced that 'The Socialist party is trying to unleash all the rancours of the working-class crowds in an onslaught on the rest of the nation: what attitude must we assume towards them ...? Can we assume by ourselves alone the task of containing or opposing this movement?' His difference with Michele Bianchi, the chief exponent of the 'anti-demagogic' tendency, was a question of tactics rather than of fundamental principle.[35] Not all the intellectual proletariat, of course, followed the Futurists, their most colourful representatives. For the numerous journalists, would-be poets or dramatists and out-of-work publicists, the *fasci* offered the chance of a career and the recognition which had eluded them.

Outside and beyond these limited, highly politicized, socially 'marginal' groups, support for Fascism in its first stages came mainly from the petty bourgeoisie of employees and shopkeepers; the movement especially attracted the youth of this class, who found in it a substitute for the emotional excitement of war to which they had come either late or not at all. To the petty-bourgeoisie, and even the professional classes, faced with a serious decline in living standards and with their social function denied by proletarian socialism, Fascism offered not only psychological reassurance, but a means of overcoming the fatal defect of disorganization which rendered them helpless in the face of the pressures from the forces of organized capitalism on the one hand, and the trade unions on the other. This point was made by Marsich, who, while he proclaimed himself an elitist, not too worried about numbers, also urged at the Second Congress that the *fasci* should concentrate on appealing to 'intellectual workers' and employees.[36] The syndical State, by making organization universal and compulsory would, it was hoped, end the disadvantageous position of the middle classes, who would in fact become the arbiters of disagreement between capital and labour.[37]

Finally, a few industrialists and men of property were from the beginning willing to participate actively in the *fasci*, as the instrument of the anti-bolshevik crusade. Usually, however, the capitalists stayed in the background. As early as 1919, Mussolini was receiving large donations from the Milan business world. These were not given so much to the movement in general as to Mussolini and the *Popolo d'Italia*. The finances of the *fasci* remained formally separate from those of the *Popolo d'Italia*. This situation, and the independence it gave to Mussolini, is of critical importance to an understanding of early Fascism. It meant that even the higher cadres of the movement were kept to some extent in ignorance of the commitments entered into by their leader, who at the same time commanded the financial resources which were indispensable. The powerlessness and rapid disillusionment of the left-wing elements in the 1919 *fasci* must be seen as in part a consequence of this situation.[38]

Mussolini from the outset presented his new 'anti-party' as a national movement, above class.[39] Just as the description of 'combatants' could range from Diaz to the private soldier, the ambiguous concept of the 'producers' included capitalist and worker alike. The class struggle, according to Mussolini, must be subordinated to the 'necessities of production', as well as to the greatness of the nation.[40] The defence of the vitality of capitalism and the possibility of class reconciliation was linked to a programme of imperialist expansion.[41] It was characteristic of the ethics and theory of the new syndicalism, that it substituted for objective legal or economic categories, capable of being precisely and unequivocally identified, moral and qualitative distinctions which could be easily manipulated. According to Agostino Lanzillo, for example, the State was not composed of 'citizens', but of 'producers and parasites', 'creators and destroyers', 'poets and materialists', etc; it was easy to see which side Fascism would be on.[42] The syndicalist argument that the abstract concept of the 'citizen' should be replaced by the concrete concept of the 'producer' in fact opened the door for all kinds of arbitrary political discriminations and exclusions. The battle of 'producers' against 'parasites' might seem to suggest the defence of labour against finance; but it could also serve as a slogan for the industrialists' resentment of the parliamentary class.

At first sight, the advanced programme and ex-revolutionary leadership of the Fascist movement might seem to be unattractive to capitalist backers, and indeed some of the more short-sighted, or honest, were discouraged. But these same factors also meant that it could offer more; it was the only instrument which might serve to 'channel the revolutionary forces into the national camp'.[43] It was this claim which differentiated the *fasci* from the Nationalists or the various minor anti-bolshevik leagues. The economic ideas of Mussolini and the Fascist movement were not new or original, except perhaps in the manner of presentation. The anti-State tradition of syndicalism was used by Mussolini and by other Fascists, notably the former individualist anarchist Massimo Rocca, the leading economic propagandist of Fascism in 1921-2, to cover the defence of free enterprise and the demand for the dismantling of wartime controls. In his S. Sepolcro speech Mussolini had already declared that: 'As regards economic democracy, we stand on the basis of national syndicalism, and against the interference of the State in so far as this desires to assassinate the process of the creation of wealth.'[44] Previously the *Popolo d'Italia* had given full and favourable publicity to the national rally of the industrialists of Bergamo in January. The objective of Mussolini and his friends was not merely to capture the industrialists' favour, but to seek to stir up their discontent, and to use them as a force to weaken and eventually overthrow the parliamentary class, described by them as the accomplice of 'bureaucratic oligarchy' or 'state bolshevism'.[45]

Mussolini's speech at the Second Congress of May 1920 only made more explicit the conservative significance of his earlier statements. 'We are in a full regime of State collectivism'; it was time 'to deprive the State of all the functions which render it dropsical and vulnerable, reducing it to that Manchesterian conception which assigns it four functions: that of the soldier, the policeman, the tax-collector and the judge.'[46] This was indeed a capitalist utopia. How could this position be reconciled with the national-revolutionary, democratic, innovating pretensions of Fascism? It was not easy. There was, in fact, during 1921 a sharp conflict between the *liberisti* and those who wanted the movement to adopt the 'Charter of the Carnaro', the corporate constitution drawn up for Fiume by D'Annunzio, with the help and advice of De Ambris. For Massimo Rocca, the question of free enterprise was the essential reason for the rejection of the ideas of D'Annunzio's followers, with their vision of a revolutionary alliance with the extreme left, and of a front extending 'from demagogues to aristocratic rebels'.[47]

The early *fasci* were an entirely urban movement. Mussolini himself believed that the rural world would long remain impenetrable to Fascism. One might suspect that it was a mark of the unimportance attached to rural problems that the Fascist land programme for the Second Congress was entrusted to the radical De Ambris, at a time when the retreat from the positions of the first programme was evident in other sectors. De Ambris did not in fact attend the Congress, and his report was not discussed, although Mussolini was nevertheless careful to make the reservation that no 'single formula' for the agrarian problem could be accepted.[48] In spite of this unpromising start, it was in the agrarian regions of Italy that Fascism during 1921 became a mass movement.

Militarization and the Origins of Squadrismo

The programme of the *fasci di combattimento*, Mussolini had said, was 'contained in the name'. The spirit of the 'dynamic minority' could only be truly expressed and tested in the piazza; it was by their aggressive tactics that the *fasci* drew attention to themselves, won publicity, and so were eventually able to lead the movement of reaction. The novelty of Fascism lay in the military organization of a political party.[49]

The first nucleus of the Fascist military organization can be seen in the personal bodyguard of unemployed *arditi* which Mussolini recruited to garrison the *Popolo d'Italia*. The Arditi Association, founded by Ferruccio Vecchi, had close ties with Mussolini; it was subsidized by him, but also directly by banks and industrialists.[50] The armed force of the *arditi*, therefore, was more an instrument at Mussolini's personal disposition than a military expression of the Fascist movement, which had no control over the Association. The first famous exploit of *squadrismo* was the burning of *Avanti!* on 15 April 1919. This seems to have been an almost spontaneous and unplanned action; the mass of those who took part were young officer-students who were not formally organized by the Fascist movement, but the leaders were Vecchi and Marinetti.[51]

During the summer of 1919 Mussolini personally took steps to promote the formation by the *fasci* of 'armed groups composed of 200–250 sure, tried and well-armed individuals'.[52] This first attempt to expand the paramilitary organization of the movement must be seen in relation to Nationalist plots for a *coup* and for the expedition to Fiume. The squads were to have a subversive, *putschist*, national-revolutionary function. However this proved to be a dangerous policy from Mussolini's own point of view; his associates, particularly Ferruccio Vecchi, were angered by his caution and demanded immediate action.[53] After the Fiume expedition their complaints were vehemently echoed by D'Annunzio himself.[54]

There is no doubt that during 1920 the secretary Pasella and the central leadership of the movement came to see the formation and training of armed squads as the most important activity of the *fasci*. On 18 July 1920 Bresciani, the founder of the Verona *fascio*, wrote to Pasella that he had formed two squads 'according to instructions received.'[55] This shows that the organization of the squads was not simply spontaneous, but encouraged and organized from the centre. Even more revealing is a letter of 26 October from Pasella to Gaggioli, one of the founders of the Ferrara *fascio* : 'A particular word of applause for the constitution of the fascist action squads, which represents – given the moment and the characteristics of our organization – our essential task.'[56]

The purpose of these squads was no longer to serve as support for a *putsch* ; resistance to 'bolshevism' was now their only function.[57] The end of the Fiume adventure, when the *fasci* failed to move a finger in D'Annunzio's defence, was the proof of this transformation. Fiume had acted as a powerful magnet to the military adventurers who thirsted for drama at all costs ; however among the mass of demobilized officers there were many who, for economic even more than political or psychological motives, were ready to play a more pedestrian role as the local organizers of the Fascist squads. It is a sign of the subordination of the political aspects of the movement to the military that the Central Committee instructed the local *fasci* to choose demobilized officers as their political secretaries wherever possible.[58] In the autumn of 1920, there was a new Fascism which was 'essentially *squad-rismo*';[59] the movement became, in the eyes alike of members, supporters and opponents, identified with the armed terrorist reaction against the Socialist party and the unions.

The first victory of *squadrismo* was in Trieste and Venezia Giulia. In these borderlands, national and social issues were inextricably linked. 'Bolshevism' was accused of conspiring with the enemy against the newly won 'integrity of the nation'.[60] It was even easier here than elsewhere to disguise reaction as patriotism. At the beginning of 1920 Francesco Giunta, previously active in the Florentine combatants' association, was despatched by the Central Committee to direct the Trieste *fascio*. In April-May 1920 the para-military organization of the squads was already well developed, on the pretext both of aiding D'Annunzio and of responding to a possible *coup de main* by Slavs and Communists acting in confederation against Trieste.[61] The commanders of the squads were all officers either still under arms or in course of demobilization. To each group leader was assigned the task of the surveillance and defence of one zone of the city, which had been divided into districts 'opportunely based on military criteria' ; each group was constituted by thirty to fifty volunteers, ex-combatants or young men of the people. The organization had an information service, a health service and a transport service, with lorries furnished by a lieutenant still on active service.[62] The later provincial *fasci* could not hope to copy the 'military criteria' employed at Trieste, a city still under military occupation ; later provincial *squadrismo* was generally a much more informal affair. However even the mass *squadrismo* of 1921 to some extent made use of military tactics and principles, at least in its major actions : rapidity of movement, achieved by the use of lorries furnished by the *agrari* or the Army itself, enabled the squads to concentrate in force and defeat their enemies in detail.

In 1922, when once again the objective of the conquest of State power came to the fore, military organization was improved.

A climate of almost hysterical fear and nationalist exaltation deliberately fostered by the Press, prepared the way for a campaign of terror; the excuse was found in the incidents at Spalato in July 1920, when two Italian officers were killed. In retaliation, the Fascists burned the Slav headquarters in the Balkan Hotel. Following this victory, the squads began for the first time to intervene with decisive effect in labour disputes; the first 'punitive expeditions' were mounted against centres of Slav resistance in the countryside.[63] This pattern was to be repeated elsewhere: first the war of nerves, provocation and the inflammation of public opinion; then the dramatic action against an enemy headquarters prominently located in the city centre; afterwards the wholesale destruction in detail of Socialist political and economic organizations throughout the province, supported by the foundation of blackleg labour unions.

The myth of *squadrismo*, as well as its reality, was a powerful and enduring influence on Fascism. The *squadristi* felt, with some reason, that they were the true Fascists, and the *picchiatori* or men of the '*manganello*', were generally distrustful of the politicians, the 'talkers'. The sordid facts behind *squadrismo*, the dependence on official police connivance and funds from industrialists or agrarians were forgotten; and the squad leaders, often from the humblest petty-bourgeoisie or the *lumpenproletariat*, with varying degrees of good faith regarded themselves as the incarnation of a populist Fascism, close to its original wartime inspiration and free from manipulation by 'parasitic' bourgeois or politicians.[64]

The leaders of Fascist extremism used and to some extent shared these feelings; but they were, and had to be, 'politicians' too, so that in reality the anarchic and destructive forces of *squadrismo* were only faced with a choice between different types of manipulation and control.

The Mass Movement: Urban and Agrarian Fascism

The great expansion of Fascism in the winter and spring of 1920–1 completely altered the structure and dimensions of the movement. The terrorist offensive of the action squads was accompanied by a great increase in recruits and sympathizers. Successful violence brought popularity, because to a large section of public opinion it appeared as a legitimate reaction to the threats and abuses of revolutionary Socialism, and as the defence of injured patriotism. However the relationship between terror and consensus in the Fascist movement is not simple. The movement of provincial *squadrismo*, although originally encouraged from the centre, was 'a chaotic ensemble of local reactions'.[65] The speed and nature of its development were neither foreseen nor entirely welcomed by Mussolini and the national leadership.

Squadrismo soon revealed itself as a Frankenstein monster, uncontrollable by its inventors.

During 1921 Fascism experienced the most serious internal conflict of its whole history. There seemed to be two alternative lines of development open to the movement for the exploitation of its success. On the one hand, as Mussolini and his collaborators wished, it could try to consolidate the enthusiastic support won among the middle classes and the petty-bourgeoisie, and to become a great 'middle party'; the terrorist phase would give way to a political phase. On the other hand, the para-military bosses of provincial Fascism saw its future in the continuation and perfection of the methods which seemed to be working so well; the domination of the masses was to be achieved by terror and by control over the labour market, exerted through the new trade union organizations which had sprung up at the instigation of employers and *squadristi*. The 'two Fascisms' of 1921 roughly coincided with a social division between urban and agrarian Fascism.[66] The two had been united by their common anti-socialism, but the coincidence of aims between the urban petty-bourgeoisie and the agrarians was neither complete nor lasting. Fascism in the cities continued to be closer to the 'Fascism of the first hour' of the ex-combatants and students, to whom the excesses of agrarian Fascism soon began to seem repugnant. These urban *fasci* were relatively homogeneous in social composition, and their transformation into a political party did not appear absurd or impossible. Agrarian or provincial Fascism, on the other hand, was far more heterogeneous; large numbers of peasants and labourers joined the movement, but no permanent tie of common interest or conviction bound them to the agrarians, who had every reason to fear that the restoration of normal political conditions would lead to the disbandment of their mass following, which resembled the rank and file of an army more closely than that of a normal party.

Agostino Lanzillo, one of the most influential intellectuals in the movement of 1919, gives a particularly clear description of the 'two Fascisms'. He believed that Fascism was destined to become a party of the centre, representing the middle classes. It should defend the taxpayer and the consumer, the true representatives of the general interest. However it could not fulfil this function until it abandoned violence and changed its relationship to other parties and classes. Lanzillo contrasted the Fascism of the cities, 'a romantic movement', which even if it had an imprecise programme, was still 'inspired by general and reasonably well-defined leit-motifs both in internal and foreign policy', with agrarian Fascism, which he described as 'a cruel and implacable movement of interests'.[67]

However this distinction between the 'two Fascisms' is undoubtedly somewhat schematic. 'Urban Fascism' has generally been used as a designation of the Fascism of the big cities; one can in fact observe the existence of an 'industrial Fascism' in the smaller manufacturing centres which resembled agrarian Fascism in tactics and motive. Again, in the provincial cities whose economy was tied to the agriculture of the surrounding province, the boundaries between 'urban' and 'agrarian' were by no means clear-cut. The *squadristi* who first took Fascism into the countryside came from the cities.

In the smaller provincial cities of the North the movement at first relied almost exclusively on students and young ex-officers.[68] Often the first nucleus was formed by members of republican, Mazzinian or democratic youth circles, the sons of the anti-clerical petty-bourgeoisie who had inherited the romantic patriotism of the 'historic' left. The Brescia *fascio*, for example, recruited its first members from the 'Roberto Ardigò' student circle ;[69] in Reggio Emilia it was a group of republican students who were the first activists. Their leader, Amos Maramotti, is a typical example of these early, romantically inclined student Fascists, drawn to the movement by a compound of the love of adventure and patriotic indignation : during the war he had tried to escape to the front, but was sent back home because he was too young. In March 1919 he became president of the local students' association, previously a-political, and immediately organized an anti-Wilson demonstration. He was killed in 1921 during the attack on the Turin Camera del Lavoro and became one of the movement's most famous 'martyrs'.[70] Elsewhere, more overtly nationalistic organizations took the lead ; at Mantua the cradle of the Fascist movement was the patriotic students' association 'La Terza Italia', founded in 1917 to contribute to resistance on the 'home front'.[71] For all these groups, whether republican or monarchist, the war had become a symbol of the conflict of generations. The Fascist movement was the ideal vehicle for their pseudo-religious cult of sacrifice and heroism, and seemed to satisfy at the same time the urge for a clean break with the past.[72] The diffusion of Fascism among the students was also aided by the lack of an effective national organization which could express both their general political views and their immediate interests. In the absence of such a body, many students recognized the *fasci* as a substitute, and found that the *Popolo d'Italia* was the newspaper which best expressed their feelings.[73] The pleasures of defying discipline and breaking up the lectures of unpopular professors could be indulged extensively under the name of Fascism ; however the movement in the universities and schools was not a 'student revolt' in the modern sense, even if it shared some of the same psychological motivations. The professors and scholastic authorities were generally sympathetic to the aims, if not the methods, of the movement, and in spite of the external appearances of revolt and a certain advance in 'student power', it did not, obviously, further the autonomy of the student body. But Fascism (and not only in the early years) manipulated with success the vague instincts of rebellion and the desire for more freedom of expression, which were current in schools and universities dominated by a heavily authoritarian tradition.[74] Rather than a serious revolt, student Fascism was more like an extension of the licensed indiscipline of the student carnival, the *'Feste Goliardiche'*. The Fascist use of the *beffa*, or practical joke, shading off from harmless acts of insolence into serious cruelty, grew out of these traditional student 'rags'.

These small groups of students and ex-combatants who formed the first *fasci* in the provincial cities would have had little more than a marginal importance if they had not found a link with wider circles of society. The *fasci* of 1919, almost without exception, failed to achieve this. Many local *fasci* were first founded in the summer and autumn of 1920; but even where they had existed previously, they often underwent a radical transformation at this time.[75] Fascism succeeded in exploiting a patriotic and class reaction to socialism which in great part had spontaneous origins outside the move-ment. Two events, the occupation of the factories in September 1920 and the local elections of November 1920, help to explain the timing of this 'revival of the bourgeoisie'. The shock of the occupation and the imminent danger of the conquest of local power by the revolutionaries pointed to the need for a united action of resistance. In most cases, the Fascists still only had a marginal role in this revival and re-organization of the political forces of the bourgeoisie; Mussolini did not wish to repeat the fiasco of the 1919 general elections, and seems to have been content that their participation as candidates should be slight. Instead, some *fasci* (or their members) received considerable sums of money for the services which they rendered as armed guards during the campaign.[76] Where older liberal and democratic groups were slow to act it was often the combatant associations, rather than the still unimportant or non-existent local *fasci*, who took the lead in promoting and organizing the union of 'anti-subversive' forces.[77] The *fasci*, however, won wide sympathy by appearing to act (often sincerely) as a 'patriotic' rather than a 'political' association. They were active in the organization of patriotic rallies; events like the anniversary of the march on Fiume (4 September), or the entry into Rome (20 September), were exploited to win publicity. In Reggio Emilia the ceremony for the return of flags from the front provided the opportunity and stimulus for the foundation of the *fascio*.[78]

In the city of *Bologna*, however, the *fascio* assumed a more central role. Bologna, the capital of the whole rich agricultural region of Emilia, was dominated politically by the Socialists, as was the surrounding province. The leadership of the Socialists had passed at the end of the war to the *massimalisti*, who talked a lot about the imminent revolution but made few serious preparations. The economy of the province was not wholly agri-cultural; there were a higher number of industrial and white-collar workers than in most regions of Italy.[79] But the local industries, especially sugar, were often based on the utilization of agricultural produce. Moreover, Bologna, as the capital of the region, was a natural centre for the organiza-tion of the *agrari* of all Emilia. Consequently 'urban', 'industrial' and 'agra-rian' elements all had a share in the rise of Fascism in Bologna, the capital of the new provincial Fascism. Bologna is also a university city: and for a long time the *fascio*, later to become the most important in Italy, stood or fell by the activity of the large student population. In Bologna, the dominant mood among the students was definitely nationalist rather than democratic. This probably reflects a reaction to the strength and aggressiveness of the Socialist party. The leaders of the *fascio* in 1919, on the other hand, were Republicans, like the brothers Mario and Guido Bergamo and Pietro Nenni, at that time editor of the local democratic interventionist newspaper, the *Giornale del Mattino*. Their programme called for a democratic revolution to be carried through by a constituent assembly.[80] The monarchists and the Nationalists immediately withdrew their support, and most of the students sided with them. 'The students, the very young, who had put themselves at the disposition of the *fascio*, and who for the greater part are Nationalists, or tend towards Nationalism, are re-organizing their Italian League of Youth. . . . They had come to us because they knew that they would have a good captain for their demonstrations.'[81] The Italian (or Latin) League of Youth was a Nationalist-inspired organization; it was in its rooms that the Nationalists Cesare Tumedei and Dino Zanetti, who had led the secession from the *fascio* in the name of 'the glorious monarchy of Savoy', organized an anti-Bolshevik league.[82] Without student support, the Bologna *fascio*, one of the most decidedly left-wing in Italy, led a miserable existence. The democratic credibility of the *fascio* was not improved when the Bergamo brothers allowed it to fall into the hands of a certain Lieutenant Garibaldo Pedrini. Pedrini was still in active service, and he was almost certainly acting as an agent of the local Army Corps command. This episode, though without important consequences, is an interesting proof of the benevolence with which the Army viewed the *fasci*, even at a time when the civilian authorities were still rather distrustful of their 'subversive' tendencies.[83]

When in the spring of 1920 Mario Bergamo and his group finally broke with Fascism, the leadership of the Bologna *fascio* passed to Leandro Arpinati. Arpinati was born in a small town of the Romagna, son of a fiercely anti-clerical innkeeper who gave him a 'Socialist' baptism. This background was remarkably similar to Mussolini's own, and the two men were friends. Unlike his leader, however, Arpinati had been a genuine member of the working class; before the war he worked as an electrician for the railways. With Mario Gioda (the founder of the Turin *fascio*), he was one of the small group of anarchists who had supported intervention: in 1919 he tried to address an assembly of railwaymen to persuade them to oppose the proposed international general strike, but he was driven from the hall.[84] These experiences had made him into a tough-minded political fighter with few illusions or inhibitions. He had no sympathy with the intransigence of the Bergamo brothers, and under his direction the *fascio* soon showed itself ready to collaborate with the rich bourgeoisie. The latter had at first stayed aloof, but after the general strike of April 1920, called in protest against the killing of eight workers by the *carabinieri* they became frightened and angry enough to turn to the small and combative group of ex-servicemen and students. In response, on 8 April there was founded the 'Bolognese Civil Defence Association'; this organization asked the *fascio* for help in the creation of a 'civil volunteer force' for action in case of strikes.[85] This initiative, and the collaboration of the *fascio*, had parallels in other cities, notably Milan, where a general was among the promoters.[86] Arpinati wrote to Pasella:

It is perhaps superfluous to say that I would have wished to adhere without ado . . . but several of our good friends are not of the same opinion. They are offended by the presence of a few 'sharks' in the Council itself, and they think it a good reason for not joining that these same men never replied to the earlier appeals launched for the same purpose. It is certainly true that these Bolognese *bourgeois* (and to say Bolognese is to say apathetic and cowardly) never made a move until, with the last strike, they felt themselves menaced in their own security and their own pockets; but should we, for this reason, not accept the *money-arm* which is so necessary for our battle, and which these bourgeois (granted, from fear alone) are offering us at this moment?[87]

Pasella agreed with Arpinati's judgement, although he warned him against the possibility that the offer might be a trap set to discredit the *fascio*.[88] His reply makes clear that Arpinati's policy was in line with the directives of the national movement. The stark clarity of Arpinati's letter needs little comment; he was willing to commit the *fascio* to the service of the interests of men whom he continued, secretly, to despise. Similar feelings of contempt for their respectable backers and employers were undoubtedly to remain characteristic of the mass of *squadristi*, who looked to men like Arpinati to provide some outlet for their resentments. This was to be one of the permanent sources of tension in the movement.

In Bologna, where the Socialist threat was particularly pressing, the old established bourgeoisie recognized, earlier than elsewhere, that they were incapable of organizing their own defence unaided; they needed the support of those groups who, like the nationalistic students and the 'heretics' of the revolutionary interventionist movement, were psychologically prepared for 'the departure from legality and the repudiation of the liberal mentality'.[89] It was the function of these small 'elites' to convince the mass of middle-class citizens and the property-holders that the *fascio* was the most effective centre of resistance. In a town like Bologna, it undoubtedly took some courage at first to overcome the fear of provoking the anger of the masses. But, little by little, the Fascists succeeded in exposing the hollowness of the revolutionaries' threats. The Fascist offensive at the end of the year was preceded in Bologna and elsewhere by a phase which can best be described as one of reconnaissance. On 1 May, a day when the streets were normally abandoned to the working-class movement, 'our patrols,' Arpinati wrote, 'made various sorties, crossing the city by the principal streets to the sound of *Giovinezza*, but without ever meeting resistance. . . . I am convinced that they [the Socialists] will never make a revolution.'[90]

During the summer of 1920, however, the *fascio* lapsed into inactivity again. The reason for this was that most of the students had gone home for the holidays. The initiative which led to the revival was in fact taken by a group of students, led by Mario Ghinelli, who had stayed behind in the city. They wrote to the Central Committee of the *fasci* to protest against the passivity of Arpinati. Arpinati replied that 'I had withdrawn from the movement in disappointment, although I was determined to take up my modest labour again on the return of the students to Bologna.' The *fascio*, in spite of the contacts established by Arpinati with bourgeois politicians, still led a precarious and marginal existence, dependent on the enthusiasm of student activists.[91]

The 'take-off' period for provincial fascism began in the autumn of 1920. At this time the Bologna *fascio*, and a number of others, were reconstituted on an entirely new footing. The new *fascio* was the result of an agreement between the leaders of the old *fascio*, principally Arpinati and several other 'political and patriotic associations of the city'. In a meeting on 20 October they decided, 'to reconstitute the *fascio di combattimento* on a broader base, with the chief purpose of forming a strong organization capable of opposing the acts of violence which the extremists of the PSU and the anarchists were committing in the city and province, offending the liberty of the other parties and in general of all the citizens who do not belong to the Red organizations. In this meeting the statute of the association . . . was compiled and approved and the *direttorio* of the new '*fascio*' was named'.

This radical transformation, whereby the *fascio* merged with older patriotic associations, was the key to its sudden emergence as a force of major political importance.[92]

In November 1920 the counter-offensive began. 'A few bands of youths . . . had been able to check the revolutionary movement; they were now joined by the best section of the citizens, the rich, the agrarians and the traders . . . little by little the movement of defence became a movement of offence, and while formerly the red domination had to be suffered, now the *fascio* rules.'[93]

After their disastrous defeat in the great agricultural strike of 1920, the Bologna agrarians had repudiated the more moderate, liberal, leaders of the national Confederation of Agriculture and turned to those who would promise action. If the State would not defend them, they would organize their own defence.[94] The *agrari* and the sugar manufacturers, equally interested in the restoration of order in the countryside, provided the funds which were indispensable for success. But the rise of Fascism in Bologna and in the whole of the Po Valley was not simply a self-defence movement of the *agrari*, although this aspect became more and more dominant with time. At first the agrarian reaction only succeeded because it was backed by a united movement of the urban middle classes against socialism. The conquest of the rural areas began with punitive expeditions carried out by the Fascists of the city; this was the pattern not only in Bologna but in most provinces of the Po Valley, and also in Tuscany and Umbria. At the end of 1920, economic hardship as well as the threat of socialism brought about the mobilization of the middle classes behind Fascism.

'A strange crowd forms under the porticoes, gathers in the cafes on the piazzas.' It is composed of the demobilized ex-officers 'who have sought and not found employment'; it is 'a compound of repressed hope and desperation', of forgotten heroes 'convinced that they can harangue a community as they harangued a battalion in the field': of 'public employees scarcely able to eat compared with whom a peasant, a league organizer, a trade union secretary is a gentleman, of swarms of brokers, shopkeepers, and contractors, hit by the slump, who detest with a deadly hatred the labour and consumers' co-operatives,' of 'students and young graduates' with no clients and grandiose ideals, convinced that their misfortunes were due to the 'sinister plots of senile politicians', of bands of 'incredible adolescents, boys aged from 16 to 19, envenomed by the bad luck which made the war finish too soon . . . because they wished to go and see it, and do great deeds; educated to admire gunpowder and to give blows by 5 years of fighting exalted by the adults; pupils of the sensational film, enamoured of every disturbance': and finally of 'bands of ex-revolutionaries who had become war enthusiasts in 1915 and without union ties . . . anxious to recapture a position of command'.[95] This 'crowd' made Fascism into a mass movement, soon swelled by opportunists of all classes who sensed that the tide had turned. In the spring of 1921, the *fascio* of the city had a membership estimated at between 5000 and 8000.[96] The conquest of the province from the powerful organizations of the Federterra (the Socialist agricultural workers' federation) was a slow and difficult, as well as violent process. As it proceeded, and new provincial *fasci* were formed, the agrarian element steadily increased in importance.

In the province of *Ferrara*, the domination of the movement by the agrarians was more rapidly achieved and more complete than in Bologna.[97] The Ferrara *fascio* was founded only in October 1920. It first drew attention to itself by tactics similar to those employed in Bologna. Forty Fascists (about the total membership) 'in military order . . . with a great tricolour banner at their head', crossed the centre of the town 'marching in martial fashion', before assembling in the main square 'to protect the freedom of speech of the Fascist orators'. The object of this demonstration was 'with forty Fascists, to make a show of having four hundred'. Early exploits included parades under the windows of Socialist leaders, and the removal of red flags from city offices.[98] This boldness of the Fascists soon attracted the notice of the agrarians, who first began to employ them to break the boycotts imposed by the Socialist League organizers on recalcitrant landlords or farmers, or on workers and peasants who disobeyed union regulations.[99] After the first punitive expeditions, the Fascist movement began to recruit members not only from the city but from the surrounding villages. The expansion of numbers was extremely rapid; on 19 November 1920 the *fascio* had only 300 members, but for the rally of 20 December in which, for the first time, the Fascists of the province were to be concentrated in the city, 2–3000 were expected.[100] By January 1921, the movement had won the almost unanimous support of the bourgeoisie; the attempt to disarm the squads provoked the wealthy citizens to make their sympathy public: 'they joined as supporting members of the *fascio*, and inscribed their sons as *squadristi*.' The leader of the *agrari*, Vico Mantovani, in a somewhat disingenuous attempt to deny the predominant influence of his class on the Fascist movement, protested that 'the resources of Fascism are notoriously to be found in the wallets of every trader, industrialist, farmer or patriot'.[101]

The influence of the Agrarian Association was resented and contested by the founders of the city *fascio*; many of the 'Fascists of the first hour' – students, employees and ex-officers – suffered a real crisis of conscience. Their anti-Socialism, although grounded in middle-class resentment, had been legitimized in their own eyes by a sincere and fanatical patriotism; they realized that Fascism was becoming the tool of crude class interest, and of groups whose attitude to the national cause was highly suspect:

The true significance of Fascism (here at Ferrara) having been misunderstood ... numerous Popolari and liberal elements have entered the *fascio*, who have brought (this is the limit) the support, more official than otherwise, of no less a body than the Agrarian Federation. Moreover, and perhaps as the result of a deal, the Agrarian Association is the financier of the *fascio*, which is monstrous and discredits us – naturally – to the advantage of our opponents. So at Ferrara the *fascio* is no more nor less than the bodyguard of the profiteers.

The question of Fiume marked the watershed between the two conceptions of Fascism. 'The gentlemen of the Fascist-Liberal crowd are afraid of losing the friendship of the government, or rather of the Prefect'; for the agrarians, Fiume was an unwelcome and embarrassing distraction from the true local aims of Fascism.[102] As one supporter of the movement, Senator Niccolini, remarked: 'At Rome the *fasci* may mean Fiume, and in Venice Gabriele D'Annunzio, but in Bologna and Ferrara they mean liberation!'[103] The national leadership responded immediately to the protests of the urban Fascists. As has been seen, Pasella had raised no objections to the earlier use of the *fasci* as strike-breaking auxiliaries: quite the contrary. The scruples he now displayed therefore raise an important problem.

In substance, the question is the same as for the conflict over the Pact of Pacification. The success of Fascism was founded on the unstable alliance between the urban middle class and the agrarians. At the outset, the former must have appeared to the leaders of the movement as the more essential and valuable component. Mussolini himself had not predicted the success of Fascism in agricultural areas; he had written, 'Fascism seems destined to remain an urban phenomenon.' Both he and his entourage were accustomed to dealing with industrialists; but the agrarians were something different, unfamiliar monsters of the backwoods. They were more easily identifiable, more dourly reactionary, and their support was more compromising. The leader of a small *fascio* in Umbria had written: 'We have no resources at our disposal because here, in a wholly agricultural region, we cannot call the few landed proprietors to form part of the *fasci* without provoking criticism.'[104] It is true that in Emilia the situation was different: tenant farmers, some of them new men, were more important than the large landowners. On the other hand, the involvement of the *fascio* with the official agrarian associations, rather than individual sympathizers, made the problem in a sense still more acute. There was an obvious danger that many of the early and most combative members of the movement would secede in disgust; Mussolini, Rossi and Pasella were well aware of the discontent aroused by their own passivity over the Fiume question, and it was necessary to do something to combat the accusations of betrayal which arose from the rank and file.[105]

There is also another aspect to be considered. The leaders in Milan recognized the purely local roots and character of the upsurge of provincial Fascism, and feared that it would escape their control. They viewed the local reaction as a means towards the seizure of power, whereas for the provincial notables it was an end in itself.

One of the aspects of the new Fascism that most disturbed Pasella was the financial autonomy gained by the local *fasci*, directly subsidized by the agrarian associations as well as by other sympathizers.[106] This point, absolutely critical for the relations between the central leadership and the local *fasci*, was also the one on which the Central Committee found it hard to secure even nominal compliance.

When they intervened at the beginning of 1921, the Central Committee insisted that the Ferrara *fascio* adopt a new programme on the land question. Marinoni was able to persuade the Federazione Agraria that the support of Fascism was worth the price of concessions. Groups of landowners agreed to grant several thousand acres of land to the peasants on long leases; with the *fascio* acting as intermediary, the Fascist movement could then claim that whereas the Socialists could only advance the mirage of a future collectivization, they were getting immediate results.[107] They could play on the latent preference, never extinguished by Socialist ideology, for individual as opposed to collective ownership of the land. This propaganda tactic had an enormous effect in dividing and weakening Socialist opposition; it might not have succeeded by itself, but combined with terror and the threat of unemployment, it was extremely effective. The discipline of the leagues, in order to avoid blacklegging, had been extremely harsh; and many individual workers had suffered. Others had tolerated restrictions only in the expectation that, this time, the revolution would really arrive. Fascist propaganda was also very much aided in Ferrara by the fact that before the war the revolutionary syndicalists (including Pasella and Michele Bianchi), rather than the Socialists, had led the agitations; Socialist loyalties were less firmly rooted than in Bologna and many other provinces, and the disposition to believe in the demagogic promises of Fascism greater. The concessions made by the agrarians were greater in appearance than substance. The leases were nominally intended as the first stage towards the permanent grant of the plots of land to the peasants on a quit rent; however the eventual passage of land to the peasants was conditional on such severe provisions relating to the annual amortization payments, and the responsibility for natural or other disasters, that the rights of the tenants were very precarious. In other cases the slogan of 'giving the worker an affection for the land' dictated the transformation of wage labour into leasehold or sharecropping contracts; this was a tendency which some of the agrarians had long favoured as a means of securing greater social stability.[108]

The Fascist movement sought to exploit and extend this success in its national propaganda. The new agrarian programme published on 27 June 1921 declared that 'the *fasci* propose in principle that the land should belong to him who works it. Our task is the gradual creation of a new agrarian democracy'. However this imposing declaration was somewhat qualified by a list of reservations, some of which were technically justified. Most significant was the defence of the 'large industrial farm'; the programme declared these to be 'generally healthy', and admitted that: 'The large farm . . . could not be divided without increasing expenditure and diminishing income, with grave loss to society. . . . Technical skills cannot be improvised.'[109] This reservation in fact made it clear that the Fascist 'tendency' to favour peasant proprietorship did not involve any serious threat to the active capitalist farmers of Emilia and Lombardy.

In succeeding months, while the movement continued to appeal to the peasants by promising the abolition of wage labour through the extension of small property and profit-sharing, the reservations and cautions with which the promises were hedged round were continually increased. When the programme was presented to the regional Fascist meetings, it met with some opposition and criticism; in Piedmont, Lombardy and the Veneto in particular the impossibility of a general solution, applicable in all cases, and the defence of existing property relations, were heavily stressed.[110] It does not seem that these modifications met with the disapproval of Pasella. Indeed, in Emilia, where the regional assembly on the contrary gave a more radical emphasis to the programme, it seems that this was not what he or Mussolini desired. An agricultural 'expert', Carlo Zuccoli, had submitted a special report to the assembly of the Modena *fascio* with the intention that it should be presented to the Congress. This made no mention of the division of property, but called for 'the maximum industrialization through the present forms of production'; as regards distribution, the programme limited itself to talking vaguely of 'association and collaboration between the three great factors of production: manual labour, mental labour and capital'. However the assembly amended this motion, adding a recommendation in favour of the division of property (either through co-operative or individual ownership). 'You will understand,' Zuccoli wrote, 'that I could not accept this amendment which contradicts and denies the whole of the report.' Pasella replied (without mentioning the amendment) that the report 'in great part corresponds to my way of thinking'.[111]

We see from this example that the local pressures were not all in one direction. In fact, in Emilia, where the expansion of the Fascist movement had been most rapid, the urban middle-class Fascists, anxious to combat the predominance of the agrarians, were often sincere in their desire to win the rural masses over by real economic concessions. On the other hand, the attitude of the landowners, once victory over the Socialists was assured, became more rigid and they started to retract their earlier promises.[112] Ferrara was the first province in which the Fascists made their breakthrough, and nowhere else does the grant of land seem to have been carried out on such an extensive scale. However examples are reported from north Lombardy, the Veneto and Cremona province; further research might reveal other instances.[113]

The success of Fascist propaganda in the countryside was not without danger for the agrarians, as the movement acquired a large number of followers who might be expected to take the statements in favour of wage earners and small peasant property seriously.[114]

The envoy sent by the Central Committee to Ferrara, Ottavio Marinoni, was able to announce after a month the substantial success, as he believed, of his mission: 'the radical change of the executive committee of the *fascio*' and the appointment of a new political secretary seemed to guarantee the change of attitude which he had inaugurated. The new secretary was Italo Balbo, until this time a member of the Republican party, 'a boy full of enthusiasm, endowed with the necessary qualities to occupy the post'.[115] The sequel was to show that Marinoni's confidence was misplaced. Certainly Balbo proved an able leader, and his fiery Mazzinian rhetoric served to give Ferraran Fascism a certain varnish of radicalism; like Grandi in Bologna, he enthusiastically backed Mussolini when the latter proclaimed the 'republican tendency' of the movement. But on the central issue of relations with the Agrarian Federation, Balbo betrayed the hopes of the group of city Fascists who had favoured and helped to bring about his appointment.

Balbo was later among the most intransigent opponents of the Pact of Pacification with the Socialists.[116] This time the secession of the anti-agrarian group led by Gaggioli and the young industrialist Barbato Gattelli could not be averted. The *direttorio* of the city *fascio*, on which they were in the majority, resigned on 5 October 1921, with a manifesto of protest against 'the bourgeoisie of exploiters'. Later Gaggioli and his friends left the *fascio* altogether.

In a meeting of the city *fascio*, on 22 October, Barbato Gattelli succeeded in passing a motion calling for a reconciliation with the dissident group of Gaggioli and Brombin, for greater autonomy of the *fascio* from the provincial federation, and for the transformation of the movement into a party.[117] The national reconciliation between Mussolini and his opponents brought with it a temporary compromise also in Ferrara; but the conflict between city and province soon revived. It was only finally resolved by the decision of a Commission of Enquiry headed by De Vecchi on 5 September 1922; this condemned without reserve the conduct of the city *fascio*:

... the *direttorio* of the *fascio* of Ferrara, violating the most elementary obligations of discipline, believed that it had the right to live in isolation and virtual independence from the superior provincial organs and to attempt to carry on secessionist propaganda of its own in the province. It even attempted to have discussed in a public assembly, contrary to an obvious duty and an explicit prohibition, the matters which form the object of this enquiry.... It is factious ... and fundamentally contaminated by that demagogy which finds in the pitiless honesty of Fascism, the friend and not the betrayer of the humble, its most natural enemy.[118]

The conquest of the province by the squads had modified the balance of power to the disadvantage of the early city Fascists. Marinoni, during his mission earlier in the year, had already seen the danger, from the point of view of the Central Committee and their local allies, in the proposal to constitute a confederation of the *nuclei* of the province. The influence of the agrarians, although present on the executive of the city *fascio*, was 'much more accentuated', for obvious reasons, in the *nuclei* of the countryside.[119] The formation of a provincial federation later in the year here as in other regions gave the *agrari* the upper hand in the direction of the local movement. Power within the federation became increasingly centralized and authoritarian. The *direttorio* of the provincial federation suppressed the general assembly, thus freeing itself from control by the mass of the members: and finally the political secretary, Balbo, in turn freed himself from control by the *direttorio*.[120]

The transformation of the internal structure of the Fascist movement was directly linked to changes in its social composition. 'Inner-party democracy', in which the leaders were elected and revoked and their decisions criticized by the general assembly of all the members, was workable in the cities, with their more or less homogeneous middle-class membership. But in the agrarian provinces, after the destruction of the Socialist Leagues, large masses of agricultural workers, 'attracted by promises of protection versus the claims of the owners', had become members of the *fasci*, and in these circumstances free discussion would have been fatal to the leaders of the movement. The true reason for the excommunication of Gattelli and his group of city Fascists seems to have been their attempt to mobilize the masses in the province against their agrarian bosses.[121] The result of the acquisition by Fascism of a base among the masses in the countryside was, paradoxically, to destroy such democratic characteristics as it had previously possessed. The protest of the city Fascists against the agrarians underlined the importance of what was described as a 'completely new precedent in national politics';[122] in other words, the process of the concentration of power at the top, which eliminated, first, the role of the ordinary rank and file member, and secondly, in many cases, even that of the restricted oligarchy of *dirigenti*. This process went hand in hand with the militarization of the movement, which entered a new phase at the end of 1921; a rigid, mystical cult of discipline and the leadership principle increasingly suffocated the original tolerance of individualist rebellion. Here are to be found the origins of the local tyrannies of the so-called *ras*.

One of the best descriptions of the social composition of the Fascist movement in the larger cities is given by Agostino Lanzillo, in an article already quoted:

... the opinion that the Fascist party should become the political instrument of the middle bourgeoisie is founded on the present composition of the Fascist party in the great cities ... the *fasci* in Milan are composed in the very great majority of employees, small rentiers and lesser and middling professional men. And what is still more important is that the members of similar organizations are, in the majority, men new to political activity. The scant parliamentary education shown in Fascist assemblies, the prevalence of sentiment, the disorder in discussion, are the results of the absolute lack of political experience among the masses gathered together under the Fascist emblem. Fascism is composed in the large cities of new men. They formed the crowd which before the war watched political events with indifference and apathy and which has now entered the contest. Fascism has mobilized its forces from the twilight zones of political life, and from this derives the unruly violence and juvenile exuberance of its conduct.[123]

Lanzillo's contention that Fascism succeeded in mobilizing the previously indifferent or apathetic is supported by a cursory examination of the election results of 1921. The votes gained by the *Blocchi Nazionali* in regions where Fascist candidates participated do not reflect merely the use of coercion; this had a distinct influence on the result only in one or two agricultural regions, the provinces of Ferrara and Rovigo, or Perugia, where the offensive of the squads had been particularly successful, or in isolated centres. But in many cities and small towns the gains were not due (or only in part) to a fall in the Socialist vote, as would presumably have been the case if coercion had been the decisive factor; and instead the greatest contribution was made by the influx of new voters.[124] The participation of the Fascists in the 'national' blocs makes it impossible to determine the precise extent of their support; but it is only reasonable to suppose that the greater part of these new voters were in fact Fascist sympathizers, swept along by the violence, crude but persistent propaganda, and patriotic sentiment well calculated to appeal to the politically inexperienced. The point is of some interest for the analysis of Fascism in general; it parallels, though admittedly on a very reduced scale, a process which is well known in the case of Nazi Germany. Lanzillo's impression of the social composition of the movement in the cities is confirmed by such scattered data as we possess. An analysis of the *squadristi* of the city of Arezzo shows that roughly fifty per cent came from the lower middle class of shopkeepers, traders and employees, and another twenty-five per cent was made up by the professional classes and students.[125]

The Fascism of the big cities, however, was not identical in composition to that of the smaller manufacturing centres. An examination of Fascism in Liguria will demonstrate this point. Liguria was the most highly industrialized region in Italy; it was above all a centre of heavy industries (steel, the manufacture of armaments and shipbuilding), and production had expanded rapidly during the war. The most influential leaders of reformist Socialism and the trade unions (among the oldest in Italy), in contrast to those of other regions, had supported the war, forming a breakaway group known as the *Socialisti Autonomi*. The extraordinary Captain Giulietti, the friend and financial backer of D'Annunzio, and his Seamen's Union had their headquarters in Genoa. It was, in fact, the one region where the tradition of Mazzinian patriotism still had a strong hold on sections of the working class. However the mass of new immigrant workers sucked in by the war industries, many from Tuscany and Sardinia, tended to be much farther to the left. Against them, the autonomists stood for the rights and privileges of the established, native, skilled working class.

The opportunities for Fascism to penetrate the working class in 1919 therefore appeared more promising in Liguria than anywhere else. Most of the early *fasci* were in fact founded by working-class activists. The Ligurian Fascists also formed the most coherent left-wing group in the early movement; when, after the elections of November 1919, the question of forming a *Blocco Nazionale* with the bourgeois parties was raised in the Central Committee, three out of the five decided opponents of the idea, Mecheri, Buttafava and Sommovigo, were all representatives of Ligurian *fasci*.[126] The first regional meeting adopted a republican and revolutionary motion proposed by Mecheri, and also, even more significant, applauded the refusal of the Federazione Mare to transport supplies to the Whites in Russia; the Nationalist members seceded in disgust.[127] However early hopes for the development of the movement were not fulfilled. Even the interventionist and Republican left and the UIL became suspicious of the overall direction taken by the Fascist movement as a whole; and these suspicions were confirmed by the opposition of Mussolini and Pasella to the railway and electrical strikes in early 1920.[128] The *fasci* of 1919 withered and died, and had to be started again from scratch in 1920; this second attempt was successful, but on a different basis. The manifesto of the new Genoa *fascio* did not mention the programme of the movement; instead it announced simply that the *fascio* stood for 'the defence of the last National war to the bitter end, for the exploitation of Victory, for the resistance and opposition to the theoretical and practical degeneration of politicizing Socialism'.[129] The Spezia *fascio* was revived with the help of a Signor Italo Lucca, partner in a firm of agents who represented several important industrial concerns: he promised to secure the help of the local newspaper *Il Tirreno*.[130] The movement had abandoned its earlier radicalism; it was now subsidized by the industrialists and supported by the papers which they controlled. A distinction, however, should be made between the Fascism of the city of Genoa, which can be described as typically 'urban', and that of the Riviera manufacturing centres. The latter ('Industrial Fascism') was not only subsidized but sometimes organized and controlled by the employers. The industrialists could use their influence at a time when jobs were short to enrol their own employees and workers. For example, the secretary of the *fascio* of Cengio, near Savona, was the son of the manager of a chemical factory; he explained that on account of his position, 'I had to manoeuvre prudently and figure as little as possible, so as not to provoke a chorus of hostile abuse.'[131] The success of the Fascist movement in the industrial regions of Liguria was greatly advanced by the economic crisis which hit the armaments industry with particular severity; the *fasci*, thanks to their influence with the industrialists and the funds at their command, functioned as employment agencies and were undoubtedly able to recruit large numbers of unemployed workers.[132] Propaganda for an aggressive foreign policy and high armaments as a cure for unemployment may have had some appeal not only for industrialists but for workers hit by the crisis.

The *fascio* of the city of Genoa on the other hand, like the *fasci* of other big cities, was a relatively homogeneous organization; it did not recruit much from the working class, but had a good base among the white-collar workers and the petty-bourgeoisie, and the less prosperous professional classes, especially among the newcomers to the city who coveted and resented the superior position held by the respectable, established 'native' bourgeoisie. It was also more independent in its attitude to business; although financed by the shipowners, it preserved contacts with their greatest enemy Giulietti.[133] In this, the local Fascists had the encouragement of the Central Committee, who were keen that Giulietti's considerable following should be absorbed into the movement and were willing to risk offending the employers with this end in view. Ideologically, the Ligurian *fasci* followed the lead of Genoa during the crisis of early 1921; they backed Mussolini on the issue of the 'republican tendency' and the Pact of Pacification.[134] However the repercussions of Mussolini's surrender to the agrarian bloc were soon felt; the attempt to preserve the independence of the *fascio* from the ship-owners was abandoned, and it became their tool for the destruction of the Socialist dockworkers' unions and co-operatives. The invasion and sub-jugation of the port of Genoa in August 1922, however, was not the work of the city Fascists, but of squads concentrated from the industrial towns, from rural Piedmont and from the marble quarries of Carrara. Once the union monopoly of work in the docks had been broken by force the Fascists could win support in Genoa from casual labourers excluded from work by the regular co-operatives of the stevedores and coalheavers.[135]

The expansion of Fascism in rural areas was stimulated and directed by the reaction of the farmers and landowners against the peasant leagues of both Socialists and Catholics. In provinces such as Alessandria, Pavia, or Arezzo, where no Fascist movement existed until late 1920, the agrarian associations were directly responsible for its formation.[136] After an initial phase in which this reaction was mainly dependent on the middle classes of the larger towns, the movement began to win an increasing number of adherents in the countryside and small towns. Mussolini, who at times during 1921 spoke of agrarian Fascism almost as harshly as outside critics like Missiroli,[137] by 1922 saw the need to admit the predominant role which the countryside now played in the movement, and to give it a theoretical justi-fication. Fascism, he said, was not 'agrarian' but 'rural'; 'the agrarians are one thing, the *rurali* another. The agrarians are great landowners, and except for laudable exceptions, strongly conservative; the *rurali* are share-croppers, leaseholders, smallholders, and wage labourers. Between Fascism and the agrarians, there is bad blood.' He interpreted rural Fascism as an individualist revolt versus the threat of collectivization.

The sharecropper or the leaseholder tries with all his strength to become an owner – and he has succeeded on a vast scale in these last ten years. . . . The peasants are conquering the land by their own strength. It is clear that these serried phalanxes of new small owners cannot but detest Socialism. Instead, they have everything to hope for from Fascism and nothing to fear. . . . Here, in a certain sense, is the prodigy awaited for centuries. During the Risorgimento the *rurali* were either absent or hostile. The unity of Italy is the work of the intellectual bourgeoisie and of some of the artisan classes of the cities. But the great war of 1915–18 recruited the *rurali* in their millions. However, their participation in events was on the whole passive. They were once again dragged forward by the cities. Now Fascism has transformed this rural passivity . . . into active support for the reality and sanctity of the nation.[138]

At first sight, an examination of the social composition of the rural *fasci* would seem to give credit to Mussolini's able defence. They were not merely composed of landowners and farmers, or local shopkeepers, or the 'semi-rural bourgeoisie', of professional men and rentiers who eked out their income from other sources with the rent of a farm or two; the majority was often composed of peasants. During 1921, the later distinction between membership of the syndicates and membership of the party or the *fasci* may not always have been observed, and the membership statistics collected by the secretariat should therefore be treated with some caution.[139] However there is evidence that even the active branch of the movement, the squads, recruited peasants; besides the masses of workers or tenants who passed to the Fascist organizations under direct physical coercion or economic pressure, it seems clear that there was a large minority who played a more active role.[140]

Fascism in Tuscany and Umbria developed more slowly than in Emilia. Like Emilian Fascism, it began in the cities and radiated out into the countryside. Even more than in Emilia, the movement became subjected to the influence of the *agrari*. Many of the local *fasci* were founded by landowners or their agents. In one sense, however, Tuscan Fascism was less 'rural' than Emilian. In the Po Valley Fascism was able, after its first victories, to profit from the existence of structural unemployment, and even more from the effects of the slump, which drove many industrial workers back to the land to seek employment.[141] It could also play on the interests of small proprietors, leaseholders and sharecroppers against the *braccianti*, in regions where the former were a relatively privileged minority.[142] The structure of Tuscan agriculture was quite different. Here, sharecroppers were in the majority; on the other side, large property was still widespread, and the class of capitalist tenant farmers was non-existent in much of the region. Unemployment, both structural and temporary, was a less serious problem in rural areas than in the North. The Fascist movement found it harder, for these reasons, to divide the peasant masses and absorb a part of them.[143] To subdue the *mezzadri*, it was compelled to rely to a greater extent on recruits not only from the urban middle classes but from the '*bas-fonds*' of the cities, including professional criminals.

Local industry in Tuscany often played a major role in Fascism. In the Valdarno the Fascists absorbed the gangs of bullies who had been employed even before the war in electoral campaigns by the radical deputy and managing director of the big iron-works, Riccardo Luzzatto.[144] The Piombino *fascio* 'benefited from the wholehearted support of the directors of the chief local industry', the large steelworks also belonging to the *Ilva* combine.[145] In the province of Carrara the movement was created by the owners of the marble quarries, who were threatened with expropriation by the commune.[146] The movement began with the middle classes, but it was soon able, with the help of the industrialists, to enrol a large number of blackleg marble-workers, who formed the bulk of the squads used in the attack on Genoa. The Carrara *fascio*, in fact, was mainly working class in membership, though not in leadership.[147]

From Movement to Party

The 1921 elections concluded the period of Fascism's most febrile growth. It was now necessary for Mussolini to take a fresh look at the movement, and to attempt to re-impose a measure of central control. The grave dangers which we have seen in Ferrara existed in many other provinces; it was necessary to give some satisfaction to the left wing of the movement, and to all those who suspected that Fascism was falling under the tutelage of the old ruling class.

The 1921 conflicts within Fascism turned on three major issues: the reaffirmation by Mussolini of the 'republican tendency' of the *fascio*, the Pact of Pacification, and the transformation of the movement into a party. The lines of demarcation on these three questions were not identical. On the republican question, Mussolini had the support not only of the majority of the 'fascists of the first hour', but also of the new leaders of Emilia like Grandi and Balbo. The Bologna *fascio* had been threatened by a sharp conflict between republicans and monarchists; this was ably averted by Grandi who, while defending the a-political character of the *fasci*, which meant in practical terms that they would welcome members of all political parties, at the same time proclaimed himself a 'Mazzinian'.[148] The majority of Fascists in Bologna seem to have had vaguely republican sentiments. However neither Grandi nor Mussolini were really pledging themselves to anything concrete; and the democratic values which in 1919 were still associated with the republic in the minds of a number of Fascists, were now obscured. Nevertheless the move aroused considerable opposition, especially from those parliamentary deputies who had owed their election to Liberal or monarchist support.[149]

However the *fasci* themselves in most regions supported Mussolini. In Venice the decided republicanism of Marsich triumphed over considerable monarchist opposition; in Liguria, Tuscany and Naples, the *fasci* did not support the monarchism of their deputies.[150] Apart from Piedmont, where monarchist sentiment was strong,[151] opposition was confined to those provinces in which the conservative agrarians dominated the movement directly and without need of intermediaries, and where urban Fascism was weak.[152] But one cannot speak of the agrarian bloc as wholly hostile on this occasion; where demagogic and syndicalist tactics had been followed, as in Bologna, Ferrara, or Cremona, the republican tendency had strong support.

The line-up was quite different on the Pact of Pacification. The Pact had a parliamentary origin and the majority of the Fascist deputies were in favour. The moderate, monarchist right (Acerbo, and even De Vecchi, in spite of his agrarian connections) backed the idea; so did Massimo Rocca, who had conducted an especially lively polemic against the republican tendency. For all these men, the Pact of Pacification and the demobilization of Fascism spelt a return to a kind of normality; they believed that in spite of Mussolini's vision of an alliance with the Popolari and the Socialists, the place for a parliamentary, non-violent Fascism would be on the right.[153] Without abandoning the republican slogan, Mussolini in fact shared most of the views of men like Rocca. The most profound division in the Fascist movement cannot be described adequately in terms of 'left' and 'right'; it was rather between those who conceived of the movement as one of 'elites' and those who exalted the new, mass movement.[154] This division roughly coincides with that between urban and agrarian, or 'provincial', Fascism; the *raison d'être* lies in the difference of social composition, analysed above. The elite conception appealed strongly to the middle class, who felt that they were differentiated from the mass; in the cities it could be maintained, even after the movement's expansion. Instead the agrarian movement was marked by violence, concentration of authority, and the cult of the charismatic chief, combined with an exaltation of the force of numbers.

A third division was that between political and military Fascism. The ex-officers, who were the campaigners, the leaders of the squads, naturally opposed pacification, while the political secretaries and propagandists were more likely to be favourable. Pasella raised the question of the supremacy of the political organs over the squads at the 1921 Congress; the creation of the party was intended among other things to secure this end.[155] But as the range of activity of the squads expanded and their organization became more systematic, the prestige and influence of their leaders within the movement grew; in Mantua with Arrivabene, in Lucca with Carlo Scorza, and to a certain extent even in Florence with Tamburini, the organizers and commanders of the squads succeeded in establishing their control, directly or by alliances, over the political organs of the movement.[156] Where the anti-pacifiers won, the consequence was often the subordination of the political arm of the movement to the squads. During 1922, this shift became general and resulted in the defeat of the tendency represented by intellectuals like Lanzillo, or old Fascists like Mario Gioda. It should be emphasized that this distinction between *squadristi* and politicians is only applicable at the level of provincial leadership; in fact the military leaders tended to have the support of the moneyed sympathizers, whereas with the mass of *squadristi*, even if the Pact was not in itself welcome, loyalty to Mussolini often took precedence over other considerations.[157]

Attitudes to the Pact were also affected by the outcome of local power struggles and rivalries. Thus in Cremona province Farinacci had at first attacked the political secretary of the Crema *fascio*, Lieutenant Bianco, for his excessive dependence on the local agrarians, but in 1921 the positions were reversed. Farinacci became the leader of opposition to the Pact and Bianco's hostility to Farinacci led him to support it.[158]

The opposition to the transformation of the movement into a party was generally connected with hostility to the Pact and to Mussolini's leadership; however the 'national-revolutionaries' and those early Fascists who had come to believe in the permanent, rather than tactical, value of the 'anti-party', were also hostile.[159] The opposition to the change from movement to party was led by Dino Grandi and Piero Marsich. Farinacci did not concern himself directly with the question.[160] Grandi presented the purpose of the Fascist movement, with elevated rhetoric, as the 'redemption of the masses and their conversion to the national ideal'; Fascism would be the instrument for realizing the Mazzinian ideal of national unity. The State was to be transformed into 'a great and powerful institution of syndicates'. The formation of a political party might not be helpful to this end.[161] But Grandi, a far from inflexible character, was willing to accept Mussolini's offer of a compromise. The ambivalence of Grandi's attitudes, in practical terms on the extreme right, theoretically on the left, of the movement,[162] reflected the bastard origins of Fascist syndicalism in violence, and the symbiosis between terrorism and the recruitment of the masses. These dual functions found institutional expression in the foundation, alongside the party, of the Militia and the syndicates. On the other side, Mussolini and Massimo Rocca now in substance stood for a cautious and noncommittal conservatism. Corporate representation had been the one 'novelty' of the Fascist programme; but Mussolini's enthusiasm for it had temporarily evaporated. It was too much bound up with the Charter of the Carnaro and the D'Annunzian mystique. Instead he accepted the views of Massimo Rocca who saw the mission of Fascism as the defence of free enterprise and even free trade. This new liberalism was bound up with the defence of the middle-class consumer and tax payer.

For Dino Grandi the question of the Pact was uppermost and that of 'party or movement' secondary; for Piero Marsich, the leader of the Fascist movement in the Veneto, it was the other way round. Marsich opposed the Pact primarily not as a representative of agrarian interests, but because he wished to keep Fascism utterly intransigent and free from parliamentary compromise; the movement should somehow remain 'above politics' and national. His 'syndicalism' also predisposed him against the Pact; he believed that syndicates should be formed on the basis of the 'category', not the 'class' (i.e. should unite employers and workers), and should be regulated by the State.[163] For this programme, which strongly resembled that of the Nationalist Rocco, to be fulfilled, it was necessary that the Socialist and other 'class' organizations should be destroyed. In the Venice *fascio* Marsich had the support of most of the bourgeois sympathizers and of the other organizers of the movement; but the majority of the *squadristi* were loyal to Mussolini.[164]

When Grandi had accepted the party in exchange for Mussolini's tacit abandonment of pacification, Marsich was left isolated. In March 1922 he wrote an open letter to Bianchi deploring the party's involvement in parliamentary crises, and he followed this up four days later with a statement which evoked the spirit of the March on Fiume as the principle which should guide Fascism: 'It is necessary that our party should return to the purity and clarity of its origins in order that Fascists, legionaries, *arditi*, and all the best, most sincere national forces may gather together. . . . When a policy of transactions and compromises prevails, we must re-affirm our honest intransigence.'[165] This message by implication exalted D'Annunzio at the expense of Mussolini. The revolt of Marsich had serious repercussions in the whole of north-east Italy, where the D'Annunzian mystique was especially powerful, and among the *arditi*. Augusto Turati, the leader of Brescia Fascism and future secretary of the PNF, seems to have been involved in the scheme for a secession in favour of D'Annunzio.[166] But without support from Grandi the revolt was destined to failure; the defeat of Marsich marked the re-establishment of the authority of Mussolini over Fascism, and the virtual elimination of the D'Annunzian and 'national-revolutionary' opposition within Fascism.

During 1922 Mussolini moved further to the right. In economic doctrine, this was unnecessary; even if the industrialists were by no means prepared to accept the end of protectionism, they had great enthusiasm for the rest of the free enterprise package which he was selling. But to preserve the sympathy of conservative groups, it was necessary to accentuate the stress on order and authority. The title of Mussolini's review, *Gerarchia*, was in itself a manifestation of the new stress on 'hierarchy' aimed at consolidating the sympathies of those circles in the Army, the bureaucracy, the magistracy and business, which had applauded the anti-Socialist reaction but were perplexed and nervous at the continuation of violence and illegalism, now sometimes directed against the institutions of the State itself. G. Lumbroso promised that although violence 'for the moment takes an illegal form, when the Fascists are in power it will assume instead the aspect of a defence and strengthening of the State'.[167] Mussolini's article in the second number of *Gerarchia*, 'Which way is the world going?', went further. It tried to place Fascism in the context of a world-wide 'epochal' reaction against democracy. It marks the moment when Mussolini first frankly espoused the reactionary tradition which Nationalism had always admitted, and spoke with a sneer of the 'principles of 1789'. He presented the end of political democracy and the restoration of a more authoritarian form of government as the natural consequence and integration of the defeat of economic democracy: 'It may be that in the nineteenth century capitalism needed democracy; now it can do without it. . . . Democracy in the factory has lasted only as long as a bad dream. What has happened to the German *Betriebsräte* (factory councils) and the Russian factory councils? Now it is the other democracy, the political one, which is about to end, which *must* end.' This was a short guide to politics for the benefit of the business man. Mussolini, however, was concerned even now to differentiate Fascism from more traditional counter-revolutionary movements. The 'hierarchies' that Fascism would create would not be the weakened and discredited forms characteristic of elites in decline but the vigorous and healthy expression of new, ascending forces of courage and vigour.[168] Fascism was to be a 'Paretian revolution'; had not the illustrious sociologist prophesied the advent of a class of lions, not afraid to use force and imbued with the 'instinct for aggregates', or in other words conservative, traditionalist values? And had Fascism not adopted his economic principles of free trade and free enterprise? Surely this was proof of the consistency and modernity of Fascism. When one considers the qualifications of the Fascist leaders, who were not, with the exception of De Stefani and a few others, men of particularly notable technical expertise, one may be rather surprised that their claim to be the new ruling class received as much favourable attention as it did. But the rhetoric which had exalted the wartime generation, and the feeling that it was time for a change and that youth and inexperience were a kind of virtue after the fumblings of the old leaders, gave the claims some credibility, even in the eyes of intelligent men. One of the central problems of Fascism after the March, however, was to be the reconciliation of their 'technocratic' promises and aspirations with the existence of a huge party and a large class of hastily created leaders. The tension between the enthusiasm of party loyalists and the expertise of bureaucrats, soldiers or managers, is a problem which afflicts all revolutions, and Fascism was no exception.

The new accent on 'hierarchy' was also found in the first statute of the Partito Nazionale Fascista; the preamble declared that 'the Partito Nazionale Fascista is a voluntary militia placed at the service of the nation. In its activity it is sustained by these three keystones: order, discipline and hierarchy'. This phraseology made something of a concession to the anti-party mentality. However the constitution of the PNF still somewhat resembled that of other parties. The directive organs (the Central Committee and the *Direzione*) were to be elected by periodic congresses of the whole party; at the lower levels, the provincial *direttori* and secretaries were to be nominated by general congresses, and the same was true of the single *fasci*. In the last case, the draft statute provided explicitly for voting by secret ballot.[169] In fact if this mechanism, as we have seen, often functioned poorly at the provincial level, at the summit it was still necessary for Mussolini to consult the other members of the *Direzione*. Even after the Marsich affair, they still counted for something. But the preparations for insurrection inevitably led to a greater concentration of authority and to the temporary passage of control over the movement to the para-military commands; this situation had important repercussions on the structure of the party after the March on Rome.

4

THE MARCH ON ROME

Mussolini's rise to power was made possible by the crisis of confidence in the Liberal regime. The urban middle class, from which alone the Liberals could have received mass support, had shown itself particularly susceptible to the appeals of Fascism. However while the Liberals showed clear symptoms of decay, the errors and hesitations of the Socialists and Popolari had prevented them from inheriting the role of the dominant political force. The result was government by a series of uneasy compromises, without force either in Parliament or the nation and unable to end the virtual state of civil war which existed in much of Northern and Central Italy. The Government's loss of authority also aggravated the economic crisis, and the restoration of State finances and business confidence provided yet another theme in the growing chorus of demands for a 'strong government'. The crisis of 'public order' and the crisis of Parliament interacted at each stage to make their solution more difficult: no one could find a political formula which would enable both these obstacles to be overcome.

These were the conditions which made Fascist victory possible; but they did not make it inevitable. Although the progress of the crisis continually narrowed the range of choices, right up till the morning of 28 October the outcome remained uncertain. In the final stage, much depended on individual decision and temperament.[1]

Giolitti's dissolution of Parliament in 1921 proved a disastrous error, even admitting the difficulty of the situation in which he found himself. First, as mentioned above, it favoured the collusion of the administration with the Fascists; secondly, it alienated the Popolari, who knew themselves to be, with the Socialists, the intended victims of the operation; thirdly, it increased the strength of the anti-parliamentary and anti-democratic forces of the right. The Popolari and the Socialists were not much reduced in numbers, so that the net effect of the elections was to weaken the democratic and liberal centre. Giolitti resigned after a debate on foreign policy in which he obtained only a bare majority. It is doubtful, however, whether this vote was really decisive: more important was his knowledge that he would soon lose the support of the Popolari.[2]

For the Government of Bonomi, who succeeded Giolitti in July 1921, the central problem was that of 'pacification'. The possibility of a Fascist seizure of power still appeared remote: but the presence in the nation of a powerful and continually expanding movement, whose determining characteristic was the use of violence, posed a clear threat to the Liberal State. To restore peace, either the Fascists had to be forcibly disarmed, or they had to be induced to accept a compromise, and to bring their illegal activities to an end in return for a share in Government responsibility.

Bonomi promoted the 'Pact of Pacification' between Fascists and Socialists. Initially, the prospects for pacification looked good. The excesses of the 'punitive expeditions' had begun to revolt public opinion, and even police sympathies could no longer be counted on. This hastened Mussolini's acceptance of the pact. The hope of an easy and bloodless solution was soon dispelled by the revolt of the agrarian *squadristi* against Mussolini's decision; but the consequent crisis in the Fascist movement nonetheless gave Bonomi a very favourable opportunity for re-establishing the authority of the State. Instead, he was unable to secure the enforcement of the Pact, or even to prevent the squads from extending the range of their activities further. Mussolini's opponents Balbo and Grandi were able to organize the 'march on Ravenna' of three thousand armed Fascists. This not only represented a victory for their strategy over Mussolini's, but was also, in the words of Balbo, the proof that '*squadrismo* could be transformed from a local into a national phenomenon'.[3]

Bonomi was certainly not the man that the situation required. He was one of those politicians who reach the top because they do not arouse strong feelings: his undoubted ability to compromise was not balanced by the possession of an adequate residue of political courage. When Bissolati had challenged Sonnino over the Adriatic question, Bonomi had failed to support him: and his equivocal attitude at that time had allowed him to remain on good terms with the military leaders and the nationalistic wing of the interventionists. However his attitude towards the Popolari and to Giolitti was equally conciliatory. In his ambition to please everybody he did not exclude from the range of his sympathy either the reformist Socialists, his former colleagues and friends, or the Fascists, who had helped in his electoral campaign at Mantua. The good will and the knowledge of what had to be done were there, but once the rosy vision of a general reconciliation had been dispelled, only inflexible determination and vigour would serve: and these were not Bonomi's qualities.

After the reconciliation between Mussolini and Grandi had restored the unity of the Fascist movement, Bonomi made one more attempt to restore law and order. On 21 December he sent a circular to the Prefects authorizing them to dissolve any armed organizations in their area, and to prosecute their members : but he left the initiative for the application of these measures to the choice of the individual officials. It was hardly likely that they would take such a dangerous responsibility on their own shoulders. The Fascists, meanwhile, moved to counter the threat by announcing that all members of the party would henceforward also be members of the squads; this meant that the latter could not be dissolved unless the Fascist party was outlawed as well. Bonomi failed to take up the challenge, and the result of his ill-judged move was therefore further to discredit the authority of the State. The chief effect of the Bonomi circular was to encourage the Prefects to suppress the working-class defence movement of the *arditi del popolo*.

The weakness of Bonomi cannot, however, be attributed only to his personal failings. While all the groups of the centre paid lip-service to 'pacification', and in a sense perhaps actually desired it, they perceived that the Socialists were likely to benefit more than the Fascists from the impartial restoration of order, and this consequence was not so universally acceptable. In fact Bonomi's failure demonstrated that impartiality was not enough. There were really two alternatives, two conflicting political solutions to the problem of Fascism ; Bonomi had avoided the choice. One was the formation of a broad anti-Fascist coalition, which had to include the reformist Socialists if it were to be effective, either in Parliament or outside ; the other was the inclusion of the Fascists in the Government on the condition that they renounced, or at least greatly reduced, their illegal activities. The best opportunity for the absorption of the more moderate and politically responsible elements of Fascism had clearly been missed : 'instead of a Fascist secession, which would have allowed Mussolini and his friends to find a place in the State, the end of the year witnessed the unification of Fascism in the battle against the State.'[4] Meanwhile the Socialists continued to refuse their support to the democratic alternative. In these circumstances, there was not much hope of constructing a more strongly based government.

At this point the parliamentary situation took another turn for the worse. The cause was the hostility between the Democrats and the Popolari. The latter had obtained a bigger share in the Bonomi cabinet than in previous ministries, and in particular they had obtained the Ministry of Justice, which dealt with Church-State relations; the Democrats held that this Ministry should never have been allowed to fall into the hands of a party connected with the Vatican. Risorgimento orthodoxy, the anti-clericalism of the masonic lodges, the desire of Giolitti to return to power, and the conservative interests which were opposed to the Popular programme of agrarian reform, made common cause in the denunciation of the Bonomi government's subservience to the PPI, and through it to the Church.[5]

The Democrats provoked the resignation of the Bonomi ministry and Don Sturzo countered by the famous 'veto on Giolitti', which prevented him from forming a government.

After two weeks of crisis, in which abortive attempts were made either to create an anti-Fascist coalition or to form a 'ministry of concentration' containing both Fascists and Socialists, the Popolari, out of fatigue more than for any other reason, accepted the candidacy of Facta, one of Giolitti's most faithful lieutenants. The only result of Sturzo's veto was thus to give power to an inferior substitute for Giolitti; Facta was commonly regarded as a caretaker who would eventually make way for the return of his chief. Naturally, at the same time, the 'veto' increased Giolitti's dislike of the Popolari. In the new Government the right, represented by the conservatives Riccio and De Capitani, gained in strength; and this signified an even greater tendency to appease Fascism.[6]

The Fascist movement was able not only to launch a new offensive against the Socialist party and the trade unions, but also to extend the practice of mass rallies and the 'mobilization' of the squads, with the purpose of intimidating government officials, or, if they remained firm, of putting pressure on the Government for their removal. The first rehearsal of the new tactics was at Ferrara in May 1922, when the Fascists concentrated an army of 30–40,000 labourers in order to compel the Government to finance new public works. Two weeks later they scored a still more significant triumph. In the key province of Bologna, they succeeded in getting the Government to transfer Mori, the most able and determined of the Prefects, who had been responsible for co-ordinating the action of the police in the whole region of the lower Po Valley. The Government had twice negotiated with the Emilian Fascists and had sacrificed its own representative to appease their discontent. Neither Giolitti nor Bonomi had fallen so low.[7]

There now existed a kind of power vacuum. The Facta government, entirely lacking in authority, was kept alive by the stalemate between the major political forces. None of them were able to impose their solution.

The first real initiative to overcome the deadlock came from the left. The new Fascist offensive and the catastrophic weakness of Facta in the Mori affair induced the reformist wing of the Socialists to make, at least, an attempt to end their isolation. On 1 June 1922, the parliamentary group by a 46–20 majority declared their readiness to support a ministry 'which would ensure the restoration of law and liberty'. The reformists were backed by the CGL.[8] This brought a response from the PPI: the party executive declared that co-operation with the Socialists was a real possibility, although it depended on their programme. They called on the Government to take note that the mere fact that such an alliance could be contemplated should give it a new freedom to restore the authority of the State.[9]

On 13–15 July 1922 Fascist bands led by Farinacci occupied Cremona, forcing the resignation of the local administration and sacking the house of the left-wing PPI deputy Miglioli; the Government's failure to react precipitated its crisis. This time it was the PPI who introduced a motion of censure on the ministry and Turati who replied by an announcement of his willingness to support any government which would defend liberty against Fascist violence. Mussolini, highly alarmed at the turn events were taking, promised his support for a 'ministry of pacification' under Orlando, with the inclusion of the Socialists.[10] The way seemed clear to an anti-Fascist ministry: but it was blocked by a letter from Giolitti to the editor of the *Tribuna*, Malagodi, which asked rhetorically: 'What good can come to the nation from a *connubio* of Don Sturzo – Treves – Turati?' By this letter, Giolitti made it quite clear that he did not intend to support any coalition formed to fight Fascism. Even if provoked by Sturzo's veto, this decision must bear a heavy responsibility for all that followed. The Socialists then made up their minds that they were willing not only to support but to join the Government and Turati in person called on the King: but it was too late. Giolitti's intervention had shifted the centre of gravity of the crisis to the right, and the Popolari, under pressure from the Vatican, now abandoned their original veto on the inclusion of the right-wing parties.[11]

The Socialists completed the disaster by carrying out the unfortunate idea of a 'legalitarian general strike'. Some months before, the various unions – Socialist, syndicalist and Republican – had formed a 'Labour Alliance' to combat Fascism; it now seemed to Turati that the time had come to throw the force of organized labour into the battle in a last attempt to influence the outcome of the parliamentary crisis. This idea of combining strike action with parliamentary negotiation might once have been effective, when the Socialists were on the offensive: but in the circumstances of July 1922 it had precisely the opposite effect to that intended. A new Facta government was hurriedly formed under the threat of the strike;[12] and all the old bourgeois fears of political blackmail by organized labour were revived, cancelling the moral advantages earned by the reasonableness of the parliamentary Socialist party. The Fascists, once more disguised as 'defenders of order', seized the opportunity and counter-attacked with complete success; their most dramatic and important victory was the expulsion of the Socialist *giunta* from Milan town hall. From this time on no political leader imagined that a new government could be formed without the Fascists: the problem was now whether their participation would be in a subordinate or a dominant role.

The anti-Fascist coalition was broken by the double defeat. The reformist Socialists formally seceded from the PSI at the beginning of October. It was too late to make much difference, and Serrati was unfortunately right when he called their hopes of collaboration with a bourgeois government 'empty and unreal',[13] although the responsibility for this in large part rested with his leadership. For the extreme left, the prospects were certainly no brighter. The strike weapon had been tried and failed; the 'Labour Alliance' broke up, pessimism settled on most of the militants and their leaders, and Mussolini was able to conclude that he had won his battle on this front, and that a Fascist seizure of power would meet with no serious resistance from organized labour or revolutionary groups. The Communists, and the majority of the *massimalisti*, who controlled the most militant groups of workers, continued to insist that the crisis of the bourgeois state was no affair of theirs.[14]

More concrete possibilities still remained for a great national ministry of pacification. Mussolini could still not afford to oppose this idea openly; he approved, and may even, for motives which remain obscure, have suggested, a tripartite agreement with Nitti and D'Annunzio. A strange accident, when D'Annunzio fell from a window after a quarrel with his mistress, put an end to this unlikely negotiation; but D'Annunzio remained one of Mussolini's most serious worries. The poet had imagined a new role for himself as the man of peace, the 'spiritual' healer of wounds who would restore national unity: and this could not be dismissed as pure fantasy. He was still formidable because of his ascendancy over the 'combatants', including many Fascists, and because he had his own para-military force, the legionaries. After the collapse of the Labour Alliance, the contacts between trade union leaders and D'Annunzio were multiplied; a number of minor organizations officially accepted his protection, and several CGL leaders put their trust in him as the only man who could obtain reasonable terms of peace from the Fascists. The keystone of this odd alliance between D'Annunzio and labour was the powerful autonomous Seamen's Union whose president, the adventurous Captain Giulietti, financed the poet out of his secret funds. Finally Facta, who had long cultivated his friendship, was anxious to give him an opportunity for action: between them, they agreed on a plan for a grand patriotic rally of disabled ex-servicemen on 4 November to be addressed by D'Annunzio. There was not, it seems, any very precise design behind this piece of political theatre. But both Facta and D'Annunzio hoped to create a moral climate in which Fascist violence could no longer be disguised by patriotism, and in one form or another thus to bring an end to the civil war.

There is no doubt that Mussolini was really disturbed by the prospect of a spectacular return of D'Annunzio to the centre of the political stage. Only when he believed that he had eliminated the threat by a direct agreement with D'Annunzio did he feel strong enough to make an assault on the State. On 16 October Mussolini brought off one of his master strokes; he signed a pact with Giulietti and the Seamen's Federation, and in return obtained from D'Annunzio the demobilization of the legionaries, who had been massing at Fiume. This gave Mussolini the confidence to proceed. However D'Annunzio was not definitively excluded from the game by this able manoeuvre. The plan for the 4 November rally continued to go forward.[15]

At the beginning of October the Fascists occupied Trento and Bolzano, forcing the resignation of the Government commissioner, and in the same days the regulations of the Fascist Militia were published. The Government failed to respond to either of these acts of defiance: it was evident that it could not survive long after this humiliation, and the search for a new ministry began in earnest. Mussolini, for his part, had completed his final

82

test of the State's capacity for resistance; he was now ready to listen to his more impetuous and radical supporters, who had long been urging a 'march on Rome' to sweep away the debris of the parliamentary regime.

What Mussolini most had to fear was the return of Giolitti. While the eighty-year-old statesman stayed at his Piedmontese home in Cavour, his friends, notably Camillo Corradini and the Prefect of Milan, Lusignoli, worked to prepare his comeback.

Mussolini could only keep Giolitti out by simultaneously negotiating and preparing for the mobilization of his private army. The decision to 'march on Rome' was taken in a meeting at Milan on 16 October, attended by Mussolini, the party secretary Michele Bianchi, the three leaders of the Militia, Balbo, De Vecchi and General De Bono, and two other retired generals, Ceccherini and Fara. The danger of a Giolitti ministry was Mussolini's chief argument for immediate action. 'Giolitti believes he can offer us two portfolios; but we want six or nothing. So we must put the masses in action to make an extra-parliamentary crisis and come to power. He would give orders to fire on the Fascists, as he did with D'Annunzio.' The three generals and De Vecchi all argued for delay; they urged that time was needed to perfect the Fascists' military organization and to 'work' the Army. They were all in reality preoccupied by the risk of a conflict between Mussolini and the monarchy. Even if Mussolini won, this would be a danger from their point of view. Bianchi and above all Balbo, who had no such worries, gave Mussolini the moral and political support he needed: indeed it was their determination which later held him to the path of insurrection when he hesitated. Balbo saw the psychological and technical advantages of immediate action: 'Today we enjoy the benefits of surprise. No one yet believes seriously in our insurrectionary intentions. In other words, in 6 months our difficulties will be ten times as great.'[16]

Giolitti, and with him all the other Liberals, were used to the leisurely tempo of old-fashioned parliamentary politics; they did not realize the vital importance of the time factor, and they did not succeed in unmasking the true character of Mussolini's politics, which consisted in the simultaneous use of intrigue and negotiation for a *combinazione*, and of the mobilization of his forces for direct action. By his apparent readiness to compromise Mussolini spread confusion and undermined the determination of those men who were still capable of offering resistance. Moreover, his negotiations kept open a line of retreat for him, in case his plans for insurrection should be discovered. The genuine disagreement between moderate 'legalitarians' and extreme 'insurrectionists' in the Fascist movement helped him to preserve this flexibility. Mussolini, unfortunately, had penetrated many of the secrets and habits of the Italian Liberals and played upon their rivalries, vanities and predilection for dignified delay; while they, on the other hand, failed to understand the 'rules' and tempo of his game, dictated by a different mentality and set of experiences.

Giolitti's conduct in the last stage of the crisis was oddly passive. Undoubtedly, he was weary of the intrigues and petty difficulties of parliamentary life. At eighty, rest was welcome. However a psychological explanation of his failure to bar Mussolini's way is not altogether convincing. If he showed himself curiously reluctant to act, this was not, I would suggest, because he had abandoned ambition. Fatigue, and perhaps scepticism of Mussolini's real intentions, blended with constitutional punctilio and a kind of vanity. He expected to be welcomed as the saviour of Italy in her most difficult hour, and would not move before he was assured of his designation by a 'regular and unambiguous decision'[17] of those parliamentary groups for which he showed such scarce regard. He wished, in fact, to be sure of almost unanimous support, and he was disposed therefore to be very patient with the Fascists. It was also true that to provoke a government crisis could give the Fascists just the opportunity they needed if a successor ministry was not ready to take over instantly.

The result, in any case, is that Mussolini's bluff worked. During October, Mussolini negotiated with everyone in sight: with D'Annunzio, with Giolitti, with Nitti, with Orlando, with Salandra, and with Facta. Each was made to feel that Mussolini desired and needed him for the new, decisive *combinazione*. On the whole, Mussolini was remarkably successful in keeping each of his interlocutors in ignorance of the advances he had made to the others; however in the case of Giolitti and Facta, given their common connections, his double game was exposed. Mussolini's agents had simultaneously been telling Giolitti that he must take over, and suggesting to Facta that the Fascists would like to join a new government with him as leader. On 13 October to counter the effects of this disclosure Mussolini and Bianchi were forced to pretend that they had decided in favour of a Giolitti ministry. However they said that they would prefer to delay action until after the Fascist Congress, scheduled for 24 October at Naples. We know that Giolitti agreed to this request. In the next ten days, it is true, his suspicions were aroused. By 23 October he had come to the conclusion that a change of ministry was urgent, and was even ready to consider forming a government without the Fascists.[18] But the loss of time could only have been remedied if he had decided to come to Rome immediately.

Facta could have precipitated events himself by resigning. It must be admitted that Facta saw himself and his government in a very different light from that in which it appeared to other people. What they saw as weakness, indecision and the humiliation of the State, he saw as a 'real miracle' of peaceful persuasion which had earned him universal gratitude. In this world of fantasy, the theatrical idea of a grand rally of reconciliation and patriotism presided over by D'Annunzio could enter, but the insistent rumours of blackshirt mobilization made small impression. Did Facta play a deliberate double game? Certainly he was misled by his little vanities, and with all the information of the government at his command, he failed to warn Giolitti to urgent action. But his reluctance to leave power had a real cause in the procrastination of Giolitti and, at the last moment, also in the intervention of the King.[19]

Why did the King intervene ? It would seem from the few hints dropped by that most taciturn man that he was already irritated, and with reason, by Facta's imbecile optimism and constant delays. In addition, by a lapse which if not deliberate was certainly at least Freudian, Facta had failed to keep him informed of the Giolitti-Mussolini negotiations. Yet Facta's negotiations with Mussolini on 26 October, of which he had informed the King, need not be construed as treachery to Giolitti. With Giolitti still in Piedmont, Facta's argument of the need to gain time was reasonable. The ministry could not resign in the face of the reports of Fascist mobilization, by now impossible for even Facta to ignore, until they were quite certain that a successor was ready.[20] On the other hand Facta's omission to inform the King about the Giolitti negotiations really does seem culpable, and undoubtedly added an extra factor of delay ; but without Giolitti's own hesitation and acceptance of the Fascist tempo it would not have been decisive.

One of the 'Quadrumvirs' supposed to lead the March on Rome, De Vecchi, still had misgivings. At the last moment he made an effort, supported by Dino Grandi and Costanzo Ciano, to avert the March and to bring about the formation of a conservative-Fascist ministry headed by Salandra. De Vecchi and Grandi would not have been sorry to see Mussolini's freedom of action curtailed by a compromise. Their initiative, unlike earlier over-tures, did not form part of a deliberate plan of deception ; it was taken with-out Mussolini's knowledge or agreement. However the effect of their action worked in Mussolini's favour ; De Vecchi and Grandi convinced both Salandra and Orlando that the Facta government must resign immediately to avert a Fascist insurrection ;[21] but in reality they were powerless to arrest the plans for the March at such a late stage, when Michele Bianchi and Balbo were determined not to compromise. The only man who could still call a halt was Mussolini himself : at the last moment, his nerve almost failed him and it was only the determination of Michele Bianchi which held him to his resolve.[22]

The plan for the March on Rome had been drawn up in a secret meeting on 24 October in a Naples hotel. The plan called for the occupation of public buildings throughout north and central Italy as the first stage in the seizure of power ; in the second stage three columns would concentrate on the roads leading into Rome, at S. Marinella, Monterotondo and Tivoli, and converge on the capital. If the Government resisted, the Ministries were to be occu-pied by force.[23] In reality, the March on Rome, in the strict sense, was a colossal bluff. The city was defended by 12,000 men of the regular army, under the loyal General Pugliese, who would have been able to disperse the Fascist bands without difficulty. Many of the Fascists failed to arrive at their points of concentration; they were travelling by train and were stopped by the simple expedient of taking up a few yards of track. Those who did arrive were poorly armed and they were short of food. They could do nothing except hang around miserably in the torrential autumn rain. The grandiose 'pincer movement' on Rome could never have been carried out with any chance of success.[24]

Anti-Fascist historians have quite rightly devoted much attention to puncturing the myth of the March on Rome, as part of a general depreciation of the 'revolutionary' claims of Fascism. However it should be remembered that the seizure of power by 'force' in a modern State is never possible, except when the army or police carries out the *coup*, unless the will to resist of the Government forces has been undermined. Even the Bolshevik Revolution could only succeed because the soldiers of the regular army would not fight for the established government. This does not mean to say, however, that power would simply have fallen into the hands of the Bolsheviks without the determined action of the small groups of Red Guards. The problem can be clarified better by reference to the famous book by Curzio Malaparte, *Technique of the coup d'état*. The exaggerations and inaccuracies of this work have often been pointed out; the notorious thesis of Malaparte that 'what governments have to fear are the tactics of Trotzky, not the strategy of Lenin' was angrily rejected by Trotzky himself as superficial, and the description of the tactics owes much to fantasy. Although Malaparte sensed well enough the importance of disorder, or the existence of what can only be termed rather vaguely a revolutionary atmosphere, he did not unfortunately allow this perception to modify his thesis.[25]

Nevertheless if one refuses to accept Malaparte's view of coup technique as a kind of magic, effective in all historical circumstances, his book can be read with profit. There *is* a 'technical' element in the seizure of power, and it is likely to be more important in the case of a movement like Italian Fascism, whose motive force was weak, both ideologically and socially, when compared with that behind the major revolutions. Malaparte was right to call attention to technique, even though he overrated its importance. The March on Rome can best be viewed neither as a 'revolution', nor as a simple piece of mass choreography, but as psychological warfare. Within the complex of the Fascist operations of the twenty-seventh and twenty-eighth, it is helpful to distinguish the March on Rome proper, which was not, and could not have been, carried out until all possibility of resistance had vanished from the 'first act' of the plan, which consisted in the seizure or isolation of prefectures and police headquarters, railway stations, post and telegraph offices, anti-fascist newspapers and circles and Camere del Lavoro. This programme corresponds more or less to Malaparte's description of the objectives of the new style of *coup*, except, of course, that it was only carried out in provincial centres and not in the capital itself. Neither Balbo, with his romantic temperament, nor Mussolini, who remained all his life surprisingly ignorant of military affairs and logistics, were likely to be altogether hard-headed in their plans; yet there are indications that the seizure of power in the provinces was, realistically, viewed by some Fascists at least as the vital stage in the insurrection. The Prefect of Naples reported to the Government on 26 October that:

From a trustworthy agent comes the following report on the Fascist action; there exist 4 different plans, to be put into effect subsequent to general mobilization: first, a converging March on Rome, the occupation of public offices, buildings, etc.; 2nd, simultaneous occupation of offices and public services of principal cities which would be held as hostages; 3rd, a feint converging manoeuvre on Rome to compel the concentration of larger contingents with object of carrying out instead the 2nd plan; 4th, mobilization ordered only with purpose of impressing public opinion and putting pressure on members of government and thus reaching objectives without striking a blow. He added, however, that he had some reason to believe that now it was a matter of plan no. 3.

According to the record kept by Balbo of the meeting at the Hotel Vesuvius on the twenty-fourth, officially, the first of these alternatives was adopted.[26] However the third alternative, which the Prefect's informant believed to have been adopted, was so much more realistic that it does seem probable that, in the minds of some Fascist leaders, the first phase was really the most important in the operation. Was Mussolini himself of this opinion ? He had certainly only committed himself to the operation in the belief that the Government and the Army would not put up an effective resistance. One cannot, therefore, take his military proposals too literally. It is probable that, while leaving the detailed execution to his subordinates, he regarded the occupation of the provincial cities as an important security and bargaining point, in case his assessment should prove wrong. What needs emphasis is that the March on Rome was almost inconceivably ill-planned if the intention really had been to seize the central State machine by force – when the only way would have lain in a rapid *coup de main*, not in a ponderous concentration. But politically it was essential to avoid surprise. The Government and the King could not be threatened too directly; they must instead be put in a position where they would have to take a positive initiative to restore order.

Where Malaparte's interpretation is best founded is in his criticism of the Government's counter measures. These, thanks to the competence of the War Minister Soleri and General Pugliese, were, as we have seen, adequate for the protection of Rome. But in the provinces it was a different matter. General Pugliese himself, anxious to avoid bloodshed, had pointed out that to prevent the concentration of large masses of Fascists, it would be necessary to co-ordinate his dispositions for the defence of Rome with a general plan for the whole of Italy. Such a plan was never drawn up. The Government's instructions to the Prefects were that they should hand over their powers to the local army command in case of grave disorders.

The defects of this system were that it left the initiative in the hands of the Fascists, and that the assignment of responsibility for preventing the take-over of public buildings and other strategic points was likely at the critical moment to be uncertain. Unless the Prefect was unusually astute and handed over power to the Army before the Fascists went into action, both he and the local military commander would find themselves in a difficult position. The Prefect might well feel reluctant to order the police to open fire or to take other decisive action, when he knew that his instructions allowed him to evade the responsibility for repression; on the other hand, the military commander would take over without full knowledge of the political situation or the forces at his disposal, and would be forced to expel the Fascists from strategic points they had already occupied, rather than merely defending them.[27]

The importance of the 'technical' defects of the Government's measures is shown by at least two contemporary documents. The first is the letter in which Camillo Corradini informed Giolitti of the start of Fascist mobilization on 27 October. Corradini, as a former Under Secretary of the Interior who before that had been a permanent official of the same ministry, had an unrivalled knowledge of the workings of the Government machinery in the provinces. His comments are therefore especially worthy of note :

The uncertainty is greatest among the police and prefectoral authorities. The Government has prescribed resistance including in case of necessity the use of arms. In other words the Government does not see the insurrectionary character of this whole movement, since in such a case it cannot be a question of a mere matter for the police, but of a real movement which should be treated as such, and therefore arrest of the leaders, military government, etc. If this doesn't occur there will be minor disasters, victims without any result, and with the certainty that sporadic acts here and there will not prevent the favourable results of the insurrection and will only embitter and increase the movement. That is my impression. At Rome they don't understand a thing, and what is worse they give uncertain and contradictory information. At Milan, for example, they are in doubt even as to whether the telegraph and telephone offices should be guarded and they telephone from Rome that protection should be confined to the offices dependent on the Ministry of the Interior, as if these offices, cut off from their communications could represent anything, and as if this powerful centre of life could do anything without its own means of communication.

The failure to provide for the defence of the communications system is here singled out by Corradini in terms which suggest the partial validity of Malaparte's analysis, which in this particular was based on his own direct experience of the Fascist occupation of Florence.[28] The second document is the record kept by General Pugliese of his meeting with Facta, the Minister of the Interior, Taddei the War Minister, and Soleri on the night of the March (27–8 October). Facta and Taddei, faced with the reports from Perugia and Florence of the occupation of the prefectures, telephones and post offices, 'expressed their pained surprise that the armed forces should not have been able to prevent this'. 'The commander of the division replied firmly that this could happen only on account of the lack of precise orders on the attitude to be taken when faced with Fascist violence.' Pugliese pointed out that his suggestions for liaison between the military and political authorities had not been taken up, except for Rome, and that 'therefore the arbitrary Fascist occupations at Perugia and Florence regretted by the ministers Facta and Taddei were the responsibility of the political authority, which, having retained the powers for the protection of public order and absolute control over all the local armed forces, during the whole day of 27 October had been unable to prevent them or to react, and had allowed trains loaded with militia to leave undisturbed for Rome.'[29]

From a strict military or strategic point of view all this was no doubt irrelevant; not only in Rome, but in the great northern cities, Milan, Genoa, Turin, and even in the Fascist stronghold, Bologna, the authorities, alerted in time, were able to maintain control of the situation without much difficulty. However the Fascist action was successful in creating an atmosphere of confusion and an impression of the widespread collapse of State power which during the critical night of 27–8 October could not fail to have a grave psychological effect. For this we have the testimony of Facta's *chef de cabinet*, Efrem Ferraris :

. . .at the Viminale, the telephones which linked the prefectures to the Ministry gave no respite and after midnight the news became alarming. In the night I witnessed, in the silence of the great rooms of the Viminale, the disintegration of the authority and power of the State. On the large sheets of paper which I kept in front of me, there grew ever thicker the names of the occupied prefectures that I was noting down, the indications of invaded telegraph offices, of military garrisons who had fraternized with the Fascists, providing them with arms, of trains requisitioned by the militia which were directed, loaded with armed men, towards the capital.[30]

Thus at Perugia the Prefect surrendered to the Fascists ; at Florence the prefecture was not occupied, but it was cut off and unable to communicate since the Fascists had occupied the railway station and the telegraph office.[31] At Pisa the occupation of the prefecture was prevented, but a large number of Fascists were able to leave undisturbed for the point of concentration ; elsewhere in Tuscany this was the general pattern, and the Tuscan Fascists were also able to acquire a notable quantity of arms, including machine-guns.[32] In the Po Valley, except at Bologna, the situation was not much better. At Cremona, Farinacci was anxious to prove himself second to none in decision and toughness. His squads were the first, with those of Pisa, to attack. They began by cutting off the electric light, and in the subsequent darkness and confusion they surprised the police station and the prefecture and occupied all the other key points. Later on, the prefecture was retaken by the Army and it was here that the Fascists suffered their heaviest casualties, eight dead and thirteen wounded. But reinforcements arrived from the province and the situation remained confused, without the military being able or willing to re-establish complete control.[33] At Mantua, the Prefect claimed that after a brief skirmish between the *Guardia Regia* and the Fascists, he was compelled to give way by 'the preponderance of the Fascist forces', several thousand strong and armed with machine-guns.[34] In Alessandria the Fascists broke into the barracks, capturing rifles and machine-guns, and seized the public buildings, holding the Prefect prisoner.[35] In Bergamo, in Venice and almost all the provincial capitals of the Veneto, and in Trieste, the Fascists seized the post and telegraph offices, and often the prefectures as well.[36] The South on the whole stayed quiescent until victory was certain, but the *ras* Caradonna occupied Foggia, disarming the local garrison and seizing large quantities of arms.[37]

It is true that from an orthodox strategic point of view all these local and unconnected successes were irrelevant: but to conclude that 'the seditious movement not only had not been victorious, but must be considered a complete failure on the military plane'[38] is surely to miss the point. The military and political planes of action were not separate but complementary and the partial successes of the military movement had their importance.

We must now return to Rome, the central government and the King. All that has been said does not, of course, alter the fact that this was the point of decision. At 8 pm on 27 December, when the King arrived in Rome from his country residence of S. Rossore, he told Facta that the Crown must be able to decide in full liberty, and not under the pressure of Fascist rifles. His determination to resist seemed evident. It was not out of character; Victor Emmanuel III had behaved as a correct constitutional monarch, and in 1919 he had courageously resisted Nationalist and anti-parliamentary pressures. To more than one visitor, he had then repeated that he was ready to take a rifle and go down into the piazza in order to defend parliament against a hypothetical military coup.[39] But by October 1922 everything looked very different. The long and painful parliamentary crises had had their effect; in the last stages of the parliamentary crisis of July the King had scarcely concealed his impatience at the protracted failure to find any effective government. In the month before the March, the insouciance of Facta had also deeply perturbed him; on 14 October he had urged Facta to summon Parliament immediately[40] and, reading between the lines, it is easy to see that he was irritated by the Prime Minister's persistent neglect to consult him or keep him fully informed. Twice, on 24 and 25 October, Facta assured him that the project of a March on Rome had been abandoned; this was not calculated to give the King much confidence in the Government's preparations or power of decision. He was bound, in addition, to be preoccupied with avoiding a violent conflict, especially when all the leading Liberal politicians had shown themselves persuaded of the necessity of giving the Fascists a share in government.[41]

Nevertheless, on the evening of the twenty-seventh, he still saw his duty, in plain terms, as resistance. Why did he change his mind ? To this central question, whose importance vividly illustrates the role of the individual in historical crisis, the answer cannot be certain. The King was an extremely taciturn man, not given to indiscretions, and the reasons for his volte-face remain a mystery : one can only guess at them.

The explanations which Victor Emmanuel gave of his refusal to sign the emergency decree in 1945 are vitiated by their purpose as Royalist propaganda : and all his retrospective statements, indeed, are marked by a desire to put his decision in the best light possible, according to the different dates when they were offered. The excuse that he quite literally ceded to *force majeure*, convinced that the garrison of Rome was too small and too unreliable to resist the Fascist attack, will not hold. However some part of these several statements may be helpful in understanding the King's state of mind : 'At difficult moments everyone is capable of indecision . . . few or none are those who can take clear decisions and assume grave responsibilities. In 1922 I had to call "these people" to the Government because all the others in one way or another, had abandoned me' ; on other occasions the King spoke of his desire to 'avoid bloodshed given the news from the provinces which were already in the hands of the Fascists', and said that if he had acted otherwise, 'it would have been civil war'.[42] Both these elements in his apologies do seem to correspond to what we know of his feelings and of the actual situation in 1922 ; in a telegram of 26 October to Facta he had spoken of his desire 'to avoid shocks' by 'associating Fascism with the Government in a legal form' and we have seen that he had some reason for believing that Facta had deliberately left the unwelcome burden of decision to him.[43] On the night of the twenty-eighth itself, Facta's conduct was extraordinary. First he offered the resignation of the Cabinet to the King, a gesture which goes some way further towards excusing the latter's hyperbolic assertion that he had been 'abandoned' : then, with rather excessive sang-froid, Facta retired to bed.[44]

It seems plain that the King's decision must have looked greater and more serious at the end of the night than at the beginning. If the Government counter-measures had been immediately effective, if the occupations had been prevented or the leaders of the movement arrested, the proclamation of martial law might have resolved the situation without a general conflict : by the morning this had become much more doubtful.

By themselves, these considerations might not, however, have been enough to make the King give way. Probably if he had been sure of the loyalty of the Army, he would have given orders for the troops to re-establish order.

With the failure of the civil power to act in time, the Army also found itself, like the King, in a position of unwanted responsibility. Certainly some generals did their duty, even in spite of their personal sympathy with Fascism ; this was true, for example, of General Sani, commander of the

Bologna Army Corps. But the Army commanders were bound to be influenced by the strong Fascist sympathies of a great part of the officer corps,
and the presence in the Militia of a good number of retired and half-pay
generals. Finally, there is good reason to believe that Marshal Diaz himself,
the president of the Army Council and virtually Commander-in-Chief, was
more closely involved with Fascism. He was in Florence on the afternoon
of 27 October, when the Fascist mobilization started; there does not seem
to have been any pre-arranged agreement between him and the leaders of
the movement, as Balbo had to intervene hastily on his arrival to prevent
the local squads from assaulting the prefecture, where Diaz was the Prefect's
guest. 'Instead I told them to organize a great demonstration for the Duke of
Victory in the streets of Florence where he would pass. I ordered them to
make contact with the Fascist railwaymen in the station ... to prepare at all
costs a train to take Diaz to Rome at any moment he might desire.'[45] It is very
interesting to note Balbo's concern that Diaz should be in Rome. Diaz left
Florence finally, by train, on the afternoon of the twenty-eighth : but, aside
from the fact that, as De Felice points out, the King could have consulted
Diaz indirectly, it seems likely that the Marshal may in fact already have
made a secret journey to Rome on the evening of the twenty-seventh.
Salvemini noted in his diary that 'Diaz was at Florence on the afternoon of
27 October; he had received favourably a demonstration of enthusiasm by
the Fascists, and had conceded an interview to the Florentine newspaper
La Nazione in which he had expressed his full faith in the Fascist movement,
and had rushed *by car* to Rome to inform the King that the Army would not
fight against the Fascists.'[46] This version receives confirmation in the
Giornale di Roma of 29 October : this also reports that Diaz came to Rome on
the twenty-seventh by car. The newspaper adds the circumstantial detail
that the owner of the car was the Liberal deputy Dino Philipson, who was
prominent among the financial backers of Fascism. Whether they actually
saw the King remains uncertain : but if one accepts that he came to Rome,
and more or less secretly, it could hardly have been for any purpose other
than influencing the outcome of the crisis. The story of General Pecori
Giraldi, told two years later, becomes more credible :

'The Marshal replied that in that night His Majesty had questioned numerous
personalities. Among these was the Marshal of Italy, Diaz, and also himself. The
Sovereign was gravely preoccupied about the attitude that the Army would take.
To Marshal Diaz he addressed the precise question : "What will the Army do ?"
"Majesty", replied Marshal Diaz, "the army will do its duty, however it would be
well not to put it to the test". I – added General Pecori Giraldi – made almost the
same reply'.[47]

The King was bound to be doubly anxious about the attitude of the Army
in view of his fears that his cousin the Duke of Aosta, who had turned up in
Umbria, suspiciously near the scene of operations, might have designs on
the throne.

But when all objective elements, the indecisiveness of the government, the partial success of Fascist tactics, the open collusion of some generals, the advice of Diaz, the fear of the Duke of Aosta, have been added up, there remains a margin of doubt which must be ascribed to the character of Victor Emmanuel. By temperament he was a pessimist, and he had little confidence in either his advisers or his subjects. He was keenly conscious that, more intelligent than the general run of monarchs, he did not have the presence or the warmth to inspire personal devotion. Finally his sceptical nature doubted, not altogether wrongly, the solidity of the Kingdom of Italy ; the old lands of the Crown of Savoy were one thing, but not all Italians were Piedmontese or Sardinian.[48] All authority depends on confidence ; and the King, rational to a fault and with a low opinion of man in general, had none. He gave way, one can suggest, because to him the evidence of his solitude had become overwhelming : the only man who could do anything was convinced of his impotence.

5

MUSSOLINI AND HIS ALLIES

The Mussolini Government

One must recognize that in the March on Rome Mussolini imposed his will and his vision; that is, his understanding of the effect of his own actions and of the general configuration of social and political forces was superior to that of his opponents, who were all acting in the dark. But as soon as one passes from Mussolini's chief and overriding aim, the winning of power, to the plans he formed for its consolidation and use, the picture becomes different. Mussolini's designs could not ignore either the limitations posed by established political conventions or, on the other hand, those set by the history and character of his own movement. The ambiguity of the March on Rome, a violent armed movement prepared by political intrigue and legitimized by royal investiture, deeply marked the character of the subsequent period. One cannot use organizations for long without also being used by them; and Mussolini's own personal freedom of action was restricted both by the resistance of the old order and the State machinery, and by the demands of the new.

The King, when he revoked the *stato d'assedio*, had not believed that this committed him to making Mussolini Prime Minister and, in fact, on the evening of the twenty-eighth he invited Salandra to form a government.[1] But this was an ingenuous illusion. The King's decision left the State powerless and Mussolini complete master of the situation. With every hour the chaos grew and the Fascists tightened their hold on the machinery of the State. The Prefect Lusignoli and the Milanese industrialists soon made contact with Mussolini and discovered that he would not now consider serving under Salandra. They then realized that delay was disastrous, and that a prompt invitation to the Fascist leader to form a government was the only way to salvage something of their aims from the wreckage. Their urgent messages eventually persuaded Salandra to give way and he had the

94

mortification of learning from his own friends that his candidature was impossible.[2]

Mussolini arrived in Rome peacefully by wagon-lit on the morning of 30 October. He presented himself to the King in his black shirt, and is said to have announced: 'Majesty, I come from the battlefield – fortunately bloodless.'[3]

The formation of the Mussolini ministry was a defeat for the Crown, the Liberal right and the Nationalists, who would all have preferred a government headed by Salandra. But the worst fears of the conservatives had not been realized. They had got back into the game, and imposed themselves as intermediaries and guarantors of the agreement between the King and Mussolini. Their wishes and pressures were reflected in the composition of the ministry. The right had been seriously alarmed by the first reports of Mussolini's list of ministers. These pointed towards a ministry of national pacification, with the collaboration of Democrats, Popolari and trade union leaders. The Nationalists and the friends of Salandra were not even mentioned.[4]

The most important modification in the ministry was the abandonment of the idea of including one or two prominent members of the CGL. If Mussolini had succeeded in his aim, he would have acquired greater independence from the tutelage of the old right and of big business; and, by forcing the reformist Socialist PSU either to co-operate or to risk the alienation of the leaders of the trade unions, he would have greatly weakened the opposition. His gain in prestige would also have been great, and perhaps deserved: he would have had the credit for an act of generosity. Besides these general motives, it seems likely that the promise to include representatives of organized labour had been at the centre of Mussolini's efforts to neutralize the hostility of D'Annunzio to the March on Rome. The poet had, we have seen, taken the trade unions under his protection, and had assumed the role, dangerous for Mussolini, of the pacifier of discord. The agreement between the Fascists and the Federazione del Mare was not regarded by D'Annunzio as an isolated bargain, but as a test case for his more ambitious policy of reconciliation. By accepting his services, and those of his political entourage, as mediators, Mussolini not only allayed their suspicions; he was also preparing to 'steal D'Annunzio's clothes' and to confine him to a subordinate position.[5]

On 29 October Acerbo, acting on Mussolini's instructions, contacted Baldesi, who agreed to accept the offer of a place in the government on behalf of the PSU, after a hurried consultation with his fellow deputies.[6] This was not an official party decision: the *direzone* of the PSU was not summoned, and Matteotti, the secretary of the party, was unflinching in his hostility to any form of co-operation with Mussolini.[7] However if Mussolini had maintained his offer, it would have been difficult for the PSU not to accept the *fait accompli*. Mussolini seems to have changed his mind about the offer to the trade union leaders during his journey from Milan to Rome. It is uncertain who persuaded him to drop the idea; it may have been the spokesmen of the Milanese industrialists De Capitani and Benni. In any case, Mussolini certainly decided that his gesture of reconciliation would place too great a strain on the fragile coalition of forces which made his success possible.[8]

Albertini had advised Salandra to give way to Mussolini on the grounds that 'Once he is at Rome, he will be much more subject to influence.'[9] His prediction was correct. The composition of the ministry which was finally formed on 30 October was conservative rather than revolutionary; it satisfied neither the extremists of the Fascist movement, like Michele Bianchi,[10] nor those who had hoped that this would be the moment for Fascism to return to the paths of democracy or syndicalism. It had a right-wing bias, but since it contained representatives of both the Popolari and the Democrats, it could expect to command a parliamentary majority.

Mussolini in person held three ministries; the Premiership, the Ministry of the Interior and the Foreign Ministry, although in theory his tenure of the last post was only temporary. The conservatives were very unhappy about the trouble which the inexperienced and aggressive Mussolini might cause in foreign affairs, and they tried hard to get him to relinquish the Foreign Ministry to Salandra; but on this point he remained adamant.[11]

The rest of the cabinet was made up of three Fascists, one Nationalist, one Liberal, three Democrats, two Popolari, two military ministers and the philosopher Giovanni Gentile.[12] The critics of the new ministry noted that Mussolini had not carried out his promise of turning to expert personalities outside parliamentary politics, with the exception of Gentile. Mussolini had intended to give the Treasury to the eminent economist Luigi Einaudi, but at the last minute he dropped the idea, probably due to fear of provoking the hostility of the circles which Einaudi had castigated in his free trade campaigns.[13] The *Corriere della Sera* (to which Einaudi was a regular contributor) commented sourly that 'no one will ever be persuaded that it was necessary to shelve the constitution, evoke the Paris of Louis Philippe, occupy Italy with a partisan militia, and demand arms from the barracks', in order to arrive at such a ministry. 'Against the universal expectation of seeing in the government men of the highest skills, experts where experts are needed, the new ministry in more than one case shows the old defect of the subordination of a higher necessity to the lower necessity of parliamentary combination.'[14] But the mediocre quality of much of the Cabinet made Mussolini's figure stand out all the more by contrast.

The Fascists for their part were discontented with their share. Michele Bianchi and other extremists had pressed for an all-Fascist ministry, while Ciano and De Bono had hoped to be given the service ministries.[15] But below cabinet level the Fascists obtained greater satisfaction and influence. Mussolini's two under-secretaries, Finzi and Acerbo, enjoyed more power than many ministers, and important special jobs were created for Bianchi (Secretary-General at the Ministry of the Interior), Edoardo Torre (Commissioner for the railways) and Ciano (Commissioner for the merchant marine). The decisive levers of power in the Ministry of the Interior were all securely in Fascist hands: General De Bono was compensated for his disappointment by getting the job of Chief of Police.

The big question-mark which hung over the formation of the ministry was whether the Popolari would participate. Without their support, Mussolini could not count on a parliamentary majority. As a disciplined party, they were less susceptible than the Liberal groups to individual bribery and pressure. The majority of their members, and even their deputies, were anti-Fascist in sentiment. However the party existed in the shadow of the Church, whose powerful presence soon made itself felt.

The *Osservatore Romano*, commenting on the Pope's letter to the bishops invoking 'the pacification of souls', remarked that 'We observe, with the greatest satisfaction, how the intentions of the supreme authorities, the will of the parties, and he who is now called to form the government, have up till now conformed to the pious exhortation of Pius XI.' The article mentioned with approval both the King's decision not to impose the *stato d'assedio* and the intention of Mussolini to obtain the co-operation of men of all parties. If the Popolari had rejected Mussolini's offer, they would have exposed themselves to the accusation of having hindered the 'pacification' which the Holy See desired.[16]

The decision to join the Government was taken by the *direttorio* of the parliamentary group, assembled in haste in a Roman villa. Don Sturzo and the *direzione* of the party were faced with a *fait accompli* which they accepted without enthusiasm.[17] Besides the attitude of the Church, there were unquestionably serious arguments in favour of the PPI's policy of appeasement. If the party went into opposition immediately, they would give the Fascists the chance to dissolve Parliament and hold elections before the excitement of the insurrection had subsided. By joining the ministry, the PPI could put Mussolini's sincerity to the test and perhaps obtain some protection for their unions and party branches against the squads. Mussolini claimed that in forming his cabinet he had dealt only with 'men' and had refused to negotiate with parties or groups: but in the case of the Popolari his assertion was not altogether justified. It is true that the PPI itself did not regard its ministers as official representatives of the party, since the power of decision was vested in the *direzione* and not the parliamentary group: on the other hand, there is no doubt that Mussolini consulted De Gasperi as president of the group, and that the Popolari did impose definite conditions for their participation. The clerical *Corriere d'Italia* implied that Mussolini had given assurances that he would return to legal and constitutional methods, and that he 'intends to maintain the system of proportional representation, save for such improvements of form as are suggested by experience'.[18] However if the Popolari believed that Mussolini would be bound by a promise to maintain proportional representation, they were soon to be disillusioned.

Mussolini had shown himself conciliatory in his choice of ministers. However he was not to be cheated of the psychological advantages of 'revolution'. He insisted that the Fascists should be allowed to stage a victory parade through Rome, and he carried this point against the opposition of the King, who had requested their immediate demobilization.[19] An imposing celebration was necessary to establish the myth of the invincible uprising. The parade, however, was headed by the Nationalist blueshirts, who had been ready to fight the squads only three days before. Even more important than the myth of revolution was the myth of unity, of the harmony of all 'national' and patriotic forces. Once he had given the Fascists their hour of glory, Mussolini turned his efforts to creating the image of a stern, impartial ruler, ready and able to impose discipline even on his own followers. He sent a message to the officers of the Rome garrison ordering them to desist from holding a demonstration in his honour: 'The national army cannot and must not applaud or disapprove. It must only and always obey faithfully.' These 'sacred words' made an excellent impression on orthodox monarchist opinion. The message would, however, be more impressive if it were certain that any intention to hold such a demonstration had ever really existed.[20]

The anniversary of victory fell appropriately for Mussolini's purposes. The provincial Fascists were hastily bundled out of the capital, for fear they might mar the occasion by unseemly behaviour. For the first time, the ceremony of the Unknown Soldier was celebrated by a religious as well as a civil ceremony: this pleased the Vatican and the clericals.[21] The reconciliation of religious and patriotic sentiment, in the past so often in conflict, was to be a staple of Fascist propaganda. The *Giornale d'Italia* described the solemn occasion for the edification of the *benpensanti* who might still have doubts about Mussolini's decorum:

Benito Mussolini to-day has an austere expression, his forehead is paler than usual, the lines of his face drawn, but composed in an expression of delicate grief. He is dressed in black and looks straight in front of him. He climbs the steps at the head of the chosen throng and when he has arrived in front of the Altar of the Nation, by the imperishable tomb, he stops suddenly. Without turning his head to scrutinize the faces of those present, as is his custom, he kneels down – notwithstanding the fact that the marble was wet from the recent rain – and closes his eyes, and prays. In that attitude of true fervour he seems like a priest. Someone bursts into tears. It is an old Garibaldian who is leaning on the right-hand altar. A woman's sob is heard. It is the mother of a combatant.

The French diplomat M. Charles-Roux, who witnessed the scene, commented dryly 'the spectacle of a row of gentlemen in civilian dress, top-hat in hand, kneeling in the open air – would have been slightly too theatrical . . .

for a Parisian public. In Italy, and in Rome, it is not considered excessive.'[22]

The Fascist claim to embody patriotism was subtly advanced by such means. Marshal Diaz and Admiral Thaon di Revel took the salute on 4 November together with Mussolini, and the former later declared that 'this year the commemoration of victory has had a higher significance'.[23] The Liberals were encouraged by the composition of the ministry and other signs to believe that Fascism would wither away and finally be absorbed into a broad conservative coalition, but in trying to deny the movement's specific and partisan character and assert their own importance they actually helped it to usurp a monopoly of patriotic feeling. Liberal journals helped to diffuse the impression that 'Fascism is patriotism': no more, no less.[24]

This atmosphere of harmony did not please the men of the party. They sensed that the 'revolution' was losing momentum. Both Michele Bianchi and Farinacci had hoped for an immediate dissolution of Parliament and new elections, but they were disappointed. Instead Mussolini chose the solution of demanding that the Chamber vote him 'full powers' for administrative and financial reform. It was easier for him to make this request since the urgency of reorganizing the bureaucracy and reducing expenditure was generally recognized: indeed, formally speaking, the Chamber had already delegated full powers for bureaucratic reform to the Government before the March on Rome. Moreover the Popolari had been foremost in complaining that political pressures had stifled all attempts at reform.[25] However the full powers which Mussolini requested were considerably more ample than those envisaged by any preceding schemes: they comprised taxation, and the ability to reorganize all state organs except the legislature, including the magistracy, the army and the schools. There were no indications as to the directions, conditions or limits of reorganization. The exercise of patronage and punishment were largely removed from parliamentary control and the potential power of the executive greatly increased.[26]

The request for full powers was made, ironically, in the name of liberal economics. The eminent economist Maffeo Pantaleoni suggested that opposition to the grant of full powers was confined to 'the most authentic representatives of bureaucratic parasitism'. He was confident that Fascism would not slip up on 'the parliamentary banana-skin': 'if the present legal forms get in the way, a new legality must be created.'[27] With such encouragement, it is no wonder that Mussolini felt confident.

Mussolini's habit was to alternate blandishment and menaces, 'the carrot and the stick', appeals to revolution and to order. When he addressed the Chamber of Deputies on 16 November he reverted to the revolutionary style.

'For the second time, in the brief space of a decade, the Italian people – or the best part of it – has overthrown a ministry and given itself a government outside, above and against all parliamentary designations.' Mussolini was here referring to the precedent of the 'radiant days' of May 1915 : while the presentation in terms of an antithesis between 'people' and 'Parliament' was only to be expected, it was surprising and significant that he omitted at this point all reference to the role of the Crown in both crises. He was intent on showing that he owed his position not to royal investiture but to 'the rights of revolution'. 'I add, so that everyone may know, that I am here to defend and strengthen to the utmost degree the revolution of the blackshirts . . . with 300,000 young armed men prepared for anything . . . and ready to execute my commands with religious devotion, I could have castigated all those who defamed and tried to smear Fascism. I could have made this grey and gloomy hall into a bivouac for my legions. . . . I could have barred up Parliament and formed an exclusively Fascist government. I could have : but at least for the moment, I did not will it.' In forming the ministry, he claimed, he had not been guided by any concern with securing a parliamentary majority, and if full powers were refused him, he would dissolve the Chamber immediately.[28]

In all this there was a large element of bluff. This was exposed by Turati. Turati accepted Mussolini's challenge. He remarked that at least with the extremists one knew where one was, while Mussolini's apparent show of generosity concealed more insidious dangers. Fascism, he said, had not followed 'the necessary logic of revolution', and Mussolini had compromised with the '*camarillas*' which he professed to despise. The offer not to dissolve Parliament was equivalent to telling the Chamber that 'it can go on existing if it doesn't live. It is the substitution of despotism for democracy with the addition of ridicule.'

Turati's stand was not foolhardy. It had a political as well as a moral justification. Fascism was not yet all-powerful : and Mussolini wanted to avoid a direct confrontation on the issue of dictatorship versus parliamentary government. It would be better to face new elections than for the Chamber voluntarily to accept a subordinate role. However Turati had few illusions that the Democrats would listen to his appeal. He claimed for his party 'the inheritance of all the principles which you are abandoning and which we will not abandon'.[29]

The Democratic groups had all decided before the debate to vote in favour of the Government. In two letters written to Carnazza and Malagodi, Giolitti had indicated his favour for the new Government, and this was a decisive factor.[30] The Social-Reformists of Bonomi also decided to vote for the Government, but this decision concealed fundamental differences of opinion within the party over the attitude to be taken towards Fascism. The split between pro- and anti-Fascists was shortly to lead to the party's dissolution.[31]

The only real revolt against Mussolini's speech came from the Popolari. The *direttorio* of the parliamentary group voted only 5 to 4 in support of the Government. During the debate the quadrumvir De Vecchi shouted

'Eunuchs!' repeatedly at the Popolari and refused to apologize when called to order. This provoked the President of the Chamber De Nicola into announcing his resignation. This gesture was effective and seriously alarmed Mussolini: De Nicola was a moderate and generally respected figure. Mussolini's reactions show his desire to avoid a crisis which would have shown up Fascism as an enemy of the constitution. In a conciliatory second speech he appealed to De Nicola to withdraw his resignation, and he accepted the Liberal gloss on his earlier anti-parliamentary statements. They were to be interpreted only as a criticism of this particular Chamber, and not of parliamentary institutions. He even held out olive branches to D'Aragona of the CGL and Cao of the Sardinian Action Party, who had both voted against the Government. This skilful tactical retreat prevented a rebellion among the Popolari. However the attitude of the PPI continued to be a stumbling-block. De Gasperi rebuked Mussolini for suggesting that he and not the King determined whether Parliament should be dissolved, and reiterated his determination to defend proportional representation.[32]

One might have thought that the conservatives would have seen the danger of encouraging Mussolini to free himself from parliamentary control. However the right, carried away by their hatred of the mass parties, were exultant at Mussolini's brusque way with the latter's representatives, and only concerned lest the presence of the Popolari in the Government should limit his freedom of action. The *Giornale d'Italia* was disconcerted to hear that Mussolini was inclined to put off the question of electoral reform: 'the electoral law must be passed and it is necessary to strike while the iron is hot. Beware of the foxes of Montecitorio, Mr Mussolini ... the Popolari hold onto proportional representation as if to their mother and they will do anything to conserve it.'[33] The first crack in the resistance of the Popolari came in the Cabinet of 15 November when their two ministers agreed to a 'revision' of the law: but later in the month the PNF *direzione* issued a statement warning that the party should not expect early elections, and delegating the task of drawing up an electoral reform to Michele Bianchi.[34] This decision showed that Mussolini had decided not to force the tempo and had decided that it was easier to govern with the old Chamber than it would be with a new one. He could rely on self-interest, fear and the honest desire to avoid conflict to keep the deputies in line, and the progressive consolidation of Fascism in the nation would go hand in hand with the weakening of parliamentary prestige and the will to resist. At the same time, the deputies were handicapped by the knowledge that the Chamber was unpopular and discredited: in case of resistance, its record would have left it wide open to the accusation that it was making effective government impossible.

Similar difficulties prevented the non-Fascist majority of the cabinet from acting as a check on Mussolini and the Fascists. In the first place, some of the ministers had naturally enough been selected on account of the personal sympathy which they had shown for Fascism. Instead of applying pressure or restraint on behalf of their parties, they were used by Mussolini as levers to bring about the latter's disintegration. This was the role which the Minister of Labour, Cavazzoni, played in regard to the Popolari. Cavazzoni, Teofilo Rossi and De Capitani were all the representatives of powerful economic interests which Mussolini was willing to protect. In addition, several of the ministers showed their readiness to use Fascism as a means of settling old scores. Thus when Sforza, the ambassador at Paris, submitted his resignation in a published telegram, giving as his reason that 'foreign policy cannot be conducted on the basis of sentiments and resentments', it was not Mussolini but Di Cesarò who demanded that he be punished for his indiscretion.[35] As a nephew of Sonnino and the President of the 'Pro Dalmatia' association, Di Cesarò had been among the most violent opponents of Sforza's Adriatic policy. Above all, the persistent antagonism between the Popolari and the Liberal and Democrat groups prevented their making any common stand, inside or outside the cabinet. But the weakness of Mussolini's colleagues and partners also reflected the state of public opinion. The reaction against a series of long government crises, with their accompaniment of laborious negotiations for the precise distribution of ministries between the various parliamentary groups, enfeebled the parties' capacity to resist or bargain. When the Minister of the Treasury, Tangorra, died, his ministry was amalgamated with De Stefani's, and the Popolari could claim no compensation for the loss of their most important portfolio. The composition of Mussolini's first government was less important than the fact that the new rules of the political game allowed him to modify it at his own discretion. Only the military ministers and Federzoni, whose sources of power lay outside Parliament, were indispensable.

The First Steps towards Dictatorship

One of the legacies left over from the period before the March on Rome was the programme of a national pacification to be achieved under the aegis of D'Annunzio. The 'spiritual' authority of D'Annunzio was recognized, at least overtly, by all patriotic circles; the relationship between him and Mussolini in consequence was rather like a parody of the relations between Pope and Emperor, or prelate and King. The latter had the force, but he had to be careful about applying it.[36]

D'Annunzio's ideas for pacification centred on the field of the trade unions. The idea of a great reconciliation between all the different political shades of union was associated with the ideology of the 'national revolution'. The pact was to be the prelude to the inauguration of a 'Parliament of labour'. The D'Annunzio syndicalists took the initiative for the creation of a 'costituente sindacale' (constituent assembly of unions); besides the syndicalists De Ambris and Angelo Olivetti the committee contained the former

CGL secretary Rinaldo Rigola.[37] The official leadership of the CGL, meanwhile, took up a conciliatory attitude towards the new Government. The CGL journal *Battaglie Sindacali* commented that the unions had no reason to regret the end of the impotent Liberal State, and welcomed the new possibilities opened up by the breach in the old order.[38] Mussolini's alliance with the old conservatives was seen as the chief obstacle to progress. The trade unionists believed that they could assist the victory of the 'revolutionary' elements of Fascism over the reactionaries. This optimistic perspective was not shared by the politicians of the PSU. The secretary of the party, Matteotti, and Claudio Treves attacked the unions for their readiness to come to terms with the government without reference to the general problem of political liberty.[39]

D'Annunzio's personal interest in the new schemes for reconciliation was fired by Zaniboni, a romantically inclined Socialist ex-officer and deputy who had become one of his disciples. Zaniboni and Gino Baldesi, who had not forgotten that Mussolini had almost made him a minister, undertook to establish liaison between D'Annunzio, Mussolini and the CGL. D'Annunzio wrote to Mussolini on 1 December: 'Before retiring I should like to offer to the Nation a broad and devout union of *all the workers* (D'Annunzio's italics). The divine voice said to the Seraph . . . (do you remember ?): "Of all these morsels make thou one offering".'[40] On 2 December Zaniboni and Baldesi saw Mussolini, who received them kindly. According to Zaniboni's account of the conversation, Mussolini told them that: 'I lack the skilled technicians of organization, who are almost all in the Confederation of Labour. I like your initiative and none of us will hinder you.' Baldesi and Zaniboni reported their success to D'Annunzio and all seemed set for the agreement. With his irrepressible sense of theatre, D'Annunzio looked forward to a solemn meeting in the gardens of his villa the Vittoriale. The trade union leaders would sit on marble seats, like ancient senators, and swear peace and friendship. This strange ceremony was to take place on 21 December 1922.[41]

Mussolini, however, could not speak for his followers. On 7 December he left for London, and in his absence the revolt against the proposed pacification triumphed easily. Farinacci and Rossoni, the leader of the Fascist unions, made common cause against the possibility of an agreement. Faced with the threat of a general mobilization of the squads of northern Italy, Mussolini hastily retreated. From London he sent a telegram to Farinacci which completely endorsed the latter's point of view: 'Rest assured that the attempted fraud will be exposed and the deception unmasked. Fascism has won by meeting its enemies head on: it is too intelligent and too strong to be hoaxed or outmanoeuvred. The remaining vague illusions will be dispersed and those enemies who have not laid down their arms will be inexorably and finally crushed.'[42]

When Mussolini returned from London he was faced by a dangerous disagreement between party and Government. The Liberals on their side had attempted to turn this situation to their profit by suggesting that Mussolini would find it easier to conduct foreign policy if he had someone experienced like Lusignoli to look after the Ministry of the Interior for him. Mussolini reacted violently to this suggestion. At the Cabinet meeting of 15 December he inveighed against the 'tiny minorities of politicos' who were disturbing the peace, and demanded authorization 'to act by whatever methods I may hold necessary against anyone, of whatever party, faction or sect, who seeks to introduce disturbance and disorder into the nation, which has an absolute need of calm and discipline'. There was talk of ill-defined conspiracy, and sinister cliques – 'called, turn by turn, high finance, plutocracy, freemasonry, socialism, trade-unionism, labourism, pseudo-Fiumeanism, Sforza-type diplomacy, and the higher bureaucracy' – were accused of 'trying to foment divisions within the *fasci*'.[43] All this served to create an atmosphere of alarm and to justify repressive measures. On 18 December De Bono gave orders to the Prefects to investigate the activities of the anarchists and subversives who had infiltrated D'Annunzio's legionaries; this was the signal for a general crackdown. The legionaries' armed squads were finally broken up, and De Ambris with other trade unionists were harassed until they decided to go into exile. D'Annunzio, after an initial protest, left his followers to their fate, though he continued to protect Captain Giulietti and his seamen.[44] The action against the legionaries was shortly followed by a drive against the Communist party. On 30 December Mussolini personally gave orders for the arrest of Bordiga, Gramsci and all the other members of the Central Committee, excepting the two deputies who were covered by parliamentary immunity. The party went underground, but in the spring of 1923 the police succeeded in arresting the greater part of the leadership, including hundreds of local organizers. There was a mass emigration of 'subversives': many thousand Socialist and Communist workers left Italy to escape the repression.[45]

On the night of 15 December, after the cabinet, Mussolini called a meeting of Fascist leaders : out of this meeting there emerged a new institution, the Fascist Grand Council. By the creation of the Grand Council Mussolini served two purposes. First of all, the new organ was intended to co-ordinate the action of the party and the other Fascist organizations with that of the Government. At the same time, the creation of the Grand Council was a revolutionary act. It has been characteristic of modern single-party regimes that they set up a network of 'parallel institutions' beside those of the existing state; the Grand Council was a 'parallel' Fascist cabinet, and its deliberations were soon recognized as more important than those of the official cabinet. In its first meeting the Grand Council defied constitutional orthodoxy by declaring that it left the decision on the date of new elections to Mussolini; it was the Crown's prerogative to make this decision, on the basis of the advice tendered by the cabinet.[46]

The Grand Council, moreover, decided on the creation of a second revolutionary institution, the Militia. The Militia was also to have dual functions: that of disciplining the anarchic forces of *squadrismo* and bringing them under the control of the Government, and that of a 'parallel army', or at least police force, under Mussolini's exclusive control. The significance of the Grand Council and the Militia was played down by conservative apologists, but more far-sighted observers saw the dangers inherent in the new institutions. The liberal *Stampa* remarked that dictatorship could be tolerable so long as it remained faithful to the old conception of the temporary grant of exceptional powers to one man in order to resolve a crisis in the State; but what now threatened was instead the permanent dictatorship of an organized party.[47] The creation of the Militia was accepted by the conservatives and the Crown in the name of 'normalization', as a means to curtailing the violence of the squads. However the problem of bringing Fascism within the constitution could not be reduced to that of ending illegal violence. The conservatives refused to face up to the more insidious danger of the creation of a quasi-legal tyranny in which the repressive mechanisms of the party would be taken over and sanctioned by the State.

The Liberal Party

From the March on Rome until the crisis of June 1924 caused by the murder of the Socialist leader Matteotti, the dominance of Fascism was ensured by Mussolini's ambivalent tactics. Each advance in Fascist power was justified as an instalment of the price which must be paid for the desired 'normalization' of the movement. This concept of 'normalization' was the last expression of the hope which persisted among the Liberals that the effervescence of passions produced by the war would subside, and reason would once again prevail. The Fascist movement, whose political and ideological content was so elusive, could, it seemed, be best defined as an exalted state of mind brought on by victory and the fear of revolution. In their optimistic view it was destined either to vanish or to be transformed and absorbed. However at the same time the concept of 'normalization' implied a positive role for Fascism, that of making possible a general social, political and financial restoration. The Liberals believed that by loyally seconding the efforts of Mussolini and his government, while calling, discreetly but repeatedly, for the end of the 'imposition' of the movement upon the powers of the State, both ends could be achieved.

The first step towards the 'canalization' of Fascism into constitutional channels had already been taken when the King summoned Mussolini to form a government; it remained to complete the work by giving him a secure parliamentary majority, which would obviate the need for violence. But there was more to 'normalization' than concern for law and the constitution. Although conservative economic interests had no reason to complain of Fascism, there were aspects of the movement which were disquieting for the conventional wisdom. Free enterprise, the defence of property, the balanced budget : Mussolini had espoused all these canons of Liberal individualism with a vehemence which delighted the doctrinaire economists and reassured the industrialists. But was the structure and ethos of a mass movement compatible with these orthodoxies ? There was room here for doubt : the violence of the *squadristi*, while it had been nourished by agrarians and industrialists, was undisciplined, unpredictable and not always respectful of property. In defending Parliament, the Liberals were also concerned to defeat the schemes of the 'national-syndicalist' ideologists of the movement for a reform of the constitution on corporate lines, which might have unwelcome repercussions in the economic sphere. The conditioning of Fascism by conservative economic interests, in this first period, was still often carried on under the name of liberalism.[48] But it remained to be seen what would happen in the case of a conflict between the two. Even by 1924, at the local level many representatives of agrarian and industrial interests had come to decide that they could influence Fascism best from within. In this way, the social and economic assimilation of Fascism continued, and proved, in a sense, anything but illusory ; this process tended to destroy the class foundation which had underlain the differentiation of the Liberals, representatives of the grande bourgeoisie, from the Fascists, whose most enthusiastic support came from the petty bourgeoisie. In those areas of the South where Fascism had hardly existed before the March on Rome, Liberal strength was undermined more slowly, but in a similar way, as the 'grand electors' and clienteles deserted their deputies and colonized the *fasci*. Those leaders of liberalism who continued to defend their political ideals were left in increasing isolation. Mussolini's policy towards Liberal and Democratic groups was well expressed by the slogan 'collaboration with men but not with parties'. This distinction, first made during the formation of the Government after the March on Rome, was revived at the time of the negotiations for the Government list in the 1924 elections.

Mussolini could not, however, altogether avoid acknowledging the existence of other parties. In the first half of 1923, in practice he recognized the Liberal party and the Democrazia Sociale as allies, though with significant reservations.[49] But his overriding aim was to absorb individuals of influence or talent, and to destroy the autonomy of organized parties. From September 1923 onwards he even tried, in a sense, to apply this policy to the Fascist party itself. But the form taken by Mussolini's strategy of absorption was also shaped by the character of the 'constitutionalist' groups or parties, strong in personalities and weak in organization. For a time, Mussolini even favoured the movement towards Liberal unity ; he suggested that when it had really been achieved, a federation with the Fascist movement would become possible.[50] This approach was not really inconsistent with the general aim of Mussolini's policy of absorption. It still had the object of destroying the Liberals' independence. A federation would have had advantages for Mussolini. It would have consolidated his power, especially in Parliament, made Fascism fully respectable, and allowed him to act as arbiter between Liberals and Fascists without being wholly dependent on either. The 'organizing impulse' in liberalism had come from the right; its most persistent propagandist, Albertini, became, it is true, also the most tenacious Liberal opponent of the regime, but it is significant that the agrarian, anti-democratic Liberals of Bologna and Tuscany, whose contacts with Fascism were very close, were the first to federate their associations. One of the leaders in the movement for Liberal unity was Senator Tanari of Bologna, a landowner distinguished by the warmth of his sympathy for Fascism.[51] The Young Liberals, with their imitation squads in khaki shirts, were best organized in Tuscany. In Lombardy and Liguria the industrialists, more conservative than those of Piedmont, were dominant, although the left was not without support.[52]

The idea of a Fascist-Liberal federation came to nothing because of the individualism of the Liberal deputies and their leaders. In Parliament, the Liberals were divided into groups; the *Democrazia* (forty-one deputies), led by Giolitti, and also containing Orlando and De Nicola; the minor Liberal group of Salandra (twenty-one deputies in 1922), and the *Democrazia Liberale* (twenty-four deputies), whose leader was the Calabrian De Nava. Most of the deputies in these three groups became members of the Liberal party. However the powers of the new party organization created by the Congress of Bologna (8–10 October 1922) remained more theoretical than real. The secretary, Alberto Giovannini, and the central executive, who were not deputies, were quite incapable of imposing their decisions on powerful personalities such as Giolitti or Salandra, or even on figures of the second rank who could rely on the strength of their local clienteles for election. This was particularly true in the South; in the North and Centre of Italy the effort to replace the old network of autonomous associations – 'liberal', 'monarchist', 'constitutional' or 'democratic' – by a modern party structure with a central executive and local branches had been generally successful, but at the Congress of Bologna, out of a total of 78,000 members, only 1,200 came from the Mezzogiorno (1,000 from Naples) and none at all from Sicily.[53] Political conflict in the South was still polarized around the personal interests of the deputies or local factions, and rival associations were often, as Giolitti put it, literally 'on an armed footing', one against the other. The boundaries between 'liberal-democrats' and radicals, or 'social-reformists', were of little or no real significance; local alliances and enmities cut across the nominal party divisions, and Southern deputies were therefore reluctant to accept a centralized discipline. The three democratic constitutional groups which were outside the Liberal party were all overwhelmingly Southern in their composition and had little internal cohesion. In the South, overt and acknowledged conservatism was surprisingly rare. Except in his native Apulia and in Naples, Salandra had few Southern supporters; the majority of his group was composed of spokesmen of Northern industrial and agrarian interests.

The Liberals were a 'cadre party'; their strength was not in numbers, but in technical capacity, experience and local influence. They were the traditional ruling elite. As the right-wing *Giornale d'Italia* wrote, 'Fascism has the ardent youth, the enthusiastic and numerous masses, the decisive and strong-willed energy, but it will be much stronger if it is supported, as it deserves, by the intellectual element and the experts in the various fields of public life, of whom there is a wealth in the Liberal party.' The force of liberalism could not be measured by the number of the party's organized members alone. 'Liberalism is the doctrine and the mentality of the leading members of all walks of national life: economic, technical, bureaucratic, administrative, etc.'[54] At the same time, the Liberals were not such a tiny handful as the Fascists sometimes liked to make out. Apart from the vast personal clienteles of the Southern politicians, the new party could command a fair number of adherents in several regions. Piedmont, the home of Italian liberalism, provided by far the most numerous contingent: 49,000 out of a total of 78,000.[55] In the rice-growing plains of Alessandria and Novara provinces, which belong geographically with Lombardy and the Po Valley, and in the hills of the Monferrato, agrarian Fascism was dominant, but the Fascists had made little inroad by 1922 into the Liberal strongholds in the heart of old Piedmont. The great majority of Piedmontese Liberals still followed their old chief Giolitti with devotion, although in the city of Turin Gino Olivetti and the *Lega Industriale* had become very influential. Here, but not elsewhere, the Liberals could claim to have quantity as well as quality.

The bargaining power of the Liberals and their capacity to maintain their independence from Fascism was weakened by their 'governmentalism'.

The journalist Mario Missiroli, explaining why the Liberals would never refuse their votes to the Government, remarked, with slight exaggeration, that 'in every provincial capital the local leadership of the Liberal party resides permanently in the Prefecture'.[56] This weakness was even more pronounced among the constitutionalist groups in the South. Southern politicians needed government patronage to keep their clienteles together; a leader who openly opposed Fascism would therefore expect to see his following dwindle rapidly.

A more profound reason for the enfeeblement of the Liberals lay in the changes brought by industrialization, accelerated by the war, universal suffrage, and proportional representation. The cultured professional classes had always been the backbone of the Liberal elite; the ideal Liberal deputy was a lawyer who also gave lectures as a *libero docente*, who could season his speeches with quotations from Dante and the classics (all, of course, taken as examples of *italianità!*) and references to his Risorgimento forebears, and who also possessed a steady income from the lease of a farm or two. These men would know about law, the classics and the price of wheat : but not so much about industry. The war, bringing on new men who had made quick fortunes, had shaken the social ranking order inside the bourgeoisie, and the free professions had lost influence. In the big industrial towns they were plainly subordinate to the industrialists, but in the provincial cities they still tried to hold on to their old position. The sense of their declining power and status led many of the professional classes to welcome the advent of Fascism at first with enthusiasm ; while their sons at school or the university joined the squads. The attitude of many Liberals to Fascism was, literally, paternal : 'almost all the sons of the Liberals are in Fascism, with their fathers' consent'.[57]

The pathos of postwar Italian liberalism comes through most vividly in the writings of the free trade economists, Einaudi, Giuseppe Prato and others. With their insistence on free enterprise, their individualism and hostility to the large trusts who battened on Government favours, and their defence of the consumer and of the stability of money, they were the ideologists of the rentiers and professional classes who suffered so heavily in the postwar inflation. Besides this, there was in Einaudi and Prato, in spite of their economists' concern with industrial progress, a deep attachment to pre-industrial values, to the civic tradition. One result of the introduction of proportional representation and universal non-literate suffrage had been to end the privileged position formerly enjoyed by the small provincial towns and the old cities as against both the fast-growing industrial towns and the countryside. Einaudi argued that this inequality was one of the advantages of the old system, the modern *città tentacolari* (metropolitan areas) were under-represented, but :

Are these true cities ? No. At the centre there exists the old city, *where the true citizens live*, those who feel an attachment to their birthplace, who want it to be great and beautiful, who are ready to make sacrifices for the sake of coming generations. *All around, there is the encampment.* There live in the encampment all those who have come in search of fortune, those who have abandoned their land and family to look for new. These are men who all deserve all the protection the State can give ; but I find it hard to believe in their fitness to choose the governing class. *They are the new barbarians*, who aspire to the fine things of the earth ; desirous of enjoyments and impatient of the necessary sacrifices. [There should be a compulsory ten years residence qualification for the right to vote in local elections ; as for general elections], ten years are not enough for the immigrants in the highly populated regions to acquire the right to rob the old, less peopled regions, rich in tradition and experience, of their rightful representation. The 200,000 inhabitants of the poor constituencies are a mass in ferment, in which those stratifications, those ties which bind the single man, through the family associations, corporations, to the State, have not yet had time to form, . . . [and they were worth less than the 30,000 of an old city]. When the small rural constituencies speak, it is the history of Italy that is speaking through their mouths.[58]

The Liberals, a purely bourgeois party in leadership and spirit, had once been able to count on a large deference vote, at least in the countryside. But, outside the South, a worker's vote was now more likely to go with the political colour of his union than with that of his employer. One of the problems the new Liberal party discussed was that of propaganda among the working class and the possibility of founding their own unions; the discussion revealed little optimism or enthusiasm.[59] Here was the decisive weakness; the Liberals had not, and would not, recognize the principle of collective action and organization by the working classes. The right was ready to recognize that here Fascism had improved on all previous models. The Liberals had lost control of the workers, first to the Socialists, and later, in the countryside, also to the Popolari, and therefore had been unable to impose their principles which, like the Fascist, demanded collaboration between classes. While 'the Liberals and Democrats negotiated with the working classes through the contractors of the proletarian movement (Socialist or Clerical), Fascism instead acts directly, after it has succeeded in diffusing national sentiment, respect for the State, and class collaboration among the masses.'[60] However nothing is perfect in politics, and the Fascist efforts at union organization aroused alarm as well as respect. The more old-fashioned industrialists disliked even the new unions, and feared that their connections with the governing party would make them a lever for State interference. This fear was reinforced by the perception that the Fascists might use the union weapon to break the independence of employers whose politics were Liberal.[61] Liberal resistance to absorption by Fascism was actually stiffened in some regions by the industrialists' desire to preserve the balance of power in labour relations and to prevent the growth of a new 'monopoly', this time Fascist.

Up till October 1922 the attitude of many Liberals had been more favourable to Fascism at the local level, where the anti-Socialist activities of the squads were seen as indispensable, than at the national level, where the movement's pretensions were thought excessive. After the March, the position was reversed. At the centre, the majority of Liberals, whatever their criticisms, found co-operation with Mussolini and his government possible and sometimes rewarding. But in the provinces the hard facts of the Fascist drive for power were inescapable. The old ruling class naturally resented the efforts of the rough new masters – often immigrants and 'barbarians' too – to dispossess them, and there was much friction.[62]

The Elder Statesmen

Giovanni Giolitti received the March on Rome with his habitual calm. If privately he may have expressed irritation at the indecision and possible bad faith of Facta in preventing his return to power, he regarded the turn taken by events as far from irreparable or even necessarily unfortunate. From his long experience of government he had learnt to trust in the swing of the pendulum; he had both benefited and suffered from the processes of slow erosion which gradually reduce the popularity of ministries. Fascism, which owed so much of its appeal to the mystery of the new, the unknown and the undefined, would, he felt, not be an exception to this general law of politics : 'when the sum of its mistakes . . . exceeds those made by the Socialists, the Popolari and the Nittians' it would disintegrate and fall, almost automatically. In the meantime, his advice was : 'Patience, patience, patience ! The theory of Tolstoy !'[63] When out of power, Giolitti had seldom practised an active opposition. It had normally, instead, been his practice to wait in silence and apparent neutrality until the unpopularity of his successors and the pressure of his friends created an overwhelming demand for his return. This habit of dignified withdrawal added to his prestige and enabled him to present himself, when the time was ready for his return, in a new light, with a fresh vision and programme. Now, after the March on Rome, in a situation which left him little scope, it was natural that he should retire to the sidelines. But this did not mean that he became an isolated or impotent figure ; his vast network of friends, supporters, and clients in Parliament and in the bureaucracy, kept him informed and continued to look to him as their leader.[64] He was the epitome and representative of those forces and qualities which most Fascists instinctively detested, but of which they had need ; self-discipline, experience and technical competence.[65]

At the outset, his approval for the new Government was sincere. His deception by Mussolini had not cancelled the sharp resentment which he felt against the Socialists and the Popolari, who had earlier impeded his return to power. 'You Socialists', he told them, 'have always been without courage ! That is why you didn't come into the Government.' 'This Chamber', he replied to the deputies who complained to him of Mussolini's 'bivouac' speech, 'has the Government it deserves. It proved unable to give itself a government, in several crises, and the nation has given itself a government instead.'[66] He saw in the victory of Fascism a necessary consequence of the impotence of Parliament produced by proportional representation. The Government's demand for full powers, and later the electoral reform law, were both justified by him as expedients necessary for the formation of a strong government.

At the same time, he certainly did not regard Fascist measures as permanent contributions to the art of government. They were necessary and legitimate only as means to the liquidation of the postwar crisis, which had proved so resistant to treatment. The complicated artificiality of the Acerbo law was, to his functionalist mind, a good proof that it would not long remain in force, and then the way would be open for a return to single-member constituencies. For Giolitti, Orlando and others of their following the *uninominale* had come to have a value out of proportion even to its undoubted practical importance. It stood for the good old days, when local notables and 'valiant professional men' addressed themselves directly to their constituents, and personal worth counted for more than party machines. It was a symbol of 'normalization' in its implicit sense of a return to pre-war institutions and values.[67]

However, whatever might be true of some of his supporters, Giolitti himself was too conscious of historical change to believe possible a simple return to the past. He still kept his evolutionist faith in gradual progress. This had not been destroyed by the rise of revolutionary movements because he optimistically believed that time and contact with the realities of government would soften their intransigence, while their realistic aspirations could and should be fulfilled. He believed, as he had earlier of Socialism, that Fascism would be tamed and transformed by the acquisition of responsibility and power, within a stable framework. Fascism was not as surprising or novel a phenomenon as some observers seemed to think 'You are amazed that a *5th Estate* is coming up with exceptional rapidity; in reality, it is one of the most common phenomena of history. After a violent agitation (and what has been more violent than the last war?) there comes a wave of extremely youthful St Justs, Napoleons, Hoches, and thousands of unknowns. True merit establishes itself and remains in the front rank, the others disappear, and then the world recovers its normal rhythm.'[68] Giolitti's concept of political renewal was in this respect not far from that of Pareto; the old and exhausted ruling class was to be regenerated by the absorption of a new combative elite: 'Italian political life needs new blood.'[69] To the pessimist Pareto, however, politics were an unaltering cyclical process of degeneration and renewal, whereas for Giolitti the 'normal rhythm' was one of slow progress, and the absorption of new elites was itself a cumulative process in which new strata were automatically lifted out of oblivion and given a share in Government and social benefits.

Giolitti's optimism did not imply, as with some other Liberal leaders, an abdication of his independence or his powers of criticism. He was willing to support Fascism, but not to identify himself with it. He refused with firmness all suggestions that would have compromised this independence; it was his intention that ultimately Fascism should be absorbed by liberalism, not the reverse, and as long at least as the former had not shown that it accepted the rules of parliamentary government, he was resolved to allow no confusion between the two. In answer to the various offers of intermediaries and the rather clumsy overtures of the government, he opposed a suave detachment broken only by occasional shafts of his characteristic sarcasm. 'Sooner', he remarked, 'than accept from Mussolini the offer of a place in the Senate, he would have preferred to resign from being a man.'[70] The practices of Mussolini's first year of government must, on the whole, have encouraged the sceptical side of his co-operation. It is true that in foreign policy, where the worst might have been feared, Mussolini, by reaching an agreement with Jugoslavia, showed himself ready to follow the lines set out by Giolitti and Sforza. The financial situation, too, continued to improve. However Giolitti was not ready to concede that Mussolini had worked miracles. He would, when the time came, point out quietly that the positive achievements of Fascism were the continuation of policies which he had set in motion; there is reason to think that he was not deaf to the detailed criticisms which were furnished him by friends such as Sforza and Camillo Corradini.[71]

There was an element of realism in Giolitti's cautious refusal to speak out clearly or join the opposition. As he remarked, 'before putting someone with his back against the wall, I wait until I am the stronger'.[72] There was nothing much he could do until the Matteotti crisis gave him a favourable opportunity. But for his realism to have been truly effective, it would have been necessary for his assumption that Fascism, in its present form, was ephemeral and would with time grow weaker rather than stronger to be justified. He was quite correct in forecasting that the 'errors' of Fascism would rapidly disillusion public opinion and in dismissing the philosophy of government and technical skills of Mussolini and his collaborators as inadequate, by his standards; what he did not, however, take into account was that when he evaluated the probable duration of Fascism, and its effect on the minds of the Italian people, by these criteria he was judging a new and ruthless movement of 'totalitarian' intentions by the standards derived from an experience of parliamentary democracy.[73] This is understandable, as there were in fact no precedents to guide him, but it remains true that by his support, although less wholly than with the other leaders of liberalism, he contributed to the consolidation of the new regime in its first and most vulnerable phase.

The chief rival of Giolitti as the leader and interpreter of Italian liberalism, Antonio Salandra, was much less reserved in his collaboration with Fascism. In public at least, he was ready to go all the way with Benito Mussolini, to the point of announcing himself to be 'an honorary Fascist'. Such unsolicited warmth took even the Duce by surprise.[74] In spite of this, Salandra in fact stopped short of a total surrender to Fascism. When Gentile applied to become a member of the Fascist party, on the grounds that Fascism was now the true liberalism, Salandra took care to mark the difference by joining the Rome branch of the newly organized Liberal party, which previously, with the individualism characteristic of the old parliamentarians, he had not cared to do.[75]

Paradoxically enough, Giolitti's pro-Fascism had the same roots as his pro-Socialism: common to both was 'an anxiety . . . the thought that the Italian political class was too small in number and faced with the risk of exhaustion, and that therefore it was advisable continually to call new social strata to take part in public affairs'.[76] Salandra shared the anxiety, but he had never accepted the remedy. Before the war, his thoughts had run on the 'senility' and decay of liberalism, and he admitted the need for rejuvenation, but he

clung with single-minded obstinacy to belief in the Liberal bourgeoisie
as the only legitimate depository of power. The crisis, he felt, had come from
slackness and weakness, from the enfeeblement of the authority and prestige
of the State by parliamentarianism, and the tendency to compromise with
socialism, the new vigour which he, too, sought was to come from the return
to a 'pure' liberalism, free from democratic taint and given emotional force
by an appeal to national pride.[77]

Salandra was a believer in the 'ethical State', which would govern by the
aid of an 'authoritarian morality': there was to be no neutrality or democratic free thought in the schools, and religion was to be used frankly as an
aid to securing obedience. But there seemed to be a lack of coherence and
of inner confidence in this belief in the State. He rejected Sonnino's paternalist reforms; they might be all right in a rich country, but in Italy there was
no 'margin' for them. His was a conservatism at heart as monotonous and
arid as the outlook over the Apulian plains from which he came. It is not
altogether surprising that at times he seems to have been attacked by doubt
about the viability of his enterprise; was liberalism, he once asked rhetorically, 'the dream of a summer night'?[78] There were times when it might
seem so.

In the years after the war, which he had hoped would unite and rally the
nation behind his principles, he suffered instead from the extreme unpopularity of all those associated with the *intervento*. In Parliament his
speeches were shouted down by the triumphant Socialists:[79] and the
Liberals, instead of resisting the tide, abandoned themselves to even worse
confusion and compromises with the spirit of the enemy. Fascism, therefore,
appeared as a providential deliverer. Once again Salandra could dream his
dream. This time, it took the form, only in externals different, of the resurrection of the right as an 'organized force', under his patronage. His aim
was a union, on equal terms, of the Fascists, the Nationalists and the
Liberals of the right.[80]

After the March on Rome, the perspectives altered. Salandra's appreciation of the March on Rome was cool, and barely concealed his chagrin at
the way he had been shouldered aside by Mussolini.[81] It was not possible
any longer to hope that the Fascists would accept his leadership: the aim
was corrected slightly. It was now necessary to combat the tendencies of
the movement to sectarianism, and to persuade Mussolini 'to leave the closed
world of the *fasci* to assume the role of leader of a historic right'.[82] The class
feelings of Salandra and his touchy sense of personal honour were not always
respected by the rough crew of parvenus who now dominated the political
scene. His susceptibility was injured by Mussolini's contemptuous reference
to the 'Gods of the parliamentary Olympus', who were now 'relics of the
past', on the day after his appointment to the League of Nations.[83] Were
not the Fascists, or many of them, adventurers of dubious origins? This was
not only a judgement on their social class, either: the Mussolini clique

itself, and many others, were 'exiles . . . from demagogic organizations', and consequently needed watching.[84] Behind the official facade of agreement, a certain distrust survived.

But it was not, for the time being, politically decisive. There was too much in common. For Salandra and his friends Fascism was simply the 'injection of energy' that the governing class needed.[85] The Fascists in the majority had the same ideals as the Liberals: only their methods were different. To believe in both an 'authoritarian morality' and in the absolute freedom of private property was a difficult combination, but one which Fascism seemed to be on the way to achieving. When Mussolini put forward his theory of force and consent as an alternative to the Liberal philosophy of government, the conservative *Giornale d'Italia*, more than objecting to the substance, tried to point out that his criticisms had been sent to the wrong address. The cult of liberty which he attacked was not theirs: 'the Liberals of whom we speak were authoritarian precisely because they were Liberals'; it was not liberalism but 'social-democracy' which had been overthrown in 1922.[86]

However there was still a serious divergence between conservatives like Salandra and the Fascists. Fascism claimed to be a revolution, while Salandra interpreted it as a restoration. He opposed changes in the formal structure of the State, remaining faithful to the old programme of a 'return to the Statute'. What he wanted was 'constitutional government', which meant government according to the letter of the Statute, as distinct from the spirit in which it had later been interpreted. In his electoral speech of March 1924, he described the practice of parliamentary designation of the Prime Minister as a mere custom, not grounded on constitutional authority. The 'designation' could be interpreted in many ways, according to the changing political situation, 'of which the sovereign is the uncensurable judge'.[87] The Fascists, of course, went along with this programme so far as it tended to emancipate the Government from dependence on a freely elected parliamentary majority. But to restore the independence of the Crown, which was Salandra's aim, was not at all what Mussolini wanted. The devices first of pseudo-parliamentary government and, later, of the State party, were necessary to give him security *against* the Crown. The constitutional reform proposed by Michele Bianchi, although superficially it resembled Salandra's in setting up a kind of 'Chancellorship' reminiscent of the German example, really differed profoundly in that it would have made the Prime Minister virtually independent of the Crown once he was chosen.[88]

Luigi Albertini was a friend and political ally of Salandra. No other Prime Minister, not even Sonnino, had received such full approval and support from him. But, whereas Salandra took Prussian conservatism as his model, the ideal of Albertini was English parliamentary government.[89] While he, too, regarded Giolitti's system as degenerate, he refused to identify the root of the evil with 'parliamentarianism'. Instead, he believed, the trouble came 'not from the use but from the paralysis of parliamentary institutions',[90] and a satisfactory reform could not be confined to the creation of an efficient executive, but must also restore legislative control over its operations. For a long time, Albertini was reluctant to acknowledge the substantial difference between his parliamentarian orthodoxy and the 'constitutionalism' of Salandra. In 1909, Salandra had written that parliamentary government, with all its defects, was still superior to any other. Could it be, Albertini asked, that he had changed his mind? Surely, he reasoned, Salandra's understanding of the evolution of law and the State was too well grounded for that, even if some of his followers were suspect.[91]

The opposition of Albertini to Giolitti had always had a moral as well as a political foundation. His severe and somewhat rigid mentality found the normal compromises of everyday politics repugnant. He wished the *Corriere* to be as he imagined *The Times* to have been in its heyday, the voice of public opinion – the moral conscience of the nation, even – and consequently no political obligations should be allowed to obstruct him in his first duty, that of providing clear information.[92] With such a temperament and such an uncompromising belief in the freedom of the Press as an absolute value, Albertini was not likely to adapt himself to Fascist methods of government.

The relations of the *Corriere* with Fascism went through at least three stages. During 1918–19, when the *Corriere* took a leading role in the polemic against Sonnino and the annexationists, Albertini's attitude to Mussolini was one of decided hostility. He disliked both his extreme nationalism and his demagogy, and he was strongly opposed to the idea already supported by some of his Milanese friends, of an electoral alliance between the Fascists and the Liberals.[93]

But he applauded the initial stages of the Fascist reaction of 1920–1 : it was, for him, the only alternative to anarchy, a necessary consequence of the absence of law, of the fact that 'the authority of the State had dropped to zero'.[94] The *Corriere* did not oppose Fascism until the eve of the March on Rome, although its reporting preserved a level of objectivity not found in most of the Liberal press.[95]

Albertini could not regard the private use of violence as anything but a provisional expedient: his solution for the crisis lay in a firm and austere conduct of government which would make Fascist violence impossible, and also unnecessary, by resisting all claims and agitations which were outside the law. But in practical terms, Albertini often helped the Fascists: his unremitting campaign against the Socialist administration of Milan helped to prepare public opinion for the occupation of the municipality. He still did not approve the result; the State, he argued, ought to have used its legitimate right to suspend administrations which were financially insolvent and thus forestall illegal reaction. During the last months before the March on Rome, his distrust of Fascism was growing. He realized, after Finzi had sounded him on his views, that the Fascists would stop at nothing and were prepared to use force in order to come to power. In his Senate speech of 13 August 1922, he warned that Fascist violence must now be considered a danger to Liberal institutions. 'There are those who are pleased at the fear which Fascism has put into so many people. I feel all the humiliation of this.' Moreover, though he advocated giving the Fascists a chance in government, his reasoning was sceptical rather than enthusiastic : 'the best way to remove every pretext for violence is to call on the Fascists to prove their capacity to direct public affairs, and to keep the promises by which they have attracted so many converts into their ranks.'[96]

For some Liberals, Fascist violence became respectable when it was exercised by the institutions of the State. But there was more to Albertini's criticism than a simple desire to see the work of repression entrusted to the policeman rather than to the blackshirt ; he sharply condemned the arrest of the Socialist leaders Nenni and Serrati in March 1923 as unjustified and unconstitutional.

The foundation of the Militia finally confirmed Albertini's sense of the incompatibility of liberalism and Fascism. He saw with astonishment that his fellow Liberals were disposed to overlook insults and to avoid the definition of their own principles in order to preserve their entente with Mussolini. His motto, on the contrary, was : 'Better alone than in bad company.' His 'pure' liberalism, which had rejected the Giolittian compromise with socialism, was equally severe towards the surrender to Fascism. Like other anti-Fascists, he came in fact to feel that the one benefit Fascism might bring was a revelation of the true nature of men and parties : the crisis was needed in order 'to lay bare the souls behind the various pompous names'[97] of the political groups. He was a conservative, certainly, according to English usage : he tended to forget later that in November 1922, while criticizing Mussolini's threats to Parliament and the maintenance of the squads, he had approved his economic and administrative programme.[98] But liberalism was for him a method of government; his definition was both less abstract and more intransigent than that of Salandra. He had, really, no prospects or strategy to offer – at least until 1924; but what he could provide was a certain illumination of the practices of Fascism and an astringent criticism of his fellow Liberals, of their tendency to 'close their eyes to reality' and to shrug off all violations of political and personal liberties as 'transitory' phenomena which need not be taken seriously. He saw that unless a stand was made it was Fascism which would end by absorbing official liberalism, not vice versa : while Mussolini boasted of the 'further developments of the revolution', the Liberals were afraid to reaffirm their principles, or even to face up to defining them. 'Up to what point does the Liberal party identify itself with Fascism and is it disposed to follow it ? If the identification is complete, then it no longer has features of its own. If support . . . has to be unconditional, differentiation is useless, and it is not sincere to assert that one has kept one's independence when one has sworn supine obedience.'[99]

It was not that Albertini refused totally the idea of co-operation with a government led by Mussolini. But such co-operation must be between equals, and must not represent either unconditional surrender or a deliberate confusion and falsification of the real character of liberalism and Fascism.

The importance of Albertini was in his influence on public opinion. The Fascists, who repaid his opposition by personal attacks of peculiar frequency, recognized the harm which the *Corriere* did to them. It was the main obstacle to their complete conquest of middle-class opinion. What Albertini also desired, however, was to preserve an independent and organized Liberal party, which could serve as a counterweight to Fascism. Here, as we have seen, he was less successful.

The Nationalists

The central position in the 'national right' was occupied by the Nationalists. The Liberals looked to them to act as a restraining influence on Fascist extremism; unlike the *squadristi*, they were led by 'men of order', a cultural elite who knew their Latin.[100] The Nationalists had, like the Liberals of the right, disdained contact with the masses, at least until 1922, and they had no party machine to rival the Fascist. They were, therefore, hostile to the attempts by the PNF to gain ascendancy over the organs of State, which they saw as inefficient, perhaps socially subversive, and certainly destructive of the ordered hierarchies which they wished to preserve and strengthen. All this, and above everything their loyalty to the monarchy, seemed to make them the natural allies of Salandra and the pro-Fascist Liberals. However in their doctrine, with its open scorn of parliamentary institutions, the Nationalists, especially Alfredo Rocco, had repudiated the Liberal State. The qualities which they shared with the Liberals enabled them to serve as their substitute. They provided a coherent philosophy of government, and their strong ties with the elites of business, the armed forces and diplomacy, decisively helped Mussolini to circumvent the Liberals and to destroy their pretensions to be the indispensable mediators who alone could instruct Fascism in the arts of government.

The March on Rome had left a legacy of distrust between Nationalists and Fascists. Intelligent observers believed that here one could already see the next crisis in the making, as Mussolini and his more radically minded friends chafed against the curbs imposed by Federzoni and his allies. They thought that the Nationalist leader might well come out on top, thanks to the backing of the top brass in Army and Navy.[101] Federzoni himself, in a speech on 16 November, claimed that the Nationalists had been 'the guarantee . . . against any danger of – even involuntary – demagogic deviations'.[102] However, in spite of this, it was not difficult for the Nationalist leaders to see that they had a doubtful future except in close alliance with Mussolini, and that the situation offered a golden and probably unique chance of imposing their ideals on government. The friction between the two movements had become really dangerous in the South, where it had served as a cover for the eternal contests between local parties. The *fasci* were often founded by the 'outs', the opponents of the local mayor and council, who would then defend themselves by organizing their supporters into a Nationalist group. As the latter had their own para-military formation, the *Sempre Pronti*, conflicts were frequent and violent.[103] The only way to suffocate local hostilities and to prevent them from causing a serious rift between the Nationalist leadership and Mussolini was evidently some kind of formal merger or federation. On 24 December Federzoni took the step of writing to Mussolini to assure him of his desire that the two movements should fuse.[104] Negotiations dragged on for some time, as the Fascist claims were predictably sweeping and seemed to some of the Nationalist leaders to involve the unconditional surrender of their own association. Mussolini refused to accept the proposal of Alfredo Rocco that the Nationalist association should remain in being as a subordinate organ of the PNF, with special functions in the field of propaganda, and that one-third of the places in the directive organs of the party should be reserved for ex-Nationalists. The Nationalists, in fact, had to accept their complete liquidation as an organization; but, in their case the marriage of 'doctrine' with 'force' was by no means wholly unfavourable to the former.[105] The ex-Nationalists were to acquire an influence within Fascism out of all proportion to their numbers.

Opposition to the fusion, in fact, was more vigorous on the Fascist side. The extremists of the party often saw the Nationalists as the Trojan Horse for all the forces who sought to tame Fascism and subordinate it to the State. Many Fascists of republican sympathies disliked their 100 per cent monarchism, and the Freemasons, very numerous among the higher cadres of the Fascist movement, feared that they would bring about a growth in clerical influence.[106]

The most violent opposition of all came from the leader of Neapolitan Fascism, Aurelio Padovani, and other southerners who believed that the new movement could serve as a force of regeneration by sweeping away the old clienteles. Although their own ranks were heavily infiltrated, they saw Nationalism in the South, with reason, as the instrument by which the old discredited politicians could hold on to power. At the back of all these quarrels there was a temperamental divergence, reflecting differences in the methods of recruitment, in class composition, and in the historic origin of the two movements. Alfredo Rocco, the most cogent theorist of Nationalism, had loftily announced in 1919 that it was 'not a disordered movement of *exaltés* worshippers of war, but . . . a complete and organic conception of society and state'.[107] This was not specifically aimed at the Fascists, but it might well have been. The Fascists, on their side, were proud that they had been guided by instinct rather than cold reason; as the syndicalist Guido Pighetti had pointed out, the Nationalists had been certain in 1914 about whether to fight but not about which side to choose, and in this they had shown themselves inferior to the democratic interventionists.[108]

However the moderate and monarchist wing of Fascism, men such as Massimo Rocca and Bottai, or the minister Giuriati, were warm in their support for the fusion: they shared with the Nationalists a tendency to deprecate the role of the PNF.[109]

Radical Fascists, and outsiders such as Mario Missiroli, had hoped that once in power Fascism would reveal its original democratic inspiration, too long hidden by necessary compromises; these illusions were rudely dispelled by the Nationalist-Fascist fusion.[110] The Grand Council decided to make membership of the *fasci* and the Freemasons' lodges incompatible; this measure, which affected probably the majority of its own membership, had little practical effect, as most of the lodges continued to enjoy the advantages of secrecy – but it was an important moral victory for the Nationalists over the forces of anti-clericalism.[111] The fusion was also, less obviously, a blow to the Liberals. The more far-sighted among the Liberals already saw the danger that the Nationalists might absorb their role in providing and organizing the elite support which was needed to complement the mass movement. The Nationalists had operated rather like a reactionary version of the Fabian society. 'Permeation' had been their most effective method; their ideas had taken hold in the universities, the law courts, the army and navy, and the civil service. They knew how to talk to the Church, the King and big business. With their guidance and help a new governing class could be created to sustain the dictatorship.

6

NORMALIZATION

The Acerbo Bill

Mussolini had delayed the contest for electoral reform in order to strengthen his own position and weaken that of his opponents. As the Fascists penetrated new regions where they had previously been weak, especially in the South, and seized control of local administration by force and fraud, the dangers of opposition, under any electoral system, became increasingly evident.[1]

The major obstacle to any scheme of electoral reform lay in the Popolari. The party was attached to the system of proportional representation by both conviction and self-interest: as a centre party, with support spread more evenly over the country than that of the other parties, they benefited most from it electorally. During the winter of 1922–3 its opposition to change stiffened, as relations with Fascism generally deteriorated. The secretary of the party, Don Sturzo, rallied his forces and successfully held off the challenge of the clerical and conservative wing. The conservatives had had a near monopoly of the party's press, which was controlled by a trust headed by Count Grosoli and linked to the Vatican and to the Banco di Roma. To break this hold, the anti-Fascists founded their own newspapers. *Il Popolo*, edited by Donati, was close to Sturzo's own views, and *Il Domani d'Italia*, edited by F.L.Ferrari, was the organ of the left.[2] In his own writings and speeches Sturzo, although he was reticent about the problem of the PPI's participation in the Government (of which he had always disapproved), was not afraid to open a vigorous counter-attack against the Fascists and their allies in the Catholic world. Few other political leaders at the time spoke so frankly. In his Turin speech of 20 December 1922 he attacked the pretensions of Mussolini to 'work miracles', and remarked on the conflict between the Fascist movement's code of personal loyalty to the leader and the legal order of the State. He was not deceived by Fascist talk about the regeneration of the South, and correctly forecast that the movement would soon be mastered by the old clienteles. All in all, his vision of Fascism was acute and discriminating : he was equally free from the conservative–liberal illusion that Fascism could be used to restore social order without affecting the constitutional order, and from illusions that democratic or syndicalist tendencies would gain the upper hand. Sturzo's firm and scarcely veiled anti-Fascism had the support of the great majority of the members of the party. Even at the highest level, among the deputies, where the desire to compromise was strongest, his position was reinforced by the growing perception that the Fascists conceived of collaboration as a one-way process. [3]

The suppression of the regional autonomy of the Trentino showed beyond doubt that Fascist ideas on 'decentralization' had nothing in common with the PPI's programme. [4] Locally, the Fascist drive against the party and the unions continued unabated. Agrarian Fascism, having broken and subdued the Socialist leagues of labourers, now turned its chief attention to organizations of sharecroppers and small tenants, the classes who formed, with the peasant proprietors, the base of the PPI in the countryside. Even the clergy were not spared, and incidents in which priests were maltreated were frequent. [5] Mussolini's policy, which was to conciliate the Church and Catholic Action while attacking only political and trade union organizations, was not easy to apply locally ; if some of the bishops were already inclined to respond favourably to the carefully calculated favours which he granted to the Church, in the North of Italy the majority of the parish priests shared the hostility of their parishioners towards Fascism. [6]

Sturzo's position, however, was still extremely difficult. He could not afford to identify himself openly with the left of the party, who demanded that co-operation with Fascism should cease forthwith. To have done so would have laid him wide open to the charges of being an obstacle to the pacification of the nation ; the only chance of satisfying the base of the party while not going against the known desires of the Vatican for a conciliatory attitude lay in the adoption of a 'centre' position. The platform of the 'centre', led by Sturzo, did not demand that the Popolari should take the initiative of passing to the Opposition : but it made clear that co-operation could not be unconditional, and that the party's autonomy and programme, including proportional representation, must be defended. In this way, the responsibility for the break would fall on Mussolini. [7]

The leaders of the Fascist party, even before the Congress of Turin, showed that they would be satisfied by nothing less than the root and branch destruction of the PPI. Sansanelli, who had succeeded Bianchi as party secretary, declared after the March Grand Council that 'we consider the PPI as a source of ambiguity which is dangerous to our national life'. *Cremona Nuova* stated the Fascist viewpoint even more bluntly. Since Fascism had both won over the peasant masses and taken upon itself the defence of the interests of the Church, the PPI had lost both its useful functions and therefore had no right to exist.[8] Mussolini and Cesare Rossi pursued a slightly less intolerant line, but one which would have had even more fatal results for the Popolari. The party's co-operation could still be accepted, but only if the left was expelled. In effect, they demanded that the majority should capitulate completely to the minority of the extreme right, who in the meantime were preparing to secede if Sturzo refused to comply.[9]

The Congress of Turin (12–14 April 1923) was a triumph for Don Sturzo; his speech was loudly applauded, while Pestalozza, one of the right's spokesmen, was booed with equal vigour. The victory of Sturzo put Mussolini in a dilemma which he had probably desired to avoid. He could not accept the continuation of the alliance without admitting the validity of pluralism and respect for the existing constitution; and he would have had to abandon the plan for electoral reform. He and the Fascists were in too weak a position with regard to Parliament and public opinion to accept such a compromise, which would rapidly have entailed a retreat on other fronts as well. But to break with the Popolari was certainly not without dangers; it would mean that he could no longer count on a parliamentary majority.

Mussolini summoned the PPI ministers and under-secretaries on 17 April and delivered an ultimatum, which, however, left them a loophole for escape. If the parliamentary group voted a clearly collaborationist motion and dropped the conditions set by the Congress, this might, he suggested, clarify the situation. The group duly promised that 'the co-operation of the PPI will, as in the past, be inspired by complete loyalty to the head of the government', and although it also promised 'fidelity to the party' (PPI), this seemed to meet what was desired.[10] The headline of the *Popolo d'Italia* announced 'The vote of the Popolari group – Full solidarity and loyal collaboration with the Fascist government.'[11] Three days later, Mussolini shocked the Italian political world by brusquely 'accepting' the resignation of Cavazzoni and his colleagues. Mussolini had hoped that if he got a favourable vote from the parliamentary group this would be enough, aided by pressures from the Vatican, to cause the resignation of Sturzo from the leadership. But the Vatican, on this occasion, refused to intervene, and even discreetly supported Sturzo. Mussolini hesitated before making his decision; he was in an angry and vindictive mood, but he may have been tempted by the possible tactical advantages of delaying the break. His final decision to reject the offer was taken under strong pressure from the leaders of the party; on the evening of 20 April Giunta, Michele Bianchi and Finzi paid a call on him to protest that the Popolari deputies had promised collaboration only with the Government, and had not mentioned the Fascist party. Farinacci, whose reaction had also been immediately hostile, saw Mussolini on 23 April, just before he made his decision.[12]

To the intransigents of the PNF the expulsion of the Popolari was only the first step; they hoped that Fascism would soon govern alone. 'The revolution is not complete', Michele Bianchi announced: the Government, since it did not owe its power to the Chamber, could not be liquidated by parliamentary or constitutional methods; in fact, the heir of Fascism could only be a party 'antithetical to ours, but like ours extremist and anti-parliamentary'.[13] Logic was on the side of the intransigents, and Mussolini had undoubtedly taken a decisive step towards full dictatorship. But characteristically he did not himself follow up the logical consequences of his action. This would have involved risks which he thought he could avoid. To avoid the dangers of a conflict with the Crown, Parliament must still be put to use.

The launching of the electoral reform scheme was further delayed by disagreements within the Fascist movement. At the beginning of February Farinacci came out for the *uninominale*; the *Agenzia Volta*, controlled by Cesare Rossi and Bianchi, immediately attacked his proposal.[14] Why did Farinacci support a proposal which at first sight one would have expected to come from the moderate, pro-Liberal wing of Fascism? There can be no doubt that the answer lies in the distribution of power within the Fascist movement. Farinacci, as the spokesman for the *ras*, saw that the adoption of the *uninominale* would make it easier for them to maintain their autonomy and would make central party or governmental control more difficult. Michele Bianchi, although an 'intransigent' and a believer in the power of the party, as secretary of the PNF had a contrary interest. To the attacks of his opponents, who accused him of wishing to perpetuate the despised methods of Giolittian Italy, Farinacci replied that the effect of the *uninominale* would be very different from formerly. The choice of candidates would be determined by the 'judgement of the provincial Federation', which would avoid the revival of personalism.[15] This made it evident that Farinacci's objective was to uphold the supremacy of the local party machines. When the polemic revived in April, its implications for the relations of power within the party became even more obvious: Farinacci, observing that the *Agenzia Volta* communique announcing the party's decision in favour of the majority list system had been issued during Mussolini's absence from Rome, counter-attacked by suggesting that Bianchi and Rossi, as 'the only interested parties' must have acted on their own responsibility. He demanded an appeal to the party at large by means of a referendum among party federations and deputies. 'I, who am not chained to Rome, know the views of the party on this issue very well.'[16] In his attack on the secret decision-making of Mussolini's entourage, Farinacci expressed resentments widespread among the provincial Fascist leaders; however his opposition, based on local and internal party considerations, did not indicate a general political strategy. The alliance between Farinacci and Liberals like Orlando on the electoral reform question plainly had no general political consistency.

The Fascist committee set up to report on the question gave several reasons for rejecting the *uninominale*. First, it clashed with the character of Fascism as a mass movement aiming at the 'integration and unification' of all classes and regions, and would allow too much scope to local and personal interests. Here it touched on a perennial weakness of the *ras*, the contrast between their interests and the nationalist, authoritarian, unitary ideology of Fascism. Second, it would create a danger of disagreement between the various national forces.[17] This was probably the most important consideration. In the North and Centre, in the regions of Fascist strength, the system would favour the intransigents (and might lead to the almost total exclusion of the Liberals), but in the South it would strengthen the traditional leaders of the clienteles. It would therefore accentuate the political divergences within the Government majority, favouring both the retention of independence by the Liberals and intransigence on the part of the Fascists. In regions such as Campania, where Fascism was challenging the power of the former political class and the contest was very much in doubt, the resolution of tensions would be very difficult, given the dependence of the old leaders on local followings. Under the regional majority system, the composition of differences would be easier. The final rejection of even the regional system in favour of a single national electoral college (though with regional lists) was presumably motivated by the fear that even the former would allow too much bargaining power and independence to the old parties, while not excluding the possibility of opposition victories. It might seem redundant to look for reasons for the Government's adoption of the national list system, so evident were its advantages. The Government gained practically unlimited power over the choice of two-thirds of the members of the new Chamber. But, in fact, the decision seems only to have been taken at the last moment. There were fears that the scheme would prove too much for the Liberals and the Southern deputies to swallow. The *Gran Consiglio* in its resolution of 25 April still spoke only of 'wider constituencies.'[18] However the break with the Popolari greatly accentuated the danger of an actual defeat for the Government in certain regions, and at the same time made doubtful the possibility of a smooth passage for any reform scheme. Moreover, events in Sicily and the South, notably the monarchist demonstrations of the *soldino*,[19] had shown the dangerous weakness of Fascism. Lastly, the internal crisis of Fascism brought with it a serious danger that whole regions might follow a dissident Fascist leader, such as Padovani in Campania, or De Vecchi in Piedmont.

The true importance of the Acerbo scheme which stipulated that two-thirds of all the seats should go to the list with the highest number of votes, was not so much in the technical provisions of the premium, but in its moral effect. It discouraged all shades of opposition, and more especially attempts by the allies of Fascism to assert their independence. Before the introduction of the measure, the *Stampa* commented that 'the fundamental question of principle now is not and cannot be that of the electoral system, but that of the very existence of Parliament and of parliamentary government'.[20]

The Acerbo Bill, however, involved such a radical modification in the system of representative government that, even if honestly applied, it was hardly compatible with parliamentary government as it had previously been understood. Amendola, answering the arguments of those Liberals who argued that it was necessary to accept the bill to avoid the worse evil of constitutional reform, remarked that 'it is *itself* the constitutional reform';[21] it marked the first *legal* alteration of the fundamental features of the representative state. The battle over the law therefore had high symbolic value as a measure of the determination of the defenders of parliamentary liberty. It was the first decisive test of strength that Mussolini had had to undergo and its outcome was critical for the consolidation of the regime.

The first hint that Mussolini favoured a national majority list came in the *Popolo d'Italia* on 19 May. The idea was attacked by Albertini in an editorial three days later. However on 23 May Cesare Rossi admitted that Mussolini had his doubts, and meanwhile soundings of the possibility of some compromise with the Popolari continued.[22] Mussolini's evident hesitations aroused hopes that the bill would not be introduced at all. On the other side the Liberals unanimously declared their opposition to the national college. Orlando came out against it on 23 May, and he was followed by the strongly pro-Fascist Casertano and by the *Giornale d'Italia*.[23] An anonymous Liberal, whom some assumed to be Giolitti but who was in reality the paper's editor, Frassati, gave an interview in *La Stampa* headed 'How to co-operate' which struck a very optimistic note. The Fascists, he said, must soon choose between the path of revolutionary violence and that of a return to the constitution. 'The method . . . of keeping two irons in the fire is possible only for the duration of the full powers granted by the Chamber.' But it seemed that Mussolini had seen the dangers of the revolutionary path.

To be persuaded of this, one need only observe the efforts that he is making inside his own party . . . the incorporation of the *squadristi* into the national militia, the punishment of the refractory, the elimination of men who were very well-known in the party, the clear assertion that the authority of the State resides in the Prefects and not in the representatives of the party, the recognition, even if for the moment it is only formal, of the Statute and the authority of the King.

'At this moment', he said, 'Mussolini finds himself truly in the position of the mythical Hercules at the crossroads'; but there were many signs that he had seen and chosen the path of reason and a return to the constitution. The Liberals should therefore grant their co-operation, because it alone could enable Mussolini to surmount the difficulties in his way without violence; but in return for their aid they must demand 'firm guarantees' for the restoration of all the fundamental liberties.[24]

For a brief moment, the Liberal world revived, in the belief that the internal crisis of Fascism would force Mussolini into a closer relationship with his other allies. These hopes were based on the action which Mussolini had recently taken to assert the supremacy of the State over the party and to discipline the extremists: the re-assertion of the authority of the Prefects, the abolition of the Fascist *alti commissari*, and the disgrace of leading *squadristi* and intransigents such as Calza-Bini and Padovani.[25]

Casertano was active at this time in trying to organize a broad coalition among the governmental deputies of the South, who were encouraged by the defeat of Padovani and the victory of the old clienteles.[26] The aim was, by emphasizing their loyalty to Mussolini, to create a bloc around his person, and thus to advance the submersion of Fascism in an indistinct conservative coalition. It was Farinacci, as usual, who voiced the alarm. He made clear that he was willing to stomach the suppression of the intransigent Padovani in the name of party discipline, but only so long as this did not signify a general trend towards the abandonment of the true Fascists in favour of the 'flankers'.[27] His scarcely veiled threats had an immediate effect. On 22 May it had been announced that Mussolini would speak to the Chamber of Deputies, but the extremists put pressure on him to change his mind. After a violent attack by Michele Bianchi on the Chamber on 30 May, the speech was definitely cancelled, and the Fascist press underlined the calculated rebuff to Parliament.[28] Instead Mussolini addressed the Senate on 8 June. Previously on 2 June he had made his final decision in favour of the Acerbo Bill.[29] His speech confirmed the new rigidity of the Government's attitude. At the same time the Popolari confirmed their opposition. The brief moment of calm had passed, and Mussolini, under the influence of Farinacci, had made one of his characteristic changes of course. He would now take the hard line. In fact the crisis of Fascism, from which the Liberals had understandably hoped to profit, probably ended by making Mussolini's position more rigid. The dramatic attack by the Fascist deputy Misuri on the whole system of party domination, transcended the previous local bickerings and marked the emergence of an acute conflict between moderate and extremist views of the role and purpose of Fascism.[30] Mussolini's anger at his own party was turned outwards against the other political groups, accused of trying deliberately to disintegrate Fascism and profit from its divisions. These accusations again probably coincided with his actual sentiments. A sceptical distrust of the future often induced Mussolini to be temporarily reasonable, but it was almost invariably in the end overpowered by his vocation for suspicion and his feeling of insecurity, which, if it did not encourage faith in the future, still more militated against satisfaction with the present. As with the expulsion of the Popolari, the play of both temperament and external pressures drove Mussolini further along the road to dictatorship. On this occasion, however, the role played by Farinacci and the extremists was probably more decisive; Mussolini knew that he was powerless to subdue opposition without them, and their blackmail outweighed the strong pressures for a more conciliatory stance.

How was the bill to be passed? It was essential to keep the Liberals in line. There were signs of disturbance : the Southerners, especially Orlando, might seize on the introduction of a single national electoral college as an opportunity for creating an opposition based on regional feeling. The Liberals exerted strong pressures behind the scenes for the modification of the project. But the Liberal decision in favour of co-operation was firm, and their leaders were prepared to subordinate their open dislike of the measure to their general view as to the expediency of avoiding conflict. Fascism, however, could still only count on the support of the Right, the Giolittians, and the Democrazia Sociale.[31] In the last case, although the deputies were pretty unanimous, the strong opposition of the party members in some regions was a real problem. Bonomi and Amendola were hostile, as well as the Popolari. The attitude of the last was crucial. If the group held firm and united in opposition, it would be very difficult for the bill to pass. If it could be persuaded to abstain, then there would be no difficulty. But it was just possible for the bill to pass even if the majority of the Popolari opposed. It might scrape through by a narrow majority if the twenty or so pro-Fascist deputies of the PPI defied (or seceded from) the party and voted for the bill, and if at the same time the majority of the deputies of the Nitti group and the former Social Reformists could be won over. Here the tradition of governmentalism was of assistance. The Social Reformist group had gone into liquidation, leaving its members free. The Nittians were no stronger. Nitti had withdrawn from the arena, and most of his followers were unwilling to sacrifice themselves. The group had no more real political consistency. Only a handful of old faithfuls grouped themselves around Amendola, while the opposition of the Palazzo Giustiniani freemasonry, led by Alberto Beneduce, helped to keep a few other Democrats in line.[32]

If the bill were to be passed only as the result of an obvious compromise, Parliament would at least have made an important assertion of independence. Mussolini's strategy, although it was not in his nature ever to close the door entirely, aimed at total victory without concessions. This was the result of the pressures exerted by the party intransigents in late May.

Mussolini's tactics for passing the bill had two aspects. One was an appeal to conservative opinion by the reminder that without Fascism the monarchy would be threatened by revolution from the left, and by suggestions that Fascist intentions could be adequately summarized by the old concept of a 'return to the Statute'.[33] This was backed by a frank appeal to social conservatism, as in his speech to the Senate. But simultaneously, in accord with the ideas of Farinacci, he used the threat to mobilize Fascism for the 'second wave'. This side of the operation did not only involve the threat of force. For the first time since he became Prime Minister, Mussolini went on a tour of the provinces and addressed a whole series of Fascist rallies. These mass rallies were treated as a demonstration of the popular foundations of Fascist power ; Mussolini appealed to the crowd as the embodiment of the popular will.[34]

The propaganda of the respectable backers of Fascism was aimed not only at conservative opinion in general, but directly at the Crown. The encroachment of Parliament upon the prerogative of the monarchy was stressed. 'All the efforts of Parliament have been directed to one purpose: to substitute parliamentary sovereignty for royal sovereignty ...'; the questions of the royal prerogative in foreign affairs and of the 'imposition' of ministers on the King by the parliamentary groups were raised again. The President of the Senate, Tittoni, while admitting an 'abstract' preference for proportional representation (he had been one of its early supporters), thought that its abolition was justified as a means of restoring the unperverted constitution.[35] But Mussolini still submitted to the necessity of monarchism with a bad grace. Cesare Rossi tells that he had great difficulty in restraining Mussolini from raising the spectre of a return to republicanism as an element in his other, popular, mass appeal. He pointed out that it was too late for this to carry much conviction.[36] Fascism also exploited the fear that it could win elections under any system by a reign of terror, and that therefore it would be better to be conciliatory and to allow the reform to pass, thus, it was hoped, removing the necessity for violence.

The dilemma of the non-Fascists was real. It would be wrong to think of the vote on the Acerbo Bill as an issue which involved only a simple moral choice. Even among the Socialists, not a few secretly hoped that the bill would pass. It would have been useless to win a purely parliamentary victory, which could have had no result except to lead Mussolini to put into action his threat of turning the Chamber into a 'bivouac'. On the other hand, defeat in the Chamber might have broader consequences. Fascism, in the midst of a grave internal crisis, did not appear monolithic or unshakeable. Rejection of the bill would have weakened Mussolini's position in relation to the Crown, and harmed his prestige. It would have multiplied discontent and the possibilities of a 'fronde' among his supporters. Approval, on the contrary, would dishearten the Opposition and would allow Mussolini to use parliamentary and legal methods as a cover for the transformation of the State, which, once the majority was safe, could be carried through without any formal break in constitutional continuity. The King and his advisers would become inevitably still more hesitant and reluctant to take action. For these reasons as well as for the sake of morality and dignity, Turati and Amendola argued that even death by violence was preferable to slow extinction as the result of an abdication in the face of threats. The rejection of the bill, Turati wrote, 'would perhaps have been civil war; but it would have been the beginning of a solution'.[37] Against their arguments stood the illusion that Fascism would die a 'natural death', caused by its internal stresses. Many Liberals hoped that the passing of the bill would reconcile Fascism with the constitution, and would make Mussolini more reasonable.

The resistance of the Partito Popolare to Fascism was much firmer than that of the Democratic and Liberal groups. This was not only a matter of the superior solidity of its organization, nor even of the hostility of the grass-roots associations of the peasantry to the agrarian reaction of the *squadristi*; there came into play also the tradition of resistance to the State, in marked contrast to the Liberals' traditional dependence, which had been inherited from the struggles of the nineteenth century. This inheritance, however, had been profoundly transformed by the Christian Democrats of the early twentieth century, and by Luigi Sturzo, whose opposition to the centralized State had much in common with the criticisms once expressed by the federalist and autonomist Left. On the other hand, the thinking of the Vatican had changed also. Pius x had allowed the political strength of the Catholics to be used as a prop by the Liberal state; this was not only conceived as an alliance against the feared advance of 'atheistic Socialism', but also as a means by which the Catholics could gradually and discreetly reassert their influence without shock or social upheaval. Such an approach was only possible when combined with the severe control of lay militancy by the ecclesiastical hierarchy. Benedict xv had instead allowed the PPI to achieve autonomy, at least in theory, from the organization of the Church; the safest policy for the Vatican in the years of postwar turbulence seemed to be one of formal disengagement from the internal affairs of Italy. But both the strong right-ward trend of 1921–2, and the personality of Achille Ratti, elected pope as Pius xi in February 1922, modified the situation.

Pius xi looked with disfavour on some of the exuberances of a part of the Popolari left, and was determined to reaffirm the strict hierarchical control of the Church over Catholic Action, which had been strongly affected by the vigorous independence of the political party. Just at this time, the Popolari were accused by all sides of making government impossible; the Vatican soon let it be known that it did not approve the intransigence of the party, which was an obstacle to the 'pacification of souls': or, to put it more plainly, to the formation of a united conservative front. The victory of Fascism was, from the Church's point of view, both interesting and alarming: interesting, because Mussolini made no secret of his willingness to negotiate substantial concessions, whether in educational policy or in the field of financial and legal relations between the State and Catholic institutions, in return for the polite benevolence of the Church; alarming, because of the 'instinctive anti-clericalism'[38] of the Fascist movement, which often broke out into threats and violence against the clergy, and against the institutions and practices of Catholicism.

Mussolini, as usual, played ably on both hopes and fears. The Vatican had no desire now to return to the magnificent isolation it had once voluntarily assumed and still maintained in name, and to the thinking of Pius xi and the Secretary of State, Cardinal Gasparri, the PPI began to appear as an increasingly dangerous liability. However there were other elements in the attitude of the Vatican; it had to consider its position at the head of an international Church, and the possible long-term dangers, both at home and abroad, of open support for Mussolini. Consequently Pius XI and the Curia moved at first with extreme care and caution; they wanted above all to be certain that Mussolini's experiment would last before compromising themselves; and they were bound also to take account of the strong hostility to Fascism of the great majority of the lower clergy, and even of a number of bishops. At the time of the Congress of Turin, Mussolini, and still more some of his entourage such as Finzi, who was in close touch with the aged and conservative Cardinal Vannutelli, misjudged the situation badly. They believed that the Vatican would come out openly in favour of the foundation of a new 'National-Popular party', which would have co-operation with Fascism as its *raison d'être*.[39] The Vatican was impressed, perhaps somewhat reluctantly, by the unity and strength shown by the PPI: and Sturzo, with assistance from the more flexible De Gasperi, had been skilful enough to leave the responsibility for the break to Mussolini. The *Osservatore Romano* gave a favourable judgement on the restored unity of the party; and the cooling of the Vatican's attitude to Fascism was widely remarked.[40] When the Acerbo Bill was introduced, De Gasperi and the parliamentary group of the PPI once again showed themselves inclined to compromise: after Donati had attacked them with vigour in *Il Popolo*, Sturzo's line once again prevailed, and on 14 June the group decided to oppose the bill.[41] The propaganda offensive now launched against the PPI was not confined to the Fascist press; it was the Liberal *Giornale*, which on 18 June addressed a warning to 'those beyond the Tiber'. Two days later the *Idea Nazionale* admonished the Vatican that it could no longer shelter behind the screen of non-intervention. These new attacks and the rising tide of Fascist violence were decisive. On 25 June an article by Monsignor Pucci in the right-wing *Corriere d'Italia* suggested, with as much clarity as the discreet modes of the Church allowed, that Papal favour had been withdrawn from Sturzo and the PPI. In these circumstances, it was a tragic and fatal handicap that Sturzo was not merely a devout Catholic, but a priest. The dilemma between political and religious duty would have been acute even for a layman; but for a priest it was impossible to ignore the will of the Pope, once it was known. De Gasperi made a last gallant attempt on behalf of Sturzo; his forced retirement would, he said, 'make the Catholics once again political minors, in comparison with those of other nations', and it would 'give credit to the opinion that the Holy See intervenes directly in Italian political life, so that every government will think itself able to get its own way by means of religious interests'. The second argument was well chosen; but it was no good. In early July Fascist threats came to a crescendo. An *Agenzia Volta* communique threatened 'exceptional and definitive measures' against Sturzo and the Popolari; they were accused of moral responsibility for the death of Fascists who had been killed in various political brawls. In secret, threats were made that the churches of Rome would be occupied by the Blackshirts. The following day Sturzo gave in his resignation; whether there had been a new direct order from the Vatican, or whether he had simply drawn the inevitable conclusions from earlier suggestions, is not known. But, in substance, one can be certain that he was left no choice except to resign or risk the consequences of open disobedience to the Church.[42]

With Sturzo's resignation the mainspring of resistance was broken. He had hoped that the group was now too deeply committed to abandon its firm stand. However on 12 July the *Agenzia Volta* returned to the attack; it accused Sturzo of continuing to direct the policies of the party as before his resignation. On the same day, Filippo Meda dealt a grave blow to the unity of the party by an open letter which criticized the party's intransigence.[43] Meda was no lover of Fascism; he was instead typical of those distinguished Catholic politicians, experts in administration, who shared the accommodating mentality which pervaded the pre-war political world of Giolitti.

The bill was not passed without a rising crescendo of threats from the Fascist side. Mussolini appeared at the start of the debate wearing a black shirt; on 19 July, carefully planned demonstrations were staged in the cities of Tuscany and Umbria and Catholic circles in Florence and Pisa were devastated.[44] As the Fascists recognized that they were lacking a clear majority in Parliament, the ominous signs multiplied. Terzaghi, the first Fascist spokesman in the Chamber, and a moderate, exclaimed: 'You are more here inside but we are more outside.' He warned the Opposition that it should be grateful that Mussolini controlled the movement: 'our movement without its leaders would be perhaps a little worse and more dangerous than you imagine.' The other note in the chord was struck by Giunta, who insinuated that the Opposition was stimulated by a clique of international bankers, afraid of the revival of 'imperial Italy', and declared that Militia, unions and party were all ready at Mussolini's orders, 'to march in any (!) direction'.[45] The Opposition leaders increasingly feared that if the bill were rejected, the Fascists would break into the Chamber and a general 'second wave' would begin in the provinces. The armed guard at the doors of Parliament was replaced by members of the Militia,[46] although Turati believed that the President of the Chamber, De Nicola, had a detachment of *carabinieri* ready inside the building to repel any attack. The Chamber, however, did not simply give way to *force majeure*. In the first place, there is a question which must, being hypothetical, remain without a certain answer. Could Mussolini have afforded an open and decisive break with legality at this stage? The chief danger to his emerging regime, as the Matteotti crisis was to show, lay in his losing control over the violent tendencies of his followers and in making martyrs. The King would not have been impressed by the sight of Blackshirts in the Chamber. Mussolini's tactics in dealing with the Crown were gradualist: he wished to avoid playing the 'high game'. Instead, as he remarked: 'We must pluck the chicken without making it squawk.'[47]

The Opposition leaders recognized the decisive importance of Victor

Emmanuel in the crisis. Both Amendola and Turati openly appealed to the King not to allow the passage of a reform which would radically reduce his freedom of choice and manoeuvre. If the bill passed, Amendola said, the Crown would no longer be able to act as 'an arbitrator between the parties' and, shorn of political functions, would be reduced to the status of a 'symbol . . . a heraldic decoration'.[48]

The refusal of Victor Emmanuel to reform the electoral system by decree has already been mentioned: there is evidence that he disliked the Acerbo Bill and that his mood was by no means altogether favourable to Mussolini at this time. But it is necessary here to distinguish the question of the dissolution of Parliament from that of reform by decree; most of the contemporary indiscretions suggest the hypothesis that the King would not have been prepared to refuse the former. Such a refusal would inevitably have entailed really decisive and positive action; at least an interlude of military government would probably have been necessary. Victor Emmanuel did not like to take such heavy responsibilities; as at the time of the March on Rome, what still most favoured Mussolini was not the King's sympathy, but his deeply rooted pessimism and sense of inadequacy.[49] However it seems probable, though in the state of the evidence not certain, that Victor Emmanuel did not remain wholly passive during the crisis. Mussolini showed his usual flair for knowing when to stop. He had screwed up tension to the maximum, and he could now afford to relax it. But this relaxation may not have been wholly spontaneous. It seems likely that the moderate and conciliatory tone of his speech to the Chamber, which was full of suggestions of 'openings' in all directions, owed something to the inspiration of the monarchy. Victor Emmanuel believed that if violent conflict was avoided, Mussolini could still be induced to take the path of 'normalization'. It seems likely that he was reassured by the attitude of the Liberal elder statesmen; after all, three ex-Prime Ministers, Giolitti, Salandra and Orlando, had agreed to vote for the bill. The King was prepared to make concessions to avoid a crisis. He agreed to approve the hastily prepared decree limiting the freedom of the Press (which was, however, suspended for a year); as the Opposition saw, if he was not prepared to reject this, he would certainly not be prepared to refuse a dissolution.[50] It may even be that in exchange for promises of good behaviour at the last moment he withdrew his veto on the passage of the law by decree. The Opposition therefore was not only disorientated by Mussolini's able tactics, but disheartened by the evidence of the King's weakening.

Mussolini's speech was not altogether insincere. With his habitual realism, he took account of the obstacles posed by the Crown and his Liberal allies, and also of the help which they were prepared to give. His scepticism and indifference to programmes meant that it cost him little to jettison the doctrinaires of his party, with their ideas for constitutional reform by Chancellorship or technical councils. Similarly, when he promised 'the transformation of Fascism into an organ of administration', he was certainly sincere, in so far as he wanted a movement more disciplined and subordinate to his own wishes. However the concrete example he gave of the process of normalization and the transformation of the essence of Fascism is highly significant. 'It is incredible how the *caposquadra* (squad leader) changes when he becomes a councillor or a mayor.' Given the methods by which this 'transformation' was generally achieved, this actually identified normalization with the piecemeal conquest of State power, which did, admittedly, involve a change of spirit in passing from 'irregular' to official and bureaucratic forms. Mussolini also played on the self-interest and fears of the deputies. He promised that the elections would be delayed and that there would be no violence. Although he kept the first promise, the belief that violence could be avoided because the law made it unnecessary proved fallacious. It ran contrary to the deep need felt by Mussolini and the Fascists to secure overwhelming popular support through the plebiscitary tactics characteristic of modern dictatorships. The law merely gave the Government security and, by putting the result beyond reasonable doubt, increased the psychological pressures to conform. The example of local elections, in which abstentions had frequently not been tolerated even when there was no opposition, should have served as a warning.

However Mussolini also struck a higher note. 'This is the moment,' he said, 'in which Parliament and nation can be reconciled. But, if this occasion is passed by, tomorrow it will be too late, and you feel this in the air, you feel it in your spirit.'[51] This appeal proved effective. The abstention of a man like Amendola did not signify that he had been convinced of Mussolini's honesty, but it did mean that he felt that he had to be given the benefit of the doubt.[52]

The crucial decision was that of the Popolari. By a margin of only two votes (41 to 39) the parliamentary group of the PPI decided to abstain; this made the passage of the bill a certainty. Several of those who voted for abstention probably did so in the belief that this was the only way to preserve the unity of the party; but their hopes proved illusory. While the left of the party loyally accepted the majority decision, Cavazzoni and eight other pro-Fascist deputies declared their support for the Government. Mussolini had made no concrete concessions, and De Gasperi's assertion that he promised to allow substantial amendments to the law had no real basis. But he had seemed to offer the Popolari, like his other opponents, a respite from terror and administrative harassment, and this was enough to undermine their resolution. In fact, the PPI did not secure immunity from persecution by their retreat. On the contrary, the next months saw a new round of violence against the party and the unions. The murder of the priest Don Minzoni by Balbo's thugs took place little more than a month after the vote in the Chamber.[53]

The ability shown by Mussolini in bringing about the passage of the bill through Parliament undoubtedly impressed the King, whose opinion of him became more favourable than before. Previously, in a conflict between Fascism and the parliamentary Opposition, it would have been the former who would have had to violate the constitution; but henceforward, whatever errors Fascism made, it would have a constitutional foundation for its powers. In 1924, the time was to come when violent moral revulsion against Fascism was to bring it very close to disintegration, but the formal position would by then have altered in Mussolini's favour, and the King would be required to exercise his initiative without clear constitutional guidance. Both Amendola and Salvemini recognized, as they had not done before, that now Mussolini was likely to stay in power for a long time.[54]

The discussion of the details of the bill took place in a much calmer atmosphere. The crisis was over, and the Opposition was a prey both to discouragement and to renewed optimism about Mussolini's intentions. 'The fear of winning' was now uppermost, and the proposal of Bonomi to establish a 40 per cent minimum quotient for the majority list was defeated in spite of the support of the PPI.[55]

The Elections

At first, it seems that Mussolini was in half a mind to delay the elections indefinitely and to ask for the grant of full powers to be extended for another year. With characteristic caution, he called a new session of the Chamber, presumably with this in mind, and then dismissed it again after three days. What caused this volte-face? It seems that the relations of Mussolini with the constitutional groups had taken a turn for the worse. On 27 November, when the Cabinet met to discuss the question of the prolongation of full powers, Di Cesarò, the leader of the Democrazia Sociale, while agreeing to the idea on his own behalf, gave warning that his support did not imply that of his group or friends.[56] Two days later, the devastation of Nitti's house by a gang of Fascists caused general indignation; the renewal of full powers suddenly appeared in doubt. A third contributory factor was the increasing discomfort felt by the President of the Chamber, De Nicola, at his position.[57] The debate on the renewal of full powers was, besides, eagerly awaited by the Opposition leaders: Amendola and Turati had consoled themselves after the passage of the Acerbo Bill by agreeing that this would be 'the true moment of decision', when they could give battle.[58]

Behind all these minor incidents there can be seen the general hostility of the Fascists to free parliamentary discussion, their vulnerability to moral or financial criticism, and their desire to avoid publicity.

Even after he had sent the Chamber home again, Mussolini delayed officially announcing his decision for another month. It is probable that he was concerned not to make an irrevocable choice until he felt that he had the PNF itself in hand: the elections of the new *direttori* of the *fasci* took place in December, and involved a contest for influence between the *ras*, the party secretary Giunta, and Mussolini's own entourage.[59] In fact Mussolini must have eventually concluded that the general elections, so far from being a risk, could be very useful in his struggle with his own party. He was, at the same time, concerned to establish beyond any doubt that the decision to summon the elections was entirely a matter for himself, the Cabinet and the King against the efforts made by the party to have the question discussed in the Grand Council. The Liberals reacted vigorously to this suggestion, as unconstitutional and derogatory to the monarchy. The affair was a sign of the tensions between the normalizing allies of Fascism and the extremists.[60]

The Opposition was unable to unite so as to present at least a theoretical alternative to the Government. This failure, however, was partially justified by the hopelessness of the struggle. Indeed in all the opposition parties, from the Popolari to the Communists, some asked whether the best policy would not be a general abstention in protest against the climate of oppression already evident at the outset of the electoral campaign.[61]

The Communists took the initiative of proposing a 'proletarian bloc' with the two other Socialist parties; however the position of the party was that 'Fascism has opened for the proletariat a period of permanent revolution', and, accordingly, the bloc must have as its programme the socialist revolution and not merely the restoration of political liberty.[62]

The appeal, in fact, was intended only to embarrass the Socialist parties by placing on them the responsibility of refusal. There would have been some political logic in a bloc between the PCI and the PSI; but the PSU could operate far more effectively as part of a non-revolutionary opposition which was willing to subordinate other issues to the restoration of liberty.

The Communists were certainly in the right when they argued the need to organize opposition outside Parliament, but one of the main propaganda themes of Fascism had always been the identification of all opposition with 'Bolshevism', and it is clear that the parties which accepted the parliamentary system had nothing to gain and a great deal to lose by in any way making this confusion legitimate.

This was the idea which inspired the approaches of Amendola to Turati; but in spite of the real rapprochement between the PSU and the constitutional opposition, the vague project for opposing a 'liberty bloc' to the Government list never came to anything. Even the constitutional opposition remained divided between the followers of Bonomi and those of Amendola.

Old jealousies and distrusts helped to divide the Opposition; but still more fundamental was the unwillingness to challenge Fascism openly.[63] If one considers only the formal provisions of the electoral law, one might come to the conclusion that the Opposition had only its lack of unity to blame if it conceded victory from the outset. But, when seen in its political context, there can be no doubt that the electoral system considerably altered the nature of the elections. Certainly in an atmosphere of freedom and of the impartiality of the organs of State, there would have been some validity in the argument that the failure of the Opposition to unite proved that the 'national' coalition was the only political force of sufficient cohesion to govern. But where such pressure was exercised to discourage all opposition, it is hardly surprising that the Government had no competitors for supremacy.

Nevertheless the formation of a 'liberty bloc', if it would not have affected the results, would have at least made an impact on public opinion. The absence of a broad opposition coalition assisted Fascism to present itself as the only 'national' force capable of governing the country.

The Liberals, and even, officially, the Popolari, had hoped that the elections would serve to legitimize Fascist power and to close the revolutionary parenthesis. But the intransigents of the PNF had no intention of accepting this interpretation, and at the outset of the campaign Mussolini came down on their side. The Grand Assembly of Fascism on 28 January inaugurated a new style of mass rally. It was held, for the first time, in Piazza Venezia, and the old appeal to the 'revolutionary' crowd was now blended with pompous official ritual of the type more associated with a military review than a party meeting. This created the atmosphere of adulation, awe and obedience which was to be the one instantly recognizable attribute of all Fascist regimes. The crowd outside in the piazza welcomed the arrival of Mussolini, announced by three blasts of the trumpet and the royal march, with repeated shouts of '*alalà!*'[64] Inside the Palace, all the dignitaries of Fascism, from provincial union organizers to ex-Nationalist senators, gathered together to hear the word of the Duce. Mussolini's speech was extremely aggressive. He attacked the Opposition as 'criminal' and once more accused them of responsibility for the attacks on individual Fascists. The constitutional opposition in particular were 'among the most turbid, dangerous enemies of the Fascist party and government'.

By refusing to dissolve the Militia ('he who touches the Militia will get a dose of lead'), he destroyed hopes that he would abandon 'force' for 'consent'.

Mussolini's speech disappointed and discontented his allies. To satisfy his own party, he once more returned to the criterion of 'men and not parties'; he gave warning that Fascism would 'firmly reject every proposal of electoral or, still more, political, alliances with the old parties'. He played ably on the disorganization, division and localism of the constitutional groups : 'the Democrazia Sociale may be worth something in Sicily, but it is completely unknown in the Po Valley. The Liberal party may represent something in the great cities but there are enormous agricultural expanses where the Liberal party is not even minimally represented.' He described Giovannini, the organizing secretary of the Liberal party, as 'an out-of-date Don Quixote in search of the undiscoverable Dulcinea of the liberal idea . . . his labours show . . . that between liberalism and organization there exists an absolutely unsurmountable personal disagreement.' But he added that, 'all those who willed or fought the war, or behaved well after the war, those who are of some personal worth and are at any rate honest men' could find a place in the government list.[65] His show of intransigence, therefore, was more verbal than real. Provided they accepted his personal supremacy, members of the old parties were welcomed in the government list. With reason, Piero Gobetti saw the elections as the triumph of a new '*trasformismo*';[66] Mussolini hoped, by denying autonomy to the allied parties, to absorb them into a unified government majority. This would have been a reasonable aim if he had not at the same time denied the Opposition the right to exist. When he addressed friends or neutrals, he would ask for a straight choice, in the name of honesty; but in the next breath he would demand that opposition should be 'technical' rather than based on principle. The desire of Mussolini in reality to obtain the co-operation of the old politicians was clearly shown by the sequel.

The Liberal party lived down to Mussolini's expectations. The central executive, torn between the determination of the right to find places in the *listone*, and the desires of the left to be free to run their own lists, took no decision at all. The only consolation for 'poor Giovannini' was that he was included in the list himself. For the purposes of the elections, the party ceased to exist as a unified force.[67]

The party of the Democrazia Sociale reacted differently. The party could not claim a brilliant past; one unkind critic had suggested as its motto 'safety and portfolios'.[68] No group depended more on Government favours to hold together its clienteles; it was no accident that the Ministry of Posts and Telegraph, with little political importance but plenty of jobs attached, had been controlled by them in three consecutive governments. But the very weakness of the party and its lack of a great tradition or great men, such as the Liberals claimed, made for a certain determination in defending its collective existence, if only out of self-preservation. The influence of the Masonic lodges, once favourable to Fascism, had by now become a powerful force making for hostility; and in Sicily, where the Democrats had most of their power, there existed a strong under-current of autonomist feeling, which the party hoped to exploit. Already in August 1923 a slighting reference by Mussolini to the radical hero Cavallotti, and the rumour that the Ministry of Posts was about to be abolished, had caused a first crisis; on that occasion, however, Mussolini had agreed to recognize the collective merit of the party, and had declined to accept Di Cesarò's resignation. Di Cesarò had probably been saved by the attacks made on him by Farinacci, at that time particularly rebellious; Mussolini had no desire to appear to give way to his pressures.[69] As we have seen, the difficulties were only temporarily shelved, and by November the party was once again preparing to pass to the Opposition. However Di Cesarò remained in the Government and it seemed likely that self-interest would dictate a continuation of the alliance at least for the election period.

Mussolini's speech, however, reopened the disagreement, and with it endangered the whole electoral strategy of Fascism in the South. Di Cesarò resigned from the Government on 3 February.[70] Ironically the demand of the Democrazia Sociale to obtain recognition as a party was a serious obstacle just because of the confusion and personalism of southern politics. Di Cesarò was a personal and political friend of Orlando, and several of Orlando's own personal followers and henchmen had joined the Democrazia Sociale group in parliament. Southern politicians, and especially Sicilians, were governed by concepts of 'honour' and patronage, deeply rooted in Mediterranean societies; as in the Roman Republic, a leader's 'honour' was impaired if he could not obtain jobs for his clients. Orlando, while he did not mind about 'party', did mind about his friends and was disturbed by the possibility of a rupture between the Government and Di Cesarò. Since no nationwide 'friendly' lists were to be recognized, and the Democrazia Sociale would not consent to limit itself to one region, if Di Cesarò headed an independent list there would be a bitter and probably violent contest, and Orlando would incur the odium of being involved in an unequal battle with his own friends.[71] Without Orlando, the Government list might make a bad showing in Sicily, and if he defected, De Nicola might retire too, with equally serious results in Campania, where Amendola and his friends had their strongest support. The elections could still be won, in the South, by fraud and violence; but without the cover afforded by the eminent names of liberalism the nature of the enterprise would be transparent, and the result might be the formation of a regionally-based opposition especially dangerous because loyal to the monarchy. Since Giolitti early made clear his refusal to enter the Government list, it looked as if all the leading Liberals, except for Salandra, who obligingly chose this difficult moment to confirm his support for Mussolini, might dissociate themselves from the national government.[72]

After ten days of complicated negotiations, however, Orlando changed his mind and was persuaded to stand. His Sicilian friends, alarmed at the possible loss of government favour, had urged him to join the list; and the Calabrian deputy, Luigi Fera, an influential leader of the Democrazia Sociale who was critical of Di Cesarò's obstinacy, also gave favourable advice.[73] Orlando saw his mission as the reconciliation of all the 'national' forces of Sicily and the South. But this was not his only objective; he hoped that his acceptance would have more than local significance. His grand design was to exact, in exchange, the recognition by Fascism of the supremacy of Parliament. His illusions were no doubt encouraged by the various intermediaries between him and the Fascist government. It seems that Orlando had meant to accept only on conditions, and to delay definite acceptance until the conclusion of the expected agreement between the Government and the Democrazia Sociale, perhaps even till he knew the names of the other candidates. He set out his constitutional ideas in an open letter to his supporters: his acceptance, he declared,

... would signify ... that the Government party in whose company I would present myself to the electoral body, while maintaining its own aims and ideals, was already in agreement on this point ... that the constitution through which the unity of Italy was formed, while susceptible of progressive modifications ... should be considered as sacred and unalterable in its essential spirit, and that therefore the citizen should not legitimately have to obey any other sovereignty than that of the Parliament of which His Majesty the King is part and head, on which depends the guarantee of civil liberty and the whole organization of the state.

A summary of the letter was released to the Press, and the Fascist electoral committee immediately announced the news of his candidature.[74] He was now irremediably compromised, and would find it difficult to withdraw if his conditions were not met. Not only did the negotiations with the Demo-crazia Sociale break down, but he was unable to secure the places he had hoped for for his friends. Worst of all, his declaration of constitutional faith fell on stony ground. It was violently attacked by the extremist *Impero* and above all by the eminent economist Senator Pantaleoni : 'it will never be permitted that the mafia and the *camorra* should return to rule in Italy' ;[75] an official communique issued on the eighteenth called off these attacks, praising Orlando's 'honesty and sincerity', but it was far from encouraging to his view that he had concluded a kind of treaty with the Government. His statement, it said, was not to be regarded in a 'commercial' light as one side of a contract ; there was, in fact, disagreement between his views and those of Fascism, but 'it does not relate to essential questions, only to a question of method. ... The past is a common heritage. In the future each will act according to his convictions and the necessities of the moment.'[76] It was precisely on the 'question of method', however, that Orlando had hoped to secure agreement.

Orlando's attempt to set bounds to his co-operation with the Government would have been more impressive and more difficult to evade if it had been backed by any united demonstration on the part of those who professed to share his principles. But the personal structure of Southern politics, based on the clientele, made the idea of effective national action impossible. It was evident, moreover, that in Orlando's attitude questions of principle were all too closely bound up with personal loyalties and vanities and even with much darker interests. He was at the same time defending the Statute and the Mafia,[77] and neither cause reinforced the other.

No more successful were the less ambitious attempts of the President of the Chamber, De Nicola, who headed the list in Campania, to ensure that the electoral campaign should be conducted without violence.[78] At the last moment, faced by a well-timed challenge from the Communist candidate Bordiga to accept a public debate, he withdrew from the contest. 'I cannot', he wote to Mussolini 'either transform an important meeting into an in-evitable brawl, nor refuse a debate ... without adding to all the other accusations that of having run away from a hostile invitation.'[79] De Nicola had, in fact, been reduced to a 'high state of nervous exhaustion' by his desperate efforts to keep his personal honour intact, and at the same time not to offend anyone.[80] Bordiga's invitation represented the challenge of reality to a master of political casuistry, a challenge which, not for the first time, he evaded.

The elections marked the lowest point in the bankruptcy of Italian liberalism. But Mussolini's success in compromising the leaders of liberalism was perhaps too complete. There was little confidence left in the future intentions of the Government.[81]

If Mussolini's only purpose had been to discredit the old order he would have succeeded admirably : but by associating with it he destroyed, for the time being, the myth of Fascism as an innovating force. The South gave little active support to Fascism until the regime was firmly established.

The normal purpose of elections is to offer a free choice between political alternatives, or at the very least to obtain a free expression of the nation's opinion. Mussolini and the Fascists quite openly denied that the elections of 1924 could be viewed in this light, or that the power of Fascism was dependent on their result. It was only to be expected that the party intransigents would devalue their significance. Farinacci remarked that 'for us Fascists the general elections are only an episode. Abroad, however, they must signify that the Fascist government is not based on violence, as our adversaries affirm, but on the consent of the nation.'[82] But similar statements came also from more official sources. Mussolini himself advised Fascists not to pay too much attention to 'these paper games', and declared that 'legions are worth more than constituencies'.[83] The elections, in fact, in spite of the existence of an opposition, had the character of a plebiscite, a propaganda demonstration of popular support and national unity.[84] Such plebiscites have been a characteristic of modern dictatorship.

The conduct of the elections was still more illegitimate than their context and purpose. The Government had an enormous advantage in all forms of propaganda, with the important exception of the Press. Here, the Government was at a disadvantage in quality ; it had the support of no single newspaper with the prestige of the *Corriere* or *La Stampa*. However it made up to some extent by quantity. The chief Rome newspapers, *Giornale d'Italia* (somewhat grudgingly), the *Tribuna* and the *Messaggero* were all benevolent : so were important regional newspapers like the *Resto del Carlino* of Bologna, the *Nazione* of Florence, and the *Mattino* of Naples. Mussolini tried to restrain Fascist attacks on the newspapers during the election campaign, and the more important of them preserved a degree of liberty, although frequently their sale was boycotted or their copies burnt at the railway stations.[85] *Il Popolo* and *Il Mondo* were both allowed to denounce Fascist violence and electoral frauds with considerable frankness. The Communists, whose Press in 1923 had been almost totally driven underground, were able to publish their new daily, *l'Unità*. This relative liberty, however, did not extend to the

humbler provincial Press; this had always been less able to withstand
Fascist pressure, and the few newspapers which remained independent were
forced into silence.[86] It was characteristic of Mussolini's whole strategy
during the elections to allow considerable freedom in the big cities where it
would catch the public eye, and to apply heavy pressure in the obscure and
unnoticed provinces.

The Fascist propaganda machine was not notably efficient by the standards
later set by the fully-fledged totalitarian movements. It suffered particularly
from a shortage of trained speakers, a legacy of the prevalence of terrorist tactics in the rise to power.[87] The Fascist movement, had, however, developed
a systematic and centralized organization for the collection of funds, such
as was possessed by no other party. In spite of this, party finances had been
in a bad state at the time of the March on Rome, but control of the Government brought a fresh flow of money from the banks, insurance companies
and industry. For the elections the Government was able to obtain a massive
official contribution from the Confindustria and the Associazione fra le
Societa per Azioni; they formed a central electoral fund financed by a
regular levy on the capital of their members.[88] The regional committees were
left to raise money from agrarians and traders and special contributions from
individuals, especially candidates.[89] Sometimes contributions were the
price of special economic favours. The captains of industry were present in
force in the Government list, led by the President and Secretary of the
Confindustria, Benni and Gino Olivetti. They included Motta and Donegani, respectively from the Edison and the Montecatini, the most powerful
enterprises in the hydro-electrical and chemical sectors; another great
electrical magnate, Ponti of the SIP; Marzotto of the famous dynasty of
textile industrialists from the Veneto; the President of the Lega Industriale
of Turin, Mazzini; and the Ligurian shipowner Biancardi, as well as a
number of lesser figures.[90] The support of the industrialists as a class was
given, in most cases, to the 'national government' rather than to the Fascist
movement; the most important men of the Confidustria were still members
of the Liberal party. While undoubtedly the enthusiasm of many industrialists for the restoration of 'order' was spontaneous and unfeigned, this was
not the only factor on which the Government could count. Agnelli remarked
that the industrialists are 'Government supporters by necessity',[91] and this
was certainly true of the hydro-electric, shipbuilding and armaments industries, with their dependence on Government contracts and special
legislation. The promise to restore the telephones to private hands had also
been effective, and the replacement of Di Cesarò by Costanzo Ciano, one of
the Fascists most closely linked to industrial interests, removed the difficulties caused by the former's resistance to what he considered the excessively
hard bargaining of the would-be buyers.[92] Even when they secretly had
strong reserves about some aspects of Fascism, the praise of the industrialists
for the national government was consequently fulsome. Their collective

support, financial and otherwise, if not exactly decisive, certainly contributed greatly to the functioning of the plebiscitary machine.

The report of the secretary Ciano to the Grand Council on 14 March declared that three million pamphlets and one million manifestos had been printed and distributed. Particular attention had been paid to the South, and especially to those provinces where the Opposition had positions of strength (Amendola in Salerno, Nitti in Potenza, Di Cesarò in Sicily). The propaganda effort was planned and centralized; local federations were sent draft manifestos to copy, and individual propagandists were given 'precise instructions about the arguments on which it is necessary to insist most in speeches and meetings'.[93] The tone and content varied according to the region. There was a prevalent emphasis on the moderate and conservative aspects of the new government's policies; the appeal was to security rather than to mass enthusiasm. The 'politics of favours' for which Giolitti had been attacked with such moral fervour was not discontinued; the South was wooed, as before, with large promises of public works. Although the achievement of a balanced budget was hailed as one of Fascism's great triumphs, Mussolini did not scruple to criticize the austerity of De Stefani's financial policy in order to gain popularity, and to promise lighter taxation.[94]

A particularly great effort was made to neutralize the opposition of the Popolari by emphasizing the work of the Government on behalf of the Church; the pamphlet 'Religione e clero nell' opera del Governo Fascista' seems to have been in much greater demand than any other.[95] But the central element in the Government's propaganda was, of course, the appeal to patriotism. From Fascist posters the stern figures of arditi, viewed in full face, pointed their finger at the citizen to demand his vote as a patriotic duty; their resemblance to Kitchener's famous recruiting poster is not altogether accidental. In foreign policy, Mussolini had timed his success perfectly. The official celebration of the annexation of Fiume, accompanied by a warm message of gratitude from the King to Mussolini, fell in the middle of the electoral period.[96]

It is difficult to judge the effectiveness of the Fascist campaign. But it seems likely that, in the absence of a real contest, and with Mussolini himself taking rather little direct part, the general mood of the public was somewhat dull and apathetic. This was especially true, in spite of Fascist efforts, in the South. The Liberal leaders were too reserved in their support to do much for the government list except lend their name, and the hostility of the real Fascists to them was ill-concealed. When Orlando made his election address in Palermo, he was received by the local Fascists with 'glacial coldness', and their attitude towards Orlando was matched by that of the inhabitants towards the Fascists. The Prefect had to report that the electoral procession passed through the streets 'without demonstrations of sympathy or solidarity, a new circumstance for patriotic demonstrations in an environment that has always been prone to explosions of enthusiasm'.

A later report remarked that the campaign had failed to stir the *lumpen-proletariat* of Palermo from their depressed indifference, which could only be overcome by 'the traditional bank-note'.[97] Similarly in Naples De Nicola confessed, when his turn to speak seemed imminent, that 'given the environment here ... I cannot be too Fascist'.[98] In the hinterland of Sicily and the South, success or failure was generally determined as before by the local notables and by government pressure. In the North and Centre of Italy, bourgeois and middle-class opinion was undoubtedly in the great majority behind the Government; in the oppressive climate of conformity prevalent in small provincial towns the member of the Opposition, or even the non-Fascist, was already cold-shouldered. As an attestation of the spirit in which the electoral campaign was conducted in the areas of Fascist strength, the following passage from the *Assalto* of Bologna is very eloquent: 'Cervia, 29 March: First Fascist electoral meeting.

'The Fascists and the workers of the union ... *formed into a military column*, preceded by the municipal standard ... and by all the banners of the *fasci* ... crossed the city in a long procession, accompanied by patriotic hymns, to reach the theatre.' This sort of militarized display probably impressed the uncommitted and a-political but the memory of coercion was still too recent for the effect on most peasants or workers to be favourable. The mentality and practices of the local Fascists were an insuperable obstacle to attempts to win over the working classes by persuasion. In the countryside, the government had alienated the *mezzadri* and the smallholders by the new tax on agricultural income; Mussolini had here failed to take the advice of Pareto, who had suggested that this was the direction in which Fascism could most easily expand its support.[99]

Neither the state of public opinion nor the efficacy of Fascist propaganda can be inferred from the results of the campaign. The use of violence, police repression and electoral fraud was on such a large scale that the expression of the popular will was radically falsified. It is a myth that Fascism was victorious in 'free elections'. The right of free speech was generally denied, except in a small number of cases, when the dominant party 'agreed for particular reasons either of place or person'.[100] The Opposition was not allowed to discuss some subjects at all. Mussolini gave orders forbidding attacks on the Militia, or on the tax on agricultural income.[101] It was not Mussolini's policy to silence the most well-known party leaders, such as Amendola or Turati: like the partial freedom of the Press, this was a necessary façade. Even then, the fact that he had to intervene specially (and in the case of Amendola without success)[102] to enable them to obtain a hearing is significant of the general climate. But the Fascists could not permit the Socialist parties to carry on propaganda in their former strongholds without endangering their own hold. How could a 'free' electoral campaign be actively conducted by the Socialists in Bologna? Or by the Popolari in Cremona? Open meetings or distribution of literature were impossible; yet clandestine propaganda was attacked with even more violence as sinister and subversive.[103]

The Socialist candidates Di Vittorio and Vella were banned from appearing in Bari, the centre of their electoral region, and the Prefect De Vita, a Fascist appointee from the regular army, took no action.[104] Matteotti estimated that in all only sixty to a hundred PSU candidates could circulate freely in their constituencies : some were not even able to stay in their own homes. The worst crime was in Reggio Emilia, where the PSI candidate Piccinini was taken from his home and shot.[105] The police not only allowed a free hand to Fascist terror, but themselves intervened actively.

The Socialists and Communists suffered most from Fascist terror because they were the chief local enemies of the *ras*. But the official policy of the PNF was more complicated and more Machiavellian. A communiqué of the PNF *direttorio* on 28 February announced that 'the PNF will conduct the election campaign with the greatest rigour ... against all the subversive parties and in particular against the PSU and the PPI and similarly against the other groups of so-called social and constitutional opposition.

'The graduation of the intensity of this struggle will be established at an opportune time by the responsible organs of the Fascist party.' The 'scale' of hostility, in fact, was : (1) PSU ; (2) PPI ; (3) Republicans, PSI and Communists ; (4) the constitutional opposition ; (5) Democrazia Sociale and ind   ᵗ Liberals (both of whom were, nominally, not in opposition).[106]
It   ᵗe that the really 'subversive' parties (Communists,
P   ᶠᵒʳ the moderate PSU and PPI. This was a
c   which saw the middle parties
                                           ᵗ the Fascist move-

                                                    he clergy
                                                    l activity.
                                                    sions, and
                                                    ed to make

                                                    re of intimi-
                                                    ε results were
                                                    written while

                                                    the popular will.
                                                    ε Prime Minister
                                                    sts were to obtain
                                                    here in which the

                                                    State apparatus are
                                                    The last communal
                                                    l and substituted by

Commissari regi and *prefettizi*; so even the polling-booths will be entirely staffed by partisans of the Government. No appeal will be possible against any form of violence used by the Fascists in the elections, since the Courts of Appeal are only charged with collecting and adding the figures sent in by the single polling-stations; and the only judge will be the *Giunta delle Eleziont* . . . which will be the emanation of those same 356 deputies whom the President has personally nominated.[108]

Matteotti's predictions were fulfilled, and with interest.

The mechanism for the presentation of the lists was complicated, and lent itself to abuse. Three hundred signatures had to be collected before a list could be presented; in six out of fifteen regions an attempt was made to prevent by violence the collection of signatures for the PSU list. Another, rather curious rule dictated that no list could be presented in only one constituency; this rule was manipulated to prevent the presentation of the dissident Fascist list of Padovani in Campania.[109]

Throughout the campaign, and especially on polling day, the Government pursued dual policies, one for the great cities, where there was a relative order and freedom, and one for the countryside and the smaller towns, where the local *ras* had a free hand.[110] It is this 'dual policy' which explains how the Opposition got 33 per cent of the votes. The argument that the size of the minority vote proves that elections were free is invalid because it does not take account of the deliberate unevenness with which coercion was used. The voting reflected this two-sided policy. Almost everywhere the Opposition did better in large towns than small, and in the provincial capitals better than in the rest of the province. This cannot be explained on the basis of previous political loyalty; in parts of Lombardy and in the Veneto the countryside had traditionally given more votes to either the Socialists or the Popolari than the towns, where the bourgeois parties were relatively stronger. The relative freedom of the large cities existed both because of concern for the propaganda effect on foreign comment, and also because the Fascist party was less effective as an instrument for control and coercion in a metropolis, where it was difficult to isolate all possible centres of opposition. However this freedom did not always extend from the centre to the working-class quarters on the outskirts, and in the Fascist heartlands even the largest cities, Bari, Bologna and Florence, were strictly controlled. In none of the other large cities, except Rome, did the national list obtain an absolute majority: in Milan it had 38.4 per cent of the vote (16,000 less than the combined vote of the working-class parties), in Turin 36·6 per cent, in Genoa 47·2 per cent, in Venice 36·5 per cent, in Naples 49·6 per cent and in Palermo 30·4 per cent.[111]

Fascist tactics must, in fact, also be differentiated by region. It was in the North that the Opposition had its greatest successes; this reflected the resistance of the working class, and also the fact that urban Fascism was less ruthless than agrarian in its methods. The middle-class vote may have been affected by the anti-Fascism of *La Stampa* and the *Corriere della Sera*.

The Po Valley and central Italy (Tuscany and Umbria), in contrast, were the regions where an absolute control was exercised by the Fascist movement. Compared with old-style methods of police pressure, the extra-legal, 'total' coercion of the Fascist movement was much more effective. It was based on the forced organization of a great part of the population, and it had an enormous network of intimidation and espionage at its service, from political secretaries down to the humblest *squadristi*, which was all the more effective because it was somewhat unpredictable. The importance of the movement, as distinct from the organs of the State, in bringing about favourable results, is shown by the fact that the areas where its unity was undermined by serious dissidence were distinguished by a comparatively high vote for the Opposition.

The vote in these regions was controlled by several methods. First, as Matteotti had warned, the Fascist conquest of local government meant that they had the right to appoint nearly all the scrutineers. The presidents of the polling-stations, often retired officers, were very likely to be Fascists. The electoral law provided a supposed guarantee in the presence of representatives of the opposition lists; but this was rarely allowed. So, in many cases, there was no check on the method of voting or of counting results. The Militia were often entrusted with the duty of 'surveillance' and the preservation of order at the polling-stations.[112] In smaller centres, where personal opinions were well known, opponents could simply be warned not to vote or turned away. Open voting was frequent. These methods were, however, supplemented by a more refined technique invented by the Prefect of Bologna, Bocchini, who here showed the talent which was eventually to make him Chief of Police. Every voter received, through the party or the syndicate, instructions on for whom, and in what order, to cast his three preference votes for individual candidates. By examining the results of each electoral district, one could then check who had carried out their instructions and voted for the Government list and who had not. The 'Bocchini system', or 'rule of three' was widely applied in Emilia and probably also in Tuscany.[113]

Another widespread, usually effective method, was the threat of post-electoral reprisals.[114] Indeed, even without explicit threats, it must have been common knowledge that a high opposition vote might have serious consequences. In fact several towns or even whole areas where the Opposition did unexpectedly well were the victims after 6 April of full-scale terrorist campaigns. The most notorious was in the Brianza, the region round Monza, north of Milan; this was one of the strongholds of the Popolari and the Catholic trade unions, and it returned the lowest vote for the Government of any district in Italy.[115]

This post-electoral violence was in most cases the result of the chagrin of local Fascists, who felt that they would be blamed for not delivering the goods; in the case of Milan province, it seems likely that the setback was also felt by the national organizers of the election campaign, notably Cesare Rossi, who had a hand in organizing the reprisals. Mussolini, however, who won his victory, saw this outbreak of terrorism as putting the whole value of the elections in question, as well as placing a fresh strain on his relations with the Church. There is no doubt that it was carried on in defiance of his instructions.[116]

Finally, in the South the methods employed were simpler and more blatant; the figures were often totally arbitrary, thanks to fraudulent counting and the interception of voting certificates then used by Fascists who voted many times over. There was a very long tradition in the South of fraud and intimidation by the State and by the local bosses acting in collusion; but Fascism undoubtedly used such methods on a much vaster scale and with more brutality than any previous government.[117]

7

THE PARTY AND THE STATE (I)

Mussolini was borne into power on the shoulders of a mass movement. The decisive role of the party and its auxiliaries in the seizure of power distinguishes the Fascist regime from all those authoritarian states which owed their existence to the support of traditional ruling groups, or to the Army. It follows that the relationship between party and state was of critical importance in determining the ultimate shape and character of the regime.

All definitions and explanations of the phenomenon of totalitarianism have recognized the existence of the mass party, or movement, as one of its central features.[1] In the totalitarian regime the mass party serves as a conductor which transmits the ruling ideology and imposes it on all spheres of life. The party sets in motion a mutually reinforcing process of coercion and mass enthusiasm leading to fresh coercion. It is informal in its operations and is not bound by bureaucratic or legal rules. It utilizes social control as well as arbitrary police action. In this way, it creates a terror whose workings are unpredictable, and which therefore allows no safe retreat into autonomy or non-involvement. The principle followed is 'the punishment of those who might rebel, rather than those who do',[2] and even passivity can be taken as a sign of disloyalty. No one can be sure of meeting the changing demands of the regime, which succeeds in making anxiety an institution.[3] In authoritarian regimes the 'good citizen' is the patient, obedient subject; in the totalitarian regimes he is required to participate, and special rights and privileges are reserved to those who demonstrate their active commitment by joining the party. In the first case, the concept of good citizenship is a bureaucratic one, derived from the experience of administration; in the second case it is ideological and political, derived from the experience of party conflict.[4]

In a totalitarian regime, therefore, either the party must be recognized as the dominant institution, with the right to exercise command over the equivalent levels of the State administration, or else the State machinery must be pervaded by its values and modes of conduct. The formal delimitation between party and State spheres of action and powers will tend to be blurred and imprecise.[5] In an authoritarian state, on the other hand, the party's role will be defined and limited. It will be regarded as subordinate to State authority, and its own members, when invested with governmental functions, will tend to conform to bureaucratic expectations. These models are intentionally abstract and are intended as aids to understanding, not as rigid formulas, and one should be prepared to admit that the reality of actual historical cases is untidy, and will seldom fit either definition perfectly. Such a reservation is particularly necessary in the case of Italian Fascism.

The Interregnum

Mussolini came to power without a precise programme for the reconstruction of the State. Amid the general confusions and contradictions of Fascist thinking, however, some clear guidelines can be discerned. Mussolini, with his stress on 'hierarchy', promised the restoration of a strong central authority, and more generally the defence of the principle of authority within all institutions. On the other hand, the creation of some form of corporative or technical representation was canvassed by several groups within the movement as the means of remedying the evils of 'parliamentarianism'. These prescriptions had somehow to be harmonized with each other, and also with the claim of the Fascist party to constitute the new ruling class. There was no real consensus within the Fascist movement on what needed to be done, and Mussolini himself, faithful to his pragmatic style and convinced of the need to go cautiously to avoid conflict with the monarchy, was not as yet ready to impose a solution. Fascism was therefore slow to create an institutional foundation for its exercise of power. At the party's National Council in August 1924, a delegate was to ask: 'What is there on which one could base the formula "We shall not turn back". Nothing !'[6] Fascism had in fact created one new institution of unquestionable importance, the Militia ; but even that had a somewhat uncertain status and future. Mussolini's most general statement of his concept of government at this time grew out of the need to justify the Militia's existence. 'The Government shows clearly that it tends towards government not by violence, but if possible, and as far as desirable, by the consent of the citizens. Naturally the Government itself keeps the necessary force in reserve, in the MVSN, in order to have force as well as consent.'[7] This somewhat jejune formula of 'force and consent' was further developed in an article published in *Gerarchia* in March 1923. Force, Mussolini argued, would always be necessary for government, since consent could never be permanent or total. Hence the party in power had an 'obligation' to fortify its position, since otherwise the State would be weak and unstable. This was an authoritarian rather than a totalitarian conception, since it admitted the inevitability of opposition.[8] This cautious and non-committal philosophy was clearly only a provisional solution. Pareto, whose writings probably gave Mussolini the idea of the 'force and consent' slogan, nevertheless perceived that regimes do not live by pragmatism alone. 'Fascism', he remarked with approval, 'is a party of facts, not of theories'; but he added, 'it will not remain so for long.'[9]

'The Fascisms marched on Rome. . . . In Rome we have to found Fascism'; this was Giuseppe Bottai's frank appraisal of the divisions within the movement.[10] During 1923-4 the most clear-cut of these divisions was that between the revisionists and the intransigents. The intransigents, dissatisfied with the compromise which had underlain the formation of the Mussolini government, wanted the radical elimination of non-Fascists from political life; the revisionists wanted to reconcile the 'revolution' with historical continuity, and urged a policy of reconciliation with at least some of the other parties.

The provincial *ras* were the backbone of intransigence. Their aggressive rhetoric disguised the defence of acquired positions; Bottai described it as 'the conservatism of revolution'.[11] They profited from the institutional interregnum which made possible and necessary the persistence of violence and illegality. The most intelligent could see that this state of affairs could not be prolonged indefinitely, but they had no real theory to put forward which could legitimize their power. In the controversy with the revisionists, perhaps because he was on the defensive and knew that Mussolini was against him, Farinacci was far from advocating the supremacy of the party over the State as an ultimate goal. In a striking and revealing phrase, he protested that 'when Fascist illegality becomes the law of the State, we shall have no more reason to insist. Then the political secretaries and the *fiduciari* could be dismissed, and Fascism could be normalized, or, rather, statized; as in the provinces it would have the prefects and all the other authorities as its defenders.' In concrete terms, he demanded strict control of the Press, the institution of the *confino* (political exile), the grant of legal status to syndicates, with the creation of a system of obligatory arbitration of labour contracts by the 'political and judicial organs of the State', and the restoration of the death penalty, 'for those whom the Fascist revolution has spared'.[12] These demands, which anticipated many of the most important 'reforms' of 1925-6, did in fact constitute a comprehensive programme for the adoption by the State of the chief functions of illegal party action. The party's most conspicuous activities after the March consisted in the intimidation of the Press, the *bando* (or prohibition to reside in a province, imposed on political enemies) and the use of terrorism against irreducible opponents. The party also, in conjunction with the corporations, imposed the settlement of labour disputes and partially controlled access to employment. If these last functions, as well as those of repression, were to be absorbed by the State, the party would be bound to wither away, unless it could make good a claim to determine government policy. There was therefore a sense in which the aims of the extremists were inherently self-defeating.

The small group known as the 'revisionists', led by Massimo Rocca and Bottai, had a quite different conception of political life. They did not desire the suppression of all political liberties, although Bottai was later to acquiesce. At the same time they saw that the *status quo* favoured the *ras*, and so they pressed for constitutional reform and the creation of new institutions. Their goal was an authoritarian, rather than a totalitarian system, one of 'limited pluralism'.[13] Weak within the movement, they enjoyed the support of most of the intellectual and conservative fellow-travellers of Fascism. The first saw them as fellow-spirits and enemies of the brutal anti-intellectualism of the *ras*; the latter approved of their relative gradualism and tolerance. More important, they had the sympathy of Mussolini. The difference between the revisionists and the intransigents was that the first wanted reform of the party to precede reform of the State; the latter, while in theory admitting the necessity for the 'normalization' of the party, wished to postpone it until control of the State was complete. Every modern revolution (using the term in a restricted and purely political sense) creates a conflict between the 'old guard', or enthusiasts, who demand the integral fulfilment of its aims and spirit and a monopoly of important positions to ensure that it is not betrayed, and those within and outside the revolutionary movement who side with the claims of the 'experts', whose skills are essential for the running of government. This conflict, in the case of Fascism, was reinforced by tension between the elitist strain which was dominant in early Fascist ideology, and the practical needs of mass organization.[14] The revisionist-intransigent dispute can be interpreted in terms of a cleavage between 'elite Fascism' and 'mass Fascism'. It is significant that Bottai attacked the organizer as a human type; he referred contemptuously to his provincial opponents, both *ras* and syndicalists, as 'the cattle-raisers'. For these well-bred Fascists, the externals of mass Fascism were too reminiscent of Socialism; Bottai admitted his distaste for the 'shirtless Italy of the rallies', and the 'peasant rhetoric of the Sunday meeting'.[15]

The revisionists were at their best in their uninhibited and often perceptive criticism of the party. But there was a practical dilemma which they were unable to resolve. Their moderate, neo-liberal views demanded that they press for greater freedom of expression, and this implied, as well as the tolerance of other national groups, the creation of an inner-party democracy. Opposition to the *ras* still existed among the 'Fascists of the first hour' in cities like Turin. Gioda, Pietro Gorgolini and Rocca, the representatives of the old group of city Fascists, were united in condemning the excesses of the squads, who obeyed only their commanders and defied the authority of the *fascio*. They denounced the squads' responsibility for the horrifying *fatti di Torino* (Turin incidents) of 18 December 1922, in which eleven workers were murdered and another twenty-six severely injured. Their attitude was endorsed by Mussolini, but his support did not prevent De Vecchi from expelling Gorgolini from the *fascio*, to which he was readmitted only in November 1923.[16] The events of 1921–2 had already shown that the balance of numbers and power within the movement had shifted towards the agrarian pole, and also that in the rural areas the forces working against inner-party democracy were too strong.[17] Moreover, as elitists, the revisionists were not prepared to use 'demagogic' tactics to appeal over the heads of the *ras* to their following. The revisionists remained an isolated minority; the mass of provincial *squadristi* distrusted them, and identified with the violent and exalted tone of their local leaders, to whom they were also bound by ties of loyalty and interest. Consequently their only real chance of power lay in the strengthening of the personal control exercised by Mussolini over the movement. In the first revisionist crisis of September–October 1923 this became evident; only the dictatorial decision of Mussolini saved Rocca from expulsion by the *Giunta Esecutiva* of the PNF. The thesis later advanced by Rocca, that the formation of an oligarchy within the movement was a decisive stage in the process by which 'Fascism became a dictatorship', is incomplete and misleading.[18] The two chief revisionists were in fact divided in their view of the party's future. Bottai was for inner-party democracy (but not until a radical purge had changed the composition of the movement), whereas Rocca believed that the party could only fulfil its functions of restoring the authority of the State and serving as the nucleus of a new elite if it was 'hierarchically organized at the orders of the Duce'.[19] In spite of his expulsion in May 1924, it was Rocca who was the true prophet of the final shape and role of the party.

The failure of Rocca brought with it the defeat of the only concrete programme for giving some substance to Fascism's technocratic claims. To remedy the movement's shortage of skills, Rocca proposed that technical groups, or *gruppi di competenza*, should be formed, both at the national level and within the single *fasci*. These groups were to form part of the movement; but it was hoped that they would serve as a medium through which experts would be drawn into the movement and involved in its work. More ambitiously, they were intended to bring about the fulfilment of a kind of conservative version of Marx's famous prophecy that politics would be replaced by 'the administration of things'. 'Economics tends to absorb politics, including foreign policy ... if the situation today is ripe for a revolution, it is ripe for the revolution which will substitute, in whole or in part, ... technique and technicians – bourgeois and workers – and syndical and technical organs for the bureaucracy, the politicians, and the demagogues, who are united in exploiting the nation.'[20] However Rocca was soon to learn the force of politics. The 'Groups of Competence' conflicted with the vested interests both of the party bosses, who saw in them a threat to their newly appropriated power, unless they could simply be used to further their own interests; and with those of Rossoni and the heads of the corporations, who paid lip-service to the same technocratic conception, but wanted the mediation and representation of interests to take place within the orbit of their own organization. In short, the improvised oligarchy of the movement naturally resented the claim of the Groups to provide the cadres of the new ruling class. However the leaders of the movement lost a chance when they failed to develop the *gruppi di competenza*. Fascism, like other modern mass movements which have aimed at the total takeover of the State, created for this purpose a number of parallel institutions; the Cabinet was matched by the Grand Council, the Prefect by the Federale, and the Army by the Militia. In this scheme of things, the *gruppi di competenza* were intended as an alternative or at least supplement to the state bureaucracy. They would ensure that by the side of 'the cold and passive action of the bureaucratic organizations' there would be a place for 'spontaneous initiative'. It was thus inevitable that they would meet with obstruction and hostility from the state bureaucracy; with only lukewarm party support, they were soon reduced to insignificance.[21]

The failure of the *gruppi di competenza* meant that Fascism continued to be deficient in administrative and economic skills. This permanently prejudiced the party's chances of success in its contest for supremacy with the state bureaucracy, and was seriously to weaken the position of the intransigents in 1925–6. But in 1923–4, as has already been suggested, the party leadership showed little interest in legal methods of reforming the State. This helped to ensure the defeat of the anti-bureaucratic, decentralizing programme of middle-class Fascism.

Relations between the Fascist movement and the central bureaucracy of the state were at first marked by a considerable degree of mutual hostility. All bureaucracies must be adaptable to the demands of political power; they are not supposed, in normal times, to question its purposes. On the other hand their plasticity is, or should be, limited by a concern for rules, order, precedents and accurate information. They are wedded to a particular mode of action rather than to a particular set of goals. The values of the early Fascist movement were in sharp conflict with the bureaucratic ideal. Fascism too stressed modes of action; and the Fascist 'style' could be defined as the antithesis of the bureaucratic, exalting risk against security, inspiration against rule. The sources of this revulsion against bureaucracy were not exclusively psychological or cultural; it also derived force from the middle-class resentment of the growth in state powers.[22] The ideology of free enterprise was reinforced by the remnants of the anti-state heritage of syndicalism, and by the old republican distrust of centralization; bureaucracy, like Socialism, appeared to be one of the objects of antagonism which could unite right and left in the Fascist movement. For Agostino Lanzillo, it was this antagonism which above all inspired trust in the validity of Fascism's claim to provide the new ruling class: 'the ignoble tyranny of bureaucracy, i.e. of organized mediocrity, will be destroyed.'[23]

The bureaucracy was much less homogeneous than it had been in 1914. The frequent changes in government had led to revived competition between rival political cliques; both Salandra and Nitti had made deliberate attempts to break the personal hold of Giolitti over the bureaucracy and to advance their own protégés. Nevertheless his influence remained great.[24] The senior positions in the hierarchy of the key Ministry of the Interior were still held by men who had been promoted to the rank of Prefect during the halcyon days of Giolitti's rule; they were, however, approaching retirement age by 1922. The passing of this generation, it is fair to suggest, would ease the acceptance of new masters and methods. Under Giolitti the bureaucracy had approached the status of a true governing class, since the boundaries between the civil service and politics were fluid, and many officials, like Giolitti himself, passed from the administration to the Chamber or the Senate, and to high governmental office. Giolitti had helped to create an elite of high officials who were honest, expert and often endowed with genuine political foresight. There was a danger in this, however; political skill and ambition could overreach themselves and some Prefects, in imitation of their master, acquired too much of a taste for complicated and risky intrigue. The consequences can be seen in the ultimately disastrous role of the Prefect of Milan, Lusignoli, during the negotiations before the March on Rome.[25]

The war had brought other and more profound changes. The great increase in the functions of government had inevitably brought with it a very rapid expansion in the numbers of civil servants and other state employees. There seems to be little doubt that this quantitative growth was accompanied by a decline in quality. Now that the bureaucracy held the keys to profit for many industries, and especially for the sinister host of *ad hoc* speculative ventures which sprang up to exploit the necessities and opportunities of the war and postwar periods, the temptations for corruption were greatly increased. This may never have been absent at the lower levels; but testimony suggests that before the war corruption had been rare among the higher ranks. The economist Riccardo Bachi believed that there had been a marked deterioration, due to 'the extensive contacts during the war between the bureaucracy and the world of business'.[26] Furthermore, after the war the instability of governments and the overloading of the legislative machinery encouraged the usurpation of power by the permanent officials of the Ministries. The continued use of the decree-law was a clear symptom of the retention by the bureaucracy of the wider scope and discretion which it had originally been granted under the stress of war.[27] However too great a concentration on these recent changes should not be allowed to obscure the importance of the more permanent defects in the Italian bureaucratic system, which were political in nature.

The crucial defect was the failure to establish bureaucracy as above party. The attempt to create an equitable system of promotions by instituting a permanent committee of 'independent men' had been a failure.[28] A French study of the Italian bureaucracy in 1892 noted that ministers 'enjoyed an almost unlimited authority over their subordinates', and that 'political custom authorized great abuses of the power the government has over its employees'; ten years later a legal encyclopaedia drew attention to 'the lack of a law governing the relationship between the civil servant and the state, which would once and for all put an end to the multiform and arbitrary rules and regulations of the ministers.'[29] The civil servants themselves complained bitterly of political favouritism, disciplinary abuses, and inadequate judicial safeguards for their independence. The supreme administrative tribunal, the *Consiglio di Stato*, unlike its counterpart in France, never seems to have functioned as a proper organ of control over the legality of administrative actions, or as a means of protecting subordinates against the illegitimate demands of their superiors. The politicians of the Risorgimento had in fact been faced with an almost inescapable dilemma; political interference had at first been a necessary precaution against the perpetuation of habits of reaction and sloth inherited from the old regimes.[30] The fear that the bureaucracy might get the upper hand led to the development of the *gabinetto* system, whereby each minister chose his own personal 'cabinet' of immediate advisers. The *capi-gabinetti* were often the most influential men in the administration; the attacks of the interventionists in 1917 on Orlando's *capo-gabinetto* Camillo Corradini, at the Interior Ministry (later Giolitti's Under-Secretary of the Interior) testify to the great importance of the office.[31] Since elevation to these positions of influence was coveted, this system tended to create clienteles of aspiring or grateful officials attached to particular politicians. This weakened the impartiality and, except during Giolitti's period of dominance, the homogeneity of the administration. Another feature which, more than any other, impaired public confidence in the administration was the influence of Freemasonry.[32] Undoubtedly Masonic ties were important as a means of gaining promotion; this was a fatal point of weakness which was to give the Fascists the excuse they needed for introducing political discrimination.

Not all critics of the bureaucracy were persuaded that Fascism was likely to make good its reforming claims. A. Monti, the author of a particularly acute survey of the problem published by the *Rivoluzione Liberale*, did not believe that the anti-bureaucratic programme of Fascism should be taken too seriously. It was in conflict with the facts of the situation, and had not the Fascists constantly exalted the importance of facts over theory? The vaunted individualism of the Fascists had not prevented the party from organizing its own civil and military hierarchy on a large scale, with official ranks; it employed a multitude of 'people on stipends, irresponsible and engaged in ceaseless activity'. Moreover, like all successful parties, it was under pressure from the mass of its active supporters to secure them government employment, and to prevent 'the dismissal of a single labourer, provided he is a Fascist'. It was an ominous circumstance that Fascism even before the seizure of power drew a large number of recruits from the middle and lower ranks of the administration, local and central. But the most decisive of all considerations was the superficiality of Fascist thought and knowledge. 'I cannot but despair . . . when I hear the newly qualified accountants or the law students of the PNF treat the gravest technical problems with such an air of disdain and frivolity . . . and when I think that *this* is after all the ruling class that Fascism will soon bring to the government, and which will come to grips with the old foxes of the Ministries.'[33]

Certainly the commonplaces of the Futuristic cult of speed and youth were not much help when it came to formulating concrete proposals for reform. However one or two serious and well qualified advocates of bureaucratic reform were attracted into the orbit of Fascism. Notable among these was Ettore Lolini, an official of the Finance Ministry and a member of the national *gruppo di competenza* for the public administration. His first writings on the subject had appeared at the end of the war in the Combatant journals *Volontà* and *La Nuova Giornata*, the organs of those groups of officers who saw the war as the premise for a radical reform of the ruling class in the interests both of democracy and *liberismo*. Lolini's aims were to increase the independence of the bureaucracy from partisan pressures, and thus to make it more just and impartial in its dealings with the citizen, and to improve its efficiency and comprehension of the needs of society. The means to these ends were to be the reform of the *Consiglio di Stato* to provide better safeguards for the subordinate against his superiors, decentralization, and the collaboration of representatives of the syndicates in local government.[34] But even if the powerful obstacle presented by the passive resistance of the higher bureaucracy could have been overcome, how likely was it that Fascism would espouse such a programme ? The claim (believed by many) that the end of 'parliamentarianism' would restore impartiality to the administration was soon belied by the influence of the dominant party on the administration : decentralization was permitted only in the sense of a technical rearrangement of functions, and when it did not contradict the tendency to a concentration of real powers and the restriction of regional or local autonomy : and the rules which ensured the unlimited subordination of officials to the minister, while freeing them from any legal responsibilities to the citizen, not only remained unchanged, but were applied with greater rigidity and ruthlessness than ever before.

When considering the attitude of the bureaucracy towards Fascism, a distinction should be drawn between the staff of the ministries in Rome and the Prefects. Although evidence is too slight for a definite conclusion, it would seem probable that the former were less well disposed towards the Fascists than the latter. The Prefects (and still more their subordinates) saw Fascism first as a deliverance from Bolshevism and later as a reality with which it was necessary to come to terms. Menaced and shaken in their authority, they were impressed by Mussolini's promises of the restoration of order. In the South, where the Prefects retained their old prestige, some nonetheless welcomed the coming of Fascism as a force which would free them from an irksome dependence on the deputies and their clienteles.[35] Under the Giolittian system the Prefect had been trained to recognize the necessity of conciliating the dominant political force of the province; from 1921 onwards this worked in favour of the secretary of the *fascio*, as it had formerly worked in favour of the reformist deputy or trade union leader. Of course class sympathies made a difference; but one should not assume that they were usually decisive. The same Prefect who, in 1919–20, aroused the fiercest Fascist protests on account of his benevolence to Socialism, might later distinguish himself by his Fascist zeal. The Prefect was no ordinary official, bound by a strict code; he had wide discretionary powers and was expected to use them on behalf of the Government. The Roman bureaucracy had more reasons to distrust Fascism. Their powers, and particularly those of the economic ministries, were the object of criticism, and their interests were threatened by the programme of economy and the reduction of state personnel.[36]

Prefect and Party in the Provinces

The peculiar flexibility and efficiency of the institution of the Prefect as an instrument for securing compliance with the will of the Government could hardly fail to be recognized. On the other hand, it was almost impossible to carry out the declared aim of Mussolini to restore the authority of the Prefects in their provinces while the process of the expansion of Fascist power continued. The Prefect could not effectively control or restrain the operations of the party, if at the same time it was his task to secure its supremacy in the province in the interests of the Government. While it was the complicity of the State organs which made possible the success of Fascist action, this latter still had an indispensable function which could not at this stage have been performed by the Government itself; the suppression of political liberties could not as yet be carried out officially, except in a few cases. Coercion still had to be largely informal, and the importance of the party and its armed auxiliary, the Militia, remained.

The relationship between government and party organs in the provinces was complex and it requires detailed analysis. First of all, it is necessary to distinguish between the very different conditions prevailing in the various regions of Italy. The special conditions prevailing in the South, where with the exception of Naples, Apulia, and one or two other provinces, the movement had remained extremely weak up till the March on Rome will be considered later. In the North and Centre the local *ras* in the months after the March on Rome exerted a decisive pressure to counteract and stifle the tendencies to compromise whose existence they suspected in the central government.

In most of the Po Valley (as in Tuscany and Umbria) the party's task after the March was to consolidate positions of power already acquired, and to eliminate the few pockets of resistance which still remained. For example, in the province of Bologna the followers of the Socialist Massarenti still held out with heroic tenacity in the agricultural town and district of Molinella. During the March on Rome the Fascists had occupied all the Socialist co-operatives, and the Prefect had underwritten their action by appointing a commissioner to administer them as an interim measure. However there were rumours that they might be restored to the Socialists as part of the negotiations for a general pacification between the various organizations of labour which was to take place under the aegis of D'Annunzio. This alarmed the local *ras*, who immediately brought pressure to bear to prevent such a solution : on 4 December Baroncini, the *federale* of Bologna, telegraphed to Michele Bianchi :

Molinella represents the only non-Fascist point in the province of Bologna. . .it is necessary not to be preoccupied by the lying legalitarian statements of leaders already guilty of grave acts of violence . . . the resistance and salvation of Molinella Socialism would represent a point around which the Bolognese subversives could polarize, as well as a constant danger to our political and union movement. Please communicate my telegram to the ministers and under-secretaries concerned, exerting opportune pressures.[37]

Elsewhere, the willingness of ministers to make concessions to individual deputies, in the hope of encouraging the tendencies in their parties favour-able to Fascism, ran up against a similar barrier in the interests of the local Fascists. The rumour that Mussolini was contemplating a deal with the Republican deputy Macrelli whereby the dissolution of the communal councils of Forlì and Cesena, controlled by his party, would be avoided, brought a protest from the local Fascist leader Amadeo Mazzotti. He urged on Mussolini 'the *necessity* that the old administrators should be removed from the Commune (Cesena), so as once and for all to have done with an administrative course which keeps the masses, organizations, and co-operatives tied to the Republican party through the public works and the resources of the Commune.'[38] The communal councils were duly dissolved. Relations with the Popolari posed a more serious and general problem Aldo Finzi, the Under-Secretary at the Ministry of the Interior, was sus-pected by the intransigents of having too marked a tendency toward pacification where the Catholic party was concerned. Finzi's personal relations with the Church were excellent ; his marriage was conducted by the aged and reactionary Cardinal Vannutelli. It is true that like other Fascists, he desired the disintegration of the PPI and its replacement by something more amenable ; but he may have feared that the violent methods of the provincial Fascists, who made little distinction between the organizations of the PPI and those of Catholic Action, would alienate the Vatican and Catholic opinion. In any case, Finzi at first seemed disposed to acknowledge the appeals which the Popolari, now officially partners with the Fascists in the Government, made to him for protection.[39]

The Prefects, however, were frequently unready to carry out the letter of the instructions which they received from Finzi. Instead they often served as a mouthpiece for the provincial Fascists' view of the necessities of the situation. There were good reasons for this, as will be seen. Thus the Prefect of Ravenna frankly admitted the cause of party expansion as an overriding consideration which made pacification impossible. The Fascists, he wrote, justified their aversion to the Popolari, still strongly entrenched in the district of Faenza, by alleging that the latter were 'extremist'; however the true motive was to be found in their conviction that 'they cannot secure the triumph of their party in a future general election, or . . . in that for the reconstitution of the Provincial Council so long as the present communal administration remains in power', and in 'the obstacle presented by the white organizations to the development of Fascism and the national syndicates in the territory of Faenza. . . . Fascism, which has remained weaker than in the other parts of the province, does not see the possibility of creating a solid base without trying to weaken the white organizations and to conquer, in part, the political positions held by the Popolari.' The 'amicable agreement' proposed by the Popolari, therefore, would have the effect of 'tying the Fascist party hand and foot.'[40]

Why did the Prefects act often rather as advocates of the local party than as obedient executors of the instructions of the central government? The answer is that they had no confidence that their superiors would back them up if it came to a showdown with the party. The 'Brescia incidents' of December 1922 show what happened when the local Prefect did not act with sufficient alacrity to further the expansion of Fascist power. The 'incidents' had more than a purely local significance; they were intended by the leaders of agrarian Fascism as a warning to the central government and as a demonstration of their strength, and they were successful in this aim, aided by Mussolini's absence in London, which weakened the authority of the central government at a critical moment. The roots of the affair lay in the determination of the Fascists to break the hold of the PPI on the province, in which they had been the strongest party, and especially to promote the growth of the Fascist unions at their expense. The crucial question was whether the Fascists could impose a new tenants' agreement of their own making on the peasants. In this aim they naturally had the support of the majority of the employers and landlords; however it seems that some agrarians, loyal to the PPI or nervous of allowing the Fascists complete control, were reluctant to admit the national syndicates' claim to a monopoly of labour representation. The Brescia squads were slow to disband after the March on Rome; when, on 8 November their leader, Augusto Turati, finally announced their demobilization, 'in obedience to the orders of the Government', he added ominously, 'For us to remain quiet it is necessary that the authorities should act with the utmost energy. And it does not seem to me that such is their intention.'[41]

The specific issue which created tension between party and Government was the presence of Professor Bianchi in the *cattedra ambulante* (travelling lectureship) of agriculture. Bianchi, besides being a PPI sympathizer, was an object of particular hatred to the agrarian Fascists because he was the author of the *lodo Bianchi* which had given official sanction to the daring co-partnership ideas of the leader of the Cremona peasant movement, Guido Miglioli. The removal of Bianchi from his position was also a matter of particular urgency for the Brescia Fascists because he had agreed to act as patron and arbitrator of a new agreement between the Catholic tenants' association and the proprietors.

In early December matters were brought to a head by a conflict between Fascists and Popolari in the village of Capriolo, which ended in reprisals being taken against the local priest. The reactions in Rome were unfavourable. The *Popolo d'Italia* published a communiqué highly critical of the local Fascists, and the Director of Public Security, General De Bono, promised redress to the Bishop of Brescia, who had protested against the outrage on one of his clergy.[42] The Brescia Fascists replied by ordering the mobilization of the squads, in open defiance of the central government. What is more, the leaders of agrarian Fascism threatened to extend the mobilization throughout most of northern Italy. Cesare Forni, the commander of the squads of north-west Italy, wrote an open letter to Mussolini which was little short of an ultimatum; the squads, he threatened, could not remain inactive 'while the ignoble class of deserters ... yells its invectives against the actions of your blackshirts, and men of the government, too soon forgetful of the October days, give way to them'.[43] Faced with this threat, the Government capitulated completely. De Bono recognized that he had lost control of the situation, and called on Farinacci to act as a mediator between the Government and the rebellious Brescians. Farinacci, of course, was entirely in sympathy with the latter. The price which he exacted for his good offices was the immediate appointment of the President of the Cremona employers' association as the Inspector charged with carrying out an 'inquiry' into the administration of the *cattedra ambulante*. His role in the affair did much to confirm his prestige and status as the leader of intransigent provincial Fascism. His astuteness may be contrasted with the naïve and incorrigible extremism of Cesare Forni, which was to lead to his expulsion from the movement a year later.[44]

The most curious feature of the affair was that the Government had not, in fact, shown any great reluctance to bow to the party's wishes where Professor Bianchi was concerned. Finzi had already asked the Under-Secretary for Agriculture, Corgini, to arrange for his dismissal on 9 December, before the demonstrations, and Corgini had ordered an enquiry. The radical mistrust of central government action displayed by the Fascists reflected a disagreement not so much about ends as about means. Another party spokesman, the deputy Buttafochi, wrote to Finzi :

I do not hesitate to report to you that in the Bianchi case, in the case of the notorious man of the Soresina decision, the Government, that is Corgini, has not acted in a Fascist way. Faced with such a man, a *Fascist* government does not order an enquiry, as any ordinary democratic government might do, but acts to free the province in a matter of hours from a man who was a tenacious and subtle enemy of Fascism.[45]

The Brescia Fascists, it is true, had intended to drive home the point that 'in Rome one collaborates with the Popolari, in Brescia one doesn't' ; but beyond this more or less rational aim their actions were also motivated by a characteristic impatience with legal and administrative procedures. The party's most significant victory was the removal of the Prefect. The latter, conscious of party hostility, had in fact represented the Fascist case to the Ministry sympathetically : but he had hesitated before the radical breach of regulations which was demanded, and was consequently found guilty of not having acted 'in a Fascist way'. His removal was a proof that obedience to orders did not guarantee a Prefect against the displeasure of the local party.[46]

The Brescia events from this point of view were not unique. The most distinguished of all the Prefects, Lusignoli, fell a victim to party hostility when he was retired in May 1923. Certainly his was a special case. Mussolini himself can be presumed to have had little desire to see the continuance in an important office of a man to whom his political debts were embarrassingly large, especially after the attempt made to launch his candidature for the Ministry of the Interior. However his forced retirement was the direct consequence of a complaint from the Milan *fascio*. The Milanese Fascists had the authoritative support of the administrative secretary of the PNF, Marinelli, who transmitted their grievances to the Government.[47] The removal of Lusignoli was the premise for a more aggressive policy on the part of the Fascist group in the town council. Shortly afterwards, they forced their Liberal allies to join in voting a resolution condemning the *Corriere della Sera*.[48]

It is understandable that in these circumstances the proclamations by Mussolini and De Bono of the Prefect's supremacy over the party should have been received with some scepticism. Under the democratic regime the Prefect had been used to the necessity of meeting the wishes of the governmental deputies : now, they adapted themselves to the more violent demands of the *ras*. Some at least had received explicit instructions 'to proceed in agreement with the members of the Fascist party'.[49] Mussolini's statements on the authority of the Prefect were not reflected in his personnel policy. One need not conclude that they were wholly insincere ; the principal explanation of the inconsistency is that he did not usually concern himself with the details of appointments and transfers.[50] In the central administration of the Ministry of the Interior the moderate views of Finzi and De Bono were counter-balanced by the presence of Michele Bianchi, for whom the special post of secretary-general had been revived. This was the one instance, and a very important one, in which the party obtained a foothold in the key positions of the state administration, for Bianchi combined his State functions with a leading role in the party.[51] The influence of the party on appointments and transfers can be seen not only in the cases where Prefects were transferred under pressure from the party ; just as significant was the fact that no attempt was made to transfer those officials whose subordination to the *ras* was notorious. In fact, the provinces of the most powerful *ras*, such as Farin-acci's Cremona or Renato Ricci's Massa-Carrara, were those in which the Prefects enjoyed the most stable tenure.[52] In the case of Massa-Carrara, a memorial from one of Ricci's enemies gives a convincing picture of the subservience of the Prefect :

... he is in the hands of Ricci, to whom he owes his salvation in the periods both before and after the March on Rome . . . he persists in turning a blind eye to what is happening in the province . . . he denies the existence of the *disperata* (Ricci's private squad) . . . he thinks above all, and indeed I would say exclusively, of reaching the age limit which will entitle him to the maximum pension . . . he is unable to find those responsible for murders.[53]

Such situations were difficult to change ; where the Prefect could be relied upon to defend the *ras*, the *ras* could be relied upon to defend the Prefect, and the Government would shrink before offending him and creating another centre of dissent.[54] After the Matteotti crisis the Government virtually admitted that their handling of appointments had encouraged the sub-servience of the Prefects to the party.[55]

Mussolini, on his return from London in December 1922, resolved the grave crisis in party-Government relations by granting a large measure of satisfaction to the discontented Fascists. He showed himself prepared, one may wonder with how much sincerity, to accept the conspiracy theories current in the movement, and to lay the blame for its growing malaise and dissensions on the subtle manoeuvres of opponents and perfidious allies.[56] The concession of an amnesty for crimes committed in the service of the nation met one of the most pressing demands of the *ras* and the *squadristi*, besides introducing an ominous principle of political discrimination into the laws of the State.[57] Farinacci and the intransigents were satisfied by the rejection of any idea of conciliation with the labour movement and a new vigour in the repressive action of the police. Many Fascists had begun to doubt the reality of the 'revolution' ;[58] the inauguration of the Grand

Council and the decision to set up the Militia did something to assuage their disillusionment.

Mussolini's aim in setting up these new institutions was to resolve the urgent and difficult problem of co-ordinating the action of the party with that of the Government and the organs of state. Formal leadership of the party, before the creation of the Grand Council, still lay with the collegiate *direzione*. The inclusion in the Grand Council of the Fascist ministers, and also of Finzi, Acerbo, De Bono and Rossi, made it, unlike the old *direzione*, an expression of both party and Government. Moreover, whereas the *direzione* had been an entirely elective body, the Grand Council's composition could at least in part be determined at Mussolini's pleasure. The superimposition of the Grand Council as the supreme organ of Fascism was made easier for Mussolini by the divisions within the leadership caused by the March on Rome. Michele Bianchi and the para-military leaders blamed the *direzione* for having hindered the execution of the March by attempting to control the activities of the revolutionary Quadrumvirate; in particular, they accused Dino Grandi of undue scepticism and of deliberate indiscretion designed to prevent the insurrection.[59] Grandi was excluded from the Grand Council, and received an office of only secondary importance. Significantly, he sought to make amends for his excessive moderation before the March by writing an article in *Gerarchia* which announced the need for a 'second revolution', in which Fascism would 'conquer the State'.[60]

The creation of the Grand Council, if it strengthened Mussolini's position at the head of the party, did nothing to ensure discipline or compliance with official directives on the part of the local organs of Fascism. The party demanded a grip on the levers of power, and here too Mussolini had to make concessions in return for obedience. Two alternative approaches to the problem of co-ordinating the party and the State machine were tried in the period between December 1922 and May 1923. The first was to entrust Fascists with high offices in the State administration. In an interview published on 19 December (while the *fatti di Torino* were in progress), Finzi promised the appointment of a number of Fascists as Prefects and chiefs of police as well as in other branches of the administration. Finzi's statement was undoubtedly an attempt at appeasement in the face of the party offensive, and, in particular, of the severe criticism of his own personal action at the Ministry of the Interior.[61] In the outcome, no civilian Fascist leader was made a Prefect or a chief of police until much later. It is true that the retired generals and colonels who were appointed to several posts could claim to be Fascists, but it seems probable that the original intention had been to appoint party men in the narrower sense of the term.[62] There was a persistent rumour that Farinacci himself was offered a prefecture at this time; but presumably he had no desire to allow himself to be bought off so easily.[63] Why the idea was dropped it is hard to determine. Conservative resistance may have been influential in limiting the choice to the military;

there was some precedent for their employment in civil office, and they were already, of course, servants of the Crown. The appointment of men like General Gandolfo did not alarm orthodox opinion.[64] On the other hand, certainly one of the reasons why few Fascists entered the administration at this stage was the difficulty of finding suitable candidates ; even the *direzione* of the party was forced to admit that 'the State is not yet entirely in the hands of the Fascists because, as there are few men in our party qualified to hold important offices, it is necessary to await the appearance of new technical and intellectual talent.'[65]

The Grand Council meeting of 13 January 1923 created a new rank in the party, the *alti commissari*. They were entrusted with authority over the Fascist party in whole regions or groups of provinces ; and they were drawn from among the most powerful of the local *ras*. Several, including the leader of Campanian Fascism Aurelio Padovani, were also zone commanders of the Militia, and so concentrated both para-military and political authority in their hands. Moreover, although there is little direct documentary evidence on this point, the Liberals asserted that these 'proconsuls' had claimed authority over the State as well as the party, and welcomed their abolition at the end of April as a great victory for the cause of normalization.[66] The State had no regional machinery, and the authority of each Prefect was confined to his own province. Consequently the creation of a regional Fascist authority put the Prefect at a disadvantage. However these concentrations of power had disadvantages for the holders also. They were too extensive to be in most cases really effective ; provincial particularism was a strong force in the Fascist movement, and it was difficult for a regional leader to impose his authority over the whole area. Nevertheless the reason for their abolition was not their inefficiency, but Mussolini's fear of their success. The *alti commissari* collectively formed a council which held several meetings ; this was a more authoritative body, in terms of membership, than the central *direzione*, and it discussed questions of general policy as well as internal party affairs.[67] To institutionalize the power of the leading *ras* and to allow them to form a collective leadership, in view of their character and past history, would have been very dangerous for Mussolini. One would imagine that the *alti commissari* had originally been more or less imposed on him by the party ; it was a sign of his growing confidence that in April he was able to revoke their powers. Both the internal crisis of the party and the support of the Nationalists may have aided him to give the intransigents their first major rebuff.[68]

However the party had to be compensated for the abolition of the *alti commissari* by a renewal of the promise that Fascist leaders would be entrusted with state functions. A first cautious step was taken with the appointment of Piero Pisenti, the former *alto commissario* for the Friuli region, as Prefect of Udine.[69] The experiment was not a success. Two incidents during Pisenti's term as Prefect illustrate the shortcomings of the party man as an executor of Mussolini's political strategy. One of the keystones of Mussolini's policy was to avoid any unnecessary conflict with the Church, while working to intimidate and isolate the PPI. A good-neighbour policy was particularly advisable in the Friuli, a region noted for its Catholic piety. However Pisenti, who in his days as *alto commissario* had called for a purge of the clergy, 'infected with Austrianism', found it impossible to suppress his anti-clerical instincts. When the Vicar-General of the Archbishop of Udine made a courtesy call on Pisenti to request his presence at the opening of the Dioscesan Eucharistic Congress, he was disagreeably surprised to find the Prefect far from benevolently disposed. 'The *signor Prefetto* limited himself to the declaration (which he did not put in writing) that in principle he permitted the Congress, but that he reserved the right to communicate four or five days previously if he will permit the procession, which is an essential part of the Congress.' The Archbishop, in protesting to Finzi, added that he had reason to believe that the local Freemasons were preparing to create a disturbance which would serve as a pretext for the last-minute prohibition of the procession. Pisenti vigorously denied the implication of complicity with anti-clerical sectarianism; but his denial was accompanied by significant reservations which made plain that the Archbishop's complaints were not without foundation.[70]

Pisenti's high-handedness was not only felt by the Church. He contrived also to offend the *fiancheggiatori*, in the person of a local worthy, Senator Fradeletto. The Senator, a professional patriotic orator, was prevented from delivering a speech in commemoration of the resistance of Fort Osoppo in 1848 by the threats of a group of local Fascists: 'and I have learnt', he protested, 'that your excellency (Pisenti) allows or tolerates this.' Pisenti replied very brusquely, informing Finzi that the choice of Fradeletto as orator had displeased the Fascists, and therefore, in order to assure 'the fervent unanimity of all national political forces in the ceremony it was decided to cancel the speech. . . .'[71] Two years later, such an action would not have been controversial, but in 1923, with elections in the offing, government representatives were not supposed to behave in this way to respectable supporters of the national cause. Pisenti resigned his appointment in December 1923 and stood for Parliament in the elections of the spring; it seems that as a 'career Fascist' he had lacked the flexibility and tact which the trained professional Prefects usually possessed in a high degree.[72]

The *Ras*

Some of the factors which made for the appearance of the *ras* have already been mentioned in the last chapter. The rise of these local dictatorships was accompanied and assisted by the growing dominance during 1921–2 of the military over the political wing of the movement. It is significant that many, though not all, of the *ras* started their careers as commanders of the action squads, only later coming to control the strictly political offices. Thus Scorza, for example, appointed commander of the Lucca squads in early 1921, soon succeeded in pushing out the original political secretary, Della Maggiora, and the whole group of founders of the *fascio*. Della Maggiora, according to his account, had favoured the use of persuasion or corruption to ease the passage of Socialist unions to Fascism, whereas Scorza preferred to rely exclusively on the simpler methods of terrorism. 'When Signor Carlo Scorza was elected political secretary I very soon had to recognize that he aimed at establishing a real dictatorship, eliminating whoever dared to contradict or in any way criticize him and the two others who had made themselves masters of the Council of whom one is an ex-gaming house keeper.'[73] This evidence, though prejudiced, is likely to be accurate; the success of Arrivabene and Moschini in Mantua seems to have represented a similar victory for the para-military wing of the movement. However some of the *ras*, such as Farinacci himself and Baroncini at Bologna, owed their position more to organizing ability than to their control over the squads.

The social origins of the *ras* were not homogeneous. Cadets of well-established aristocratic or land-owning families are to be found alongside ambitious parvenus. The *ras* was very often a recent immigrant to the province where he exercised his rule; Farinacci and Scorza were both of southern origin; Pala and Lantini were equally despised by the old Genoese establishment as 'foreigners': Ricci was of very modest origins (his father had risen from plumber to tax-collector),[74] but Arrivabene and Barbiellini both belonged to families of local fame. Nearly all, however, were extremely young for the positions which they had come to hold, and their technical qualifications and education were usually unimpressive.

The Prefect was the highest state authority in the provinces. When he identified himself with the interests of the local Fascist leaders, it was difficult for the other organs of the State not to follow his example. In consequence, the most successful of the *ras* were able to wield a power that was almost total within the boundaries of their province. 'The Prefect, the provincial medical officer, the magistrates' bench, the law courts, everything is at their disposal, they command and rule over everyone with incredible abuses, threats, and provocations ... it would be useless to waste so many millions paying prefects, policemen and authorities of all sorts, if these are then to be dependent upon the *fasci* of the various cities';[75] this heartfelt cry from an 'old Fascist' in Carlo Scorza's Lucca could have been echoed in many other towns or provinces. In Piacenza, Barbiellini was accused of having created a 'medieval tyranny'; the Prefect and Chief of Police were his instruments, 'and therefore the authority of the central government is nil'. Justice was equally impotent; it was impossible to bring an action against anyone who enjoyed the protection of the leaders of the federation.[76]

At the base of the whole system, a multitude of petty bosses in the villages and small towns imposed their own parochial tyranny. Some of these held their position as clients of the provincial leaders, but others, men of local influence or *squadristi* notorious for their violence, like Carosi in the province of Pisa or Regazzi the boss of Molinella, were powers in their own right.[77] In many provinces no single leader was capable of imposing his authority, and the movement was split into feuding factions. This, indeed, was the typical situation; the power of all but a few of the provincial *federali* was unstable. This was particularly true in the more important provinces; the *fasci* of the large cities were usually in conflict with the provincial federation. The most secure of the *ras* were those who dominated smaller and more homogeneous provinces; Barbiellini in Piacenza, Arrivabene in Mantua, Scorza in Lucca, Ricci in Massa-Carrara, and of course Farinacci in Cremona were among the most notable. One should not exaggerate the self-sufficiency of these local potentates; they were only secure if they possessed friends at the centre who could be trusted to repulse intrigues and repress rumours. The combination of power in the provinces and influence at Rome was difficult to achieve; even Balbo, whose prestige made him almost invulnerable, found it difficult to delegate his power over Ferrara satisfactorily. The *ras* maintained their power, over Fascist and non-Fascist alike, by terror, backed in some cases at least by an efficient spy system. The Militia, with the help of the police, prevented any revival of organized opposition; but its existence did not eliminate unofficial *squadrismo*. The *ras* kept their own private gangs for use especially against rivals within the party. In Carrara the *disperata* squad served as Ricci's private bodyguard; it was 'an armed and organized unit of blackshirts, with a uniform elegantly edged in white thread, and supported by another unit of cavalry, commanded by Signor Guido Fabbricotti'. Many of the *disperata* had criminal records.[78] Barbiellini had ten or fifteen thugs at his personal disposition; his henchmen were almost certainly responsible for the murder in 1924 of a disabled ex-serviceman, Lertua, who had imprudently accused him of having organized an attack on the Milan Socialist deputy Buffoni.[79] Barbiellini also employed a large number of spies; in Mantua Arrivabene's network of informers had permeated all the government offices and established surveillance over the telegraph and postal services.[80] Balbo, in anticipation of the procedures of the American crime syndicates, preferred to use a 'foreign' gang from Perugia to suppress his personal enemies in the Ferrara party. But the murder of the anti-Fascist priest Don Minzoni was the work of local Fascists, who sheltered in the house of the secretary of the Argenta *fascio*, Maran. Later Balbo complained that the *federale* of Ferrara was not sufficiently active in trying to secure Maran's release from arrest after he had been charged with complicity.[81]

The finance of the *fasci* by industrialists and *agrari* had originally, of course, been voluntary and individual. However at a second stage several agrarian associations took to imposing on their members the payment of regular and specified dues to the movement. The *ras* were quick to exploit this opening. The next step was for them to demand the payment of these dues as an absolute right, irrespective of the collective or individual wishes of the proprietors. Previously, of course, a landowner or farmer who objected to supporting the *fascio* could always resign from his association; but once Fascist power was secure, refusal to pay could bring a beating. This method of self-financing can be described as a very successful form of protection racket.[82]

Direct taxation was usually reserved for the *agrari*; but even the industrialists who had been more cautious about imposing collective obligations on themselves could nevertheless be squeezed by more indirect methods. Ricci forced the local railway line to lower its tariff for the transport of marble by 17 per cent, and the owners of the marble quarries were ordered to pay the difference between the old and new price to the Fascist federation.[83] There was a shifting boundary between this type of operation in the interests of the party, and more sordid operations aimed purely at personal enrichment. The general of the Militia, Bresciani, was suspected of lending his protection to a *maison de tolerance*; and the Consuls Tamburini and Galbiati were involved in dark episodes of violence for private ends.[84]

However the major *ras* had other objectives than mere profit. In their dealings with industrialists and agrarians they were also inspired by considerations of power. Their intolerance of dissent and the insecurity of their position drove them on, even where it was not their conscious aim, towards total control of all aspects of life within their district. This meant freeing themselves from the tutelage of their financial backers and forcing them to accept alliance on the *ras*'s own terms. Rival centres of power could not be tolerated. Ricci used his position as *alto commissario* 'to exert a direct influence over everything and everyone, in the life of the *fascio* as in the provincial federation, in the communal administration, the organization of industrialists and the life of the unions'. This meant in the first place jobs for the boys. Patronage and intimidation were mutually reinforcing; the *ras* could threaten their enemies because they could reward their friends. Local government was the first objective. The mayors of the larger communes often entertained the dangerous belief that their superior age and experience gave them the right to run things their own way. They were soon forcibly reminded that they owed their position to the party and its *squadristi*; the latter moved into the town hall, installing their own offices alongside those of the commune, dictated decisions on all 'political' matters, questioned even purely administrative decisions, and eliminated the mayor from his traditional role as the mediator of patronage with the central government. When the mayor of Carrara visited Rome, Ricci, 'after having expressed amazement that I had not warned him of my departure, later informed me that by the terms of an agreement concluded with the Prime Minister I was to prepare a report for him every month on the business to be concluded with the Ministries in the Capital, which I should not visit in future.'[85]

Control over the smaller communes was simpler to achieve, and they could be filled with reliable clients. When Barbiellini was in trouble in April 1924 the mayors of seventeen communes and the President of the Provincial Council threatened to resign simultaneously in protest against his suspension as *federale*.[86] But so long as the holders of economic power remained fully independent, the control of the *ras* was incomplete. This was true even within the party : industrialists or agrarian leaders might, and often did, finance dissident tendencies.

The *ras* consequently sought to impose their power even in the economic sector : the opponents of Barbiellini complained that 'the Fascist federation wishes to command even in private firms'.[87] Ricci, who went furthest in this respect, tried to dictate prices and wages in the marble industry, and threatened to use the Militia to enforce his orders. He had the backing of a group of industrialists, who may perhaps have rigged the prices in their favour : but the majority of the class seem to have been decidedly hostile to his interference. Against them, Ricci sought to mobilize mass support by promising a wage increase and attacking the egoism of the industrialists. The *fasci* of Carrara and the marble-producing zone, as well as the *sindacati*, contained a large proportion of unemployed marble-workers, and this must have encouraged Ricci to use demagogic tactics. He hoped not only to frighten the industrialists but to broaden the social base of the movement among the stably employed majority of the working class, who had remained hostile. This line of policy was to culminate in the calling of a general strike in late 1924.[88] The *masse de manoeuvre* provided by the *sindacati* was regarded by the *ras* as a valuable instrument of political pressure and blackmail, not only against the industrialists and agrarians but against government or party superiors. In April 1924, faced with an inquiry, Barbiellini proclaimed a general strike, apparently with success, in protest against his opponents in the Militia. But such tactics were risky ; on this occasion the *ras* may have lost more than he gained, as his initiative infuriated Mussolini.[89]

The best-known and certainly the most powerful of the *ras* was Roberto Farinacci. Intensely ambitious, vain, half-educated, and consumed by jealous resentment of the cultured classes, Farinacci represented, almost to the point of caricature, the aspirations and motives of that legion of obscure provincial enthusiasts who were the backbone of Fascism. He has been judged both as a disinterested fanatic and as a corrupt careerist : the truest judgement would be that his own personal advancement and the fortunes of the movement formed for him an inextricable whole.

Ironically enough Farinacci began his political career as a follower of Bissolati. Unprepossessing and awkward, Farinacci seems to have understood that he could only make his way as a follower of more glamorous and eloquent figures. It seems in the light of history both tragic and grotesque that the first leader he attached himself to was the idealistic Bissolati. The choice is easy to understand ; Bissolati was by far the brightest star in the little firmament of Cremona. Already in his relations with Bissolati, Farinacci began to employ a technique which he was to perfect in his dealings with Mussolini; his endless and embarrassing professions of loyalty cloaked the pursuit of a policy often at variance with that of his leader.[90]

In July 1915 Farinacci joined the local Freemasons' lodge. This was an almost obligatory step; it gave him access to the small group of patriotic, anti-clerical notables like Professor Alessandro Groppali who were to provide him with money, advice and contacts. His enemies later insinuated that his joining the Freemasons at this time also had a more immediate and discreditable purpose: that of using their influence to secure exemption from military service at the front. There does not seem to be any proof of this, and as an official of the railways Farinacci had good grounds for exemption, yet the truth was not exactly heroic. He did one year's military service in a regiment of telegraphists, and was never nearer than four miles from the front line. As a skilled telegraphist and official of the railways, he had good grounds for exemption from the more dangerous branches of service; however his military record was for Farinacci yet another mark of inferiority, which he tried to live down by showing himself, in peacetime, the most aggressive and indefatigable of all combatants for the nation.[91] Unlike the majority of the *ras*, Farinacci belonged to the original nucleus of 1919. By late 1920 he was already, in fact, a well-known figure in the movement; his ability as an organizer was recognized and the Fascists of other provinces asked for his advice and assistance. He was one of the first local leaders to extend his operations outside the restricted circle of the provincial capital and to organize *fasci* in the smaller provincial centres.[92] However it does not seem as if during 1919–20 he had, any more than the other leaders, anticipated the growth of agrarian Fascism. His main clientele seems still to have been urban; in particular he used his experience as a former stationmaster to build up a clientele among the railway staffs and to create a force of blacklegs for use against the railwaymen's unions. The first provincial 'nuclei', in fact, were all founded in towns which were on the railway.[93]

At first, indeed, Farinacci seems to have shared Pasella and Mussolini's distrust of a movement under too exclusive agrarian influence; he wrote to the central committee that he had heard that the Padua *fascio* 'stinks a bit of the *agraria*'. Moreover a delegation of agrarians from Cremona complained to Cesare Rossi about the uncertain Fascist attitude towards the agitation of Miglioli's Catholic peasant leagues.[94] However it is clear that during the next months Farinacci and the agrarians did conclude a firm alliance; Miglioli's movement, unlike the Socialist leagues, was still in the ascendant, and the spectacle of Fascism in other provinces, especially Ferrara, may have convinced the *agrari* that the Fascist acceptance on paper of a radical land programme was a necessary expedient. Part of Farinacci's force after 1921 is to be explained by the strength of the resistance which he encountered;

the Miglioli movement, because it received some sympathy and support in respectable official quarters, remained a serious threat when the power of the Socialist leagues was plainly in full retreat. This meant that Farinacci became the natural spokesman for all those who wished to treat the Popolari as irreducible enemies, on a par with the Socialists. In this matter character and conviction reinforced local necessities; Farinacci's anti-clericalism was sincere and deep-rooted, and he even went out of his way, on more than one occasion, to proclaim himself an atheist. The necessities of the struggle against Miglioli also helped Farinacci to achieve an unusual degree of discipline and centralized power in the province.

Cremona was one of the richest agricultural provinces in Italy. Its medium-sized, heavily capitalized dairy farms were often held up as models of efficiency. It was on the active agrarian bourgeoisie, most of whom were tenant farmers who leased their farms from absentee landowners, that Farinacci based his power. However the role of industry and the banks, as in other Po Valley provinces, was important. The Sperlari family, who controlled an important firm of sweet manufacturers, and the directors of the Zuccherificio Agricolo Lombardo were among Farinacci's influential backers.[95] Still more important was the financial support provided by Count Lusignani and his agricultural credit bank in the neighbouring province of Parma. Lusignani was an adventurer who needed political cover for his risky business ventures; he stood as a candidate on the national list in 1921, but he was not elected, and thereafter he leant heavily on the backing of Farinacci.

Farinacci's rising influence within the Fascist movement eventually brought him to the attention of far more important groups of capitalists in Milan and Rome. It is not possible to say with any precision when these contacts began; it is possible that the 250,000 lire found to start the publication of Farinacci's daily newspaper, *Cremona Nuova*, still came mainly from local sources.[96] But it is clear that a year later, in early 1923, Farinacci, who liked to pose as the honest provincial, was nonetheless active in the financial intrigues of the capital. His influence must in fact already have been considerable; when the Government stepped in to salvage and reorganize the Banco di Roma by a remarkable coup he got his candidate Carlo Vitali appointed as the new managing director.[97] It may be that besides his political influence Farinacci could already count on the support of one of the richest of Milanese industrialists, Senatore Borletti. Borletti, who had been one of the most conspicuous backers of D'Annunzio and the extreme Right during 1919, certainly financed Farinacci in 1926 and later: though direct evidence is lacking for the period 1922–4, it is significant that when Borletti bought out the owners of the radical *Secolo*, with the purpose of transforming it into a pro-Fascist newspaper, the successful candidate for the editorship, Giuseppe Bevione, sought Farinacci's patronage for his appointment.

The possession of an efficient daily newspaper gave Farinacci an advantage which no other *ras* possessed. Balbo, his chief rival for leadership of the intransigent wing, did not acquire one until 1925. Indeed, as the *Popolo d'Italia* came to represent more and more exclusively the official viewpoint of the Government, Farinacci in the *Cremona Nuova* could claim to be the chief spokesman for the party.[98]

As one of the *alti commissari* in early 1923, Farinacci was able to intervene in the affairs of the provinces bordering on his own. Parma Fascism was in perennial crisis, thanks to the intrigues of rival factions of Freemasons, tension between the city Fascists and those of the province, and between the syndicates and the *agrari*. The 'subversives', whose morale was high after their successful defence of the Oltretorrente quarter in July 1922, were still a force to be reckoned with. Farinacci, requested by Mussolini to clear up the mess, agreed, but only on condition that the secretary, Ezio Ponzi, who had concluded a local pact of pacification with the Opposition, was sacked, and that the Government agreed to make the necessary transfers of officials.[99] This episode is highly revealing of the relations between Mussolini and the party: it shows how in spite of professions to the contrary, in the interests of party efficiency and the extension of Fascist control he was forced to take measures which would increase the power of the *ras* at the expense both of State authority and of those Fascists who, like Ponzi, had backed him during the crisis of 1921.

Farinacci had already intervened decisively in the province of Brescia during the crisis of December 1922. A more permanent reason for intervention was provided by the presence of D'Annunzio at Gardone. Augusto Turati, the leader of Brescia Fascism, was a former legionary who had seriously considered joining Marsich in a D'Annunzian revolt against Mussolini's leadership during 1922, and therefore could not be entrusted with the task of surveillance over the *Comandante*.[100] The new Prefect of Brescia, Arturo Bocchini, realized that Farinacci would be a powerful protector likely to advance his career, and therefore consulted him with deference on all important decisions. His spies reported on D'Annunzio's doings not only to Mussolini but to Farinacci as well. What Mussolini thought about this is not wholly clear. Although he certainly knew that Farinacci received direct reports from Gardone, he did nothing to put a stop to it. It seems that on balance his suspicions of D'Annunzio outweighed his suspicions of Farinacci.[101]

The alliance between Farinacci and the Prefect Bocchini was for both men of more than purely local significance: Farinacci repaid Bocchini by urging his promotion. Having failed in the attempt to get him appointed head of the personnel division of the Interior Ministry, he continued to press for his transfer to a more important province. At the end of the year Bocchini's loyalty to Fascism was finally rewarded with the key post of Bologna; in spite of his contribution to the fall of the *ras* Baroncini, Farinacci remained his assiduous patron. In the critical days after the murder of Matteotti, he urged that Bocchini, 'a practical and intelligent man who would perform excellent service for your government', should be appointed De Bono's successor as chief of police.[102] Farinacci was right about Bocchini's ability, but from another point of view he had judged his man poorly. Ironically, Bocchini was to play a leading role in liquidating the pretensions of intransigent Fascism.

Elsewhere, Mussolini and Bianchi, in spite of their reservations about Farinacci, employed his services as a trouble-shooter to deal with some of the frequent crises in the Fascist movement. He was entrusted with the difficult and extremely important task of reorganizing Roman Fascism in July–August 1923. In reporting the conclusion of his mission, he announced that he had purged 40,000 members, mainly 'scum that had come to us after the March'. Surprisingly, Farinacci did not in this instance use his powers to favour the old *squadristi* of Calza-Bini, but instead 'made great use of the Nationalists, because Roman nationalism has a history, and must not be confused with the nationalism of the provinces'.[103] At first sight, given the mutual hostility of Farinacci and the former Nationalist leaders, this looked like a present to his enemies; but Italo Foschi, one of the ex-Nationalists promoted by Farinacci, later became his ally, and so it seems as if Farinacci was fairly successful in extending his influence over Roman Fascism in spite of the enmity of such important figures as Bottai and Federzoni.

Farinacci was the head of a vast and diversified clientele. He assumed the defence of important interest groups and widened his influence through strategic alliances with other Fascist leaders. The most important of these alliances was with Edmondo Rossoni and the Fascist syndicates. Rossoni needed party support both against the proponents of a deal with the CGL, such as Cesare Rossi, and the orthodox *liberisti*, such as Corgini, and Farinacci was willing to identify with the cause of integral syndicalism. Of more limited importance, but still useful, was his entente with Edoardo Torre, the *commissario* of the railways. This helped him to maintain his influence among his old comrades of the important Fascist railwaymen's association, which was working hand in hand with Torre to secure the 'fascistization' of the railways. When the Minister of Public Works, the Demosociale Carnazza, proposed to hand back the Cremona branch line to private enterprise, Farinacci organized meetings of railwaymen to protest, and with Torre's support soon got Mussolini to rescind the measure. He thus at the same time reasserted his right to determine all policy decisions affecting the interests of Cremona province, assumed the role of the railwaymen's protector, and dealt a sharp rebuff to the hated *fiancheggiatori*. Not content with his success, he accused Carnazza of a deliberate manoeuvre designed to cast discredit on Mussolini. 'To the world of Fascism we utter the warning: Be vigilant! . . . We cannot permit even the remote possibility that the name of the President should be compromised. . . . Let there be around the President a corps of pure Fascists as his vigilant and uncontaminated sentinels.'[104] This is a good example of Farinacci's characteristic and oppressive style of loyalty.

In spite of his financial connections it would be correct to view Farinacci as a defender, first and foremost, of agrarian interests. The rhetorical defence of the 'healthy provinces' against the corrupt capital reflected not only the *ras*'s grievances against the Government but the concern of the agrarian bloc, who noted with alarm the growth in the influence of industrial and allied banking interests over the Fascist movement. Even the non-Fascist agrarian associations acknowledged Farinacci as a protector against the industrial lobby. One of their leaders, the deputy Ducos, wrote protesting to him about the damage which would be done to agricultural interests by the proposed amalgamation of the Ministries of Agriculture and Industry in a single Ministry of the National Economy: 'The Associations charge me with the task of bringing home the danger to you and turn to you for protection. You will be able to make their voice heard at Rome.'[105] The almost official position which Farinacci enjoyed as spokesman for the agricultural interests is perhaps even more clearly illustrated by a letter which was addressed to him by F. Guarneri, secretary-general of the ASIA, calling for a truce between agrarians and industrialists during the negotiations for the commercial treaty with Germany.[106] However the backing of the agrarians was ultimately a liability as well as a source of strength to Farinacci, for it was bound to alienate the industrial establishment.

The local dictatorship of the *ras* was only the extreme form taken by the power of a party based on the use or threat of organized violence. The more successful local chiefs performed several positive functions for Fascism as a whole, and therefore for Mussolini. Their coercion was effective, and they imposed order, or at least silence, stifling political opposition and economic disputes. They were also able to mount an impressive show of force, to mobilize in mass meetings or processions a large and enthusiastic following. It is true that Mussolini himself could do this even more effectively, and yet the plebiscitary tactics of Fascism, as well as the coercion, were still dependent on the existence of a solid and permanent following which would not disperse on the day after a speech by the Duce. Charismatic rapport was not enough without the backing of an organized movement.

On the other hand the rule of the *ras* had features that were undoubtedly less welcome to Mussolini. It alienated neutrals and respectable public opinion; it interfered with the orderly creation of new institutions; and it was a direct limit on Mussolini's own power. Mussolini's discontent with the party grew for all these reasons: but the main cause for his mounting irritation was the inability of the party to give itself a stable and efficient form of organization, or to control and limit the ever more frequent outbreaks of internal conflict.

Dissidents and the 'Crisis of Fascism'

The deleterious effect of competition for office, the massive influx of new and opportunist converts, and the centrifugal forces liberated now that the need to combat adversaries was less pressing, all made themselves felt after the March on Rome in the form of an alarming growth in dissension within the federations and the single *fasci*. The *direzione* of the PNF, 'in consideration of the situation of Fascism in the nation and especially in relation to the attempt of men of other parties and with a varied past to invade or disintegrate Fascism', was forced to ask the provincial *direttori* not to refer conflicts to it without urgent necessity, as their constant appeals for arbitration 'are preventing it from exercising its regular functions as the supreme political organ'.[107] The frequent repetition of these warnings during the next few months shows their futility; the *direzione* was powerless to check the outbreak of local quarrels.[108] With varying accents of hope or dismay, contemporaries spoke of the 'crisis of Fascism'.[109] The fundamental causes of this crisis, as the dissident Fascist Gaetano Lumbroso observed, lay in the mentality which Fascism had encouraged in its devotees, in the exaltation of the principle of leadership and of prompt and violent action.[110] The good Fascist was the man who could secure obedience by whatever means he chose. In spite of the unprecedented bureaucratic and military organization of the movement, the effort to inculcate the complementary principle of disciplined submission to orders from above had not been nearly so successful. Giuseppe Bottai remarked that 'while homogeneity is more or less possible in parties formed around a rigid and precise programme, it is almost impossible in a party whose recruitment stemmed from an atmosphere of passion. While strong feelings are active, it is possible to unite different types of men ; calm revives their disagreements.'[111] The crisis reached its culmination during the months of April and May 1923 : in the Marche the movement was split into two by Silvio Gai's decision to expel all members who had joined since the March on Rome :[112] in Rome, the followers of the former political secretary and *alto commissario* for Lazio, Calza-Bini, invaded the offices of the *fascio*, now controlled by his opponents :[113] and in the provinces of Pavia and Alessandria the bitter dispute between the followers of Forni and Sala on the one hand and Torre on the other broke out into open violence.[114] The cases of Misuri and Padovani were even more serious ; although they had their origin in local disputes, they nevertheless both expressed reactions of genuine political and ideological importance, which gave birth to 'dissident Fascism'.

The phenomenon of 'dissident Fascism' had no single cause. Its origins were local and various, in the clash of personalities and the competition for power. However some of the more important dissidents did express objections to the prevailing policy which were not merely parochial in their implications. In fact these dissidents were just the tip of the iceberg. Their openly expressed criticisms often give a valuable indication of feelings and views which were in all probability widely distributed within the movement.

For convenience, one can roughly distinguish three important types of dissidence. The first is that of the pure conservatives : it includes the Tuscan *fasci nazionali*, Misuri in Umbria and Corgini in Reggio Emilia. These criticized Fascism from the standpoint of an orthodox monarchic authoritarianism. Their polemic harked back to the 1921 controversy over whether Fascism should become a party, or remain a kind of armed auxiliary force, open to all 'patriots'. Misuri and Lumbroso, the spokesman of the *fasci nazionali*, had both then opposed the foundation of the PNF. Like the revisionists, they demanded the restoration of State authority and the elimination of illegitimate party interference ; Misuri even went so far as to demand its total dissolution. They were associated with those groups of agrarians who resisted the forced absorption of their associations by the corporations, and they were in general highly critical of the 'demagogy' of the Fascist unions as well as the indiscipline of the mass party.[115] Dino Perrone Compagni, the chief of Tuscan agrarian Fascism in 1921-2, wrote that 'it distresses me to see Fascism become Bolshevism'.[116]

The second type can be described as that of the extreme agrarian intransigents, and is represented by Cesare Forni and his friend Raimondo Sala. Here, local rivalries are without doubt more important in the explanation. They became leaders of dissident Fascism because they lost out in their struggle for local power with Torre, backed by Giunta, who was secretary of the PNF during the decisive phase of the conflict towards the end of 1923. However there was also a more general question involved. Forni, like the conservatives, put his loyalty to the agrarian associations above his obedience to the movement's directives, and opposed the party's line on the development of the corporations and the co-operatives. On the other hand, his position cannot be identified with that of Misuri, because he was an 'intransigent', hostile to compromise with the old political class and on the side of the PNF against the State. For this reason Farinacci, implacably hostile to Misuri, defended Forni.[117]

The third type is that of the radical intransigents. These, such as the Neapolitan leader Padovani and the 'free Fascists' of the Marche, were 'revolutionaries' who, like Forni, opposed the subordination of the movement to State authority, and attacked Parliament and the spirit of compromise. They were the sworn enemies not only of the Liberal *fiancheggiatori* but of the Nationalists. But they also attacked Fascism for following a reactionary policy, hostile to the interests of the working class and the petty bourgeoisie. The 'free Fascists' of the Marche, who declared that 'Fascism is movement, not stasis' (a typical intransigent pronouncement), expressed the protest of the petty bourgeoisie, particularly the rural, against the influence of large industry and the banks. Locally, this issue hinged on the 'insidious offensive' of the 'false Democrats' led by the electrical industrialist

Tofani; nationally, on the maintenance of protective tariffs and the tax on agricultural income. This kind of radical criticism inevitably extended to the structure of the movement itself. The 'fetishism' practised by Fascists with regard to Mussolini, the cult of blind discipline, the false intransigence and real corruption of the *ras*, and the frustration of inner-party democracy by intimidation, the usurpation of powers, and the growth of bureaucracy within the movement; all these were summed up in the slogan of the defence of the 'spirit of 1919' against the influence of the Nationalists, reactionary, pro-clerical, and tied to the protectionist interests of heavy industry. Mussolini, they complained, had 'imposed a hierarchy on Fascism', and 'changed its content'.[118]

These dissident movements, diverse and opposed as they were in their social and political motives, nonetheless found some common ground. The common denominator was in the resentment felt by the less successful of the old *squadristi* against the new oligarchy, both the provincial, agrarian *ras* with their hangers-on, and the 'fixers' of metropolitan Fascism, allied to high finance. On the other hand, the continuing strength of the leaders of the official intransigents, such as Farinacci, was dependent on the mobilization and diversion of similar resentments, under such slogans as the provinces against Rome, and the *squadristi* against the *politicanti*. In this way the *ras* could combine the defence of their recently acquired positions with a pseudo-radicalism which gave some satisfaction to their followers.

8

THE PARTY AND THE STATE (II)

Party Organization and the Revisionist Campaign 1923–4

The 'crisis of Fascism' gave the *fiancheggiatori* a chance to press their criticisms of the subordination of the State administration to the party. They seized eagerly on signs which suggested that Mussolini might be willing to repudiate the extremists. The April session of the Grand Council, besides abolishing the *alti commissari*, took other decisions which were welcomed by orthodox Liberal opinion; the verbal intemperance of De Vecchi and other extremists was rebuked; an attempt was made to separate command in the Militia from authority in the party, and a purge both of party members and of Militia cadres was announced.[1] In May 1923, the disgrace of Padovani and the recognition by the new directive organ of the party, the *Giunta Esecutiva*, of the separation of party and State authority in the provinces, gave still further satisfaction. However these decisions were partially counterbalanced by others which were more pleasing to the party: the revival of the idea of 'Fascist Prefects', the solemn condemnation of the Popolari, and the order that all party members should *ex officio* belong to the Militia. Moreover the reorganization of the party leadership, which abolished the old *direzione* and substituted a new *Giunta Esecutiva*, represented a concession to the provincial bosses. The difficulty of establishing an efficient organ for the control of the party resulted in large measure from the distrust existing between those who held functions at the centre and those who held power locally, dramatized in terms of the conflict between Rome and the provinces.[2] When 'centralism' prevailed and the direction of the party was entrusted to a restricted group working full-time, the leadership tended to lose contact with the grass roots and responsibility was divorced from power: when 'provincialism' had the upper hand and influential local chiefs took part, they used the position to strengthen their baronies, and the danger of disobedience to the directives of Mussolini and the Government increased.

The new *Giunta Esecutiva* included Farinacci, along with two other provincial chiefs, Lantini and Zimolo, and confirmed the exclusion of the moderates Grandi, Rocca and Postiglione. Its composition ensured that any purge of membership would not work to the detriment of the *ras*'s following. Liberals pointed to the danger that the new '*fiduciari provinciali*' would play the same role as the old *alti commissari*, though in a reduced area; this fear, in spite of the *Giunta*'s formal recognition of State authority, proved largely justified. The decisions of the *Giunta* also, predictably, reinforced the authority of the provincial secretaries and thus the autonomy and the 'cult of personality' of the 'little Duces'.[3]

The end of May 1923 saw the climax of the offensive of the 'normalizers'. On 29 May the dissident deputy Alfredo Misuri rose in the Chamber to deliver a detailed denunciation of the party's illegal interference with law and the administration; at least six other Fascist deputies, moderates or ex-Nationalists, publicly congratulated him on his speech.[4] The response was immediate: three hours later he was assaulted from behind and cudgelled by a picked squad of Fascists led by the Bolognese Arconovaldo Bonaccorsi, acting, it seems clear, on the orders of Mussolini himself.[5] In any case, his refusal to condemn the aggressors and the forced resignation of the Under-Secretary Corgini, one of Misuri's sympathizers, showed beyond any doubt that the Liberals' hopes of dividing Mussolini from the party and from his entourage were still illusory; the accentuation of the crisis of Fascism, on which they had counted, in fact convinced him of the necessity to call a halt to criticism and restore morale by showing his solidarity with the movement. This is not to deny that Mussolini acted on sudden impulse in ordering the attack on Misuri; however the sequel showed that policy as well as resentment had dictated a return to the hard line.

Attention shifted during the following months away from the internal feuds of Fascism and towards the struggle over electoral reform. The contest itself helped the movement to recover a measure of unity; Fascist aggression was once more turned outwards, towards the movement's enemies, although local disputes remained frequent. Slowly, too, a natural process of selection and consolidation led to greater stability.[6]

The next serious crisis in the Fascist party was not caused by local feuds, but by far-reaching disagreements over policy. The first 'revisionist crisis' in September 1923 revived some of the issues raised by Misuri. This time, however, Mussolini sided with the critics and entered into open conflict with the provincial leaders. After the passage of the Electoral Reform Bill he felt reasonably secure, and he could afford to cultivate neutral public opinion. The *ras* were in the way, and on a number of issues his decisions and theirs were in conflict. The most explosive issue, as in November–December 1922, was that of relations with the CGL. During the final stages of the debate on the Acerbo Bill, Mussolini had renewed his overtures to the trade union leaders. The ideas of pacification and of the participation of a union representative in government were once more the subject of discussion. This profoundly alarmed the *ras* and their agrarian supporters. Nor was this the only point of friction. As spokesman for the party, Farinacci criticized Mussolini's new government appointments. Sicilians from the old political class and 'experts' with an anti-Fascist past were being preferred to true Fascists; the appointment as Under-Secretary for Agriculture of Arrigo Serpieri, 'a man who in the agrarian conflicts of the Po Valley was our bitter adversary, to the point of assuming the role of defender of the agrarian reform of Miglioli and Dr Bianchi', touched agrarian Fascism on the most sensitive nerve.[7] Mussolini resented this interference and Farinacci's continual implicit reminders of his dependence on the forces of provincial Fascism. The future of the Militia was an even more important bone of contention. Farinacci published an article on 16 August criticizing the tendency to transform the Militia into an a-political military force, and demanding that it remain 'what it is according to its nature and its origins in squadrism : a body of political police at the disposition of our *Duce* and of Fascism'. This article brought an angry response from Mussolini; the controversy foreshadowed the more serious crisis in the relations between the two men which took place in September.[8]

These various problems formed the background to the revisionist crisis. However this had as its central issue the future role of the party. Massimo Rocca accused the party of coming between Mussolini and the nation : and the ministerial *Corriere Italiano* went still further, calling for 'the reconstruction on a new basis of the disciplinary structure and rules of the party, in short for its recreation *ex novo*'.[9] Farinacci took up the challenge in his speech to the provincial council of Cremona on 17 September 1923, in which he made public his criticisms of Government policy and of the new course of the Militia, threatening to provoke a mass resignation of the Consuls.[10] This was a tactical error, and Mussolini was able to call Farinacci's bluff, but the intransigents' counter-offensive continued. Farinacci acted in concert with Baroncini, who was specially active in trying to promote the formation of a 'united front' among the *federali* of the Po Valley.[11]

The *ras* hit back hard, accusing the revisionists of involvement with the shady financial dealings of the capital ; Baroncini claimed, in reply to Rocca, that it was 'Roman' corruption and not provincial authoritarianism which had disgusted public opinion. This line of attack was effective ; the *ras* could point to the connections of the revisionists' campaign with notorious 'fixers' like Filippo Naldi and Carlo Bazzi, and they could play on agrarian grievances against the political influence of protectionist lobbies like the sugar trust, which financed Finzi's newspaper the *Corriere Italiano*. They claimed to be defending the interests of farmers and consumers against the intrigues of a 'Judaeo-Masonic' clique.[12]

The *Popolo d'Italia* came down heavily on the side of the revisionists. On 18 September one of its columnists commented that all Fascists who were in good faith would agree with Rocca's criticisms. The points in the revisionist critique which it singled out for special emphasis were the party's insensitivity to broader issues, and especially those of foreign policy, and, by contrast, the exaltation of Mussolini's infallibility. The revisionist controversy advanced the cult of Mussolini as a superman who needed no collaborators.[13]

However the two Fascist leaders who probably stood closest to Mussolini, Rossi and Marinelli, were distinctly more cautious in tone. Both minimized the gravity of the crisis, and Marinelli described the dissolution of the party as 'unthinkable', on the grounds that in many regions it constituted 'the true basis of social order'.[14] The party must therefore accept a subordinate function as the instrument and not the determinant of government policy, and concentrate on practical tasks of administration. On the internal structure of the party Rossi held views which agreed with the substance of the revisionist criticisms. He spoke as a representative of the urban Fascism defeated by Farinacci and the agrarians in 1921. He believed that the model for reform could be found in the organization and practice of Milanese Fascism, where internal democracy still existed and the *direttorio* was assisted by a consultative council drawn from the *gruppi rionali* (ward groups), where the stress was on organization rather than violence and indiscriminate recruitment was avoided. He threatened the *ras* not only with the revival of free elections in the *fasci* and federations, but also with a 'centralist' reform of the *Giunta Esecutiva*. For the sake of efficiency, he argued, the *Giunta* should be composed exclusively of permanent residents in Rome.[15]

Mussolini and his personal clique saw the revisionist campaign as a means of securing a reform of the party leadership to make it more amenable and to reduce provincial influences. The *Giunta Esecutiva* invited reprisal by expelling Rocca, and Mussolini seized the opportunity to order its members to resign. Michele Bianchi, who had presided over the Executive as general secretary, became the target of Mussolini's anger and had to resign along with the other members.[16] The fall of Bianchi, unlike that of the rest of the Executive, had not been desired or foreseen by Rossi, who had perhaps hoped to win him over to his side.

Mussolini's decisions undoubtedly marked a notable victory for the revisionist outlook. Yet the victory had its limitations, as was soon made plain. Mussolini recoiled before the prospect of a decisive break with the dominant faction in the movement, such as full support for Rocca would have implied. Early in October 1923 he received the two leaders of the *ras*, Farinacci and Baroncini. This marked the beginning of a reconciliation with the intransigents which was symbolically confirmed by the announcement on 11 October that the celebrations of the first anniversary of the March on Rome would begin in Cremona.[17]

The Grand Council met on 13 October. Rocca's expulsion was formally revoked, but he was suspended for three months, 'for contributing to the degeneration of the polemic', a decision which cannot have failed to give some satisfaction to his enemies. The programmatic resolutions which were voted by the Grand Council also showed some evidence of a desire to compromise. In July the discussion of the Militia had finished with the declaration that Fascism could not do without it 'until the State has become integrally Fascist, until, that is, the succession to the former ruling class has been completely realized in all the administrations and institutions of the State'. The new programme sketched out in the October meeting confirmed this declaration : and the party was further reassured by the affirmation that it had 'scarcely begun its historic mission, which is that of giving the nation a new ruling class'. However the revolutionary force of Fascism's claim to constitute the new ruling class was considerably diminished by the recommendation that 'the party must make continual efforts to increase its political and moral efficiency by a cautious and qualitative work of proselytism, with an opportune sifting of unsuitable elements, and with the admission on request or *ad honorem* of all those who intend to collaborate in the reconstruction of national life.' This made clear that, as far as possible, the old ruling class was to be absorbed, not destroyed. The programme sketch further laid down the duty of the party to collaborate with the Government 'without public polemics', and finally, the previous solemn declarations of the independence of the Prefect from the party were reaffirmed and strengthened by the statement that 'the Prefect is responsible only to the Government, and must therefore act with absolute liberty within the limits laid down by the law.'[18] The new secretary of the party, Francesco Giunta, bluntly told his subordinates that they must be content with a role of reduced importance : 'it is time that the party realized that its only task is that of assisting the work of the Fascist government. It is time, that is to say, that Fascism recognized that with the coming of the Fascist government it has already achieved its ends as a party, and must from now on pursue its ends as a government.'

It was, however, the practical decisions on party organization which had the greatest importance. The old *Giunta* was replaced by a new *direttorio* of only five members, who would all reside permanently in Rome. Francesco Giunta replaced Bianchi as secretary; the other members of the *direttorio* were Cesare Rossi, Marinelli, Bolzon and Teruzzi. The inclusion of both Rossi and Marinelli in a directive body of only five members weighted it heavily in favour of Mussolini's personal entourage. However it is certain that in the measures for reorganization Mussolini had to compromise with the provincials. A draft for the composition of the *direttorio*, drawn up by Mussolini or with his approval, included besides Rossi, Marinelli and Teruzzi, the names of Michele Bianchi, Polverelli, Alfredo Rocco and Maurizio Maraviglia, the last as general secretary.[19] Of these, Polverelli was an old associate of Mussolini and leader-writer of the *Popolo d'Italia*, and Rocco and Maraviglia were both ex-Nationalists. The time was not yet ripe when Mussolini's design of putting the party leadership in the hands of a combination of ex-Nationalists and his personal clique could be realized. The party undoubtedly gained by the changes and particularly by the substitution of Giunta for Maraviglia as general secretary.

It was not only in the composition of the *direttorio* that the objections of the provincials made themselves felt. Farinacci and a group of *fiduciari* suggested an innovation in the structure of the party which greatly reduced the 'centralist' character of the reform. The new *direttorio* appointed by the Grand Council was only granted provisional status, and was to remain in office only until 12 January 1924. The provincial secretaries would then meet together under the name of the *Consiglio Nazionale* and propose a list of names for the permanent *direttorio*, from which Mussolini would then make his choice.[20]

Mussolini, however, did not keep the terms of his bargain with the provincials. Neither he nor his clique were satisfied with an arrangement which might restore the leadership of the party to a group of unknown nominees of the provincial secretaries. The meeting of the *Consiglio Nazionale* was postponed, and in the meantime Parliament was dissolved. When the meeting did take place (29–30 January 1924), therefore, it was overshadowed by the election campaign, which Mussolini used as a pretext for confirming the 'provisional' directorate in office. The *federali* were given no chance to state grievances or express their views on policy; afterMussolini and Giunta had spoken, the assembly, according to the disingenuous report published in the *Popolo d'Italia*, 'showed such lively enthusiasm, such warm agreement ... that the Rt Hon Mussolini, who had previously expressed the desire for a full discussion of the action of the Directorate of the Party, saw plainly that the debate would be useless'. But Mussolini's own speech revealed that all had not been in reality so harmonious : 'the provinces should not pay any attention to gossip, or to the wicked insinuations of our opponents, who attempt to devalue the work of persons who are near to me and of the highest rank in the party hierarchy.' 'The Duce answered that he had no counsellors, still less evil counsellors. He gives his attention to the smallest details and watches over the execution of every action of the Government and the party ... he knows even his most distant collaborators well.'[21] The myth of the omnipotent and all-seeing Duce was invoked by Mussolini himself to shield his entourage from criticism.

Predictably, however, Mussolini and his friends had much less success in their attempts to strike directly at the roots of the *ras*'s power in the provinces. Here the prospect of general elections worked in favour of the provincial bosses. The *ras* knew how to control their districts and they would deliver their votes by fair means or foul; moreover, it was essential that the party should remain as far as possible united, and that the threat of dissidence, made more serious again by competition for inclusion in the list of parliamentary candidates, should be circumscribed. In any case, long before the election campaign Mussolini and his collaborators had shown signs of a failure of nerve in their dealings with the *ras*.

The personal commitment of Finzi to the cause of normalization deserves belief; his attitude to the *ras* was less ambivalent than that of Mussolini himself, and his hostility to them was amply repaid. One grateful correspondent spoke of 'your holy crusade against the *ras*'.[22] Among the *ras* Baroncini had held a position second only in importance to that of Farinacci. His efforts in organizing the *fasci* and the unions of Bologna had earned a public tribute from the Grand Council, and even in November, when his loyal Prefect, Aphel, reported that he intended to resign unless he received some reassurance that the Duce had not lost confidence in him, the Duce duly obliged.[23] His fall in December was thus a major event, and at first sight a great victory for Finzi's 'crusade'; but the real causes of his downfall were more complicated and less creditable. One of the chief architects of his disgrace was none other than Augusto Regazzi, the brutal boss of Molinella, whose excesses had first provoked Finzi's protest. His latest crime, the murder of a peasant, Pietro Maran, had for once been publicly exposed. Yet at the height of the revisionist controversy, Finzi telegraphed to the Prefect of Bologna asking him to see that 'excessive sanctions' were not taken against Regazzi and his accomplices.[24]

The ambiguous significance of Baroncini's fall becomes apparent. Unquestionably his position was deliberately weakened and undermined by the central government, first through public criticism, and then by the replacement of the Prefect Aphel by Bocchini who, it is fairly clear, was given instructions to work for his overthrow. On the other hand, the Government deliberately refrained from pressing their attack on him, and indeed prevented his resignation until they were assured that a powerful opposition group had been formed behind Grandi. This local opposition was certainly not motivated by sympathy with the Government's normalization campaign; apart from purely local and personal rivalries, which made the Fascists of Imola, for example, prefer their co-citizen Grandi, it was in fact inspired by agrarian and industrial interests, who objected not to Baroncini's violent methods but to his radical postures. Baroncini wished to make the party and its dependent institutions into an independent economic force, which would impose the 'interests of production', if need be, even on the landowners and small industrialists.[25] Although he had always co-operated with Regazzi and the extreme wing of the agrarian reactionaries in their onslaughts on Molinella, it is probable that the August offensive had been designed to answer the criticisms which this wing of the party had already voiced of his leadership, and to unite the 'province' against the interference of government. The agrarians were successful in defeating Baroncini, but they did not succeed in replacing his influence by that of Grandi. The quarrel among the provincial Fascists gave Arpinati, who still controlled the city *fascio*, the chance to play the decisive role. Although an intransigent, Arpinati was also an old friend of Mussolini, who put far more trust in him than in either Farinacci or Baroncini. The outcome of the Bologna affair, therefore, strengthened Mussolini's grip on the party by restoring the leadership of perhaps its most important federation to an ally, but it was not a victory for normalization or revisionism.

The revisionist crisis did have some local repercussions. It encouraged urban Fascist groups and leaders to contest the dominion of their opponents, entrenched in the provincial federations, and it gave private citizens the courage to protest to the Government about some of the more bizarre excesses of the *ras*. One leading *ras*, Barbiellini, offered his resignation. However it was not until April that his opponents finally brought about a crisis which led to his fall.[26] In Turin the attempted expulsion of Rocca caused Mario Gioda and his group of old urban Fascists to denounce their fragile agreement with De Vecchi; in this case the revolt was temporarily successful. Gioda was re-elected secretary of the Turin city *fascio* in December, and he succeeded in getting rid of the friends of De Vecchi and the Nationalists who had previously formed the majority of the *direttorio*.[27]

However in Liguria the revisionists were definitely unsuccessful. This was in part because of the complicated interrelation of industrial with political feuds. Rocca himself and his ally Giuseppe Mastromattei, who represented the founding group of Genoese Fascism, were supporters of the Perrone brothers, the Ansaldo and the former directors of the Banca di Sconto. Pala, Lantini, and the new dominant faction in Ligurian Fascism, on the other hand, were in the pay of the Odero shipbuilding firm and the interests linked to the Banca Commerciale. The Ansaldo group, since their financial disaster, supported the *sindacati* in the hopes of weakening their opponents, and even defended the cause of Captain Giulietti. Rocca thus appeared locally as the friend of bankruptcy and of what almost amounted to 'subversion', whereas his opponents had the backing of one of the most powerful capitalist groups, whose support the Government, as well as Ligurian Fascism, desired. This was a grave weakness in Rocca's position, which did much to aid his final defeat in May 1924.[28]

The situation in Florence was unusual in that here it was the provincial federation who supported Rocca and the city *fascio* which stood for the intransigents. This probably reflects on the one hand the peculiar tradition of plebeian violence of the *fascio autonomo*, led by Tamburini and glorified by Malaparte, and on the other, the weight in the provincial federation of the respectable upper classes, who wished to avoid violence and had misgivings about the Fascist 'masses'. Even here, however, the attack on the provincial secretary Zimolo for his part in expelling Rocca was led by Ezio Lascialfare, one of the urban old guard, who had played a leading part in the reconstitution of the Florence *fascio* in 1920.[29] On the whole, however, the result of the revisionist campaign did not shake the power of the provincial oligarchies. The party elections of December 1923 disappointed the hopes of Cesare Rossi for a spontaneous 'revision' of the leadership from below. In part, this was due to the insufficient energy showed by Giunta in securing the freedom of vote and discussion; but one must also reckon with the fact that the structure of provincial Fascism made plebiscitary methods almost obligatory. Moreover Mussolini and the Government were hesitant about encouraging the dissidence of the city Fascists, except where they could call on reliable leaders such as Gioda and Arpinati. In Parma, for example, the Government turned a deaf ear to appeals from the Corridonian syndicalist faction and aided the victory of the agrarian wing, which had close connections with Farinacci.[30] We have already noted a similar contradiction in the attitude of the *Comitato Centrale* at the time of the Pact of Pacification. The need to keep radical tendencies under control was even stronger than the wish to dismantle the strongholds of the *ras*.

The failure of revision from below meant that new methods had to be found to reduce the party to obedience and to secure the position of Musso-lini's friends. Giunta was not by temperament or past history a very satis-factory secretary to preside over a new course for the party. He was not without a certain sympathy for the *ras*, and he succeeded, even more than his predecessors, in discrediting the authority of secretariat and *direttorio* by using his powers to eliminate his personal enemies and advance his friends. Rossi and Marinelli therefore decided, presumably with Musso-lini's knowledge and approval, that their objective in the next stage must be to eliminate Giunta. Moreover they still had to face the threat of the *Consiglio Nazionale*, which was scheduled to meet once the elections were over. They now put into action a plan of remarkable subtlety. To the general surprise, at the last minute Rossi decided not to stand for Parliament; Marinelli had never been a candidate. On 15 March 1924, while the electoral campaign was still in progress, the Grand Council passed a somewhat vaguely worded motion against 'the combination of offices'. In their next session, after the elections, the Grand Council interpreted this motion as signifying that 'the combination of party office with government office is not admitted'; no deputy could hold office either in the central *direttorio* of the party, or as provincial secretary. This 'incompatibility resolution' gave a dominating position to Rossi and Marinelli who, not being deputies, formed part of the new 'provisional' directorate of four, together with the ex-Nationalist Forges-Davanzati and Alessandro Melchiorri, neither of whom had previously formed part of the leadership.[31]

The reconstruction of the directive organ of the party, before which Mussolini had hesitated in October, could now be said to be complete. In addition, as the many provincial secretaries who had been elected deputies now had to be replaced, the meeting of the *Consiglio Nazionale* to ratify the *direttorio* could again be postponed till June. In the meantime, the *direttorio* would be able to exert all its influence in the choice of the new provincial

secretaries. The circular of the new *direttorio* to the provincial federations
on 29 April warned (somewhat ineffectively) that there must be no discussion
of the incompatibility resolution, and added that the election of substitute
provincial secretaries must be 'a simple expression of the will of the single
fasci (or federations) who are not bound by any previous manifestations'.
The same circular attacked 'that litigious and paralysing localism, which is
so often overrated and held to be the quintessence of Fascism'.[32] The
incompatibility ruling marked the climax of the long battle to reduce the *ras*
to order and to put Mussolini's own entourage in control of the party.
Whether the manoeuvre of Rossi and Marinelli could have succeeded
remains a matter for speculation, since the murder of Matteotti abruptly
cut short their progress and opened a new phase in the history of Fascism.

The Party in the South

The causes which produced the rise of Fascism in the North and Centre of
Italy were largely absent in the South. The most convincing proof that
Fascism was essentially and literally a reaction can be seen in the fact that
before 1922 it took root only in those areas of Italy where there was a strong
Socialist party. This point stands out with especial clarity in Southern Italy.
Southern Fascism suffered from the lack of an enemy. In Apulia, in Naples
and its environs, and in the provinces of Syracuse in Sicily, all regions in
which (in decreasing order of intensity) socialism had made a real impact,
a Fascist reaction more or less on the northern model duly followed.[33]
Elsewhere in the South there were only isolated pockets of Socialist, and
consequently Fascist, strength, as for instance in the mines of Iglesias in
Sardinia. It is true that Fascism did gain a number of converts among the
petty bourgeoisie of the larger towns, especially in the spring of 1921, when
it looked as if the movement might be a useful vehicle for electoral success.
However these *fasci* lacked the dynamism of their northern counterparts
and never succeeded in attracting more than a small fraction of the middle
classes, who remained in the majority indifferent to the movement.

When in the summer of 1922 it became clear that there was a very strong
likelihood that the Fascists would get at least a partial share in the government, the *fasci* at last began to multiply throughout the South, and after the
March on Rome their growth became precipitous.[34] But this growth reflected the traditional governmentalism of the South, and the desire of
personal clienteles to jump on the bandwagon before their opponents.
A Calabrian Prefect, trying to explain why the numerical expansion of the
party should be viewed with some scepticism, put his finger on the difference
between northern and southern Fascism :

In the rest of the province the *fasci* have a larger following, but since there could
be no reaction to Bolshevism where there was none, they are based essentially on

local contests, and I ask myself how far they are really worthy of confidence . . . the Fascists are not always united or in agreement, since in essence the aim of most of them is to substitute new *camarillas* for those already in existence.[35]

Politics in the South had always centred on the contests between rival personal factions for the control of the town halls and the distribution of central government favours : Fascism had to adapt itself to this traditional mode of politics. Already in the North Socialist and Popolari communal administrations had been ejected by force; southern faction leaders reasoned that the prestige of Fascism and its influence on the Government would authorize them to use similar tactics against their enemies. For this reason, it is reasonable to assume that the first Southern *fasci* were usually founded by the local opposition, the 'outs': the party which wanted to dethrone the one in power transformed itself into a *fascio* with the intention of obtaining by violence what it could not obtain by legal methods. The situation was further complicated by the emergence of the Nationalists as a major force. What happened was simply that where one faction founded a *fascio*, its rival responded by putting its men into blue shirts, thus denying the former their hoped-for monopoly of patriotic zeal.[36]

Intimidation had always played a great part in Southern politics. This took the form not only of the recruitment of bands of thugs for specifically political purposes – the notorious '*mazzieri*' denounced by Salvemini – but also, in certain regions, of an alliance between the politicians and the forces of organized crime. The March on Rome opened new prospects for the use of violence under 'patriotic' colours. Fascists and Nationalists rivalled each other in their haste to recruit the members of the underworld. In a speech to the provincial Fascist Congress of Bari on 28 December 1922, Starace issued a warning remarkable for its frankness : 'Do not let yourself be led astray by the stupid prejudice that the convicted criminal dressed in a black shirt is an element of strength.' The aim of Fascism should be to assist the 'rehabilitation' of criminals : 'But the black shirt must not be worn by them. . . . I have witnessed a very sad phenomenon. In a place where neither a *fascio* nor a nationalist branch existed, at the moment when their foundation was decided there was a race to see who could come first in recruiting the experienced hooligans.'[37]

There was, however, another side to Southern Fascism. The officers and students who were mainly responsible for founding the first *fasci*, before the movement became generally fashionable in the South, saw in the old clienteles their principal enemy. Another and contradictory consequence of the weakness of the mass parties in the South was, in fact, that it left room for Fascism to exercise a more radical function than was possible in the North. It could, that is to say, attempt to become a populist movement which would mobilize the masses directly and eliminate the mediation of the old politicians. The young Fascist officers might fulfil a somewhat similar role to that performed by the military in certain underdeveloped countries in breaking the hold of a restricted and corrupt parliamentary class. In the immediate postwar years the ex-combatant movement had in fact made itself the vehicle for the new aspirations aroused in the petty bourgeoisie and at least a part of the peasantry by the war : might Fascism not take up its heritage ?[38]

The idea of a Fascism that would see its *raison d'être* primarily in the uprooting of the old clienteles was personified by Aurelio Padovani. Padovani was a sincere idealist ; he had kept intact, in all its ingenuous simplicity, that romantic faith in the redemption of Italy which had inspired so many young officers, whether they followed Mussolini, D'Annunzio, or even Salvemini. His ideal was that of an authoritarian but radical dictatorship. Although the force of Fascism in Naples was undoubtedly, as in the North, derived from its violent anti-Socialist offensive, and the movement had been lavishly financed by rich traders and industrialists, Padovani had preserved a real degree of independence from his backers. He favoured a vigorous development of the Fascist unions ; if these made little headway among the workers in the steel and engineering industries, who remained faithful to socialism, in the docks and among the workers in the paper and textile factories of the Liri Valley, where class consciousness was less developed, they were able to acquire a considerable following. All this displeased the local bourgeoisie ; but even more alarming was the determination with which he sought to impose his line of rigid and intransigent exclusion of the old clienteles upon the Fascist movement elsewhere in Campania.[39]

It seemed at first as if this strategy had the wholehearted support of Mussolini : in his interview with the Neapolitan newspaper *Il Mattino* just before the March on Rome he had declared 'The task of Fascism in Southern Italy is that of breaking up personal clienteles and political localism', and in his famous speech at the San Carlo theatre he sounded the same note.[40] On the other hand, the leaders of the Fascist movement showed an ominous evasiveness when Padovani tried to initiate a serious discussion of policy. At the meeting held in Rome on 7 September to discuss the problems of the South, Padovani attacked those northern Fascists who conceived of the movement's role in terms of a work of 'colonization'. Instead, the aim of the party should be to help the South to stand on her own feet and thus to bring about her 'political and moral resurrection'. This could only be done if the movement remained on guard against the 'pseudo-Fascism' of opportunist converts. Massimo Rocca replied that the redemption of the South was an 'essentially technical problem . . . of roads, railways and land reclamation'. There was certainly much truth in this, and indeed one of the grave weaknesses of Padovani and his like was that they showed little understanding of such questions ; but Rocca did not explain how the solution of the problems he mentioned would be compatible with the general programme of financial retrenchment which he also advocated, and on this as on later occasions the appeal to technical expertise served as an excuse for avoiding difficult political choices. At the Naples Congress itself in October 1922, which was supposed to be a proof of Fascism's new interest in the South, the debate on Southern problems for which Padovani pressed, with the support of Farinacci, was first delayed and then cut short by Michele Bianchi.[41]

After the March on Rome Padovani built up an impressive concentration of powers. As *alto commissario* and zone commander he exercized supreme authority over both party and Militia throughout Campania; the subordinate *federali*, Tecchio at Naples, Di Lauro at Caserta and Adinolfi at Salerno, were all his friends and political allies, and the leaders of the *sindacati* were devoted to him. Unquestionably Padovani still had no rival to his authority over Campanian Fascism; the critical question was rather the importance of the whole movement and its relevance to Mussolini's political needs. Padovani drew his strength from Naples and, in lesser measure, from the other large cities of the region. In the rural areas, the old traditions of private agrarian or electoral terrorism and the *camorra* were successfully revived under the name of Nationalism. Moreover Padovani's intransigence could not prevent the Fascist movement itself from being infiltrated by the traditional clienteles. He and his lieutenants intervened energetically to check this process, reprimanding and dissolving those local *fasci* where the degeneration was most flagrant; but very often they could only succeed in replacing one clientele by its rival. Old supporters of Nitti and influential Freemasons were prominent among his own personal following.[42] He had no ties with the peasantry who remained for the most part under the dominion of the old bosses.

The Nationalist-Fascist fusion brought about Padovani's downfall. Even after the national agreement, he remained naïvely confident that his devotion to Mussolini would be rewarded by the latter's support. He refused to admit the local Nationalist leader Paolo Greco and his rural clienteles to the party. Forced by Padovani's stubbornness to choose between him and his opponents, Mussolini repudiated his loyal lieutenant. His resignation from the party and the Militia provoked a massive demonstration of solidarity, but he refused for the time being to organize a secessionist movement and ordered his supporters to rejoin the movement.[43]

Padovani was sacrificed to the needs of Mussolini's general political strategy. His intransigence had been an obstacle not only to the fusion with the Nationalists, but also to the winning of the votes of the Southern deputies, which Mussolini needed so badly for the passage of the Electoral Reform Bill. Moreover, by the time of the Padovani crisis, Mussolini was in possession of information which might well lead him to be sceptical of the possibilities of a true Fascist movement taking root in the South. There was the character of the people to be considered: compared with their northern counterparts, the masses of the South had given little trouble. They were still in the main docile, traditionalist, and politically ignorant. They could be relied upon to give their passive acquiescence to any government, provided certain prejudices were respected. Such were the views which Mussolini heard from his informants, and there was much truth in them.

The affair of the *soldino*, on the other hand, showed that the misery of the South could be exploited by the opponents of Fascism. The Fascists suspected Orlando of complicity, but this was almost certainly unjust.[44] However the old political leaders, while they did not, probably, take any part in organizing the demonstrations, nonetheless could not avoid expressing a certain satisfaction. Indeed they were the political victors, for the time being. They could appear as the champions of the injured feelings and interests of their various regions, and their warnings against the 'incomprehension' and impatience of the young Fascist hotheads received impressive confirmation. It was, of course, in Sicily that the regionalist card could be played most effectively; as in Sardinia where, however, the old politicians were no longer in control, strong resentment had been aroused by the highhandedness of a movement and government which appeared as an artificial foreign transplant. But everywhere, even on the mainland, the 'peculiar susceptibilities', or the 'special psychology', of the natives could be adduced as a reason for leaving the *status quo* undisturbed. Against the sure prestige of great and respected names such as Orlando or De Nicola, what had Fascism to offer? An 'idea': but in the South ideas were judged by the reputation of the men who put them forward.[45] Here there was an almost inescapable dilemma. Intransigence meant the search for the 'new man' not compromised in old party struggles; but this usually meant the promotion of 'men whom no one respects', 'youths of undoubted faith but no moral authority'.[46] Since scarcely any career was independent of politics, it was indeed generally reasonable to equate the absence of political ties with either inexperience or deserved obscurity. These were fatal handicaps in the South, where personal status and popularity were all-important, and public opinion did not share the Fascists' messianic belief in the virtues of youth. Moreover Fascism in this first phase had not offered the South much in concrete terms: financial retrenchment had hit public works badly, and it was observed that while work on the new harbour of Messina was suspended, funds were still found for the construction of the first autostrada, from Milan to Como. At a lower level, in the dark undergrowth of politics, Fascism was not at first much better placed. It could only win votes or support through the medium of the indispensable *grandi elettori* – mayors, landowners, town clerks, successful lawyers and other notables, and the organizers of co-operatives. The same was even true of the exercise of violence, at least in those regions where organized crime had long been a political factor. *Squadrismo* was not impressive in a countryside which knew the Mafia.

An intransigent Fascism would risk alienating this powerful class of intermediaries, who would be able to play on the fears of the 'amorphous mass' of respectable opinion, or on popular monarchist sentiment, already aroused by the daring republican pronouncements of Padovani and a few others. Instead, a Fascism which appeared in governmental guise, in which the party was reduced to a secondary role, had much more possibility of success. The *grandi elettori* could be depended upon to join the winning side in large numbers once they were assured of the stability of its victory, and the remainder could then be isolated and eliminated without difficulty.Moreover the slogan of 'strong government' and the myth of the Duce had a natural popular appeal. 'Mussolinism' could succeed where Fascism, in any more specific sense of the word, had failed. Perhaps the particular situation of the South was not without its effect on the increasing tendency of Mussolini during 1923 to bypass the party and present himself as the friend of all 'good Italians'.[47]

There remained, however, the problem of how the sickly Fascist movement in the South could be kept going and made reasonably stable. The Padovani crisis, demoralizing as its outcome must have been to the handful of sincere Fascists, in a sense simplified the problem, except in Campania where it left a serious and long-lasting heritage of dissidence. The attempt to ignore the old personalist parties had in most cases led to nothing except confusion. Starace had denounced Sicilian Fascism as 'opaque': the *alto commissario* Villelli had bravely replied that it had been 'luminous' until corrupted by association with a government in which notorious members of the old order like Carnazza and Di Cesarò took part, but his answer was not convincing.[48] The intransigents saw as their task the building of a 'new, young, ruling class', but where were the elements from which this could be constructed? The inexperience and lack of influence of the first Fascists usually led them to become the dupes and instruments of the old clienteles, with the result that their faction struggles were carried on within the new movement. This result, in turn, discredited Fascism and strengthened the prestige of the old leaders.[49]

However the more intelligent of the intransigents were able to produce telling criticisms of the course taken by Fascism in the South. Fascism failed to evolve a consistent strategy towards the other political groups, or to put forward a programme which would arouse enthusiasm. One critical issue was that of relations with the combatants. Admittedly in most regions the combatant movement had lost its original capacity for innovation, and its fragments had been absorbed into personal groupings of the familiar type. But the structure of Southern politics had not been wholly unaffected by the social changes consequent upon emigration and the war.[50]

In some parts of the South there had been extensive changes in the distribution of landed property and in the level of wages; these had permitted a great expansion in the number of peasant proprietors.[51] The uncertainty of property rights and the legislation in favour of co-operatives occupying uncultivated land had the same effect as labour troubles in the Po Valley in inducing the old owners to sell out: but many of the situations brought into being by the peasant occupations of land remained unresolved.

Some land was still occupied illegally, or pending the settlement of litigation ; many owners who wished to avoid the alternatives of sale or dispossession had granted favourable leases to the peasant co-operatives. Social change, however, did not, as the optimists had hoped, bring the breakdown of the old political structure in the South. However if the patron-client relationship remained unimpaired, at least the nature of the services expected from the patron had changed and broadened. Even the rudimentary degree of organization achieved by his clients meant that he was forced to take account of interests that were not those of individuals, but of collectivities or even classes. The corollary of this is that, while Southern politics remained based on personal interests, ties and antipathies, it would be a mistake to regard all clienteles as perfectly equal in value. Some had a strong bias towards the interests of the peasants ; others, towards those of the landowners. Fascism was pushed and pulled in opposite directions. One might have expected that the leaders of the Fascist movement would have exercised a strong preference in favour of those groups where the combatant element was still prominent, and would have discriminated against those headed by neutralist Giolittian deputies. But any such principle was soon abandoned. In so far as any principle of discrimination was adopted, it worked against the combatants. Fascism showed a conservative bias, in part dictated by divisions of national politics. 'Nittians' were (with many personal exceptions) treated as the enemy No 1, and Social-Reformists were also suspect. While the majority of the deputies in these groups were in fact pretty conservative, they also contained most of the younger politicians and the patrons of combatants and peasant co-operatives.

The only region in which Fascism opted decisively for an alliance with the combatants was Sardinia. Here the circumstances were exceptional. The young officers who led the combatant movement had been able to mobilize large masses of the peasantry behind a programme of regional autonomy, and had founded the Sardinian Action Party, which won four out of twelve seats in the 1921 elections. The local Fascist movement was weak, and the actions of the Sardinian *squadristi* only succeeded in arousing sympathy for their opponents. Mussolini soon came to appreciate the risk that a repressive policy might provoke a serious popular revolt. With characteristic flexibility, he repudiated the local Fascists and sent General Gandolfo to the island with the aim of dividing and absorbing the forces of the Action Party. This policy was highly successful. In the province of Cagliari most of the cadres of the Action Party passed over to Fascism, and Gandolfo was able to claim that he had ensured the triumph of the 'young forces' over the 'old cliques'. But this was an exceptional result, not paralleled in other regions.[52]

The history of Fascism in Sicily shows clearly how the movement came to rely for preference on the most conservative elements in society. In the island the impact of the social changes described had been considerable, greater than on most of the mainland. But the new political climate brought about by the March on Rome restored the confidence of landed property and halted the process of the formation of new peasant property. The 'national government's' decided opposition to 'bolshevism' in any shape or form brought immediate benefits to the great landowners; the bill for the division of the *latifondo* was dropped, and the Prefects began to take a more severe view of land occupations. However the aristocracy and landowners of Sicily, while they might give credit to Mussolini for the improvement, were nonetheless slow to acknowledge the merits of Fascism as a movement, or else their Fascist sympathies found no easy means of expression within the contorted structure of island politics. The old parties, which were really alliances of clienteles, resisted Fascist penetration and absorption more stubbornly than elsewhere in the South. The organizers of the Fascist movement marched confidently into a labyrinth where no path led in the expected direction. They were faced by an intricate network of personal alliances and temporary coalitions formed for the pursuit of electoral success or governmental favour. The results were grotesque. Neither Mussolini nor the busy agents of the national movement, such as Starace, who descended periodically on the island for tours of inspection, could make the movement either independent or strong. Although in Palermo and elsewhere a limited alliance was eventually concluded with the combatants' leaders, it was generally agreed by Fascist critics as well as by opponents that the movement had failed to inherit their popularity. Fascism was content in the end to live and let live, and to rely on opportunist converts to supply it with a following. 'The convert St Paul was one of the greatest apostles of Christianity,' so why should Fascism reject the help of the old politicians?[53] In Agrigento, the former Democrazia Sociale deputy Abisso became the leader of local Fascism. In this case, since he was the patron of the combatant co-operatives, they obtained the movement's protection.[54] However in Messina, the local landowner and agrarian deputy, Crisafulli Mondio, was made *federale* after a particularly gloomy set of failures which culminated in the affair of the *soldino*: he was hostile to the combatants.[55]

The case of Catania will serve to illustrate, in an extreme form, the comedy of errors typical of Sicilian Fascism. The politics of Catania had for some time been polarized around two old and well entrenched factions. One of these, headed by the Carnazza brothers, was of the most orthodox type, based on government influence, local wealth and inherited family prestige. Gabriele Carnazza was one of Giolitti's most faithful Southern supporters, and he had been a minister in his government during 1920–1. The rival faction had more unusual sources of strength. It could trace its origins back to the one great movement of social protest which the island had known since unity, that of the *fasci* of 1892. After the movement had subsided, first broken by repression and then undermined by emigration, a relic survived in the shape of the extraordinary personal popularity enjoyed by one of its leaders, De Felice Giuffrida. When De Felice died, his vast clientele, if not his personal charisma, was inherited by Vincenzo Giuffrida, who had been one of Nitti's young men in the civil service, flanked by two other deputies, Macchi and Saitta. They had gained a firm grip over the local combatant movement. The *giuffridiani*, as this faction were now called, did not rely on popularity alone to counter the superior financial resources of the Carnazzas. De Felice's terrible bands of goatherds had long enjoyed notoriety, and the faction could count on a large armed following in many of the communes around Catania.[56]

The supporters of Giuffrida controlled the communal council of Catania ; the Carnazza faction therefore used the March on Rome as a pretext for carrying out their own local coup. On 31 October the town hall was unexpectedly occupied by a group of 'Fascists and Nationalists'. Other Nationalists occupied the offices of the provincial council and the city hospital, and on the following day a group of 'legionaries and *arditi*' occupied the neighbouring town hall of Giarre. All these actions had the support of the Prefect, Flores, a prominent client of Nitti, who seems to have turned decisively against his former allies, perhaps in an unsuccessful attempt to live down his past. Flores reported that two hundred Giuffrida supporters, 'mainly goatherds', had held a demonstration of protest against the Fascist party, and that the trade unions were preparing to retake the town hall by force.[57] On 2 November he asked the Ministry for police reinforcements to help defend the town hall, and reported that he had sent fifty *carabinieri* with a machine-gun to Palagonia to forestall 'an imposing concentration' of Giuffrida's combatants.[58] His attempt to present these incidents as the product of a straightforward conflict between Fascists and anti-Fascists was not, however, altogether successful. The deputy Saitta denounced the activities of 'the partisans of the Minister Carnazza and his brother Carlo, notorious neutralists', and his protest seems to have had some effect on Finzi, who urged impartiality and the restoration of the occupied town halls on the Prefect.[59]

When Starace arrived to carry out an inquiry for the party, he had no difficulty in realizing that the Carnazza faction had made a take-over bid for Fascism. Asked by an interviewer, 'What can you tell me about the devotion of the *carnazziani* for Fascism ?', he replied, 'The deception has been cleared up, unmasked : Fascism at Catania is now going forward on its road, without concerning itself with this or that leader of the now obsolete clientele parties.' He even showed a slight preference for Giuffrida, whose forces, he said, were superior to those of Carnazza.[60]

Starace's optimism about the progress of Fascism did not prove justified. The Prefect at first prudently agreed in forecasting the sure success of a Fascism independent from the factions, but he observed that 'internal crises in the party, inevitable in the period of consolidation, have for the moment kept at a distance from it those persons most conspicuous for wealth or culture.' His own efforts were directed to securing the support of the agrarians and the traders.[61] Flores' strategy, designed to make Fascism into the party of the rich and the *benpensanti*, was at variance with the policy of the *alto commissario* of the PNF for Sicily, Gennaro Villelli. Villelli, the founder and organizer of Fascism in Messina, seems to have wished to pursue an intransigent line, like Padovani in Campania, but without the latter's prestige or resources.[62] The attempt to create an intransigent Fascism, independent of the clienteles, led only to chaos and confusion. Personalities were all-important in Sicilian politics, and the leaders of the Fascist party did not possess the indispensable 'moral authority'. Their internal feuds gave the Prefect his chance to eliminate the influence of Villelli and once more assume the uncontested direction of policy. The party was weak: 'nor for the moment can it be reinforced by the adherents of His Excellency Carnazza, since, by another grave error of local Fascism, its leaders persist in believing that they must oppose His Excellency Carnazza, despite the fact that his friends have always maintained an extremely correct attitude, and have not only not hindered Fascism in any way, but have instead in every way favoured it.' The only remedy was to entrust the direction of the *fascio* to a delegate chosen by him personally, who must be able to act freely without being subject to the 'interference of provincial or regional delegates'. The Prefect in fact demanded, and obtained, *carte blanche* for the reconstruction of the Catania *fascio*; it was entrusted to Colonel Liotta, an outsider whom Flores had previously installed as *regio commissario* for the temporary administration of the commune.[63]

However the new Fascism of the Prefect was no more successful. By this time the Giuffrida party, realizing that independence was unprofitable and fearing the passage of Macchi to Fascism, had changed tactics. They now encouraged their supporters to join the movement, and there was a rush of communal councils, combatant associations, unions and co-operatives to declare their sympathy for Fascism.[64]

Matters were now further complicated by the question of the Nationalist-Fascist fusion. The inexperienced Liotta was easily deceived and failed to check the influx of Giuffrida supporters. At Catania the Nationalist association was the creature of an extremely rich local deputy and landowner, Count D'Ayala. In the 1920 local elections, when Giuffrida and Carnazza had temporarily agreed to forget their differences and join forces, D'Ayala had unsuccessfully attempted to oppose them. However when the Giuffrida party broke with Carnazza in 1921, the latter allied with D'Ayala. The news of the fusion thus threw the Giuffrida party into dismay. The passage *en bloc* of the Nationalist branches to Fascism threatened to destroy their newly acquired strength within the movement. The new *fasci* in the rural areas included many of Giuffrida's most active followers, 'hardened fighters, quick to use their fists', who felt that the time had come to show strength under their new colours. On 21 April 1923, an enormous mob of Giuffrida supporters, most of them nominally enrolled in the *fasci*, occupied the city of Catania as a demonstration of protest against the fusion and in support of the existing secretary of the *fascio*, Ferro. It took the intervention of the disciplined Fascist Militia of the neighbouring province of Syracuse and the appearance of an armoured car manned by the *carabinieri*, to restore order.[65]

The 'March on Catania' spelt the downfall of Flores, never well-liked by the Government. However his policy triumphed. During later 1923, under the guidance of Starace, the party definitely allied itself with Carnazza, and collaborated with him closely over the question of the dissolution of the provincial council. In return, Carnazza himself joined the party at the beginning of 1924: he was an important convert to Fascism, since his defection weakened Di Cesarò and his Democratici Sociali just at the time when they were about to break with Fascism. The Government recognized his authority even outside his province; the Prefect of Syracuse (where the Fascist organization was strong) was ordered to keep in touch with him 'so as to find the right political line'.[66] An interesting comment on the choice made by Fascism in allying with Carnazza rather than Giuffrida comes from an authentic *diciannovista* Fascist and Futurist, Guglielmo Jannelli: 'behind De Felice there was the People, behind Carnazza there is Calculation, the Joint Stock Company, the Bank'.[67] The triumph of Carnazza was marked by the elections of 1924, in which he headed and organized the government list and wrote himself a record number of preference votes.

In the west of Sicily the Fascist party was still weaker than in the east. For this was the country where the mafia ruled. The dominance of the mafia restricted both the functions and the social support available for the creation of a Fascist movement. It guaranteed the suppression of peasant unrest and the maintenance of a kind of order, and it drew its strength from the rural middle class (the *gabellotti*) and the professional classes. The first Fascists announced their intention of fighting the mafia, but this proved a task for which the party was ill-fitted. The mafia was not a monolithic organization; there were murderous feuds between rival *cosche* (gangs), each boasting its own political patron among the deputies. Consequently, where the party attacked one mafia network, it served the interests of its rivals, who were able to use the fasci for their own purposes.

In the province of Trapani the situation was particularly confused. There was a contest between the 'old mafia' and the 'new mafia' of younger men who had made their mark during the war. The Fascist party in attacking the old mafia soon became involved with the new. The provincial secretary, Pellegrino, was reported by the Prefect 'to favour, albeit in good faith, persons notoriously affiliated to the mafia'.[68] However, the Prefect's own favourite, Avvocato Rubino, a 'worthy professional man', with 'widespread backing' was not above suspicion either. His candidature on the government list in the 1924 elections was supported by the mafia of Salemi and Trapani.

It seems reasonably certain that the leading figure in Palermo Fascism, Alfredo Cucco, himself had close ties with the new mafia.[69]

Mussolini for his part early saw the prestige to be gained by a campaign against the mafia. The Prefect of Palermo reported to him in May 1923 on the measures advisable. However, so long as elections continued, the campaign could only be half-hearted. The votes controlled by the mafia were too useful. Moreover, the mafia could to some extent play on Sicilian pride and suspicion of the North in order to mobilize popular support. The mafia put it about that the government 'has treated Sicily like a colony'[70] by withdrawing arms permits and threatening to introduce deportation.

For the time being, a kind of truce existed between Fascism and the mafia. The old mafiosi disliked Fascism. They were bound by personal ties to the liberal politicians, and they saw the threat inherent in the Fascist belief in strong government. In 1924 when Orlando joined the government list he found it hard to keep his *capi elettori* in line. However, the mafia had clearly every interest in seeking an accommodation with the government party so long as it was possible, and where local loyalties were not too strong, it usually did so. Fascism on its side accepted the support of the old deputies and of other 'respected' men. As late as 1925, the government still found it necessary to enlist the support of rival mafia leaders in the contest against Orlando and his supporters. The truce was disturbed by occasional embarrassments: during the 1924 elections the secretary of a local *fascio* interrupted a meeting of the pro-government candidate Pasqualino Vassallo with a cry of 'Down with the delinquents', which was interpreted by the rt hon. Pasqualino Vassallo as 'an offence to his friends'.[71]

Once elections and collaboration with the liberals had come to an end Mussolini had his hands free. In his campaign against the mafiosi he could count on the support of the landowners, whose rents they had intercepted. Moreover, the upper stratum of the mafia, the lawyers, doctors, and other professional men who had protected and profited from its criminal activities, were willing to abandon the more notorious criminals to their fate. The Prefect Mori broke the mafia by the use of ruthless police methods, including torture. This was an achievement which undoubtedly won Fascism a good deal of popularity and prestige. However, the mafia had been driven underground and not destroyed. The mentality and social relations which were the foundations of its power survived.[72]

The Fascist party failed to evolve a consistent or convincing strategy for the South. On paper the numbers of the *fasci* continued to grow, but only a small part of this expansion was due to genuine political commitment. The former Nationalist Nicolò Castellino, in a long memorandum on Fascist propaganda in the South, warned the leaders of the party against taking apparent successes too seriously.

First of all it is necessary to take note that up till now the work of propaganda in all that vast zone has been almost nil; the ease with which Fascist branches have arisen everywhere, even in small and remote villages, must not deceive us and make us believe that . . . the movement of national revival has been profoundly felt and that the Fascist idea therefore has won numerous and secure converts; unfortunately this is not so . . . almost everywhere there is a complete lack of knowledge of the ideas and principles which inspired the triumph of Fascism. The Fascist branches have multiplied and the battalions of blackshirts and blueshirts populated every angle of southern Italy for other reasons: the love of novelty, the romantic fascination of *squadrismo*, the spirit of imitation, and, above all, the aim of conquering local government.[73]

The weakness of the party in the South could hardly fail to make its relations with the State very different from those prevailing in the North and Centre. It is true that it was not unknown even in the South for a Prefect to be removed from office because he fell foul of the local Fascist leader :[74] but such occurrences were less frequent than in the North. Vice versa, it was not long before the Prefects began to acquire a growing influence over the local organization of the party, amounting in several cases to a real supremacy.

The Prefect in the South was still the pivot around which political life revolved. However this does not mean that his life was always easy or enviable, or that he relished his position as the broker of political influence. In the sleepy provincial capitals, 'where political life is carried on within a space fifty yards square', the Prefect was every day exposed to the interference of the deputies in the most minute details of his administration ; he was not always even master in his own house, since the lesser officials of the Prefectures often had close ties with the local politicians, who would be able to prevent their transfer or punishment, and it was impossible to satisfy one faction without discontenting another, with the result that he lived in a state of continual insecurity. 'The difficulties of the environment are such that it is impossible to preserve the necessary calm' ; 'I have asked to be removed from this hell even by enforced retirement' : it is hard not to acknowledge a note of genuine exasperation in these *cris de coeur*. There may, therefore, have been much sincerity in the hopes expressed by some Prefects that the advent of Fascism would lead to the end of the old systems of interference and corruption, and the realization of the impartial ideal of 'justice in the administration'.[75]

Unfortunately the failings of the Fascist movement were such that the Prefects' favourable expectations were not fulfilled. The new masters claimed the same rights of surveillance as the old, if not more, and the intrigues of the old clienteles, reproduced within Fascism, perpetuated the state of insecurity. Fascism, in short, was not what it ought to be ; and the more active Prefects, despairing of the possibility of normal collaboration with a movement so ill-organized, protean, and unstable, decided that the only remedy was to take it in hand themselves. 'It is necessary to intervene . . . to rectify errors . . . to form a true Fascist consciousness' :[76] this task could not be left, it was implied, to inexperienced hands. Flores' essay in prefectoral

Fascism at Catania was a resounding failure; but the precedent was none the less copied. Sardinia was a special case: Gandolfo, a Fascist official in the full sense of the term, acted as a kind of commissar uniting both party and State authority. Sardinian Fascism was in a sense largely his creation, since he had imposed the policy of absorption of the Sardisti which gave the movement a largely new leadership. Elsewhere after long contests the Prefects succeeded in ousting assertive or unpopular *federali* and imposing their own candidates for the direction of the movement. In October 1923 in Benevento, Clinio Ricci, one of the last surviving *federali* who had remained faithful to Padovani and his aims, finally fell victim to the Prefect's hostility; in Trapani, the *federale* was reported to be sustained and controlled by the Prefect; in Girgenti the *federale* Dima was slowly undermined and the Prefect succeeded in having his re-election quashed.[77] The Prefects had a natural preference for the rich and respectable, the *benpensanti*, and their influence on the development of Fascism in the South could hardly fail to be a conservative one. It was in the South that the model for some features of the later regime can first be found; the transformation of Fascism from an aggressive ideology, powered by *ressentiment*, into a tranquil official cult, the bureaucratization of the movement, and its subordination to the State.

9

EMPLOYERS AND UNIONS

Fascism can be viewed as a product of the transition from the market capitalism of the independent producer to the organized capitalism of the oligopoly. By a remarkable irony, while Fascism as a political movement originally gave expression to the revolt against the emergent forces of organized capitalism,[1] Fascism as a regime furthered its development and provided it with a theoretical justification. According to the definition of the Nationalist theorist Alfredo Rocco, 'the Fascist economy is . . . an organized economy. It is organized by the producers themselves, under the supreme direction and control of the State.'[2]

The link between the beliefs of the revolutionary syndicalist intellectuals and the final shape of corporativism is tenuous. The early syndicalists were free traders, suspicious of State action: mature corporative ideology was protectionist and *dirigiste*. However there was one thing in common between syndicalism and corporativism. This was the recognition of the importance of the new 'intermediate associations' between the citizen and the State whose rise accompanied the development of capitalism and mass politics.

In the postwar period, the problem of the role of interest groups in the formation of policy became a matter of general concern. Already in the period 1908–14 there had been increasing criticism of the incompetence of Parliament to legislate on technical, and especially economic and social, matters. The reformist leaders of the trade unions, used to negotiating wages directly over the table with employers, believed that the same methods should be applied to legislation, and that devolution to 'technical' bodies which directly represented the interests involved would ensure both quicker and better decisions.[3] After the war, however, the problem took on a new dimension. The great growth in the economic activities of the State and in the size of the bureaucracy during the war made it acute. Another novelty was the emergence of the Confederation of Industry (Confindustria) as a powerful and centralized pressure group, where previously there had been only the unco-ordinated initiatives of individuals or regional industrial associations. The secretary of Confindustria, Gino Olivetti, declared that 'the future is with organized classes'.[4]

There was general agreement over a wide spectrum of political opinion that parliamentary control was insufficient to check the collusion between the bureaucracy and organized industrial interests. The practice of legislation by decree-law enabled bureaucrats and industrialists virtually to elude parliamentary control altogether. It was easy to denounce this 'conspiracy' to defraud the tax-payer, the consumer and the peasant: but hard to find a solution.

The general dissatisfaction with orthodox parliamentary methods of control helped to create a fashion for syndicalist or 'guildist' schemes of representation. Mussolini spoke of this idea as the 'novelty' which was needed to give éclat to the Fascist programme; the CGL called for 'a constituent assembly of labour', and for the creation of a supreme economic council to control national production.[5] The industrialists on their side demanded the devolution of economic legislation to elected technical councils.[6] Some free trade spokesmen, like Salvemini, felt that the devolution of economic legislation to elected professional councils was the only way to break the stranglehold of the bureaucratic-protectionist *camarilla*.[7] Former anarcho-syndicalists like Massimo Rocca or Lanzillo who joined the Fascist movement believed that only the corrupting influence of politics prevented the laws of economic science from working correctly. They believed that in a syndically organized state conflicting interests would reach a natural adjustment; they saw the future Fascist state as a self-regulating technocracy, with the 'expert' as the final arbiter. These 'experts' would be drawn from the middle classes, who would thus acquire a decisive influence on economic decision-making.[8]

The most distinguished of the Liberal economists, Luigi Einaudi, had also at first seen the solution in direct bargaining between the representatives of interest groups. He had welcomed the rise of the trade unions and the agrarian and industrial associations because he thought that it would lead to the formation of 'a new, bold young class of entrepreneurs, farmers and workers, who will no longer put all their hopes in the State, but will have confidence in themselves . . . in the virtue of their own organizations.'[9] This was excessively optimistic. The regional associations of agrarians and industrialists had been formed primarily to fight wage claims: but the chief purpose of the national confederations was to exert greater leverage on government policy. Within the Confederation of Industry heavy industry soon became the dominant influence.

By 1919 Einaudi had come to recognize these truths, and he consistently opposed the argument that economic legislation should be left in the hands of the interested parties. The syndicalists and technocrats argued that professional representation, unlike the parliamentary system, would ensure that all interests were adequately and fairly represented; Einaudi replied that this would not be so. Councils of 'experts' would be, still more than Parliament, the natural allies of the bureaucracy; the system of professional representation would crystallize the existing relations of power and new industries would find it hard to make their voice heard, and the delegation of power to councils of workers and employers would increase their tendency to seek agreement at the expense of the consumer.[10]

Fascist propaganda assumed the defence of the middle class and the farmers against the 'parasitic' and protectionist alliance of labour and capital, 'demagogues and speculators'. This propaganda owed much to Pareto. Pareto's contempt for the Italian parliamentary system had its origins in his faith in the scientific validity of free trade principles. It followed, for him as for other free trade economists, that the good cause could only be defeated by a corrupt conspiracy. Even those economists like Einaudi, Giretti and De Viti De Marco, who remained faithful to Liberal political ideals, were attracted to Fascism by the movement's espousal of the cause of private enterprise, and the hope that it could break the nexus of interests which maintained high tariffs and high State expenditure. The young Ernesto Rossi, later to be one of the most tireless and courageous opponents of the regime and its social and economic policy, was at first drawn to Fascism by patriotism and by the moralistic fervour of his free-trade, pro-agricultural views.[11]

Liberismo, associated with the belief in sound money and a balanced budget, was the middle-class ideology par excellence; it reflected the interest in stable prices of the groups with fixed or inelastic incomes, rentiers, pensioners, civil servants and to a lesser extent employees and the professional classes. It was also compounded with that suspicion of the big firm, the big organization, and the machinery of government which, in its more extreme and paranoiac forms, has always provided much of the motive power for the Fascist movements.[12] The stabilization of prices was an aim which Fascism could not afford to forego; for the majority of middle-class Fascist supporters it was the essential task of the movement, and if it was not fulfilled many would return to Democratic sympathies. At the same time, small businessmen and traders, hard hit by the slump, shared the resentment of other middle-class groups against the 'policy of favours' for large industry. In particular, the Nationalistic attack on the policy of the big banks and international finance must have been popular with these groups. Small investors who had lost in the crash of the Sconto were encouraged to blame their misfortunes on the servitude of the Government to the Banca Commerciale, formerly associated with both Giolitti and Germany.

The middle classes and the agrarians were the backbone of the party, which often gave voice to their economic demands. However, corporative or syndicalist ideas, as Einaudi predicted, proved favourable to the interests of large-scale industry. The realization of the corporate State went hand in hand with the triumph of the great pressure groups over the middle-class Fascism of the party.

National Syndicalism and the Programme of Heavy Industry

The most coherent doctrine of 'national syndicalism' was to be found in the writings of the Nationalist Alfredo Rocco. The theory of Rocco was in stark opposition to the liberalism of an Einaudi. For Rocco, in fact, liberalism had been rendered obsolete by the dawn of a new age, the age of organization. 'The isolated individual, the inorganic and amorphous masses of individuals, who still dominate the whole of our political life, are worth nothing.'[13] Economic individualism and the law of supply and demand were just as outdated as the political principle of one man, one vote. The anarchy produced by the unrestrained conflict of powerful interest groups was not the consequence, he held, of the existence of 'syndicates', but of the false concepts of Liberal individualism which forced the State to remain neutral and disarmed. The State should recognize the importance of the syndicates, and 'should absorb them and make them its organs'. They were to be universal, obligatory and strictly controlled; rules for their conduct were to be laid down by the State; strikes and lock-outs were to be outlawed, and wage disputes were to be settled by special courts of high magistrates who would substitute the conscious determination of a 'just wage' for the impersonal workings of the law of supply and demand.[14] The programme outlined by Rocco was, in all essentials, that finally adopted by Fascism. The originality of Rocco's doctrine lay in the marriage of the doctrine of the omnipotent State as the source of all law and the point of reference for all values with the doctrines of corporativism, which originally had evolved out of the resistance of privileged classes to the growth of modern, centralized government. The 'intermediate association', for De Tocqueville a necessary check on the power of the State, which would otherwise overwhelm the isolated individual, for Rocco was instead to be a cog in the machinery which would ensure his subordination. The corporative principle meant that the individual must be subjected to the 'collectivity', and the collectivity to the State.

It is untrue to suggest that the ideas of Rocco were in absolute conflict with those of the Fascist syndicalists. Sergio Panunzio, perhaps the most authoritative among Fascist writers on the topic, agreed with Rocco in seeing the syndicates as subordinate organs of the State. There was, however, a significant difference in their conception of the process by which the corporate order was to be achieved. Panunzio hoped, unlike Rocco, that the shape of the new compulsory syndicalism would be evolved by and within the national syndicate movement: legislation would only complete the 'spontaneous work' of social forces.[15]

Rocco's corporativism was logically associated with protectionism and the theory of the controlled market. Unlike Liberal economists, he welcomed the rise of the trust and the cartel as a healthy reaction against anarchic *laissez-faire* individualism.[16] The formation of the Confindustria was correctly interpreted as a sign of the greater unity and coherence brought by the process of industrial concentration.

The Nationalists were the prophets of the new capitalism. They had hit upon a real deficiency in orthodox Liberal theories, even if their own economic proposals were often inspired by a naïve faith in the possibilities of national production overcoming all obstacles of location and comparative cost.[17] The association between the Nationalists and the trusts was not disinterested, or coincidental. Their paper, the *Idea Nazionale*, was financed by the steel and armaments industries; before the war, their chief patron was Dante Ferraris, a leading manufacturer of artillery and explosive shells.[18] In 1920 Rocco himself acquired the controlling interest in the paper, but the money was found for him by the Parisi Bank, which was linked to the Perrone brothers, who controlled the great Ansaldo armaments combine. During the summer of 1918, the Perrones had also come to terms with Mussolini. Immediately after he had concluded an agreement with Ansaldo for the finance of the *Popolo d'Italia*, Mussolini changed its title from 'a Socialist newspaper' to 'the newspaper of the combatants and the producers'.[19] Heavy industry, and the Perrone brothers in particular, were thus directly responsible for the diffusion of the ideology of 'productivism' or 'national syndicalism' by Mussolini as well as by its inventors, Rocco and Corradini. It was in the steel and armaments industries that the formation of trusts and the process of concentration was most marked. The problem of over-production had led the Banca Commerciale to promote the foundation of a steel trust in 1911, under the leadership of the Ilva combine.[20] The rapid expansion of wartime industry produced the formation of great integrated industrial complexes: while Ilva moved from steel production into engineering and shipping, Ansaldo did the reverse. Both of these firms at the height of their power had a capital of about 500 million lire; Ilva employed 50,000 workers, Ansaldo 111,000.[21] Behind these giants came Fiat, Breda and Terni, all of which had similarly expanded and diversified their interests. The banks were closely involved in this process of concentration; but while Ilva fell under the control of the Commerciale, in the case of Ansaldo the chief shareholders, the Perrone brothers, were successful in winning control over their main creditor, the Banca di Sconto.[22] This set the precedent for the fiercest and most unscrupulous financial battle of the postwar years, when the Perrones attempted to capture the greatest of all the banks, the Banca Commerciale itself. This attempt failed; but it had the result of creating two irreconcilably opposed groups in industry and finance.

The bitter hostility between the Commerciale, its friends and clients on the one hand, and the Ansaldo – Banco di Sconto complex on the other had important political consequences. The Commerciale faction comprised the industrial establishment, the authoritative and respected leaders of industry whose advice was sought by the Government, men like Ettore Conti and Silvio Crespi, Alberto Pirelli and Giuseppe Volpi, all of whom at one time or another held important public offices. If it was certainly not true, as his opponents asserted, that Giolitti was the creature of the Commerciale, the mutual ties between him and the bank were undoubtedly strong. The Credito Italiano, on which Agnelli, the founder of Fiat, had an important influence, also supported Giolitti.[23] On the other side, led by the Perrone brothers, were the majority of the new plutocracy of arms manufacturers, contractors, speculators and dubious adventurers operating in the twilight zone between industry and politics. This is, admittedly, too schematic a picture. The Commerciale had never abandoned a shrewd diversification of interests and was accused by its opponents of favouring the textile and other consumer goods industries at the expense of the industries vital for national defence; but the root of the rivalry with the Sconto was nonetheless in the conflict within the steel, shipping and armaments sectors, in which the BCI also had a very great stake.

The same qualification is necessary in relation to the political alliances of the two groups. The conflict between Giolitti and the Commerciale on the one side, and the Nationalists with the Sconto on the other, was clear enough. It dated from the days of intervention, when German and French capital were involved on the two sides. However the Perrone brothers, more surprisingly, also had ties with Nitti, a fact which certainly did not prevent the Nationalists from opposing the latter, but which did on the other hand help to exacerbate the conflict between him and Giolitti.[24] The relationships between economics and politics did not, as some historians appear to have thought, follow a tidy pattern in which given sectors of industry or combines were represented by corresponding parties. One should rather think of the industrialists as intelligent gamblers, who would for preference place bets on more than one runner in the political race.[25]

Nevertheless the difference in line, policy and outlook between the Banca Commerciale and the Sconto groups is clear. Giuseppe Toeplitz, the managing director of the Commerciale, wanted to restore the international economy, and viewed with some equanimity 'the deflation of those industries artificially expanded during and after the war'.[26] The men of the Sconto, who were no match for the Commerciale in the smooth manipulation of political contacts, revived the old interventionist war-cries of the crusade of 'national industry' against disloyal, international, pro-German finance. In internal affairs they accused the Commerciale of carrying on a 'secret and independent' policy during the occupation of the factories, by bringing pressure to bear upon the industrialists to give way and accept Giolitti's solution, and even of directly subsidizing the 'enemies of the bourgeoisie' in the extreme parties. Abroad, the sins of the bank were even greater; the Perrones attacked Toeplitz for:

. . . carrying out a plan of his own for expansion in the Balkans, unconnected with any national co-ordination of banks and industries . . . sinking hundreds of millions of national savings in countries in complete dissolution, which cannot be markets for our expansion because they are included in the sphere of influence of nations stronger than ours . . . he does not forward a national foreign policy, but leads our foreign policy towards goals which could even be anti-national.

In contrast, the Perrones pointed to 'Our ideal of an Italy which would be an end in itself, with a programme of union and greatness, reconstruction and expansion.'[27]

During the war, the need for expansion of production at all costs and the total failure in the first years to create an efficient check on the prices of military contracts and their accurate fulfilment, had led to a general 'worsening in economic psychology'. The rigorous calculation of costs and of comparative productivity had been made unnecessary by monopoly conditions and the possibility of retrieving economic mistakes through political pressure. The Perrones and many other industrialists failed to adjust to peacetime conditions. They continued to use their resources to finance a rapid and disorderly expansion, dictated by the search for quick, speculative profits rather than by the rationalization of their industrial structure; an alternative policy of investment designed to reduce costs and raise productivity would have eased the transition. The armament and steel manufacturers placed their hopes in the perpetuation of a high level of expenditure on arms, in high tariffs and, like Stinnes in Germany, in the continuance of an uncontrolled inflation which would wipe out their debts.[28]

The worldwide deflation of 1920 was fatal to the great armaments combines; the Banca di Sconto, controlled by Ansaldo, continued to pour new funds into the industry when the beginnings of the recession were already evident. After this, the Nationalism of the Perrone brothers and their spokesmen took on a more subversive note. Fascist attacks on the hidden hand of international finance capital, apparently motivated by petty-bourgeois resentments, were often inspired by the unsuccessful business rivals of the dominant oligarchy grouped around the Commerciale. It is significant that by 1922 the establishment-minded Nationalists seem to have abandoned their old allegiance and to have contracted ties with the Commerciale. The financial groups involved in the Sconto and Ansaldo, who retained considerable private resources, and the Banco di Roma, which was also approaching bankruptcy, put their money on the Fascist party:[29] they were threatened not only with ruin but with criminal prosecution for fraud.

The Industrialists and Fascism, 1919-22

In spite of their internal conflicts, the political self-confidence of the industrialists as a class grew greatly in the period 1910-20. The founders of the Confindustria and the Association of Joint Stock Companies were sharply critical of the pre-industrial mentality of a great part of the political class, made up predominantly of lawyers and professors.[30] The Government's attitude to labour relations was the point, naturally enough, of greatest friction. The movement of association among industrialists had at first been largely successful in its original and primary aim, that of checking the growth in the power of the trade unions. While this successful reaction continued, the attitude of the industrialists was complacent, and their leaders approved Giolitti's tolerant attitude to the labour movement. But the worsening of the economic situation and the success of the industrialists' reaction helped to radicalize the working classes and Giolitti, with universal suffrage imminent, became alarmed. The intervention of the Government to present a general lock-out in the Turin engineering and metallurgical industries of 1913 was regarded by the industrial leaders as a violation of the theory of neutrality in labour disputes.[31] This conflict marked the beginning of a change in the attitude of the industrialists towards the Government.

In the postwar period, there was a crescendo of complaints from industry that the Government was willing to buy social peace at their expense, and had sabotaged all efforts by the class to contain the offensive of labour. In 1919 the Confederation of Industry at first favoured a conciliatory policy, supporting the eight-hour day and schemes for profit sharing: but in response to the radicalism of the labour movement it soon returned to a tougher stance.[32] The climax came with the occupation of the factories, which revived many industrialists' suspicions of Giolitti and the political class in general. Some, it is true, appreciated the virtues of Giolitti's pacifying tactics; but the maintenance of his promise to bring in a bill for working-class participation in management kept opposition active. The Lombard industrialists proposed to boycott the law if it were ever passed.[33]

Public opinion demanded that those who had made huge profits during the war should be forced to bear a large part of the costs of postwar reconstruction. This demand, which was advanced not only by the Socialists but by the ex-combatants and by the early Fascists, was strenuously resisted. Industry succeeded in defeating the first attempt, by Nitti, to introduce a scheme for the compulsory registration of shares in their owner's name, and his project for a capital levy. But Giolitti, more determined, pushed these measures through; unfortunately, whereas in 1919 they would have helped to restrain inflation, in late 1920 they undoubtedly accentuated the general fall in investment. Resistance to these fiscal measures combined with the question of workers' participation and the general need to restore labour discipline to harden the mood of industry and to increase industrial support for Fascism.[34]

During 1921–2, the situation changed. The slump enabled the employers to recapture the initiative. Strikes were ineffective in a period when unemployment was growing and leading militants could be victimized. In industry, the direct effect of Fascist terror was in the main a secondary factor.[35]

However the more diffuse effects of the rise of Fascism, the 'revival of the bourgeoisie' and the general swing to the right, were undoubtedly crucial. Socialist pressures on the Government to restrain the employers' counter-offensive might have been successful, as in the past, had there been no countervailing threat from the Fascists. By the end of 1921, in any case, the industrialists had achieved many of their objectives; a new tariff marked the victory of the protectionists, Giolitti's legislation had been tacitly shelved, and new subsidies had been granted to the shipbuilding industry. By no means all, or perhaps even the majority, of the leading men of industry were prepared to concede that they owed these results principally to Fascism; they felt rather that their own methods of organization and influence had finally paid off. However the economic crisis continued: the fall in investment was accompanied by an unstable lira. All respectable opinion was united in demanding the return to a balanced budget in order to restore international confidence. The industrialists were determined, however, that the restoration of State finances and the stabilization of the lira which they invoked should not be achieved at their expense, and that, indeed, taxes affecting industry should be lightened to aid the recovery. They demanded a massive reduction in 'unproductive' State expenditure, to be achieved by the dismissal of redundant State employees and the reduction of wages. Now that the industrialists had recovered the initiative, they were even more critical of the weakness of the State as an employer. The spring and summer of 1922 saw a sustained offensive by the industrial associations to secure fiscal concessions and economies in the State administration; otherwise, they protested, general ruin would result.[36] In Parliament the campaign was conducted by an *ad hoc* formation, the Alleanza Economica Parlamentare, which besides the leaders of the industrialists and the agrarians included a number of Fascist deputies. The Fascist programme adopted all the main demands of the industrialists.[37]

De Felice has demonstrated that a large amount of the money which sustained the Fascist movement consisted of modest contributions from individual sympathizers, traders, small businessmen, professional people, etc., and this is a valuable corrective to the old and oversimplified idea that it was created and financed by a handful of powerful industrial magnates.[38] However De Felice's study, which is based on the records kept by the administrative secretary of the *fasci*, Marinelli, tends to underrate the importance of industrial support for Fascism. The regions of greatest Fascist strength – the Po Valley and Tuscany – contributed very little to the central fund administered by Marinelli: the backers of the movement financed the local *fasci* exclusively. Although in these regions the influence of the agrarians was predominant, this does not mean that subsidies from local industry were unimportant. There is evidence that the sugar industry in Emilia and the Veneto, the marble industry in Carrara, the shipowners of Livorno and the iron and mining industries of Piombino and the Valdarno all contributed heavily to the growth of Fascism.[39] In addition, it is certain that even in the highly industrialized regions of the North, although they were more amenable to control from Milan, the *fasci* received subsidies from industry which were not remitted to the Central Committee. This was the case in Liguria, in Piedmont and in much of the Veneto.

During 1922, the refusal of the local *fasci* to contribute to the central fund became general, so that Marinelli was handling a smaller proportion of the movement's total resources than previously.[40] However during the summer of 1922 subsidies from industry probably did decline somewhat, on account of the economic crisis, and also because the defeats already inflicted on the Socialists had led to 'diminished concern'.[41]

In addition, the finance of the *Popolo d'Italia*, which remained separate from that of the Fascist movement, was assured first by the Perrones, and later by the rival armaments magnate Max Bondi of Ilva and by a variety of other Milanese industrial interests.[42] It has often been suggested that light industry was less interested in Fascism than heavy industry,[43] and certainly in 1919–20 the Fascists, like the Nationalists, received most help from the war industries, who were directly interested in keeping up a high level of armaments expenditure. However with the expansion of provincial Fascism, other industries took a hand. For the textile industries, interested in exports, the reduction of labour costs was a still more urgent necessity than for the metallurgical industries which could offset higher costs by higher tariffs. Many textile factories were still dispersed in the countryside and recruited their labour force from peasant families. All the industries based on the transformation of agricultural produce (food, sugar, silk and hemp) had moreover an indirect interest in the level of agricultural wages. For this reason, it seems likely that light industry was closely involved with provincial Fascism.

In the first phase of the Fascist movement, it was the local *fasci* who were often bypassed and discredited by the fund-raising activities of Mussolini and the agents of the Central Committee, over whom they had no control. However with the expansion of provincial Fascism this relationship was often reversed. New leaders emerged, like Costanzo Ciano in Livorno, or Banelli in Trieste, who were the representatives of local industrial and commercial interests.[44] The Fascist movement was not directly subordinated to the leadership of the Confindustria : it would be vulgar Marxism to think so. One can speak in general terms of an alliance between industry and Fascism : but on both sides, in industry and in the Fascist movement, there were some who viewed the alliance with feelings ranging from suspicion to outright hostility. The Fascist movement was, rather, penetrated by a multiplicity of industrial and commercial groups, whose interests were only partially identical, and in some matters often in sharp conflict. The subterranean struggle fomented by these groups within Fascism helps to explain the growth of feuds within the party.

The Confindustria made use of Fascism to add strength to its pressure on the Government for concessions in economic policy ; but its leaders did not wish to identify their position too closely with that of the movement. The attitude of the secretary of the Confindustria, Gino Olivetti, and of the major industrialists of Turin remained faithful to the maxim that 'Fascism is one thing and industry another'. Olivetti rejected the idea that industry owed its salvation to Fascism ; he argued that the crisis had instead been surmounted by the determination and organization of the industrialists themselves.[45] The more optimistic and progressive industrialists believed that the idea of a revolution in industry had died a natural death, and that a sound working relationship could be established with the reformist trade unions, who now had the allegiance of the mass of workers. They were well aware that only a very small minority of the industrial workers, at any rate of those engaged in modern, large-scale production, supported Fascism, and they feared that the attempts of the movement to extend to the industrial cities the kind of coercive recruitment which had proved effective in the countryside would only lead to exasperation, disorder, and a revival of the revolutionary tendency.[46] These views were not, however, shared by all industrialists ; a number, to start with, the future President of the Confederation, Benni, had made direct use of Fascist help in re-establishing control over their own workers.

The two tendencies were substantially agreed in pressing for the immediate inclusion of the Fascists in the Government, but the Confindustria was not a party to the March on Rome, which at first came as a shock. The vague conservative fear of disorder, the fear that the movement might either fail, leading to a left-wing reaction, or if successful, take a republican direction, the concern with foreign opinion, which might be unfavourably impressed, and the strong residual doubts which remained of Mussolini's respectability and reliability, all combined to make the responsible 'captains of industry' favour a peaceful solution.[47]

It is true that the leaders of the Confindustria exerted pressure on Salandra to withdraw, in order to hasten the formation of a Mussolini government, but this was on 29 October, at a time when the issue had already been virtually decided. They were motivated not by a preference for Mussolini as Prime Minister, but by a desire to shorten the revolutionary interlude. Senator Conti refused to accept the Ministry of Industry, 'not desiring to participate in a government born of revolution', while another leading electrical industrialist, Giacinto Motta, had hoped that the March on Rome would be resisted by force.[48] However when the new Government had been formed and had received Royal investiture, the industrialists began to feel less nervous. In a fulsome communiqué they declared that they were willing 'to place themselves totally at the disposition of the Mussolini ministry'.[49]

The measures taken by the new Government soon showed an overriding desire to conciliate the interests of industry and property. The satisfaction with the national Government which the industrialists expressed in their public utterances was sincere and unfeigned. Industry, however, continued to look with some unease on the tumultuous and uncontrollable expansion of *squadrismo*; there were signs that this might even invade the sacred sphere of economic enterprise. The Chamber of Commerce of Naples, guilty of support for Nitti, was forcibly occupied; and it seems that some Fascist unions succeeded in creating squads of their own.[50] Aside from these marginal disturbances, there was a more general dislike and fear of open terrorism. Terror was at odds with the rationality of modern industry. In a city like Turin, the industrialists were proud of the superior quality of their work-force, and aware that it had one weapon of protest always to hand, namely emigration to the factories of France or Switzerland. The *fatti di Torino* provoked a collective protest by industry. A strong delegation visited Mussolini, and he promised that 'as for calm and public order, which are essential prerequisites for the improvement of Italian economic conditions ... the Government would safeguard them with the greatest rigour, and would not allow any persons to substitute themselves for the State.'[51]

The tactic of the industrialists was to give support to Mussolini personally and to favour the strengthening of his authority over the movement: the newspapers which they controlled dissociated his image from that of the party. The dangerous tendencies of the Fascist movement were at the same time to be tamed through 'action in detail to soften the new authorities'. The means of persuasion at the disposal of the industrialists' political arm, the Società Promotrice, were consequently increased.[52] It is difficult to show in detail, but impossible to doubt, that the work of corruption and influence was highly successful in the long-term.

However it was the other aspect of the industrialists' policy, the direct entente with Mussolini, which paid the greatest immediate dividends. The instrument was Benni; he was elected to the presidency of the Confindustria at the beginning of 1923. Benni owed his election to the excellent relations which he had already established with Mussolini in Milan and his well-founded reputation as a friend of Fascism.[53] Benni made a curious contrast with the secretary of the Confederation, Gino Olivetti. Whereas the latter was a man of wide learning and general intelligence, cynical and astute, Benni was an uneducated philistine who appeared obtuse.[54] It is noticeable that self-made men like Benni tended to be more enthusiastic about Fascism than industrialists from secure upper-class backgrounds like Agnelli or Ettore Conti.

The Agrarians

The industrialists, while supporting Fascism, had in the main preserved a certain distance from the movement. This was less true of the agrarians, who were far more committed to the success of the movement. One reason why this was so was because the agrarians never had an organization of their own comparable in efficiency to the Confindustria. The rise of the employers' organizations in agriculture roughly paralleled the same process in industry, but with important differences. The farmers and landowners were more individualistic and more backward-looking in their attitude to labour relations, and many showed scarce interest in association. The representatives of the vast, but diffused, bloc of agricultural interests could never exert an influence on public policy comparable to that of the industrial leaders. This failure created a strong resentment against the Government; the agrarian class were therefore less concerned than the industrialists with maintaining order and continuity, and more ready to back the Fascists in demanding a clean sweep.

The agrarians were far more reluctant than the industrialists to come to terms with the labour movement during the era of Giolitti. It was much harder for the agrarians to maintain their profit margins, given the pressure to relieve structural unemployment, than it was for the industrialists. However here too difficulties could be turned to good advantage, and the lavish government grants for public works to alleviate unemployment benefited not only socialist co-operatives, but employers and land reclamation companies. Although labour relations were inherently more unstable on the farms of the Po Valley than in the factories, most of the leaders of the agricultural trade unions before the war were moderate and reformist. They cultivated good relations with the Government, for if public works grants were sometimes useful to the employers, they were a matter of life and death for the unions and their members. The mass of workers drawn to the region by the land reclamation programmes had to be found work; government help was essential to tide them over the winter months, when normal agricultural operations did not require surplus labour.[55] But if the efforts of official leaders were insufficiently successful, then their followers might turn to revolutionary syndicalism, which in the countryside meant violence. The opposition between the reformists and the syndicalists was matched by a similar conflict of mentalities among the employers. Some agrarian leaders, like the industrialists, accepted the Giolittian system: in the province of Bologna, a stronghold of the reformist unions, many landowners and farmers tacitly refrained from using their money and influence to combat Socialism, in return for a quiet life. To quote Cavazza, the first President of the Confederazione Agraria, the object of organization was to achieve a 'balance' in the relations between capital and labour; the agrarian associations, he warned 'must never assume an *a priori* stance of resistance';[56] before the war, the agrarian elite, the more enlightened of the nobles and other large landowners, on the whole supported this moderate and optimistic view, unless they happened to belong to a province dominated by the revolutionary syndicalists. But the active entrepreneurs, often leaseholders rather than owners, were not so easily persuaded to take a remissive view. Their champion was Commendatore Lino Carrara, the man who broke the

1908 syndicalist strike in Parma province led by De Ambris. Carrara, as early as 1909, spoke of organizing 'an inter-provincial corps of volunteers', and of undertaking 'pacific propaganda' among the workers, 'pacific as long as it is permitted to be so, because sometimes it might even be active propaganda and this is no bad thing at all.'[57] Here there was already an anticipation of agrarian *squadrismo*. Men like Carrara or Vico Mantovani, the leader of the Ferrara agrarians, were essentially capitalist entrepreneurs, with interests not only in agriculture but also in banking and in large-scale speculative reclamation projects. They grew industrial crops like sugar-beet and hemp, and were in close touch with the industrialists of the corresponding sectors; Carrara opposed any reduction in sugar tariffs, although many agrarians were hostile to them.[58] There were signs even before the war that Carrara's arguments for a more aggressive policy were gaining ground; as in industry, the advance of the employers' organizations made possible a tougher line and even the attempt to retract earlier concessions.[59]

After the war, although many agricultural labour unions remained in reformist hands, they did not escape the general radicalization of class relations. Indeed it seemed to the agrarians that men like Massarenti, the famous leader of the Molinella unions, who was, politically, a reformist, were their most dangerous enemies; they had built up an unshakeable structure of unions and co-operatives where the more impetuous revolutionaries had failed. The leaders of the Catholic peasant unions in Cremona and upper Lombardy, who put forward demands for the participation of workers in farm management with a share in the profits, were also particularly detested by the agrarians; their claims might in the last analysis be preferable to collectivization, but they were more dangerous because they were advanced as immediate requests and not deferred till after the revolution. The Catholic programme was even more unwelcome because it appealed to classes of workers like the *salariati fissi* and some of the *mezzadri* who had stable interests in the land they worked, and who had therefore been slower than the casual labourers to enter unions. Even the moderate agrarians, who were prepared to make economic concessions, were not prepared to compromise with proposals which radically limited the management functions of owners and farmers.[60]

The nucleus of the Confederazione dell'Agricoltura (founded in 1920) was formed by an organization known as the *interprovinciale*, which had its centre in Bologna and its master-mind in Lino Carrara, who for a time succeeded in capturing the important local newspaper, *Il Resto del Carlino*, as his mouthpiece.[61] The *interprovinciale* was purely concerned with resistance to wage claims. But, as in the case of industry, the 'summit organization' or Confederation had a different function. It was intended as a political pressure group which would provide the badly needed co-ordination of agricultural interests and secure a more favourable government policy, not only on labour relations but on taxation and tariffs.[62]

The disastrous defeat suffered in the 1920 Bologna strike produced a crisis in the agrarian organizations. One of the causes of the dispute had been the Socialist refusal to recognize the agrarian association, and the claim that the wage agreement should be negotiated with individual employers. This claim had been justified in economic if not in political terms by the indiscipline of many farmers who, even when they were members of the association, refused to carry out its decisions. After the Socialist victory, many farmers lost faith in the association and withheld their contributions. The disaster broke the influence of moderates like Cavazza and also helped to create a rift between the *interprovinciale* and the national Confederation. The latter became the scapegoat for the defeat : its leaders were accused of appeasement tendencies and of having failed to influence the action of the Government which, by requisitioning the crops, had caused the burden of the stoppage to fall on the employers.[63] The initiative passed to the local agrarian leaders, who turned to Fascism to give the protection which neither the State nor their own Confederation had afforded. The feeling that 'Rome' had sold the 'provinces' down the river was a powerful sentiment which found expression in the later polemics within Fascism. 1921 did not remove the tension between the provincial and national leaderships, since the success of the agrarians' local counter-offensives was not matched by a similar gain in influence on the Government, where the Popolari remained a serious obstacle. At the Congress in February 1921, Donini, the director of the Confederation, argued that the time had come to return to 'normal' relations with the unions, now chastened by experience of the Fascist reaction. He was attacked by the representatives of Reggio Emilia and Pordenone (Friuli) for not having understood 'the concept of class collaboration'. This meant the reverse of what it might appear to do : class collaboration signified the refusal to deal with the Socialist and Catholic unions, and the granting instead of exclusive recognition to Fascist or other unions under the employers' own direct influence. Once again the spokesman for the intransigents was Lino Carrara : his motion, he said,

. . . does not contain a protest against the Government. Such protests are useless. We must find in ourselves, and in our own strength alone, the means to obtain those remedies which honest criticism and clear reason indicate. I do not believe we can expect much from the Government. . . . We must deprecate the gravest and most imminent of all dangers . . . that of peace at all costs. We have already had wartime defeatism ; we must prevent at all costs the victory of peacetime defeatism.[64]

Soon after this Mussolini himself became guilty in the eyes of the agrarians of 'peacetime defeatism' when he concluded the Pact of Pacification. This reinforced the agrarian suspicion of politicians. Unlike the industrialists, many agrarians sympathized with Fascist intransigence and distrusted compromise. However even the agrarians did not identify totally with Fascism : in Parliament a separate agrarian group was formed, and as the power of labour declined, their old aspirations to complete independence tended to revive.

The Fascist Unions

During 1919 the Fascist movement made no attempt to organize unions of its own. Mussolini tried instead to work in alliance with the Unione Italiana del Lavoro (UIL), the organization of the interventionist syndicalists, whose most prominent leaders were De Ambris and Rossoni. However, in January 1920, the Fascist movement broke with the UIL when the latter supported the railway and postal strikes, and instead gave its blessing to the blackleg unions formed to combat the strikes. These were the nucleus of the Federation of National Unions founded on 27 February.[65] At first the membership of these unions was confined almost entirely to white collar workers, including teachers. At the same time a Fascist lawyer, Sileno Fabbri, succeeded in forming an Italian Confederation of Intellectual Labour, comprising members of the free professions as well as employees. In the autumn the first large-scale squadrist offensive, in Venezia Giulia, was accompanied by the promotion of the 'Sindacati Economici Nazionali'; this set the pattern for the later development of the Fascist union movement.[66] When the agrarian reaction got going in Emilia, it was soon followed by the constitution of unions of agricultural labourers. These unions were not formally part of the Fascist movement, but they were usually organized and led by Fascists, and they were entirely dependent for their success on the terrorism of the squads and the discrimination of the employers in their favour.[67]

The local 'Sindacati Economici' in Emilia and the other regions of Fascist strength prospered: but the national organization, the Confederazione Italiana Sindacati Economici, which had been founded in November 1920 with the railway organizer Isidoro Provenza as its secretary-general, was a failure. He and the CISE were accused of 'bolshevizing' and repudiated both by Mussolini and Michele Bianchi, who wished to bring the unions under the direct control of the party, and by the local *ras*. The objective of Mussolini and Bianchi was to curb the independence of the provincial bosses. Originally, they had made use of the syndicalist polemic against the exploitation of the unions by parasitic political parties, but now this viewpoint was explicitly repudiated by Bianchi.[68] On the other hand, the provincials, though critical of the CISE, wanted the unions to remain independent of the party, because they wished to prevent the national secretariat from interfering in their affairs. They also opposed calling the unions 'Fascist', because they were aware that this would make recruitment more difficult; not only the Socialists, who anyway joined under compulsion, but the important minority groups of ex-Combatants and Republicans might be alienated.

The *Convegno* held at Bologna in January 1922 tried to reconcile the two opposing viewpoints, defended respectively by Michele Bianchi and by

Balbo, Baroncini and Rossoni. It was Dino Grandi who suggested an acceptable compromise; the unions should not be called Fascist, and they should admit non-Fascist members; however the new federation, 'although remaining materially outside the party, should maintain close relations with it, follow its directives constantly, and its leaders should be exclusively Fascist'. If the unions remained quite independent and a-political, they would end by falling under the influence of other parties, as the CISE had done; on the other hand, for the good of the party, union and party membership should be kept distinct. Otherwise 'too many people would enter our ranks ... which are already suffering from the grave disadvantages of a ... facile work of conversion'. What transpires from this is the determination of Grandi (shared by several of the other speakers) to keep the working-class organizations in their place; they were neither to enjoy independence nor to be allowed any influence on the party.[69]

The head of the new organization, which assumed the name of the Confederazione Nazionale delle Corporazioni Sindacali, was Edmondo Rossoni. Before the war Rossoni had emigrated to the USA, where he made his name in the American revolutionary syndicalist movement, the International Workers of the World. In 1913, however, he returned to Italy, and the following year he joined the interventionists. Ironically enough in 1919 he led the opposition within the UIL to the policy of co-operation with the *fasci*, which was defended by De Ambris.[70] As late as May 1921, he was still critical of the Fascist movement: but financial or other inducements led him to desert the UIL shortly afterwards and to take over the task of organizing the Fascist unions of Ferrara.[71] Given his position, it was natural that Rossoni should at first side with Balbo and the *ras* and defend the traditional syndicalist doctrine that the unions should remain independent of party control. However he had no illusions about the dependence of the 'national' unions on the *fasci*: 'without the action of Fascism, which has broken the hegemony of the reds and the whites, and has created a new moral atmosphere in a great part of the country, our union movement would not exist.' Consequently his efforts to defend the autonomy of the corporations were only half-hearted. At the first Congress of the Corporations in June 1922, he did not oppose the motion which gave the *direzione* of the party the right to be consulted over all appointments of union officials.[72]

Mussolini had promoted the founding of the corporations more because he disliked the independence of the organizations already in existence than out of any real enthusiasm. He had not yet given up the idea of coming to an agreement with the CGL, once this had detached itself from the Socialist party, and on the other hand he feared that the new unions would cause difficulties with the employees. These fears were not groundless. In agriculture, in spite of the fact that the new contracts concluded with the corporations were highly advantageous for the employees, there were several conflicts between the agrarians and the unions in the summer of 1922.[73]

The Fascist movement expected the agrarians to provide jobs for the labourers under its protection; this had been easy enough when the latter were only a minority, but as the numbers in the unions grew, it became harder to find work for all. 'Elitist' Fascists and free-enterprise economists both accused Fascism of copying the 'demagogic' tactics of its opponents.[74]

The Prefect of Bologna, while admitting that for the moment the entente between the Fascists and the agrarians was still very much in force, believed that eventually a conflict would be inevitable 'and in the hour of crisis the Fascists will be on the side of the big battalions'.[75] This was not a wholly fanciful idea; on occasions, the local party did side with the unions against the employers. The most notorious example, which caused a great scandal in conservative circles, was in the province of Siena, where the federation ordered the occupation of farms belonging to landowners who had refused to take on a quota of unemployed labourers belonging to the unions.[76] Mussolini was sufficiently alarmed by the reaction to these outbreaks to give explicit reassurances. At the June Congress of the Corporations, he emphasized the need to avoid repeating Socialist errors; Fascist syndicalism must be 'qualitative, not quantitative. We cannot reject the masses, but we must not go too far out of the way to seek them.'[77]

Mussolini and Rossoni often claimed that the national unions represented 'the aristocracy of the proletariat'. In 1919, when Mussolini had hailed the 'productive strike' of the metalworkers of Dalmine as the dawn of a new syndicalism, there had been some reality behind such slogans; the attempt then had been to appeal to the feelings of superiority and the pragmatism of the skilled workers and to separate them from the mass of new unskilled labour.[78] But in 1922 the social composition of the Fascist unions was entirely at odds with the concept of the heroic working-class elite which their leaders had derived from revolutionary syndicalism. The mass of the membership came from the agricultural labourers of the regions under Fascist control; next in numerical importance were the workers in the docks, where fierce competition for employment induced many casual labourers to join the unions and even the party. The Fascist unions also enrolled a considerable number of workers in the transport, municipal and service sectors: but among the workers in large-scale industry they had little success. Where industrial unions existed, they were company unions closely dependent on single employers. The labour aristocracy of printers, engineers, metallurgical workers, builders, etc., remained obstinately faithful to the CGL. It was, in fact, on the least qualified and the least politically conscious among the manual workers that Fascism imposed its control.[79]

There was, however, another important element in the corporations besides the casual labourers and the victims of terror; they also included the new organizations of the white collar workers and the free professions. The representation of these 'intermediate classes' or 'brainworkers' was the chief boast of the Fascist union movement. Their presence distracted attention from the embarrassingly poor quality of the working-class recruits. The organization of these white collar groups was spontaneous, and there is no reason to doubt that most of their members had genuine Fascist sympathies; however many public employees were also moved by more opportunist motives to attach themselves to the strongest political force as a means of gaining preferment, or exerting pressure on the State and the communes for higher salaries. Fascist propaganda also exploited with some success the grievances of the ex-Combatants, supporting their claims for preference in employment and quicker promotion, and played on the resentments against the employment of women or foreigners and the preference given to foreign goods.[80]

In industry, the Fascist unions had to contend not only with the distrust and hostility of most workers, but with the dependence of the *fasci* on the employers for financial support. Some of the latter had favoured the constitution of blackleg unions as a weapon against Socialism, but now that the danger was past, they preferred to keep the new organizations weak. At Monfalcone, near Trieste, one of the earliest centres to have a 'national' union, a correspondent complained: 'As for trade unionism, let's not even talk about it. At Monfalcone there are more than 2,000 disorganized workers who would all have joined the unions if someone had carried out a little propaganda, but the *fascio* is directed by the management of the shipyard which has every interest in leaving them to their own resources and does not desire trade union propaganda to be carried on.'[81]

But the Fascist unions sometimes played a more positive role from the employers' point of view. Even before the rise of Fascism, industrialists who were exerting pressure on the Government for State contracts or subsidies had already often used the threat of creating unemployment and provoking strike action as a means of pressure; the connivance, real or imaginary, of the unions in these tactics was one of the main accusations made by the *liberisti* against the labour movement. The Fascist movement offered an opportunity to revive and perfect this technique; for now, behind the obedient manoeuvrable unions, there was also the far more menacing force of the squads, ready to intervene in defence of 'their' workers, if the Government did not give way.

When the Orlando shipbuilding company of Livorno, and the Terni firm with which it was financially associated, were in grave difficulties, the Fascist movement came to their rescue. On 30 May 1922, the secretary of the Fascist unions of Livorno wrote to the Central Committee of the *fasci* pointing out that if the party could force the Government to make concessions which would avoid the crisis and closure of the Orlando firm, the influence of the local Socialist deputy Modigliani, founded largely upon his past successes in dealing with governments, would be shaken.[82] For the moment, their efforts were unsuccessful; the Orlando works were closed. But in the negotiations which finally led to the re-opening of the Orlando shipyard and of the Terni works, the threat of Fascist mobilization was decisive in persuading the Government to yield to the companies' demands for the promise of new arms orders, the reduction of claims for arrears of taxes, and the cancellation of fines for delay in fulfilling government contracts.[83] From the Fascist point of view, such agitations had a dual purpose : they not only pleased the industrialists, but also enabled the Fascist unions to make some headway among the workers. It is significant that the Prefect of Terni in 1923, in appealing to the Government to check dismissals, referred to the 'merits in relation to the PNF' of the workers in the arms factory 'whose work force . . . was the first, in that almost wholly subversive centre, to help the national movement and which represents the central nucleus of the fabric of the national unions.'[84] The only way in which 'class collaboration' could be made a reality was if the unions aided the employers in their efforts to exploit the taxpayer and the consumer. The development of the corporations thus reinforced the subservience of local Fascist leaders to specific industrial interests. This was an obstacle to the fulfilment of the programme of the *liberisti* for the abandonment or scaling-down of unprofitable industries which were dependent on State assistance.

Integral Syndicalism

During 1923 a serious conflict broke out between the Fascist movement and the old employers' associations. Primarily, this conflict was not over social issues but over power ; it was caused by the Fascists' attempt to subject all interest groups to a process of totalitarian co-ordination. At the beginning of 1922 the principles of 'class collaboration' inspired the formation of the first Fascist organizations of employers. An employers' federation was formed in Cremona during February, under the patronage and control of Farinacci ; at about the same time, two young Fascists, Gino Cacciari and B. Fornaciari, founded a Provincial federation of *agricoltori* at Bologna. The foundation of these organizations, soon copied in other provinces, enabled Fascism, their founders claimed, to create an 'absolutely new and original form of union movement, which could give a real meaning to the concept of 'class collaboration'.[85] We have learnt to look with scepticism at this concept ; however the claim that the setting-up of a Fascist employers' organization marked a new departure is not altogether untrue.

After the March on Rome co-operation between the Fascists and the agrarian associations became more difficult. Victory revived the old agrarian spirit of indiscipline and short-sighted avidity ; the organizers of the Fascist labour unions found that it was difficult to secure compliance even with the new, less favourable labour contracts which they had imposed on the workers. On the other hand, 'agriculturalists' like Cacciari and Fornaciari saw that in the long run it was in the interests of the agrarians to possess an organization which could act as a counterweight within Fascism to the workers' unions.

They recognized that the latter were necessary not only as a simple coercive mechanism, but to provide a safety-valve for discontents which might otherwise explode in desperate revolt. 'Class collaboration', to be effective, needed the presence of an employers' representative who could exercise surveillance over the work of his opposite number, who might otherwise be tempted to revive 'demagogic methods', and also some degree of genuine co-operation to allay the causes of discontent. The task of the corporation, formed of both employers' and workers' unions, would be 'to keep all the forces of production permanently in touch with each other through its technical organs, in order to prevent conflict'.[86] From the ideological and political point of view, the advantages were more obvious. The *ras* now aspired to dominate the whole life of the provinces over which they ruled; for this aim to be fulfilled it was necessary to break the employers' independence and bring them within the orbit of the party. At the same time, 'class collaboration' did not have the same meaning for all Fascists as it had for the agrarians. The programme of 'integral syndicalism', or the formation of corporations in which employers and workers would be equally represented, required that the organization of the two sides should be at least apparently on the same footing. Party leaders like Farinacci or Gino Baroncini for these reasons seized on the new idea. Their aims were not the same as those of the old agrarians: each was trying to use the other, and however large the area of agreement, the issue of power, of ultimate control, divided them. The agrarians, or at least the more old-fashioned of them, wanted 'freedom' to do as they liked in hiring and firing workers,[87] and the more ambitious also wanted to retain local political predominance; the Fascists wanted to create a system of total control in which all interests would be organized and subordinated to the movement.

In some provinces (e.g., Ferrara), the old agrarian associations were astute enough to see the way the wind was blowing and simply converted themselves *en bloc* into 'Fascist' organizations, thus conserving their influence. Elsewhere, however, the two organizations subsisted side by side, in a state of mutual rivalry which during 1922–3 tended more and more frequently to become active hostility. Apart from the reasons suggested above, and the influence of purely personal jealousies between old and new organizers, another factor was involved. The formation of the Fascist organizations represented a further stage in the revolt against the traditional leadership of the agrarians. The war had brought with it a passage of property from the hands of large landowners not only to peasant cultivators but, perhaps in even greater measure, to a new class of small entrepreneurs. It was this newly made agrarian bourgeoisie which was the backbone of Fascism: 'the anti-Bolshevik reaction in the countryside must have had its social foundations in the rise of this new class . . . very different from the old torpid and absent class of landowners.'[88] The leadership was now claimed by the representatives of these new men, and by the important class of agricultural experts and farm managers, ranging from the graduates in agriculture, of middle-class origin, numerous in Lombardy and Emilia, to the more modest *fattori di campagna* often by origin successful peasants. These agricultural managers identified themselves particularly closely with Fascism; their ideal was a 'managerial revolution' in which they, as the guardians of the interests of technique and production, would represent both employers and workers.[89] In provinces such as Bologna, the Fascist movement also actively undertook propaganda among the intermediate classes in the countryside, smallholders, leaseholders and sharecroppers, whose interests obviously diverged from those of the large landowners.[90]

After the March on Rome, the Fascist drive to organize entered a new phase. The old *interprovinciale* was dissolved, and the Fascist unions of 'agriculturalists' were united in a federation centred at Bologna. The chief patron of the organization was Gino Baroncini, the *federale* of the party. It seems that Baroncini was genuinely worried by the breakdown of contractual labour relations which threatened to result from the victory of agrarian Fascism. The purpose of the foundation of the FISA (Federazione Italiana Sindacati Agricoltori) was to have an organization that would guarantee the application of contracts between employers and workers.[91] The Minister of Agriculture, De Capitani and his Under-Secretary Corgini, both faithful interpreters of conservative agrarian interests, succeeded in suppressing the official government committees for arbitration and negotiation in agricultural disputes. This return to the 'anarchy' of free enterprise was opposed by most local Fascist leaders.[92]

Baroncini had worked in the interest of the agrarians to destroy the red unions. He agreed with them on the need to restore discipline in labour relations, and to lower wages. But the mass following of Fascism in the unions and even to some extent in the party was held together by the promise of preference in employment. If the agrarians, as seemed possible, returned to a short-sighted individualism, and consulted only their own preference about whom to employ, the Fascist organizations would be severely weakened.[93]

Baroncini believed in 'productivism' and 'class collaboration'. These were both slogans adopted by the agrarians, but he gave them a different meaning. The *fasci*, not only in Bologna, but in Cremona, Ravenna and most of the Po Valley provinces, refused to abolish the *imponibile di mano d'opera*, or labour quota, which had been one of the main conquests of the unions before the war. It is true that it was usually lightened; but the Fascist attitude was still in sharp disagreement with that of the agrarian associations, who demanded its total abolition in the name of the freedom of the entrepreneur. In fact the Fascists even on occasion continued one of the most criticized features of Socialist practice, the imposition of a labour quota during the harvest and other peak periods of activity on peasant cultivators and sharecroppers, and the discouragement of the exchange of labour between the families of the latter, in the interests of the landless labourers.[94]

In several provinces, Fascist policies were directed towards reducing unemployment in the interests of social stability. The experts of the movement favoured the concession by the large farmers to the labourers of small plots of land, which they could cultivate during slack periods. This scheme, which critics attacked as likely to lead to a diminution in productivity, was to be accompanied by a programme for the intensified mechanization of agriculture and the creation of new industries for the transformation of agricultural produce.[95] A Ravenna Fascist, Mazziotti, tried to create a national organization to finance projects for the relief of unemployment under the name of the Comitati delle Opere, but the one serious enterprise which he founded was soon in financial trouble and had to be wound up.[96] Such ambitious exercises suffered from the naïve belief that economic problems could be solved by efforts of the will, and also from the attempt to make quick speculative profits through the exploitation of political influence.

Although the local unions of employers and workers were entirely distinct, they both formed part of a unified national Corporation of Agriculture. This was the first institution in which the principles of 'integral syndicalism' were embodied. Even though this innovation may have been more formal than material, and may have made little difference to the actual conduct of labour relations, it was none the less stubbornly resisted by the agrarian associations. The agrarians resented the idea of being bound by decisions reached in concert by the representatives of employers and workers, even if the latter were represented only in name. The agrarians of Parma protested that the new organization 'proposed to regiment every kind of economic activity, whether that of worker or employer, in unions which would finish by suffocating all free individual initiative. Is this Fascism ? It does not seem to us possible. At the most, it may be the Fascism of Racheli, but it is certainly not that . . . of Mussolini and the *Popolo d'Italia*'.[97] The agrarians also called attention to their undeniable merits in promoting Fascism and they did not lack defenders within the ranks of the party. The most influential agrarian spokesman within Fascism was Corgini, the Under-Secretary of Agriculture, who had been an organizer of the Reggio Emilia agrarian association, as well as one of the founders of local Fascism. In his speech on 24 December 1922 to the association, he defended the principle of freedom of organization against monopoly, and criticized the dangerous influence of 'facile organizers, and especially those who have brought with them a heritage of past errors'. Mussolini was present; and in conjunction with the interview he had granted three days previously to the President of the Confederation of Agriculture, Bartoli, this was taken to mean that he had repudiated the idea of integral syndicalism.[98] However whatever assurances Mussolini may have given, he did not halt the offensive of the Fascist organizations.

The party backed Rossoni's programme of integral syndicalism. On 24 January 1923 the *direzione* decided that members of the party should belong only to Fascist organizations.[99] This was a declaration of war on the independent employers' associations. The Confederation of Agriculture protested against 'the determined and tenacious hostility shown to them (the agrarian associations) by the local Fascist organizations'. Like the parties of the Government coalition, it found that collaboration at the centre was no guarantee of tolerance at the grass-roots level; 'the body of the Confederation in the provinces is subject to such pressure that it is deprived of all possibility of an independent existence.'[100] The conflict was fiercest in the provinces of Parma and Reggio Emilia, where the agrarian associations were particularly prosperous; closely linked with banks and marketing consortia, they were the major centres of local economic power. In Parma, the agrarians were able to recover from an initially unfavourable situation by exploiting the rivalries within the Fascist party, particularly the conflict between different branches of the Freemasonry.[101] In Reggio, on the other hand, Corgini and his faction were decisively defeated; both locally and nationally he found himself isolated.[102]

Where, on the other hand, the local agrarian association speedily detached itself from the Confederation of Agriculture, the influence of its leaders might remain predominant: in Ferrara province the alliance between Mantovani and Balbo remained as close as before. The Fascist trade union organizer Granata, a native of the province who had worked with Michele Bianchi in the latter's revolutionary days, was horrified at the state of affairs in Ferrara, which he described as 'agrarian slavery'. The agrarians of Ferrara retained their own squads, which were not incorporated in the Militia, and displayed a complete contempt for the maintenance of labour agreements; little or no effort was made to relieve unemployment, in contrast to the situation in Bologna.[103]

The question of taxation was another cause of conflict between the FISA and the old agrarian associations. Although the agrarians had gained very considerably from the redistribution of local taxes carried out by the *fasci*, they were restive at having to pay the new tax on agricultural income, and also at the revision of the assessments for the old land tax.[104] In addition, many Fascist party federations continued to tax the proprietors for their own upkeep, and this caused added friction.[105] The FISA was in an awkward position: it felt bound to support government policy and to demand that the agrarians should drop their protests in the name of discipline. However the FISA was able to reconcile loyalty to Fascism with the interests of its members by accusing the bureaucracy of wilful error in the application of the taxes. The FISA functioned as a regional rather than a national pressure group: its protests seem to have been effective, since the tax burden was redistributed in a manner which grossly favoured the rich regions of the Po Valley where Fascism was strong at the expense of backward regions like the South, Sicily and Sardinia, where the agricultural interest was less well organized and less committed to Fascism.[106] During 1923 the FISA was clearly winning in the Po Valley, while in the South the old agrarian associations were more successful in resisting absorption.[107]

The party's decision on the question of employers' associations threatened not only the Confederation of Agriculture but the Confindustria itself. Although no national organization equivalent to the FISA existed in industry, it was clear that Rossoni with party support intended to extend the programme of integral syndicalism to all branches of production. The Confederation of Commerce announced its official adherence to Fascism on 18 February 1923;[108] however this formal act of discipline seems to have had no binding effect on the Confederation, which was able later to repudiate the decision and return to independence. But in the provinces, single federations of traders and small industrialists began to pass to the corporations; only large-scale industry remained more or less unaffected.

It was natural that the Fascist industrial unions should follow the Corporation of Agriculture in the attempt to achieve an integral organization of employers and workers. If industry remained independent, the agrarians would become restive at their unequal treatment. The basic problem, moreover, was the same in industry and agriculture. It was put bluntly by the representative of the Naples unions, Bifani, in the meeting of the Consiglio Nazionale of the Corporations on 10 November 1922: 'In the South the workers are with us, but we find ourselves faced with opposition from the industrialists. We ask Rossoni, therefore, what line of conduct we should take up when faced with industrialists who close their factories in order to re-engage their workers on onerous conditions? The masses up till now are with us, but for how long?' Rossoni had no answer to Bifani's question except to say that 'we will hold a lightning enquiry'.[109] Although the Confindustria urged the respect of existing wage agreements, many industrialists, profiting from the depressed state of the labour market and also from the virtual ban on strike action imposed by Fascism, carried out arbitrary wage reductions.[110] One method frequently employed to circumvent resistance was to dismiss skilled workers and then hire them again at rates for unskilled labour.[111] Sometimes the industrialists refused to recognize the Fascist unions. The important Montecatini chemical firm cut short negotiations with the Fascist unions at Ravenna by a lock-out.[112] On the other hand, there were cases of direct and blatant collusion between industrialists and the Fascist unions. The most notorious example was in the Naples textile industry in March 1923. The workers were 'represented' by Preziosi, who in return for selling them down the river was made editor of the Naples daily *Il Mezzogiorno*, which was the property of the leading textile manufacturer Bruno Canto.[113]

Rossoni was confronted with a problem for which he had no ready solution. On the one hand, if he was to build up the corporations into a serious organization of some political weight, he could not afford to rely exclusively on coercion by the party. Moreover it was still uncertain how far these methods would be effective in industry, especially where skilled labour was essential and relatively scarce. Some measure of protection had to be afforded to the workers to gain even their grudging and half-hearted adherence. On the other hand, Rossoni had no illusions about the likely fate of Fascist unionism under conditions of free competition. The active cooperation of the party and the good will of the Government were essential to his success.

On the first score, Rossoni was highly successful. The threat of an agreement between Mussolini and the CGL in November 1922 (revived in July 1923) brought into being the alliance between Rossoni and Farinacci, with other leaders of agrarian Fascism. The Rossoni-Farinacci axis was of the highest importance for the internal structure of Fascism. Those agrarian Fascists like Cesare Forni or Corgini who opposed Rossoni and his plans, and old-fashioned syndicalists who wanted more freedom for the unions from the party, alike protested unsuccessfully against the alliance between union and party bosses. The position of the corporations was much less secure in relation to the Government. De Stefani, as well as the Liberal ministers, was no friend to the unions, and the Prefects were always ready to underwrite complaints that the corporations were reviving the regrettable methods of the subversives. But that was not all: Mussolini's own attitude could hardly have been less helpful. When the corporations undertook strikes or other direct action to enforce their claims, he frequently intervened to condemn their indiscipline: yet at the same time he was irritated by their lack of success among the industrial workers, and consequently continued to hanker after an agreement with the CGL as the only organization capable of delivering working-class support. The Fascist unions, unlike the party, were expendable. Mussolini showed interest and concern with labour problems only on those rare occasions when his vanity was satisfied by a request for his direct arbitration. He was pleased to extend his protection to the ultra-moderate leader of the printers' union, T. Bruno; he tried also, with less success, to arbitrate between employers and workers in the Rome building industry.[114]

The secretary of the Confindustria, Gino Olivetti, in an acute analysis of the motives behind the campaign for the 'integral corporation', explained that the more intelligent of the Fascist union leaders, including Rossoni himself, recognized that the discipline enforced on them by the Government condemned them to a position of inferiority. This was reinforced by the strong value attached in Fascist propaganda to the avoidance of strikes. Yet how could employers be brought to reason without strikes? The only alternative was to force employers and workers to accept a 'single discipline'.

The employers' unions thus become a condition *sine qua non* of Fascist union activity. If they are removed, the whole system will be unbalanced and in danger of collapse. Caught between the political needs of the Government and the resistance of the independently organized industrialists, the Fascist unions would have no possibilities of life, let alone development, once the force of suggestion of today's exceptional political situation has passed away.

The union leaders were also moved by reasons of self-interest : while the mass of lesser union organizers showed little interest in the question, as they saw the task of the common organization essentially as the regimentation of the masses, 'the general staff, on the other hand, are most sensitive to the question because they intend to make their career in the field of the employers' unions, which they think would bring a far greater yield than the unions of workers.' A typical complication here was that the few organizers who had already created unions of traders, shopkeepers and small industrialists, were hostile to the inclusion of large industry in the orbit of the corporations, because it would have lessened their own importance.[115]

The first meeting of the Grand Council in December 1922 promised that the freedom of organization would be maintained : but in the very important debate held on 15 March 1923, the leaders of the party backed Rossoni. Michele Bianchi tried to remove the misgivings of those who feared that the Fascist unions, particularly in agricultural regions, would be tempted to revive Socialist methods once they had achieved a monopoly ; the guarantees against this, he said, lay in their 'absolutely dictatorial' procedure, and in the control exercised by the party. 'As is well known, the general secretary, Rossoni, is the delegate of the Fascist party and the choice of local leaders is entirely subject to his discretion. It is not therefore the leader who has to submit to the masses, but the masses who have to submit to the leader.' Bianchi also threw out the suggestion that Fascist unionism should be based on the single firm, 'the most natural environment for co-operation'. This would have meant something like the Nazi 'plant community' with the industrialist as leader ; however Rossoni and his subordinates, who were interested in building up a large centralized bureaucracy, did not show any interest in this idea.

Farinacci, for his part, advanced a thorough-going totalitarian justification of the corporation. 'As Fascism's word of command is directed solely to obtaining unity of purpose, it is therefore natural that the Fascist employers should wish to achieve this unity, in so far as it is possible, in the syndical field also.' Farinacci and Rossoni proposed a joint motion which was passed unanimously, except for the abstention of Corgini ; this recognized the corporations as 'one of the aspects of the Fascist national revolution, whose requirements and discipline they obey unconditionally' ; and while paying formal respect to the earlier decision against the establishment of a monopoly, declared it necessary 'that workers' technicians and employers should be brought together under the aegis of Fascism by an intense work of propaganda and education, since only through a single discipline and a common faith is it possible to obtain the effective collaboration of all elements of production in the supreme interests of the Nation'. Fascists should consequently belong only to associations which formed part of the corporations.[116]

This meeting of the Grand Council was the high-water mark of integral corporativism. Mussolini had given the idea his formal approval, and had rebuffed Corgini and the independent agrarians :[117] but his support seems to have been dictated much more by a desire not to go against the general sense of the meeting than by any real enthusiasm. Olivetti and Benni rushed to repair the breach. They were received by Mussolini on 20 March : Benni was able to report to a meeting of the *Giunta Esecutiva* of the Confindustria that Mussolini had said that 'in the interests of the nation, the Confederation must not be touched, and the Fascist corporations must remain in contact with it and maintain excellent co-operative relations'.[118]

Rossoni was ordered by Mussolini to negotiate with the Confindustria leaders. His direct bid for the integral corporation was thus checked, but he did not give up hope. While formally acknowledging the independence of the Confindustria, in practice he tried to encourage the regional union secretaries to work for the inclusion of the industrialists in the Fascist employers' associations.[119]

The continued uncertainty of Fascist policy towards the employers' organizations was reflected in the Grand Council decisions at the end of April. On the one hand, the motion voted denied that the corporations were aiming at a monopoly : but 'we refuse also the syndical monopoly of the old employers' and working-class organizations'. The obligation for Fascist members to belong only to the corporations was restated.[120] Nonetheless relations between the Confindustria and Fascism continued to improve. Olivetti and Benni saw the necessity of establishing a closer and more formal relationship with Fascism if the threat of forced inclusion in the corporations was to be averted. In July for the first time they attended a meeting of the Grand Council in person.[121] On the Fascist side, this was an admission of the industrialists' strength ; it was the first time that the representatives of an independent, non-Fascist body had been allowed to present their case in person. The revisionist crisis which brought about a decline in the power of the party, also weakened the corporations. In the autumn and winter of 1923, the trend was towards a return to conservative orthodoxy and away from the totalitarian claims of the movement, in economics as in politics.

The Fascist unions reacted by becoming more aggressive in their attitude to labour disputes. Rossoni and the Confederation decided to launch a general offensive against the industrialists. Unfortunately for them, with a very poor sense of timing the leader of the unions in Turin, Bagnasco, chose to open the attack on the eve of Mussolini's visit to the city. Mussolini was furious, although his suspicion that Agnelli had in reprisal deliberately arranged for the workers of Fiat to give him a cold reception caused him to direct some of his anger onto the industrialists.[122] The Fascist unions of

Genoa also started a serious agitation, threatening a strike of metallurgical and dock workers.[123] But this new attempt to put pressure on the industrialists was a failure. One result of Mussolini's visit to Turin was to convince him that the majority of workers in industry were still implacably hostile to Fascism, and that consequently it would be foolish to allow the unions to imperil good relations with the employers.

The Grand Council declaration of 15 November 1923, besides settling the specific local disputes started by the unions, signified a complete victory for the point of view of the Confindustria. Rossoni was forced to recognize that the Confindustria represented the majority of industrial interests and to promise that he would not encourage 'the division or diminution of the technical and moral efficiency of the organization'. In return, the industrialists agreed not to have official dealings with other unions, and subscribed to a rather vague undertaking to set up some sort of consultative machinery. The industrialists were also reassured against the dangers of union militancy by the assurance that the unions would continue to be directed from above by their secretaries, who would be chosen by the central Confederation in agreement with the party. Any undesirable attempts to introduce democracy into the workings of the Fascist unions would therefore be stifled.[124] Having established their superiority, the Confindustria could afford to make concessions. On 19 December the industrialists concluded a formal agreement with the corporations, the 'Pact of Palazzo Chigi', in which the two Confederations pledged each other mutual support. Mussolini remarked that 'Rossoni will not mind if I observe that the attempt at integral syndicalism in the industrial field has not been a success.'[125] With this agreement Rossoni, at the price of subservience to the industrialists, won a limited victory. If the employers refused to negotiate except with the Fascist unions, the CGL would be rendered impotent.

The Palazzo Chigi agreement showed the shape of things to come. However in immediate practical terms it was not effective. Mutual distrust between industrialists and Fascist organizers continued, and the permanent committee set up to ensure liaison between the Confederations worked badly.[126] The Matteotti crisis destroyed the agreement, and the whole question had to be thrashed out again in 1925. In agriculture, the terms of the November Grand Council decision were much more favourable to the corporations, although even here they obtained less than they had hoped. The FISA was granted official recognition on a par with the Confindustria, but even the Fascist agricultural workers' unions were left free to make contracts with any other existing farmers' organization. In spite of this clause, the FISA was in a strong position. In most provinces of the North and Centre it had won over the majority of the employers, and many local agrarian associations had been dissolved under pressure from the party. It seemed as if the Confederation of Agriculture was nearing the point of unconditional surrender. But at the last moment the leaders of the

Confederation, Bartoli and Donini, averted the collapse by a personal appeal to Mussolini. On his instructions, the Confederation was merged with the FISA. This, though technically a victory for the latter, in fact forced them to give important posts to a number of the old agrarian leaders and disrupted the unity of the federation. The merger was not a success.[127]

The CGL and Fascism, 1923-4

During 1923 the destruction of the non-Fascist unions continued. Where fair competition was still possible, the Fascist unions made few converts. The elections to the *commissioni interne* and to other working-class bodies showed the limited extent of Fascist penetration, especially in the larger factories; where a free vote was taken, the Fascists' share did not exceed 10–15 per cent.[128] The Fascist unions in consequence, relied on the well-tried methods of intimidation. To the brutality of the squads there was now added state pressure: Prefects might confiscate the funds of a union or co-operative, or hand over their offices to the Fascist union on the pretext of public order or the changed political situation, in spite of some attempts by Finzi to restore them to their legitimate owners. The situation was worst in agriculture: all attempts to revive the Socialist leagues were met with open terror, and attacks on the Catholic unions multiplied after the Popolari left the Government. But similar methods were used even in industrial areas. Tough *squadristi* rather than specialist labour organizers were often entrusted with the task of getting the Fascist unions started. A typical example of their methods comes from Busto Arsizio in the industrial belt north of Milan, where the future Militia Consul Aldo Tarabella was in charge. On arrival he called on the secretary of the Camera del Lavoro and told him it was his intention to 'speak frankly': 'I have been sent to Busto to form a Fascist trade union organization: I accepted the job on the condition that there should be no restrictions or obstacles of any sort to my action. For me, you are the greatest obstacle and therefore, as you are an honest man, I give you warning that I cannot allow you to continue to concern yourself with trade union organization at Busto.'[129] The next stage was often to declare that meetings of other unions would be allowed only if a representative of the *fascio* were present: from this it was a short step to giving the members of the union a choice between dissolution and the transfer of their organization *en bloc* to the corporations. Understandably, many chose the latter alternative in the hope that this would leave them some rights of self-defence.[130]

The CGL leader Azimonti, reviewing the situation at the end of January 1923, concluded that 'competition between trade unions ... has had its day'.[131] The results were disastrous for the standard of living of the working class. In a period of economic crisis, they were left without defence: money wages declined appreciably, while the cost of living remained almost unchanged. The fall in real wages was greater during 1923 than in any subsequent year of the Fascist regime.[132] In spite of the Fascist projects for corporate representation, the Government destroyed those consultative bodies through which the unions had been able to make a contribution to the formulation of policy. The Labour Ministry was abolished, and with it the Consiglio Superiore del Lavoro, on which the unions were represented: the project for a new Consiglio Superiore della Produzione e del Lavoro was not put into effect. The State contribution to unemployment insurance was withdrawn. On the other hand, the eight-hour day was made compulsory by law, but since the unions were unable to supervise the application of the law, it was widely violated by the employers.[133] As if to make the hostility to the working-class movement clear by a crowning symbolic act, Fascism suppressed the celebration of Labour Day on 1 May. The 'birthday of Rome', 21 April, was supposed to be a substitute for the old holiday: but for some years to come groups of workers demonstrated against the change in spite of police and Fascist repression.

It is against this background that the renewed approaches from Mussolini to the union leaders must be seen. After the fiasco of December 1922, Mussolini had not given up the idea of reaching some kind of *modus vivendi* with the organized working class which would allow him effectively to neutralize Socialist hostility and thus diminish his dependence on the right. The CGL leaders on their side had been rendered cautious by the disappointments of November and December 1922 and the ensuing disasters. There were several shades of opinion among them, ranging from the scepticism of Buozzi, the head of the still formidable FIOM, to the optimism of men like Emilio Colombino and Baldesi, who still believed that Fascism might swing to the side of labour. In general, even the gravity of their defeats had not altogether destroyed the belief that the storm must pass; the union leaders saw Fascism as an irrational phenomenon which must sooner or later come to terms with 'reality'.[134] This meant the acknowledgement of class conflict and of their own role as representatives of the workers. They were, of course, perfectly right in pointing out that the Fascist slogans of class harmony and obedience to the superior interest of the nation were illusory and had done nothing to remove the causes of class conflict: but they had their own illusions, bred by a naïve form of economic determinism. 'Strikes have disappeared simply because the economic period which encouraged them . . . has disappeared'; they would become possible again when conditions improved.[135] In this comforting perspective, politics and violence could be conjured away as irrelevant and ultimately ineffective.

The first definite overtures from the Government to the CGL came on the eve of the vital vote on the Acerbo Bill; it was suggested to the moderate trade unionist Colombino that he might enter the ministry. This in itself seemed enough to discredit the approach as a mere tactical manoeuvre to divide the Opposition. D'Aragona nevertheless responded by declaring that he was voting against the bill not as a trade union leader but as a Socialist deputy: this concession was made to avert the threat of an intensified Fascist offensive against the unions, not to prepare the way for active co-operation.[136] However this encouraged Mussolini and Finzi to go further. In his speech to the Chamber, Mussolini said that he would like to entrust a ministry to the 'direct representatives of the organized working class'.[137] Colombino had an audience with Mussolini. The CGL and Turati had hoped that he would be offered an under-secretaryship: since he no longer held an official position in the union leadership and was ready to leave the PSU, his acceptance would not compromise them and might bring benefits. However the offer Mussolini made was different; 'more generic, but also larger, i.e., that of putting the new Ministry (National Economy) which would embrace Public Works as well, in the hands of the CGL: if the latter did not agree to co-operate he would be bound to put it instead in the hands of industrialists and representatives of the Corporations.'[138] This put things on a more serious but more difficult footing. D'Aragona realized that he could not make an official agreement with the Government until a degree of liberty had been restored to the unions. On 24 July Mussolini saw a delegation of trade union leaders including D'Aragona, Buozzi and Colombino. The conversation was cordial, but revealed some of the difficulties in the way of any agreement. D'Aragona and Buozzi insisted that the restoration of the unions' freedom of action was the fundamental problem: Mussolini on his side seems to have revived the suggestion that the solution was to be found in a unified confederation of all the unions independent of the parties.[139] The danger of this proposal was evident, and had grown since December 1922 with the advance of the corporation. Independence from party would not give much security, as unity could only be imposed by the influence of the Government, which would really control the new organization. But the door was left open for further negotiations, and on the whole the CGL leaders drew moderately optimistic conclusions from the interview. The plan which seemed to offer the best prospect of reconciliation was that of the formation of a 'labour party', supported by the unions but non-Socialist. The *Popolo d'Italia* came out in favour of this scheme, and on the union side there were several favourable responses.[140] At the same time, however, Buozzi and even Baldesi sounded a note of distrust. The former remarked caustically that the basis of a political agreement would be hard to find because Fascism had as yet no programme.[141]

If Mussolini were sincere, the unionists had nothing to lose from some sort of pact, since their situation was already desperate. The only alternative policy, secretly advocated by the Left, was that of working within the Fascist unions at the ground level.[142] But one cannot reasonably blame the reformists for attempting to explore other possibilities: the 'infiltration' thesis, though it ultimately might prove necessary, was clearly a counsel of desperation. It roused great resistance among the rank and file, and had little ultimate chance of success, given the Fascist unions' hierarchical structure and effective subordination to the party. During the next months the union leaders watched anxiously for signs of improvement. While their chief desire was to see the end of party terrorism, they also judged the intentions of the Government by its record in social legislation. Corporativist or syndicalist ideas of reform, put into cold storage during the first half of 1923, were now once again the object of serious attention. The Cabinet discussed a draft bill for the legal enforcement of labour contracts on 7 July, but the form of the measure, was not disclosed. Were the benefits of the new legislation to be extended to all unions alike, or were they to be confined to those recognized by the Government: and in the latter case, would this mean giving the corporations a monopoly? Was union membership to remain voluntary, or was it to be made obligatory for all workers, as Sergio Panunzio suggested?[143] Even in industry, the CGL unions were habitually being denied the right to conclude regular collective agreements.

Towards the end of August the CGL held a conference to discuss the new developments and decide policy. In spite of the strong attacks from the left, supported by some of the reformists, the majority of the conference agreed with D'Aragona that the possibility of an agreement could not be ruled out. Apart from announcing that the CGL was ready to provide any form of 'technical' co-operation requested by the Government, D'Aragona made plain that he would not object to a union leader joining the ministry, although he would have to do so as an individual and the CGL would remain formally independent. He also hinted that if the Socialist parties tried to block the agreement, he would be ready to found a labour party.[144] A new decree in early September seemed to give evidence of the Government's good intentions. The freedom of competing unions to conclude contracts and have them legally registered was explicitly recognized: the *Battaglie Sindacali* commented that 'the Government's action was not dictated by faction.'[145] Simultaneously, a decree set up a new consultative body, the Consiglio Superiore dell' Economia; however neither its powers nor its composition were settled. If it were to be given the power to propose and draft legislation, then it could serve as the instrument by which the CGL could exercise 'technical co-operation'.

The optimism of the union leaders was soon shaken. The Cabinet on 15 September agreed on a proposal to give the Prefect powers of supervision over the affairs of associations maintained by the contributions of workers. It was not quite clear whether this was meant to apply only to co-operatives or to unions as well; given the commercial nature of co-operatives, the large funds which they often controlled, and the existence of undoubted cases of corruption, to allow the Prefects to inspect their accounts would not have been wholly unreasonable.[146] The unions were still able to talk to Mussolini. Early in October he saw D'Aragona, Azimonti and Colombino: this meeting marked an apparent example of 'technical co-operation' in action. Mussolini promised to revise the law on labour contracts to take account of the views of the CGL, and assured the trade union leaders that the vigilance decree would apply only to co-operatives. He also agreed to slow down the dismissals of railway workers.[147] The cardinal question, however, remained that of the freedom of the unions and other working-class organizations to operate without fear of action by the *squadristi*. In early August, Mussolini and Finzi persuaded the local Fascists to call off hostilities against the Socialist co-operatives of Reggio Emilia, which had been the most flourishing in the country. Although the co-operatives lost their independence, they were saved from destruction or outright seizure. This agreement alarmed and angered the *ras*, and was attacked in the strongest terms by Baroncini and Farinacci.[148] Their polemic with Finzi was the prelude to the revisionist controversy of September; there is no doubt that the issue of relations between the Government and the old working-class organizations was one of the main causes of the new crisis in the party.

The Fascist movement reacted to Mussolini's conciliatory gestures, as in 1921 and December 1922, by intensifying its offensive against labour. Even the new course which Mussolini set for the party did not, as might reasonably have been expected, benefit the unions. There was no significant diminution in the number of violent incidents; relations between the union leadership and the Government worsened significantly when Mussolini brushed their complaints aside. On 20 October a communiqué from the government-controlled *Agenzia Stefani* dismissed union grievances as 'generic': in the two conversations which Mussolini had 'conceded' to the CGL, 'the only act of violence denounced by the latter was one which is said to have been performed on some pieces of furniture in a trade union office ... at Cagliari ... before the March on Rome.' This frivolous and contemptuous response caused the CGL to draw up a long memorandum setting out all the acts of interference and suppression of liberty committed by the Government and the Fascist movement. A few days later Mussolini, in a speech to the foreign press, claimed that 'the Government has never pursued an anti-worker policy.' This was too much: in reply, the union spokesman Azimonti listed, as well as the suppression of liberty and the breaking of wage agreements, the question of the dismissal of railwaymen and the Fascist record on social legislation.[149] The CGL leaders, it is true, still reaffirmed their readiness to co-operate in a meeting of 26–27 November: but for the moment any chance of a serious agreement was dead. The Consiglio Superiore dell'Economia proved a disappointment; it was only given advisory powers and its composition was left to the discretion of the Minister.[150] Finally, at the beginning of the New Year, the vigilance decree was published, and contrary to Mussolini's promises, it did include the unions.[151] The memorandum of protest which the CGL presented to Mussolini at the beginning of 1924 summed up the failure of 'technical co-operation': in spite of Mussolini's repeated promises, the unions had won no respite and the interests of the working class had been systematically ignored. The CGL had 'passed from disappointment to disappointment'. The memorandum concluded that 'If the Government does not take measures to secure minimum guarantees for our operations, the CGL must consider itself as virtually suppressed.'[152]

After this confession of failure, the further gestures of appeasement made by the CGL leaders cannot so easily be justified. They declared that their members were free to vote as they liked in the general elections. It would have been better to say nothing. It is true that very probably Mussolini intended to make another approach to the unions after the election. But the experience of 1923 had convinced the more resolute among the union chiefs that the hopes of a compromise were illusory: Buozzi, who had been ready to talk in July, in April 1924 declared himself flatly opposed to any further contacts with Mussolini.[153] To conclude that the new attempt would have led to a serious change in the policies of the Fascist government and the direction of the movement appears hazardous.

Left to himself Mussolini no doubt would have liked to come to terms with the CGL. In the 1920s the Spanish dictator Primo de Rivera achieved a *modus vivendi* with the Socialist unions; in Argentina, Peron was to show that a dictator who came to power with a 'Fascist' programme could construct a successful government formula on an alliance with labour. Why, one might ask, could Mussolini have not done the same? After all, unlike De Rivera or Peron, he had a Socialist past which still could be exploited for popularity. The question has only to be posed to make the differences evident. First, Mussolini had come to power over the ruins of union liberty in the countryside and small towns; the destruction of the working-class movement had been the essential activity of the Fascists up till 1922. Secondly, in order to win power, the Fascists had created a huge political, syndical and para-military machine whose interests and structure were directly opposed to the revival of independent working-class action. Mussolini, without an independent power base in the Army, could not afford to weaken his organized support: and in consequence, though he could reach limited agreements with individuals, he could not in fact permit the revival of conditions which would allow unions or mass parties to function freely.

10

THE MATTEOTTI CRISIS

The Murder of Matteotti and its Consequences

The moderate Fascists and their Liberal allies alike hoped that the elections would signify the end of the interregnum; Fascism, having acquired full constitutional legitimacy would be able to renounce the use of illegal violence. However whereas the Liberals regarded the Fascist task as that of restoring the authority of the traditional state, even the revisionists in the party were dissatisfied with the *status quo*. Indeed, as we have seen, it was from them that there had come the most concrete plans for institutional reform. With the end of the period in which it had been easy to justify provisional and irregular measures, it became harder to postpone the basic choices. Would the new legislature bring about the return of Fascism to the constitution, or would it be the constituent assembly for the new Fascist state?

The early days of the new Parliament revealed the fragility of the grounds on which the normalizers' hopes had been based. On the one hand, the Opposition used the parliamentary rostrum to denounce in circumstantial detail all the irregularities of the recent election. The beginnings of the new Chamber showed that Pareto had been right, and that the Opposition, with its mandate confirmed, could embarrass the Government more easily than it had in the old, even if it was now only a minority. As well as the question of the elections, the threatened revelation of financial scandals involving prominent personalities hung over the party and the Government. Giacomo Matteotti, who had led the attack on the validity of the elections, was also rumoured to have prepared a dossier exposing these cases of corruption.[1]

On the other side, Mussolini had to reckon with the hostility to Parliament which was current in his movement. The party as a whole was uneasy at the thought that the elections might actually give new life to the despised institution. The Fascists of Bologna drew the conclusion from the first sittings of the Chamber that the electoral experiment had failed. If the Opposition had shown itself both simple-minded and treacherous, the majority had been 'unprepared and inadequate'. 'Closure, then, and full powers' : the Duce should not compromise with the old forms of government but 'dedicate some days of his laborious existence to the study of a new form of organization which will unite the representatives of knowledge and labour'.[2] The idea of functional representation lived on, and the elimination of Massimo Rocca from the scene made it easier for the intransigents to consider with favour the idea of setting up Technical Councils, though not of course in such a form that they would represent a third force independent of party and unions.

The expulsion of Rocca, which took place in May 1924, was a sign that the *ras* still had a notable capacity for resistance to Mussolini's campaign for greater discipline. It is true that Rocca helped to bring about his disgrace by attacking the Finance Minister De Stefani, in alliance with the dubious adventurer Carlo Bazzi, editor of *Il Nuovo Paese*. A year previously, Bazzi, a great friend also of Cesare Rossi, had described the demand that the Commission on War Expenses should publish its evidence as 'syphilitic demagogy'.[3] His anger can be explained by his activities as organizer of the National Syndicate of Co-Operatives, which were reputed to have brought him a profit of four million lire. Since part of this profit helped to finance the March on Rome, he was entitled to claim consideration as a national benefactor : however Mussolini was not prepared to sacrifice the competent and incorruptible De Stefani.[4] The result of the second revisionist polemic of May 1924 was undoubtedly a victory for Farinacci as well as De Stefani ; the former was once again able to claim that he was the champion of provincial honesty against '*affarismo*'.

The most immediate and serious problem, however, remained that of the Opposition. Their refusal to admit the legitimacy of the Fascist victory undermined the whole foundation of the strategy of Mussolini and Cesare Rossi. In a sense, the Matteotti crisis can be said to have begun even before the tragic murder of the Socialist leader, with his speech to the Chamber on 30 May. The salient feature of the crisis was to be the secession of the Opposition from Parliament, known as the 'Aventine'. The 'Aventine secession' condemned to failure the idea of an assimilationist, outwardly legal, constitutionally conservative, form of Fascism. What is important is to note that the idea of such a secession was already current in the first week of June 1924, before the murder. It was prompted by the abuse and actual physical intimidation of Opposition deputies by the Fascists within the Chamber of Deputies. Government sources accused Matteotti of being one of the leading advocates of secession, though it is doubtful whether this was in fact the case.[5] On the Fascist side, Matteotti's speech immediately brought about the formulation of a contingency plan to deal with a possible secession. Cesare Rossi, as head of Mussolini's Press Office, sent a circular to the pro-Government newspapers ordering them to unmask the 'concerted plan' of the Opposition to prepare for a secession : 'These plans are destined seriously to compromise the long hoped for and now achieved normalization of national life, because of the inevitable and legitimate reaction that the Fascist movement will at the right moment unleash.'[6]

The murder of Matteotti was not simply an unforeseeable accident. There is plenty of evidence that both Mussolini and his entourage had personally arranged for a number of assaults on individual opponents. In December 1923 Amendola had been set upon and beaten in the street : according to the later confession of the *capomanipolo* of the Militia, Perrone, who led the assault, 'When I was given the name of the Rt Hon. Amendola I was taken aback – the affair made me nervous – but I was personally able to ascertain that His Excellency Mussolini himself wished that it should be carried out.'[7] These assaults, organized in the offices of the Viminale by members of the *Comando Generale* of the Militia, differed in character from the usual terroristic activities of the *squadristi*.[8] They were directed against a small number of individuals who had resisted or embarrassed Mussolini in his tactics of absorption ; it is significant that the victims were not usually communists or *massimalisti*, but dissident Fascists (Misuri or Forni), Democrats (Amendola, Gobetti) or Reformist Socialists (Matteotti). Misuri had exposed the realities behind the fine phrases about the supremacy of State over party : Amendola and Matteotti, besides leading the Opposition in Parliament, had exerted a notable influence respectively on the independent ex-combatants and the CGL leaders, groups which Fascism was anxious to absorb.

On 10 June bystanders on the Lungotevere Arnaldo Di Brescia in Rome saw five men force another into a car, which then drove off. When the disappearance of Matteotti was reported, the car was rapidly traced : it turned out to belong to Filippelli, the editor of *Corriere Italiano*, formerly the mouthpiece of the under-secretary Finzi, but now inspired by Rossi.[9] There were bloodstains on the car, and the obvious conclusion was drawn that Matteotti had been murdered, although his corpse was not discovered till months later. Further inquiries revealed the assassins to be Amerigo Dumini, a notorious Florentine *squadrista*, closely associated with Cesare Rossi, the equally dangerous Milanese '*ardito*' Albino Volpi, G. Poveromo, Viola and Malacria.[10]

It is not my intention to go over all the facts relating to the murder and to the enquiry. It will be enough to say that the evidence does not allow a certain conclusion about the degree of Mussolini's responsibility. However it seems unquestionable that the attack on Matteotti was ordered either by Mussolini himself or by the two leading members of his entourage, Cesare Rossi and Marinelli, on their own responsibility. Any other hypothesis would make it impossible to explain why Rossi, previously a devoted supporter of Mussolini, should have accused him of having ordered the crime : either his accusation was justified, or else he was trying to shield himself. But it is very unlikely that Rossi and Marinelli would have arranged to kidnap Matteotti unless they had believed that Mussolini wanted it done. One perfectly plausible explanation lies in what one might call the 'Becket hypothesis' : Rossi or Marinelli may have interpreted one of Mussolini's outbursts of violent invective as an order to make Matteotti disappear, or even to kill him.[11] The second problem which cannot be resolved with certainty is whether whoever gave the order really intended Matteotti to be killed, or simply 'given a lesson' : there would have been only a very doubtful political advantage in the latter course, given Matteotti's well known courage, but the hypothesis can still not be ruled out. Calculating as he was, there was an impulsive side to Mussolini's temperament which sometimes led him to seek vendetta without weighing the consequences. But whether it was Mussolini or his advisers who gave the first order, and whether the murder was planned or partly accidental, it is clear that the initiative came from Mussolini's immediate entourage. Farinacci was fond of pointing out with some unction that the 'savages' of extremist Fascism could not be saddled with responsibility for this crime. This apparent paradox can be easily explained in both political and psychological terms. It was the moderates, and not the extremists, who had reason to fear Matteotti's attempt to deny the legality of the elections and the possibility of a secession : the *ras* had no use for Parliament, and would benefit (as the sequel showed) from actions that would make compromise harder. Seen in this light, the conciliatory speech delivered by Mussolini to the Chamber of Deputies on 7 June is not really evidence against his involvement in the crime. The more he desired to prevent a showdown and to exert his powers of persuasion on the more vulnerable members of the Opposition, the greater the motive he had for desiring the disappearance of a man whom he knew to be unshakeable. From a psychological standpoint, it is likely that those who had been trying to give Fascism a veneer of parliamentary legitimacy would be the most angered when this was called in question. There is first-hand evidence of Cesare Rossi's uncontrollable rage at Matteotti's speech.[12]

In the days after the murder, Mussolini and his entourage were taken by surprise by the rapidity with which suspicion spread. A full dictatorship could easily have suffocated or diverted the enquiries; but the existence of an independent press and magistracy, and the formal respect of parliamentary privilege, made this impossible. Mussolini had profited from the complaisant attitude of the members of the old political class, disposed to overlook acts of violence and violations of the law providing they were not forced on their attention. But premeditated political murder, in Rome, while Parliament was sitting, was another matter. The nobility and courage of Matteotti's character made an immense impression.

In the Chamber on 12 June, Mussolini returned an evasive answer to the deputies who urged that greater efforts be made to find out Matteotti's whereabouts. At this moment the Republican Eugenio Chiesa burst out 'Then, he is an accomplice!' (*Allora è complice*).[13] Seldom have three words had a greater immediate effect. Temporarily, they broke the spell imposed by fear and caution: Mussolini was in the dock. In the next few days his conduct was extremely indecisive: several eye-witnesses describe him as in a state of mental paralysis.[14] His closest collaborators were equally incapable of formulating a concerted strategy and of recovering the initiative: their mutual distrust was too great, and all cohesion in Mussolini's entourage rapidly disappeared amid a welter of conflicting accusations. Spontaneous demonstrations in favour of the Opposition broke out in the streets, which was something that had not been seen for a long time. Mussolini, probably at the party's suggestion, tried to throw the blame onto Finzi and to present the murder as the result of plutocratic intrigues. The idea that Jews (Finzi was Jewish), Freemasons and the Banca Commerciale were responsible for the murder is too characteristic of the 'paranoid style' of Fascism to be taken seriously. Some Fascists took the inevitable further step of suggesting that the crime was in fact the outcome of a subtle plot which had aimed deliberately to discredit Fascism.[15]

On 13 June the Fascist ministers in the Cabinet intervened with decisive effect. De Stefani, Oviglio and Federzoni, followed on the fourteenth by Gentile, all threatened to resign unless Mussolini got rid of his morally suspect subordinates, that is to say, Rossi and Marinelli as well as Finzi.[16] They also demanded the broadening of the ministry. The threat from the moderate elements in his own Cabinet was reinforced by the danger of an intervention by Victor Emmanuel. After initial resistance, Mussolini agreed to hand over the vital Interior Ministry to Federzoni, although he delayed making other changes. The appointment of Federzoni, if it considerably diminished Mussolini's liberty of action, may ultimately have worked to his advantage. It encouraged the illusion that he was safely under the control of the Crown and the moderate and legalitarian right. The bland and cultivated Federzoni reassured those *benpensanti* who feared the unpredictable brutality of the Fascists.[17] Even many of the Opposition believed that at the right moment Federzoni would join with the Liberals in imposing on Mussolini the choice of resignation or the liquidation of the Fascist movement, and if he chose the latter alternative, his fall would still not be long delayed.

After the first days, Mussolini's position rapidly improved: on 17 June he had his first audience with the King since the murder, and nothing happened. Turati is a witness to the change of atmosphere: 'the day before yesterday we were the victors almost without knowing it, and he was beaten and knew it. Yesterday they had already taken heart.'[18] The Opposition had lost their first and perhaps best chance to act: however only with the advantages of hindsight can one say that they were definitely wrong in trusting to legal methods to overthrow Fascism. To have called a general strike would have run the danger of alarming the bourgeoisie and the forces of order, and driving them back into the arms of Fascism. Carlo Sforza was in favour of arresting Mussolini by a *coup de main*. A small and determined group of conspirators could possibly have carried out such a coup; but where was such a group to be found ? One of the few men who had the necessary dash and resolution was Zaniboni, the Socialist war hero and friend of D'Annunzio, but Zaniboni's discretion was not equal to his courage. As he disarmingly confessed in his memoirs, 'the role of the professional conspirator did not suit my temperament'.[19]

A more practicable proposal was that the Opposition should form themselves into an anti-parliament and deny the validity of the majority's mandate. This move would have thrown the onus of action onto Mussolini and the Fascists at a time when their resolution had been shaken. The King and the conservatives would not have been able to remain inactive and hope for a pacific solution. It is clear, however, that this plan would have had to have been put into action immediately to have had a chance of success. When the Communists proposed it in November, the time was long past, and indeed they themselves brought forward the proposal in order to embarrass the other parties rather than because they seriously thought it could work.[20]

Turati was in favour of taking some decisive action, probably of this nature, in the first days; but he was restrained by Amendola and Gronchi, with the majority of the constitutional opposition and the Popolari.[21] On the night of 12 June they announced that they would abstain from taking part in the work of the Chamber, but the definitive decision to secede was taken only two weeks later. The 'Aventine' secession, even without the constitution of a rival authority, was a dramatic gesture which had a strong moral effect. But the maintenance of the secession, once the initial effect of the crime and the protest had worn off, led the Opposition into a blind alley. The idea that a dignified but essentially passive protest would bring about the fall of Fascism was a dangerous illusion. Like many illusions, it was the result of a compromise between incompatible aims. Amendola and the other Aventinians wished to make a clean break with Fascism, but they also put their trust in a legalitarian strategy which required for success either the intervention of the Crown, or the disintegration of the Fascist majority, or both. It should have become clear to them in the months which followed that their return to the Chamber would greatly increase the chances of overthrowing Fascism by legal methods. Instead, by remaining outside Parliament, they gave the King a pretext to wash his hands of the situation.

At the same time, the Aventine parties did not succeed in presenting themselves as a credible alternative government. This was not altogether their fault. Amendola and Turati, though often in disagreement about tactics, co-operated cordially, and a coalition between the Reformist Socialists, the constitutional opposition and even a part of the Liberal party, headed by Albertini, would undoubtedly have been possible. A really stable coalition, however, would have also needed the support of the Popolari. In July, feelers from both sides showed that the leaders of the PPI and the PSU were ready for such an alliance. But at this point Pius XI made known his opposition in unequivocal terms. The idea of co-operation between a Catholic party and the Socialists where there was no absolute necessity for it showed, he said, 'dangerous immaturity'.[22] Subsequent statements made clear that he regarded this directive as binding. The Pope's intervention was doubly serious because it implied not only a criticism of the projected coalition with the Socialists, but a withdrawal of his trust from the PPI itself. The Pope intended to reassert his authority and to deny the existence of an autonomous sphere of political action within which Catholics were not subject to ecclesiastical discipline, which Benedict XV had instead been prepared to concede. In August the Vatican, not content with having forced his resignation, ordered Don Sturzo to go into exile. It is ironic that the first major political exile should have left Italy in obedience to the commands of the Church.

Yet it is only fair to say that there was much apparent evidence to sustain the hope that time would bring about the collapse of Fascism through isolation and internal disintegration. Once the Opposition had agreed to trust to strictly legal methods, it was necessary for them to play a waiting game. The Crown would not intervene so long as Mussolini still enjoyed respectable conservative support, and the Liberals were unfortunately still disposed to extend further credit to Mussolini. They believed that the purge of the Viminale and the appointment of Federzoni were sufficient guarantees, and they were afraid of the threat of a revival of subversion. The rapid worsening of living standards among the workers and peasants brought about by Fascism gave a sharper edge to these fears. Giolitti had no desire to see the triumph of an Amendola-Sturzo-Turati combination; moreover, the surprising turn in the political situation appeared to confirm the wisdom of 'the theory of Tolstoy'. A little longer and Fascism would disintegrate, without the need for violent measures : such a pacific solution would avoid the risk of a swing to the opposite extreme. On 26 June the Senate, which unlike the Chamber had not been packed by Mussolini, voted confidence in the Government by 225 votes to 21, with 6 abstentions. This large majority reflected the traditional conservatism and dislike of political initiative natural in a body of men mainly distinguished by age, wealth and past government service. However the decision to support the Government was not confined to relics of the nineteenth century or retired Prefects : the leading representative of Italian culture, Benedetto Croce, voted with the majority. He told an interviewer that while Fascism 'should give up the claim of inaugurating a new historical epoch, we should not expect, or even hope, that Fascism should fall suddenly'. It had 'done much good', and created new 'interests' which might not always be admirable, but which could not be ignored. 'We must therefore give Fascism time to complete its process of transformation.'[23]

The dangers of such a comfortable and passive trust in the natural evolution of events were soon demonstrated. On 1 July a cabinet reshuffle brought in two right-wing Liberals, Casati and Sarrocchi, and a clerico – moderate, Cesare Nava. However the conditional approval of the conservatives was only one of the elements which enabled Mussolini to stage a recovery. The other was the revival of the movement, led by the provincial intransigents. The group of men on whom Mussolini had relied to bring the party under his personal control had been totally dispersed and discredited by the murder and its aftermath. Rossi and Marinelli were under arrest, Finzi and De Bono had been forced to resign. The intransigents seized their opportunity to reverse the trend of the previous six months. Even more than the disgrace of Mussolini's entourage, the logic of the situation helped to bring about the intransigent revival.

The Militia

The MVSN had originated in the need to give an occupation and a legal status to the mass of the *squadristi* after the March on Rome.[24] Even before the March the squads had, at least in theory, been transformed into a revolutionary army, with a regular hierarchy of command. But this Fascist Militia, although it eased mobilization for the grand manoeuvres of 1922, was something of a façade. 'The whole *esprit de corps* of the blackshirts was concentrated in the squad.'[25] The squads had their own names, their own banners and sometimes special membership cards, and they owed allegiance to a particular leader, who was chosen informally. The origins of many squads are to be found in a loose, informal relationship between a group of adolescents, somewhat resembling that of a youth gang. Rivalry between different squads in the same city frequently turned to hostility. Primary ties of kinship or friendship were important in creating a feeling of camaraderie among the *squadristi*. The existence of this 'small group solidarity' served to protect the Fascist from the feelings of impotence and ennui common among those in the grip of large, impersonal bureaucratic organizations; they seemed to allow the individual to achieve both integration and independence. At the same time, of course, the violence which was the essence of *squadrismo* allowed an outlet for aggression.

The influence of the squadrist mystique survived the formation of the Militia. The 'style of life' which Fascism held up for admiration was military in its inspiration; but the values which were especially emphasized were not those of the regular soldier but of the volunteer. Italy had no military heroes who could rival the fascination of Garibaldi. The volunteer tradition, emptied of any serious democratic content, survived within Fascism in the form of a penchant for individualist heroics and a belief in improvisation. It was difficult to reconcile the cult of informality and allegiance to 'natural' leaders with the new requirements of discipline.

In the Fascist Militia (before the March) the commands up to the rank of consul were either elected from below or appointed by the local party organization. There was strong opposition among the '*squadristi*' to the abandonment of this method in favour of appointment from above.* The foundation of the MVSN could only be effected with the co-operation of the *ras*, whose prestige was needed to convince the leaders of the individual squads to submit to the discipline of the new organization. Consequently, although a number of retired officers of the regular army were introduced into the highest ranks, at a lower level the Command was very cautious in replacing the old leaders. 'It kept, one could say, nearly all the consuls in office. The consuls were the pivots of our squads; it was around the consuls that they grouped themselves. The consul was the man who enjoyed the absolute confidence of his followers. ...' In short, the consuls remained the backbone of the Militia, and they were mostly old Fascists; they supervised recruitment and thus ensured that the old *squadristi* were predominant among the rank and file.[26]

The generals of the regular army regarded the creation of the MVSN with some suspicion. They appreciated the function that the Militia would play in relieving the army of responsibility for public order; it had long been a military grievance against the Liberal governments that they had allowed so much routine police work to fall on the shoulders of the troops.[27] But the army commanders were at the same time aware of the possible dangers inherent in the creation of a large para-military force recruited on a political basis, and outside their control.

Before the March on Rome, the Fascist party had identified itself to some extent with ideas of army reform. The ex-combatants and reserve officers had derived from the experience of the war a good deal of distrust for the traditional wisdom of the regulars and the higher commands. Fascism, founded as it was on the 'combatants', could not ignore this state of mind, and was therefore concerned to project a radical image. The party adopted the old democratic programme of the 'armed nation'.[28] In practical terms, this meant the proposal to reduce the period of conscription and the numbers of the regular army, while taking measures to ensure that manpower and industry could be mobilized with rapidity in the event of war. This programme was strongly opposed by the majority of the generals and regular officers, who saw in it a threat to their careers.

The military establishment feared that the creation of the MVSN might be the first step towards the realization of the 'armed nation'. Part-time military training was an essential feature of this programme, and the MVSN was intended by De Bono and Mussolini to perform this function. The

---

* Only the officers from the rank of consul upwards were in permanent paid service. The rank and file of the junior commanders instead remained in civilian occupations and served only as and when they were summoned. The consul commanded a legion, at full strength about 1,500 men.

opposition of the generals, in alliance with the Nationalists, to the creation of the Militia was only overcome by Mussolini's conciliatory tactics. In return for the Army's agreement to allow the constitution of the Militia, he agreed to drop all projects of military reform and to confine the new organization to police functions. The deal must have been fixed in a conversation between Marshal Diaz and Mussolini on 26 December 1922; on the next day, the Cabinet meeting which discussed the foundation of the MVSN also decided to raise the period of conscription from twelve to eighteen months. This signified the rejection of the 'armed nation' idea. Diaz also imposed the abandonment of the project to constitute a single Ministry of National Defence, with authority over all three services and power to plan arms production.[29] This scheme had been proposed by General Douhet, the famous theorist of aerial warfare, who enjoyed much support in Fascist circles and had obtained the post of Commissioner for Military Aviation.[30]

However distrust between the Army and the MVSN remained. The regulars viewed the pretensions of the jumped-up Militia commanders with professional disdain.[31] Diaz politely but firmly squashed the suggestion by De Bono and De Vecchi that the officers of the Army and the Militia should exchange salutes.[32] It was the problem of rank which did most to create bad blood between the officers of the two corps. The Militia commanders enjoyed extremely favourable treatment; the pay and bureaucratic status of Balbo as 'Commandant General' was equal to that of the commander of an Army corps, while the consul was equated with a colonel. It was a scandal, in army eyes, that such dignity should be granted to wartime subalterns, or even to retired regulars who now obtained ranks in the Militia higher than those of their contemporaries who had stayed in active service.

The essential function of the MVSN as originally devised was to protect the government of Mussolini by armed force. It swore loyalty to Mussolini alone, not to the King. In the aftermath of the debate on the Acerbo Law, De Bono put forward a plan for the transformation of the Militia into an organization with military rather than political functions. Its numbers should be reduced to 100,000, its commands should be entrusted exclusively to former regular officers, and it should take over the task of pre-military training. The De Bono plan also revived the idea of a single Defence Ministry, to which the MVSN, like the other armed forces, would be subject. The July 1923 Grand Council, however, threw out De Bono's plan and reaffirmed that the Militia's essential function was that of 'a great political police'. The terms of the Grand Council motion emphasized the intransigent inspiration of the decision; 'Fascism cannot renounce the armed force of the blackshirts ... until the state has become integrally Fascist, until, that is to say, the Fascist ruling class or one loyal to Fascism has succeeded the ruling class of yesterday in all the administrations and institutions of the State.'[33]

It seems certain that Mussolini had given his approval to De Bono's scheme; in his speech at the close of the electoral reform debate he had hinted that the anomalous position of the Militia would shortly be regularized. Undoubtedly Mussolini was favourable to the gradual replacement of the riotous *squadristi* by career officers; this was all part of his programme for bringing Fascism under control. But one cannot tell how far he was really unwilling to acquiesce in the Grand Council's unexpected decision; it would seem reasonable to suppose that he might have had reservations about surrendering his unfettered personal control. His whole policy at that time was one of gestures rather than firm commitment. In January 1924 he declined to adopt a scheme drawn up by the Chief of the General Staff, General Ferrari, for 'gearing' the Militia to the Army, on the grounds that he did not intend 'to rob the Militia of its Fascist character'.[34] However there is no doubt that during and after the revisionist crisis (September–October 1923), the question of the Militia became one of the many points of conflict between Mussolini and the intransigents. Mussolini did not intend to let either the party or the Army dictate to him if he could help it.

Any attempt to define the MVSN's relationship with the Army aroused strong opposition among the Militia commanders. They had won their positions by the 'rights of revolution', and 'natural ascendancy', and they were suspicious of any transformation which might lead to the requirement of higher technical qualifications for command. Farinacci threatened to resign, together with a number of other commanders, because they were required to take an examination.[35] Moreover it was almost certain that the Army would demand as the price for any agreement the reduction of the Militia officers to a rank more or less equivalent with that which they had held in active service. On the other hand, the Army leaders continued to suspect the Militia's ambitions to usurp its training functions and to claim autonomy in time of war as well as peace. They were still troubled by the spectre of the 'armed nation'. Moreover a section of the officer-corps feared that to give the Militia responsibilities in the field of military education might open the door to the fascistization of the Army itself.[36]

The Matteotti crisis heightened the tensions inherent in the position of the Militia. Pressures from conservative and Army circles for the re-definition of its status and functions became more insistent; but the intransigents argued that the Militia had been created for just such a crisis as now threatened, and that it was therefore essential to preserve its Fascist character unaltered. To the minds of simple and violent men, it might well seem that the time had come to pass from menace to action. Besides the desire to justify their existence, more selfish motives urged the Militia officers to resist strenuously the pressures for normalization. These threatened not only their rank, money and status, but still more basic privileges. The Militia officers had enjoyed near immunity from the penalties of the law. They had no legal right to avoid arrest by the civil powers, but in spite of the opposition of the Ministry of Justice it became standard practice to allow the Militia to carry out the arrest and imprisonment of its own officers. This 'military arrest' was often a synonym for complete liberty. In spite of his much vaunted legalitarian scruples, De Bono sanctioned this state of affairs.[37]

During June the Militia performed important services for Fascism. At 5.40 pm on 13 June Mussolini ordered the mobilization of six legions, in Rome, Perugia, Florence, Bologna, Ferrara and Milan. Although definitive evidence is lacking, it seems likely in view of the general demoralization of the Roman Fascists, which was noted by all observers, that in Rome the mobilization was a failure. Between 14 June and 16 June the anti-Fascists had a chance to control the piazza. However in the provinces matters went differently. At midday on the fourteenth, 1,600 men had already been mobilized in Florence, and 1,200 in Milan, and though the response was slower in the other cities this was probably the result of confusion rather than panic.[38] By 17 June, taking the State visit of Ras Tafari of Ethiopia as an excuse, Mussolini was able to concentrate the provincial Militia in the capital. At this point, the likelihood of violent action or even successful mass demonstrations by the Opposition had evaporated. By 19 June two complete legions, the Florentine and the Perugian, were in Rome, and other squads were continuing to arrive. The influx of *squadristi* was halted by Federzoni, who feared that they might get out of hand, with disastrous results.[39]

The mobilization of the six legions was not the only step taken. The *Comando Generale* of the Militia secretly gave orders for the assignment of both arms and ammunition to the individual Militia units throughout Italy. Previously the arms had been kept in the custody of the army or the *carabinieri*. The distribution of arms and ammunition was contrary to regulations, and cannot be interpreted as an orthodox provision for the security of the State against subversion. As the Militia was short of barracks, many arms had to be stored in the officers' private houses, where they were exposed to the risk of theft. The purpose can only have been to subtract the Fascist private army from the last vestige of control by the other organs of the State, in view of a possible conflict, or at least to heighten the threat of civil war. Significantly, the local army commanders, the Prefects and Federzoni tried to put obstacles in the way of the Militia's armament.[40]

Mussolini referred jocularly in his speech on 25 June to the 'absurd rumours' of a planned Militia coup.[41] But in fact these rumours had some consistency. There is no evidence that Mussolini himself favoured such a move: it is more probable that after he had set the machine in motion it developed its own momentum. At Perugia the rumours of a possible '*coup de main*' by the Militia on the night of 21 June were serious enough to cause the Prefect to take 'precautionary measures' in concert with the local garrison. It is not clear, however, whether the fear was of a coup in the sense of the occupation of public buildings and communication centres, or merely of a punitive expedition against the opposition.[42]

On 19 June tens of thousands of *squadristi* gathered in Bologna, and this was the prelude to a much bigger rally in the same city three days later, when 50 or 60,000 Fascists, mainly from Emilia, assembled. This was the first of a series of regional rallies designed to raise morale and show strength. Of the leaders who addressed the rally, Dino Grandi took a fairly moderate line. If he indulged in revolutionary rhetoric about the possibility of a new March on Rome, he also declared himself in favour of 'a profound revision' of the party. Balbo, however, significantly recalled the earlier rally held by the Emilian Fascists in July 1921 to protest against the Pact of Pacification, when 'we affirmed that Fascism was an idea and not a man'. Even if he went on to say that 'not Fascism but Italy now has a single face . . . that of Benito Mussolini', the warning was more important than the obligatory words of devotion.[43] Balbo was making clear that the provincial Fascists did not intend to allow Mussolini to conclude peace at their expense. After the rally the Fascist leaders held a secret meeting. A number of the participants spoke in favour of a violent counter-offensive or 'second wave', but more cautious counsels prevailed.[44] In general, it was the Militia officers who were for 'acts of force' while the party officials were more reconciled to playing a waiting game. It must be remembered, however, that in some provinces (e.g. Florence, Ferrara, Ravenna) the Militia dominated the party.

After the Bologna meeting the danger of an attempted coup receded; the Militia passed from conspiracy to more open pressure tactics. On 30 June Balbo organized a 'grand review' of the Militia commanders of Emilia, Tuscany and the Veneto, and afterwards telegraphed to Mussolini on their behalf declaring that 'the Militia remained the guardian of the Duce and of Fascism.'[45] This was a thinly veiled collective protest against the idea that the Militia should be placed under Army control. Even the projected ceremony in which the Militia would swear loyalty to the King had to be postponed.[46] In a circular of 5 July, Balbo advised the Militia officers to be patient and not to fear for their jobs or their political function.

Our nerves must always be in order, more than ever at this time. . . . I have the firm conviction that those higher officers and generals who are able to keep their units in a state of splendid efficiency, and who have been promoted in the examinations, will not be touched. The Militia will not lose its character . . . if it were lost it would die of apathy. The *Comando Generale* is informed by these ideas and cannot legitimately depart from them. I therefore beg officers not to write me too many private letters.[47]

Balbo's confidence was justified. A new decree modifying the regulations of the Militia appeared on 1 August, after it had been approved by the commanders.[48] In substance, there was little to discontent them. The Militia remained at the direct orders of Mussolini except while it performed functions of pre-military training. Its Fascist uniforms, symbols and nomenclature were untouched. Recruitment, although it was nominally opened to non-Fascists, remained under the control of the consuls. Finally, a small concession was made to the Army by the ruling that outside the service MVSN officers would enjoy the same rank as they had had in the Army: however within the Militia they could continue to exercise functions of command superior to their nominal rank. Nevertheless, a feeling of discontent and uncertainty about the future persisted among the former *squadristi*.[49] On the anniversary of the March on Rome, the Militia finally swore loyalty to the King. The oath was an important gesture of reassurance to the monarchy, which had good reason to fear the well known republican sympathies of Balbo. But it did not satisfy the Army leaders or conservative opinion, who regarded it as merely the prelude to a satisfactory settlement which would render the Militia politically innocuous.[50]

The Consiglio Nazionale: Mussolini between the Fascist party and the Liberals

The impression made by the murder of Matteotti had been far greater in Rome and other great cities than in the provincial towns, where Fascist control was tighter and the climate of violence more oppressive. Fascists who left Rome for the provinces, like Costanzo Ciano, experienced 'a sense of relief'.[51] The Fascists of Florence, Ferrara or Cremona remained confident; the débâcle of Roman Fascism simply confirmed what Farinacci and the other *ras* had been saying for a long time, namely that it was untrustworthy and corrupt.

Mussolini himself saw the need to favour the provincial extremists. Once his panic was over and the immediate threat of dismissal had been removed by the interview with the King, the Senate vote and the Cabinet reshuffle, Mussolini turned to rally his own forces. Only the enthusiasm of the provincial masses and the armed force of the Militia could give him the strength he needed to resist the pressure for his removal. But Mussolini's commitment to the intransigents was only temporary; his strategy still conformed to its characteristic pattern of alternating menace and conciliation. He seconded the revival of the movement in order to restore his bargaining power; he had not yet abandoned all hope of compromise.

However this time Mussolini's customary strategy proved inadequate. The party and even the Fascist unions acquired a new independence from the Government as a result of the crisis. Michele Bianchi spoke for the dissatisfied and the critics of Mussolini's leadership when he suggested 'that the party should acquire a certain autonomy'.[52] The vigorous revival of provincial Fascism, in part born of fear, was reflected in the foundation of a number of new journals which expressed the intransigent viewpoint. This was particularly a Tuscan phenomenon; July saw the appearance of the Florentine *Battaglie Fasciste*, a paper mainly characterized by the crudest type of abuse and physical threats, and the more intellectual *Conquista dello Stato* and *Il Selvaggio*, edited respectively by Kurt Eric Suckert, better known as Malaparte, and Mino Maccari. The mood of the provincial Fascists was often openly critical of Mussolini; an editorial on 19 July in *Il Selvaggio* remarked that 'the evil of Fascism is idolatry. We have come to identify the idea with the man without thinking that men can change and make mistakes and ideas are immortal.' They blamed the crisis of Fascism on the continuance of old style parliamentary politics and the refusal to make a clean break with the past.

If the intransigents showed new vigour, the situation also gave a new stimulus to the legalitarian critique of the revisionists, whose chief spokesman was now Bottai. Bottai called for a purge of the violence and the dishonest, the repudiation of 'the revolution of arms and blood', and the 'restoration of normal contact between governors and governed', both in the party and the nation. But, as has already been observed, the demand for greater internal democracy in the party was not likely to produce the results for which Bottai hoped. 'The knowledge on high of what the lower levels are doing and thinking'[53] was more likely to lead to a decisive break with the constitution. The Florentine Fascists sent a delegation to Mussolini on 11 July to convey to him the decision of the provincial federation in favour of complete intransigence. This was the first of a series of ostentatious visits by provincial Fascists to the capital. Bolognese Fascism had been relatively moderate at the end of June, under the influence of Grandi. But Grandi, back in favour, was made Under-Secretary for the Interior, and Arpinati, who had been temporarily incapacitated by a car accident, reassumed control. From this time on, Bologna joined the other 'capital of Fascism', Florence, in demanding extreme measures.

Suckert and the *Selvaggio* spoke for the mass of discontented petty bourgeois and ex-combatants who felt that the 'revolution' which they had made had been betrayed. Suckert saw the task of Fascism as that of making possible 'the effective participation of the masses of ex-combatants in government'.[54] The 'revolutionaries' of Fascism, though they recognized the failings of many party chiefs, their lack of culture and often of honesty, none the less had to make a fetish of the party. They identified it with that 'heroic democracy', or reign of force, virility and will, which was their ideal.[55] It is hard to relate these vague aspirations to concrete political aims, although the *Selvaggio* wanted a revolution against the lawyers and the *commendatori* and the re-establishment of the community of the trenches. It was the impossible dream of a society which could repudiate class distinctions but recognize true natural merit. 'There were no class differences at the front.'[56] Suckert had some ideas for positive reform: Parliament should be replaced by technical councils and an assembly chosen by indirect election through the provinces and the communes.[57] This programme reflected both syndicalist and Republican ideas, but it still appears something of an anticlimax after all the bold talk of revolution.

The new provisional *direttorio* of the party hastily appointed on 16 June included Farinacci and one or two of his supporters. Although Farinacci was once more in the ascendant, after a period of near disgrace, his influence was not yet dominant. It was contested by the ex-Nationalists, two of whose leaders, Forges Davanzati and Maraviglia, were members of the *direttorio*. The former, as the senior member, was the nearest the party had to an official leader. Forges and Maraviglia defended 'extremism' and refused the idea of a reconciliation with liberalism or 'the democratic state'; but at the same time they insisted that the emphasis should be on constitutional change rather than on violence.[58] This was the position which was closest to Mussolini's own. But Mussolini also gave strong encouragement to the syndicalist intellectuals and the more radical trade union organizers. He wanted to restore the credibility of Fascism as a serious political force; it must therefore acquire a new look and undertake institutional reform. This line would give some satisfaction to all sections of the party. The intransigents would be pleased by the prospect of a 'revolutionary' break with liberalism, and the revisionists by the emphasis on constitutional change rather than violence.

Mussolini's speech to the Grand Council on 22 July,[59] even though he declared himself an 'anti-normalizer', did not altogether please the extremists. They disliked his praise of the Nationalists, and still more his suggestion that a kind of inspectorate should be set up 'to supervise the political and private activity of the leaders of the party', possibly headed by someone outside the party. This was in substance a revisionist proposal, and it got a predictably poor welcome from the *ras* and their supporters.

Mussolini saw that he needed to go further if he were to regain the confidence of the party. On 30 July he sent an open letter to Arpinati, congratulating him on his recovery, in which he referred sarcastically to 'the idea that we should become good Liberals, heirs of that Risorgimento, in which, if I am not mistaken, besides the Liberals, there took part Republicans, like Mazzini and Garibaldi and even Socialists like Pisacane'.[60] This letter, as much for the choice of recipient as for the message, was taken as a clear option for the intransigents and the Fascist left. The *Consiglio Nazionale* of the Fascist party, which lasted from 2 to 7 August, was an important event, unlike many such meetings. The composition of the assembly (all *federali* and Fascist deputies) favoured the extremists. Mussolini's opening speech praised the solidity of rural Fascism, in contrast to that of the cities. 'Men of the provinces ... I want you to carry your rough spirit into the over-populated cities. ... We must make Fascism a prevalently rural phenomenon. All the remnants ... of the old parties have taken refuge in the cities.'[61] This was the first time that Mussolini had taken sides openly with the agrarian wing of the movement. The *Consiglio Nazionale*, in fact, achieved the political rehabilitation of the *ras*. The meeting was a personal triumph for Farinacci, who from now on became unquestionably the leading figure in the party.[62]

The new *direttorio* was elected on a regional basis, which ensured the predominance of the intransigents, who had insisted strongly on the adoption of this method. Farinacci shared the leadership with Forges Davanzati, who were the two members of the *direttorio's* executive committee charged with responsibility for general political questions.[63] Forges Davanzati in his opening speech had criticized 'localism' and demanded that the party should follow the Government's directives with discipline. There must be no repetition of the situation in September 1923, when the party was 'disorientated by internal polemics' at the very time when Mussolini was occupied with the international crisis of Corfu. This argument, typical of the Nationalists, was clearly aimed at Farinacci as well as the revisionists.[64] However Forges' speech was out of key with the prevailing spirit of the assembly, which was concerned to affirm the rights of the 'revolutionary' provinces. The revisionists were on the defensive. The view of the majority was expressed by Bastianini, who re-christened the opposing points of view 'integralist' and 'neo-liberal'. 'The neo-Liberals are for making Fascism parliamentary and the Fascists are for making Parliament Fascist.' Farinacci was also successful in putting paid to any idea of a purge, or the creation of an independent inspectorate to watch over the party.[65]

The practical issue of control over the party was of more concern to the extremists than the theoretical issues also discussed by the assembly. Nevertheless the general conclusions of the *Consiglio Nazionale* were also of great importance. The council voted a motion in favour of institutional reform proposed by Corrado Marchi: as was usual in Fascist gatherings, formal unity was preserved and the motion was signed by both Farinacci and Bottai. In its original form, the motion clearly embodied the views of 'revolutionaries' such as Suckert; it spoke of 'the necessity to develop the revolution by the insertion of new forces which are the expression of the provinces of Italy in the old and by now exhausted organization of the demo-liberal state through the transformation of the existing institutions and the creation of new institutions which will bring the Fascist revolution to the complete conquest of the State.' However the motion was watered down in response to the strong objections raised by conservatives outside the party and the ex-Nationalists within it. The final text eliminated the reference to the 'provinces', omitted the vital phrase 'the conquest of the State', and carefully blurred the distinction between the revolutionary overthrow of the existing parliamentary constitution and a partial modification of it.[66]

Mussolini had exerted himself to paper over the cracks in the party, and to persuade the wild men that while he was on their side about ends, they must trust him as to means. 'We must chloroform ... the Opposition and the Italian people. The state of mind of the Italian people is this: do anything but let us know afterwards. Don't tell us every day that you want to bring in firing squads. That annoys us.' Mussolini's closing speech, of which the most important parts remained secret and were not released to the Press, was certainly one of his most able performances.[67] But the unity achieved was precarious, and Mussolini had paid a higher price for it than he intended. The Liberals had watched the revival of Fascist violence with growing disillusionment. The *Giornale d'Italia* (now the property of the Liberal party) at first took the line that it was the duty of the Liberals 'to sustain the government . . . in the task of the purge of the Viminale and the liquidation of provincial *rassismo*', adding that the 'country' would deprecate any radical change in the political situation. But from 30 June onwards its tone became more sceptical. The Liberals still accepted Mussolini's promises, but they began to ask whether he were not the prisoner of his followers. 'Many have wondered if his strength is not a myth which does not correspond to the reality.'[68] The menacing tone of the Fascist press, the activities of the Militia and the mass rallies gave the alarm. The publication on 8 July of the decree, prepared a year previously, restricting the freedom of the Press, further disillusioned the Liberals. The explicit threat that the Liberal party would withdraw its support appears for the first time on 11 July.[69]

The *Consiglio Nazionale* widened the breach still further. Its resolutions marked, in fact, the formal break between Fascism and the Liberal state. Mussolini's own speeches, following on the other proofs of sympathy for syndicalism and extremism that he had given, exasperated his allies. It was the *Consiglio Nazionale* which finally turned Salandra against Mussolini: only his friends held him back from declaring his opposition.[70]

Fascism was rapidly approaching isolation. At the Congress of Assisi (27–29 July) the ex-combatants' association had voted in favour of its own autonomy, and for 'the absolute condemnation of illegalism'. At the *Consiglio Nazionale*, Mussolini and other Fascists brusquely rejected the attempts at explanation offered by the combatant deputies Viola and Ponzio S. Sebastiano. The latter had identified with the revisionists in the PNF; but by November they were convinced that there was no place for them in a party dominated by Farinacci. The defection of the combatants was a serious loss; even more than Liberal hostility it threatened to bring about the disintegration of the Government's majority, since their example could easily affect the more moderate or irresolute Fascists.[71]

On the other hand, the attempt to soft-pedal the revolutionary significance of the *Consiglio Nazionale* resolution irritated the integralists who had genuinely believed in its importance. The major result of the resolution was the creation of a constitutional reform commission of fifteen members. Suckert complained that 'the Jacobin mountain has finished by giving birth to fifteen *girondin* mice, in the majority either ex-Nationalists or Hegelian excrescences'. The only radicals in the commission were the syndicalists Olivetti and Lanzillo, both personally recommended by Mussolini and Rossoni.[72] The provincials of the party, always short of experts, were unrepresented, although the agenda reflected their preoccupations with the hidden hand of international finance. The extremists and the Nationalists had formed a common front against the Freemasonry, but demands for the foundation of a 'Fascist bank' were peculiar to the party. They were probably inspired by the perennial hostility of the old Banca di Sconto and Banco di Roma factions against the Commerciale.[73] In any case, it seemed evident that the commission would be slow in its procedures and cautious in its conclusions. Meanwhile the *squadristi* clamoured for the 'second wave' of violence with increasing vehemence. Mussolini himself had perhaps not ruled out the possibility of a sudden blow at the Opposition, but he needed to preserve the forms of law. It seems likely that he toyed with the plan of involving the Opposition leaders in a fake conspiracy to overthrow the Government by force. Turati at the beginning of September warned of the possibility that the Government was 'preparing some monster conspiracy trial', and it is probable that the existence in Mussolini's personal files of a fantastic account of a conspiracy has something to do with this. The link is provided by the activities of a Captain Umberto Bellini, almost certainly an *agent provocateur*.[74]

At the beginning of September the problem of relations with the Liberals came to a head. Mussolini showed more than usual inconsistency by giving an interview to Vettori, the editor of the *Giornale d'Italia*, which was intended to be conciliatory, and some days later (before its publication) threatening in a speech to the miners of Monte Amiata 'to make the Opposition into straw for the Fascist encampments' if they tried anything on.[75] The Monte Amiata speech produced an immediate reaction from the Liberal ministers in the Government. Casati was determined to resign but was eventually persuaded to stay by his colleague Sarrocchi, a wholehearted pro-Fascist.[76] However the incident did not end there. One of the results of the near-crisis was to convince the leaders of industry of the need to intervene on the side of the Liberals and the normalizers.

The murder of Matteotti had shaken the industrialists profoundly. Like the other groups of 'flankers', they doubted whether Mussolini could survive the crisis. Although some industrialists still identified themselves unreservedly with Fascism, the majority were uneasy. They were prepared to concede support to Mussolini only on the terms laid down by the Liberals; there must be an effective normalization and the extremists must be brought under control. At the Grand Council meeting of 22 to 24 July Mussolini had threatened a three-pronged offensive: support for strikes undertaken by the Fascist unions, the establishment of the corporation as a legal State institution, and the introduction of a scheme to give workers a share in profits.[77]

On 6 August, in an article in the *Corriere* entitled 'The silence of the industrialists', Luigi Einaudi accused the employers of keeping quiet about the political situation because they valued the 'tangible benefits' conferred on them by the Mussolini government more highly than liberty. Albertini had suggested that Einaudi write the article after he and Amendola had failed to persuade the Confindustria to issue an open warning against the 'second wave': In the ensuing controversy, a former president of the Confindustria, Silvestri, replied that industrialists were busy people with 'a horror of politics' who had supported Fascism as 'the lesser of two evils'; but some other industrialists took a less favourable view of co-operation with Fascism.[78] In fact although Einaudi did not succeed in getting the Confindustria to break its official silence as Albertini had hoped, his appeal was at least partially successful. Gino Olivetti appreciated the moral weakness of industry's neutral stance, and was furious with Silvestri for his ill-judged and stupid reply.

At a meeting of industrialists summoned to discuss current labour problems, Olivetti unexpectedly took the initiative of calling for a discussion of the Confindustria's attitude to the party and the Government. Although the president Benni shared Silvestri's views, the majority of the industrialists sided with Olivetti. Olivetti feared that the political inertia of industry would allow the victory of the corporations in alliance with the extremist wing of the party.

It is not possible that at such a grave moment all that the industrialists have to say is that they are not interested in politics because they have to work from morning to evening in their factories. If it were so, I wouldn't be able to rule out the possibility that one fine day they will wake up and find the black flag of the corporations flying over the factories. I don't want to see that day: there is no need to believe that the black flag is better than the red. Therefore we must do something; we must go to the head of the government and tell him that things can't go on like this. Mussolini will understand that we want nothing but the re-establishment of legality: without a peace which is inspired by profound motives and not imposed by bludgeons, not even industry can work and prosper.[79]

Olivetti won general support for his idea. He was given a mandate to draw up a memorandum for presentation to Mussolini: on 9 September it was delivered by a delegation composed of Olivetti, Benni, Conti and Alberto Pirelli. The memo began by expressing gratitude for the 'confidence' and stability restored by the Government: but it went on to make severe criticisms. The Confindustria leaders declared themselves in favour of 'freedom of labour and organization', and opposed the idea of the legislative discipline of labour relations. This section of the memo concluded with an obvious reference to Mussolini's so-called 'swing to the left': it called for 'the greatest possible elimination of political influence from the economic field with the guarantee that the State will not surrender its authority and force, or use it in favour of one or other class, especially for contingent and opportunist reasons of the moment.' The industrialists, however, did not confine their criticisms to the field of labour relations. The memo went on to attack the whole structure of Fascist party domination; it called for impartial administration of the law, 'free from private or local political influences', and attacked the lack of preparation and corruption of much of the Fascist governing class. 'A new ruling class may be in the process of formation but it has not yet been formed.' All this led up to the familiar recommendation that Fascism must accept expert advice and welcome 'the active co-operation of all those in the national parties, who are willing ... to work for the achievement of a concrete payment'. The political purpose of the memorandum was to get Mussolini to make concessions which would make it possible for the Liberals to continue to co-operate.[80] In this it was successful: during the next three months Mussolini became more moderate in his tone both on political and industrial questions.

Temporarily, Olivetti had succeeded in calling Mussolini's bluff. However he did not believe that the industrialists had the power by themselves to decide the issue of the political struggle. With realistic pessimism, he admitted that Mussolini's decision would be governed by the attitude of the monarchy. The majority of industrialists, moreover, still clung to the idea of appealing to Mussolini's good sense: if faced with a stark choice between opposition and surrender, the industrialists could hardly fail to reflect on the practical consequences of provoking government hostility and risking the revival of the left. Olivetti himself advised the industrialists that 'if there are clear signs that he intends to remain and govern by force, make yourselves small, let drop any question of unity, scatter and don't expose your flank to a frontal attack (sic) by Rossoni, who has not forgotten his 1923 defeat and is waiting for his time to come.'[81] Hence the Confindustria would not publicize its dissent, beyond leaking a few calculated indiscretions to the Press. Individual industrialists like Ettore Conti and his fellow magnates of the electrical industry, Motta and Ponti, opposed the Government: and Conti was active together with Alfredo Lusignoli in trying to organize support for Giolitti's succession.[82] But other industrialists like Benni and Donegani, the head of the important Montecatini chemical firm, worked on Mussolini's behalf. The industrialists had an important influence in persuading Salandra to delay his break with Mussolini, and in splitting his party against him when he did so.[83] After September, the fears and divergences of the industrialists prevented them from finding a common voice or programme, and their influence on events was not decisive.

The Third of January

At the Congress of Livorno in early October, the majority of the Liberal party voted for a motion demanding the restoration of the constitution and freedom in local government, and criticizing the Militia. Salandra and the right remained officially loyal to the Government, however, and the Liberal ministers still did not resign from the Cabinet.[84] But Fascism was rapidly becoming isolated, and with the re-opening of the Chamber on 12 November the crisis entered a new phase. Giolitti declared his opposition to the Government on 15 November, and there were defections from the majority both among the Liberals and the Combatants. Salandra, though he voted for the Government, admitted his 'perplexity'. His speech on 22 November was a severe attack on the Fascist party, on the Press decree and on the suppression of the freedom of local government.[85] It is at this point that the leaders of the Aventine should have begun to query the wisdom of remaining in proud isolation. But the Opposition remained passive. Amendola put his faith in the revelations contained in the memorandum of Cesare Rossi, which he possessed. He believed that the effect of these on the King would be decisive.

Mussolini tried to disarm the growing opposition among the conservatives by a 'new course' of conciliation and promises of legality. He believed that he had at all costs to try and prevent the passage of Salandra and the Right to the Opposition, because of the effect this might have on the King. So he made another volte-face, and his earlier encouragement of the provincial extremists and the left-wing syndicalists was now revoked. The Liberals were reassured that the work of the fifteen 'solons' of the constitutional commission would not lead to fundamental changes in the Statute.[86]

In the Grand Council meeting of 20 November Mussolini's new directives came up against strong opposition. The party was now informed that 'the revolutionary period of Fascism has closed', and that its duty was to obey the Government without discussion. At the same time, hints were thrown out that if the party caused trouble, Mussolini could do without it. On 27 November Franco Ciarlantini, a member of the *direttorio*, declared that 'Fascism is not a phenomenon which can be exhausted by the fortunes of a party. . . . The present form of Fascism may last for one year or five.'[87]

On 30 November Mussolini addressed a circular to the party. Special regional meetings throughout Italy were summoned to receive the message. The circular called for the conciliation of the Government's allies and the end of illegality and *squadrismo*. The party would have to be purged: 'it is necessary to liberate the party from all the elements who are unfitted for the new settlement, from those who make violence a profession.' Most of the Southern regions, where the moderates predominated, received the circular with discipline and even genuine approval; but in the heartlands of Fascism its reception was stormy. The circular was not openly rejected, but in Tuscany, Emilia and Lombardy, the Fascists made their opposition known. At Bologna, Mussolini's message 'was received with notable coldness, by the assembly and there were even some expressions of disagreement'. The Prefect reported that the tendency which favoured 'normalization' had triumphed over that which wanted 'a second wave', but this did not mean quite what it might seem. The 'normalizers' in fact demanded 'legislation which would safeguard the claims of Fascism'; they were prepared to obey the Government only if it undertook a more aggressive policy. In Milan, Farinacci, loudly applauded, said that although he had every intention of obeying the Duce, 'it must be kept in mind that since the Opposition aims . . . to put Fascism on trial a policy of force without weakness or compromise is necessary'. Criticism of the Government was so strong that Arnaldo Mussolini tried to throw responsibility on to the *direttorio*, saying that it, and not the Government, should have guided the party. This was hardly consistent with the sermon of absolute obedience to the Government which he had just preached in the *Popolo d'Italia*.

The Tuscan meeting was even more hostile. Although there were the usual ritual expressions of loyalty to the Duce, the participants 'showed a state of mind tending towards extremism', and the meeting closed without voting a motion. The consul, Tamburini, organized a noisy demonstration of 500 Fascists, who tried to attack the Liberal newspaper *Il Nuovo Giornale*, and openly threatened disobedience.[88]

The 'revolutionaries' of Fascism, whose hopes had been raised by some of Mussolini's earlier utterances and by the *Consiglio Nazionale*, were naturally foremost in expressing disillusionment. The *Conquista dello Stato* threatened an alliance with the extreme left and the proletariat against Mussolini, whose circular was described sarcastically as a 'sincere act of constitutional faith'.[89] This threat need not, of course, be taken seriously, but it is still indicative of a state of mind. However the dominant note in the reactions to the circular was not that of idealism or blind enthusiasm, but fear. The vital preoccupation of the provincial Fascists was immunity from prosecution. They were afraid that Mussolini might try to save his skin at their expense, and voiced loud complaints against the magistracy 'which is said to have ordered excessive arrests' and against Federzoni. 'Either everyone in prison, or no one': this was, underneath the revolutionary rhetoric, the heart of the matter.[90] The demand that the party should enjoy greater independence from the Government, which Michele Bianchi and others had voiced in early July, now became general. It was not confined to the provincial extremists or revolutionaries; even moderates or revisionists believed that the salvation of the party and Fascism could only be achieved by greater independence from the Government. Bottai complained that 'the confusion . . . between the actions of the party and the Government has caused the party to be corrupted, in both ideals and practice, by the necessary diplomacy of the art of government.'[91] Opposing factions in the party had come to share a distrust of Mussolini's leadership, authoritarian in style but uncertain in aim. They were willing to put up with his constant 'zig-zag' so long as it brought success, but failure brought smouldering dissatisfactions to the surface.

Mussolini was probably sincere in his message to the party. He may well have still thought it possible to escape from his more compromising supporters and to remain in power as the leader of a composite conservative bloc. But even if the hesitations of Salandra and the Liberal right had not yet entirely disappeared, the reaction to Mussolini's new peace offensive did not encourage such hopes. The views of the Liberals and the other forces of order were summed up by the severe comment of the *Giornale d'Italia* on the circular to the party; between June and the present there had been 'a whole series of actions and speeches by the Rt Hon. Mussolini himself which form an absolute contrast with the spirit which animated his speech to the Senate in June, or the present letter . . . the Prime Minister in yesterday's document as in his recent speech to the Chamber, appears not as a man of decided conviction, but rather as one constrained to change tactics in order not to lose power'.[92] It had taken a long time for the Liberals to reach this conclusion, but it was now irrevocable. Fascism was in danger of losing the support of the elites who had helped it to come to power. At the Senate debate in early December, the Government was attacked by prominent representatives of industry (Conti), the bureaucracy (Lusignoli), and the Army.[93]

For the time being, Mussolini was left without a real policy; he kept going only by a series of expedients, which did not halt the development of the crisis of confidence either in his own ranks or among his former allies.

At this time the problem of the Militia once again became acute. Balbo, who had become interim Commander-in-Chief of the Militia after De Bono's resignation, was forced to resign in turn by the revelations which came to light during his libel action against the *Voce Repubblicana*. Mussolini annoyed the extremists by accepting Balbo's resignation, and at the same time displeased the respectable by writing him a letter of comradely sympathy. He would almost certainly have replaced Balbo by a general of the regular army even without the scandal; but he got no credit for doing so under pressure. However Balbo's successor, General Gandolfo, combined a Fascist past with the necessary military antecedents.[94]

The Balbo affair seriously alarmed the hard core of the Militia officers. They recognized that Mussolini was likely to give way to the pressure of the Army by filling the higher ranks with former regular officers, ending the disparities of rank, and opening recruitment to non-Fascists. The consuls wished to preserve the Fascist character of the Militia and its local links with the party. They regarded it as 'a real absurdity' that officers should be transferred from one zone to another, as in the regular army. The Militia was a force held together by old loyalties rather than formal discipline: 'the Militia in Emilia and Romagna is formed by old *squadristi* who obey none but their present officers because they were once the leaders of the old action squads.' It was the Militia commanders, therefore, who were the most decided opponents of Mussolini's new directives. Whereas the party men were prepared at least to concede that repression and 'revolution' should be carried out prevalently by legal and administrative measures, the Militia made no secret of their readiness to use force. Balbo advised his supporters to prove their obedience 'one last time': but if the Opposition did not accept 'this last message of peace', then 'we are ready to make the war cry of the first days of Fascism sound again'.[95]

On the other side, however, Mussolini was faced by growing military criticism. The extent of the Army's disapproval was revealed during the Senate debate in early December. The Generals Giardino, Zupelli and Caviglia denounced the reforms of the Militia as insufficient and revealed the truth about the distribution of arms in June. Giardino pointed out that the independence of the Militia presented a serious threat of civil war, or at least a brief period of uncontrolled violence. 'The Army must always be the strongest ... of all the forces which exist in the nation'; if its superiority were doubtful, then 'the peace of civil society' could not be guaranteed. Giardino's speech was highly damaging to Mussolini, but it unwittingly revealed one of the factors that was to work in his favour. There could be no question, of course, of the Army's ability to handle the Militia in a prolonged conflict. But the menace of civil war was serious. It must not be forgotten that the Army was not altogether united; there were still some high-ranking officers, like the commander at Florence, General Gonzaga, who might be prepared to help the Fascists. This was more than enough to make Victor Emmanuel hesitate before the risks involved in forcing a showdown.[96]

Important meetings of Militia officers took place at Ferrara on 9 December and at Bologna the following day. The Emilian consuls agreed reluctantly to accept a settlement which would subordinate the Militia to the Army, providing that they were guaranteed security of tenure. But this guarantee was not forthcoming. On 20 December the new commander, General Gandolfo, announced his decision to replace all zone commanders who had not attained the rank of brigadier in the regular army. The consuls felt that they would be next, and there were one or two desperate men among the directly threatened zone commanders. The commander of the Umbria-Marche zone, Agostini, was an old henchman of Balbo's, and the *Voce Repubblicana* trial had revealed that he had organized and led a special punitive expedition against the dissident Fascists of Ferrara on Balbo's behalf. The evidence suggests that he had a leading role in the June plots for a local or national coup.[97]

About the middle of December a conspiracy of the Militia began to take shape. The danger that the Militia would act was obvious even to the Opposition: on 16 December Anna Kuliscioff wrote to Turati that 'if it is true that the army is almost disarmed and arms are with the Militia instead of in the military magazines ... the hypothesis is not too fantastic that some coup of great importance is being prepared'.[98]

Between 17 and 28 December there were a number of semi-clandestine meetings of the consuls, some with Agostini, at Bologna, Ferrara, Florence and Perugia. There is no certain evidence of Balbo's involvement, but the *Voce Repubblicana*, which had good sources, reported his participation in the earlier meetings. It also published a telegram from Grandi to Balbo: 'Yours received, remain Ferrara. Keep very calm. Show yourself able to wait in silence. ...'[99] Balbo seems to have heeded this warning to the extent of avoiding open involvement from this time on, but there is more than one reason for believing that the Consuls regarded him as their leader. First of all, he had already established his claim to the leadership in the eyes of the old Fascists in the Militia in June and July; his forced resignation had only made him more popular. Secondly, his temperament, bold to the point of rashness, and his republican sentiments make it likely that he was prepared to risk a confrontation with the monarchy and its forces. Mussolini's later attitude is indicative. He hated and at times despised Farinacci: but he feared Balbo, because he knew that he had the courage and charisma of a true leader. It is highly probable that Agostini, who was Balbo's 'trusted friend', served to maintain liaison between him and the rebels in the Militia. There is good reason, therefore, to believe that Balbo, while staying in the background, knew and approved of the movement of the Consuls.

Events in the Chamber of Deputies meanwhile heightened the impatience of the Fascist party. The new Press Censorship Bill had to be withdrawn; this was a grave sign of the weakness of the Government. An open split began to appear between the moderates among the Fascist deputies and the extremists. It is almost certain that Victor Emmanuel, convinced that the Government was about to collapse, at this point began active soundings to see if a peaceful transfer of power could be arranged. In the Senate debate his former ADC General Brusati had voted against the Government, and the Minister of the Royal Household, Mattioli Pasqualini, had left the hall in order not to have to vote. These were clear signs of disapproval. On 15 December Senator Pompeo di Campello, one of the Gentlemen of the King's Household, approached Raffaele Paolucci, an ex-Nationalist deputy and war hero. Pompeo di Campello suggested that Paolucci write to the King and urge on him the formation of a government of 'national concentration', with the participation of all the former Prime Ministers, 'including Mussolini if he accepted, without him if he showed himself intransigent'. Paolucci wrote the letter, and in addition he started to gather support among other moderate Fascists for this solution.[100]

The Giunta episode advanced the split in the Fascist party. The magistracy asked for permission to open proceedings against Giunta, one of the Vice-Presidents of the Chamber, for his part in organizing the attack on the dissident Fascist Cesare Forni. His friends staged a demonstration in his favour and when the Liberal deputy Boeri showed his disapproval by leaving the Chamber, Mussolini called him back and told him that, since he had been elected on the government list, he ought to resign. This outburst nearly caused the Liberals to withdraw from Parliament. Giolitti and Salandra both refused to attend the sittings so long as Giunta remained Vice-President. Mussolini climbed down, ordering that the resignation offered by Giunta should be accepted. This brought about an open revolt of the extremists, led by Michele Bianchi. Behind the scenes Giunta himself and Edoardo Torre organized a meeting of 'old Fascist' deputies for 'the defence of the ideals and the political and moral programme of Fascism'.[101]

The formation of this extremist caucus precipitated a similar move by Paolucci. Forty-four deputies met at his house and agreed, with one exception, to support 'a policy of conciliation and normality within the Constitution', and to send a delegation to Mussolini to demand the end of the Militia's police functions, the purge of the party and the restoration of single-member constituencies. Most of the moderate group were from the South, where party organization and loyalty counted for less than personal ties. As Salandra and his group were also on the point of declaring their opposition, the Government's parliamentary majority was close to disintegration. Unfortunately the continued absence of the Aventine opposition prevented them from taking full advantage of this situation.[102]

Mussolini meanwhile bought time by one of his most skilful manoeuvres. He took the wind out of the sails of Paolucci and the moderates by hastily introducing a bill for single-member constituencies. This pleased the Southerners and wrung words of approval from Salandra and Giolitti. Alarm at the thought of having to face new elections weakened the resolution of the Liberal right and the Paolucci group.[103] On the other hand, the new electoral bill was interpreted by the extremists and intransigents as yet another sign of Mussolini's surrender to the old ruling class. Suckert and the *Conquista dello Stato* became their spokesmen, and the titles of the articles he published on 21 and 28 December are eloquent : 'Fascism against Mussolini ?', and 'All, even Mussolini, must obey the warning of integral Fascism'. In more guarded language, Farinacci warned the Duce that the obedience of the party was conditional on his adoption of a 'strong' policy.[104]

On 27 December *Il Mondo* published the Rossi memorandum, which exposed the responsibilities of Mussolini for the attack on Amendola and other acts of violence. 'We have a Prime Minister charged with common crimes. No nation can tolerate that such a situation should be protracted' : the comments of the Liberal press make it clear that after the publication of the Rossi memorial Mussolini had no choice but to react immediately or to resign. On 29 December he learnt that Salandra had resigned from the presidency of the budget committee ; this meant that the withdrawal of the two Liberal ministers from the Cabinet was imminent.[105]

Mussolini therefore took the initiative by summoning the Cabinet unexpectedly on 30 December. The decisive role in the events of this day was played by Federzoni. In the morning he agreed to support Casati in demanding the resignation of the ministry, but when the Cabinet met in the afternoon he changed his mind. Casati must have hoped to receive support not only from Federzoni, but from the two military ministers, and even perhaps from the moderate Fascists De Stefani and Oviglio, but in the event he was backed only by his fellow Liberal, Sarrocchi. Apart from preventing the break-up of the Cabinet, the attitude of Federzoni and the military ministers meant that Mussolini could be sure of the police and the army. Although he was refused a formal grant of emergency powers, the majority of the

Cabinet agreed to take 'the necessary measures' to restrain the Opposition press campaign. Federzoni also gave orders to search the houses of the members of the *Italia Libera* opposition group, 'excluding deputies'.

Mussolini had used the threat of the Fascists to intimidate the waverers, declaring 'that he will oppose any successor with all his forces – impression that he would even descend into the piazza'. He persuaded Casati and Sarrocchi to delay their resignation in exchange for a promise to use only legal methods of repression, and was thus able to begin the reaction with the apparent agreement of a united Cabinet. This was an important advantage. However Mussolini's measures were essentially defensive and they did not amount to the adoption of a general strategy of repression.[106]

Consequently they did not avert the threatened extremist revolt. On 31 December a delegation of thirty-three consuls of the Militia called on Mussolini to demand that he act with vigour against the Opposition, and see to the release of the Fascists in prison. Their leader, Tarabella, handed him a letter from Tamburini. 'I am at Florence to prepare and put into effect the rally that the *direzione* has requested . . . either you, guided by God, pursue a grandiose programme, as we hope, or we before becoming an object of ridicule will engage battle.' In Florence, Tamburini was as good as his word ; thousands of armed Fascists from the province poured into Florence, and parties of the Militia and *squadristi* wrecked the printing presses of two newspapers, the Masonic lodge, the 'circle of culture', and a number of lawyers' offices. Similar outbreaks followed in Pisa, Bologna and elsewhere.

The consuls had openly threatened Mussolini, while the *direttorio* of the party acted with more circumspection. It is clear from Tamburini's letter and other evidence that Farinacci, Renato Ricci and the other extremists on the *direttorio* planned the Florence rally with the intention of forcing Mussolini's hand. But it is doubtful if Farinacci knew or approved of the consuls' open challenge. The consuls had in fact planned their action before the 30 December cabinet meeting, and some at least among them were resolved to carry their rebellion further if Mussolini did not give the necessary assurances. The story that Edoardo Torre tried to persuade the consuls to replace the Duce by a leader who belonged to the Freemasonry of the Piazza del Gesù seems far-fetched but is confirmed by documentary evidence.

Both Balbo and Farinacci had been members of this branch of the Freemasonry. However Torre's attempt to exploit the revolt of the consuls was probably impromptu, and certainly ill-prepared. Tarabella and Galbiati, two of the leaders of the consuls, were so scandalized that they founded an 'anti-Masonic order'. It is unlikely that Farinacci thought of taking Mussolini's place, though Balbo might have contemplated carrying out a real coup if Mussolini had shown signs of weakness.[107]

The 'movement of the consuls' and the violent offensive of the provincial Fascists in Florence, Pisa, Bologna and elsewhere made it necessary for Mussolini to go forward on the path to complete dictatorship. For the next three or four days the situation remained extremely uncertain. The Opposition still hoped that the King was only waiting for the resignation of the Liberal ministers in order to intervene.

On 2 January Mussolini sent his Under-Secretary Suardo to ask the King to sign a decree for the dissolution of the Chamber, with the date left open. Victor Emmanuel, who had seen Mussolini earlier in the day, was taken by surprise and was reluctant to consent. He even hinted that he might consider abdication rather than perform an act which he considered unconstitutional. At the end of the conversation he relented and agreed to sign the decree providing Mussolini came to see him in person : however in the interview which took place later in the evening between Mussolini and the King, the latter still evidently raised some objections. The communiqué, which was only issued on 7 January, said that the Chamber 'may' be dissolved after the approval of the new electoral law. This suggests that Mussolini had not pressed his request and Victor Emmanuel had in fact reserved his signature, while giving Mussolini to understand that he would not refuse the dissolution on a more suitable occasion.[108] On 1 January the two sons of the Duke of Genoa had sent telegrams of New Year greetings to Federzoni and to the commander of the Militia, General Gandolfo, and there were rumours that once again the Duke of Aosta was intriguing with the Fascists.[109] The danger of a conflict within the Royal House may have weighed on Victor Emmanuel's mind. But the most important reasons for his inactivity probably lie elsewhere. Above all, he took a formal view of the constitution. He disapproved of the Aventine and refused to act unless either the majority of Parliament or the majority of the Cabinet turned against Mussolini. He was also afraid of civil war. Finally, there is some reason to suppose that the publication of the Rossi memorandum and the threat of further revelations may have had an effect opposite to that which the Opposition intended. Like Salandra and other conservatives, he was very distressed by the damage done to Italy's reputation by the Opposition campaign. The King must have been reluctant to believe that a Prime Minister whom he had appointed, and decorated, had been responsible for crimes of violence. In consequence, he may have tended to blame the Opposition rather than Mussolini for lowering Italy's reputation. This was the justification which the Government had originally advanced for their restrictions on the Press.[110]

Mussolini had not got all that he wanted, but he had sounded out the King and he concluded that it was safe for him to go ahead. On 3 January he took the decisive step of assuming personal responsibility for crime and terrorism. 'I declare . . . that I, and I alone, assume the political, moral and historical responsibility for all that has happened. . . . If Fascism has been a criminal association, if all the acts of violence have been the result of a certain historical, political and moral climate the responsibility for this is mine', and he challenged his opponents to indict him. This was what the consuls and other extremists had above all demanded; solidarity with all those accused of crimes in the service of Fascism. 'Either everyone in prison, or no one.' The conflict could only be settled by force : and he promised that 'in the next forty-eight hours . . . the situation will be cleared up all along the line'.[111] Mussolini profited from the outbreaks of Fascist violence in the provinces, in order to justify police repression as the only way in which to avert a reign of terror. This was an effective threat.

No one could now have any doubts about Mussolini's intentions. Nevertheless, in the final hour of the crisis both the Liberals and the Aventine opposition showed a fatal indecision.

On the morning of 3 January Salandra and Giolitti had met in the house of a friend. The two elder statesmen had for some time come to an understanding to agree to forget the past, but this was the first time that they had met face to face on friendly terms. Salandra asked Giolitti what he thought about the idea that they and Orlando should call on the King. 'Giolitti excluded the idea : it would be known; it would seem like a *pronunciamento* ; it would compromise the Crown directly if the latter followed another road ; I did not insist.' To the last, Giolitti remained a faithful servant of the King, concerned to protect him from disgrace even when he was failing in his duty. One cannot tell if a direct appeal by the three Prime Ministers would have had any effect on Victor Emmanuel, who was certainly informed indirectly of their views, but it would have been worth trying. Salandra for his part warned Giolitti that 'it would be perhaps wise not to insist on a vote today because a part of the Right would certainly remain with the Ministry'.[112] He knew that within his own group De Capitani and other representatives of industrial and agrarian interests were preparing to desert him. On 28 December the Lombard Liberal association, including a number of leading Milanese industrialists, had voted confidence in the Government. After Mussolini's speech, the Salandra Liberals met, and to his chagrin only nine out of twenty-four or twenty five present agreed to vote against the Government. 'No one praised Mussolini's speech or had words of affection for him. All were animated by a double fear : of the subversives if the pressure of Fascism should be removed ; of the Fascists themselves if not held back but unleashed by Mussolini.'[113]

The Giolitti-Salandra meeting, therefore, had failed to reach any positive conclusion, and the defection of Salandra's followers started the collapse of resistance. Paolucci warned Salandra that though about thirty Fascist deputies shared his feelings, it was not possible for the moment to get them to vote against the Government. Faced with the defection both of his own supporters and of the moderate Fascists, Salandra advised Giolitti to avoid a vote. Giolitti accordingly withdrew his motion of censure and this made a fatal impression of weakness. Meanwhile the Aventine remained inactive. Their manifesto of protest was not issued till 8 January, a whole five days after Mussolini's speech. Even at this stage, their return to the hall might have revived the political struggle. As it was, Mussolini was the only man who had shown himself capable of taking any action to resolve the crisis, and this made him the victor almost by default.[114]

After the sitting of the Chamber, Mussolini, Federzoni and Ciano met the chiefs of the police and the *carabinieri* to arrange for their measures of repression. Circles and clubs were closed; branches of opposition parties were dissolved; the *Italia Libera* organization of ex-combatants was suppressed altogether; and even wineshops suspected of serving as the meeting place of 'subversives' – were closed down. The measures amounted to a suppression of the freedom of assembly and association, coupled with a widespread use of arbitrary arrest. All these measures were made 'legal' by reliance on the Prefect's wide discretionary powers for the maintenance of public order. At no time during the repression did popular reaction cause the Government serious difficulty. Even in the big cities there was no effective protest. On 5 January the Militia were officially mobilized in Milan, and from this time on the Blackshirts acted as auxiliaries of the police.[115]

During these first days the Opposition were by no means altogether dismayed. Giolitti thought that the ministry was 'a walking corpse', and it was only when the King allowed the resignation and replacement of Casati, Sarrocchi and Oviglio to take place without a murmur that their hopes began to fade.[116] The King had not been informed by Mussolini of his 3 January speech, and had probably been shocked by it; but he refused to take any responsibility upon himself. This made dictatorship inevitable; in the long run Victor Emmanuel's passivity was also fatal to the monarchy.

Aftermath

The third of January marked the beginning of Mussolini's dictatorship from a political point of view. The Opposition never recovered, and after the first few days the continuing discussions about whether the Aventine should return or not became of little practical significance. The parties lingered on : the first party to be banned altogether, in October 1925, was the PSU, Matteotti's party. The pretext was provided by Zaniboni's attempt to shoot Mussolini, which had been carefully staged by *agents provocateurs* (Zaniboni was, rather incongruously, a PSU deputy).

The Popolari deputies attempted to return to Parliament in January 1926, but were driven out by Farinacci and the Fascists. Finally, after a new attempt on Mussolini's life on 3 October 1926, all opposition parties were suppressed and their reconstruction forbidden by 'the law for the defence of the State'. The Aventine deputies were declared to have forfeited their mandate, together with the Communists, in spite of the fact that the latter had returned to the hall. Gramsci and a number of other Communist deputies were immediately arrested. During 1925–6 the Communists had worked hard to build up a clandestine organization, and they had become in consequence the only opposition group who caused the Government serious concern. But even they were unprepared for the passage from semi-clandestine to completely undercover conditions, and the new and more efficient police administration created by Bocchini wrought havoc among their cadres.[117]

The one-party state had been formally established. A flicker of legal opposition still remained alive in the Chamber with Giolitti, and in the Senate. Due mainly to intra-party disputes over the form of representation, it was not till 1928 that the Chamber was finally dissolved, to be replaced by a new body nominated by the Grand Council. The Senate, thanks to Royal protection, could not be transformed and on rare occasions such as the approval of the Lateran Pacts in 1929, still held debates that were worthy of attention.

If, however, Mussolini after 3 January became more and more able to ignore the political opposition, this did not mean that all politics was conducted within the Fascist party. Autonomous institutions survived: and as well as the party, Mussolini had still to reckon with the views of the Crown, the Army, the Church, big business, and other interests. Even old conservatives like the President of the Senate, Tittoni, kept some influence. In fact the history of 1925–9 is in large part the history of the process by which Mussolini eliminated the Fascist movement's resistance to the measures by which he achieved a stable *entente* with these institutions.

THE DEFEAT OF THE PARTY

With the defeat of the Opposition, relations between party and State entered a new and critical phase. The Matteotti crisis had reversed the process by which, before June 1924, the importance of the party as an independent force was being eroded, and the outcome had shifted the balance clearly in its favour. It remained to be seen whether the party, more especially the intransigent wing, would be able to use their victory to consolidate a position of hegemony not only over the other parties but over the administration; whether it would determine the shape of the new regime.

It is not accidental that 1925 saw for the first time (in any country) the elevation of the word 'totalitarian' to a central place in the political vocabulary.[1] The new term served Mussolini both as a programme and as a justification, as the synthesis of Fascist aspirations and as a new theory of legitimacy. At first the adjective had no fixed point of reference; in so far as Fascism was proclaimed 'a total conception of life', it might be assumed that the movement was to be the 'totality' within which all other institutions were to move. However when Mussolini devised the formula 'everything within the State, nothing outside the State, nothing against the State',[2] it became clear that this was not the use to which the new concept would be put. The idea of the 'totalitarian State' served in fact to emphasize the necessity for a *single* hierarchy in which State authority would be supreme and the party would be subordinate.[3] Although Fascism invented the concept of 'totalitarianism', it diverged in this respect from the pattern of later totalitarian regimes. For the rational bureaucratic ideals of centralized control, differentiated function and technical qualification for office, the totalitarian regimes have substituted respectively (1) a conflict between parallel hierarchies of party and State with ill-defined responsibilities; (2) the unification of separate administrative and political functions under local autocrats; and (3) political loyalty as the only basic requirement for all office-holders, and services to the party as the criterion for promotion.[4] The early practice of Fascism had conformed markedly with this pattern in the first two instances : only in the third was it deficient, since the Fascists had not purged the central bureaucracy. During and after 1926, the regime reverted towards the bureaucratic model. There was a restoration, though not complete, of centralized State control and of the orderly division of administrative and political functions. In spite of the imposition of a loyalty oath, the party offensive against the neutral, technically qualified, career civil servants, was checked.

The Secretariat of Farinacci

After the defeat of the Opposition, Mussolini's most urgent need was to recover full control over the party and to co-ordinate its action with that of the Government. The confidence of many Fascists in the infallibility of Mussolini's leadership had been shaken : and the mutual distrust between the leaders of the party and Federzoni remained. Police and party were often united in the work of repression ; but this did not satisfy the provincial extremists. The orthodox police measures ordered by Federzoni did not go far enough for them. They complained that government repression had spared the leaders of the Opposition. They wanted police action to be auxiliary to the terrorism of the revived squads, and not the other way round.[5]

Federzoni, on his side, wished to minimize the scope of repression to avoid unnecessary political risks, and saw the party as a disturbing element which was delaying rather than assisting the restoration of public order. Federzoni even took direct disciplinary measures against the participants in the 'second wave'. His energetic intervention secured the arrest of fourteen Fascists in Bologna for the devastations of lawyers' chambers, and disciplinary measures against the *carabinieri* who failed to protect them.[6] He refused to exempt the Fascist party from the general ban on public meetings ; in spite of this, the *direttorio* sent a circular to the provincial federations giving orders for 'a revival of party activity' by means of a series of meetings and rallies.[7] Mussolini supported him, and the *direttorio* had to climb down, but this incident only increased the ill humour of the integralists.

Suckert in the *Conquista dello Stato* continued to insist on the difference between Fascist 'dynamism' and governmental reaction; his exuberance provoked Federzoni into ordering the sequestration of the number of 1 February. The measure did perhaps have some effect, as the tone of the *Conquista* from now on became more subdued. However Suckert's reply to Federzoni, which claimed that his views were approved by the party leadership and echoed by important provincial groups, was to the point.[8] Federzoni could not accept his implied challenge and sequestrate the journals of the Bologna or Florence federations, which were equally outspoken.

The most aggressive extremists were still the Florentines. They complained of bureaucratic sabotage and an undue preoccupation with Parliament, instead of with the solid achievements of Fascism, 'the support of the masses' and 'the organization of labour'. 'The Duce must realize that our action and obedience and even our discipline are conditional on the realization of the Fascist programme. On the road of normalization he may perhaps find other support but not that of the Fascism which is truly Fascist.'[9] This sounded dangerously like an ultimatum, and Mussolini seems to have been convinced that it was prudent to appease the integralists further. On 15 February Farinacci was appointed General Secretary of the PNF.[10]

It was a measure of the changed relations between Mussolini and the movement that he should have agreed to the nomination of Farinacci, a man whom he secretly disliked and even feared. But at this point Farinacci was less dangerous to Mussolini than Balbo, whose impetuosity, desire for action, and access to armed force had made him the spearhead of the movement's revolt at the end of 1924. Farinacci, by contrast, eager as he was to exercise power, realized that in the last analysis Mussolini's authority over Fascism was unshakeable. To destroy it would have meant destroying the movement itself. His relations with Mussolini continued to be those of servant and master ; but under the name of obedience he would pursue his own policy, designed to make himself indispensable. He had already imposed himself on Mussolini as the self-appointed embodiment of the party's collective conscience; he would procure its obedience, but on condition that the Duce's will was in harmony with his own interpretation of the humours and necessities of the Fascist mass. The Duce would rule : but Farinacci would be his oracle.

This meant ensuring party supremacy and eliminating the other, counter-vailing influences on Mussolini. On the other hand Mussolini had no intention of allowing Farinacci to establish himself as a sort of permanent vice-Duce. He saw the appointment as a means of making the poacher into a gamekeeper. Farinacci was to be condemned to work against his own interests and even for those of his enemies.

Farinacci's authoritarian temperament did not easily tolerate discussion and dissent. This did not displease Mussolini, who was anxious to curtail the newly found intellectual independence of the 'kulturized youths',[11] both integralists and revisionists. The appointment of Farinacci soon restored conformity in the party. Intellectual dissent was firmly suppressed, and 'barrack room discipline' descended on the party.[12] The third Congress of the party, held at the end of June, gave a most remarkable demonstration of the newly enforced unity. No discussion was permitted, and one of the dominant notes of the Congress was anti–intellectualism. Mussolini preferred 'the *squadrista* who acts to the impotent professor', and Farinacci confirmed the lesson. The new ruling class had been formed 'in life and battle', and had repudiated the false idea 'of 'a knowledge superior to party, of liberal knowledge, that is to say neutral and superior to life'.[13]

The imposition of ideological discipline was accompanied by an expansion of the powers of the secretariat and a development of the party bureaucracy. The *direttorio* declined in importance as a collective body ; it was to have only consultative functions, and to meet when the Secretary chose. The Congress confirmed the subordination of the *direttorio* to the General Secretary, by giving Farinacci the power to nominate its members.[14] The offices of the central party administration were reorganized ; after the upheavals of 1924, the outlines of a permanent bureaucratic structure began to emerge. The Fascist deputies were subjected to severe discipline. Many of the newly elected members of 1924 had shown undesirable normalizing tendencies, especially in the South, where they had shown themselves mainly intent on building up their personal clienteles, and where the concept of party loyalty had remained elastic. In the first eight months of his secretariat Farinacci expelled one former minister and five other deputies from the party : all deputies were placed under the exclusive control of the party organization, and were forbidden to have relations with the Government, except through the medium of the secretariat.[15]

Each member of the secretariat was given a specialized function ; the secretariat was divided into two branches, one for politics and party discipline, the other for relations with the corporations. The first was headed by Mazzolini, the second by Melchiori and A. Turati. Of the other members of the *direttorio*, Renato Ricci was made responsible for youth organization, while Forges Davanzati and Masi shared the responsibility for culture, propaganda, and the universities. Within this last department, Masi headed a special office for the investigation of Freemasons. The ex-Nationalist Maraviglia had suggested in July 1924 that 'territorial' organization was inadequate, and that the party should also create a 'functional' organization with specialized departments, and the reform of the *direttorio* embodied this principle. The central bureaucracy of the PNF became more powerful from now on.[16]

However although Farinacci undoubtedly laid the foundations for the monolithic and hierarchical centralization of the party under his successors, it would be wrong to think that this was exactly his aim. In fact he remained bound to the sources of his power in the provinces. He encouraged the leadership principle locally as well as at the centre ; elevating the provincial secretaries above their *direttori* ; but this was a measure designed to strengthen and generalize the dominion of the *ras*, whom he explicitly held up as the model for the successful exercise of party office.[17] The structure of the party which he desired was still to be based on local 'feudalism' ; the assault on the provincial chiefs is a feature of the last months of his secretariat, and was inspired not by his own wishes, but by those of Mussolini. The forces of provincial Fascism could not accept centralization, and this was one of the contributory causes of their defeat.

To strengthen his position, Farinacci tried to recapture and elevate the alienated or disgraced representatives of intransigent Fascism. This meant not only the rescue of a typical *ras* such as Barbiellini,[18] but offers of reconciliation to two of the most prominent dissidents, Cesare Forni and Padovani.

Forni accepted,[19] but Padovani still refused to rejoin the party in spite of a strong revival of his supporters.[20]

Conditions seemed more favourable than ever before for the intransigents. The Matteotti crisis had greatly increased the tensions between Fascists and *fiancheggiatori*. Moreover the very failures and frustrations of the party tended to heighten the irrational fears and propensity to violence of its followers. The extremist mood must have also owed something to the serious financial inflation of 1924-5. If the inflation had been a factor in weakening Fascism during the Matteotti crisis, when many of the petty bourgeoisie and middle classes had turned in disillusion to the Aventine, it had probably also strengthened extremism at the expense of the relatively moderate wing of Fascism. Farinacci became the leader of a new reaction of 'rentiers' against 'speculators'; this time the battle was fought out within Fascism. With the appointment of Giuseppe Volpi as Minister of Finance in July 1925, the business establishment entered the Government. The old Giolittian coalition of interests – the Banca Commerciale and its dependent industries, the protectionist lobby, and the higher officials of the bureaucracy – was opposed by a loosely structured front consisting of the fixed income and salaried groups, the agrarians, the free trade interests and the neglected industries of the South. The financiers connected with the old Banca di Sconto and the new Banco di Roma also supported Farinacci because of their antipathy to the Commerciale, Volpi, and Federzoni.[21] The industrial working class had largely been eliminated from the struggle. The only organization which, to a very limited degree, represented their interests, the Fascist unions, played a very contradictory role, which will be examined later.

In a climate of assumed ideological and political uniformity, there is little room for the open clash of programmes and principles. Even interests are usually masked. The political contest becomes a series of factional struggles, the true motives of which are often concealed. This was true of the intransigents and their opponents.

In the provinces 1925 saw a new offensive by the intransigents against the local notables, the grande bourgeoisie, who had backed Fascism and to a large degree controlled it. The men of the organization, mainly petty bourgeoisie, often 'foreigners' and so doubly excluded from the cohesive network of the ruling families, now turned against their former patrons, the men whom Farinacci's lieutenant and propagandist Masi called 'the surviving feudatories of Italian society'.[22] Social resentment and suspicion of wealth and culture gave an added edge to ambition. Some of the intransigents had already been successfully assimilated or had come to terms with local society. The really successful *ras*, like Balbo, Arpinati or Ricci, out of jealousy and a consciousness of achieved position became less and less committed to support of Farinacci and his line. But in regions where the intransigents were weaker, where clerical, conservative or Nationalist influence was strong, or where no single effective leader had emerged, Farinacci could succeed in building a new and more extensive following, though only by working through existing local factions. It was in Friuli, Trieste and parts of the Veneto, in Liguria and even in some areas of the South rather than in the Po Valley, the classic territory of the *ras*, that Farinacci acquired his new power base.

Under Farinacci the party made a second and more serious attempt to conquer the South. In the big cities of the *Mezzogiorno* -- Naples, Bari, Catania and Messina -- the tension between the party and the old notables was particularly acute. The notables were backed by the Prefects, who viewed with alarm the disruption of their cosy alliances. In Bari the party expelled the influential Commendatore De Bellis, who was a power behind the chief local newspaper, the *Gazzetta di Puglia*, and a member of the Bank of Naples board ;[23] in Catania, Masi, acting as Farinacci's special envoy, stirred up the forces hostile to the Carnazza party which was still dominant in the *fascio* and the federation. The local extremists in Catania published a news-sheet simply called 'Farinacci ! Farinacci !'[24]

The party's 'southern strategy' was masterminded by Preziosi and Michele Bianchi ; with their aid an alliance was forged between Farinacci and Southern industrial interests. The industrialists of the South shared Farinacci's antipathy to the Banca Commerciale and its vast network of allies and dependents. They regarded it as the pivot and symbol of those forces which held back the development of the South in the interests of northern industry, and the appointment of Volpi as Minister of Finance inflamed their suspicions. They were therefore anxious to co-operate with the party in an attempt to gain control over the key posts in the State, the economy and society. The most important of all these was the Bank of Naples. The industrialists accused the Bank of pursuing restrictive credit policies and thus stifling development. Farinacci, on his side, as we have already seen in the case of the Bank of Rome, was well aware of the strategic importance of the great financial institutions. For the party leaders, indeed, it was a critical battle ; in the words of one of Farinacci's southern informants, 'if Fascism does not fill the post with its own man, the party can demonstrate and wave flags, but the masters of Naples and the South will be the others.'[25]

The party fought, and lost, a second critical struggle in Naples. Since 1923, a long and bitter war of words had been waged between the *Mattino*, edited by the Scarfoglio brothers and friendly to the local Giolittians and the Banca Commerciale, and the *Mezzogiorno*, edited by the Fascist private enterprise, anti-Masonic propagandist Giovanni Preziosi. Preziosi thought that he now saw a chance of eliminating the more successful *Mattino*'s competition altogether. He was backed by the new *federale*, Vincenzo Tecchio, a follower of Padovani, and by Farinacci, who wanted to inflict a defeat on the old politicians and their moderate allies within Fascism, for whom the *Mattino* was a mouthpiece. In December 1925 they sent an ultimatum ordering the proprietors of the *Mattino* to abandon the newspaper, and tried to impose a boycott on sales. But they were outmanoeuvred ; Mussolini agreed to a financial *combinazione* which would ensure the loyalty of the *Mattino*, but without placing it under direct party control. The party resisted stubbornly ; Tecchio refused to give up the boycott on government orders, replying that he took orders only from Farinacci. Farinacci himself expelled the millionaire film-magnate and deputy Barattolo, the architect of the *combinazione*, from the PNF. Farinacci then attempted to mobilize his wealthy backers, both northern and southern, to win financial control of the new *Mattino* ; but the Neapolitan Union of Industrialists, supported by the Confindustria and probably with a shrewd idea of Mussolini's attitude, backed out. The *Mattino* continued to exist, and this check was one of the clearest signs that by the turn of 1925–6 the power of Farinacci and his friends was on the wane. In fact it was after his defeat on this question that rumours of his impending resignation became current.[26]

The conflict between the intransigents, the new men, and the old notables was nowhere sharper than in Trieste. Trieste, the birthplace of *squadrismo*, had one of the strongest Fascist movements before the March on Rome. In spite of this, from 1923 on the party fell increasingly under the domination of a group of ex-Nationalists led by the deputy Suvich. The real power still lay with the Nationalists' patrons, the great capitalists ; not only Suvich, but also the most important of the early Fascist leaders, Banelli and Giunta, were in their pay, and this explains why the latter failed to oppose the rise of the Nationalists.[27] Although Trieste was in economic difficulties, the insurance and shipping companies of the city were of much more than local importance. They were the centre of a powerful and cohesive network of financial interests, whose influence ramified throughout Italian business. They had business ties with the Nationalist leader Enrico Corradini. Politically, however, they remained vulnerable.[28] Their record of Italian patriotism under the Austro-Hungarian monarchy had been dubious, they kept strong links with the German-speaking world, and many of them were Jewish. This cosmopolitan group of financiers was obviously liable to excite the suspicion and rage of the 'pure' Fascist. The intransigents' greatest strength was among the *regnicoli*, those born in Italy, who resented the exclusiveness of the native Triestine bourgeoisie. Their furious nationalism, with anti-semitic overtones, was a weapon against the pride of the cosmopolitan civic aristocracy. Their most influential representative was Giorgio Masi, a schoolmaster who was the most trusted collaborator of Farinacci in the national *direttorio* with special responsibilities in the propaganda field.

The first crisis in Trieste Fascism was caused by the aggressive tactics of the *federale* Captain Lupetina, a former leader of irredentist students who was known as 'the Farinacci of Trieste'. He humiliated the mayor of the city by forcing him to kneel down in the piazza to show his gratitude for Mussolini's escape from assassination ; this episode was followed by an attack on the Freemasons. Lupetina named eight Freemasons, who occupied important public or economic positions, and demanded their resignation. They included the President of the Savings Bank and a leading official of the Lloyd Triestino shipping company.[29] The business world did not approve of this interference in their own affairs and several of the *direttorio*, including the editor of the local Fascist newspaper, opposed Lupetina. Federzoni intervened, transferring the Prefect, Moroni, who was on good terms with the Fascist leaders, an action which was 'generally interpreted as a change of policy with respect to the local *fascio*'. The new Prefect earned the applause of 'leading citizens, representative figures of politics, commerce and industry, the Press and public officials', but was virtually boycotted by Lupetina and the *squadristi*, who wanted to 'pursue to the utmost limit the battle against the Freemasons and for the Fascistization of the city'. Masi complained that the Prefect 'took his orders from Suvich', and that his opponents put all their hopes in the Viminale. He could not understand why Suvich, recently rewarded with a place on the board of one of the chief insurance companies, the Riunione Adriatica di Sicurtà, kept up the struggle. With ill-concealed resentment, he wrote to Farinacci that 'I am not greedy for his money or his friends . . . But the party, no, that I won't give him.'[30] 1926 saw a desperate jockeying for position between the rival factions. Renato Ricci, dispatched to Trieste as *commissario*, pursued an ambivalent line. By this time he had become personally hostile to Farinacci and he was suspected of selling out to the industrialists. For this reason he was replaced by one of Farinacci's personal lieutenants from Cremona, Moretti. However the sequel was to show that Ricci, if he was not favourable to Masi and Farinacci, did not believe that the industrialists should control the *fascio* either.[31]

In the neighbouring province of Udine, Farinacci intervened even more brusquely to break the hold of the industrial interests. Here, Farinacci had the support of the old Fascists of the provincial capital, led by a former railway official, Ravazzolo. In January 1926 Moretti, dispatched to Udine with full powers, started to carry out a ruthless purge of his opponents. These were led by Pisenti, the former *alto commissario* and Prefect, whose power base was among the textile manufacturers of Pordenone, and the mayor of Udine, Spezzotti. Spezzotti was typical of the notables whom the intransigents tried and ultimately failed to dislodge. He was a textile industrialist and wholesale clothing merchant, an assiduous and successful office-seeker with excellent business connections. He had been mayor of Udine since 1919, and had not joined the party until April 1923, although in view of the 'sympathy' he had shown, his membership card was backdated to 1921. He was later to be described as 'notoriously the man who pulls the strings of the whole political and economic situation of Udine'.[32] Moretti forced the resignation of Spezzotti, and expelled Pisenti. This campaign led to a new clash between the intransigents and Arnaldo Mussolini, who as usual assumed the defence of the moneyed men. He even defended Pisenti against the criticisms of those who pointed out that he had evaded military service, remarking that it was only a 'simple question of convenience' if a *federale* had or had not fought in the war.[33] It is, of course, true that Farinacci himself was hardly above reproach in this respect. None the less, Arnaldo's denial of the necessary relationship between Fascism and wartime heroism was unusually frank ; not often were the real priorities of official Fascism so clearly revealed.

There was something desperate in Farinacci's last minute provincial offensive in early 1926. He was conscious that he was likely to lose his office very soon, but no doubt he believed that he could remain the real arbiter of party policy, as he had been in the past, even after his resignation. He may even have believed that he could create such a powerful faction within the party that he would be able to force his return. However what could be done in a hurry could be undone in a hurry. In spite of the resistance of the rank and file *squadristi*, Farinacci's measures were in most cases successfully reversed after his fall.[34]

The defeat of Farinacci

The party's drive for supremacy in the State could only be successful if it managed to infiltrate and subvert the central ministerial bureaucracy. The Matteotti crisis seemed to have opened the way for such a process. The bureaucracy, sensitive to changes in the political climate, had become notably more reluctant than previously to grant Fascist requests. Mussolini, who earlier in the year had defended the bureaucracy from party accusations of disloyalty and obstructionism, now showed his dissatisfaction.[35] In the first half of 1925, there was full agreement between Mussolini and the party on the need for measures to secure the regime's control over the civil service.

Rocco struck the first legislative blow at the independence of the bureaucracy with the bill on associations (introduced on 12 January 1925), which made it illegal for public officials to belong to secret societies. This measure hit the bureaucracy where it was morally weakest. The illegitimate influence of the Masonic network in the civil service had long been the subject of criticism. However the law contained a clause which forced civil servants to declare if they had ever belonged to secret associations in the past, and this gave Government and party a powerful weapon.

The attack on Freemasonry was only the prelude to the more sweeping measure introduced on 28 May which allowed the dismissal of officials who showed their 'incompatibility with the general political directives of the Government'. The introduction of this bill, as Mussolini himself emphasized, was a decisive step in the progress of Fascism from a 'government' to a 'regime'. The bill was virtually retroactive, since proof of past membership in opposition parties was considered reason for dismissal.[36]

The party campaign against the bureaucracy had Mussolini's blessing. It helped him to intimidate any would-be opponents. He seemed to have adopted the party viewpoint when he publicly expressed regret at having failed to carry out a 'pitiless purge' of the administration immediately after the March on Rome. However the party had its own aims and its agitation did not cease with the introduction of the bill, although it became less vocal. In the April Grand Council meeting Federzoni admitted the existence of a 'programme of the party' on the problem of the bureaucracy. While promising that the Government would take action along the lines the party desired, he stressed 'the absolute necessity of preventing the indispensable renewal of the administration from giving occasion or pretext for unjust persecution'; the aim must be to reinforce 'the authority of the responsible powers'. This was a cautious warning of the dangers of undue party interference. Federzoni's position at this time was delicate and somewhat isolated; it seems that even Rocco, though an unbending defender of State supremacy, was prepared to countenance a more thoroughgoing purge than Federzoni desired, and therefore did not give him effective support against the party.[37]

The seriousness of the Fascist threat to the bureaucracy was much increased by the very considerable following which the party had won in the lower and middle ranks of the civil service, and among local government officials. Aldo Lusignoli, the secretary of the Corporation of Employees, demanded that the 'obstructionists' among the top civil servants should be replaced by loyal Fascists promoted from below or brought in from the provinces.[38] The suggestion that there should be a massive intake of local officials into the central government administration was particularly dangerous; it would have allowed the *ras* to gain a foothold in the ministries by 'recommending' their clients. The party's attempt to undermine the ideal of an objective and technically qualified bureaucracy received support from surprising quarters. Lolini, the chief spokesman of early Fascism on the problems of bureaucracy, was led by his frustrations as a reformer to take up an extremist position. The old bureaucrats, ready to serve any master, must be replaced by 'men of proven Fascist faith'. Enthusiasm was more important than culture; Lolini laid the blame for the insufficient Fascist ardour of the higher officials on the education they had received in the university law faculties. These were guilty of forming a cultural mentality 'pervaded by mechanistic rationalism', and a belief in objectivity and legal norms.[39]

The party played an active role in the purge of Freemasons and anti-Fascists, receiving information and singling out victims. It tried, though with rather less success, to place its own candidates in the key positions in the administration. Most serious of all, the party set up its own political groups within the ministries, under the control of the *direttorio*; their dissolution, on 26 November 1925, was one of the most significant consequences of Farinacci's political defeat.[40] Until that defeat the central bureaucracy was seriously menaced by the party's inroads.

In the spring and summer of 1925 the party had pretty much its own way in the provinces. Federzoni was on the defensive, and he was powerless to check the renewed outbursts of violence from the party. The Prefects were still very reluctant to offend the local party bosses. Friendly Prefects were protected by the party, who expected to be informed before the Ministry of the Interior took any disciplinary measures.[41]

In these circumstances Federzoni's efforts to suppress terrorism were still largely unavailing. The root of the problem remained how to restore the confidence of the State authorities. It is true that in April Farinacci issued a circular warning the federations against the unnecessary continuation of local and sporadic acts of violence; as a counterpart he demanded repressive legislation.[42] However the old sequence of provocation, reaction and reprisal continued, and it only needed the excuse of a dead or wounded Fascist, whatever the provocation, for all restraint to be dropped. In late May, a particularly grave series of reprisals took place in the Polesine, with repercussions in other parts of the Veneto and Lombardy. Balbo, whose Ferraresi were actively involved, defended these outrages with notable candour, and Farinacci too excused them.[43] This period reached perhaps the low-water mark of Federzoni's control of the situation. He had just had to consent to the appointment of Teruzzi as his under-secretary. Although Teruzzi's abilities proved quite insufficient for the role, he was expected to act as party watchdog and controller and at the time his appointment was regarded as a serious setback for Federzoni.[44]

Federzoni, however, did not give up. He assiduously collected evidence on the revival of the squads, and with a clear political purpose, took especial pains to discover if their formation was ordered and approved by influential personalities of the party and if it formed part of a definite programme.[45] This patient preparation of the evidence put him in a position to exploit to the utmost any error that his opponents might make. One feature of Fascist violence, as in the past, which was politically inconvenient, was the attack on Catholic institutions. On 23 June an attack on a religious procession in Rome drew a strong protest from the Pope; a month later the *Osservatore Romano* carried a long article on violence concluding with the phrase '*Nihil violentum durabile*'. The Vatican, moreover, let it be known that soundings for a Concordat could not be pursued until the Fascist regime showed itself able to control the lawlessness of its supporters.[46]

The revival of the squads dated back to the summer of 1924, as we have seen. Some of the squads then formed had later been dissolved, but the greater part remained in existence. Their terroristic purpose was thinly disguised by a variety of subterfuges. In Genoa they were known as 'Ward sporting circles'; in Turin they were organized by the so-called '*Mutua Squadristi*', who pretended to be an organization for the assistance and employment of the old fighters; in Bologna they were grouped round the *Casa del Fascio* and the various *Circoli Rionali*. Particularly ominous from the point of view of the State was the revelation that in certain areas the squads were tending to usurp the functions of the police, not only in the repression but in the investigation of crimes.[47] The one way in which the squads could have made themselves into a permanent institution was by assuming the role of a political

police force. There can be no doubt that Farinacci approved and even insti-
gated their formation. He regarded them as an indispensable weapon for the
permanent intimidation of the party's enemies; moreover the morale of the
party was closely bound up with *squadrismo* and the exercise of irregular
violence. It is significant that the activity of the squads remained particularly
notable in the large cities (Turin, Genoa, Rome) where a strong working-class
opposition to Fascism existed. In working-class quarters the *fasci* held on to
their primary repressive function. A *fascio* which 'dominated' a particularly
troublesome area was excused any number of irregularities.[48]

However the causes for the persistence of *squadrismo* were also to be found
in the internal politics of the movement. Sometimes the prevailing reason lay
in the rivalries between individual Fascists; in one or two cases rival squads
were formed by the leaders of the party and the Militia. In Mantua, the *ras*
Arrivabene and Moschini promoted terrorism and the myth of *squadrismo*
mainly as a weapon against the notables, who were trying to undermine their
dominion.[49] This local and anarchic nature of *squadrismo*, a legacy from its
origins, made it difficult for Farinacci to manipulate or control from the
centre. Moreover an increasingly sinister air of corruption enveloped the
squads. Private quarrels, blackmail, protection rackets and straight theft were
among their activities.[50] In short, the local Fascist leaders had a vested
interest in maintaining the climate of tension and fear which alone justified
and permitted their arbitrary rule, and which allowed them to suppress not
only opposition but internal criticism. This interest largely coincided with
Farinacci's own strategy.

The fear of Bolshevism, however, was no longer so credible as in the past.
The *fasci* and the squads needed a new enemy; they found one in the Freemasons. The Freemasons were a secret organization, penetrated however by
the Fascists. Their secrecy made them the perfect object for what Hannah
Arendt has called a 'counter-conspiracy'. The strength of the Freemasons
was in the respectable middle class, in the bureaucracy, the professions and
the world of business; an attack on them would therefore serve the purposes
of a demagogic extremism – the reality or threat of exposure could be used to
discredit the local notables, or make them submissive. Such were the motives
which probably inspired the launching of a new Fascist press campaign
against the Freemasonry in September 1925. The situation was, however,
complicated by the Masonic connections of many Fascists, and the rivalry
between the two Freemasonries of Piazza Giustiniani and Piazza del Gesù. It
seems that although the Grand Master Palermi had officially dissolved the
Piazza del Gesù Freemasonry, some kind of link between its members may
have remained. Both Farinacci and Tamburini, ostensibly leading 'anti-
Masons', were strongly suspected of keeping up the connection.[51] The
campaign, therefore, was directed exclusively against the anti-Fascist
Freemasonry of Piazza Giustiniani.

The temperature of the anti-Masonic campaign rose abruptly when the

Voce Repubblicana published the documents of Farinacci's entry into the Freemasonry in 1915. The Freemasons were accused by Farinacci of trying to 'disintegrate Fascism'.

There was every reason why the campaign should have exploded into brutality at Florence sooner than anywhere else.[52] The 'October incidents' fittingly closed the period which began with the mobilization of the Florence Fascists at the end of 1924. The political defeat which the intransigents now suffered had, unfortunately, lesser consequences than their former victory, but it was also in its way decisive. During 1925 the Florentine Fascists had taken on the air of guardians of the revolution. 'The Florentine *squadristi* are asking: who is the man who is betraying Fascism and the Duce . . . ?'[53] In any absolutist system, the way to square rebellion with loyalty is to claim that the leader, Czar or monarch, has been misled and betrayed by his advisers. Alone among speakers at the Party Congress Tamburini sounded a note of dissent and barely concealed insolence towards Mussolini; he complained that the Militia was being diluted by the entry of men of doubtful faith, and demanded 'a return to the origins'. Then he added: 'You Farinacci, understand our spirit. I am sorry that the Duce is not here to listen to the voice of the *squadristi*!'[54] 'The revolutionary will of the *squadristi*' in Tamburini's version willed some very sordid happenings; there is no need to labour the point. What, however, must be stressed is the populist and demagogic tone of the propaganda of the Florentine Fascists. There was something here of the totalitarian dynamic of 'permanent revolution' or at least permanent terror; new enemies were found to replace the old. 'Fascist propaganda has turned from the ignorant masses to enter the universities and the temples of justice;[55] violence was to be turned against the elites of law and culture and the anti-Masonic campaign was to provide a blanket justification for personal persecution. On 12 September 1925 the Florentine *fascio* announced that the Freemasonry of Torrigiani 'had declared war to the uttermost against Fascism'; one of the hallmarks of totalitarianist propaganda is to attribute or project your own intentions onto your enemy.

The Florentine Fascists made no secret that they expected to take matters into their own hands. The bludgeon and not the handcuffs were to have the last word; and the Fascists were to decide for themselves who was or was not a Freemason; 'In this struggle . . . we may hope that the Government will not hinder us.'[56]

A fortnight later the climax of the press campaign came with the publication of a Masonic circular calling for foreign help. 'We accept the challenge. From today no time must be given to the Freemasonry or to the Freemasons. The devastation of the lodges has become a joke. We must strike at the Freemasons; in their persons, in their goods, in their interests'; the communiqué was signed by the *direttorio* of the *fascio*.[57]

The Florence incidents started on 25 September. A number of Freemasons, or of individuals accused of belonging to the organization, were attacked and beaten up. They included several employees of the municipal government, traders and the manager of a factory at S. Giovanni Valdarno.[58] One can see from the list of victims that the rationale of the violence lay in reducing the independent elements in the bourgeoisie to the same state of powerlessness and dependence that the working class had already been forced to accept. But these incidents were only a prelude to the real outbreak; on 3 October a group of Fascists broke into the house of a Freemason, who killed one of them in self-defence. This was a signal for the unleashing of a general reign of terror. The next day the violence spread to Prato and other provincial centres, where a number of shops belonging to reputed Freemasons were attacked, as well as the Combatants' and Catholic circles. Further reprisals were planned. The Prefect reacted by signing an order for the mobilization of Tamburini's Militia legion, which was entrusted with the task of watching the gates to prevent the entry of troublemakers![59] This was to put the wolf in charge of the sheepfold.

The '*fatti di Firenze*' of October 1925 were not wholly a local or spontaneous episode. During their course they rapidly degenerated into episodes of private violence and blackmail; it seems likely that a mafia-type situation existed in the wholesale grocery trade, and that the squads intervened, under cover of the anti-Masonic campaign, to suppress competition. But the incidents had none the less been carefully prepared by a concerted propaganda campaign; it was, after all, likely that somewhere a persecuted or harried opponent would react and give the excuse for massive reprisals.

On 5 October after energetic orders from Mussolini and Federzoni, Farinacci arrived in Florence to impose discipline. Here he made a serious if perhaps inevitable mistake. He stuck to his usual line and excused what had happened as the result of the 'legitimate exasperation' of his comrades. Farinacci's only hope of avoiding the storm would have been to take strong measures against Tamburini and the Florentines on his own initiative, but he hesitated before the claims of political consistency, or *omertà*.[60] Meanwhile Mussolini had summoned the Grand Council in haste, and it met on the night of the fifth. Mussolini launched an all-out attack; the nervous pencil jottings for his speech which survive in the record convey vividly his fury and scorn. He started by attacking Farinacci where the latter believed himself strongest; as an organizer and disciplinarian. In the months since the Rome Congress, Mussolini alleged, there had been no improvement in the compactness of the party; in the provinces local 'chaotic situations' and 'provincial *commissari* who don't settle anything' continued to be the norm. Federzoni and Rossoni, as leader of the unions, were singled out by contrast for praise. Farinacci and the party, he suggested by implication, were the only failure. His speech rose in crescendo; from organization he passed to the more explosive topic of *squadrismo*: 'there must be an end to it', it was now 'grotesque and criminal'; at best it 'represented the aspirations of local leaders to hegemony'. He threatened 'to carry out another 3 January against the degeneration of Fascism'.

'Making a second Matteotti out of Pilati (one of the victims killed in the incidents) only just avoided. Bondinelli – a tradesman – a dangerous enemy of the regime ? The murderer – we can admit that – is killed. But the rest ? It is not Fascist, not Italian – not timely, chivalrous or surgical violence.

'Devastation of lawyers – Freemasonry ? and what about the Catholic circle of Pistoia ? and the Faenza notary ? . . . And all this under the eyes of 10,000 English and Americans.

'Decided to suppress by all means in power. Devotion to the Duce ?'

'*The most anarchic party* in Italy is the Fascist – useless papers – useless periodicals – bought by schoolboys and women. We must have the newspaper of the party – a daily order-sheet. Millions spent uselessly. . . .[61]

Mussolini, in fact, had widened his attack from the specific incidents to strike at the root of Farinacci's policy and the party's claims. He saw that the moral turpitude of the Florence incidents as well as the evidence collected by Federzoni, had left Farinacci exposed and isolated, and seized his chance. His indignation was genuine ; one must give Mussolini credit for a sincere desire to avoid the creation of a permanent climate of terror. At the same time, he was probably moved by alarm as well as by repugnance.

Mussolini's speech shows that one of his chief preoccupations was with foreign opinion. The continuation of lawless violence was compromising the prestige of the regime abroad ; this had consequences which were not confined to the field of diplomacy. Against the background of an already serious financial crisis, they greatly contributed to diminishing the confidence of foreign investors ; moreover the good opinion of the English was needed for the settlement of war debts.[62] Such repercussions, in turn, were bound to affect the attitude of conservative circles in Italy which were still powerful – in the first place, industry, and more doubtfully the Army and the monarchy : all those forces, in short, whose preference for a Federzoni government was no secret. It is not unlikely that if Mussolini had now taken on these forces he might, as in January 1925, have found that they would back down rather than face a head-on clash ; but it would have been a big risk and it was one he did not now need to take. Instead, against the party he could count on the support of Federzoni, Rocco and Volpi, i.e., the State machine and the leaders of industry and finance.[63] It was this coalition which triumphed in October 1925 ; but Mussolini, by putting himself at its head, retained and even increased his room for manoeuvre.

It is probable that after Mussolini's onslaught Farinacci offered his resignation ; to avert this and to save his face the Grand Council ended by voting a motion of confidence in his work. Much more important, however, was the approval of the motion for the immediate dissolution of the squads. This decision was kept secret, since the existence of the squads had always been denied by official sources.

Mussolini's outburst in the Grand Council marked a turning point ; yet by itself it settled nothing. Once before, in the revisionist crisis, Mussolini had delivered a similar, if milder, general rebuke to the party and its leaders ; on that occasion, his attack had not been followed through by adequate reorganization and consequently his 'new course' had had little practical result. Mussolini's own ambivalence on the question of law had then been largely responsible. Now his dependence on the party was less because the opposition was weaker. Another factor of importance was the presence of Federzoni at the Ministry of the Interior. Up till this time he had been hamstrung by the uncertainty of Mussolini's support ;[64] now, however, he was able to see to it that Mussolini's orders were carried out faithfully and efficiently at least by the organs of the State.

The policy of Federzoni and Rocco offered an alternative to party control which promised to be more efficient and more reliable. Their aim, of course, was not any ideal of impartial administration. Their problem was, instead, that of how to secure political reliability without having to employ the party as a watchdog. One part of the solution lay in the care with which the ex-Nationalist ministers conciliated the feelings and interests of the administrative elite, as far as was consistent with their claim to absolute political unanimity. Rocco, in his speech introducing the law on the bureaucracy, described himself as a 'functionary', and excused the imposition of political discrimination by the conservative argument that it was only necessary because of the 'social democratic perversions' of the last twenty years. He made out that his aim was to restore the conditions of the golden age before Giolitti, 'when officials did not engage in politics'.[65] The other half of the solution was to increase the powers of the Prefects still further, giving them the chief role in the surveillance of the other branches of the administration. To the party's claim that it alone could carry through 'the fascistization of the State', Federzoni replied that the Prefects, as political officials, were the natural instruments for the purpose. The 'prudence and precision' of their operations would ensure that the necessary purges were carried out smoothly and without the need for terror and the anonymous denunciation.[66]

There remained the problem of how to restore discipline in the party. In the week following the Grand Council meeting, there were several attempts to imitate the deeds of the Florentine Fascists. In Rome, where Luporini and a group of Florentines had been personally active in stirring up trouble at the beginning of October, the Fascists assaulted the headquarters of both the Freemasons, Palazzo Giustiniani and Palazzo Gesù, on 12 October. This incident led to the forced resignation of the secretary of the Rome *fascio*, Foschi. Serious acts of violence against the Freemasons and the opposition were also committed in Bari ; in Modena, Forlì and Genoa the police restrained the Fascists with difficulty.[67] The order to dissolve the squads met with predictable resistance and incredulity. The Modena Fascists demanded 'direct confirmation' of the order by the *direzione* of the party and the Militia command. The case of Turin was even more serious. The regional *fiduciario* Gianferrari declared that he had had instructions from Farinacci not to dissolve the squads, and called the Grand Council's decision in question on the grounds that the motion had not been put to the vote.[68] This attempt to deny Mussolini's absolute authority over the movement, together with the news that the leaders of Turin Fascism had rushed to Cremona for direct consultations with Farinacci, revived the Duce's anger.

My orders are not voted, they are accepted and executed without murmuring or reservations, because the Grand Council is not a little parliament and in the Grand Council there have never – I repeat never – been votes of any sort ... it is high time to make the necessary distinction : the Fascists with the Fascists, the criminals with the criminals, and the profiteers with the profiteers ; and above all it is necessary to practise moral intransigence, I repeat moral.[69]

Mussolini forced Farinacci to capitulate and himself to execute the policy which he had opposed. Mussolini finally imposed his views on the party in a meeting of the *Consiglio Nazionale*. The news that this body, where the intransigents were at their strongest, was to be summoned, caused some surprise and perplexity among non-Fascists ; they believed that it would be simply a rubber stamp for the confirmation of the directives of the Secretary.[70] But Mussolini attended the *Consiglio* in person, and neither Farinacci nor the *federali* dared to raise any protest in his presence. Farinacci read a list of 'ten commandments' which must have been dictated by Mussolini. The *federali* must purge and discipline the party cadres : *fasci* in which there were disturbances of order were to be dissolved ; all squads were to be disbanded, and an enquiry carried on into the normal moral as well as police record of all members. Finally, a significant blow against the squadrist spirit, no arms or bludgeons were henceforward to be carried in processions, and black shirts were to be worn only on authorized occasions. The only concession to the intransigents was made on the question of the Militia ; the dissolution of the squads was sweetened by a promise that the party would 'demand the appointment of commanders worthy of the tasks and traditions of the Militia'.[71]

The document ended with a promise that the party would put pressure on the Government to see that all positions in the government apparatus were staffed by reliable men. In theory, the position of the party remained unchanged ; only illegal action was condemned, and the promise was still held out that in exchange the Fascist spirit would permeate the State organizations ; but in practice, the result of the *Consiglio Nazionale* represented an act of submission by Farinacci. The acid test of these new resolutions was Florence : unless an example were made of the Florentine extremists, the new code of conduct would be worthless. At first contradictory signals suggested that Mussolini might again in practice permit a compromise solution.

On 9 October the Prefect of Florence, in a last desperate attempt to save his position by demonstrating the energy and honesty which he had failed to show during the crisis, warned the Government that the situation was still out of control, and would remain so while the present leaders were in office.

If the *fascio* and federation were not quickly dissolved 'a magnificent opportunity will end by being wasted'.[72] But even so, in recommending a list of
candidates for the provisional *direttorio* he excluded the moderate deputies
Lupi and Marchi on the grounds that they were 'strongly opposed by
Tamburini'. The Government took the Prefect's warning to heart; but not
quite in the way he had intended. Both he and the chief of police were removed,
and a special *commissario* was despatched to reorganize the party.

The man chosen to carry out the vital mission of restoring order to Florentine Fascism was Italo Balbo; it seemed at first sight very doubtful that
Balbo would crack down on Tamburini and his friends. Balbo, however,
showed himself resolute and straightforward in carrying out the policy
Mussolini desired. The intransigents were not united; Suckert, who for
reasons that are obscure had fallen out with Tamburini and the other Florentine leaders, was suspected of being the *eminence grise* who advised Balbo to
take a firm line. Tamburini at first believed that he could ride out this storm
as he had done in the past. He recognized, with a certain shrewdness, that
the time for tough, uncompromising defence of his position was over; he
made a show of being perfectly willing to accept the nomination of the
moderate Marchi as *commissario*, insinuating, however, to Farinacci, that it
might not be in his best interests to agree. 'We, provided you are pleased, *will
obey anyone. I repeat, however, provided it pleases you, as the most Fascist
of all Fascists, and not you in your official character of general secretary of
the Fascist party.' When it became clear that Farinacci could not respond to
this appeal, Tamburini fell back on the tactic of trying to see that the new
commissario in federation and *fascio* would be flanked by advisory committees,
in which his friends were well represented. If the old *fiduciari di zona* were
maintained, and so long as Marchi took their advice on expulsions and
admissions, his following might still stay substantially intact.[73]

Tamburini's other residual strength was that his formal position of leadership was not in the party, but in the Militia. Balbo purged a number of
Tamburini's 'Fascists of pure faith', men like a certain Sorbi, 'repatriated in
1920 from Trieste as a police measure, who belongs to the Militia without
having any other occupation . . . extremely violent', but when he left, perhaps
speeded on his way by Tamburini's protests to Farinacci, the work was
incomplete. The old and politically inexperienced General Secco who was
left in charge of the *fascio* was quite ineffective; both Marchi and the Prefect
came to the conclusion that all changes in the party would be fruitless if the
problem of the Militia was not grasped firmly. The zone commander General
Ceccherini was 'completely tied and enslaved to Tamburini'. Ceccherini
refused to carry out the order from Rome for the dismissal of the other
Consul, Onori, and instead succeeded in having the order temporarily
revoked.[74] Only at the beginning of December were Tamburini and Onori
finally dismissed. Tamburini was sent into a well-cushioned exile in Libya.
The old Florentine Fascism, as Tamburini asserted in a letter to Mussolini,

was dead.[75] The new *commissario* Marchi and the Prefect, acting in close alliance, promoted members of the aristocracy to a new controlling role in the *fascio* ; from now on social and political status were to go together. Marchi's most spectacular move to change the structure of Florentine Fascism was to admit all 420 members of the former 'National Liberal Party'.[76] The editorship of the *Battaglie Fasciste* was taken on by the revisionist Gherardo Casini. Tamburini retained a strong personal following among Florentine Fascists. In 1928, a demonstration of 1,500 sympathizers greeted him on his return to Florence and the Prefect reported that 'his position is still the most lively and combative' ; even as late as 1931 Tamburini had to disavow another attempt at a demonstration in his favour.[77] But the changes of 1925–6 were not to be reversed.

In Florence it had proved impossible to deal with the problem of terrorism without a complete restructuring of both the Fascist party and the Militia. In no other way could the web of intimidation, complicity, and *omertà* be broken. If the Florentine machine of Tamburini was an extreme case, both more criminal and more powerful than others, the same difficulty also existed elsewhere. After October 1925 the majority of the squads were dissolved. There were exceptions ; in Genoa the 'sporting circles' were only unmasked by Bocchini in May 1926, or so he claimed. But the heart of the problem was not necessarily touched by the dissolution of the squads. These had usually been in origin highly informal organizations, bound by personal ties of *camaraderia* and personal loyalty, coming together when specific needs or opportunities presented themselves ; little communities gravitating round a particular cafe or brothel. It followed that the problem of *squadrismo* could not be solved by organizational measures alone ; so long as the 'spirit of opposition' to official directives survived, and so long as individuals within the Fascist movement preserved their old ties, the squads could reappear in times of crisis or excitement as if by magic. At Trieste, for example, one of the most turbulent cities during 1926, the Prefect remarked that there were no formal groups left after the dissolution of the local *selvaggi* of the Masi faction, but that this made little or no difference, since there were still leaders who could mobilize 'thirty or forty enthusiastic youths with a nod'.[78]

This explains why in many places *squadrismo* could not be eliminated from Fascism without eliminating a great number of the *squadristi* themselves, and indeed without destroying the vitality of a movement so largely founded upon the use and cult of violence. It is clear at the same time that the elimination of *squadrismo* was not complete. *Squadrismo* lost its political significance and also its psychological function as an outlet for the enthusiasm of youth ; at the other extreme, the forms of *squadrismo* which were practically indistinguishable from ordinary crime were also greatly reduced. Crimes of violence, in fact, diminished in number from 1926 on, reflecting a general stabilization and lessening of the acute tensions of the postwar period. But in rural districts and in some working-class areas the squads remained as an instrument of intimidation directly or indirectly controlled by the employers : and in the smaller *fasci* some local leaders continued to use the squads as a prop for arbitrary personal power.[79]

The decline of Farinacci's prestige after October 1925 was evident from a number of signs ; the revival of the intellectual opposition centred round Bottai and the *Critica fascista* ; the growing challenge to his authority from influential leaders such as Balbo, Arpinati and Ricci ; and direct attempts to damage him morally and politically, by exposing and attacking his less desirable connections. Already in October new complaints had reached Mussolini about the activities of Count Lusignani ; when yet another crisis broke out in the Parma party, Farinacci's attempts to hush it up and protect his friends were unsuccessful. Ricci, given powers to reorganize the Parma federation, like Balbo in Florence, acted against the Secretary's interests. Farinacci was forced to stand by inactive ; he could not afford further to antagonize Mussolini by intervening on behalf of a man whom the Duce made no secret of despising.[80]

The beginning of 1926 saw a revival of debate within the party. Both revisionists and intransigents spoke out frankly. Conformity was not fully restored until November 1926, when the crisis in the party can be said to have been finally resolved. The participants in the debate recognized that the coming period would be decisive in defining the role of the party in the regime. The intransigents held that the party, as the vigilant custodian of the Ideal, had the duty of correcting or stimulating the operations of the State machine. The party-State issue returned to the centre of political discussion in January 1926, with the publication in the Florentine newspaper *La Nazione* of an article by Ermanno Amicucci criticizing the party. Amicucci was not a revisionist, but a writer of impeccable orthodoxy and the secretary of the Fascist Journalists' Union ; no doubt about the significance of his criticism remained when Arnaldo Mussolini himself came to his defence in the *Popolo d'Italia*.[81] Farinacci, while denying the truth of Amicucci's accusation that some provincial *federali* still gave orders to the Prefects, went as near as he could to defending their interference. He could not openly assert the supremacy of the party, but he defended the right of its leaders to exercise a surveillance over the State organs which in practice came to the same thing ; 'every time a local leader has done wrong to the authorities, the party has intervened energetically, except if the Prefect has behaved in a way harmful to the regime, in which case the intervention of our representatives has been more than justified'.[82]

Farinacci and his supporters rested their case on a typically totalitarian conception of continuous struggle, or permanent revolution ; 'what must we ask from the Government if we are to serve the State ? The freedom to combat our *moral* enemies, who are now the most dangerous enemies of the State.' This process would be completed only when all Italians shared the Fascist outlook ; until then 'we will not concede rest to anyone'. The Government, without the stimulus of the party, would inevitably be affected by the 'bureau-cratic spirit' and would remain content with the purely negative achievement of keeping order. The party, as the guardian of the 'apostolic spirit', therefore had a special responsibility for the continuation of the revolution. 'Officials' could never be 'animators', only the party could defeat 'the offensive of cowardice, indifference and egoism' and combat 'moral inertia'.[83]

The intransigent view of the functions of the party in relation to the State had remained basically unchanged. In 1926 Farinacci and his allies were bringing forward new arguments in defence of the position which they had taken up in 1923; it was a question of justifying the permanent exercise of extra-legal powers which had previously been excused as the product of a transitional phase, before complete 'fascistization'. The apologia for extrem-ism, in fact, simply assumed the indefinite prolongation of this phase of transition. Even the suppression of all opposition groups (which, it must be remembered, in January 1926 still preserved a shadowy existence) could not permit any relaxation: the battle would continue against the neutrals, the indifferent, and new scapegoats could always be found. Farinacci claimed that the decline of opposition within Italy was compensated by the growing determination and unity of the anti-Fascist coalition 'beyond the frontiers': therefore vigilance must be intensified.[84] Readers of *Animal Farm* will have no difficulty in recognizing this argument. When internal opposition is subdued, the myth of foreign conspiracy becomes a necessity for the totali-tarian leader. Mussolini, of course, could turn this particular weapon against the party. His appeals for internal unity and discipline were also backed by the rhetorical suggestion of foreign encirclement.

Farinacci's views on internal party structure were changed by the new and difficult situation in which he found himself. While he had been in full control, he had permitted the free entry of new members into the party, and other intransigent leaders had criticized him for permitting this dilution of the old faithful by opportunist converts. Farinacci had always been favourable to the mass party which would impress by force of numbers, and he saw no danger in new recruits so long as old Fascists stayed on top. However after October 1925 the danger posed to his politics by the large intake of 'Fascists of the last hour' became too obvious to be ignored, and in November he decided to close the membership lists. This decision was reversed by the Grand Council on 3 January 1926; Mussolini could not achieve his aim of destroying the intransigents' hold of the party without the admission of new and more docile members to take the place of the riotous and uncontrollable *squadristi*. The importance of the Grand Council decision will become clearer if one examines another aspect of Farinacci's activities in the last months of his secretariat.[85]

So long as he had enjoyed Mussolini's confidence, Farinacci had been ready enough to talk about discipline and obedience. Now, however, with his loss of authority and the probability of his fall, he had to find some new formula to arrest his decline and revive his following. What initiatives were open to him?

The *federale* of Pavia, Bisi, advised him, 'to appeal to provincial Fascism and summon the *Consiglio Nazionale*'; but he did not make use of this well-tried device for showing his strength, probably because Mussolini would not have allowed it.[86] Instead, besides the efforts already described to create new zones of influence for himself, he was forced to appeal to the base of the party, the mass of ordinary members. A conformist, cowed party would accept any leader and present no problems to his successor : it was therefore in Farinacci's interest to encourage participation by the rank and file.

The Congress of the *fasci* of Lazio on 31 January 1926 gave Farinacci an excellent opportunity to launch a counter-attack on his critics. 'What will your Congress say ? That the party is what it is : that the intransigent line of the party remains intact. This annoys our false friends, and so, oh Fascists, we see repeated the same phenomenon as in 1923. Then, too, they said : Enough now ! The party no longer has a function. Down with this Fascism and with intransigence. And now again we see the grey press criticize Fascism . . .'; the critics were attempting to dictate the tasks of the movement to it from outside. Instead, 'Our tasks, and especially those of the leaders, consist of the exact interpretation of the will and thought of the Fascist masses.'[87] To reinforce the effect of this appeal to the Fascist masses, Farinacci was not afraid to play on direct economic grievances. The *Regime Fascista* attacked urban landlords in general and the president of their association, Commendatore Stucchi, in person, for charging unjustifiably high rents in defiance of the spirit of Fascist social policy.[88] These attacks greatly exacerbated the hostility between Farinacci and Arnaldo Mussolini, who had close ties with the Milanese property developers.

In a party whose social base was mainly among the middle classes and the petty bourgeoisie, and whose first *raison d'être* had been the containment of working-class claims, the most effective form of social radicalism lay in a defence of the interests of the consumer rather than the producer. Questions of wages and salaries were dangerous, divisive, and were left to the unions, with the party only exercizing supervision. But high rents and price rises in general hit the middle class as well as the workers ; consequently the generally respectful attitude of the party towards employers of labour contrasts with the tone of menace often used towards owners of urban property, shopkeepers and other groups on whom direct blame could be laid for the sufferings of the consumer.

When Arnaldo Mussolini subtly called in question Farinacci's boasted ability as a disciplinarian and suggested that the ruthless purges undertaken by his emissaries at Udine and elsewhere were responsible for increasing disorder within the party, Farinacci replied by a kind of defence of disorder. The internal revolutions of the party were a symptom of its continuing 'dynamism' ; a static, well-behaved party would be one which had lost its vitality.[89] Farinacci was right ; a monopolistic party needs a continued supply of fresh enemies to conquer, and once its power is well established it finds these not only among the apathetic, the neutral and the foreigner, but among the deviationists or 'heretics' in its own ranks. It was not, therefore, altogether a contradiction when Farinacci both claimed that the unity of the party was 'monolithic' and defended the positive significance of inner party feuds; the stimulation and manipulation of personal and group hostilities by the leaders is a basic device of totalitarian rule, which thrives on this apparent contradiction.

The trial of the murderers of Matteotti was the occasion of Farinacci's removal from office. Mussolini had authorized him to defend himself, but had given him instructions that the hearings must not be dramatized, and the political significance of the murder played down as far as possible. Predictably, Farinacci did not keep his undertaking, and this gave Mussolini a good excuse to be rid of him. On 30 April he was succeeded by Augusto Turati.[90]

After his fall from office, Farinacci continued to fight his successor on the same platform. During almost the whole of 1926 the situation in the party remained tense. Shortly after his resignation, Farinacci went on a tour of Venezia Giulia, where his supporters engaged in noisy and sometimes violent demonstrations. At Trieste the demonstrators shouted 'Discipline, what's discipline? Bloodshed, Bloodshed!', and manhandled Renato Ricci when he tried to bring them to heel.[91] There were several rumours that Farinacci supporters intended to carry out some kind of local coup or occupation of government buildings.[92] All this activity, real or imaginary, convinced Mussolini and Turati of the need to carry the war into the enemy's camp. They succeeded in stirring up demonstrations against Farinacci in his own province, among the Fascists of the Soresina district, always inclined to dissidence. The threat to Farinacci became much graver when the scandal of Lusignani and the Banca Agricola of Parma broke. Professor Groppali, Farinacci's *eminence grise*, and Stevani, his nominee as secretary of the Parma *fascio*, were both arrested for their involvement in the crash. Farinacci held on, raking up scandals in turn against his opponents, sealing the borders of his province off with the Militia and protesting his total innocence of any involvement with banks.[93] In July, Arnaldo Mussolini wrote Farinacci a fairly moderate letter which was intended, probably, to open the way for a reconciliation. Farinacci replied with a long letter of self-justification, blaming Federzoni, Balbo, Bottai and Suckert for the persecution which he was suffering. This reply, although more conciliatory in tone than previous utterances, cannot have satisfied the Duce.[94]

Farinacci's vainglorious assertions that the campaign against him had merely increased his popularity, and his threat that if he was not left alone in his own province, then the leaders of Fascism 'will know how to behave', showed that his attitude was still hardly submissive. Above all, Farinacci showed that he intended to keep to his own political line. A certain decline in the factional struggle within Fascism was noticed at the beginning of August 1926; but during the month Mussolini's interventions to compel Farinacci to silence became even more frequent; first it was an ominous article approving the terrorist methods of the Greek dictatorship that aroused his anger; then Farinacci's campaign against Parliament was cut short as politically premature, and finally there were Farinacci's persistent attacks on the Banca Commerciale and speculative high finance in general. By early September the patience of Mussolini and Turati was at breaking point; the latter sent Farinacci a regular ultimatum threatening him with disciplinary sanctions if he continued to go his own way. Even his friends and allies now advised him to submit as the only way to avoid the ruin of his career.[95]

It is somewhat surprising that Farinacci survived the impact of Mussolini's sustained hostility. To explain this, one needs to take into account not only the strength of his personal power base, but also the general situation in party and State. First of all, he was still not entirely isolated from the top level of the party leadership. No one in the *direttorio* could afford to declare himself a supporter of Farinacci; however it was possible to take the line that his followers should be conciliated in order to avoid a permanent and damaging split in the party. This was the position taken by Starace who, judging from his past and future history, was the member of the *direttorio* closest to Farinacci's outlook.[96] The party, even in the new and reduced role which Mussolini planned for it, could not afford to do without personalities like Starace, limited, unimaginative, dependable organization men. Secondly, the general political situation and the relationship between the party and State had not yet been stabilized. The series of attempts on Mussolini's life which succeeded each other at short intervals during 1926 weakened Federzoni and helped to keep extremism alive. After the anarchist Lucetti had thrown a bomb at Mussolini's car on 11 September the chief of police, Crispo Moncada, was replaced by Bocchini who enjoyed the confidence of the party. The PNF *direttorio* demanded the introduction of the death penalty and more efficient police measures; in the October Grand Council Turati read a motion which ended by inviting the provincial leaders 'to maintain an attentive vigilance over the conduct of all the surviving enemies of the regime'.[97]

This motion was published but not, it would seem, formally approved; the phrasing and intent seem more likely to have been dictated by the party than by Mussolini. In spite of the hostility and even hatred existing between Farinacci and Arpinati or Balbo, it seems that there was at least a tacit agreement among the intransigents to forget their differences and to act together. According to a report at the beginning of October, the extremist wing of the party was planning 'an offensive in grand style' against Federzoni, Rocco, Turati and the ex-Nationalist or moderate elements within Fascism. In so far as the intransigents had a leader, it was probably now Balbo. He was aiming to become Under-Secretary of the Ministry of the Interior or, failing that, secretary of the party.[98]

The extremists took advantage of the assassination attempts to exalt justified reprisals over legal procedures. A writer in Balbo's *Corriere Padano* defended the unreasonable excesses of exasperation as preferable to

... bureaucratic seriousness ... the principle of old age. ... A Fascist revolution which settled down quietly in the State would be a revolution that has finished. ... A revolution which may be fully victorious at home but is opposed and undermined abroad cannot be defended and sustained unless the revolutionary temperature is constantly kept high. ... The atmosphere produced by moralizing and exemplary violence constitutes in any case an infinitely more effective defence than the best organized and most careful police force. ... Heroic violence attracts youth, calmness repels them.

The same number carried a personal attack on the Prefect of Padua : evidently the supremacy of the State over the party could still be called in question.[99]

Party State or Police State?

The intransigent offensive was crowned by the resignation of Federzoni. This was not quite the triumph it seemed. As early as April, Federzoni had offered his resignation after the first of the year's assassination attempts, that of the crazy Irish spinster Violet Gibson. He seems to have assessed his own position with a certain objectivity and to have come to the conclusion that after the fall of Farinacci, Mussolini would no longer regard him as indispensable. Making a virtue of necessity he advised Mussolini that 'it is necessary to remove the impression that the Minister of the Interior has defeated the party'. Yet there is a difference between voluntary withdrawal and resignation under pressure, and Federzoni's declarations in November do not suggest that he was happy about the circumstances of his departure. He spoke of the difficulty of achieving a synthesis between the principle of authority and 'the autonomous will to command of Fascism in its revolutionary form'.[100]

However the party victory was this time an empty one, and the sacrifice of Federzoni, as he had foreseen, helped Mussolini to placate party discontent while at the same time increasing his own power. By reassuming direct control over the key Ministry of the Interior, Mussolini once again succeeded in turning an intransigent offensive to his own personal profit. Mussolini also benefited directly from Federzoni's removal to a less important post. Since the fall of Farinacci, Federzoni, as he had himself realized, was the second man in the regime, and as the favourite of the conservatives, monarchists and business, a potential danger. It would have been bad policy for Mussolini to have allowed him to retain a hold over the levers of power.

Piecemeal concessions – the removal of unpopular Prefects and the appointment, with much publicity, of a new batch drawn from the Fascist movement – at first confirmed the impression that the party had won a real victory.[101] But with the January 1927 circular to the Prefects Mussolini once more reaffirmed State authority as supreme. Unlike the earlier declarations of 1923 on the relationship between Prefect and *federale*, this circular had a real and lasting practical effect. Mussolini now possessed both the will and the means to secure compliance. The suppression of all opposition parties and of local elections made it possible drastically to reduce the functions of the Fascist party. It was no longer 'the only foundation of social order in many provinces'; that function passed to the Prefect and the Podestà.[102] Mussolini had loyal and docile subordinates both at the head of the party and as Under-Secretary of the Interior; although in 1928–9 the appointment first of Bianchi and later of Arpinati to the latter post might seem to show a revival of independent party influence, these appointments were concessions from strength and not from weakness. By then the battle had been won, and the party was a very different organization.

One of the most important landmarks in the transformation of the party was the reform of its Statute. The new Statute was discussed and voted by the Grand Council on 7–8 October. For the first time, it was clearly stated that the Duce was at the summit of the Fascist hierarchy, although in the field of policy-making the Grand Council was still recognized as the supreme organ of Fascism. The substitution of nomination from above for election throughout the party was accompanied by other practical reforms which all worked in the direction of bureaucratic centralization. The wide disciplinary powers delegated to the provincial *federali* and *direttori* were now limited; no *fascio* could be dissolved without the authorization of the General Secretary, and individual Fascists were given the right to appeal to the higher authorities against sanctions by the provincial organs.[103] Another innovation of great importance for party organization was the *Foglio d'ordini*. Until 1926, the dissemination of orders and directives within the party had been entrusted to the Fascist press. Moreover the deliberations of the Grand Council and the *direttorio* were the only binding documents issued by the central leadership; much scope therefore remained to the federations for interpretation and day-to-day decision making. The *Popolo d'Italia* often gave a lead on questions of policy; but its views, authoritative as they were, were not official and could be challenged. On local questions, moreover, the board of the *Popolo d'Italia* seems to have exercized only a loose control over its own correspondents, who sometimes preserved an independent point of view. The institution of the *Foglio d'ordini* at the end of July 1926 gave Mussolini and the secretary of the party a new instrument of control, confirmed by the Statute; Mussolini had foreseen the necessity for this since October 1925. The next stage was to reduce the party press both in quantity and quality. The numbers of party newspapers shrank (the reduction had financial even more than political reasons) and they became increasingly uniform in content. The creation of a standardized and centrally controlled system of communications is an important feature of all systems of bureaucratic control.

The most important of the changes was, however, the end of elections within the party. From now on the party was to be organized on strictly hierarchical principles; the General Secretary would nominate the *federali*, and the *federali* would nominate the secretaries of the single *fasci*. Under the new system, it was possible for the General Secretary to transfer a *federale* from one province to another at will. The ties between leaders and followers were thus severed, and the *federale* became, as Farinacci put it, 'a Prefect of the party', that is to say a bureaucratic official responsible only to his superiors.[104] This is not to say, of course, that the old system had been one of true inner-party democracy, exercized according to defined rules of procedure. Farinacci declared himself 'a constitutionalist within the party'; but the thought of Farinacci as a constitutionalist in any context was incongruous. Instead, according to Bottai's excellent description, the old system had been 'a singular form of absolute, direct democracy', in which 'the mass chose its dictators by acclamation'.[105] This plebiscitary system of manipulated spontaneity is, again, typically totalitarian; but its existence at a local level was bound to conflict with the demands of the supreme Duce.

What the intransigents were defending was not a democratic process of selection, but a particular style of leadership. So long as provincial secretaries were nominated by the assemblies, Farinacci argued, they would be 'real leaders who know how to impose their authority and exact obedience'. When nomination from above replaced election, leadership became less personal and more institutional, more bureaucratic. The *ras* could no longer serve as the interpreters of the oracle and derive a partly spurious, partly genuine, authority from their investiture by the masses. Farinacci complained that the new system would make it impossible for the Duce to hear the 'true voice' of his followers. The reform of the Statute had a depressing effect on the collective life of the party. The party 'needed an outlet'; when assemblies and congresses were suppressed, or at the least ceased to have any influence on the choice of leaders and policies, what remained? The alienation of the leaders from the rank and file, and the disillusionment and apathy of the latter were bound to grow.

By autumn 1926 even the intransigents recognized that the party would have to change its character and relationship to the State. They had revised their strategy, and their last offensive had aimed at new objectives. Formerly, they had defended the independence of the party: it must control the workings of the State machinery from outside, and remain free to exercize terror unhampered by rules. After the new Statute of the party, they discarded this conception as obsolete, at least in part. Party dominance, they saw, could now best be secured by promoting a merger between the *apparats* of party and State. Farinacci suggested that instead of keeping the *federale* as a subordinate to the Prefect, the offices should be unified so that the Prefects would control the provincial federations directly. This system, of course, could only work on the assumption that the Fascist prefect would have nothing in common with the old type of official; the Revolution would have to get rid of all those 'who still have the germs of Nittianism and Giolittianism in their bloodstream'.[107] This was a prescription for the replacement of the keystone of the State bureaucracy by a new type of wholly politicized official; unification of party and State machinery on those terms would have led to something like the German Gauleiter system.

A parallel strategy is to be discovered in the writings and activities inspired by Balbo; he proposed to conserve the influence of the party by organizing a secret political police staffed by Fascists, and organized and controlled by the provincial federations and the Militia. If such a plan had succeeded, a new and more dangerous form of institutionalized terror would have replaced the irregular forces of *squadrismo*.[107] The decision to form a Fascist secret police was actually put into effect in Ferrara; it was accompanied by the compilation of lists of proscription, of opponents who would be murdered in reprisal if an attempt on the Duce's life succeeded. Such an eventuality was, of course, hypothetical, but the existence of such lists, whose composition remained secret, was clearly an effective instrument of terror. These sinister initiatives, which were incompatible with the centralization desired by Mussolini, were, however, formally repudiated by the Grand Council on 5 November.[108]

The type of organization and the staffing requirements of the police force will eventually assume a decisive importance for the structure of a dictatorship. In the first years after 1922, the role of the police in imposing Fascism, though undoubtedly important, had been on the whole that of an auxiliary to the terrorist activities of the *squadristi*. By the standards of modern dictatorship the police still left much to be desired in its efficiency and structure.

Under General De Bono the central police administration was not significantly modified. His principal assistants, the *capo-gabinetto* Umberto Ricci and the vice-chief of police, Dante Almansi, were men trained under the old regime. Bureaucratic and political resistance prevented Fascist ideas of reform from coming to fruition. On the one hand, the bureaucracy of the Interior Ministry resisted strongly and successfully all schemes (which may have had party backing) for decentralizing control and increasing the autonomy of the Prefects; on the other hand, the programme for creating a unified police corps, officially proclaimed by Mussolini and De Bono in November 1922, was never put into effect. The one important institutional change was the abolition of the *Guardie Regie*, the special force which had been created by Nitti for riot control and security.[109] However, here as in other fields, the Fascist movement created a parallel institution in the shape of the *Ufficio politico* of the general command of the Militia. The Consul Mosconi was the most important member of its staff. However the activity of the political investigation service of the Militia during 1923–4 remained limited in scope and somewhat amateurish; it was mainly occupied in furnishing general information about the state of opinion in the population and about tendencies in the Fascist movement. The accuracy and detail of this information was in general much inferior to that supplied by the reports of the regular police.[110]

In November 1926, as a partial concession to the views of the extremists, the political police organization of the Militia was greatly expanded. Directions were given for each legion to organize its own political investigation office

(UPI). How far this police force would be under party control depended on the local relationship between the Militia command and the federation. One of the tasks of the UPI, in fact, was to provide information on the activities and internal disagreements of the Fascist movement, and their effect on public opinion. In this way they helped the Militia to function as an instrument of control over the party, or rather over the local parties. Though documentation is scarce, it appears that the chief function of the UPI was to investigate anti-Fascist activities, and also those of the Freemasons, outside and inside the Fascist movement.[111]

The State police, however, were the central and dominant instrument of control under the regime. The technical expertise of Bocchini, which he demonstrated by his success both in protecting Mussolini from assassination attempts and in destroying the clandestine *apparat* of the Communist party, both tasks in which his predecessors had failed, enabled him to triumph over his opponents.[112] Bocchini's administration is a typical instance of Max Weber's theory of the limiting power that bureaucracy and expertise can exert over political commands. In Germany, the police administration fell into the hands of an ideologically inspired elite, originating in the ranks of the party. In Italy, it remained under the control of trained bureaucrats, and this was a fact of decisive importance.

There was, at first, a real danger of party control over the political police. Turati had his own man, E. Guli, appointed as head of the political police, and it was some time before Bocchini could exercise unchallenged control.[113] He owed his ultimate success not only to his skill but even more to Mussolini's suspicion of the party. The dictator applied the classic principle of 'divide and rule' and this led him to favour the independence of the police from party influence.

The police, under Bocchini's efficient management, largely absorbed the repressive functions of the party and the squads. There is no doubt that in practical terms this was a gain for the ordinary citizen and even, perhaps, for the political suspect. The operations of the State police were more predictable and more impersonal than those of the squads : Bocchini's criteria were utilitarian rather than ideological. Prevention, not persecution, was the key word ; suspects were sometimes given discreet warnings in advance. But against these advantages must be set the final and total suppression of all guarantees for the citizen against the arbitrary exercise of police power. The reformed *legge di pubblica sicurezza* was the true 'fundamental law' of the regime ; it can be said that November 1926 saw the birth of a 'police state'. This should not be taken as an all-embracing and adequate definition, but it comes nearer the truth than talk about a dictatorship of the monolithic party.

The concept of law implies that its operations should be limited, calculable and predictable ; that it should state clearly what is, and is not, permitted ; and that it should not be retroactive. These criteria cannot be upheld unless the responsibility of the executive for its actions is recognized at least in theory.

Fascist laws and ordinances repeatedly violated these conditions. In introducing the new Public Safety Law, Rocco made explicit its character as a charter of the absolute Police state.

The function of public security is no longer to be considered as something exceptional, in conflict with the dogma of individual liberty as the foundation and aim of society. It is, on the contrary, to be judged as one of the primary functions of the activity of the State. . . . It is therefore an activity whose exercise cannot be obstructed by absurd preconceptions. . . .[114]

With this flat repudiation of all doctrines of natural law or individual rights went the abolition of all distinctions between the State as a permanent entity and the Government of the moment. The safety of Fascism and the safety of the State were treated as identical.

In accordance with these premises, all vestiges of the responsibility of the executive for its actions were annulled. The citizen was left without redress; the police were no longer required to produce reasons to justify the imposition of restrictions on liberty. The police authority, for example, enjoyed absolute discretion in granting authorization to form associations or to exercise certain professions : 'consequently the citizen has no *right* to obtain authorization, or – having obtained it – to keep it'.[115]

The institution of *confino* made possible the internal exile and confinement to an enforced domicile, for a period of up to five years, of those *suspected* of the *intention* of engaging in subversive activity. The procedures governing the operation of the *confino* were especially arbitrary. The decision to commit suspects to the *confino* was taken by a provincial committee presided over by the Prefect; the only appeal was to a committee headed by the Under-Secretary of the Ministry of the Interior. The accused could be arrested at once, before their appeal was heard, and they were not allowed either to employ a lawyer or to summon witnesses in their defence. The jurisdiction of the magistracy was entirely excluded.[116] Moreover these unpredictable and arbitrary procedures gave an opportunity for the party to interfere. It was usually the party which denounced suspects, and on occasion local leaders, like Carlo Scorza in Lucca, used the mechanism of *confino* to deal with their personal enemies.[117] It is true that regular imprisonment could not be inflicted by administrative order, as in some totalitarian regimes. The Special Tribunal set up to judge 'crimes against the State', which had the power to inflict the death penalty, preserved legal forms, even if the composition of the court made these a very slight safeguard.[118]

Unfortunately the creation of the Police state in Italy was much assisted by the inadequacy of the guarantees for liberty provided under the parliamentary system. The Fascist regime was able to build upon established institutions and precedents. *Confino* itself was an inheritance from the Liberal State: though *domicilio coatto*, as it was then known, was originally intended for use against the Mafia, the *camorra* and brigandage, governments soon gave way to the temptation to use the weapon against political suspects. However under Giolitti the application of *domicilio coatto* had been confined to professional criminals.[119] In other respects, too, the procedures of the Liberal state had left much room for arbitrary police action. The sweeping emergency measures of January 1925 were legitimized by the vague and undefined powers given to the Prefects under article 3 of the existing communal and provincial law.[120] The power of *fermo*, or preventive arrest, had always been much abused, and the attempt of the 1912 penal code to introduce the rule of *habeas corpus* had not been a success; the police and other officials were in practice almost entirely immune from prosecution for excess or abuse of their powers.[121] Even the sanctions of public opinion and parliamentary discussion, though effective in securing new political liberties after 1900, were usually powerless to check the more humdrum abuses of official authority. Nor can the trouble be traced exclusively to official attitudes, the truth is that to a vast number of the Italian people, especially in the backward rural areas, the informal exercise of power to keep the peace, based on tradition or practical intuition, appeared more comprehensible than the workings of the law, which were slow, cumbersome, and bore little relation to real needs.[122]

The Party after 1926

During 1927–8 Mussolini was largely successful in breaking the independence of the party. The change in the relations between the party and the State and the Duce is reflected in the writings of the former revisionists during this period: they came to see the need to fight a battle on two fronts. Their main effort, certainly, was still directed against their old enemies, the intransigents, over whom they were finally victorious. Under the secretariat of Augusto Turati, Bottai and his friends were at last rewarded, both morally and materially, for their persistence in criticism. Their line was accepted; they welcomed the severe purge of the party undertaken by Turati, and above all, his 'change of style', the end of that 'provincial rhetoric' which Bottai so much despised and at the same time feared.[123] However there was another side. The revisionists – less so Bottai, who was increasingly affected by orthodoxy as his influence and power grew, and more the other writers of *Critica fascista* – began to criticize with caution the new tendency to suppress the functions of the party as an effective institution of government. Their concept of the party as an elite, as the nursery of the future ruling class, was menaced by the growth of Mussolini's unrestricted personal dictatorship. They saw a new threat in Mussolini's charismatic relationship with the masses, which duplicated, on a national scale, the emotive rhetoric which they had disliked in the *ras*. Moreover some of the provincial bosses had adapted themselves with great success to the new climate. Men like Scorza, the *ras* of Lucca, who lost no opportunity for servile adulation of Mussolini, and who wrote that 'criticism only serves to confuse values', were able to salvage their personal positions and even strengthen them. The revisionists had defended the change in the party Statute as necessary to break the hold of the intransigents ; but the nomination system soon showed its disadvantages. The rigid control of the party from above would frustrate the free circulation of elites in which the revisionists, as disciples of Pareto, believed.[124]

The new attitude of the revisionists is also discernible on the question of party-State relations. Their early approval of the purge of the party and the restoration of State authority was qualified by the perception of new dangers. By the end of 1926, they were criticizing the excessive interference of the Prefects in the party. The purge should have allowed the urban elite of the first hour, the intellectuals, and the new generation to come to the front : instead the Prefects were taking over the effective direction of the party by installing recent converts in positions of leadership.[125]

The restoration of the Prefects' power had been made more palatable to the party by the promise that the prefectoral corps would be rejuvenated by new, Fascist blood. Eight 'Fascist Prefects', drawn from the party, were appointed in December 1926 ; the *Tevere* welcomed their appointment as marking a change in the Prefect's function. 'From yesterday the Prefects have assumed a function of extreme importance, that of the supreme regulators of all activity in the province ; they are no longer bureaucrats but animators ; their God is no longer the career but Fascism.'[126] This was propaganda designed for party consumption : but it is possible that Mussolini himself may have had some illusions on this score. Any conclusion must be tentative until there has been a systematic study of the 1930s, but there seems little reason to doubt that, even if the 'animators' brought in from the ranks of Fascism did bring a more zealous partisanship and less scruple about legality into the administration, on balance it was the bureaucratic ethos and the 'career' which triumphed. The numbers of 'Fascist Prefects' as opposed to career Prefects became considerable over the years ;[127] but the influence of the new men was diminished by the structure of the administration and their own growing age and respectability. Moreover, as Farinacci had foreseen, paradoxically the continued existence of the party as a separate, though subordinate, institution, worked against the ideal of the 'Fascist Prefect' becoming a reality. In the province, the *federale* was the natural and obvious rival of the Prefect ; and when the latter was himself a party man friction was not less, but more, likely. As the Prefect was almost always a stranger to the province where he was appointed, he had a vested interest in reducing the autonomy and vitality of the party organization, and when he succeeded in controlling it through his own nominees, the latter were likely to be unpopular and unrepresentative. The mutual suspicion and hostility which often existed between the Prefect and the local Fascists, particularly the remnants of the old guard, must have helped to convert the former into upholders of statist, bureaucratic orthodoxy. It is unlikely to be a coincidence that some of the most vivid and persistent complaints and warnings about the party's depression and loss of morale came from provinces where a new Fascist Prefect was in charge. For example, the leader of the *Selvaggi*, Maccari, wrote to Turati of the growing dissatisfaction in Siena province :

... who, if not the Prefect Pighetti, is responsible for having nominated to the commanding positions in Sienese Fascism men who seem to have been chosen on purpose to discredit it and bring it into ridicule ? ... during the last years he has been *modifying* Sienese Fascism by behaving like a petty tyrant out of a melodrama and by the intrigues which are natural to his character.... I am indignant at the spectacle of the methodical humiliation of a strong and healthy Fascism, and of its best members.[128]

In Reggio Emilia the former *generalissimo* of Tuscan Fascism, Dino Perrone Compagni, not content with breaking the hold of the *ras* Fabbrici and having him sacked from *federale*, pursued a relentless vendetta against him, defying Turati's nervous exhortations for a reconciliation. Fabbrici's friends in the party manoeuvred him onto the list of deputies in 1929, but Perrone still won the last round. He expelled Fabbrici from the party during the electoral campaign, which meant that he was not allowed to take his seat.[129] All Prefects, and most especially the new Fascist recruits, who had the greatest temptation and often necessity for interference, would tend to prefer as *federale* the pliable and dependent man to the efficient or enterprising.

One cause of the decline in Fascist militancy and morale after 1926 was the successful *sistemazione* of so many Fascists within the State administration, and in the new *Enti parastatali* whose number was already increasing, though not as vertiginously as during the 1930s. Together with the new Statute and the changes in the party, the increasing number of opportunities in government and other offices tended to divide leaders from followers. The successful members of the Fascist elite were no longer dependent on the solidarity of their provincial environment. The locus of power had once more shifted from the provinces to Rome. The workings of this change can be illustrated by reference to the career of a successful Fascist leader, Ferruccio Lantini.

The career of Lantini up till 1926 had been that of a local party boss. He had filled all the most important offices in the region in turn, from secretary of the Genoa *fascio* to *alto commissario* and later representative of Liguria in various *direttori*. In 1926, however, he became president of the new Fascist Confederation of Traders. He probably owed this appointment to his connections with Attilio Odero and other members of the influential Genoese business establishment. But Lantini's new position was suddenly imperilled by a grave scandal in Genoese Fascism ; the former squad leader Gerardo Bonelli, an ally and supporter of Lantini who had himself become a national vice-secretary of the party in 1926–7, was found to have given protection to a professional thief and safebreaker. Bonelli was expelled ; but he and his followers, who included most of the *squadristi*, continued to cause trouble.[130] Called upon by Turati to choose between his old friends and his new position,

Lantini made the predictable choice : 'I remember well the words of the Duce, "The past is past, we must look to tomorrow and still further ahead." My liberation from local boundaries, from narrow and particular interests has been complete and definite.'[131]

In 1923-4 a number of Fascists, like M. Rocca, who had claimed 'liberation from local boundaries', had paid for it by earning the still formidable enmity of the provincial bosses, the real controllers of the party machine. Now, from the lips of one of those bosses themselves, we hear the confession that Rome had finally conquered the provinces. The result was that even if many of the old local bosses were knocked off their perches, either because of their own insubordination or as a result of intrigue, their replacements were even less accountable to the members. Even Carlo Scorza, hardly a nonconformist or lover of free discussion, admitted that something was wrong. There was a 'crisis of silence' ; the Fascist movement was increasingly absorbed in the performance of routine bureaucratic tasks, and the indoctrination both of party members and of the neutral mass of the population was neglected. 'The leaders do not speak to their followers or to the people' ; they were passively dependent on superior authority ; they showed no appreciation of the 'psychological factor'.[132] From the point of view of the population at large, there was clearly much to be said for the change ; in Piacenza, the fief of Barbiellini, it was reported that 'they say with evident satisfaction, "Now it is the Prefect who gives the orders".'[133] Less is heard of violence, spying and intimidation ; the climate became more relaxed now that opposition was less to be feared.

Fascist theorists viewed the party as a representative institution which ensured that the masses remained in contact with the leaders : or, alternatively, as the mechanism for the creation and circulation of elites.[134] The party after 1926 failed to perform either function efficiently ; the provincial federations fell increasingly under the control of narrow, closed cliques, whose members did not necessarily possess even those rough and often criminal abilities needed in the early phases of the movement. 'All these people proclaim themselves to be masters and immovable.' 'Fascism is considered the citadel of the *arrivistes*. 'These cliques of leaders became in most cases closely intertwined with the local business establishment.[135] They might indeed be directly dependent upon it : great companies like the Terni could dominate a whole federation. More usual, perhaps, was a kind of mafia situation, in which party and business were equal partners. The party leaders exercised control and got rich by means of their business contacts ; but business in turn needed them to get things fixed, to get favours from the administration and to discourage competitors. It would be wrong to think of the turning point of 1926 as the substitution of fanatics by *arrivistes* ; the typical Fascist leader of the early period was both, and his fanaticism was inextricably associated with his personal ambition. But after 1926 pure careerism of a pedestrian kind predominated over a more adventurous and aggressive spirit ; Fascism developed a middle-aged spread. Rank and file membership in the party came to signify less and less. This was a predictable evolution, observable even in totalitarian regimes where the party or movement obtained recognition of its supremacy over the organs of state, as in Nazi Germany. The decline in active participation was most marked in the lesser provincial centres, which had provided Fascism with so much of its strength. The new Statute had provided for at least two assemblies a year in every *fascio*; but this rule was not kept. In September 1928 *Critica fascista* complained that the duty of holding assemblies was being generally neglected; in Reggio Emilia, a provincial capital, the *fascio* did not hold an assembly between June 1926 and February 1929.[136] One can imagine that the smaller *fasci* must have been even less active; they suffered not only from lack of participation by the members, but from a shortage of suitable cadres. Some *fasci* closed down altogether for long periods; elsewhere a solution could only be found in large-scale pluralism. In the Castelli Romani one local boss was political secretary of no less than five *fasci* of considerable importance, as well as *podestà* of one.[137]

In the large cities it was presumably easier to maintain a façade of participation. Florentine Fascism, in contrast to Sienese, did not sink into total apathy. After the great purges of 1925–6, it recovered, under Alessandro Pavolini, something of its old aggressive, populist image, especially among youth. Politics was not the only way of raising the temperature and avoiding apathy. Fascism had early and successfully identified itself with sport; the racing driver and the football star were endlessly exalted as the proper models for youth, bold, amoral and anti–intellectual. The astute and energetic leader could win a genuine popularity by his patronage of the local team; here Arpinati excelled, building a model 'super-stadium' and making Bologna for a time the centre of Italian football. Local folklore was also taken under party patronage.[138] Moreover, in the larger cities with their looser and more mobile social structure, the party functioned as a mechanism for social integration. The *circoli rionali*, even if they were little more than social clubs, gave their members a sense of belonging.[139] However their active membership remained chiefly petty bourgeoisie or middle class; the industrial workers, it seems, still did not feel at home in them. In Milan, Mario Giampaoli, recognizing this, tried to involve the industrial workers in the party through a new type of organization, the *gruppi aziendali*, or factory cells. This initiative met with less response than he had hoped: none the less the idea struck most of the Milanese business world as subversive, and was probably the principal cause of Giampaoli's disgrace.[140]

It is impossible to assess with any degree of accuracy the effect of the 1926–7 purges on the social composition of the Fascist party. The Communist party carried out an extensive enquiry into the social composition of the party at this date, whose results have been republished in an article by Ignazio Silone.[141] There is no reason to doubt that the information gathered by this investigation about the contemporary structure and recent conflicts in the *fasci* is substantially accurate, although naturally enough it suffers from a shortage of exact statistical data. The analysis sometimes shows the influence of the Communist polemics of the time, as for example in the thesis that most of the workers who joined Fascism came from the 'reformist categories' or working-class aristocracy, when the reverse is true. The most serious limitation, however, is that the reconstruction of the changes in 1923–5 is inevitably more speculative, and unfortunately I have not been able to find any reliable data on the composition of the party in those years.

In general, it seems likely that the predominance of the middle classes in the *fasci* became more marked in 1926–7. In 1921–2 about a third of the total membership were listed as workers or peasants, although many of these recruits had undoubtedly joined out of fear or to avoid unemployment. The results published by Silone show that by 1927 the numbers of workers and peasants combined seldom exceeded 20 per cent of the membership. My own samples of the membership in two big cities, Rome and Milan, at the beginning of 1926 show a working-class membership of only 10–12 per cent.[142] It may well have been the deliberate policy of many *fasci* to exclude unreliable proletarian recruits once the unions had been formed, and this is probably one of the reasons for the decline in working-class membership. It is also probable that many of the *lumpenproletariat* and criminals who had joined the movement were expelled in the various purges. The richer peasants who had supported the party in some provinces were disillusioned by high taxation and the 1927 agricultural crisis.

In some areas artisans, with a few skilled workers, had been active in the early *fasci*; in Alessandria province, for example, they figure quite often among the members of the *direttori* of the smaller *fasci*.[143] In the south where, though the majority of artisans were extremely poor, there was a prosperous minority who had been able to challenge the leadership of the professional classes even before Fascism, this phenomenon can certainly be found after 1922.[144] It is probable that in some areas of the South due to the weakness of the local middle class, the part played by the artisans and the richer peasants in the *fasci* remained somewhat greater than in the North, where it probably declined after 1922, though reliable information is not available.

The main conclusion reported by Silone is that the 'unproductive' middle classes (public employees and the free professions) had come to prevail in numbers over the 'productive' (artisans, richer peasants, and traders). The division made by Silone is not altogether satisfactory. It leaves out of account the very important category of white collar workers in private employment, while the classification of artisans and peasants together with the small business and shopkeeping class does not assist clarification. The class of employees, both public and private, had always been the largest single element in many of the city *fasci*; their predominance was nothing new. However it is certainly true that the number of *public* employees in the *fasci* increased notably during 1926–7. In many *fasci* they formed over half the total membership, and in parts of the South as much as 75–80 per cent. The party was invaded by a mass of civil servants, post office clerks, schoolteachers, etc., anxious to protect their careers by joining the dominant party.[145] The subordination of the Fascist movement to the State machine was undoubtedly assisted by this increased predominance of public employees among the rank and file. The survivors of the old *squadristi* were submerged by a mass of nervous functionaries, and this contributed to the decline of enthusiasm.

By 1927 the question of the social composition of the party was of less significance than previously, given the way in which the party was run. The effective leadership of the party was often in the hands of the Prefects or their nominees, usually drawn from the upper middle classes or even the nobility. The introduction of the *podestà* in place of elected local councils favoured the restoration of the influence of the 'natural leaders' of the community. The recovery of political power by the aristocracy was very marked in Tuscany, the only region where the social background of the *podestà* has been studied. It is true that the position of the Tuscan aristocracy was exceptional; only the Roman *latifondisti* exercised a comparable degree of influence. Even cities like Milan had aristocratic *podestà*, though they may often have been figure-heads. In a memorandum which he sent to Mussolini in 1930, Giampaoli remarked that the nobility had never understood Fascism, but would remain faithful so long as it received the lion's share of posts and honours. On the other hand, the new men from the party were certainly not excluded from local administration, and the separation between State and party office was not strictly observed. It was quite common for the same man to be both *podestà* and secretary of the *fascio*, even in important communes such as Perugia.[146]

The party's loss of power was bound to affect the quality of its leadership. This had never been remarkable for honesty or efficiency; but in the earlier history of the movement leaders had required at least a certain energy and capacity for survival. Now, these qualities could no longer be guaranteed. As a mechanism for the selection and circulation of elites, the party suffered from another defect. A successful career in the party was no guarantee of access to the highest levels of the governing elite. The *federale* could expect to become a deputy, but that entailed merely a gain in status.[147] The circulation of elites was hindered by the youth of the first generation of Fascist leaders. In spite of 'the changes of the guard', the younger generation found it hard to make headway, faced as they were by a well-entrenched body of leaders still in their forties or early fifties.

In spite of his distrust of many of the Fascist 'old guard', Mussolini did not succeed in replacing them by a group of faithful servants of his own choosing. He bypassed and fragmented the Fascist elite, but he did not eliminate its members or reduce them to total dependence upon him. Within the old guard, both extremists and moderates maintained their distinctive viewpoints. They were both critical of the personal and provisional character of Mussolini's dictatorship, and of the contradictory position of the party within the regime. On the one hand, Farinacci and his friends continued to urge that real political power should be restored to the party, pointing to German or even Russian models as worthy of imitation. On the other hand, the moderates complained that the party still interfered too much with the workings of the administration. The degeneration of the party and its divorce from decision-making caused some of the old intransigent group to lose faith in its efficacy. Men like Arpinati and Balbo came to share the 'statist' views of a Federzoni; these converts from intransigence were the most dangerous of Mussolini's internal opponents during the thirties.[148]

After 1932 the party, even as an idea, failed to hold the loyalty of the ablest Fascists. Turati and his successor, Giuriati, had pursued the aim of forming a select, educated party, even if this was a far cry from the reality. But Starace, during his long secretariat (1932-9), destroyed the elite party as effectively as Turati had suppressed the mass of the *squadristi* . The new huge increase in the party's numbers brought a further decline in morale and political cohesion. At the same time, while the party was losing in terms of political independence and ability to influence policy, its sphere of administration continued to expand as the regime attempted to bring fresh sectors of social and economic life under its control. The number of auxiliary organizations and semi-public institutions controlled by the party grew continually. Its activities ranged from censorship to forestry and child welfare.[149]

The party still played a leading part in the *sottogoverno* or undergrowth of government. Beside its legal activities, it continued to exercise considerable informal and illegitimate influence on the distribution of patronage and resources. The PNF transformed the system of personal *clientelismo* inherited from the Liberal state into the bureaucratic *sottogoverno* which has pervaded the Republic. The activity of the party therefore came to seem to those in the know like an inessential and harmful disturbance of the legitimate machinery of government. This was the viewpoint of the *frondeurs* of Fascism after 1936, Federzoni, Balbo, Grandi and Bottai. Their well-founded criticism also concealed their fear that the party might revive under extremist leadership, and their dislike of the demagogic aspect of Mussolini's style of government.[150]

It would be too simple to explain the continuing split in Fascism entirely in terms of the social origins of the leadership. It does seem, however, as if political disagreement was at least in part the result of social and cultural differences. The leaders of the 1938-43 opposition to the 'nazification' of Fascism (Balbo, Federzoni, Grandi, Bottai and De Stefani) were men from the same social and educational background as the majority of the old parliamentary class. They had all been to university. They were of a different milieu from the typical advocates of party supremacy like Farinacci, Starace, Scorza and Ricci, who were all from humbler petty bourgeois backgrounds and with little formal education. In 1935, out of a sample of 93 *federali*, 39 had no university degree, 25 described themselves as *dottori* without giving details, 5 were accountants and 4 engineers. There were only 5 professors and 15 lawyers; these professions had provided about half the deputies in the pre-Fascist parliaments.[151]

In July 1943 Mussolini suffered the fate he had narrowly escaped in January 1925; he was overthrown by the King with the support of the moderates of his own party. Their action had been precipitated by rash initiatives on the part of Farinacci and Scorza. The old antagonism between the two wings of the party had never been resolved, and it helped to bring about the collapse of the regime.

12

THE ORIGINS OF THE CORPORATE STATE

Palazzo Chigi to Palazzo Vidoni: the Fascist Unions and Labour Relations, 1924-5

One can distinguish three phases in the action of the Fascist unions. The first, which came to an end with the Chigi agreement, was that of the programme of 'integral syndicalism' under the patronage of the party. The second (May 1924 – February 1925) was marked by a limited return to the theory and practice of class conflict: in the third phase, the unions worked for a legally regulated corporative order under the patronage of the State.

Ideas of a new corporative order were current before 1925, but they were not practical politics. The Fascist unions had to obtain a *de facto* predominance in industry before they could demand exclusive legal recognition. In July 1923 Rossoni admitted that the time was not ripe for granting the unions legal status; it is easy to see why he took this line if one remembers that this was the period when Mussolini was coquetting with the CGL.[1] By the end of 1923, however, state syndicalism had come to seem a real possibility. The first number of Rossoni's new review, *La Stirpe*, carried an article by Sergio Panunzio which demanded that the monopoly of the Fascist corporations should be imposed by law. 'If I am not mistaken, the 2 lire coins bear the emblem of the *fascio*. . . . Would it be amazing if the Fascist union were made obligatory for all ? . . . Let us have a single, obligatory State union.'[2] But the idea was not yet acceptable to the Confindustria, who preferred to preserve competing unions and to follow a policy of divide and rule.[3]

The situation was different in the agricultural sector. The programme for the legal recognition of unions and compulsory State arbitration can be said to have had an agrarian origin. The farmers of Ferrara and Bologna called for the establishment of a 'labour magistracy' as early as 1902. Of course not all agrarians liked the idea of State intervention : where the unions were weak, the employers remained individualists. But it had significant support among the active capitalist farmers of the Po Valley, who were to be the backbone of the Fascist movement. The large leasehold farmers were particularly favourable to the idea of State arbitration because they hoped to link the question of wages to that of rents, and thus obtain reductions.[4] After 1922, the idea of the labour magistracy and the enforceable collective contract received powerful backing from agrarian Fascists like Farinacci. Even the old Confederation of Agriculture, under Fascist pressure, came out for State arbitration in November 1923, at a time when it was still firmly rejected by the industrialists.[5] The idea of the 'integral corporation' had been realized in agriculture, but the part played by the Corporation of Agriculture in the negotiation of wage agreements was very modest. The local party federations often settled disputes between the local unions of agricultural workers and the FISA without the intervention of the Corporation. However there was one significant innovation: the member unions of the Corporation were obliged to refer all disputes over the application of wage contracts to the arbitration of the magistrates.[6] In this respect the Corporation of Agriculture at least acted as a precursor of the new order, and its achievements were magnified by propaganda.

The Palazzo Chigi agreement showed how little the interests of the working class or the views of the Fascist left weighed in the balance against the arguments of the industrialists. The corporations had neither been allowed to resume the class struggle by strike action on a large scale, nor to create a new framework for the adjustment of labour disputes, with the party or the State as arbitrator. The projects of 'syndical unity' and 'pacification' had suffered no better fate. Those national revolutionaries who sincerely believed in the reconciliation of all the forces of labour had looked to D'Annunzio for leadership. By June 1924 he also had to admit complete defeat. A test case for D'Annunzio's influence was whether his protection could save the Seamen's Federation from destruction. After long and exhausting negotiations, a pact was finally signed between the shipping employers and the Seamen's Federation on 16 February 1924. Nominally this marked a success for the Commandant, but the reality was very different. The employers had stubbornly refused to make concessions so long as the Federation remained under the leadership of the formidable Captain Giulietti. Only after D'Annunzio had been persuaded to get rid of Giulietti were they willing to come to terms. But Giulietti's fall in fact made the agreement worthless. Some of his subordinates had sold out to the Fascists, and without his peculiar combination of toughness, lack of scruple and charisma, the Federation's ability to resist declined rapidly. The shipowners did not keep to the terms of the agreement, and presumably never had any intention of doing so. Their victory was all the more significant in that on several occasions Mussolini, for whom avoiding a rupture with D'Annunzio was top priority, had put heavy pressure on them to come to terms and to leave the Federation alone. In this case, the party (and the corporations) acted purely as auxiliaries of the employers. In January

1924 D'Annunzio was on the point of dissolving the legionaries (now known as the D'Annunzian Spiritual Union) : although at the last moment he decided that this would be too great a proof of subservience to Mussolini, he none the less abandoned the direction of the movement.[7] The defeat of the D'Annunzian national revolutionaries and of the Federazione del Mare was another blow to those who believed in a Fascist 'opening to the left'.

Signs of working-class discontent accumulated in the period after the elections. The results of the poll themselves showed the failure to make progress among the industrial workers ; this impression was reinforced by the sweeping victory won by the FIOM in the elections to the Fiat Works Council on 27 April. The revisionist *Nuovo Paese* commented that 'Fascism has shown more than the necessary zeal in denying its left-wing origins'.[8] On the other wing of the party, the intransigents were also agitating for a more positive approach to the working class. The *Assalto* of Bologna called for the compulsory legalization of labour contracts and criticized the recalcitrance of the industrialists. The leaders of Bologna Fascism had particular reason to be preoccupied with the need to contain and divert the pressures from below : first the agricultural labourers and then the brickworkers and other groups had broken discipline, and the revival of class conflict had put the internal unity of the Fascist party to a severe test.[9]

Inside the Fascist unions, the pressures for a change of policy were mounting. In agriculture, the employers had often been prepared to force the workers to join the Fascist unions by making membership a condition of employment ; but the industrialists were more reluctant to do this. In consequence, the Fascist unions in industry had to offer some positive inducement to the workers to get them to join. Many organizers made rash promises of wage increases or protection against unemployment : even though the majority of workers were reluctant to join and notably sceptical from the outset about the advantage of membership, nevertheless the failure of the corporations to live up to their claims produced a backlash of disillusionment and anger.[10] The new 'converts' felt that they had not only been beaten, but tricked as well. These feelings were in some cases shared by the local Fascist union officials, who were in any case forced to take account of working-class indignation if they wished to avoid an explosion. With the revival of production towards the end of 1923, the question of wage increases came to the fore again.[11]

For these reasons, Mussolini, when he spoke to a meeting of the corporations on 22 May, sounded a new note. He told them that he was not in the least worried when he heard that a Fascist union had called a strike and that he had personally brought to Rossoni's attention 'the need that the conditions of the mass of industrial workers should not deteriorate'.[12] This was a *volte face* : at the same time as he admitted the justice of the corporations' complaints, Mussolini tried to lay the blame for past failures on Rossoni.

The Matteotti crisis greatly increased the chances for working-class discontent to express itself ; faced with a possible revival of the free unions, the corporations were forced to adopt a more radical attitude. A serious rebellion against Rossoni's leadership broke out. In the major industrial centres, Genoa, Milan and Turin, the local corporations denounced the grasping and selfish conduct of the employers. Their criticisms did not spare the party and the Government; the Turin corporations complained that in their contest with the industrialists they did not get much help from the Government, the authorities, or even from the party, in which 'members of the employers' class serve with excessive authority'. Nothing had been done to check the rise in food prices or rents, or to secure compensatory wage increases, and the eight-hour day had not been observed. Collective agreements were almost worthless because individual employers violated them with impunity.[13]

The new political atmosphere encouraged a revolt of the discontented elements within the corporations, who accused Rossoni of keeping them subservient to the Government and the party. A group of old syndicalists led by Edmondo Malusardi and Virginio Galbiati formed a dissident movement with the intention of securing a change in the leadership and policies of the Confederation.[14] Rossoni claimed that the rebels had seceded and were trying to start a rival organization, but they replied that their desire was to reform the Confederation from within. They wished to end bureaucratic and authoritarian centralization, and to allow the free election of leaders by the members of the unions. Rossoni could have suppressed this group easily enough had he been sure, as in the past, of his political support. But there were persistent rumours that Mussolini, as he had hinted even in May, meant to make Rossoni the scapegoat for failure, and to replace him by someone more radical and less heavily compromised. The revolutionary syndicalist A. O. Olivetti, who had supported Fascism but had not taken an active role in the corporations, was thought to be Mussolini's candidate.[15] Rossoni's position was probably saved by his party connections. It is very doubtful whether Farinacci would have approved of the change, and his influence was now again dominant.

The hierarchy of the corporations was cautious and even hostile in its attitude to the new stirrings of radicalism. Rossoni gave an interview in which he declared that the corporations did not believe in the significance of the words 'left' and 'right', and that no return to 'demagogic systems' was intended. To check the possible radicalism of local leaders, the executive of the corporations decided to tighten up central control: in future national representatives would have to be present whenever a wage contract was being negotiated. At the same time, within the group of leaders, Mario Racheli, the head of the Corporation of Agriculture, and A. Casalini, urged on Rossoni the need for more positive action to restore morale.[16]

Nervous of the consequences of supporting strike action, the leaders of the corporations clung to the panacea of legally enforceable labour contracts. In this, they had the support of the party: *Cremona Nuova* came out firmly against strikes and called for the 'statization of the unions' with compulsory membership and a 'Magistracy of Labour'.[17] For the moment, however, there was no possibility of introducing such legislation. The Fascist unions had to use the normal methods of negotiation and, as a last resort, to go on strike. The situation of the Fascist unions seems to have been particularly tense and difficult in Tuscany. This may have been in part due to Communist efforts. In Florence, Prato, Viareggio and Grosseto province, there were major revolts among the workers enrolled in the corporations,[18] and this pressure from below helps to explain why it was in Tuscany that the longest and most serious strikes by the Fascist unions were staged.

The Valdarno miners' strike showed the new radical course of the Fascist unions in action. The Fascist unions demanded a wage increase of 20 per cent: the employers would only offer 10 per cent, and a strike was called on 4 August. It was backed both by Rossoni and by the party. The *fasci* of Arezzo province in fact financed the strike fund, and on 15 August 1924, the national *direttorio* voted a contribution of 50,000 lire. Both the party and, to a lesser degree, Rossoni had political motives for hostility to the Valdarno Company. The lignite mines were now controlled by a group headed by Senator Agnelli, who at this period was strongly suspected of working against Fascism, and in addition Senator Frassati, the owner of the *Stampa*, was a leading shareholder. Rossoni may have resented the fact that the company, like a number of others, had withdrawn its advertisements from his magazine *La Stirpe* after the June crisis.[19]

It seemed as if Mussolini's directive to the party to move to the left was being taken in earnest. Even in this case, however, there was something half-hearted about Fascist radicalism. Mussolini, while he wished to show the industrialists that the corporations were capable of action, also wished to demonstrate that he could settle disputes by his authority, and his impatience to secure a settlement was evident. At the outset of the strike the corporations and the Confindustria had agreed that supplies of fuel to the local power station (run by the same company as the mine) would be maintained: when the strikers, after they had been out a month, threatened to impede deliveries, Mussolini became nervous about the whole affair. He accused the organizer of the strike, Bartoli, of having got himself into a 'blind alley'. The Florence Fascists also intervened in the dispute: they were anxious for a quick settlement because they feared that the continuation of the strike might set a bad example to the workers of their own province, where the situation was explosive. On 31 August Mussolini received their representatives, Nenciolini and Tamburini, and expressed his hope for an early solution.

Rossoni, meanwhile, showed himself extremely compliant in his negotiations with the Confindustria. The strike was finally settled on 12 September by a compromise offer of around 15 per cent: but Bartoli was extremely discontented and refused to tell the miners to return to work.[20]

The episode showed the very limited freedom of action enjoyed by the local Fascist unions. A few days before the settlement, Bartoli had complained to Mussolini of the undue influence experted by the Mining Company 'which has penetrated in force into our camp and during the past two years has prevented your watchful eye from seeing into the deep and dark labyrinths of the said firm, where a conspiracy is being enacted against the Nation and Fascism'.[21] There is plenty of circumstantial evidence to support this flowery accusation. The influence of the former chairman of the mine, Luzzatto, on Arezzo Fascism had been extremely powerful.

In spite of a few successful episodes, the corporations' offensive was short-lived and not very effective. The party and the Government were still only prepared to back strikes half-way, and after the beginning of September, Mussolini returned to a much more conservative attitude. The Fascist unions were also in many cases paralysed by the fear that once a strike had been called, the workers would throw off their disguise and return to old loyalties. In addition, the Fascist union organizers, although they recognized that they had to act more decisively in order to hold their members, were reluctant to enter into conflict with the industrialists, because they needed their agreement to exclude the other unions from negotiation. The situation in the textile industry illustrates this point. The Prefect of Como, noted for its textile industries, explained that 'one cannot do serious work in trade union organization without an agreement with the industrialists ! In Biella, the centre of the Italian wool industry with 60,000 workers, the Fascist unions failed totally to make an impact, thanks to 'the incompetence of the organizers and the negligence of the leaders'. The industrialists, noted for their old-fashioned individualism, gave no assistance. 'They are said to prefer the Socialist unions : they believe that it would be easier to defend themselves against the Socialist unions inasmuch as they lack the support of the PNF and the Government : the contrary would occur with the Fascist unions.' In September 1924 the unions were only able to obtain a 'derisory' wage increase of 2 per cent and the Socialist FIOT, which had maintained an undercover organization, took advantage of this to resume open recruitment. In Como, the members of the Fascist unions were reported to be paying large contributions to the red leagues. In similar circumstances, the corporations were too weak to be anything but company unions.[22]

Meanwhile the general crisis of confidence in the Fascist movement had seriously affected the relations between the party and the *sindacati*.

By November, the corporation leaders feared that they and their programme were about to be disowned by Mussolini and the party : they were distinctly alarmed at the prospect of enforced autonomy. Their faith in the possibilities of class action was waning : in a 14 November memorandum they declared that it was impossible to go any further towards the goal of the 'integral corporation' without State intervention.[23] This marked a break with their earlier ideas. Afraid of being abandoned by the party, the corporations sought safety in an accentuated dependence on the State.

However during December 1924 the position was temporarily reversed.

The fear that Fascism was heading for a political disaster led to the formation of a strong current of opinion in favour of the detachment of the corporations from the party, which was a suggestion that the leaders had earlier unanimously deplored. At the same time, there was mounting criticism of Rossoni's extravagant style of life and his policies. His critics included both Suckert and Arnaldo Mussolini, with whom he had a public row at the Corporations' Congress. Arnaldo Fioretti, the head of the Corporazione Sanitaria (doctors' and nurses' union), although he had signed the 14 November memorandum, began a campaign to detach the corporations from the party.[24] On 30–31 December a stormy meeting of the *direttorio* of the corporations took place. Rossoni began the meeting by attacking his critics, whom, he said, had descended to 'incredible' levels, 'presuming to pass judgement on the tenor of life pursued by the President of the Corporations. . . .' He was firm in his loyalties : 'at this time . . . the corporations cannot leave Mussolini or the party without being stained by cowardice and treachery . . . the President declares . . . that he will not disown Mussolini at any price, although he asks Mussolini for a better understanding of the needs of the union movement'. Fioretti replied that he had not intended to attack Mussolini, although he observed that the middle-class membership of unions like his own, was severely affected by the 'moral question'. But he believed that the corporations could not act effectively unless they obtained greater independence : 'the incapacity of the corporations to defend group interests is not their own fault, but is due to the obstacles put in their way by the Government and the party.'[25]

Rossoni's critics seem to have been in the majority at this meeting : but his loyalty to Mussolini and the party paid off. The third of January discomfited the opposition within the unions. Like Farinacci and the party intransigents, Rossoni now had greater scope for action. He felt himself free to attack not only the industrialists but the government bureaucracy, and he led the successful revolt of the Fascist left against the introduction of the plural vote in the parliamentary elections. The industrialists' ties with the Liberals, formerly useful, now became a liability. The line of action decided upon in July 1924 could now be pressed with a much greater chance of success. The question of wage increases was particularly urgent as inflation had now reached an acute stage. According to the figures of the Milan Chamber of Commerce, the cost of living rose by more than 8 per cent between November 1924 and February 1925.[26] The victory of the intransigents meant that the propaganda needs of the mass party were uppermost.[27] The time was ripe for a demonstration which would convince the working-class that the new 'discipline' which the regime aimed to impose could be to their benefit. The intransigents wrote off the 1922–4 period as one of political stasis and compromise with Liberal parliamentarianism ; they could therefore also believe, with some degree of consistency, that the decline in working-class standards of living was the result of the persistence of Liberal 'anarchy' and that the economic significance of Fascism was yet to be revealed.

The essentially totalitarian aims of Farinacci went beyond merely ensuring the passive acceptance of the new regime by the workers: he wanted their active participation. As he remarked with his usual brutality: 'The working class can easily be conquered by fear; but such a conquest lasts a very short time,' while workers who were persuaded by propaganda would become 'an active part of the movement'. He believed that the Fascist workers should form an elite within the working class as a whole: 'We are not worried about recruiting the mass; let us pick the elite of the proletariat . . . and with this minority we will govern the majority.'[28]

In these circumstances, an unusual degree of unity between the aims of party, State and corporations was briefly achieved. The Grand Council discussed the problem of the unions on 23 January 1925: it passed a motion criticizing the attitude of employers who failed to understand the role of Fascist syndicalism, and recognised the need for strike action. A few days later a circular from Grandi advised the Prefects to take a sympathetic view of Fascist labour agitation.[29] However this was tactics rather than strategy: the ultimate aim of the action of party and unions was 'to resolve the problem of the incorporation of the organized economic forces in the life of the State'.[30] The idea of the integral corporation was again very much alive, though it was now clear that it would be realized within a framework of formal State control and legislative regulation.

The decisive action was fought out in the metallurgical and engineering industries. It was here that the elite of the working class, under the skilful and determined leadership of Bruno Buozzi, had put up the strongest and most successful resistance to Fascist penetration: the FIOM was still a force to be reckoned with, and it had benefited from the relaxation of pressure during late 1924. The engineering and steel industries had borne the brunt of the 1921–2 crisis: the high wages conquered by the unions in the post-war period had been slashed even more abruptly than in other industries.[31] The position of the Fascist unions was weak in most of the great centres of the engineering industry, but Brescia was an exception: there, under the protection of Augusto Turati, a *ras* with an unusual degree of concern for the corporations, the Fascist unions had won a strong position in the numerous small factories of the zone, which specialized in the production of arms. Turati, therefore, was the leading figure on the Fascist side. He could afford to be militant: elsewhere the Fascists were restrained by the fear that action might reveal the superiority of the FIOM, or else by their ties with the employers. In September 1924 Turati wanted to call a strike to prevent an agreement between the Lombard industrialists and the FIOM: but in the end the Lombard association agreed to conclude an agreement exclusively with the Fascist corporations. The Fascists made great play with this success, boasting that the FIOM had been willing to accept a lower wage increase in order to be recognized: but the FIOM countered by pointing out the deficiencies of the Fascist agreement, which had overlooked the vital question

315

of a guaranteed minimum wage, overtime, and indemnity for dismissal.[32] When the old union called a one-day strike to protest against the Fascist agreement, the response in Milan was general.

In February 1925 the FIOM resumed agitation for a wage increase, with temporary and partial stoppages of work : they did not call a regular strike, presumably out of fear that it would be suppressed. In Brescia, the workers in the Fascist unions began to take matters into their own hands ; reprisals by the industrialists heightened the tension. Turati had to act if the Fascist unions were to maintain their credibility : on 2 March, 6,000 workers came out on his orders, and in the next days the strike was extended, with the squads playing an active part in beating up blacklegs. However the great majority of white-collar workers rather unexpectedly refused to join the strike : when Fascism took to organizing working-class action, its normal middle-class supporters grew hesitant.[33] Mussolini himself received the strike with decided hostility.[34] Rossoni nonetheless pledged the support of the corporations on 10 March and threatened to make the strike general unless a new nationwide agreement was reached. The Fascist unions in some other provinces joined the strike. Following the breakdown of negotiations, the PNF officially approved the action of the federations which had supported the strike.[35] At this point, however, the FIOM intervened with great effect. At Milan and Sesto S. Giovanni the great majority of workers followed their lead and the strike, hitherto confined to one or two factories, became general. In all, more than 100,000 workers were involved.

The Fascists were now in a serious dilemma. They feared the continuation and extension of the strike which would show the strength of the FIOM to be much greater than their own : they were also afraid that the employers might punish them for starting the strike by coming to an agreement with the FIOM. From Trieste the Prefect reported that the industrialists had refused to negotiate with the local Fascist union leader, and that 'today they will start friendly negotiations with Dr Falchero, the Rt Hon. Buozzi's secretary . . . this will naturally constitute a defeat for the Fascist party and the Fascist unions, and may have damaging consequences. . . . On their side the Fascist unions cannot give orders for the end of the strike both because that would accentuate their defeat, and because they would not be followed by the masses, and above all because they are afraid that the FIOM is on the point of calling a strike of the metallurgical workers in the whole region'.[36] The dilemma could not have been more clearly stated.

On the night of 15 March, barely forty-eight hours after the entry of the FIOM into the contest, Farinacci announced that an agreement had been reached with the industrialists on a wage increase of 2·2 lire a day. Significantly, however, Rossoni admitted that further negotiations would be needed to complete the agreement. In the provinces under firm Fascist domination, such as Brescia and Pavia, the order to call off the strike was effective : but in Milan and several other places the majority of workers stayed out until forced to return by the police and the Fascist militia. In Turin, the Fascist union opposed strike action, but 40,000 workers nevertheless came out at the orders of the FIOM.[37] The settlement had been hastily imposed on both industrialists and workers by the party, with State backing. Rossoni did not even take part in the final negotiations : and he admitted that only the influence of 'political Fascism' had forced the industrialists to give way.[38] It may seem surprising that Rossoni went out of his way to publicize the unions' dependence on the party : but by doing so he was answering the critics who had attacked his past subservience. Turati, the initiator of the strike, was much less pleased : he publicly announced that the terms were unsatisfactory and that he might reopen the question if his demands were not met.[39]

The corporations had won a limited success in some areas : but the political consequences of the strike were decidedly unfavourable. Farinacci drew the conclusion that the dangers of strike action outweighed the benefits, and took the opportunity to reimpose strict party control over the corporations. The April Grand Council pronounced the strike to be an 'act of war', which should be used only as a last resort, since it benefited foreign competitors and hindered Italian economic expansion. Sympathetic strikes were outlawed : and in future all strikes were to require the approval of the central organs of the corporations and the party. The Fascist federations, as well as the national hierarchy, recovered the right to have a say in the choice of the provincial secretaries of the corporations. To make even more clear that the past period of relative independence and militancy was being repudiated, the Grand Council ordered a purge of the cadres of the union movement.[40]

The objectives and tactics of the corporations during the third phase (April–December 1925) had some resemblance to those of the first phase (1923). The relative freedom of agitation enjoyed by the unions between July 1924 and March 1925 now came to an end : on the labour front, the corporations were in retreat, and the other sensational novelty taken up by Mussolini, the idea of profit-sharing, was quietly and inconspicuously buried at this time.[41] But in exchange Rossoni could still hope for the aid of the party in realizing his essential political objectives. The coercive force of the party and the influence of the Government, rather than the bargaining power of the corporations, would play the leading role in compelling the employers to accept 'corporate discipline' and to outlaw all other unions. At the *Consiglio Nazionale* of the corporations, Farinacci in person delivered a warning to the Confindustria : 'the Confederation of Industry must return with sincerity to the Pact of Palazzo Chigi ; if it does not, Fascism will fight it to the bitter end. This is the desire of the honest majority of the industrialists themselves.'[42] Farinacci knew better than to lay himself open to the charge of reviving class war : he was careful to distinguish between the Confindustria and the industrialists as a class.

For the time being, Rossoni tried to delay rather than hasten legislative reform : he wanted to eliminate competition first, before the structure of the new corporate institutions was decided. In particular, Rossoni attacked the 'Solons' proposals for constitutional reform because they proposed to create the new state corporations on the basis of a system of registration which would give all 'producers' a vote for the election of their professional representatives.[43] Rossoni's aims were ambitious: every industry should have a 'corporative council', with powers which would not be restricted to labour questions but would extend to the planning and organization of production itself. The councils should take over many of the functions of the Ministry of National Economy. There should be 'one organization of employers and one single organization of the workers of hand and mind'.[44]

At the Party Congress of June 1925, Rossoni interrupted Bisi of Pavia when he referred to 'State syndicalism': 'do not speak of State syndicalism! It is an ugly expression: say rather that syndicalism must be inserted in the State.'[45] This touched on what was to be the critical issue of the future: if Rossoni could manage to 'insert' the corporations in the new institutions, while preserving the Confederation as an independent force under his direction, he would achieve a position of great power. On the other hand, there was the danger that 'State syndicalism' would replace what might be called 'party syndicalism', and the control over policy and cadres formerly exercised by the party would pass to the State bureaucracy. If this happened, Rossoni and his organization would be worse off than before, since the controlling power would no longer be influenced in their favour by personal and political ties.

The immediate aim of the corporations was to eliminate the *commissioni interne* and to replace them by *fiduciari di fabbrica* (factory agents) chosen by the Fascist unions. The *commissioni interne* had always been a thorn in the corporations' flesh. The power of the Fascist militia stopped short at the factory gates, unless the employer willed it otherwise. The *commissioni interne* therefore represented one of the last survivals of the free electoral system in Italian society: and they operated in an area where, without coercion, Fascist successes were especially unlikely. The corporations suffered another defeat in the elections to the Fiat committee at the end of May 1925, which gave a clear majority to the Communists.[46]

The independent attitude of the Piedmontese industrialists was the major obstacle to be overcome, and from the beginning, therefore, the Fascists concentrated their efforts on Turin. A joint meeting of the party and unions on 15 July launched the new campaign. The industrialists at first resisted both the demand for a collective agreement and the abolition of the *commissioni interne*: on 18 August, Agnelli forestalled new demands from the Fascist unions by coming to an agreement with the Communists of the Fiat committee for a wage increase. The Communists admitted, with some astonishment, that Agnelli was speaking the truth when he told them that his objective was to creat a *fait accompli* and make it impossible for the Fascist unions to intervene.[47] This unexpected manoeuvre temporarily threw the Fascists off balance. They held a series of meetings outside the factory gates in which they tried to incite the workers to demand a larger pay increase, but they could arouse little enthusiasm. Fiat replied effectively by observing that the pay increase had been given 'as compensation for the increase in the cost of living determined by the wheat duty', for which the Government was responsible. But the Fascists received timely encouragement from the jealousies of the other unions. Both the FIOM and the Catholic union, with a poor sense of the situation, voted a protest against the Fiat agreement.[48] Agnelli's manoeuvre could only delay the decision. The campaign was intensified, with violence against workers and managers, and on 30 August the most important *commissioni interne* were forced to resign.[49] But the Turin industrialists still refused to give way on the question of principle : if the Government wanted to abolish the *commissioni interne* permanently, it would have to impose its will by decree. The locus of decision now shifted to Rome, where the Metallurgical Workers' Corporation put forward a demand for a new collective contract which would ratify the abolition of the *commissioni interne* and their substitution by Fascist *fiduciari*. Negotiations took place between representatives of the Confindustria, the corporations, the party and the Government. On 25 September Olivetti told the Turin industrialists that there was no alternative but to acknowledge the determination of party and Government to impose the abolition of the commissions.[50] Moreover, the conviction that Liberalism was a dead cause and identification with Fascism inevitable had become general. The Confederation of Labour had by this time been reduced to impotence ; the great majority of the Camere del Lavoro and union federations rejected the idea of a protest strike as impracticable.[51]

The Pact of Palazzo Vidoni, concluded on 2 October 1925, recognized the Fascist unions' claim to monopoly and 'in consequence' the abolition of the *commissioni interne*. However Olivetti and the Confindustria turned the stubborn opposition of the Turin group to good account and drove a hard bargain : apart from obtaining other concessions from Mussolini, they succeeded in blocking the institution of the *fiduciari di fabbrica*. The corporations obtained neither the immediate wage increases which they had demanded, nor the recognition of the principle that in future, to avoid the need for strikes, wages should be adjusted automatically in accordance with the rise in the cost of living.[52] The terms of the bargain represented a victory both for Fascism and for the industrialists, at the expense of the workers. The employer's authority within the factory was now absolute, since the unions had no legitimate representative on the shop floor. The fact that grievances could now only be taken up through the mechanism of negotiations between the local union and the corresponding employers' association gave the industrialists an immense advantage when it came to the interpretation and execution of contracts.[53] It is only natural that the injured parties should have denounced the agreement as a general betrayal of principle.

It would be unfair, however, to suggest that this victory of the industrialists was the result of a premeditated stratagem. It seems rather that, a little like the Vatican, the Confindustria was able to drive a hard bargain precisely because it had shown some genuine independence and ability to resist. The fear that the Fascist *fiduciari* would act as the Trojan horse for Government interference in the management of business is probably the chief explanation for the hostility shown by a part of the industrialists to the Fascist claim to monopoly. But it is also true that the more progressive industrialists felt some disquiet about being a party to depriving the workers of representatives whom they would freely recognize and accept. They regarded the regulation of class conflict as more efficient than its suppression. They respected the competence of the old union men : while, on the other hand, in the words of one industrialist, the representatives of the Fascist unions were often 'individuals of the lowest quality without even that minimum of decency required for negotiations over conflicting interests'.[54]

We have seen that during 1924 several leading industrialists had joined the opposition. The most powerful opposition group was among the magnates of the electrical industry : dissatisfaction with De Stefani's tax policy was one of the factors which influenced their attitude.[55] Ettore Conti and Giacinto Motta of the Edison seem undoubtedly to have desired Mussolini's fall : but once it became clear that he was there to stay, they inevitably sought reconciliation. Far from being punished for their independence, they were able to sell their support more dearly : the appointment of Volpi as Minister of Finance was a triumph not only for industry in general, but for the electricity magnates in particular. Their dominant economic position was recognized and they obtained a corresponding hegemony in terms of power and political influence. The lesson of the events of 1925 is not that the industrialists reaped handsome dividends from their total subservience to Fascism and their connivance in its aims. The truth is more ironic : the degree of independence shown by industry was great enough to force Mussolini to make substantial concessions in order to win the support and confidence which he needed so badly for the stability of the regime.

The *Legge Sindacale*

The Pact of Palazzo Vidoni was a decisive event in the development of the Fascist regime. It modified the political balance, and made it easier for Mussolini to take a tough line with the party extremists, as he did at the Grand Council three days later. Now that the Confindustria had repudiated liberalism, the way was at last open for the introduction of the long-heralded measure for the legal recognition and control of the unions. However the Pact did not signify that all the major political problems relating to industry and corporative organization had been solved. In fact the period from October 1925 until July 1926 saw a struggle of great importance within Fascism to determine the form and details of the law on collective labour relations. The protagonists in the contest were the Confindustria and the corporations : but the independent viewpoints of the party and the agrarians also had their importance.

The Pact of Palazzo Vidoni still left the Confindustria outside the sphere of government and party control. The corporations, subject to both, bitterly resented this inequality of treatment. They still hoped to realize a form of 'integral corporation' in which the industrialists' association and their own would be alike subordinated to a single, unified system of control. The party, who disliked the political independence retained by the industrialists, supported this programme for its own reasons. It wished to transform the industrialists' association into an obedient instrument of the totalitarian regime. The Confindustria, backed by the great majority of industrialists, remained firmly opposed to entering a single organization together with the Fascist unions.

The Commission on Constitutional Reform, appointed in January 1925, had discussed the problems of corporate representation and of the legal status of the unions. The majority report was prepared by Gino Arias, a distinguished medieval historian and economist known for his studies of the Southern problem. As one might expect of a man of his background, Arias was inspired by a romantic medievalism. He claimed that the corporate constitution would revive 'the glorious spirit of our old communal civilization'. His scheme advocated the creation of a system of self-governing corporate colleges, freely elected on a basis of professional suffrage : in industry, employers and workers were each to elect one-third of the representatives, with the remaining third going to the employees and technicians.[56] As the ex-Nationalist Coppola observed, Arias' programme was an 'ideological abstraction', without any real political backing. While Coppola, speaking for the extreme right, condemned Arias' proposals as 'materialistic' and dangerous to the unity of the State, Rossoni also attacked them because they ignored the vested interests of the Fascist unions.[57] The Arias report had condemned the idea of the single 'obligatory union' as 'an artificial and anti-economic system of coercion', which would lead to the replacement of collective bargaining by administrative decree, and deprive the unions of all vitality. This criticism was very pertinent : but the Arias solution was doomed precisely because it did show some real concern for the liberties of the 'producers' and their associations. It was too conservative for Fascist tastes because it did not provide for the compulsory public arbitration of wage disputes, and at the same time too democratic, because it did not give formal sanction to their monopoly. In condemning Arias' proposals as abstract and utopian, the Fascists revealed that they were well aware of the political objections to granting any genuine form of self-government to the interest groups. On behalf of the industrialists, Benni was equally scathing in his condemnation of the attempt to control modern production through 'medieval institutions'.[58] The October Grand Council finally threw out the Arias Report and instead adopted a scheme which sanctioned the predominance of the Fascist unions.

The Fascist unions alone could be recognized by law ; although non-Fascist unions were still to be allowed a twilight existence as '*de facto* associations', without the right to conclude collective agreements.[59] The law on this point in fact simply confirmed the monopoly privileges obtained by the Vidoni Pact. The decision to set up a 'magistracy of labour' with the power to arbitrate in disputes between employers and workers, was more radical : but for the moment the feelings of the industrialists were respected, as recourse to its judgements was still to be voluntary. Where both sides could not agree on arbitration, strikes would remain legal (except in public services).

A faint trace of the earlier plans for technical councils or corporative colleges survived in the bill introduced by the Minister of the National Economy, Belluzzo, for the formation of provincial economic councils. But this reform, which amalgamated the existing provincial agrarian councils with the independent Chambers of Commerce, so far from extending producers' self-government, marked an intensification of State control. The new councils were presided over by the Prefect and were under the supervision of the Minister of the National Economy, who chose a third of their members. Belluzzo made quite clear that their task was to transmit central directives, not to serve as the expression for local or professional interests. 'The provincial economic councils should reflect in the provinces the directives which the Government intends to give to the national economy.'[60]

The Vidoni Pact had still not established relations between the Government and the industrialists on a footing of mutual confidence. Benni complained to Mussolini on 13 November 1925 that the Confindustria had not been consulted in the drafting of the new legislation, unlike the corporations and other bodies.[61] There was a political reason for this discrimination : the Confederation of Industry had not yet accepted the Fascist label. It was necessary to show that decision making was a prerogative now reserved for organizations which had formally renounced their independence. At first sight, it seems astonishing that industry should not have been consulted about a measure of such importance. However the composition of the parliamentary committee set up to examine the bill made handsome amends. It is important to note that this committee was freely appointed by the 'offices' of Parliament and that the Government did not choose its members directly. In the committees of Parliament, the technical skills of the industrialists and their allies and spokesmen had always ensured them a disproportionate share of influence. The president was Ernesto Belloni, a Fascist who had used his political influence to become an important figure in the chemical industry: no one in the party had pursued his own personal enrichment more single-mindedly, and his devotion to the interests of business was total. The secretary of the committee was Benni himself. The original draft of the bill drawn up by Rocco was consequently considerably modified in the committee.[62] The jurisdiction of the magistracy of labour was to be obligatory only in agriculture, and legal recognition could not be obtained by organizations which comprised both labour and capital.

The parliamentary debate held in the first week of December 1925 proved extremely lively. Freedom of expression was possible even in the governing party, because Mussolini had not yet made up his own mind. It was the last time that a parliamentary debate would be really decisive. The first clash of significance was between Lanzillo and Rocco. Lanzillo accused Rocco of an outmoded belief in the possibility of fixing a just price by law. He argued that wages, like other prices, must reflect the workings of supply and demand and that therefore they must be determined by free bargaining between employers and employed. Unions, by demanding higher wages, could exercise a progressive influence, forcing industrialists to improve productivity and helping to eliminate the inefficient firms unable to meet increased costs. He feared that if the magistracy were allowed to determine wages they would tend to protect the inefficient employers by fixing them at a level which all firms could afford : on the other hand, in times of economic crisis they might be insufficiently sensitive to the need to reduce wages. Unlike other Fascist 'syndicalists', Lanzillo still held fast to a belief in the social and economic uses of conflict : for this reason he defended the legitimacy of strikes, and protested against the introduction of excessive controls which would 'transform the unions into bureaucratic organs and their leaders into civil servants, so that the revolutionary spirit of the law will be frustrated'. Instead, he looked forward optimistically to the new unions taking over many of the functions of the State.

Rocco replied brusquely that 'the State cannot morally or politically renounce even a jot of the control established by the bill. The State cannot admit, and the Fascist state less than any, the formation of a State within the State. The organization must be a means to discipline the unions, not to create powerful and uncontrolled organizations which might overshadow the State.'[63]

Lanzillo had voiced the protest of the Fascism of 1919 against the doctrine of the Nationalist latecomers. But just because he was faithful to 1919, Lanzillo was by 1925 an isolated figure : he did not speak for Rossoni or the majority of the trade union organizers. Indeed his liberal view of labour relations was more likely to find sympathizers among the industrialists, who also distrusted controls.

Rossoni was still fighting on another front. He repudiated Lanzillo's criticisms of the excessive controls set up by the bill : his one overriding concern was to secure the extension of the labour magistracy to industry. He knew that he was sure of a favourable party response when he asked the Confindustria 'to declare spontaneously to the Fascist government that they do not only believe in the strong head of the Government, that their belief in the Fascist state is not merely vague, but that they have confidence also in the magistrate of the Fascist state. . . . Why do you hesitate ? Is it for technical reasons ? I hope it is only for technical reasons.' He also found an argument which would probably have impressed Mussolini : if industry were excluded, he said, the law would not make much impression abroad. Benni replied for the industrialists: 'I believe that the intervention of the magistrate in the execution of a labour agreement in the industrial field would lead to the end of Italian industry.'[64] In spite of this apocalyptic utterance, at the end of the debate Mussolini made a dramatic and unexpected intervention to impose his will on the industrialists. They were told to accept the jurisdiction of the magistracy.[65]

Mussolini's instinctive preference for the 'totalitarian solution' which extended the labour magistracy to industry was also recommended by powerful political arguments. In the conflict between Rossoni and the industrialists, the voice of agrarian Fascism intervened with possibly decisive effect. The agrarians could hardly fail to resent the inequality of their position with respect to the industrialists. Many of them shared the industrialists' old-fashioned dislike of State interference: Rossoni accused the agrarians who protested against the unequal treatment of agriculture and industry of the 'secret desire to abolish the obligatory jurisdiction of the magistracy in agriculture as well', and Barbiellini declared that the agrarians doubted whether collective contracts were feasible in agriculture and had accepted the law only out of discipline.[66] Some agrarian Fascists, however, held opposite views. The Mantua agrarian leader Giuseppe Moschini was among the most persistent spokesmen of 'integral syndicalism':[67] and Farinacci himself, though for political reasons he had to disguise his views, was also an advocate of compulsory arbitration. Benni's attempt to divide the ranks of his opponents by declaring himself opposed to the jurisdiction of the magistracy in agriculture as well was misjudged. If confined to the public services alone, the 'magistracy of labour' would hardly have appeared a significant innovation, and the propaganda effect of the law would have been completely lost.

The extension of the labour Magistracy to industry sealed the fate of the free unions. Since they could now no longer either conclude collective agreements or conduct strikes, they had lost all essential functions. Nevertheless, even the residual activities permitted to the *de facto* associations were not allowed to proceed without interference. The CGL and the pro-Catholic CIL dragged out their existence for another year, but during the winter of 1926–7 both gave up the struggle as useless.[68]

Even during the debates on the *legge sindacale*, Olivetti still tried to resist the pressure to make the Confindustria accept the Fascist label. But there was no place any more for distinctions between economics and politics: everything was political. After Mussolini's decision on the magistracy of Labour, the industrialists could no longer risk being left out in the cold without an influence on State policy. At the price of adding an adjective to its title, the Confindustria preserved its leadership, cadres and organization intact. As an 'organization of the regime', it received the right to have a permanent representative (Benni) on the Grand Council. This formal integration did not appease the enemies of the industrialists in the corporations and the party and among the agrarians. Rossoni claimed the change of title as a victory for the corporations, but added darkly that 'we shall see up to what point the appropriation of the name is licit or illicit'.[69] Rossoni might be lacking in many qualities, but one must give him that of tenacity. He still hung on to the programme of the integral corporation. He demanded a 'totalitarian solution': all corporations should be grouped together in one great Confederation. Each corporation should have three sections: capital, labour and technical. 'To silence the doubts of those who suspect the leaders of the Fascist corporations of being too labourist ... we say immediately that... the head of the Confederation could only be B. Mussolini.' As a second best solution, Rossoni suggested detaching small and medium industry from the organization of speculative joint stock capital: this, however, was not a very realistic idea. In any case, he held, the Fascist Confederation of Industry should be forced to become the Fascist Federation of Industrialists, and to recognize the 'common hierarchy' of the corporation, on a par with the agricultural employers of the FISA.[70] An even more dangerous line of attack was opened up by Moschini. Moschini demanded that the party should intervene to secure the co-ordination of the industrialists' organization. How could the regime, he asked, be confident that the Confindustria had really accepted Fascist discipline? And were the present leaders Fascists? 'Only a few have the party card and some once used to be our opponents.' His programme envisaged not only the subordination of the Confindustria to the authority of the corporations, but a thoroughgoing political purge: the party should name a commissar 'to prepare the congress for the election of new men, our men'.[71]

Industry, however, fought off the final assault by the party and the corporations. One reason for this was the decline of the party's prestige and influence over Mussolini. Although where the Confindustria was concerned Turati was no less radical than Farinacci, the defeat of the intransigents nonetheless reduced the dangers of a political purge. The worsening economic situation, which came increasingly to dominate Mussolini's thoughts, also worked in favour of the industrialists. Mussolini believed that the crisis of the lira was now the most serious danger to the regime, and was therefore unwilling to offend the industrialists without real necessity.[72]

Over the next years, the Confindustria was largely successful in preserving its autonomy. The decision of the Grand Council on 15 November 1927, which authorized the Ministry of Corporations, in co-operation with the Ministry of the Interior and the party, to carry out a purge of the Confederations, affected the Confindustria much less than the more 'Fascist' agricultural Confederation, or the workers' unions.[73] The industrial associations were formally subject to government control: and the party was also informally consulted about appointments. But against this party interference in industry must be set the reverse process: the influence which industry had on the party was much greater.[74]

The Pact of the Palazzo Vidoni strengthened the hold of the Confindustria over its own class, the industrialists themselves. After the Pact, the Confederation was recognized as the sole legitimate representative of industry in its dealings with the public administration.[75] The *legge sindacale* made the Confindustria monopoly official. The attempt to form a separate confederation of small industrialists was finally suppressed, in spite of the renewed efforts of Rossoni. The authority of the Confindustria was extended to cover provinces from which it had previously been excluded by the powerful *ras*, jealous of their local autonomy. Olivetti did not succeed in preventing the constitution of a separate Confederation of Transport, including shipping : but this was a relatively minor defeat.[76] Within the Confindustria itself, in accordance with the principles of 'hierarchy', decision-making became more centralized : a group of Turin industrialists complained of 'the dictatorship of a few over the whole of Italian industry'.[77] The concentration of power in the hands of the Confindustria leaders assisted the pursuit of a policy of industrial concentration and rationalization, which subordinated the interests of small producers to those of large concerns.

The Confindustria saw the need to 'discipline production' : but it found its own informal procedures, backed by the political and legal authority it had acquired through the *legge sindacale*, sufficient for the purpose. It saw no need to set up a cumbersome new corporate machinery. The Confindustria, backed by the majority of industrialists, was in fact firmly opposed to any extension of the corporate system from the field of labour relations to that of production. Benni appealed to the concept of hierarchy which had become central to Fascist thinking :

... the factory, in essence, is a little technical state, in which the same principles of authority apply as in the State itself. Permit me to say that just as the parliamentary state has fallen short of its aims, so the idea of the constitutional factory has been a failure. No confusion of powers is possible : the only possible hierarchy in the factory is the technical one, required by the organization of production. To insist on this principle and on its complete application seems to me to correspond perfectly to the necessities of industry, the interest of the nation, and the concepts of Fascism.[78]

Benni, no doubt, intended to remind Mussolini of his own statement condemning 'the constitutional factory' in 1922.

Benni's arguments were victorious, and Rossoni was forced to recognize the final defeat of the integral corporation. He fell back on the idea of State control.[79] It is ironic that the pressure for the establishment of the Ministry of Corporations should have come from the Fascist unions : the creation of a new bureaucratic empire, whose tasks were essentially those of surveillance over the unions, was to reduce still further the remnants of autonomy left them by the *legge sindacale*. Lanzillo's prophetic warning against the danger of excessive controls went unheeded by Rossoni. In May 1925 Rossoni hoped to obtain the key post of Under-Secretary in the new ministry, but he was foiled by Olivetti. The secretary of the Confindustria insinuated that Rossoni would take all the credit for himself and leave none for the Duce.[80] The appointment went first, in July 1926, to Mussolini's faithful henchman Suardo, and then in November 1926 to Bottai. Although he did not hide his disappointment.[81] Rossoni nevertheless continued to urge that the powers of the new ministry should be extended. Rossoni and his agrarian and party allies thought of the Ministry of Corporations as an instrument which would serve to discipline and humble the arrogant independence of the barons of industry. In addition, it might serve as the mechanism whereby the idea of the 'corporate discipline of production', and not merely distribution, could be reintroduced. Rossoni demanded that the new ministry should take over the functions of the Ministry of the National Economy, and regulate production as well as labour relations. Within the new ministry, bureaucracy should be kept to a minimum and the work should instead be carried out by advisory bodies of a corporate type.[82] Rossoni and the other labour bosses hoped that in this way they might still come to have a say in the planning of industry.

These hopes were no more fulfilled than Rossoni's personal ambitions had been. During May 1926, calculated indiscretions disclosed the text of the *regolamento* of the *legge sindacale*.[83] The full success of the employers' counter-offensive was now revealed. As Rossoni observed, the position had been reversed: it was now the employers who demanded that the corporations conform to their model. 'The regulation went beyond the law, because it brought fundamental changes in the organization of the working-class unions, demanding that the latter should be brought into line with the situation of the employers' associations'.[84] The employers had been divided into five separate confederations (industry, agriculture, banking, commerce and transport), and they argued that the corporations must follow suit. In addition, there should be three separate confederations for the free professions, the arts and the artisans. Rossoni had foreseen the danger, and in March 1926 he had argued that the employers' confederations should be united, which would have prevented the former from arguing that symmetry and fairness required the subdivision of the corporations. 'It is a characteristic of the Fascist system of organization to reduce the number of associations to a minimum.'[85] This was a good general statement of totalitarian strategy: but his attempt was shipwrecked on the rock of the Confindustria's autonomy.

However Rossoni was still able to fight back. On 18 May the Cabinet approved a 'definitive draft' of the *regolamento*, drafted by Rocco,[86] but Rossoni succeeded in re-opening the whole issue. Mussolini, though he favoured the employers, still needed Rossoni. For practical and propaganda reasons, the new law had to appear to be the result of a consensus. The unions, therefore, could exert some influence, and in the Grand Council meeting of 25–6 June, which prepared a final revised text of the *regolamento*, a number of their objections were met.[87] Rossoni kept control of all the workers' unions and even of the artists and free professions. Only the artisans had to be conceded independence. The bureaucratic controls over the operations of the unions, while they remained severe, were loosened in some particulars. In addition, the share of the compulsory union dues which went to the central confederation was increased at the expense of the local unions, and the confederations were allowed to collect their own contributions, instead of having them levied by the State tax collectors. One can imagine why this point was of special concern to Rossoni and his aides.

The 'corporative idea' had triumphed first in the organization of the agricultural classes. However this victory was more impressive on paper than in reality. The huge variety of local conditions made the creation of a unitary organization or a unitary policy far more difficult even than in industry. The achievement of the 'integral corporation' was at best a dubious and fragile affair. Rossoni had refused to allow the corporation to become autonomous and had insisted on retaining control over the agricultural workers' unions : this was an anomaly. By the terms of the *legge sindacale*, the 'federation' of Fascist farmers was transformed into a 'confederation', equal in status to the Confindustria. The feud between the old agrarians of the Confederation of Agriculture and the Fascist organizers of the FISAF had persisted after the fusion of the two organizations. After the *legge sindacale*, Cacciari was named special commissioner with full powers to purge and reorganize the agricultural confederation.[88] The 'fascistization' of the employers' associations did not inaugurate a new season of corporate harmony with the workers' unions. Once he had parity with the Confindustria and his own men were in control, Cacciari repudiated the idea of the integral corporation, and was soon in violent conflict with Rossoni.[89]

Not all the changes in the regulation were made to suit the workers' unions. If the new *regolamento* saved Rossoni's face, it also marked a very important victory for the employers over Rocco. His idea of effective, centralized State control by a caste of bureaucrats and lawyers had to be modified under the pressures of the interest groups of labour and capital. The regulation in its earlier form had given the Magistracy of Labour the right to make enquiries into the costs and methods of individual firms, which could be asked to produce their books. This idea was anathema to the industrialists, who believed devoutly in the right to keep their affairs secret both from the representatives of the workers and from the State. Benni complained that 'the procedure, which gives one of the sides (i.e., in effect to the workers) the opportunity to demand that any document whatsoever should be exhibited, gives rise in effect to *workers' control*, and moreover as it envisages an unlimited *judicial control*, constitutes a very serious danger for the peace and therefore the development of our firms.'[90] This clause was now suppressed, and with it the Magistracy of Labour was shorn of its most essential prerogative. It would be forced to accept the employers' pleas of poverty and the necessities of production at their face value, and to make its judgements in the dark. It must be remembered that the workers, after the abolition of the *commissioni interne*, had lost all rights of representation or investigation within the individual firm.

Another vital change effected by the employers' pressure was the abolition of a clause empowering the Magistracy to issue temporary ordinances while a dispute was still in progress. This meant that employers could dismiss workers or withhold their pay until the dispute was settled. The removal of the safeguard against these practices gravely handicapped the unions, leading both them and individual workers to seek hasty and unfavourable settlements, since they had no effective answer to tactics of procrastination on the employers' part.[91] It is only fair to recognize that these deficiencies in the system, which were among the features most severely criticized in later years, were not due to its principal architect, Rocco.

The deficiencies in the new corporate order soon provoked a heightening of the ever-present tension between employers' and workers' organizations. There were special problems in the transition stage. The Magistracy of Labour did not begin to function until March 1927 : but in the meantime the dispositions of the law forbidding strikes were already being applied to the obvious disadvantage of the workers. Even protest strikes against the failure of industrialists to keep to existing agreements were being punished.[92] Rossoni charged many industrialists with violating the spirit, if not the letter, of the law by deliberate delays and by pressure on workers to accept restricted local agreements, or even individual contracts, which the unions had tried but failed to make illegal.

Labour exchanges posed an even more serious problem. The industrialists had refused to acknowledge a general obligation to hire workers through the labour exchanges. The labour exchanges were managed by the Patronato Nazionale, an institution originally created to give legal advice and protection to the workers on matters regarding social legislation, insurance etc., and contracts of employment. But while the employers enjoyed absolute freedom of choice in hiring labour, it was almost impossible to keep them to their agreements. In some cases, particularly in the textile industry, the employers actually refused to employ members of the Fascist unions. Reprisals against organizers were still more frequent, in spite of the theory of class collaboration. The practice of dismissing skilled workers and re-engaging them at lower rates continued. As unemployment again mounted, such tactics met with less resistance. By continual changes in the method of job evaluation, the employers were moreover able in effect to reduce piecework rates drastically, without technically breaking the terms of the collective contracts.[93] On some of these points, Rossoni obtained apparent satisfaction. A circular from Mussolini to the Prefects on 19 November 1926 warned the employers that a widespread return to the practice of individual bargaining would be contrary to the purpose of the law, and the party reminded the employers of their duty to concede preference in employment to the members of the unions.[94] But the abuses continued nonetheless. In the summer of 1927 Rossoni complained that in Emilia, where agricultural unemployment was very severe, farmers were compelling labourers to accept reductions of 40 or 50 per cent in wages, instead of the 10 per cent laid down by the official agreement.[95]

Rossoni's complaints had another important result, It was to placate his dissatisfaction that Mussolini first suggested the idea of a 'Charter of Labour'.[96] What is, however, impossible to determine is how far this high-sounding initiative was originally intended as a real solution to the problems raised, and how far as a propaganda diversion. Rossoni and the unions took up the idea of the Charter eagerly, hoping that it would establish guarantees of the workers' rights enforceable by law. They hoped that, at least in part, the concessions won by the workers in more advanced regions of Italy would be recognized as universally valid principles and would become obligatory throughout the peninsula.[97] In the backward South, where unions had always been weak, the appeal of this idea was very considerable.

Predictably enough, however, the resistance of the employers and the advice of the experts combined to emasculate the Charter. A fierce battle took place over many of the clauses of the Charter before a compromise could be reached. The Confindustria and the other employers' organizations had to abandon their opposition to recognition of the right to yearly paid holidays and indemnity for dismissal. On the other hand, they were successful in defeating the idea of a national minimum wage for each category of worker. While they had to accept the principle that workers should be engaged through regular employment exchanges, they defeated Rossoni's demand that these should either be administered by the unions themselves or by the Patronato Nazionale. Instead, they were to be under State control. These important divergences between the employers' associations and unions were settled in the first stage of the preparation of the Charter, which was entrusted to Bottai.[98] However so many difficulties remained that, after he had submitted a questionnaire to the confederations, he had to admit failure. Rossoni's confederation drafted a text in agreement with the Confederation of Agriculture and the minor employers organizations, but the Confindustria remained intransigent. One might have expected that Bottai would have overridden its objections now that it was isolated from the rest of the employers : but instead he deferred to their veto, and submitted both their draft and the other to Mussolini for a final judgement. The procedure was all the more curious since many of the more important points of disagreement had already been settled. At this stage, the labour of preparing the text was turned over to Alfredo Rocco, whose decisive and authoritarian temperament fitted him for the task which had proved too much for the more cautious and inexperienced Bottai. Rocco produced an extremely conservative document, much closer to the draft of the Confindustria than to the other. His text, however, though it served as the basis for the final document, was in turn revised at several points by Mussolini and the Grand Council. Particularly important was the addition of a clause giving preference in employment to members of the party or unions, which was not in Rocco's draft.[99] But it was not so much in the content of the single clauses as in the form of the whole document that the 'Charter of Labour' fell short of the hopes of Rossoni and the Fascist unions. As Bottai had suggested in his memorandum, the Charter was not issued as a decree-law or as the draft for an act of Parliament, but 'more simply, as the draft of a programme . . . a formal pledge for further action by the legislative organs of the State . . . in my opinion, more than dictating specific laws, it is a question of affirming certain principles . . .' The Charter was approved only by the Grand Council and not the Cabinet, and did not take the form of a decree-law : in consequence, it remained a 'statement of intent', without binding force. Only further legislation could give its provisions practical importance, and the way was open for further dilution : on the vital question of employment, the Grand Council retreated on 15 November 1927 by recognizing the employers' 'free choice' among the workers inscribed on the lists of the labour exchanges.[100] Other principles of the Charter remained unfulfilled.

In the minds of Rocco and Mussolini, the *legge sindacale* had the purpose of transferring to the formal organs of the State the powers of arbitration hitherto exercised by the party. However the political history of the law and its application during 1926–7 show that the formal impediments created by the Confindustria to the idea of the integral corporation, and their emasculation of the powers of the Magistracy of Labour, left the new system of labour relations dangerously incomplete. It was easy to foresee that if no other organs of conciliation were available, the Magistracy of Labour would collapse under the weight of the disputes it would be called upon to solve. To avoid this, it was necessary for the Ministry of Corporations to take on much of the work of arbitration. The decisions of the Ministry were usually the result of 'conciliation', which meant a negotiated compromise between the parties to a dispute. Superficially, this procedure did not essentially differ from that adopted by a Ministry of Labour in a free system. But the context, of course, was entirely different, and since recourse to strike action was impossible, 'conciliation' usually favoured the employers, who could afford to take a tougher line. The substitution of Ministry for Magistracy also meant a shift away from economic to political criteria in the determination of wages. The decisions which were left to the Magistracy often turned out to be 'pseudo-decisions', i.e., the ratification by the court of the will of the Government. The procedure of the labour courts allowed the Government to be represented by the public prosecutor, and his arguments were usually decisive. Most of the cases brought before the labour courts in fact concerned individual complaints : the Magistracy settled only a very small number of important collective disputes.[101] However even the enforcement of existing contracts was difficult. The trade unionist Capoferri, appointed to head the Milan unions in 1930, described the situation as 'problematic – with a law which punished strikes and a labour Magistracy which was practically non-existent'.[102]

On the other hand, from the Government's own point of view the creation of the Ministry of Corporations did not solve the problems of labour control in a period of economic crisis. The need to impose wage and price reductions in line with the revaluation of the lira necessitated the return of the party as a factor in economic life.

*Peace & Justice Network
of San Joaquin County*

13

THE FASCIST ECONOMY

Fascist Economic Policy from De Stefani to Volpi

Fascism had no consistent theory about the economic system. The beliefs typical of Fascism were not so much economic theories as what might be called anti-economic theories. The Fascist belief in 'will', in the capacity of the strong man with faith to triumph over natural obstacles, implied a devaluation of the whole sphere of economic action and utilitarian motive. '*Politique d'abord*': 'Guns before Butter': the primacy of politics over economics, and war over politics, is a central tenet of Fascism. When Mussolini wound up the important debate on the *legge sindacale* of December 1925, he used the occasion for a grandiose declaration of these basic principles. 'I consider the Italian nation in a permanent state of war': if Italy accepted her state of economic inferiority as inevitable, the Italians could still 'vegetate' happily. But: 'to live for me means something different. To live for me means struggle, risk, stubbornness . . . never to submit to destiny, not even to what has by now become a commonplace, our so-called deficiency in raw materials. Even this deficiency can be overcome by other raw materials.'[1] The economy, too, would have to acknowledge the supremacy of the dictator's heroic will: that was the message, and it is no accident that it was in the same speech that Mussolini imposed the institution of the labour tribunal on the leaders of the Confederation of Industry, in spite of their dark and somewhat absurd prophecy that it could lead to total ruin.

From 1925 onwards the totalitarian vocabulary of combat was applied to economic crises. 'The battle of wheat' was followed by 'the battle of the lira', and 'the campaign for the national product', and the party was 'mobilized' for the general 'economic battle'. Industry was told to conform to the dictator's desire for unity of purpose and to form a 'common front' against the foreigner.[2] The function of this rhetoric was twofold: to divert criticism from the regime to the 'conspiracy' of international plutocrats (which

333

Mussolini knew perfectly well to be a myth)[3] and to justify the drive towards political uniformity. It is well known that totalitarianism thrives on the creation of a sense of crisis.

Mussolini's famous Pesaro speech of 18 August 1926, which determined the revaluation of the lira, and his subsequent refusal to depart from the unrealistically high figure of 'quota 90' (to the £ sterling), showed the new voluntarism in action.[4] It was a demonstration that the dictator could set aside expert advice (which overwhelmingly favoured a lower rate) if he chose : and that he, and not the bankers, would make the fundamental decisions on the future of the economy. But Mussolini's interventions were dramatic in purpose and discontinuous in effect. Between speeches, he listened to the experts and the spokesmen of pressure groups. Mussolini's policy had a dual aspect : the triumphant 'Will', so to speak, was for Sundays and mediation between interests for weekdays. The economic philosophy of Fascism in fact was beset by a basic contradiction. For against the political emphasis on will, which led to what has been called 'the command economy', must be set the Corporate ideology, which was hostile to 'politics'.[5]

It is of course true that the architect of the *legge sindacale* and the basic legal structures of the Fascist state, Alfredo Rocco, overcame this contradiction in his theoretical constructions. As a Nationalist, he believed that the recognition of syndicates or corporations could only be a means of subordinating them to the will of the State. He made quite clear that the *legge sindacale* was 'a means to discipline the unions, not to create powerful and uncontrolled organizations which might overshadow the State'.[6] But was this the last word ? Certainly, the political supremacy of the State over unions or associations was established beyond doubt. In the economic sphere, however the problem of planning remained unresolved. Political logic, as well as economic difficulties, dictated the deliberate abandonment of the conception of the free market economy governed by the laws of supply and demand. On the other hand, centralized State planning was 'socialistic' : and without a revolutionary shake-up it would be extremely ineffective, given the deficiencies of the public bureaucracy compared with the much more efficient and highly paid staff of the industrial associations and other pressure groups. Consequently, the idea of economic 'self-discipline' survived as a legacy of earlier theories to become the official doctrine of the corporative state. But, as an intelligent French commentator observed,[7] this concealed rather than solved the dilemma. If 'self-discipline' was taken literally, the directive power of the State would be severely restricted by the pressure of the institutionalized interests, which would, moreover, tend to reflect the *status quo* and proscribe innovation. The State would therefore be forced to restrict the independence of the corporations : but in this case they would become merely organs of the bureaucratic police state. In practice, the corporative state revealed a profound lack of symmetry, dictated by class interests. Where the workers' unions were concerned, Rocco's 'Statism' triumphed; they lost what limited autonomy they had ever possessed within Fascism. They became instruments for the political control of the masses, with functions auxiliary and subordinate to those of the police and the party. Instead, however, the employers in some measure realized the opposed ideal of 'self-discipline'. The legal corporations never had the practical importance in planning which was attributed to them by theory and propaganda, but the employers' associations, whose monopoly had been given sanction by Fascism, remained genuine centres of power. The Confederation of Industry in particular achieved a position of strength which was at odds with the expressed intentions of Rocco and Mussolini: it could indeed be described as 'a powerful and uncontrolled organization', which at times 'overshadowed the State'.

Before the war, the Nationalists, and particularly Rocco, had looked on the German cartels as a model for the efficient organization of industry. The war economy, in which the action of the cartels had been integrated and co-ordinated by the State in the interests of total mobilization, had impressed them even more. Rocco's programme of 1919 linked the corporate discipline of labour with the corporate discipline of production, under the supreme authority of an omnipotent State.[8] This was not just the vision of a theorist or even a party: there were industrialists who thought along the same lines. There is a remarkable, and hardly accidental, concurrence between the ideas of Rocco and those set out in a memorandum presented on behalf of the Perrone brothers in April 1924.[9] The Perrone memorandum attacked the free enterprise policy of De Stefani for neglecting the interests of the heavy industrial sector, iron and steel and armaments. They insinuated that this policy was incompatible with Fascism, both because it endangered 'defence and national independence' and because it allowed the economy to be manipulated behind the scenes by the Banca Commerciale and its industrial allies. 'Mussolini cannot submit to the present situation; he must become the master of the keys of the national economy.'

Each branch of industry should be 'co-ordinated' by groups of industrialists acting under the supervision of the Government, which would be the final arbiter in case of disagreement. The aim should be the organization of compulsory cartels in all the major industries. At the summit, a 'Grand Council of economic defence' would draw up a plan and determine the credit to be allotted to each sector. In order to break the 'monopoly control' exercised by the Banca Commerciale in alliance with the Credito Italiano, the Government should acquire a majority shareholding in the latter; even the Perrones evidently did not consider it feasible at this stage for the government to take over the Banca Commerciale itself.

This comprehensive scheme for a planned, militarized economy managed by more or less self-governing cartels or 'corporations' was more far-reaching than anything the Fascist regime put into effect even during the 1930s. Some of the ideas expressed in the project were eventually realized, and others became at least official aspirations. But the programme of the Perrone brothers and their party spokesmen was too advanced and visionary for 1926 : Rocco, presumably, realized that such schemes were not for the moment practical politics. The main interest of the Perrone memo is that it reveals how certain ideas of great importance entered the Fascist blood-stream. Distrust and fear of the Commerciale, priority for national defence, economic self-sufficiency, the controlled economy under political direction : these were feelings and aspirations shared by many Fascists, and in some measure by Mussolini himself. Industry as a whole did not share the Per-rones' enthusiasm for a planned economy. The old Ansaldo-Sconto group had been defeated and discredited, and the whole steel-armaments sector had shrunk in relative importance after the disastrous crisis of postwar reconversion. Financial and political predominance had passed to the electrical industry, and the chemical industry had also gained in importance.[10] These dynamic sectors, rather than the steel and armaments complex, were to assume a role of political and economic leadership during the years 1925–9. The postwar crisis had in fact weakened those groups which had formerly been the main proponents of an imperialist foreign policy.[11]

Confindustria policy also had to take account of the export industries (textiles, artificial fibres and cars), who were decidedly unsympathetic to the grandiose programme of heavy industry. Agnelli, Gualino of Snia Viscosa and other prominent industrialists greatly irritated Fascist opinion by signing an international business manifesto in autumn 1926, calling for lower tariffs and less international restrictions.[12] This was a deliberate reminder that Italy was part of an international system of finance and trade, heavily dependent upon the outside world for raw materials, and could not afford to conduct her economy in isolation on principles not recognized by the outside world. The Confindustria had its own policy, but it was one not of command but of consensus between the leading groups in industry. Benni and Olivetti were nothing if they did not enjoy the confidence of magnates like Agnelli or Pirelli. Rocco himself recognized, reluctantly, the barrier set to corporate ideas by the persistent suspicion of State planning still prevalent among most industrialists.[13]

In its first phase, Fascist economic policy had indeed aimed at reducing the role of the State in the economy. The orthodox economic policy pursued by De Stefani was orientated towards the restoration of Italy's place in the international economy. De Stefani believed that the fundamental problem of Italy was overpopulation in relation to her productive resources.[14] Emi-gration was one answer, and De Stefani, in contrast to the Nationalists, was convinced that it was desirable. But already the first severe restrictions imposed by the USA on immigration showed that the problem of demo-graphic pressure was destined to grow more serious. It was therefore impera-tive to restrict consumption in order to raise the rate of investment.[15] De Stefani subscribed to the orthodox wisdom of the economists and dismissed the belief that public works could create employment as an illusion. The State's services were to be essentially negative. It was to reduce 'unproductive' expenditure and to ensure free competition among workers as well as enterprises. This policy could be enforced only since Fascism had destroyed the resistance of the unions. De Stefani was well aware of this, and he tried to minimize the influence of Rossoni and the corporations. In accordance with De Stefani's ideas, the telephone companies and other State concerns were hived off to private industry. Progressive taxation and death duties were discarded as measures which would 'dry up the sources of investment'.[16]

By 1924–5 De Stefani was able to achieve a budget surplus. The Fascist achievement in balancing the budget, which was of great political significance, was less impressive than it looked at first sight. Much of the improvement was due to the end of the extraordinary charges for war expenditure which had been the main item weighing on the budget during 1919–22.[17] The timing of Fascism's rise to power was fortunate both in this respect, and because it coincided with the beginnings of the international revival from the postwar depression.[18] The main lines of De Stefani's policy were in accord with the desires of the industrial class : but one would be wrong to assume that all industrialists were equally pleased. The new Finance Minister was a man of principle, and was prepared to show a dangerous consistency. He accepted the gospel according to Einaudi, Pareto and Pantaleoni: although sectorial pressures greatly limited the extent of his innovations, the tendency of his policy was towards free trade.[19] Such a tendency was diametrically opposed to the Nationalist ideology of 'economic independence'. The policy pursued by De Stefani corresponded to the interests of the textile industries. It is no accident that his home province was Vicenza, an important centre of the cotton industry. The textile industries, particularly cotton and silk, benefited from the reduced costs of imported machinery and raw materials as well as from lower wages.[20] Engineering, too, was favoured by lower duties on iron and steel : but none the less opinion in this sector remained prevalently protectionist. The opposition to free trade was led by the iron and steel, mining and armaments industries, although in 1923 the situation of many firms was so disastrous that they were less concerned with tariffs than with direct appeals for State assistance in avoiding bankruptcy. The electrical and chemical industries, which were in rapid expansion, were also disposed to be critical of De Stefani, even though the former benefited greatly from the de-nationalization of the telephones. The electrical industry expected the State to subsidize the creation of new plant, as it had done in the past. Like the shipbuilders and the arms manufacturers, the electricity magnates argued that the State, having persuaded them to undertake costly programmes of expansion by promising subsidies, could not now withdraw its support. De Stefani, however, replied to the requests of the industry that 'these subsidies . . . must be much reduced, if not suppressed, since it is inadmissible that on the one hand the national savings should be diverted from highly remunerative employment, and that on the other hand the Government should maintain the present pressure of taxation and annually contract new debts . . . with the purpose of promoting the execution of private works which, since they require a State contribution, show that they cannot give an adequate return.'[21] This was a courageous but somewhat old-fashioned attitude; De Stefani refused to admit that the State could have a positive role in promoting economic development.

The heavy industries, with their subsidized press, still formed an extremely powerful pressure group to which De Stefani was forced, against his inclinations, to make a number of concessions, and though the 1921 tariff was reduced, the level of the duties on iron and steel remained above the pre-war level. But the greatest derogation from his principles was in the 'salvage' of bankrupt enterprises. This struck at the other pillar of his orthodox economic policy, the restraint of State expenditure. The State intervened to save the Bank of Rome from bankruptcy, and invested money in the reconstructed Ansaldo firm. Of course to modern economic opinion there is nothing inherently shocking in these measures, which could have been justified by the need to overcome a period of depression, but the Fascist government had declared a programme of rigid economy.[22] At first, as the lira remained fairly stable, the judgement of experts on balance was favourable. Moreover, De Stefani's 'productivist policy' appeared to be an undeniable success. During 1923 investments revived and a period of rapid industrial expansion set in. In 1924 industrial production passed its previous wartime peak, while home investment for the first time exceeded pre-war levels.

This revival, however, soon brought serious problems. By early 1925 the economy was showing serious signs of overheating. Imports of raw materials and foodstuffs rose rapidly, and confidence in the lira was also undermined by the unsettled question of the war debt to the USA and Britain. The lira was falling on the foreign exchanges and rapid inflation began again to eat into the income of the middle classes as well as the workers. To a considerable degree both the industrial revival and the inflation were the consequence of lavish State assistance to industry. Besides the spectacular salvages of bankrupt firms, the Bank of Italy (and indirectly, the Treasury) underwrote the granting of massive credits to the major industrial groups. The two relevant agencies, the *Sezione Autonoma Consorzio Sovenzioni su Valori Industriali* and the *Consorzio Anticipazioni*, were responsible for nearly half the total commercial circulation in June 1924.[23] According to De Stefani, the responsibility for this situation lay in large measure with the director of the Bank of Italy, Bonaldo Stringher, who was far too ready to concede credit to the Banco di Roma and other joint stock banks.[24]

The mighty Banca Commerciale, once the bulwark of stability against the inflationist Banca di Sconto, was now rumoured to be speculating on the depreciation of the lira.[25] The growing mutual suspicion between the Minister and financial circles came to a head in April 1925, after De Stefani had issued a series of decrees designed to check the speculative boom on the stock market, and to impose restrictions on dealers in foreign exchange. These measures caused a panic which only aggravated the situation of the lira, and the banks and industry became determined to secure the removal of De Stefani. In June 1925 the depreciation of the lira became alarmingly rapid: in July Mussolini gave way and sacrificed De Stefani to satisfy the demands of the Confindustria.[26]

Even before De Stefani's fall from power a major breach had been opened in his free trade policy. He had suspended the tariff on sugar in May 1923; as foreign sugar prices were then actually above the Italian level, his action caused little protest at the time. In the summer of 1924, however, revived competition from Czech sugar factories caused a disastrous slump in prices.[27] The Italian sugar manufacturers' trust refused to lower their prices because, they said, it would mean selling under cost, and by November large stocks of unsold sugar were beginning to accumulate. Meanwhile the industrialists denounced the agreement which they had signed with the Beetgrowers' Federation, suspended payment to the farmers and started to dismiss workers. This naturally caused something of a panic. The political effect of the sugar crisis was much magnified by the fact that the factories and the beet-growing areas were heavily concentrated in the Fascist heartland of the lower Po Valley, especially the provinces of Ferrara, Rovigo, Padua and Venice.[28]

The FISA as well as the industrialists campaigned for protection, warning of the dangers of widespread unemployment. In spite of the stubborn resistance of De Stefani on 11 February 1925 the Government gave in and restored a duty of 9 gold lire per quintal. But this was only the beginning: the industrialists were dissatisfied with the level of the tariff, and they refused to negotiate a new agreement with the Beetgrowers' Federation, demanding the right to bargain with individual growers. The FISA retaliated by ordering all its associates not to grow sugar beet; the financier Max Bondi complained that in Cremona and Piacenza provinces 'violence and intimidation' were being used to prevent farmers from accepting the industrialists' offers. However this conflict did not exclude the possibility of collusion between industrial and agrarian leaders. Both sides, while blaming the other's intransigence, suggested that the root of the conflict lay in the inadequacy of the tariff. Racheli, for the Corporation of Agriculture, admitted that 'the farmers know that the present tariff only allows minimum profit margins'.[29]

At the end of 1924 the Minister of the National Economy, Nava, had appointed a commission to investigate the tariff; four of its eight members had a direct interest in sugar production (Bruzzone and Risso of the sugar trust, the Rovigo agrarian deputy Casalicchio, president of the Beetgrowers'

Federation, and the secretary of the FISA, Cacciari). Predictably, it reported in favour of doubling the tariff from 9 to 18 gold lire. On 5 October 1925 the FISA sent a memorial to the Government which reported that an agreement had been reached with the industrialists, but that it would be null and void if they were not assured that the higher tariff would be introduced and maintained throughout 1926–7. The tariff increase was granted a week later; the full restoration of sugar protection was a triumph for the organized pressure groups.[30] The protests of consumers, shopkeepers and even of landlords from regions which did not produce sugar carried no weight against the powerful coalition between the Emilian agrarians of the FISA, the Fascist unions and industry.

As long as De Stefani remained in office he resisted the pressures to restore the tariff on wheat and other grains: his last refusal was in June 1925.[31] His resignation removed the major obstacle to the tariff. The activities of the wheat interest are harder to trace than those of the sugar lobby, but it is possible to suggest some of the reasons which may have led up to the decision to restore the tariff in July 1925. Unlike sugar prices, wheat prices affected the majority of all agricultural producers above subsistence level. The agricultural expert, Serpieri, in spite of his general free trade views, defended the tariff on wheat as beneficial to the whole agricultural interest and therefore to social stability.[32] De Stefani's successor, Giuseppe Volpi, a great financier associated with the Commerciale and the electrical industry, was determined to reverse the whole trend of his predecessor's policy in favour of one of high protective tariffs. In 1887, the duty on wheat (as earlier in Germany) had been the price paid by the industrialists to the agricultural interest in exchange for the introduction of tariffs on manufactured goods. It is probable that Volpi made a similar calculation in 1925: it was necessary to prove that 'the conflict between industry and agriculture had no basis in reality'.[33] The wheat tariff would silence the agrarian advocates of free trade. The sugar crisis had driven home the lesson that protection made possible 'harmony' between conflicting interests, who could reconcile themselves at the expense of the consumer.

However there were also more immediate reasons for the introduction of the tariff. The bad harvest of 1924 in Italy had caused a large rise in wheat imports: the fact that world wheat prices were unusually high aggravated the adverse effect on the balance of payments. A poor harvest was an unavoidable accident: but advocates of the tariff pointed out that the effect of free trade had been to reduce the area under cultivation and therefore greatly to increase the impact of a bad year. The protectionist policies of other nations made it risky to count on an increase in exports of manufactures to compensate for a rise in the imports of a basic necessity which could not be curtailed except by increasing home production. During 1921–4 wheat imports averaged 26 million quintals (twice the pre-war level) and accounted for 15–20 per cent of all imports. In 1925 the trade balance showed a deficit of 3,151 million lire on cereals, which was nearly 40 per cent of the total deficit.[34] There were therefore powerful arguments to justify the introduction of the duty at least as a temporary measure to correct the balance of payments deficit. The duty was set at 7·5 gold lire per quintal, or 27·5 lire at current prices. It is harder to find an economic rationale for the maintenance of the duty and its subsequent increase to 11 gold lire in 1928 and 14 in 1929. The high tariff served to protect inefficient, high cost producers, especially in the South, and to encourage the extension of arable cultivation at the expense of other crops, although it already covered almost half of all agricultural land. It is true that the 'battle of wheat' aimed to improve and intensify production through a propaganda drive, with lavish prizes for the best yields per hectare: the Government declared that it intended to raise production without extending the area under arable. However the effects of the tariff contradicted this aim. Between 1924 and 1928 the area of land under wheat increased by 347,000 hectares, the equivalent of an entire province : of this increase, 291,000 hectares was in the South and the islands, where yields were usually lowest. The effects on the balance of payments would seem to have been moderate : the saving in imports was offset by a decline in agricultural exports. Between 1925 and 1927 a surplus of 330 million lire on meat and dairy products became a deficit.

Socially the effects were certainly regressive. Small peasants, even if they grew wheat, consumed most of it themselves. On the other hand, the effect of the tariff was to raise rents. The large farmers also benefited more from the 'battle of wheat' : the rhetoric and advice on how to increase yields often passed over the head of the small peasant, who was given little help in improving his archaic methods. Suspicion that Government policy deliberately favoured the large landowners and the merchants was increased by the fact that the tariff was introduced in the month of July, at a time when small producers would have sold their crops and only those who could afford to wait would benefit from the rise in prices.[35]

Politically, the adoption of the tariff could be exploited to win over those Southern landlords, especially in Sicily, who still backed the Liberals. On 10 August, ten days before the poll in the Palermo local elections, in which Orlando was leading the last organized protest of the Liberals, the Sicilian Agricultural Society telegraphed their 'fervid applause' to the Government for the duty.[36]

The new tariffs on sugar and wheat were only a beginning. In the years 1925–7 De Stefani's policy was reversed and both industrial and agricultural tariffs were raised.[37] The propaganda and action of the regime were directed towards the development of national resources with the aim of self-sufficiency.

During his period of office Volpi never lost sight of the banking and electricity interests which he represented. He had been a trusted agent of Giolitti, and it was the old statesman who had made him the Governor of Libya and a Senator. Like Ettore Conti or Silvio Crespi, he was a member of the business establishment connected with the Banca Commerciale. The success of the Banca Commerciale and its associated industries in re-establishing their political power is one of the big facts of 1925.[38] But it gave rise to a reaction. Volpi, as an international 'plutocrat' and a symbol of continuity between the old regime and Fascism, was understandably unpopular with the party. This ideological hostility was to be of some importance during the 'battle for the lira'.

The revaluation crisis and the defeat of the Fascist unions

During the year from July 1925 to July 1926 the Government practised a policy of defending the value of the lira through Treasury purchases of lira offered on foreign exchanges. This policy, though it had an initial success, proved incapable of preventing a new depreciation of the lira during 1926 : the Treasury had to abandon its purchases as too costly and the lira sank to a new low of 153 to the pound at the end of July. It became clear that only a resolute deflationary policy could stabilize the lira. The banks, Volpi and Mussolini were all agreed on this : but on the method and extent of the stabilization or revaluation they differed. Volpi seems to have favoured a rate of 120 to the pound, and some of the bankers might have been content to see the rate stabilized at 150, but Mussolini stuck out for 90. For him, the value of the lira was a prestige question : it is no accident that 'quota 90' had been the rate when Mussolini had first come to power.[39]

Mussolini's personal policy of revaluation was initially popular in Fascist circles. Party opinion, led by Farinacci, saluted the Pesaro speech with enthusiasm as a blow against international finance and the Banca Commerciale.[40] There is evidence that Mussolini himself was impressed by a work edited by the non-Fascist economist B. Griziotti, who argued that social justice demanded revaluation. Griziotti's book had accused Fascism of allowing its original monetary policy to be deflected by the pressures of bankers and industrialists, and of having damaged the small investor, the middle classes and the workers.[41] Fascism seemed to have returned to its original function of defending the 'rentiers' against the 'speculators'; the middle classes and even the agrarians, who were to lose heavily, believed themselves the beneficiaries. However the 'Prestito del Littorio' of November 1926, which imposed the forced conversion of short term treasury bonds into long term loan stock, and also raised a compulsory subscription from state employees, imposed a new burden on the rentiers and the lower middle classes.

The Confederation of Industry had pressed for currency stabilization. It would make it easier and less onerous to obtain foreign loans, which could only be contracted previously on condition of paying the interest in gold lire.[42] However the consequences of the deflation for industry were extremely serious. At a meeting held on 3 November 1926 in Milan, the leaders of industry agreed that 'quota 90' was an unrealistically high figure.

The textile industries, interested in exports, were particularly badly hit by the revaluation policy and were the authors of the most vigorous protest. Relations between Mussolini and the world of industry and high finance deteriorated sharply. Mussolini himself seems to have come to share at least some of the suspicions of the Banca Commerciale which the party extremists had long entertained : it was no secret that the Commerciale looked with ill-favour on 'quota 90', and the connections of the Bank with Volpi made the matter more serious.[43]

But industry was able to recoup much of its losses. The leaders of the Confindustria recognized Mussolini's determination to push through the revaluation and concentrated on obtaining countervailing concessions. In August 1926, when the policy of revaluation was inaugurated, Volpi was granted wide powers to increase tariffs as he felt necessary. During 1926–7 there were considerable increases in the tariffs on iron and steel tubes, agricultural machinery, chemicals, dyes, tyres, textiles and many other goods. The naval budget allocated 60 million lire a year for four years to encourage shipbuilding. The tariff increases meant that the benefits to the consumer of lower import prices were reduced. However these protectionist measures did not of course benefit the export industries whose interests were sacrificed. The growth of the car industry, which exported more than 50 per cent of its production, was halted, and textiles also suffered.[44]

However the industrialists were even more successful in their efforts to shift the burden of the revaluation policy onto the shoulders of the workers. At first, in the autumn of 1926, Rossoni and the unions were successful in resisting wage reductions, arguing that they must follow, not precede, a fall in the cost of living. On 8 October, the Grand Council invited employers not to reduce wages before the consequences of revaluation made themselves felt.[45] At the same time, Rossoni opened a second economic front, against the shopkeepers. When he attacked 'the so-called freedom of commerce',[46] Rossoni knew that he would have the sympathy of the party. Propaganda against 'speculators' and intermediaries went down well with most rank and file Fascists. As for the Government, Belluzzo was convinced that there were too many shopkeepers and that the rationalization of the retail sector was urgent.[47] The result was the 16 December 1926 decree law for the 'discipline of commerce', which established restrictions on the opening of new shops and gave the communes the right to fix the prices of the principal foodstuffs. However the law, although applied with a certain severity, did not prove very effective in reducing prices.[48]

During 1926, in spite of several failures, Rossoni and the Fascist unions had on balance acquired greater importance than previously. In their new monopoly position, they had some bargaining power, and politically they had shown that they counted for something, even if they usually came off worst in a showdown with the Confindustria. Now that the threat from the Left had been eliminated, Rossoni had become considerably bolder in his action on behalf of the workers. The further development of the revaluation crisis, however, dealt a blow to Rossoni and the Fascist unions from which they never recovered.

Rossoni had, it would seem, made some impression on Mussolini by his attacks on the industrialists for sabotaging the working of the *legge sindacale*.[49] However it was not long before they launched an effective counter-offensive. The December 1926 memorandum on the Carta del Lavoro, signed by all the employers' confederations, charged the unions with 'following a course which conflicts with the directives of the regime' : they had adopted much of the programme of 'old style trade unionism', and their requests, if granted, would 'seriously compromise or even destroy discipline in the factory, and prevent the employer from carrying out his function as the director of production'. Some of these failings could be attributed to defects in the recruitment of the union cadres, but others were due to the example set by Rossoni himself.

> The peregrinations which the leader of the aforesaid Confederation makes through the various regions of Italy leave a trail of unhealthy excitement in the minds of the workers, who are not, and cannot yet be, completely transformed at heart ; it is an excitement which causes an insufferance of discipline, discontent and the rise of new claims ; all phenomena which occur with mathematical certainty wherever the leader of working class unionism has passed.[50]

This was the start of a campaign against union 'demagogy' which continued throughout 1927.

It is arguable that in the first phase of revaluation the defence of wages in some industries was, in fact, too successful, and that it accentuated the gravity of the crisis. By January 1927 the problem of unofficial and un-authorized wage reductions was becoming serious ; it was the smaller firms, driven by fear of bankruptcy and closure, which led the way. However more powerful forces soon followed suit. The cotton manufacturers, who had already benefited from the introduction of a nine-hour day without com-pensation obtained a wage reduction on 22 December, after their memor-andum of protest against revaluation. On 16 January, Rossoni denounced an unspecified union of manufacturers in the north for unilateral abolition of the cost of living and seniority bonuses.[51] Rossoni had at first criticized the employers for excessive pessimism, but now the unions admitted the exist-ence of a crisis.[52] The opposition to 'quota 90' was rapidly becoming general : unemployment was increasing and factories were closing. This only increased Mussolini's determination to impose his policy. It was the party which took the lead in forcing the first all-round pay cuts on agricul-tural workers. On 2 May 1927, Turati gave the signal for a general reduction in wages by imposing a 10 per cent cut on the agricultural labourers of Brescia. The unions were compelled 'to indicate to our comrades, the workers, the hard road of the necessary sacrifice'.[53] The 'sacrifice' was carefully timed.

The Charter of Labour had finally been published on 23 April, and the wage cuts started ten days later. The coincidence can hardly be fortuitous : the propaganda victory of the Charter served to divert attention from the blow which was about to fall on the workers. The first round of cuts affected over 2 million workers in industry and 500,000 in agriculture : in October 1927 the PNF directorate accepted the demands of the employers for a reduction of all wages by 10–20 per cent. The effect on the standard of living of labourers both in agriculture and industry cannot be estimated without taking into account the unofficial reductions of pay carried out by the employers. In agriculture and textiles, the total reduction of wages in some cases may have been as much as 40 or 45 per cent compared with 1926, while the cost of living fell at an estimate less than 20 per cent.[54] 'Discipline' made it impossible for Rossoni to object to the official wage cuts decreed by the Grand Council and enforced by the party : but he did protest on occasion against the failure to achieve corresponding reductions in prices. This brought down on him the anger of Mussolini, who did not want the failure of price control to be advertised.[55]

The intervention of the party was an important feature of the revaluation crisis. Belluzzo, a great believer in will-power and the effects of propaganda, had already suggested 'mobilizing' the party for the economic struggle in a Cabinet meeting of December 1925. When Mussolini took up this suggestion in July 1926, in conjunction with the Pesaro speech, he was aiming to kill two birds with one stone : he would give the party a new outlet for its exuberant energies and divert it from politics or violence, as well as using it as an instrument to enforce his directives on society. The 'economic battle' in the official view was to become the foremost task of the party : 'at a moment's notice, the Fascist party has changed course . . . it has superseded mere political polemics . . . and has turned to organizing the agricultural and industrial masses at the orders of the Government for the greatest battle that the Nation has ever decided to fight.'[56] The intervention of the party in the economic battle had some fairly comic results. In Florence, for example, the party devoted much earnest endeavour to a campaign for the Italian straw hat : dark threats were uttered against those who wore fashionable soft hats of foreign make.[57]

But the party's role in the 'economic battle' was not confined to propaganda. Farinacci and other chiefs were quick to see their chance to reassert local party controls which had been endangered by the creation of the centralized apparatus of the Ministry of Corporations and the legally recognized confederations.[58] As the economic crisis deepened, the Government leant more heavily on the party.

In May 1927 it was the party which forced through wage reductions ; in July Mussolini turned to it for assistance in intensifying the campaign for reductions in prices and rents. The secret speech of Suardo to the Fascist *federali* at Bologna on 6 July showed Mussolini's determination to carry

through the revaluation against the opposition of both employers and workers, using the party to secure compliance. The convenient fiction of a sinister
alliance between the proletariat and the plutocracy was refurbished once
again ; Suardo told the party that the enemy was 'the old economic ruling
class', but the thesis of the proletariat's complicity served to justify wage
reductions.[59] A circular of 2 August 1927 sanctioned previous local party
initiatives in the creation of new organs, the inter-syndical committees.
These marked a return to the methods of informal party control and a
temporary setback for the ideal of orderly regulation by State bodies entrusted
with formal legal powers. Their task was to act as a liaison between the
party and the unions, who were both represented on the committee. They
were presided over by the party secretary, and it is clear that their task was
to ensure that the unions obeyed the Government's political directives.
Their powers were broad and vague, covering many of the responsibilities
entrusted by law to the Ministry of Corporations : they were to examine all
important controversies regarding production and labour, to plan and draft
new labour contracts, and to exercise vigilance over the actions and policies
of the single unions. In the autumn, the provincial committees were crowned
by a central inter-syndical committee. It was presided over by the PNF
secretary Turati, and included the presidents of the various confederations,
the Patronato Nazionale, the Ente Nazionale Consumo and the Under-
Secretary of the Ministry of Corporations.[60] Soon afterwards, the committees
extended their powers further. They were to function as 'price committees'
with powers to investigate costs of production and to 'indicate' suitable
retail prices for rice, pasta and other essential foods. One might conclude
from this that the party had conquered the commanding heights of the
economy and established its own form of totalitarian *dirigisme* : but one
would be wrong. First of all, it appears that the party's action to control
prices was of very dubious effect. Whereas the party representatives often
imposed a figure for wages which the unions had to accept with discipline, on
prices they were usually guided by the suggestions of the shopkeepers and
merchants, armed with technical arguments. In other cases, where the party
secretary showed his independence by setting a price in defiance of the
traders' views, evasion and the black market rendered his decision
nugatory.

Secondly, the role of the party was linked to the revaluation crisis ;
'totalitarian mobilization', which was in any case one-sided and largely
confined to labour, was limited to the period of the economic battle. In
September 1928, when stabilization had been achieved and the pressure could
be relaxed, the party committees had to surrender their powers over prices
to the CPE (Consigli Provinciali dell' Economia). However in 1934 the party
again acquired responsibilities in this sector, only to lose them yet again in
1937.[61] Finally, it is clear that the party acted throughout as an instrument
to enforce the policy determined by Mussolini and the economic ministers :

and even then its powers of intervention were largely confined to distribution. In the control of production, at least in industry, the party had a very marginal role. Some committees tried to interfere directly in industry, and even to fill the gap left by the abolition of the *commissioni interne*; in August 1927 they were warned by Turati not 'to interfere in the relations between single firms and their dependent workers', or to attempt to regulate conditions of work inside the factories.[62] In agriculture, the party did intervene directly to plan production on a number of occasions. The PNF federations took the initiative in March 1926 in trying to limit the production of hemp, which had suffered a disastrous fall in price. However the party's efforts seem to have been ineffective : by the end of the year, the failure of the campaign was evident, and the farmers' syndicates took over responsibility for reducing the area of hemp cultivation by 40 per cent.[63]

During 1927–8 Rossoni lost ground to his critics. Through the newspapers which they controlled the industrialists were able to expose the abuses, corruption and bureaucratic red-tape of the unions without their being able to reply with equal effect. These criticisms were no doubt justified by the malpractices of the union officials, who were not responsible to their members. However the purpose was to undermine rather than improve the efficiency of the workers' Confederation in defending the workers' interests. The central organs of the Confederation were accused of obstruction because they refused to ratify the more humiliating of the local agreements for wage reductions, concluded under party pressure. As usually happened in Fascist organizations, Rossoni's subordinates sensed the weakening of his position and started to intrigue against him.[64]

While the crisis lasted, however, Rossoni and the Confederation enjoyed a precarious security. During 1927 labour unrest and illegal strikes presented a serious problem to the regime, and though this was harmful to Rossoni's prestige, Mussolini probably wished to avoid taking any action which might add further to working-class discontent. What made Rossoni's defeat inevitable in the long term was the alliance between Turati and Bottai. The Ministry of Corporations and the party made common cause against the unions. Bottai accused the great confederations of perpetuating the idea of class interest, which should have no place in the corporate State. 'The idea of a guarantee for class interests ... conforms perfectly to the destructive theses of syndicalist doctrine, but cannot be taken into consideration by the Fascist concept of the corporate State.' Accordingly, the autonomy of the recognized associations was to be reduced still further. Bottai's attack though he did not exempt the employers from criticism, was aimed principal'y at Rossoni's Confederation, the largest and most vulnerable target. Bottai aimed especially to discredit the old guard of revolutionary syndicalists who still occupied many of the leading positions in the unions : 'syndicalism must disappear'.[65] The ex-syndicalists used verbal demagogy as a substitute for the effective defence of working-class interests, rendered impossible by the action of party and Government. This offended Bottai. As in his revisionist polemics against the party bosses, Bottai stood for 'technical' qualification against charisma, for the 'open' elite against the mystifications of the demagogues who appealed to the masses. Trade union officials should regard themselves not as agitators or even organizers but 'solely as officials of the regime' :[66] within the unions, therefore, a new class of experts, closely linked to the reformed party, should replace the old leaders. Who were these 'experts'? They were, principally, the graduates and the products of the technical schools. This new managerial class was becoming more important in industry, and it already filled most of the posts in the employers' federations : the importance of the agronomists has already been mentioned. Now, the managers were to take over the unions as well : the same kind of men increasingly would 'represent' workers, employers and the State. In this limited sense, one can see Fascism in the perspective of the 'managerial revolution' : but one must be clear about the limitations. It meant much less, at least in Italy, than is suggested by James Burnham's famous book. The rights of labour, rather than capital, were expropriated : both economically and politically the managers formed a new middle class rather than a directing elite.[67]

Bottai described the existence of a single workers' confederation as 'the greatest obstacle to the satisfactory working of the central liaison organs', and demanded that it be broken up. To do justice to Bottai, it must be said that he was anxious also to reduce the power of the Confindustria. He had ambitions to make the Ministry of Corporations into an instrument for the planning and direction of the whole economy. He complained that 'corporative action' was limited by 'combinations effected in advance by competing . . . interest groups' within the confederations : this meant that the strongest groups usually imposed their will on the others. The solution must be to increase the independence of the 'basic categories', or branches of production from the confederations, whose regulating powers should be transferred to the State. Just as the State arbitrated between employers and workers, so it should arbitrate between the different branches of production.[68] Although this part of Bottai's programme was destined to remain a dead letter, his analysis was accurate and prophetic. In spite of the creation of new corporative organs, real power continued to be exercised by the employers' confederations.

The so-called 'unblocking' of the corporations destroyed what little was left of the Fascist unions' prestige. On 21 November 1928 Mussolini ordered the division of the Confederation of Corporations into seven separate organizations. Under Rossoni, the unified organization, for all its weaknesses and defeats, had counted for something in the balance of political forces. Now this was no longer true. Rossoni himself warned that :

. . . all the disgust provoked by parliamentarianism, and the just criticism of socialism and democracy will end in bitter disappointment, and inconclusive rhetoric and – worse still – a fatal reactionary illusion, if Fascism is not to have a more solid, realistic and human base. . . . The Communist utopia might still recover its deleterious influence if the new order were to show itself incapable of ensuring a minimum of economic welfare and if it ceased to be animated by an idea . . . by its myth.

Labour, he said, had achieved formal political equality with capital in the corporate order : but further development was needed before this principle acquired 'a social and economic value'.[69] The totalitarian fusion of interests remained incomplete : Rossoni was correct in thinking that the victories of capital would have consequences for the political strength of the regime as well as for the distribution of power within society. But even before the break-up of the Confederation, it had lost credibility. The revaluation crisis had destroyed any chance that the masses might view the new Corporate order with anything more than a grudging acquiescence. The understandable scepticism of the industrial workers about the possibility of defending their interests within the framework of the Fascist state, destroyed Rossoni's political usefulness. Mussolini might have been more willing to underwrite 'demagogy' if he had been convinced that it would work.

The 1929 debate on the question of 'factory representatives' confirmed the powerlessness of the unions. The experience of the first years of the corporate regime had shown the necessity for the unions of having representatives inside the factories, who could hear complaints on the spot and bring violations of agreements to the notice of their superiors. In 1928–9, especially in Milan, the unions tried to revive the 'factory representatives' : but they met with the uncompromising hostility of the industrialists. The latter argued that the Pact of Palazzo Vidoni had settled this matter once and for all and that 'the hierarchy and discipline of our establishments could not but be very seriously affected by the institution'. The appeal to the principle of a 'single hierarchy', and the veiled threat of the industrialists to reconsider their whole attitude to the corporate order, were effective. Mussolini showed quite clearly that he held the unions in slight esteem. Fioretti, the president of the Confederation of Industrial Workers, was condemned for holding mass rallies and using a 'demagogic vocabulary'. There was no need, Mussolini asserted, for the unions to act as a channel of information between the masses and the government : the police knew perfectly well what the needs of the workers were.[70]

Agriculture and 'Rurality'

In July 1923 Arrigo Serpieri became Under-Secretary in the Ministry of the National Economy. He had previously been a member of a 'Higher Technical and Economic Council' set up by the Corporation of Agriculture to study problems of credit, taxes and land reclamation.[71] Serpieri was a leading agricultural expert, and one of the most able recruits made by Fascism after the March on Rome. However his appointment was extremely unpopular with the party, who had not forgiven him for the impartiality he had shown in the past on the subject of relations between workers and employers. He never overcame the hostility of most members of the party and of the representatives of landed property: but he had the backing of Acerbo, a fellow professor of agrarian sciences, and he seems to have impressed Mussolini. After his resignation in June 1924, he remained an influential figure.[72]

Like De Stefani, Serpieri was a disciple of Pareto and saw Fascism as a Paretian revolution directed against the speculators. He recognized that the Fascist movement had been created largely by the petty and medium bourgeoisie, both urban and agrarian; like Pareto himself, he was convinced that Fascism could only find a secure social base if it succeeded in forging an alliance between the middle class and the mass of the peasantry, who were a naturally conservative and stable class.[73] There was a contradiction between the social and the economic vision of Serpieri. On the one hand, he was a paternalist who deplored the creation of a rural proletariat, dependent on wages alone, as an unnatural, quasi-industrial perversion of the harmonious order of the countryside, which had always assured the worker of a direct share in his own produce. The true rural classes were the 'intermediate groups' of peasant proprietors, tenants and sharecroppers; he wanted Fascism to take over the role of the Partito Popolare as their defender. On the other hand, as an economist, he was convinced of the virtues of free enterprise and efficient, rational capitalist farming.[74] Serpieri's recognition of these conflicting values led him to support a *laissez-faire* policy in the North and Centre of Italy, with some measures for the protection of small property. But in much of the South, Serpieri saw conditions which were equally unjustifiable either from a social or an economic point of view: large inefficient estates supported a mass of miserable semi-proletarian cultivators. The objective of policy should be to encourage the formation of regular, stable farms in place of the scattered strips and short tenancies characteristic of the South.

The great invention of Serpieri was the concept of the *bonifica integrale* (integral land reclamation). Previously, government grants for reclamation had been available only for drainage works. Under the terms of Serpieri's new bill (18 May 1924), instead, money could be sent on the improvement of a whole area, by whatever methods were most appropriate. This legislation had radical implications. It was Serpieri's purpose not only to reclaim areas formerly uncultivated like the Pontine Marshes but, where possible, to replace extensive forms of agriculture by intensive. Most southern landlords were very reluctant to insist on improvements when a good income could be had by sitting back and leasing rough pasture or arable land at exorbitant rents, made possible by the pressure of population. Consequently Serpieri's bill made improvement in the areas designated as subject to the *bonifica integrale* obligatory, not voluntary. He hoped that this would induce large absentee landlords to sell, so that land would be re-distributed by the normal mechanism of the market. The State would grant technical assistance and easy credit to groups of proprietors who were willing to co-operate in sharing the costs of improvement.[75] However Serpieri, in his distrust of the southern landlords, stipulated that if local initiative were lacking, the land could be expropriated by outside *consortia* formed for the purpose. This clause was denounced by the southern landlords' lobby as the Trojan horse which would allow the conquest of the South by grasping northern capitalists : ironically, Serpieri's policy was identified with the interests of the 'speculators'.

The leaders of the FISA supported Serpieri's measure, but they could not compel the dissident southern landlords to observe discipline. In 1925 the opponents of the expropriation clause formed a 'Committee for the pro-motion of improvements in the South and islands' : one of the presidents was Ferdinando Rocco, a brother of the Minister of Justice, Alfredo, who also sup-ported the committee. In November 1925 they were successful in obtaining the repeal of the clause. This was a notable victory for local conservative pressures over the forces making for modernization.[76]

'The battle of wheat' was the first sign of a new emphasis in Fascist propaganda on the values of agriculture and the land. Photographs of Mussolini among the harvesters or the rice-pickers, or at the plough, multiplied : the image of the Duce as the First Peasant of Italy became even more important than the earlier image of the Duce as the Modern Man. On 26 May 1927, Ascension Day, Mussolini delivered an immense, care-fully prepared speech, a general review of the regime's achievements and aims.[77] The 'speech of the Ascension' began with 'an examination of the situation of the Italian people from the point of view of physical health and of the race'. Mussolini launched into the twin themes of 'demographic power' and 'rurality'. The decline of the Roman Empire had been due to depopulation, and Italy's most precious possession was her demographic vitality. Starting from these premises, Mussolini could reach the remarkable conclusion that Basilicata was a model province because of its high birthrate – 'evidently it has not yet been sufficiently infected by the pernicious tenden-cies of contemporary civilization', and could remark that the population in the miserable slums of Palermo and Naples was 'fortunately' still increasing naturally, while that of Milan and Turin remained stationary except for immigration. The exaltation of the birthrate went logically hand in hand with the myth of unspoilt rural virtue. In the countryside, Italians had more children : therefore they must be discouraged from coming to the towns. In October–November 1928 Mussolini inaugurated a deliberate policy to restrain urban growth under the slogan 'Empty the cities'. During the 1930s further restrictions on the mobility of labour were introduced : they culminated in the 1934 law against urbanization.[78]

By an irony which may not be accidental, 1927, the year in which Mussolini launched 'rurality', was also a year of disaster for the landed economy. The crisis brought about by revaluation hit agriculture even more severely than industry. Fascist loyalties and efficient political co-ordination proved a disadvantage : the Confederation of Agriculture was unable to exert the leverage of the more independent Confindustria and on the contrary helped the Government to stifle discontent. The party was more effective in voicing the protests of the farmers : both Balbo and Farinacci were active on behalf of their constituents. Farinacci tried to obtain compensation for the capitalist leasehold farmers by obtaining a forced reduction in rents.[79] But the agrarian Fascist leaders had signally failed to predict the disastrous consequences which revaluation would have for the agricultural economy.

The 1927 crisis was not merely a passing disturbance, but a real turning point. The blow to the confidence of the capitalist farmers was great. Caution about profitable but risky industrial crops, like hemp, and a return to the practice of paying wages in kind instead of cash were among the marks of the new deflationary mentality.[80] The new peasant proprietors also suffered. Most had incurred debts in order to buy their land : the burden of the revalued debt forced many to sell in the next years, at a time when land values were falling (in Emilia they fell 50 per cent between 1927 and 1932). The result was a reversal of the trend towards greater dispersion of property, at least in the North of Italy. In the South, the law of 6 June 1927, which ordered that communal lands suitable for cultivation should be divided among peasant proprietors, favoured some extension of small property and the scarcity of credit meant that peasants had contracted less debt, and were therefore less badly hit by revaluation.[81]

In fact Mussolini's defence of 'rurality' looks suspiciously like ideological compensation for crisis. Just as the party received platonic compensation for loss of power in an aggressive foreign policy, so the agrarian Fascists were gratified by Mussolini's adoption of their own language and ideology. One of the first Fascists to denounce 'urbanism' had been Farinacci, and panegyrics to the 'moral health of the countryside' were a commonplace in the columns of the provincial Fascist press. The city was blamed for creating a shortage of rural labour, and for encouraging higher standards of consumption.[82] The agrarians had anticipated the concrete remedy : a leader in the Bologna *Assalto* in June 1926 recommended that 'whoever cannot demonstrate how and why he lives in an urban centre should be invited in the Fascist manner to obey a warrant for repatriation to his birthplace'.[83] The 1927 crisis also had a direct effect on the policy of 'anti-urbanism'. The more decisive measures taken at the end of 1928 were provoked by the large immigration of rural workers to the cities in early 1928 as a result of the unemployment in the countryside.[84]

Apart from the psychological satisfaction of seeing Mussolini acknowledge the soundness of rural values compared with those of the city, the agrarians had material reason to be pleased with any policy that would hamper the mobility of labour. The restrictions on foreign emigration worked in the same direction.[85] A leading agrarian, Marescalchi, in 1930 explained that 'To ruralize means to hold the peasants to the soil, or, if they have left it, to bring them back'.[86] It would be unfair, however, to see in the new ideology of 'rurality' merely the justification of police measures to keep the peasants on the land. Mussolini also intended to shift the balance of State expenditure from town towards country. Expenditure on land reclamation rose from 182 million lire (1927 values) in 1926–7 to 258 million in 1927–8.[87] Studies of rural economy and life received great encouragement and brought some benefits. The attempt to encourage the building of farmhouses rather than speculative construction in towns was praiseworthy at least in intention. In 1929 the Ministry of Agriculture was revived, and with Acerbo as Minister and Serpieri as Under-Secretary it must be said that it was in competent hands.

From the beginning, Fascism had been built upon the destruction of the rights of the agricultural labourers. It was only to be expected that the burden of the crises of 1927, and then 1929–33, should have been transferred to their shoulders. But less inevitable was the failure of Fascism to protect the interests of the middling peasantry. The policy recommended by Pareto and Serpieri was not really followed through, and Fascism did not acquire a true social base among the peasantry. In provinces like Ferrara the crisis of 1927 disillusioned the active Fascists among the more prosperous peasantry or small farmers.[88] Alfredo Rocco believed in the creation of a class of stable peasant proprietors who should be prevented by law from dividing their holdings. This project for the creation of an indivisible hereditary peasant holding bears some resemblance to the Nazi legislation on the *Erbhof*, or hereditary peasant homestead. However Rocco's relatively far-sighted concern with social stability was not shared by other Fascists.[89] The Fascist attitude to small peasant property was by no means wholly favourable. Mussolini in his Ascension speech noted that the experience of France showed that small proprietors tended to limit their families : and Gino Arias remarked that 'the higher standard of living of the rural population, even the diffusion of small property, as has occurred in other nations, might favour the utilitarian instinct which makes one forget the duties of the individual to the nation, and is everywhere the final cause of the demographic crisis.'[90] Even the land reclamation policy did not, as it might have done, work to the advantage of the peasants. Small proprietors were required to execute a share of the works, and they often found it hard to fulfil their obligations.[91]

The Fascists, like earlier conservatives, regarded *mezzadria* (sharecropping) as the ideal system of agriculture. Whereas peasant proprietors might limit their families to avoid subdivision of their property, since holdings were distributed according to family size and working ability, the *mezzadri* had a positive incentive to have large families. Their birthrate was in fact higher than that of other classes. The system of *mezzadria* itself, based on the sharing of produce, was praised as an example of 'social solidarity' and 'class collaboration' : 'the *mezzadria* contributes to the conservation and formation of large families living in patriarchal discipline under the authority of a single head, thus guaranteeing a healthy family life.'[92] However this enthusiasm did not signify that the interests of the *mezzadri* were defended. The pompously entitled 'Charter of the Mezzadria' was prepared by the landowners who met in the old Tuscan society the Accademia dei Georgofili. The reforming proposals of Serpieri, who wished to ensure for the *mezzadri* a greater say in the running of the farm and a share in profits, were defeated. Over the period 1919–35, the indebtedness of the *mezzadri* to their landlords tended to increase substantially.[93]

However from a political point of view Fascist rural policy was not altogether a failure. The rural and demographic propaganda did leave its mark on large sectors of the peasantry : the best study of the *mezzadri* available, while extremely critical of Fascist policy, concludes that 'in Umbria at any rate, the relations of the *mezzadri* with Fascism were good',[94] although their support was passive rather than fervent. The same would probably be true of the majority of small peasants, especially after the Conciliation. One reason behind 'rurality' was Mussolini's correct belief that it would be easier to placate the rural population than the urban proletariat. Even rural poverty and underemployment did not work wholly to the disadvantage of the regime.[95] In rural areas the Militia was increasingly recruited from poverty-stricken or unemployed labourers who needed the pay. Of course, the solution did not do much for the prestige of the Militia. But in general Fascist support in the countryside depended on the success of propaganda campaigns, not on real achievements or class interest. Such support would be unreliable in times of adversity.

The policies of 'rurality' and the demographic battle marked a significant turn away from the objectives of modernization. Even from a military point of view, Italy's problem was arms rather than manpower, and extra cannon-fodder would not prove very useful. The restrictions on the mobility of labour seriously contributed to the stagnation of the economy.[96]

Towards the Organized Economy

After 1925, responsibility for economic policy was shared between two men : Volpi and the new Minister for the National Economy, Belluzzo, a far more important figure than his predecessors. Volpi was a financier, Belluzzo an engineer, and their approaches to economic policy reflected this difference of background. Unlike Volpi, Belluzzo co-operated successfully with the party.

Before the March on Rome, though he had not been a member of the PNF, he had been a conspicuous sympathizer. He shared the Fascist distrust of international finance and speculation, which he regarded as harmful in their effects on the technical organization of industry. There was a mixture of the old-fashioned and the modern in this outlook. Belluzzo regretted the modern tendency to separate ownership and control; his ideal was the industrialist of the true old style who owned and managed his firm directly, and refused to form a limited company. But if this looks like reactionary nostalgia, Belluzzo also stood for the new class of engineers, technicians, managers and scientists. It was conventional for all Italian industrialists to describe themselves as '*tecnici*' but to Belluzzo, with his suspicion of capital where it was divorced from management, the word really meant something. He was a genuine technocrat.[97] It was the *ingegneri*, he said, who had brought about the failure of the occupation of the factories; the workers, who had abandoned Nation, Family and Religion, had bowed before Science.

Belluzzo first became actively involved with the Fascist government when Mussolini gave him the job of re-organizing the Società Ansaldo-Cogne, one of the constituent firms of the bankrupt Ansaldo combine.[98] Mussolini appointed him because of his dissatisfaction with the conduct of the new administrators of Ansaldo, who were accused of deliberately running the firm down while at the same time demanding subsidies from the Government. His task was to serve as a watchdog for State interests. Belluzzo evolved an ambitious project for transforming the Cogne enterprise (an integrated complex of iron-ore mine, hydro-electric plant and steelworks) into a plant for the production of high quality steels, such as hitherto had been lacking in Italy. This looked like a bright idea, but the plant, owing to its unfavourable situation, produced at an uneconomically high cost and required a constant flow of subsidies over the years. In Belluzzo's handling of the Ansaldo-Cogne affair one can see several elements which were to be characteristic of his work as Minister: commitment to technical achievement and the utilization of natural resources without much consideration for cost; the conviction that the State must intervene directly in the management and ownership of firms which it subsidized; and the consideration of Italian industry from the point of view of planning for defence needs.

Belluzzo soon had occasion to develop this last idea more fully. After his election to Parliament in April 1924, he became a member of the Chamber's Budget Committee and devoted himself to the study of the economic problems of defence. He drafted two important reports, on the military budget and on the problem of industrial mobilization. The first outlined the aims which military policy should pursue: the formation of a modern, mechanized army and air force, with high fire-power and mobility. He made the radical suggestion that the industrial establishments controlled by the War Minister, as well as the medical and other services, should be demobilized and entrusted to civilian administration. Private industry could produce arms more cheaply than the State arsenals, which should be restricted to the testing of experimental models. The memorandum on industrial mobilization translated Belluzzo's military concerns into directives for general economic policy.[99]

The functions of the High Command should include those of stimulating production and organizing 'a rational technical supervision' over industry. One of the novelties in Belluzzo's outlook was that, guided by his technical knowledge and the experience of the 1914–18 war, he did not see the steel industry as occupying the privileged central position which it had always claimed with reference to defence policy. Instead, he argued that it was the chemical industry which should be given top priority. Here Belluzzo, as in much of his thinking, was presumably impressed by German precedents. Although Belluzzo's hostility to the steel and sugar lobbies has led one writer to describe him as a qualified *liberista*, it would be more accurate to see in him a precursor of autarchy.[100] As in Germany, autarchy was not simply a quantitative extension of traditional protectionist trends, but an altogether new policy, in which the central emphasis shifted from the metallurgical to the mining and chemical industries. Belluzzo was against protection only where he considered it to be inefficient and unnecessary.[101] He was responsible for the law of 7 January 1926 which satisfied one of the industrialists' most persistent demands by making it obligatory for the State and local administrations to show preference for the products of national industry. Belluzzo in fact promoted State intervention to protect and foster the new science-based industries, and to develop Italian resources in raw materials and fuel. It was his obsession with the second of these problems, notably the production of iron-ore, petrol and lignite, which makes him a precursor of the policies of autarchy.

It is clear that military considerations even more than the balance of payments problem were responsible for the Messianic fervour with which he pursued the objective of freeing Italy from 'servitude' to foreign raw materials and fuel.

Economists, far from the reality of life, have often repeated that not a few industries in Italy are hothouse plants, because they cannot find the raw materials at home. I believe instead that any nation can exercise all the industries which are exercised in other nations. . . . Everything that is necessary for our defence must be studied and constructed in Italy by Italian industry.

The raw materials indispensable for defence were to be replaced by synthetics developed by the chemical industry : 'even in peacetime Italian industry must be directed towards the use of metals which can be found in Italy' : fuel resources must be developed to the utmost, and the substitution of electrical energy for coal should be encouraged. Belluzzo explicitly mentioned the need to protect the chemical industry from foreign competition : while the electrical and mining industries were deliberately to be fostered by subsidies and by the promotion of scientific research.[102]

In November 1926 the SIPE chemical combine, whose president was the Fascist deputy and *podestà* of Milan, Ernesto Belloni, asked for a loan of 50 million lire to assist their programme of co-ordinating the gas and dye industries and the production of explosives, and to help them meet the competition of the English and German trusts. Belloni described this as 'a programme of redemption from foreign domination . . . but also, and indeed principally, for the formation of the largest and strongest possible basis for national defence'. Belluzzo backed this plan against Volpi's opposition : however he insisted that the loan should only be granted as part of a general plan for the development of the war industries under the close supervision of the State. 'The Ministry of Defence should become a shareholder, albeit in the minority, of these enterprises of basic importance, contributing to an increase in their capital, and at the same time following and supervising their management through representatives on the board of directors or in the college of auditors, and find out the real costs and hence the equitable prices for State contracts.'[103] The ideas of Belluzzo here foreshadowed the development of the public sector of the economy during the 1930s, when the State came to control the lion's share of the armaments industries through the IRI (Institute for Industrial Reconstruction). The programme of State shareholding and control in the armaments industry curiously enough originated with the *liberisti*, whose suspicion of the influence exerted by private arms manufacturers on government policy led them to favour public intervention in this sector. If further operations of industrial salvage had to be carried out, the 'shareholding State' would at least ensure that the public purse received compensation from any subsequent profits.[104]

Belluzzo's ideas on import substitution appealed to Mussolini because of his anxiety about the trade deficit, which he described in May 1926 as 'the worm in the woodwork' of the economy.[105] It should be noted that the policy of autarchy in 1937–9 was also in part the result of a balance of payments crisis. In June 1926 the Cabinet decided that in order to reduce the import bill priority should be given to agriculture and mining.[106] Another factor which led to increased concern with the problem of raw materials was the development of international cartels, such as the Franco-German iron and steel cartel. It was feared that the richer nations might manipulate the output and prices of indispensable raw materials and fuel in the interests of their own producers.[107]

Italy already felt keenly her dependence on the international trusts for oil. The search for independent supplies of oil or natural gas has been one of the constants of Italian economic policy : in the 1920s as in the 1950s this was the most important objective of the Italian efforts to expand commercial relations with Russia. However the purchase of Russian oil was only one of the alternatives pursued. Italian capitalists also prospected at home and, with more success, in Albania.[108] To co-ordinate these initiatives Belluzzo created the AGIP (Azienda Generale Italiana Petroli). This was the forerunner of a new type of enterprise, which was destined to be of great importance in the future, the 'para-State' institution. The AGIP was a joint stock company for which the State put up all the initial capital. Belluzzo was a firm believer in State shareholding and supervision as a means of development. However the early history of AGIP was not fortunate. For both political and financial reasons, the acquiescence of the business establishment had to be secured, and Senator Conti was accordingly made president of the company. Disagreement soon broke out between Conti and his friends on the board, who were backed by Volpi, on the one side, and Belluzzo with his civil servants on the other. Conti argued that the first task of AGIP should be to acquire control over the various Italian oil companies already in existence. He negotiated the purchase of a majority shareholding in SNOM (Società Nazionale Olii Minerali) from Piero Pirelli, who became vice-president of AGIP on terms which were criticized as excessively favourable. Belluzzo wanted to put more emphasis on prospecting inside Italy : but at the same time his Ministry refused to allow AGIP autonomy in this field. There was a bureaucratic vested interest involved, since a whole department of the Ministry existed to supervise mines and prospecting. The first experiment in para-State enterprise thus suffered both from manipulation by private financiers with outside interests and from centralized bureaucratic control : the advantages of the formula for the conduct of public enterprise were only to be demonstrated much later.[109] The success of the 'para-State' institution in industry (under the IRI) depended on the existence of an independent class of managers distinct from both the bureaucracy and big business.[110]

Nevertheless from 1926 onwards the para-State enterprises grew like mushrooms on the rich soil of the corporate economy. They were used to develop resources which private industry found it too costly and unprofitable to utilize. In 1927 the new emphasis on agricultural development dictated the creation of SAFNI for the commerce and production of natural fertilizers. During the period 1935-9 para-State enterprises played a very important part in the policies of autarchy ; they were created for the production of coal, lignite, synthetic petrol and cellulose.[111] In this field, as in that of armaments, the importance of the para-State enterprise had been foreseen by Belluzzo. Before 1929, however, the new para-State institutions were still relatively unimportant in direct industrial production ; they had a much greater function in credit and the administration of social welfare. These functions were linked ; the social welfare institutes were used to provide capital for other public enterprises.[112]

Both the growth of the international cartels and the imposing rationalization programme of German industry convinced Belluzzo of the need for a drastic reorganization of the structure of Italian industry. Few Italian companies had the scale or expertise necessary for successful competition with the new rationalized enterprises ; only in the newer sectors, chemicals and artificial silk, did they participate in the international cartels.[113] In all countries, the rationalization movement signified the concentration of industry and an attempt to reduce labour costs by raising productivity. Belluzzo earned polite words from Rossoni for warning the industrialists that the right way to meet the pressures of international competition was not simply by slashing wages.[114]

Many of Belluzzo's more ambitious ideas found fulfilment only in the 1930s, if at all. The military aims of his economic programme were frustrated by the conservative hostility of the army establishment, who had no time for interfering civilians. His views on the organization of the economy conflicted with those of Volpi, who defended the cause of orthodox protectionism. There was a natural affinity, however, between Belluzzo's voluntarist economic philosophy and the outlook of the Duce; it is very probable that he had an important influence on the development of Mussolini's economic thinking after 1925.

A good example of Mussolini's new views is provided by his inaugural speech to the National Exports Institute on 8 July 1926. 'Italian industry should conform to the directives of the Government which is decidedly unitary.'[115] Industry was ordered to form 'a common front' in dealing with foreigners, to avoid 'ruinous competition', and to eliminate inefficient enterprises. Although Mussolini expressed himself more crudely and with less precision, his agreement with Belluzzo is evident. The values of competition were to be replaced by those of organization: Italian industry would be reshaped and modernized by the cartel and the trust.

Mussolini's 'unitary' directives, however, also showed the influence of political analogy. It was not clear how Italian exports would in fact benefit from the elimination of competition between firms, unless a policy of dumping was envisaged, and that would invite retaliation. The foundation of the Institute for Exports coincided with the beginning of their decline. Although industrial production revived during 1928–9, exports remained sluggish. The textile and food industries, where small firms were still common, provided the great majority of Italian exports. In 1929 textiles accounted for 52 per cent and food for 17 per cent, while the engineering and chemical industries, the sectors in which production grew fastest between 1926 and 1930, together only accounted for 11·6 per cent.[116] The policy of rationalization, concentration and resource development left the major export industries relatively unaffected; after 1926 government policy consistently favoured heavy industry over the consumer goods industries.

The opposition of industry to 'quota 90' elicited a Fascist counter-attack against the concepts of Liberal economics and the failures of private enterprise, and thus contributed to the formation of a new orthodoxy. This was well expounded by Arnaldo Mussolini in a September 1926 article: 'The Italian bourgeoisie has in a certain sense failed to perform its task. . . . Our potential has been little studied. *This is the century of chemicals and electricity* (my italics). We can't stay for ever in the epoch of iron and steam. We must look to the future. Private enterprise has not shown resilience in its plans, methods and initiatives. The Fascist state has intervened in its place.'[117] There was a new philosophy here of State intervention for the technical modernization of the economy serving the ultimate a-political objectives of military strength and self-sufficiency; it was a return to the authoritarian and interventionist war economy.[118] The attack on 'private enterprise' is deceptive: the reference to 'chemicals and electricity' gives the game away, for these were the sectors in which the monopoly of a few great concerns was furthest advanced.[119] The repudiation of 'private enterprise' went hand in hand with the encouragement of oligopoly; organized capitalism replaced market capitalism as the Fascist model of the economy.

The role of the State, in fact, was principally that of underwriting the 'self-discipline' of industry. The Confindustria leaders opposed the extension of legal controls by the State over industry, even when the objectives were acceptable. They were unfavourable to the institution of compulsory cartels by the State; the necessary rationalization measures were to be carried out through the agency of their own associations.[120] In pursuit of rationalization, Belluzzo gave his support to the Confindustria's promotion of mergers and cartels. In June 1927 the Confindustria obtained a very important tax concession which facilitated the conclusion of mergers between firms. The result was a startling increase in the number of these operations; from 1918 to June 1927 there had been an average of 16 mergers per year; in 1,928 there were 266, involving 5,210 million lire of capital, and in 1929, 313 (4,568 million lire). Numerous cartels were organized with Government support. Their formation provoked protests from the smaller industrialists, who complained that they were being 'coerced' and kept in ignorance by the powerful. The reality of 'corporate planning', such as it was, lay in the informal agreements concluded within the employers' associations. The corporate framework and ideology made for a new atmosphere; industrialists became less individualist and more trust-minded.[121]

Both Belluzzo and Bottai, though they assisted this evolution, were somewhat disconcerted by its results. They recognized that the power of the Confindustria and, through it, of the major industrial groups had greatly increased, and that it was the latter and not the Government who really shaped economic policy. Bottai in 1928 complained that 'the State can do nothing within the syndical organizations',[122] and some years later Belluzzo echoed his views: 'It is the confederations and not the State, who control the national economic system, and who have created a State within a State. . . .'[123]

In 1929, Bottai succeeded in reviving the idea of formal corporate control over production. The National Council of Corporations was set up as an advisory body, with the right to give opinions 'on any question which interests national production', at the request of the Prime Minister or the Minister of Corporations. However the industrialists distrusted the new institution and were successful in limiting its effective functions. Benni sided with the procedures of personal dictatorship against those of corporative planning. He recognized that by leaving the final decision, in theory, to Mussolini, the Confederation of Industry could preserve its policy-making hegemony; he therefore argued that the *ad hoc* consultation of the interests involved in a particular decision was preferable to more complicated machinery. 'When a house is burning, the head of Fascism, and the Fascist government do not wait for Byzantine discussions, even if corporative; they look directly for a way to put out the fire.' Benni's main objective, of course, was to continue to exclude the Fascist unions from any say in questions of production.[124]

Bottai won a personal victory in the Government reshuffle of September 1929. He became titular Minister of Corporations, and the long battle with the Ministry of the National Economy was resolved in his favour. The Ministry of Corporations absorbed the industrial side of the Economics Ministry, and an autonomous Ministry of Agriculture was revived. The decision was a victory for the 'ideological' arguments of Bottai over the 'technical' arguments of Belluzzo. It seemed like the fulfilment of the old aspiration of the corporativists to make the Ministry of Corporations into a Ministry of Production: however it seems doubtful if the change really brought the unified direction of the economy any nearer.

Of much more importance for the future were the changes in the structure and organization of credit. The State take-over of the great banks during the 1930s was, of course, a consequence of the slump of 1929–33, and it was not foreseen in the 1920s. During the period 1926–8, the difficulties of the banks, created by revaluation, had already made the need for a change in the system apparent. The banks had been a major agency not only in financing but in planning Italian industry. In the postwar period the Commerciale had extended its influence, particularly in the highly concentrated, capital-intensive sectors of industry, such as electricity, steel and shipbuilding, in which control of the market was easiest to achieve.[125] Deflation not only increased the existing burden of debt on the banks, but forced them greatly to increase their industrial holdings. This was necessary both in order to avoid the collapse of share values and also to remedy the grave shortage of capital from which industry suffered. The 1925 stock-market crash, followed by the revaluation, discouraged the private investor, who during the De Stefani period had momentarily abandoned his traditional reluctance to invest in industrial shares. Private investment on the Stock Exchange declined from 8 milliard lire in 1925 to 1·8 in 1927.[126]

The consequence was that the two major banks, the Commerciale and the Credito Italiano, which had avoided the postwar disasters which had brought about the collapse of the Banca di Sconto and the Banca di Roma, found themselves in turn in a very exposed position. It was the bankers themselves, conscious that they could no longer support the burden of financing industrial growth, who impressed upon the Government the need to develop alternative sources and channels of credit. The recourse to foreign credit was one of the answers ;[127] one of Volpi's main concerns as Finance Minister was to make it possible for the electrical industry to have recourse to the American market. In 1927-9 the electrical companies raised 58 million dollars on the American market. The Banca Commerciale was able to sell a large part of its shares in the electrical industry to a special holding company financed by American capital. The scheme met with strong opposition from those who feared that it would open the way to foreign control, and Volpi's support was essential in enabling his old friends in the electrical industry to carry it through.[128]

Meanwhile the State had evolved new methods of investment in industry designed to avoid a repetition of the costly salvage operations of 1922-3. This was largely the work of Alberto Beneduce, whose career under Fascism is a very remarkable story. Beneduce had actively opposed Fascism until 1925, and his belief in public intervention had Socialist rather than Fascist origins. He enjoyed the confidence of the magnates of the electrical industry, and he was a friend of both Volpi and Stringher, the president of the Banca d'Italia. Their support enabled him to overcome the initial distrust of Mussolini, who as late as 1928 protested angrily at the preference shown by Volpi for 'an anti-Fascist and a Freemason'.[129] Beneduce's master idea was that the State should raise money for industry by offering gilt-edged shares with fixed interest which would meet the investor's demand for security. This was done through 'para-State' institutions, the ICIPU, which provided direct credit to 'public utilities', in the first place the electrical and telephone industries, the CREDIOP, for the financing of public works (including the development of sources of hydro-electric power) and the Istituto per il Credito Navale. Beneduce was to be the *eminence grise* behind the takeover of the banks and heavy industry by the IRI during the 1930s.[130]

The year 1926 also saw a great extension in the powers of the Bank of Italy, engineered by Volpi. The Bank of Naples and the Bank of Sicily lost their right of issuing currency ; henceforward the Bank of Italy was the only bank of issue. The central bank also acquired the right to supervise the operation of all other banks.[131] The new system did not avoid a fresh series of bank scandals. Supervision was rendered almost nominal by the inefficiency of the Bank's auditing and the laxity of Stringher.[132] Shady promoters often obtained the protection of prominent Fascists, for example Bottai.[133] More serious still was the general crash of the Catholic banks; between 1926 and 1929 more than seventy, with over a thousand branches, failed. It was a disaster which hit the small man in industry, commerce and agriculture particularly hard. The growing centralization of credit, in agriculture as in industry, favoured the large landowner and the large firm over the peasant and the small entrepreneur.[134]

None the less, in spite of a poor beginning, the banking reforms of 1926 laid the foundations for the central control and planning of credit which have been exercised by the Bank of Italy in the postwar period. In this instance, the 'unitary ideology' of dictatorship undoubtedly did prove helpful in creating a rational structure which would aid development.

The great slump vastly accelerated and intensified the trends towards a closed economy. Agricultural interests, hit by the catastrophic fall in the price of primary products, took the lead in imposing a system of bilateral trade agreements.[135] The collapse of the great banks and their dependent industries forced the State to intervene and provided the occasion for the interventionist schemes of men like Belluzzo and Beneduce to be put into effect. De Stefani summed up the position in an article written on 10 March 1932 and republished in a book aptly entitled *The Surrender of Economic Liberalism*.[136] It was an epitaph for his own philosophy. The growth of trusts and consortia supported by the State could no longer be viewed simply as the temporary product of the crisis : 'There is a feeling that there can be no turning back.' The old economic system had been irreversibly changed by the tendency to standardization, the triumph of the assembly line over the individual, and the limitation of competition by cartels which determined the individual enterprise's range of product, market and output, and which in return eliminated risk by assuring them a fixed share of the protected market. Free competition was no longer the driving force of the new economy of manoeuvred production, and the new system required a new 'ethical and philosophical' justification. Fascism – but also Communism – had been the prophet and precursor of the new economy. Some of De Stefani's predictions were too pessimistic : but it is impressive to see a man of his outlook admit the inevitability of trends which at heart he still disliked.

Did Fascism form a peculiar type of economic system ?[137] A full answer to this question cannot be attempted here, since that would require an examination of the period of autarchy. What one might suggest is that the question has not been altogether well posed. In terms of the standard economic orthodoxy acceptable in the 1920s, that is to say by the criteria of the market economy, the later developments, whether under Fascism or Nazism or the NRA, represented a new departure. It seemed to contemporaries that the rules of the economic game had been radically changed. While only the ingenuous imagined that Italian Fascism had found a solution to the great slump, and while the evolution of the Italian economy until late in the 1930s can still be explained as an instance of a more general process of development, it is still true that Fascism found a 'myth' to make sense of the responses to crisis.

14

IDEOLOGY AND CULTURE

The Activist Revolt

Early Fascism did not possess a systematic, logically constructed doctrine of how to organize social and political relations : none the less it was marked by a particular mentality. Fascist ideology was composite, an unstable functional synthesis of the needs of various social groups. It is impossible to arrange the ideas current in the Fascist movement into one 'relatively coherent system of generalizations about nature, society and man'.[1] The distinctiveness of Fascism was, one could say, more in form than in content : it was an ensemble of new techniques of inspiration. The closest bond between Hitler and Mussolini was in their belief that the road to power lay through the mastery of collective psychology, the manipulation of mass passions ; they were both disciples of Gustave Le Bon and his 'psychology of the crowd'.[2] The vagueness of Fascist ideology, when considered in practical terms, was in accordance with the Sorelian idea of the 'myth', which in order to move the masses should be distant and incapable of immediate realization. The 'myth of the nation' was of this kind.

It is interesting to note that Pareto believed that Fascism, on account of its inconsistency, had in part failed to create a really satisfying 'faith', and would probably therefore remain 'subordinate to the great factors of social evolution'.[3]

In the long term, there was a good deal of truth in this view. But the immediate success of Fascism was rather advanced than hindered by its lack of definition. The open-ended character of Fascist ideology, in contrast to the coherence of the Nationalists, facilitated the winning of converts. This was true even among the intellectuals : men like Gentile who had quarrelled with the Nationalists over doctrinal issues could persuade themselves that Fascism corresponded to their ideals. The novelty of Fascism was that it was a political movement which deliberately set out to exploit irrational

364

instincts. It was, Ardengo Soffici said, the first political movement which had captured 'the heart and the imagination' of Italians since the Risorgimento.[4] The core of the Fascist ideology in intellectual terms was a belief in the primacy of unreflecting action, life and inspired creativity over reason and 'dead' systems of thought. Fascism stood for action not thought: but it would not be at all justified to conclude that therefore it had no intellectual antecedents. On the contrary, this mystique of action was a distinctive cultural creation. It was one of the forms taken by the twentieth century 'revolt against reason'. In modern times, continuous social change undermines the stability of categories and values; religion and tradition are discredited by science. 'No sooner have we become attached to a pattern than its social prestige melts away'; the criteria for decision become uncertain, and a growth in insecurity results.[5] At the same time, the growing rationalization of life makes self-expression difficult and produces a reaction: 'the more rationally ordered society became, the more non-rational became the needs of the individual in that society'.[6] Croce put it another way; in a society where technique and calculation are increasingly dominant, 'Man feels attached to facts, driven by facts; but depressed in his feeling of freedom'.[7]

One type of response to the crisis of values and ways of understanding the world, and probably the most familiar, is the flight into sources of irrational conviction. The promptings of the unconscious, the race, the blood, the revealed faith, are armoured against critical examination by the assertion that they are 'higher' forms of knowledge which the intellect is inherently unable to appreciate. The sources of certainty are usually held to be collective or supernatural creations, hence the inability of the individual to criticize them. In Italian Fascism, however, the part of such collective mystic faith was not at first prominent in the justifications and patterns of feeling of the movement. Mussolini presented himself not as a man of faith, but as a sceptic, a 'heretic'. The Fascist movement claimed to stand for individuality, not for the submergence of personality in a collective leviathan. All this points to the importance of another type of response to the dilemmas of modernity. The obsolescence of values and categories is accepted, and conclusions are drawn from this.

All is fiction, in varying degrees useful for promoting the purposes of life. . . . To life, to action, there is thus recognized an absolute supremacy over intelligence and reason. . . . From the premise of the equivalence of all ideologies, all equally fictions, the modern relativist deduces that everyone has the right to create his own and to impose it with all the energy of which he is capable.[8]

It would be wrong, of course, to treat this 'relativism' as necessarily corresponding to a Fascist disposition. What, however, can be said is that Mussolini made conscious use of the fashionable slogans of relativism and pragmatism. He claimed that 'our action is directly linked to the most contemporary movements of the European spirit'.[9] This pretentious claim to modernity cannot be taken at face value; with notable superficiality Mussolini lumped together Einstein's philosophy of relativity and Spengler's Decline of the West under the same heading. It would be more accurate to speak of a link between Fascism and certain specific French and Italian interpretations of the contemporary movements in thought.

In Italy the intellectual reaction of the 1900s against 'positivism', by which one should understand a determinist view of human conduct as subject to laws resembling those of natural science, was for historical reasons associated with the political reaction against reformist Socialism and radical democracy. The identification was made, explicitly and powerfully, by Croce, then at the height of his influence.[10] When the young Florentine intellectuals Papini and Prezzolini joined Enrico Corradini to produce the first nationalist review, *Il Regno*, they combined political with philosophical criticism. Prezzolini anticipated Mussolini's terminology when he described himself and the other young nationalists of *Il Regno* as 'a minority of heretics who have the courage to deride the sacred beliefs of the humanitarian religion'.[11] Papini, a voracious and eclectic reader, was ready to take an interest in any philosophy which seemed to promise an escape from the stultifying determinist certainties of evolutionary social democracy. At one time he called himself a pragmatist: but by this he understood not the empirical idea that the meaning of concepts is dependent on their practical verification, but an almost magical belief in the power of the individual will to shape external reality.[12] Papini had begun by attacking all forms of metaphysics as obsolete: but the cult of spontaneity, instinct and force itself had metaphysical foundations.

One of the spiritual fathers recognized by the new activism was Henri Bergson. Both the syndicalist intellectuals and the Futurists shared Bergson's vision of reality as a continuous, unpredictable process of creation, which could not be grasped by the rational intellect but only intuited and lived. Sorel's concept of the myth was framed in Bergsonian terms; it was 'a body of images which by intuition alone, and before any analyses are made, is capable of evoking as an undivided whole the mass of sentiments' of a political movement.[13]

Mussolini's mental tool-kit was completed by his absorption of the anti-determinist, voluntarist tendencies of the new philosophy. His was not a disinterested acceptance; like others of his generation, he saw in these ideas a weapon with which to fight the complacent optimism of the evolutionary view. Fascism, contrary to the stereotype of totalitarian ideology, was not founded upon a belief in historical inevitability, but indeed on its opposite, on a radical denial of the possibility of social prediction or the extrapolation of historical trends.[14] The clash of the two opposed concepts of history (both originating within Socialism) was never better illustrated than in the exchange between Mussolini and Turati during the debate in Parliament after the former's 'bivouac speech':

Turati: Democracy will win, because it must win, because it is history; yes, for this simple reason.

Mussolini: History does not have fixed rails like a railway.

Turati: I know, you are a follower of Stirner, the will for you is everything, and ignores the causes which determine and moderate it. The trouble is that reality is not in agreement with Stirner or with you, and economics is not literature or romance.

'The will for you is everything':[15] Turati's conception of history might be crude, but he had a point here. The belief in the primacy of the will, in the total freedom of the superior individual, was destined to flower vigorously in the climate of dictatorship. It sustained the myth and rhetoric of the new Caesarism. The ideological function of voluntarism, however, did not end there. For Fascism it was a counter-philosophy, used originally and primarily against Marxism.

The war contributed greatly to the diffusion of the activist mentality. The interventionist intellectuals conceived of the war as an assertion of will and energy in defiance of the supposed 'laws' of historical development. 'The world war has destroyed the ideology of progress as a slow ordered succession of events and institutions ... it has destroyed the bourgeois, reformist, evolutionist conception.'[16] In the postwar period, activism ceased to be merely an intellectual fashion and became a widespread state of mind. The confusion and dissatisfaction with all existing ideologies had become acute. While other parties appeared to deny the existence of a crisis of values, Fascism not only recognized but glorified it. Mussolini's attitude of tough-minded pragmatism, his claim to have seen through and 'transcended' the old ideologies, appealed to many intellectuals. They celebrated Fascism as the end of ideology, as the first realistic political movement free from both moral and intellectual preconceptions, one in which practice would precede and form values instead of the other way round. Fascism taught the Power of Negative Thinking. There were echoes here of Nietzsche's 'trans-valuation of values'; the Fascist felt himself to be the superman freed from conventional moral restraints, and this helped him to act with confidence and ruthlessness.

Though they were incompatible philosophically, activism here converged with the social-Darwinist concepts of the life force and the survival of the fittest. Both diffused the profoundly important and widespread emotive idea of life as struggle, which was made more relevant and popular by the war.[17] The spiritual attribute of 'faith' and the biological attributes of 'youth' and 'masculinity' were equally essential for the self-image of the true Fascist.

For Pareto, humanitarianism was not only ineffective but harmful, since it hindered the natural selection through conflict of the strongest and most intelligent.[18] Sorel also regarded conflict as progressive; in a curious way, he blamed middle-class cowardice and pacifism for the failure of Marxist predictions to be verified.[19] The Marxist theory of class conflict points to an eventual resolution; but Sorel's 'heroic morality of the producers' views conflict as a moralizing force and therefore a permanent necessity. Ironically, the morality of conflict united syndicalists and Nationalists; the two vanguards, instead of fighting each other, formed an alliance to urge commitment to the grandest of conflicts, war. Enrico Corradini also identified the syndicalists in Paretian terms as a popular counter-elite of 'lions'; their commitment to the national cause allowed an optimistic reinterpretation of the theory of the circulation of elites.[20] Besides the syndicalists and the Nationalists, a third group of intellectuals were important in forming the mentality of Fascism. The continuity of the activist revolt from the Libyan War through to Fascism was maintained by the extraordinary propagandist verve of Marinetti and his band of Futurists, often absurd but surprisingly effective.

Marinetti described the Futurists as 'the mystics of action': their minimum programme was 'the love of danger, the rehabilitation of violence as the decisive argument, and the advent of youth to power'.[21] No one stated more clearly than Marinetti what was to be the fundamental political intuition of Fascism: the idea of nationalism, he said, had been associated with conservatism, repression, the aristocracy and clericalism, 'linked ideas which must be brutally separated'. Instead, the ideas of nationalism and anarchism should be reconciled. In accordance with this, Marinetti recommended the replacement of the police by a body of 'heroic citizens', whose 'sense of physical dignity' would not be impaired by dependence on legal methods. The *squadristi*, even if they did not disdain the help of the police, in a way fulfilled Marinetti's idea of an 'anarchic nationalism'.[22] The illegal, spontaneous, often haphazard and arbitrary character of their repressive actions distinguished the *squadristi* from the traditional conservative believers in law and order.

For an ethic the Futurists substituted an image. The 'programme' of the *ardito-futurista* is an idealized self-portrait, a narcissistic fantasy.[23] It starts with physical description and ends in the demand for privileges. As in D'Annunzio's speeches at Fiume, the keynote of Futurist propaganda is that the brave and the strong have an absolute right to rule. The aim was the propagation of the Futurist type of man: 'we aspire to the creation of a type of man who is not human, from whom there will be eliminated moral pain, goodness, affection and love, the poisons which alone corrode the inexhaustible vital energy.'[24] Marinetti was not, perhaps, entirely serious at such moments; it was all a kind of artistic fantasy, a scandalous *jeu d'esprit*. Unfortunately, others were to be in earnest. The step from the politics of fantasy to the politics of violence is short.

In a vulgarized form the revolt against disciplined and organized thought came to serve as material for a crude anti-intellectualism. The former Futurist Mario Carli asserted that 'philosophy of whatever school, period, or tendency is anti-Fascist by nature'.[25] Farinacci's deputy Giorgio Masi asserted that 'Erudition is a dead weight . . . when it claims rights . . . over the strong and pure will' ; 'the Fascist veterans of the trenches' revolted against 'the men of culture' in the name of 'faith, will and enthusiasm' against intellect. Pragmatism was similarly degraded into a justification for propagandist distortion ; Masi observed that themes suitable for propaganda were not to be considered according to 'abstract and scientific criteria'. 'The stupid concept of objective truth as independent of our will . . . must be scorned and repudiated with violence.'[26]

Another, more important, consequence of activist thinking was the prevalence of a concept of political action which saw law and institutions in a negative light, as obstacles to the free activity of the spirit. Here Gentile made his contribution. For Gentile's actualism the State existed only as an internal reality, which was continually being created in the minds of its members. Some of his disciples derived from this philosophy the slogan that 'the State does not exist, but is made from day to day', and gave it a very practical interpretation ; they used it to defend the freedom of the Fascist movement from legal and institutional regulation. The violence of the *squadrista* appeared in this light as creative spontaneity ; the 'dynamism' of the Fascist movement was held to be 'intolerant of crystallization into fixed forms'.[27] The same ideas served as justification for the avoidance of rational discussion and Mussolini's refusal to commit himself to a clearly defined doctrine. 'The "thinker" of Fascism is and remains Benito Mussolini, since he has thought and thinks Fascism in making it.'[28]

Mussolini described the ideological sources of Fascism as 'activism in philosophy and decadentism in literature'. At first sight this looks like a contradiction. The Futurists and the rest of the activist avant-garde had little tenderness for D'Annunzio, the major representative of 'decadentism'. The latter's fascination with Byzantium might appear to have nothing in common with the avant-garde's radical rejection of the past. However one can argue that these opposites were complementary. 'In the spirit of decadence it is not difficult to recognize the profound nostalgia for a new primitivism, the expectation in a mixture of fear and hope, of a new cycle of barbarism' :[29] the Futurist rage to destroy the movements of the past and to start again from the beginning followed logically on D'Annunzio's myth of the '*finis latinorum*'. The idea of decadence and revival through barbarism is at least as old as Tacitus, but around the turn of the last century it seems to have been invested with a new strength. More than vice and corruption, it was the moral indifference and materialism linked to the spread of industrial civilization – what Weber calls 'disenchantment' – that were taken as the signs of an old age in need of regeneration.

Pareto's cyclical theory, which predicted the coming victory of the courageous plebeian 'lions' over the astute and sophisticated 'foxes', was really only another variation on the theme : and for Sorel too, humanity was sinking into decadence and could only be redeemed by a morality of heroic struggle.[30] The Fascist writer Ardengo Soffici, who noted what seemed to him to be 'the extraordinary similarity' between Bolshevism and Futurism, expressed his sympathy for the national and primitive aspects of Russian communism : if its meaning were really to be found in the intention 'to turn everything upside down in order to rediscover a simple, primitive brotherhood, to restore the conditions of existence . . . to those of the rudimentary and savage horde of prehistoric times', then 'we might even give it a hand in trying the experiment of a plunge into refreshing barbarism'.[31]

The success of the Fascist cult of youth needs to be seen in the context of this widespread concern with decay : it is rather striking how often the metaphor of the rejuvenation operation was applied to describe the effect of Fascism on Liberal Italy. In the appeal to youth, Futurism was of special importance. Marinetti succeeded in dramatizing in an easily understood form the dissatisfactions of the younger generation, in revolt against the oppressive discipline of the provincial middle-class family. The students in the postwar period found themselves in a precarious position, with their future no longer assured. This uncertainty reacted upon parental authority : the habits of obedience were no longer justified by their results. The traditional type of classical and humanistic education seemed irrelevant to a world in which figures and quantities were coming to be all-important. Middle-class ideals of regularity, thrift and caution (always imperfectly internalized) were discredited by the success of audacious speculators and the impoverishment of the rentier.[32] The writer Massimo Bontempelli observed that the cause of democratic decadence had been the respect of sons for their fathers. Now the war and technical change had created a gulf between 'the generation of gaslight' and 'the generation of the bar', which preferred boxing and football to music and literature.[33]

Futurism taught Fascism the cult of technique, speed and sport, and the direct flattery of the younger generation.[34] It gave youth a new sense of liberation from the bonds of family and society by offering the model of a new style of life. Futurism had very little real reference to problems of production : but it was a precursor of the new patterns of consumption of the age of electricity and internal combustion. Its icons were the film, the motor car and the aeroplane. Sorel had preached the heroism of the producer ; Marinetti's was the heroism of the consumer.

From Futurism to Traditionalism

Between 1920–2 Fascism ceased to be the movement of an elite of adventurers and became a mass movement of reaction. Its centre of gravity moved from Milan to Bologna and Florence. This shift is reflected in the writings of those intellectuals who can be described as the ideologists of this second and decisive phase of Fascism. The Futurists were elitist and anti-proletarian : but they had stood for innovation in religion, morals and the arts. Moreover, although extreme nationalists, they were culturally cosmopolitan. This was a fact which they tried hard to disguise : but their commitment to the idea of modernity none the less imposed a kind of solidarity with the rest of the European avant-garde, from Joyce to Gropius to Mayakovski. The intellectuals of Florentine Fascism, Curzio Malaparte and Ardengo Soffici, rejected the Futurist creed as too modern and too European. They presented Fascism as a 'counter-reformation' ;[35] the task of the 'national revolution' was to shake off the superficial and deforming influence of foreign ideologies and to return to the true values of the real Italy. In attacking Piero Gobetti and the group of La Rivoluzione Liberale, Soffici wrote that their mentality was 'anti-Latin', that is to say protestant, systematic and arid. They had failed to understand the true character of the Italian race, which 'lives more by poetry than by material things ... has more thirst for song than for figures', dislikes modern theories, and knows that 'what is good for people of another stock is of no help to it, and for this reason loves Fascism'.[36] This is all very familiar. It is the common coin of the romantic reaction in all countries, the belief in the uncorrupted, instinctive virtue of the people, which desires to obey and revolts only when misled by the intelligentsia.

There were, however, some peculiar difficulties in the way of accepting this ideology which did not exist in other countries. In France, national unity existed before the Revolution ; instead in Italy it was still difficult to ignore the anti-clerical element in the creation of the national state. Many Fascist intellectuals refused to accept the 'counter-reformation' because they felt that it implied the repudiation of the Risorgimento tradition, which Fascism instead must 'overcome' in the sense of bringing to completion.[37] From the nationalist point of view, the traditional values of the peasantry were still suspect ; Fascism patronized folklore and popular tradition, but it discouraged the use of the dialects on which local culture was founded. It is no accident that the association of Fascism with regional populism was a phenomenon chiefly characteristic of Tuscany, the one region where the dialect problem was unimportant.

Soffici, in spite of his Futurist past, can be regarded as a fairly orthodox interpreter of the European reactionary tradition. Instead Malaparte, a typical representative of the 'adventurers' of the postwar generation contre,[38] expressed to the full, more than any other writer, the confused and contradictory realities of the Fascist movement. Malaparte's real name was Kurt Eric Suckert, and there was, ironically, something Germanic in Malaparte's romantic and morbid vision of what he claimed to be classical and Latin ideals. As with Marinetti (born in Alexandria) his was the nationalism of the déraciné. On the other hand, Malaparte was neither by origin nor conviction a 'man of order' : his father, an immigrant German technician who had settled in Prato, lost his job and was forced to become an ordinary worker. This background probably explains Malaparte's attraction to the idea of Sorelian Man, the heroic producer, worker and technician in one; he had a lasting attachment to the name and notion of syndicalism.[39]

The ideological writings of Malaparte are pervaded by a basic confusion. He is attempting to reconcile the activist, syndicalist, elitist philosophy with a kind of reactionary populism. The old antithesis of progressive, dynamic minority against passive, backward masses takes on for Malaparte a new and strange ambivalence. On the one hand, he regards the passive resistance of the masses during the Risorgimento as justified, in so far as the political class were attempting to impose liberalism, a Nordic and Protestant ideal, on a southern Catholic people. He even praised the 'military strike' after Caporetto as a legitimate revolt of the neglected rank and file against the corrupt and lying society of the home front, with its empty propaganda and high profits. The more orthodox reactionaries among the Fascists were profoundly shocked by this subversive view.[40] However Malaparte himself belonged by virtue of his temperament and life-history to the 'dynamic minorities'; he had been a republican, a nationalist, a syndicalist and a Garibaldian volunteer by turns. This was a heritage which Malaparte was not willing to forget. His populism, in consequence, was only half-hearted; he could not believe in the mystic unity of the Volk. He got round the contradiction by arguing that the true, Catholic nature of the Italian people was to submit to leadership and hierarchy. The cowardice of the masses had been justified because their leaders were hypocritical and indecisive flatterers; the 'heroes', Mussolini, Garibaldi or the minority of active interventionists, had triumphed not as representatives of the popular will but as dominators who had conquered its natural inclinations. Malaparte's ideological position was undoubtedly convoluted and artificial, often studied rather than sincere. Yet his writings are still significant; in their constant alternation of opportunism and passionate rebelliousness, they mirror the confusions of the squadristi.[41]

Malaparte and Soffici were, in a sense, the inventors and theorists of the 'second wave'. The completion of the Fascist revolution, however, was not seen even by Malaparte, the more radical of the two, as a social upheaval. Rather it was to be an integral destruction of the 'modern', a change of values: this pretentious and abstract idea was accompanied by unrestrained invective against the 'vile family of intellectuals'. 'Our revolution . . . was, and is, more against Benedetto Croce than against Buozzi or Modigliani. . . . In the same way as we have burnt the houses and dispersed the families of those who were, out of ignorance and cowardice, hostile to the living spirit of our nation, we will burn the houses and disperse the families of those who are hostile to it out of culture and intelligence.'[42] The veneer of egalitarianism serves here only to support a programme for the destruction of free culture. One might think that these were the words of a fanatic; but in reality Malaparte, a cynic who appreciated intelligence even in his opponents, was only showing a horrifying irresponsibility.

The subversive side of Malaparte's attitudes became less acceptable to the official ideology of the regime after 1926. But the reactionary and populist themes developed by Malaparte and Soffici anticipated an important change which came over Fascist ideology in 1926–7. This was the central position given to the linked themes of 'the demographic campaign' and 'the struggle against urbanism'. Nothing marked more clearly the break with the early days when Fascism was inspired by Futurism than the new attitude towards urbanization and the influence of the city.

Nationalist and clerical influences can both be seen at work behind Mussolini's preoccupation with the birthrate: however to a large extent the fear of demographic decadence was a sort of ideological import from France and Germany. The startling decline of the French birthrate had given rise to a large literature, and the theories of Corrado Gini, the most notable demographic theorist in Italy, were originally based on observation of French rather than Italian experience. Gini, a professional demographer and statistician of some distinction, was a pupil of Pareto, and he was one of the 'Solons' of the Fascist Constitutional Reform Commission of 1925. His description of the 'old age' of nations which accompanied demographic decline showed a distinct similarity to the later Fascist stereotype of Liberal Italy; it was marked by a prevalence of economics over patriotism, the triumph of 'calculated egoism' and 'the sedentary character', and a growth in working-class disorders. It is also significant that the problem which led Gini to formulate his theory was that of the struggle between Italians and Slavs in the Adriatic territories.[43] From the start, the demographic issue was linked to nationalist expansion, and moreover to a conflict between races rather than states. Although it was to Gini that Mussolini turned for information when he decided to launch the 'demographic campaign', it seems that it was a German work by Richard Korherr which first aroused his interest in the problem. Mussolini wrote a preface to the Italian translation; the German preface had been provided by Spengler.[44]

The theme of the defence of 'rurality' followed logically on that of the demographic campaign, since the birthrate was much higher in the country than in the towns. Mussolini himself probably had little enthusiasm for the rural way of life, but his commitment to rural values gave satisfaction to the provincial and agrarian elements within Fascism. The regime invested a great deal of propaganda effort in the new campaigns:[45] their effect, however, is difficult to assess. Certainly there is little evidence that birthrates were affected, in spite of the notorious tax on bachelors, though prizes to mothers of especially large families and more sensible measures in hygiene and education may have done something to reduce infant mortality.

Concern with population led in fact to a more positive Fascist attitude towards social welfare: a numerous and healthy people were needed to sustain imperial expansion, or so it was held. One cannot reasonably regard the speeches about 'the health of the race', which became frequent from 1927 onwards, as yet being racialistic in the commonly accepted meaning of the term. A closer analogy would be with the 'social imperialism' current in England around the turn of the century. However the new emphasis on health, numbers and physique brought Fascist ideology closer to a racialist way of thinking,[46] although this trend was resisted by many Fascist intellectuals, who were still faithful to a 'spiritualist' or 'idealist' outlook.

The Conservative Intellectuals and Gentile

After 1922, Fascism was grafted onto the trunk of authoritarian nationalism. Even before the war, Italian culture had been deeply penetrated by the doctrines of the new nationalism. The replies to a questionnaire circulated by the Nationalist association as part of their campaign against Freemasonry are revealing : philosophers, writers and historians vied with generals and industrialists in their rejection of rationalist and humanitarian beliefs. The assertion of a common humanity was an 'unreal abstraction'; instead 'humanity lives concretely in the strongest peoples and the richest personalities' : reason and humanity were mere 'rhetorical lustre' for 'coalitions of egoistic interests', which aimed to weaken 'the moral primacy of the strongest races'.[47]

On the side of Fascism, the decline of the party and the acceptance of the supremacy of the State was accompanied by a reconciliation with tradition as interpreted by the Nationalists. Prezzolini noted that 'In four years Fascism has not only changed its political outlook ... it has gone further than that and changed its intellectual outlook.... Fascism is all for hierarchy, tradition and respect for the law.... It chooses to set its standards by Rome and the classic era ... to submit to age-old Italian institutions, and among these it includes Catholicism.'[48]

Both by personal contacts and in their writings, the ex-Nationalists performed an important function in explaining and excusing Fascism to the world of culture. Their efforts in this direction run parallel to the similar work of mediation which they performed in political or business circles. The refined humanist and literary culture of a man like Federzoni (a pupil of Carducci) was reassuring to those who distrusted the Fascists because they didn't know Latin.[49] But the intellectuals who did most to render persuasive the view of Fascism as the logical outcome of Italian tradition did not follow the strict nationalism of the *Idea Nazionale* circle. Both the philosopher Gentile and the historian Gioacchino Volpe had been frequent contributors to the Nationalist review *Politica*, but they rejected some aspects of Nationalist orthodoxy. Before 1922, Gentile called himself a Liberal, Volpe a 'National-Liberal'. This was the clue to their dubious achievement. They succeeded in presenting Fascism as a movement which had overcome the limitations of nationalism and reached a new synthesis.[50] They could thus affirm the continuity of Fascism with older cultural traditions without denying its novelty. A very important element in the historical interpretations of both Gentile and Volpe was their recognition of the positive function performed by socialism in the political education of the people. Socialism was unacceptable because it was internationalist and because the doctrine of class war weakened the national community: but its positive achievements had to be comprehended in the Fascist synthesis. Gentile and Volpe had both hoped, in common with a number of other conservative and idealist thinkers, that the war would create a truly united nation. But by 1919 it had to be recognized that the war had driven yet another wedge between the State and the people. The political consciousness of the masses had indeed been awakened, but not in the way that had been hoped. Hence Gentile, Volpe and a number of other intellectuals rallied to the Fascist slogan of 'the defence of victory'. The task of Fascism in their eyes was to revive and fulfil the unrealized war aims of the nation, not only in foreign policy but also at home: Gentile wrote that with the Fascist seizure of power, 'it suddenly appeared that the Italian people had recovered the enthusiastic unanimity which it had had on the eve of the war'.[51]

Gentile had not identified himself with Fascism before the March on Rome. However the attraction which Fascism had for him can be understood in the light of his writings during and after the war. He was obsessed with 'the urgent necessity of conquering a position in the world for ourselves at all costs', and he believed that the failure of Italy to obtain her due was the consequence of deficiencies in political education and moral unity.[52] These deficiencies must be overcome by a stringent discipline, through which alone the masses could be brought to understand the reality and value of the State. For Gentile's idealist philosophy, the State could only exist as a moral reality in the minds of the people. The Italian State was weak because its institutions remained for her masses either mere names or else external and coercive forces.[53] The moral life of the individual was not organized by the idea of the collectivity. The central problem for Gentile, as for so many writers, was that of how the higher Italy of the cultured could organize and activate the great mass of citizens and thus create a true national consciousness. This end, he felt, could never be achieved if the individualist and utilitarian view of the State as a mere night watchman was allowed to prevail. The State must instead be 'ethical', a positive educational force inspired by a belief in its own mission. Gentile himself was before all else an educator, who conceived of politics as 'pedagogy on a grand scale'.[54] He saw Italian history as a struggle by those who possessed faith, ideals, or a 'religious sense of life' to overcome the passive resistance of sceptical individualism. The antecedents of this view go back to the great nineteenth-century literary historian De Sanctis and his portrayal of Machiavelli and Guicciardini as the incarnation respectively of civic duty and sceptical self-interest.[55] In his interpretation of the Risorgimento, Gentile came to see Mazzini as the central figure because of his insistence that the individual must subordinate himself to a moral discipline, dictated by the consciousness of his duty to collaborate in realizing the 'divine design' in history. Modern Italian democrats, although they claimed Mazzini as their own, were unable to understand his true importance because of their empiricist and positivist premises. His idea of the nation, Gentile argued, was incompatible with individualism.[56] There was a great degree of truth in this criticism, but when it came to the content of Mazzini's faith, Gentile's interpretation ran into difficulties. The attempt to explain away Mazzini's humanitarianism and his belief in national self-determination and to prove that for him too, 'right is conquest', was unconvincing.[57]

None the less, Gentile's reconciliation of Mazzini with the authoritarian and nationalist tradition was influential. Younger men were impressed by his single-minded preaching of the ethical value of the nation, and by his insistence that there must be no separation between thought and action. In troubled times, Gentile appeared a more militant and therefore relevant thinker than the detached and Olympian Croce.[58] For Gentile, Fascism was the heir of the Risorgimento. It seemed to him to embody that spirit of 'religious seriousness' which he admired. This now seems an astonishing conclusion, and one must pause to ask how he arrived at it. It would be too simple to say that Gentile simply admired force and success, and believed that might is right. But by a more roundabout way his philosophy tended indirectly towards the justification of the exercise of naked power. While he insisted that all true force was moral force, he also viewed force in the tangible sense of success, as the proof of the strength of ideals. This was an argument he first employed in relation to international affairs to prove the immorality of the League of Nations, but it was equally valid for him in internal politics. Even the Fascists' brutality and persecution of opponents became in his eyes a proof of their 'seriousness', for it showed that they cared strongly enough about their ideals to wish them to be accepted by everyone. In theory, at least, Gentile entirely approved of Fascist intransigence and regarded it as a demonstration of moral force.[59] Certainly Gentile always insisted, against the Nationalists and others, that the ideal State (which was also the true will of the citizen) was always distinct from the real, actually existing State, and that the latter could and should be criticized by the standards of the former. However the political values for which Gentile showed an overriding and exclusive concern were those of patriotism, State power and national prestige. If the State was even potentially the highest value, then what could be its ethical content other than the aspiration to complete self-realization ? The way was thus open to the total identification of the citizen with the purposes of the State. Nonetheless it would have been possible to object, within the framework of this view of the State, to the Fascist method of coercion, on the grounds that it would work against the desired identification of the citizen's moral consciousness with the State's purposes. But Gentile's theory of coercion closed even this avenue. He had denied (before Fascism) the distinction between physical and moral force, and equally that between public life and inner life : he argued that it was the right and even the duty of the State to enforce moral conformity with its purposes. Physical force was justified with arguments derived from St Augustine as a means towards ultimate spiritual re-education. This doctrine, already contained in itself the seeds of totalitarianism : Gentile's thought was not simply authoritarian and conservative, because of his belief in moral unanimity as the end which coercion should serve.[60]

Gentile's philosophical defence of Fascism did not simply reflect his conservative and nationalistic ideals. Croce and Gentile had fairly similar prejudices and expectations : but Croce's views and their articulation in thought were open to revision in the light of evidence, and Gentile's were not, owing to the extreme abstraction from reality which was sanctioned by his method. By insisting on the identity of thought and action, he excluded all criteria whereby political action could be criticized. This is apparent, for example, in a comment he made on Mussolini's aims : 'the true resolutions of the Duce are those that are both formulated and put into immediate effect'.[61] Gentile intends this not as a harmless tautology but as a subject for praise. The principle of 'the unity of thought and action' in Gentile's hands actually led to their complete dissociation : the philosopher engaged in baseless speculation and the statesman acting on blind impulse could nod to each other with approval.[62] Moreover one cannot say that Gentile, like some conservative defenders of Fascism, simply ignored or minimized the new and most ominous features embodied in the practice of the movement. He shared the ideals of the epoch, activism[63] and a form of elitism which looked with approval on the spectacle of the manipulation of the masses by crude slogans. He had assimilated the teaching of Le Bon and Pareto ; Fascist 'thought', he explained, did not have to be understood by all those who joined the movement. One had to distinguish between the simple slogans for the masses 'which practically and immediately distinguish friends from enemies', create myths, arouse blind, total support, and put into motion the forces of will and feeling, and the true ideals of Fascism. The masses were mere instruments animated by the 'thought' of 'a few guiding spirits – indeed one – the Duce'.[64]

However if Gentile's ideal was totalitarian, it is only fair to recognize that this does not mean that he approved of the actual practice of the Fascist regime, or other totalitarian regimes. Totalitarianism aims at an extreme of spontaneous universal submission which can never be fully realized ; the tensions between obedience and fanatical enthusiasm, coercion and conviction, cannot be resolved except verbally, and the characteristic atmosphere of a totalitarian regime is one of bad faith. Gentile could easily stomach the early excesses of Fascism as a transitional necessity ; but could not indefinitely deceive himself about the failure of Fascism to create a true moral conformity. The man, indeed, was a great deal more tolerant than the philosopher. Gentile fought for the right of criticism to exist within the Fascist regime.[65] But just that 'serious' and 'religious' view of life which he so ardently wanted, would demand something more than the right to criticize and make minor adjustments. When faced with downright opposition and negation, Gentile simply turned a deaf ear : he refused to admit the existence of a 'religion' that was not his own, on the grounds that those who opposed Fascism had estranged themselves from the national community. He always presented the conflict between Fascism and its opponents in terms of his habitual schema, as one between 'religion' and 'scepticism', or moral indifference, and this was an evasion.[66] He was unable to cope with the problem of the clash of ideals, or to recognize the value in his own day of the capacity for resistance to power and disinterested sacrifice which he admired in Mazzini and other historical heroes.

The Regime and Culture

Fascism has frequently been described as 'the negation of culture'. If one understands by this that the development of the regime ultimately proved destructive of all the values which a 'true' culture ought to represent, then one can agree. But here, more even than elsewhere, the historian must be careful not to let moral condemnation distort historical understanding. In order to assert that Fascism had no connections with 'culture', it is necessary either to use the term in a purely evaluative way, excluding from its scope all that is judged to be harmful, or else to minimize systematically the number of points of contact between the regime and the worlds of art and literature, philosophy and history. No reasonable definition of Italian culture could exclude a philosopher such as Gentile, a historian such as Volpe or a dramatist such as Pirandello ; and to assert that their work was altogether foreign to Fascism, and their connection with it purely accidental or personal, is an act of piety which may once have served the cause of intellectual tolerance, but now seems superfluous. The history of Fascist culture cannot be understood by means of a Manichean division between that which is 'just Fascism' and that which is 'just culture', but rather in terms of the aspiration of intellectuals to mediate between the two, to achieve a reconciliation or synthesis between them.[67] Towards the end of the regime, between 1938–40, the divorce did become almost total ; but this situation must not be projected back into an earlier period. The support which the regime received from Italian intellectuals did not simply result from opportunism, but from the illusion that Fascism would provide a solution to the various problems which agitated the contemporary mind. Here, as elsewhere, it is necessary to distinguish between the 'Fascism' of the movement and the 'Fascism' of the regime. Both had their cultural interpreters ;

but they were not always the same people. The cultural movements associated with the rise of Fascism, in particular Futurism, fought a losing battle within the regime against more orthodox and traditionalist forces. However the latter could never quite destroy the residues left by the former ; Fascism, and Mussolini himself, could neither carry out a cultural revolution, nor wholeheartedly accept the interpretations of official academic culture. Hence a growing indecision and uncertainty of aim, which was only increased by the multiplication (at the end of our period) of controls and attempts at indoctrination. This uncertainty in cultural policy in large part derived from the more basic ideological uncertainty.

Fascism paid a high price for the support and approval which it won from the representatives of official and traditional culture. What it gained in respectability, it lost in conviction. Always inconsistent and empty if considered as formal doctrine, the Fascist ideology had, instead, possessed a reality and structure that was psychological, not rational. The claims to a distinctive 'style of life' and to modernity were a vital element in the mystique which sustained Fascist morale and aggressiveness. They were never, of course, relinquished ; but the demobilization of the party was matched by a similar surrender on the cultural plane, in some ways still more complete and far-reaching.

In view of the later importance of the propaganda function in the Fascist state, it is surprising to find how slowly the movement, or Mussolini's government, evolved an efficient organization for the control of culture, or for mass indoctrination. At first the initiatives of Government and party were haphazard and unco-ordinated. Not until the middle of the 1930s did the example of Nazi Germany stimulate the regime into setting up a unified system of controls under the direction of the Ministero della Cultura Popolare.

The facts of technology must here be taken into account. In 1922 the 'mass media' whose exploitation is so characteristic of the modern totalitarian regime could hardly be said to exist in Italy. There was no radio, the film had only limited audiences, no newspaper had a circulation of more than about half a million. Direct, face-to-face propaganda was still the only way in which large sections of the people could be reached, particularly in the countryside. In the South, the problems of communication posed by scarce literacy and the dialect barrier were especially acute. The Fascist regime, like the Liberal, had at first little success in overcoming them. The shortcomings of early Fascist propaganda can also be explained, however, by the character and history of the movement. Compared with the Communist parties, or even the Nazis, the Fascist movement lacked the experience of a long period out of power. The shortage of trained and tried party cadres was in part an inevitable consequence of the movement's rapid success. The reliance on the 'holy bludgeon' had not encouraged the development of more subtle methods of persuasion ; many Fascist leaders admitted, in veiled language, that the movement relied too much on coercion. The movement none the less evoked a complex of rituals and ceremonies which succeeded in evolving enthusiasm and in impressing the inexperienced. The roll-call of the dead comrades, the Roman salute, the banners and the 'songs of revolution', all helped to create a pseudo-religious mystique, and to give the Fascist a sense of identity and participation. The marches and mass rallies created a special atmosphere of virile *camaraderie* which impressed even hostile observers.[68] To the patriotic anniversaries such as that of victory and entry into the war were added those peculiar to the movement; above all, from 1923 onwards there was the commemoration of the March on Rome, which was accompanied by a mass celebrated in the open air.[69] The Army and the Church, according to Soffici, were the only organizations before Fascism which had captured the heart and the imagination;[70] and the movement drew heavily on the experience of both in assembling its own ritual.

The strategy of Mussolini after the March on Rome, however, required different methods. The main problem was not how to recruit fresh masses of enthusiasts, but rather how to impress and reassure the mass of the uncommitted, and how to retain the sympathies of conservative elites. In the effort to prove that Fascism stood for security, tranquillity and order, the type of propaganda evolved by the movement was likely to prove counter-productive. 'Fascism' during 1923–4 was presented as a kind of spiritual revolution, inspired personally by Mussolini, which had been only temporarily and provisionally crystallized in the forms of the party and movement. The 'national government' was identified with the values of patriotism, order and loyalty to the state; Mussolini abandoned the black shirt for the top hat and tails to show his respectability. The Fascist emblem appeared on state coinage and a great effort was made to appropriate the symbols of patriotism, such as the gold medals for wartime bravery.

It was not only the intransigents who perceived possible dangers in this; the views of the director of the new *Ufficio Propaganda* of the PNF, Maurizio Maraviglia, an ex-Nationalist not suspect of desiring to put the party above the State, wrote as follows:

Outside the party support for the Fascist government and for the person of the Duce far surpasses support for Fascism. . . . One of the most urgent tasks of Fascist propaganda is in fact that of persuading the nation that the personality of the Duce is, *par excellence*, of a Fascist make which cannot be understood or appreciated without Fascism. Propaganda must thus combat both the 'apocalyptic', extremist, anti-legalitarian outlook, and the revisionist tendency, which identifies Fascism with the Government, and denies the function of the party.[71]

It does not seem that Maraviglia was very successful in imposing rationality and efficiency on the party propaganda machine. The Matteotti crisis, which hit party finances, also encouraged the revival of provincial particularism. Farinacci, by bringing the party propaganda office more closely under his own control, overcame one difficulty; but the plethora of newspapers remained a problem.

The year 1925 saw a revival and extension of the ideological and cultural ambitions of Fascism. For the emerging regime, the pragmatic arguments of the first years were not enough. Mussolini and Gentile proclaimed the totalitarian character of Fascism: the task was defined as that of creating a new national consciousness, a new mode of life, a new type of Italian. No field of national life was, in theory, to be exempt; it was the 'whole man' who must be remodelled.[72] But these typically totalitarian arguments were only very partially translated into practice. Mussolini's own attitude to higher culture showed a curious mixture of cautious respect and sceptical contempt. On the one hand he believed that the damage done by martyring or reducing to silence men of real eminence such as Croce would outweigh the gain, particularly in its effect on foreign opinion; on the other hand, he believed that the existence of an independent culture could be tolerated so long as its diffusion was limited. He recognized that the position of Fascism in the world of culture was weak (it was weaker in 1925 than in 1922), and, drawing back from any drastic attempt to impose uniformity, he put his trust in a patient work of pressure and corruption.

A review like the Florentine *Solaria*, which was known to be anti-Fascist in tendency but which kept to literature and avoided politics, could continue to appear.[73] Fascism, during the years with which we are concerned, persecuted only the militant and engaged forms of culture. Independence and non-involvement were not in practice treated as criminal, although from 1926 on, for those who wished to engage in journalism or other public activities, expressions of sympathy or at least submission to the regime became increasingly necessary. Mussolini believed, with character- istic cynicism, that the carrot would in this case accomplish more than the stick. The intellectuals were to be wooed by promotions and honours. When compulsion had to be applied, as with the famous oath of the professors in 1931, its scope could afford to be very restricted.[74]

Mussolini gave frequent reassurances that literature and the arts would remain free and would not be subject to direct political control.[75] Against these statements, however, there must be set the demands made by a number of authoritative figures that culture should serve the ends of the State. In short, literature and philosophy were to remain free, but only within the limits of what was considered useful or at least not positively harmful to the regime. The National Philosophical Congress of 1926 was dissolved by the Prefect after some of the participants had produced arguments in favour of liberty and natural rights.[76] Such direct intervention was rare, but significant. The clearest and most ominous definitions of the political functions of culture came from the ex-Nationalists. They saw the task of Italian culture as the exaltation of the nation and the inculcation of 'the sense of Italian power and the necessity of expansion'. Moreover culture could only perform this function if it freed itself from 'agnosticism', 'abstract universalism', and 'submission to foreign ideologies'.[77] The suspicion of all foreign influence, leading eventually to the attempt to enforce a kind of cultural autarchy, was the most dangerous source of intolerance and discrimination in Fascist cultural policy.[78] The effects of nationalist dogma were reinforced by philistine and provincial prejudices : however cultural nationalism was not just the product of ignorance. It drew ample nourishment from the world of learning.

Underlying cultural nationalism, there was the romantic metaphysic of the nation as an Individual, whose essence must be preserved against the levelling influence of reason. A man like Gentile had no personal animus against foreign culture : quite the contrary. However he shared the 'religion of the particular', the idea that 'patriotism is an affirmation of one form of soul against other forms of soul', which Julien Benda identified as the chief source of the 'treason of the clerks'.[79] Nevertheless, in spite of the tendency towards cultural autarchy, the eclecticism of Fascist ideology and its lack of definition helped to ensure a fair degree of tolerance. To the mature regime, all philosophies were acceptable, providing they acknowledged the supreme genius of the Duce.[80] Ideological censorship cannot be effective unless it is consistent. After 1929, intellectuals often found that the expert censorship of the Church was far more difficult to evade than the fumbling attempts of the State.

Between 1922 and 1925 Mussolini had more urgent things to attend to than the relationship between Fascism and culture. Fascist cultural policy was hesitant and discontinuous, and where the arts and literature were concerned, virtually non-existent. But after 3 January the problem of 'Fascist culture' begun again to receive attention. In its new phase, Fascism could not easily ignore cultural questions. The claim to be 'totalitarian' implied a search for uniformity not only in politics but in thought and artistic expression. But such aims were still very imperfectly realized.

Franco Ciarlantini, the director of the PNF Propaganda Office, decided to draw together and publicize the scattered initiatives of the party in the field of culture by organizing a conference of 'Fascist cultural institutions'.[81] The conference met at Bologna in March 1925. The Futurists were well represented at the conference, certainly outnumbering the representatives of any other definable cultural tendency : however, in his speech to the conference, Marinetti sharply criticized its aims and organization. 'To my amazement I have not heard one indispensable would mentioned . . . art. . . . We have not come to Bologna to expound programmes of economics, politics, sociology, philosophy and banking science.'[82] He had obviously been bored – and no wonder ! – by the endless series of reports on such topics as 'the Fascist spirit in the solution of technological problems' (Ingegnere Berretta), the diffusion of Italian science abroad (Corrado Gini), the rebirth of choral music (I. Sabattini), and the cultural relations between

Italy and Latin America. With his usual vivacity, he had hit on the fatal defect which doomed the initiative to sterility : the absence of any working definition of culture. The 'Fascist intellectuals' who participated in the conference and later signed the manifesto drawn up by Gentile were a mixed bunch indeed ; alongside bona fide artists, writers and academics there were numbers of party hacks and assorted worthies, whose claim to represent 'culture' or 'the intellectuals' was to say the least of it dubious.[83] Even as propaganda, this was a great mistake. The sacrifice of quality to quantity accentuated rather than disguised the inferiority of the Fascist list of intellectuals to the signatories of the anti-Fascist Croce manifesto : a smaller but more distinguished list would have made a better impression.

The result of the two manifestoes was undoubtedly a moral defeat for Fascism. During 1925 it became the habit among Fascist spokesmen to complain that 'culture' or 'the intellectuals' had ranged themselves against Fascism. Mussolini was stung into declaring 'I have never read a word of Benedetto Croce'.[84] This was untrue: and it was not characteristic of Mussolini to minimize his cultural attainments. His cultural ambitions soon revived. 1926 was to be the 'Napoleonic Year' : and if he could not give Italy military triumphs, he could perhaps at least found an Academy. But the foundation of the *Accademia italiana* ran into difficulties. Although announced in 1926, it was not finally inaugurated until 1929. Its composition was evidence of the cautious eclecticism of Mussolini's cultural policy. By the side of 'moderns' like Marinetti, Pirandello and Massimo Bontempelli, there were traditionalists like the writer and art critic Ugo Ojetti, the composer Mascagni and a number of salon painters and neo-classical architects.[85]

During these years the cultural action of Gentile was extremely wide-ranging. His aim was to repair the bridges between Fascism and culture and to hold in check the intolerance which was rife in the party. With these ends in mind, he persuaded the party to set up the Istituto Nazionale Fascista di Cultura. As he wrote, 'after the battle of the manifestoes the Fascists in reply to the blows of their adversaries ... launched an assault against culture, intelligence and philosophy ... we ran the risk of giving credit ... to a legend which may have had a certain charm in Fascist eyes : the legend of a Nietzschean and barbaric Fascism which despised and oppressed culture.'[86] As president of the Institute he had the main influence in determining its policy; his review *Educazione politica* was recognized as the Institute's official organ, although after some months Mussolini ordered that its name should be changed to *Educazione fascista*.[87] At the same time, Gentile did not have a free hand : the Institute was formally attached to the *direzione* of the PNF, and it is clear that he had to take account of the views of the *gerarchi* of both party and State. The programme of lectures and publications which it sponsored was pretty eclectic; Gentile explicitly denied that he intended to make use of the Institute to diffuse his own philosophy.[88] Even so, the Institute was never popular with the party : Turati protested against Gentile's *ex officio* membership of the Grand Council on the grounds that the institutes of Milan, Bologna, Florence (all founded and controlled by the local party) 'engaged in much more notable activity'.[89]

The Fascist suspicion of Gentile's independence was increased by his other activities, and particularly by the way in which he carried out his responsibilities as editor of the Italian Encyclopaedia. Gentile assured Orlando in 1925 that the Encyclopaedia was 'absolutely foreign to all contests between political parties',[90] and his choice not only of contributors but of sub-editors was not partisan. Well-known anti-Fascists like the Professor of Law Francesco Ruffini, the ancient historian De Sanctis and the oriental scholar Levi Della Vida, worked for the Encyclopaedia for years in spite of violent protests from the party.[91] Croce noted with understandable satisfaction that in defending his editors and contributors Gentile was forced to resort to the distinction between theoretical knowledge and politics which he had denied in his philosophical writings.[92] By far the most stringent control over the Encyclopaedia was exercised by the Church, who demanded the right to censure all articles relating to religion.[93] In addition to the Institute and the Encyclopaedia, Gentile came to control the publishing houses of Sansoni and Lemonnier, and he was president of a number of other important cultural institutions. In 1932 he became head of the Scuola Normale of Pisa. But successful as he was in extending his influence, it was increasingly threatened by the converging attacks from the party extremists and the Church, united in their dislike of his philosophy. The Conciliation was a severe blow to Gentile's prestige, and although his co-operation with Mussolini in producing the 1932 Encyclopaedia article on 'The doctrine of Fascism' might seem to have confirmed his authority as the regime's official philosopher, the middle 1930s witnessed a rapid decline in his influence.

The Arts and Literature

Sympathy for Fascism was more widespread among creative artists than among any other section of the intellectual community. The 1925 battle of the manifestoes showed that Fascism was in a minority among philosophers, scholars or critics: but, largely thanks to the Futurist connection, among modern artists, composers, and to a lesser degree writers, committed Fascists outnumbered their opponents. Early Fascism was unusual among political movements in the closeness of its connections with the artistic avant-garde. There is no doubt that the idea of rule by the creative, dynamic elite had a natural appeal to the avant-garde and indeed to many other artists. The disparagement of pre-war Italy as provincial and unadventurous struck an answering chord among modern artists who were irritated by the cautious conformity of prevailing taste.[94]

Mussolini's association with the Futurists had done a great deal for his image. He lost no opportunity of advertising his familiarity with the modern :

the aeroplane, the racing car and even the skyscraper were pressed into service as symbols of the new Italy. 'Mussolini', in the words of Giuseppe Prezzolini, a well-qualified observer, 'is the first statesman in Italy who has ever shown any intelligent appreciation of contemporary art.'[95] There is more to this appraisal than mere flattery, even if it cannot be taken as literally true. It seems doubtful, in fact, if Mussolini had any real interest in the visual arts. On the other hand, he had a genuine sympathy for what might be called the metaphysic of Futurism and appreciated the propaganda value of the modern movement. His mistress, Margherita Sarfatti, an *eminence grise* in cultural matters, was an active patron and collector of modern art, and it was her knowledge and judgement which gave Mussolini his reputation for artistic enlightenment. The personal connections between Fascism and Futurism remained strong. Marinetti, after breaking with Fascism in 1920 and flirting with communism, found the attraction of a generous recognition of the historical importance of his own movement irresistible. The regime could count on his support. Emilio Settimelli and Mario Carli, the editors of the extremist *Impero*, were old Futurists, and their paper continued to defend the identity of the true spirit of Fascism with Futurism. Futurist contributors dominated the cultural 'third page' of the paper. Later on, *Il Tevere*, edited by Telesio Interlandi, gave space and favourable comment to Futurist writings.

The hopes of the Futurists and the connection which they made between their art and their politics were thus described by the theatrical producer A. G. Bragaglia : 'in 1919, for our groups the word "revolution" had . . . a meaning in the artistic field'. The Futurists had seen the political action of Fascism as parallel to their own, and as an infallible way to achieve their aims. The 'revolution', in art as in politics, would cut short 'the prolongation of the nineteenth century'. 'When Mussolini had Marinetti, Papini, Soffici, Palazzeschi and the other Futurists as his collaborators, he would not have hesitated to declare the art of the Futurists as the logical form for Fascist art: as Fascism itself had arisen in the Futurist intellectual atmosphere.'[96]

Fascist patronage undoubtedly made it easier for Futurism to breach the resistance of official orthodoxy; the first showing of Futurist art in the Venice Biennale was in 1926.[97] Fascist cultural policy nevertheless disappointed Futurist expectations. In a sense this was inevitable; one cannot easily conceive of the aesthetic of an avant-garde becoming the official art of a regime without losing vitality. Marinetti boasted that the Futurists had served the nation by restoring the prestige of modern Italian art in the world : he pointed proudly to the success of Futurist exhibitions, and to their influence on French and Russian art. But this claim to worldwide influence could rebound. It was easy for the enemies of the Futurists to insinuate that an artistic movement which had found enthusiastic disciples in democratic France and even in Bolshevik Russia could not be truly Fascist or Italian.

During the 1920s modern architecture became known as the 'international style'; this made it ideologically suspect, and suggested that modern art was akin to the other 'internationals' which Fascism fought. Prezzolini noted the incompatibility of Futurism with the growing Fascist respect for Rome, tradition and the Church.[98]

The abstract painter Enrico Prampolini described the tendencies against which Futurism had to battle as 'reactionary demagogy'.[99] This was a good description. Since the majority taste in modern times in all countries has been traditionalist, the opponents of Futurism could attack from two directions. To the criticism that an art which ignored tradition could not be national, they added the more pragmatic argument that such an art was bound to be restricted in its appeal and could not easily serve as an instrument for mass propaganda. The aesthetic and moral radicalism of the Futurists was something of an embarrassment. In art, as well as politics, the ideology of the elite conflicted with the needs of the authoritarian mass state which required an epic art easily comprehensible to a broad public in style and theme.[100] The Futurists posed the alternative in stark, dramatic terms: either Fascism would continue to be the companion of Futurism, or it would surrender to philistinism and artistic reaction. However there was in fact an internal schism in the modern movement in the arts. Some of its founders now believed that the conflict between tradition and innovation could be resolved in a new synthesis which could be modern, but also 'national', and that this would be the art of Fascism. Such a middle tendency really did exist among Italian artists. One side of the 'modern' was subjectivism and the search for the accurate rendering of sensations and movements; the early Futurists still recognized the Impressionists as precursors. Artists like Carrà and De Chirico, the 'metaphysical painters', however, instead became the champions of a return to a Platonic conception of art as pure form. This new aesthetic had ideological implications, which the artists themselves undertook to explain. For Carrà, French art was to be rejected as 'a form of empiricism', and 'Impressionism is the opposite of Italianism'. 'After having been sensual and materialistic, the artist is again becoming a mystic, or, which is the same, idealist, platonist and a discoverer of forms'. Similarly Gino Severini defended, in language which recalls the cultural polemics of Maurras and the Action Française, the classical ideals of 'order, certainty and balance' against the 'disorder of fantasy and instinct left to run wild'.[101]

The first attempt to lay down the principles which should guide Fascist cultural policy in relation to the arts was made by Soffici. In an article published in *Gerarchia*, he declared that since all manifestations of the spirit are interdependent, 'every political principle must of necessity have a corresponding aesthetic principle'. What, then should Fascism support? On the one hand, it must reject all those forms of art 'which we shall call philistine, which mirror a vulgar materialist or theatrical state of mind, or petty bourgeois or socialist sentiment, and which guide the spirit towards the prosaic, gross sensualism, or democratic cowardice'. There could be no question therefore of a return to nineteenth-century realism. 'Fascism is not an enemy of modernity' : however it could not commit itself to the Futurist programme either. 'We have already seen how this tendency is that which is, logically, followed and glorified by Russian Bolshevism; and this will be enough to show that it cannot be the one which best serves the general purposes of Fascism.' He urged the Italian artist once more to seek inspiration in the great native tradition of the Quattrocento.[102]

At least one attempt was made to organize a regular movement which would give substance to the idea of Fascist art. The movement known as the *Novecento* put in a strong claim for official status. Its pretensions need not perhaps be taken too seriously. The *Novecento*, whose nucleus was in a privately formed group of Milanese painters and architects, turned into an ambitious cultural operation. The group attracted the patronage of Margherita Sarfatti, and she was able to persuade Mussolini to open their exhibition in February 1926.[103] The most interesting figure of the *Novecento*, from both an artistic and a political point of view, is Mario Sironi : Sironi was a committed Fascist who drew the political cartoons for the *Popolo d'Italia* and the covers for *Gerarchia*. There is something about his sombre artistic vision which may explain the attraction for him of a movement which proclaimed itself the enemy of optimistic illusions. He belonged to the Milanese intellectual *ambiente* which had close contacts with Mussolini, as did Massimo Bontempelli, the chief literary propagandist of the *Novecento*. Bontempelli had been the only literary contributor of any note to *L'Ardita*, the monthly review published under the auspices of the *Popolo d'Italia*. Between 1926 and 1929 a number of artists of very diverse tendencies accepted the '*Novecento*' label as a passport to patronage, so that the original significance of the movement, as an attempt to reconcile classical tradition with modernity, was weakened by dilution.[104]

At the Perugia Fine Arts Academy on 7 October 1926 Mussolini announced that 'we must create a new art of our times . . . a Fascist art'.[105] This was an order : whether or not the new art would be forthcoming, it made discussion of the problem a duty. Most of the participants in the discussion, for example Soffici, rejected party control over art, even though at the end of their enquiry into Fascist art, the board of *Critica fascista* for the first time suggested the creation of a Ministry of Culture. For the moment, what was at stake was the direction to be taken by official patronage.[106] In his contribution, Soffici chiefly repeated what he had said before. However he added a more decided rejection of all forms of abstract art : cubism, which Margherita Sarfatti had described as 'classical', a term of praise, did not escape Soffici's condemnation. On the other hand, his sharpest criticisms were reserved for philistinism. 'The new authorities and the so-called new journalism have vied in revaluing the most idiotic representatives of pre-Fascist official art.' In the field of culture, he complained, the leaders of Fascism were incapable of distinguishing their friends from their enemies.[107] In fact even those Fascists who were not simply incapable of artistic judgement soon took refuge in a cautious eclecticism. The *Novecento* movement was able to attract official patronage in part because it was a compromise which seemed to bridge the gap between neo-classicism and modernity. Margherita Sarfatti spoke of the style of the classical *novecento* as 'the Fascist style which starting from here will impose itself on the world'. However she was careful not to offend the old school. The sculptor Adolfo Wildt and the architects Brasini and Piacentini, all representatives of the most trite academic classicism, received her commendation as well.[108] '*Romanità*': this was the magic word before which the moderns had to retreat. The obsession with '*romanità*' was seen at its worst in the reconstruction of Rome, which was dictated by the needs of archaeology. Mussolini ordered the Governor of Rome, Senator Cremonesi, to 'isolate' the ancient monuments, 'as the thousand-year-old monuments of our history must tower like giants in the necessary solitude' and thereby gave the signal for the destruction of some of the most beautiful quarters of the city.[109] On the other hand, the modernity of Fascism could still be a useful argument when it came to sanctioning the ravages of the property developer. The Duce's brother Arnaldo, closely linked with the great Milanese building contractors, reminded the preservationists that they must not forget 'the inevitable needs of modern life'.[110]

During 1927–9, the architects, the writers and other members of the free professions, were organized in the official *sindacati*; this gave the regime a powerful instrument for co-ordination. With the aid of Bottai, the Fine Arts Syndicates obtained control over all major public exhibitions, national and regional, depriving the various private societies of patrons of the functions which they had previously exercised. The two most important exhibitions, the international Venice Biennale and the newly instituted national Quadriennale at Rome, were controlled respectively by the secretary and president of the Fine Arts Syndicate, the sculptor Maraini and the painter Oppo. Oppo, however, showed some independence of judgement : he was cautiously favourable to the moderns, and he spoke out against academic neo-classicism and the idea of an 'imperial art'. On the whole, the organizers of the syndicates were tolerant and disposed to compromise. But the fact remained that it was now possible to condemn dissenting aesthetic views as infringements of discipline.[111]

The most ambitious and interesting ideas on the role of the artists' unions came as usual from Soffici. He saw them as the means of reviving the medieval guild organization and freeing the artist from dependence on the market. There would be no obligatory style, but different types of commissions would be allotted to different groups of artists in accordance with their talents : the syndicates would take over responsibility for town planning.[112] However as with most sincere corporative proposals, too many vested interests opposed such a scheme for it to have a chance of success.

The organization of the unions prepared the way for a much more aggressive intervention by the regime in the artistic field, beginning in 1930–2. The programme of the 1930 Venice Biennale attacked 'cosmopolitanism' and 'cerebralism' : a more important symptom was the foundation of numerous special artistic prizes by the party and the professional confederations to encourage works of art with directly propagandist content. Apart from the obvious themes of the Duce as hero and the new virile ranks of the marching Fascists, the 'corporative' social ideals of 'the defence of maternity' and 'the poetry of labour' required and received illustration. This new stress on content naturally favoured a more traditional style of painting as against formal experiment.[113] However the Futurists still played their part in the visual propaganda of the regime. The manifesto of '*Aeropittura*' ('Air painting') in September 1929 represented a successful attempt by the Futurists to show the political, or military, relevance of their art.[114] If the illustration of the regime's conservative social ideals was best performed by more traditional artists, the Futurists were still the best at projecting the image of an aggressive, technologically advanced power. The regime, by this division of labour, was able to make effective use of the available talent in the visual arts for its propaganda. Beside the art for the masses, there still existed possibilities for more sophisticated and advanced techniques, especially in the displays of the Mostra della Rivoluzione Fascista of 1932 and other exhibitions. In architecture it was, ironically, the 'rationalists' of the modern movement who took the initiative in demanding greater intervention by the State. Some of the most brilliant modern architects were convinced Fascists, like Terragni, whose best known building is the Casa del Fascio at Como, and Pagano. Another architect, Ernesto Rogers, has written that 'Terragni and Pagano were the most Fascist of us. ... We based ourselves on a syllogism which went roughly thus : Fascism is a revolution, modern architecture is revolutionary, therefore it must be the architecture of Fascism.'[115] The illusion still persisted at the beginning of the 1930s that the dictatorship was an innovating force in the arts ; it was a defender of the modern style, the architectural critic, P. M. Bardi, who proposed that architecture should become a 'state art' and that a single obligatory style should be imposed on all public buildings.[116] In fact it was the advocates of *romanità* who eventually benefited in the later 1930s from the trend towards uniformity. The alliance with the Nazis, intransigent enemies of all that was modern in the arts, was a grave blow to the moderns within Fascism, and in this case the influence of the Church worked in the same direction. However, in spite of the victory of the '*Stile Littorio*' in architecture and the style of the Foro Romano in sculpture, conformity was never complete. The rival 'Fascisms' incarnated by Farinacci and Bottai were reflected in the arts : the latter still protected the avant-garde. The personal prestige which many modern artists enjoyed as committed Fascists of an early date, and which traditionalists like Ugo Ojetti, converts to Fascism of 1925 or 1926, notably lacked, preserved for them some right of dissent. The freedom of artistic expression was often defended by the 'true' Fascists against official mediocrity.[117]

Literature is more easily politicized than art, but a recognizable 'Fascist literature' was slow in making its appearance. One reason for this is that the impact of Futurism on literature was far less considerable than it was on the visual arts or even the theatre. One can also give a more general explanation : the creative writer is more likely to be a precursor than a follower of political trends. The evolution of Papini, from blasphemous atheism and rebellion to submissive piety and the defence of tradition, foreshadowed the similar evolution of Fascist attitudes. After 1929 Papini was no longer ahead of the times : but at the same time the style of literature which he represented began to go out of fashion among other writers, if not among the general public. A Fascist literature, in the sense of a literature likely to promote Fascist values and attitudes, did exist. Its heroes were D'Annunzio and Papini, even though it would be quite wrong to measure all their work by the Fascist yardstick. But literature ceases to be such when it becomes eulogy, celebration, concealment : and the victory of Fascism perhaps for this reason helped to bring to an end one phase of Italian literature, marked by the rhetoric of national power and individual genius, even if it made it harder for the new ideals to find expression. By the end of the twenties, the young intellectuals were reading Joyce, Freud, Proust and Moravia.[118] Like all regimes with totalitarian ambitions Fascism expected its writers to be 'positive', healthy and optimistic. 'Destructive' analysis of society or morality was equivalent to defeatism. A symbolic turning-point in the relationship of Fascism with literature came with the publication of Moravia's *Gli Indifferenti* in 1928. The book, a ruthless portrayal of bourgeois hypocrisy and moral emptiness, was extremely successful with the public, rapidly running into four editions; it was defended by Marinetti, Bontempelli and other modernists of early Fascism. But it was violently attacked by *Il Tevere* and by Arnaldo Mussolini, who compared Moravia 'the destroyer of every human value' with Erich Maria Remarque (*All Quiet on the Western Front*), 'the destroyer of the grandness of war'.[119]

Most 'Fascist literature' consisted of patriotic poetry and stories of war, travel and adventure.[120] In 1928 *Il Raduno*, the official journal of the artists' and writers' syndicates, caused the more intelligent Fascists considerable embarrassment by its over-zealous celebrations of the anniversary of the death of Emilio Salgari, the author of *The Pirates of Malaya* and other best-selling adventure stories for boys. Salgari was 'one of the greatest Italian artists', 'our true teacher', without whom 'we would have grown up to be serious, methodical accountants from the age of twelve'. His influence had fortunately replaced that of the democratic Jules Verne : 'it was not science which attracted us, but adventure.'[121] This was too much for most of the regime's intellectuals to stomach; however Bontempelli, one of the regime's most sophisticated cultural apologists, had recommended 'books of adventure' along with 'a theatre of imagination, rhythm and colour' as suitable reading for Fascists.[122] But even at the level of popular entertainment the regime was fighting a losing battle. The popularity of foreign bestsellers and American films was an object of growing concern.

The old conflict between elitist urban Fascism and populist rural Fascism reappeared in the literary controversies of the late twenties. The latter were represented by the movement of Strapaese (Super-Province), which had as its leaders Soffici, Malaparte, Mino Maccari and Leo Longanesi and the reviews *Il Selvaggio* and *l'Italiano*: the former by Marinetti, Bontempelli, and the review *Il Novecento*, who were christened by their opponents 'Stracittà'.[123]

Massimo Bontempelli, the theorist of the *Novecento*, belonged to the Milanese avant-garde which had such close connections with Fascism. Many of his early short stories appeared in Mussolini's review *L'Ardita*. He accepted and propagated the idea of Fascism as the revolution of youth and masculinity.[124] Like other young artists and writers associated with Fascism, he identified the modernist revolt against social realism with the Fascist revolt against socialism. 'Realism has always been defeatist': realist literature had been preoccupied with the themes of *ennui* and the brute in man. The new 'Mediterranean' literature would instead return to a conception of art as magic, as the creation of 'myth'; it would be optimistic and 'solar'. It would be European: but the Europe would be that of Nietzsche, not the League of Nations, of Catholic Rome, not of the Anglo-Saxons.[125]

Although Bontempelli became president of the Writers' Syndicate, the *Novecento* was less successful in literature than in the arts; literature is less dependent on official patronage. Bontempelli failed to found a real school, and his own writings, elegant but rather contrived fantasies, were restricted in their appeal. The attempt to bridge the gap between the criteria of a literary coterie and those of a political regime was a failure. Bontempelli himself declared that the war had ended the function of the avant-garde and that twentieth-century art must be anti-bourgeois and popular, but this remained just an aspiration.[126] Ironically, the most important aspect of Bontempelli's activities as a literary patron was the protection which he gave to writers attacked for their anti-Fascist attitude, such as Moravia and Corrado Alvaro. Bontempelli earned his privileged status by repeated and effusive declarations of Fascist faith.[127]

The 'Strapaese' movement was much more vigorous, and it inspired the only serious attempts to produce a committed Fascist literature. The commitment of the *Strapaesani*, however, was not to the real Fascism of the regime but to an idealized picture of heroic and uncorrupted rural or small-town virtue. As Maccari wrote, 'we have taken *seriously* several points that we hold, and that have been proclaimed, to be essential in Fascism: its Catholic and rural nature, its respect for the healthy traditions of popular sobriety and wisdom, its struggle against secret tyrannies, against corruption and the reign of *Affarismo*, its help for the honest. . . .'[128] To take the ideological affirmations of Fascism seriously was bound to lead to eventual disillusionment.

The reviews and writers of *Strapaese* were closely linked to Tuscan provincial Fascism. *Il Selvaggio* first appeared as the organ of the Fascists of the Val d'Elsa, an area on the borders between the provinces of Florence and Siena. Like Malaparte's *Conquista dello Stato*, it exalted the purity of provincial *squadrismo*. For the *Selvaggi*, the Fascist cudgel was a symbol of plebeian honesty, force and virility. The true people settled their disagreements not by argument but by blows. They believed in *squadrismo* as the motive force of a moral revolution which would restore honesty and sobriety to public life and the arts. The origins of the mythology of *Strapaese* go back to Soffici's pre-war novel, *Lemmonio Boreo*. Soffici can be said to have invented rural *squadrismo* in the sense in which D'Annunzio invented the March on Rome: his hero goes about Tuscany redressing wrongs with his cudgel and the help of an honest strong-arm man, the butcher Zaccagna, who wears a black shirt.[129] Soffici at first was the ideological mentor of *Strapaese*: he was probably the author of the statement of aims which appeared in *Il Selvaggio* in November 1927. It was pretty familiar stuff about the defence of the true Italian values, which were also regional and popular, against foreign and modern corruption.[130] Clearly *Strapaese* could serve as a vehicle for the worst kind of provincial chauvinism, of a sort which official ideology found very palatable. It gave, obviously, enthusiastic support to the official campaign against urbanization and for the birth rate. Where one finds the mystique of the simple, unspoilt people, anti-semitism is seldom far behind: Soffici defended the authenticity of the Protocols of the Elders of Zion.[131] However the younger writers of *Strapaese* did not follow slavishly the lead given by Soffici and the later writings of Papini. Malaparte, Maccari and Longanesi at first differed from them in style rather than content. Their models in literature and graphic art were the burlesque and the caricature. Under a dictatorship this spelt unorthodoxy and danger: satire is always subversive.

Both Maccari in *Il Selvaggio* and Longanesi in *l'Italiano* came to specialize in the mockery of established institutions and persons, in the deflation of the pomposities, pretensions and evasions of official culture: the two reviews became favourite reading for anti-Fascists. The belief of Maccari and his friends in the healthy traditions of popular sobriety and wisdom found an echo in the young writers like Berto Ricci, Romano Bilenchi and Vasco Pratolini, who contributed to the new journal of the Florentine Fascist federation, *Il Bargello*, launched in 1929. They believed in a populist form of Fascism, which would be based on the peasant and the artisan. Pratolini repeated the 'anti-bourgeois' slogans of the Fascism of the thirties and swallowed the old myth of the 'proletarian nation' when it was refurbished for the Ethiopian war. Eventually, however, he recognized the impossibility of giving Fascism a social content and his sympathies turned towards Communism. Pratolini was to become one of the leaders of literary neo-realism after the war, together with Elio Vittorini who had also contributed to *Il Bargello*.[132]

A similar connection can be traced in other arts. Alessandro Blasetti, who directed effective films of high propaganda content on the draining of the Pontine Marshes, on Garibaldi and on the Fascist 'old guard', was recognized by the neo-realists as a precursor. Although Maccari himself strongly disliked modern architecture, the interest in the traditional forms of rural building which was characteristic of *Strapaese* was shared by Pagano, one of the leaders of the 'rationalists'. A sincere commitment to tradition could serve as a standard by which to judge the deficiencies of official culture.[133]

By the late 1930s, the ideal of a spontaneous, self-regulating Fascist culture, acknowledging limits but not under total political control, had broken down. The regime, inspired by the example of Nazi Germany, deployed a vast bureaucratic effort to subordinate culture directly to the needs of political propaganda. This made it increasingly difficult for serious literature or art to survive : however it seems that the real success of the effort to master culture was in almost inverse proportion to its apparent extension. Where indifference and conformism reigned, even formal controls lost much of their efficacy.[134]

15

PROPAGANDA AND EDUCATION

The Press

The Fascist regime was prepared to allow a degree of liberty in the pursuit of those cultural activities whose political relevance was not immediate or obvious. But those circles in the universities, or among artists and writers, whose ideas were unfavourable to the regime, were isolated from the public by the strict control established over the main channels of information. Of these, the Press was the object of by far the greatest attention. The newspapers were undoubtedly important centres of political power and in addition Mussolini's own journalistic career gave him a particular interest in the control of the Press. In this field, his attention to detail was minute and unremitting; the time which he devoted to the scrutiny of newspapers and periodicals was excessive, and distracted him from more important problems.

During 1922–4 the Press was controlled by informal methods. The Prime Minister's Press Office, directed by Cesare Rossi, was an institution of great political importance. The chief way in which Rossi extended Fascist influence over the Press was by fixing up deals with groups of financiers to purchase newspapers for the Government. This was necessary since the party press, including the *Popolo d'Italia*, had a very limited circulation. Perhaps Rossi's most important success was in arranging the purchase of the Milan radical newspaper *Il Secolo* by a group of industrialists headed by Borletti and Cesare Goldmann.[1] The paper had played an important part in the campaign against the Acerbo Bill; under its new editor, the nationalistic Giuseppe Bevione, it became entirely subservient to Fascism. The creation of the *Corriere Italiano*, which was first controlled by Finzi and later by Rossi himself, was financed by a large consortium consisting of the Fiat, Ilva and Terni firms and the shipping magnate Odero.[2] However Rossi's policy ultimately backfired. The revelation after the murder of Matteotti of the atmosphere of sordid intrigue surrounding the *Corriere Italiano* and the *Nuovo Paese* was damaging to Fascism. All Italian governments had tried to control the Press both through direct subsidies and through bargains with the owners : that Mussolini and Rossi should do so was only natural. But their action took on a different meaning in the political context of 1923-4, when papers which opposed or criticized Fascism were subjected to all kinds of intimidation. A number of newspaper offices were occupied by the squads during the March on Rome, and some were only able to resume publication after they had accepted the conditions posed by the local *ras*.[3] In general, the provincial press enjoyed little liberty after the March. The newspapers which supported the Government, such as the *Giornale d'Italia*, found that they were expected to suppress not only 'unfavourable' comment, but unwelcome news, in accordance with the constant flow of instructions which issued from the Ministry of the Interior and the Press Office.[4]

However the major opposition newspapers, as we have seen, survived. Even the Socialist press, in spite of the smashing of its printing presses and the beating of its subscribers, struggled on. In the latter half of 1924, after the murder of Matteotti, the circulation of *Avanti!* still exceeded that of the *Popolo d'Italia*. The *Mondo*, the *Stampa* and the *Corriere della Sera*, though they might have to mute their criticisms, preserved a wider circulation than any of the Fascist newspapers.[5]

Mussolini made a definite concession to his Liberal allies by suspending the publication of the decree on press censorship passed by the Cabinet in July 1923. It was only a year later that the Government finally issued the decree to counteract the growing volume of press attacks after the murder of Matteotti. The decree allowed the Prefect to 'warn' any editor who 'damaged the credit of the nation at home or abroad', 'aroused unjustified alarm in the public', published 'false or tendentious news', incited class hatred or disobedience to the law, etc. ; an editor who was warned twice inside a year could be dismissed by the Prefect, who also had the right to refuse permission for the appointment of a successor, and thus in effect to suppress the newspaper or periodical concerned. A separate decree gave the Prefects the right to sequestrate any issue of a newspaper which committed one of the offences detailed above. Whereas in the case of the more severe 'warning'procedures the Prefect had to consult a committee consisting of one magistrate and one journalist, he could order sequestration on his own responsibility.[6] This may be one reason why the Prefects at first made sparing use of their power to warn and preferred the less radical measure of confiscation ; the journalists' representative was to be nominated by the local press association, and these were still mostly controlled by anti-Fascists. In the autumn of 1923, the attempted takeover of the national Press Association by the Fascist Journalists' Union had been blocked when their candidate for the presidency, Enrico Corradini, had been defeated by Bergamini.[7] A number of press associations had protested vigorously against the new decree.[8] The general political situation during the Matteotti crisis also dictated caution ; a circular from Federzoni advised the Prefects accordingly. His interpretation probably disappointed the party, who hoped for a more ruthless application of the sanctions. Even the weapon of sequestration was chiefly used against the Socialist and Communist press, or against periodicals with a restricted circulation; the major newspapers of the constitutional opposition remained relatively immune.[9]

This immunity was abruptly curtailed by the repressive measures taken on 31 December and on subsequent days.[10] During 1925, the opposition press existed on sufferance, harassed by prefectoral sequestrations and party boycotts. The Fascist offensive to secure complete control over the Press developed three lines of attack simultaneously: legislative controls, party intimidation and agreement with the newspaper proprietors over the heads of editors and journalists. These methods were complementary; when the positive inducement of the regime's friendship was insufficient, the proprietors were pressured into submission by threats of forcible closure and the destruction of their property, while the struggle with official censorship became increasingly futile and costly. In the last months of 1925 the leading Liberal papers fell victim to these pressures. Mussolini later justified his abolition of the freedom of the Press by the argument that the newspapers had been the instruments of the outside financial interests which owned or subsidized them.[11] But in the case of the two chief Liberal newspapers, the *Corriere* and the *Stampa*, it was Fascism which destroyed the independent position of the editors and established a monopoly of ownership and legal control in the hands of the industrialists. The majority shareholding in the *Corriere* belonged to the Crespi brothers, Milanese textile manufacturers who sympathized with Fascism: but Albertini was a co-owner, with voting rights equal to theirs, and they had no power to get rid of him. In November 1925, however, after an ultimatum from Farinacci, they found a legal pretext for declaring the contract invalid and bought out his share.[12] Senator Frassati, the editor of the *Stampa*, had a majority shareholding, and the suspension of the paper for six weeks was necessary to convince him to surrender. Agnelli, who had previously had a minority shareholding, became the sole owner.[13]

The new Press Law of 31 December 1925 codified the substance of the earlier decrees. In one respect, surprisingly, it was more liberal, since it took the initiative of the 'warning' out of the hands of the Prefect and entrusted it to the public prosecutor. In fact, Federzoni found it necessary to explain that the new law did not limit the Prefect's traditional discretion in sequestrating newspapers which might cause a disturbance of public order. Administrative and police power were supplemented but not superseded by the new legislative framework.[14]

The most novel and radical provision of the 1925 law was the institution of an Order of Journalists. This measure, inspired by the corporative ideas of Rocco, made possible the total control of all journalism by the regime, since only those inscribed on the rolls of the Order would be allowed to exercise their profession. The effect of the measure, however, was not immediate; the rolls were not drawn up until February 1928. The time-lag was probably due to the need to strengthen the Fascist Journalists' Union and to collect information before proceeding to a definite purge. The Fascist Union, although membership remained voluntary, supervised admission to the Order through regional committees set up for the purpose.[15] Rocco's measures for the organization and control of journalism were, typically, modelled on the structure of the legal profession. He even created a 'higher court of justice', the Commissione Superiore della Stampa, as a counterpart to the lawyers' disciplinary tribunal. The Commissione was composed of journalists, not magistrates, and so Rocco claimed that 'it realizes both the autonomy of the class and its link with the State'; however Rocco himself, as Minister of Justice, nominated its members.[16] He thus realized his ideal of organizing the free professions into rigid, exclusive bodies, subject to a judicial discipline exercised by members of their own class, but under the control of the State.

However the new apparatus of control did not mean the end of conflict over the organization of the Press. 1927–8 saw a sustained campaign by the Journalists' Union, acting in unison with the party, to purge the newspapers of former anti-Fascists and to obtain a monopoly of editorial posts for their own members. But the owners and editors turned to Mussolini for protection against these pressures; they urged the claims of skill, continuity and solvency against those of political loyalty. Official doctrine recognized the need for two different types of newspaper: alongside 'the Fascist Press ... the political instrument of the regime', there was room for the existence of 'a national press which operates within the orbit of the State'.[17] This distinction meant that the position of the former 'independent' newspapers still remained distinct from that of the Press directly controlled by the party. The Journalists' Union urged that the owners of the independent papers should be expropriated; the secretary of the Union, Amicucci, wrote that it would be unjust to expel anti-Fascist journalists without also removing the proprietors, 'anti-Fascists themselves and often these principally responsible for a political line contrary to the Revolution and the Regime'.[18] But the movement's demands for total control and orthodoxy were unsuccessful: the position of the plutocracy remained unshaken. Reasons of economy still made it imperative that the burden of financing the Press should not fall entirely on Government and party; consequently control over the most important papers remained in the hands of industrial groups which had exercised it before Fascism. They were still able to use their papers to influence government patronage and economic policy; old Fascists complained that the regime allowed the Press to serve as the instrument of a new 'plutocratic *ras*-ism'.[19]

In the provinces, an increasing number of papers were brought under the direct control of the party federations between 1926–8. By the end of the decade nearly two-thirds of the daily newspapers outside the big cities were owned by the PNF. At the same time, the number of weekly or monthly periodicals published by the federations or the *fasci* was sharply reduced in the interests of economy and of easier political control.[20] The author of this policy of rationalization, which naturally often met with local party resistance, was Arnaldo Mussolini, who had criticized Farinacci for not tackling the problem.[21] But the new policy was only partially successful. The problem of quality remained : the local party press continued to be poorly written and produced,[22] and the political climate encouraged an ever more cautious conformity. Moreover, the party's assumption of control over more important newspapers, with large resources and a wide circulation, revealed these inadequacies still more clearly. The party showed grave deficiencies in the financial as well as the journalistic management of its newspapers. The *Mattino* at Naples was so badly managed that its entire capital was dissipated in the space of two years after the party had assumed direct control. The Bank of Naples, which had been induced by party pressure to loan the money needed to buy out the former owners, the Scarfoglio brothers, was forced to appoint its own officials to manage the business side of the paper. The outlook was so bad that overtures were even made to induce the Scarfoglio brothers to return.[23]

The demands of integral 'fascistization' and political uniformity inevitably conflicted with those of readability. In the case of the leading newspapers, Mussolini at first showed a certain concern that something of their distinctive style and character should be preserved in order not to alienate their traditional public. In the *Stampa* a conflict soon developed between the editor, Andrea Torre (formerly a Liberal deputy), and the owner, Agnelli. Torre complained that he had been put in an impossible position because Agnelli refused to allow him any say in the business and technical management of the paper, and even exercised direct control over the literary pages and the news services, arguing that Torre's responsibility was solely for the political side. Agnelli replied that Mussolini had ordered him 'to keep the paper on a line which would make it acceptable to its readers, especially those of the working class whom Fascism wanted to acquire above all others. ...' 'You, however ... acted in such a way, especially in the dispositions imparted to the journalists, as to lower the paper to the level of those which by living on eulogies and plagiarism lose their authority and lower their circulation without being of any use to the regime.'[24] This crushing retort was probably well-founded. Torre had to resign, and his successor was an unquestioned Fascist, Malaparte. He probably owed his appointment to the patronage of the PNF secretary Turati, who succeeded his protégé in 1931. In spite of being a party appointment, Malaparte found no difficulty in establishing good relations with Agnelli ; but his sarcastic and rebellious personality made him many enemies, and he was a more successful editor from a journalistic than a political point of view. Intelligence and independence were risky qualities, even in the hands of a Fascist.

Fascist journalists with the brilliance of a Malaparte were in any case few : the regime could not dispense with the assistance of highly trained professional journalists who had made their career in the free press. The most influential editorships were held either by nationalist publicists of long standing like Virginio Gayda and Giuseppe Bevione, or else by men like Ugo Ojetti or Luigi Barzini Sr. whose adherence to Fascism had remained doubtful until 1925. At the *Corriere*, the party's dislike of Ojetti contributed to his removal from the editorship in December 1927. His successor was an orthodox Fascist, M.Maffii, who had been head of Mussolini's Press Office in 1924–5 ; however his abilities were not up to the job, and in 1929 he was succeeded by Aldo Borelli, who remained editor till 1943.[25] Borelli had joined Fascism earlier than Ojetti, but he too had made his reputation as a Liberal polemicist. Even Mario Missiroli, one of the leading critics of Fascism up till 1924, found a protector in Arpinati. He was the author of the most persuasive eulogies of the Duce's social and religious policies, although it seems that Mussolini never entirely forgave him for his remarks during the Matteotti crisis. The literary pages, where a greater degree of liberty was allowed, were often the object of special editorial attention and some maintained a high standard in spite of the exclusion of those writers who were too openly unfavourable to the regime. The survival of pre-Fascist men and styles no doubt served Fascism better both at home and abroad than a more rigid ideological purism would have done. One striking concession made by Mussolini was the permission given to *Il Lavoro* of Genoa to resume publication after it had been suppressed. It was the organ of the group of CGL leaders who had made their peace with the regime, and it employed a number of well known anti-Fascists.[26] Mussolini presumably hoped that *Il Lavoro* would help to overcome working-class distrust of the regime, but it does not seem that the experiment was very successful. The Catholic press preserved a more lasting importance. Few Catholic dailies survived, but their periodicals, often directly controlled by the bishops, remained numerous.

At the outset, then, Mussolini seemed to perceive the advantages of diversity. But none the less 'the reign of boredom and uniformity'[27] gained ground, and the man most responsible was Mussolini himself. His Press Office, now under Lando Ferretti, expanded its functions rapidly during the years 1926–8. Besides serving as Mussolini's personal instrument for censorship and patronage, the Press Office was the nucleus out of which the Fascist propaganda ministry (the Ministry of Popular Culture) grew in the mid-thirties.[28] Voices in the party demanding the right of criticism were silenced, and the party press became increasingly standardized, enjoying little liberty in choice or treatment of topics. Amicucci and the Journalists' Union actively promoted this development : in his memo of November

1927[29] Amicucci wrote that 'the Union, which boasts of being the political instrument of the regime at the orders of the Duce and the party, does not associate itself with the campaign which some newspapers have launched in favour of greater freedom of criticism'. He asked that the Press Office should give journalists more careful instructions, since at the moment 'they often have to trust to good sense and flair to avoid dangerous gaffes'. The conformist mentality could hardly be better illustrated. Even the non-party papers were more and more restricted by a flow of instructions which often became obsessive in their detail. In September 1928 the Press Office issued a code of conduct which all newspapers were expected to follow. The restrictions did not only relate to political news: optimism and the concealment of disagreeable facts became obligatory in a number of other fields. News of air and rail disasters and bank failures was to be restricted and even natural catastrophes were to be treated 'with great sobriety'. For 'the moralization and education of the masses', Mussolini personally ordered 'the demobilization of the crime column, with particular reference to news of suicides, tragedies of passion, violence and sexual crimes against minors'.[30]

Il Tevere, edited by Telesio Interlandi, performed a special function of some interest. It was inspired directly by Mussolini and it was encouraged to air themes and views (e.g. anti-semitism) on which he did not wish to commit himself officially. He spoke with two voices, cautious, official, opportunistic in the *Popolo d'Italia* and the rest of the obedient flock marshalled by the Press Office: extremist, unrestrained and speculative in *Il Tevere*. He regarded *Il Tevere* as his own personal, unofficial organ, just as the *Popolo d'Italia* was his official one, and for this reason its opinions had always to be treated with respect by the other papers. The role of *Il Tevere* in cultural questions was particularly important; a writer condemned in its columns as lacking the true Fascist spirit was in serious trouble.[31] This type of informal control exercised through *Il Tevere* (and to a lesser degree some of the other extremist papers) was of great importance in creating a climate of anxiety in which journalists wrote only what they knew to be safe.

Compared with the Press, the other media in the 1920s still had relatively little importance for propaganda. The first radio stations were set up in 1924–5 and the number of radio sets licensed was only about 100,000 by the end of the decade. Most of these were concentrated in the industrial triangle, and round Rome and Naples. Only with the great expansion in 1934–5 did the radio assume the leading place as an instrument of propaganda. It then made possible a new atmosphere: the range and constancy of the charismatic relationship between the Duce and his audience could be immensely extended. Totalitarianism implies the creation of a single public: in the Italy of the twenties the technical conditions for such a state of affairs did not exist. Large sections of the population were illiterate, and modern methods of communication were still little developed.[32]

The propaganda uses of film, however, were already obvious in the twenties.

Party and State collaborated in the creation of the Istituto Nazionale Luce for the production of documentary films. All cinemas were obliged by the law of 3 April 1926 to show its newsreels with every performance; the projection of the Institute's longer educational and propaganda films was also obligatory. These last covered such subjects as 'Our war', the Militia, the *Balilla*, the *Dopolavoro*, the Opera Nazionale for the protection of Maternity, etc.[33] Feature films, however, were not yet used for propaganda, and were subject only to negative controls through censorship exercised by the Ministry of the Interior. Here again, the early thirties saw a change; state intervention, however, was not so much the result of conscious planning as of the financial crisis which had brought the Italian film industry to a standstill. It was only after State assistance had been invoked by producers, directors and performers that the regime began to show an effective interest in the production of ideological feature films. At the same time, the Public Security Law of 1931 created a more complicated apparatus of control for both theatre and cinema; the censorship committees, previously entirely bureaucratic, now contained representatives of the party and its satellite organizations. None the less, the methods of censorship continued to be haphazard and often dependent on Mussolini's personal whims.[34]

An account of Fascist propaganda would not be complete without mention of the growing regimentation of leisure activities. It was in this field, where measures of social welfare and control went hand in hand, that the policy of Fascism made the greatest impact on large numbers of people. This was an area, too, where the party retained an important function after 1926, working through its various auxiliary organizations, the *Dopolavoro*, the *Balilla*, the *Avanguardia*, and the *Fasci Femminili*.[35] The most extensive of all these organizations was the *Dopolavoro* (After-Work). Until 1925–6 the office for the *Dopolavoro*, controlled first by the party and then the corporations, had only a modest importance. Like the Fascist unions, it grew by the forcible absorption of pre-existing Socialist associations. In 1925 the *Dopolavoro* became an official para-State institution, and it grew rapidly after the foundation of the corporate order. In 1926 it still had only 280,000 members (over half among railwaymen and postmen): in 1927, 440,000; by 1930, 1,400,000. In the cities, where the Socialist associations had usually resisted incorporation, the *Dopolavoro* founded new circles which it controlled more rigidly than those which it had taken over from the Socialists. The *Dopolavoro* also absorbed the *circoli aziendali* (company clubs) which had been founded by various industrialists for their workers and employees.

The *Dopolavoro* was probably the most effective instrument of the regime for penetrating the working class; it met a real need. It was especially successful in attracting young workers; this was the age in which the working classes took to sport on a large scale, and Fascism was able to exploit the generation gap as it had earlier done among the middle classes. In the South, the *Dopolavoro*, like the Fascist unions, was a real innovation: previously no associations had existed except the circles where the notables played cards. Apart from sport, the *Dopolavoro* circles procured cheap theatre tickets, organized tours, etc. If control of the Press was one of the germs out of which the propaganda apparatus of the thirties grew, the *Dopolavoro* can be considered to be the other. It was within the *Dopolavoro* that an office for 'popular culture' was first created.[36]

Organized recreation served several purposes; first, the real advantages of cheap excursions, youth camps and subsidized seaside holidays were good material for the propaganda of the regime abroad: second, these initiatives aimed to imprint upon the popular mind (and especially on youth) an impression of the beneficence and ubiquity of the regime: third, they could be used as channels and instruments for direct political propaganda and for reinforcing social discipline. Apart from these forms of recreation, directly inspired by the State or the movement, the whole field of sport was the object of an increasing effort of co-ordination and patronage. The regime and its local leaders were quick to perceive the advantages of identification with the new heroes of football and cycling.[37] By a decree of 2 March 1927 all sporting associations were placed under the control of the National Olympic Committee (CONI), which was appointed by the Government. Arpinati became the president of the Football Federation.[38] Like most modern dictatorships, the regime was lavish in its encouragement of sport and achieved some notable successes.

Education: Universities, Schools and the Youth Movement

One feature of the original Fascist ideology which remained strong was the belief in youth. It was to the new generation that Mussolini and the Fascist leaders looked for the realization of the totalitarian ideal. The conquest of the schools and the universities therefore became an objective of the highest importance to the regime; during the period 1927–31 the party and other institutions made a determined effort to transform the educational system to serve the needs of propaganda. However the situation was complicated by the fact that a major reform of the educational structure had already been carried out by Gentile in 1923. This reform was a 'work of the regime', which it was embarrassing to repudiate; but it was not designed to serve the crude needs of a totalitarian system.

The structure of the Italian educational system had been determined by the *Legge Casati* of 1859. By the beginning of this century, the need for far-reaching reforms was evident, and the Giolittian period saw a lively debate on the functions and methods of the Italian schools. The leading role in the debate was assumed by the new teachers' associations, founded by Socialists and Democrats.[39] The Socialists concentrated their attention on the elementary schools and the fight against illiteracy; they regarded the secondary schools as the province of the bourgeoisie. But at the same time growing numbers of children from families of the lower middle class and the upper strata of the working class and peasantry began to seek the advantages of secondary education. Even the 'classical school' (*ginnasio* and *liceo*) was affected by this influx. Numbers rose and the standard of teaching suffered.[40] In the secondary schools, the revolt of the idealist philosophers against positivism had great importance in modifying the climate of opinion. Even Democrats like Salvemini favoured a more vigorous process of selection to weed out the unqualified, and admitted that this would inevitably tend to restrict the access of the lower classes to higher education. Nevertheless the idealists accused democracy and positivism of being together responsible for the decadence of education and the consequent failure to form a cultured ruling class.[41] Gentile's educational philosophy attacked determinist psychological theories, fixed rules of pedagogical technique, and the 'encyclopaedic' concept of learning as the acquisition of a certain number of facts in the name of spontaneity and the community between teacher and pupil. He gathered a small band of devoted disciples, who responded with enthusiasm to his appeal for the restoration of true human and cultural values. At first sight, Gentile's criticisms might seem to have a great deal in common with 'progressive' theories of education which stressed the need for active participation by the pupil in the process of learning. In fact he and his pupils did make a genuine effort to introduce methods which would encourage the pupil to develop his own capacities and interests, e.g., by replacing manuals with original texts.[42]

However Gentile's frequent invocation of liberty as the guiding principle of education was in some respects deceptive. Liberty, according to his idealist premises, consisted in the development of the individual's true self, which must be in harmony with the whole formed by the historically created institutions of the nation : he rejected the false 'empirical' concept of liberty as signifying the free choice of the pupil.[43] A significant debate took place at the Secondary Schoolteachers' Congress of 1907 between Salvemini and Gentile. Salvemini argued that the task of education was to teach a critical frame of mind and that this could be only done if different schools of thought were allowed to contend. Against him, Gentile reiterated his conviction that education must be unified by a single vision or philosophy. Education for him was an almost religious process of initiation. He had no love for the experimental method.[44] Gentile's own vision was conservative. He defended with intransigence the privileged status of the classical school, while his antipathy for the natural sciences prevented him from acknowledging their growing importance and intellectual function. There was something pure and sincere in his missionary insistence that the essential purpose of education was to form men and not merely to teach useful techniques, but the reforms which he urged had the effect of making the divorce between the principles of higher education, designed to form the ruling class, and those which governed the vocational schools for the masses, more absolute than before. The unifying vision of the enlightened bourgeoisie or elite was to be philosophical : but for the people, whose education stopped at fourteen, the teaching of religion was once more to have the central place. This was the old reactionary belief that religion was a good thing for the people, dressed up in Hegelian clothes. Gentile's programme failed to take into account the development of Italian society, and particularly the growing importance of technical, managerial and scientific requirements in an industrial society.[45] There was a contradiction between Gentile's educational thought and his political thought after 1925, and in fact the introduction of religion into the elementary schools was to have unforeseen consequences which his theory of the State could only view as disastrous.

The idealists accused Italian education of two principal failures: first that it had failed to select and form a qualified elite, because the higher schools and universities had lost sight of their cultural mission and had been degraded into a machine for supplying diplomas and certificates to a horde of petty-bourgeois status seekers; second, that at all levels the schools had failed to strengthen the sentiment of nationality, thanks to the positivist belief that education should be ideologically neutral and concerned only with the teaching of factual knowledge.[46] The war sharpened the divisions among the teaching profession. Patriotic sentiment was mobilized against those teachers who refused to admit the supremacy of national values. The elementary school-teachers' association, the Unione Magistrale, had always been dominated by the anti-clerical left wing of Radicals, Republicans and Socialists. In 1916, however, following attacks in the Nationalist press, the interventionist left overthrew the Socialist leadership at the Congress of Bologna. Gioacchino Volpe saw in this conversion of the Union, formerly a Nationalist *bête noire*, to patriotism, a decisive proof that the war was effectively destroying the anti-thesis between class and nation.[47] The secondary school teachers were less seriously affected by the war since the democratic interventionists were in the majority from the beginning. However the leaders of their association also came under heavy fire after Caporetto, when they criticized the excesses of Nationalist propaganda.[48] A more serious division took place after the war. The idealists, led by Ernesto Codignola and Balbino Giuliano, accused the association of surrendering to the trade union mentality and of limiting its activity to the defence of the teachers' economic interests. They founded their own group, the *fascio di educazione nazionale*, which eventually seceded from the federation. The *fascio* (the name had nothing to do with Fascism) was entirely identified with the educational philosophy of Gentile, and its leading personalities were Giuseppe Lombardo Radice and Ernesto Codignola.[49] They saw the task of Italian education as that of remedying the moral and political failings revealed by the war. Codignola saw the 'mutilated victory' as a result of the democratic ideology transmitted by the schools.

We have lost the best fruits first of our intervention and then of victory because the war found us spiritually unprepared, ignorant of the elementary conditions of the internal and international political contest ... poisoned by the ideologies we breathed in the schools and outside during the years of our mental formation, by the myths of humanitarian pacifism, of the war for democracy, of unproductive expenditure, of the national rights of small, helpless peoples . . . of the Wilsonian peace.

The decadence of Italian education was, he believed, the result of the invasion of the high schools by a new class of pupils from petty-bourgeois, artisan and skilled working-class families, who were incapable of acquiring true culture. To restore the seriousness of Italian education, it was necessary to 'chase the plebeian clientele back to the hoe and the servile labours for which it was born'.[50]

The antipathy to the organization of class interests, the conviction that only a strong state could overcome parliamentary confusion, bureaucratic obstruction and favouritism, and put into effect a policy of rational severity, and above all their bitter feelings of nationalistic disillusionment, led the men of the *fascio* and Codignola in particular to welcome the advent of Fascism. About a month before the March on Rome, Camillo Pellizzi arranged a meeting between Codignola and Mussolini, as a result of which Codignola agreed to transform the *fascio* into a *gruppo di competenza* of the PNF.[51] This alliance between the idealist reformers and Fascism was sealed after the March by the appointment of Gentile as Minister of Education.

Although some Fascist intellectuals, such as Pellizzi and Agostino Lanzillo, were convinced supporters of Gentile's views on education, the party as a whole was indifferent or even hostile to the idealist point of view. The most important practical issue in educational reform was the question of the State examination. Both Croce and Gentile wanted the various types of high school to have a uniform final examination, judged by external examiners, in order to raise standards: this measure would also allow the private schools (of which the vast majority were controlled by the clergy) to compete on equal terms with those run by the State. Many Fascists regarded this as an abdication of the State's responsibilities and a surrender to the Church. The Congress of Naples passed a resolution proposed by De Stefani, asking the Fascist deputies to reject the State Examination Bill.[52] The aim of the State examination was in fact to lighten the burden on the State schools by relieving them of a large number of pupils who would now be able to obtain the professional qualifications which they desired from the private institutions.

Gentile's reform was 'more reactionary than Fascist', in the words of Piero Gobetti, once his admirer.[53] The deliberate tendency to reinforce class distinctions in secondary education was only in part acceptable to the Fascist movement. It was one thing to differentiate the schools designed for workers from those designed for the petty-bourgeoisie: but quite another to make access to the university harder for the latter class, or to demand that children of even the upper classes should have to pass difficult examinations before admission.

For the idealist intellectuals, the fate of Gentile's reforms was a test of the regime's ability to stand up to the 'demagogic' pressures exerted by the mass of the movement in favour of a relaxation of standards. The ideal of these intellectuals was a functionally stratified society presided over by a humanist elite. They were, however, a minority within Fascism. Particularly vocal opposition to the reforms came from the Futurists, and the average Fascist, particularly of the younger generation, must have found Marinetti's idea of education much more congenial. Futurists and philistines were agreed in depreciating theory and demanding that education should become more practical, with a greater emphasis on sport and on industrial techniques. The aim of education should be not to promote 'culture' but military strength and economic efficiency.[54] The students of the technical schools resented the higher social prestige which attached to humanist education and were naturally attracted to ideas of this kind. Between 1914 and 1922, in fact, the popularity of the humanist faculties of law and letters had declined, while there had been a great growth in the schools of engineering and commercial sciences, which gave access to industry. The Gentile reform, which made it virtually impossible to reach university from a technical college, tried with some success to reverse this trend.[55] Mussolini at first supported Gentile. He described the reform as 'the greatest revolutionary act which Fascism has dared to perform in its months of power', and as the necessary condition for the formation of the future Fascist ruling class.[56] However the reform interested him mainly as a means of raising the cultural prestige of Fascism and of demonstrating the ability of his government to pass legislation which had been held up by the inefficiency of Parliament. He seems to have shown little interest in the content of the reform and in its ideological implications. So long as Gentile remained Minister, dissent within the movement was suppressed in the name of discipline, but his resignation after the Matteotti murder gave his opponents their chance. From 1925 onwards the idealists fought a losing battle against the pressures of middle-class opinion to make examinations and courses easier. The regime and the party here showed a revealing weakness: by the failure to maintain the mechanisms of selection introduced by Gentile, they lost their credibility in the eyes of serious educators and students. There was a real dilemma in Italy between the necessity of selection imposed by scarce resources, and democracy: but Fascist education ended up by being neither selective nor democratic. The character of the secondary schools as 'automatic dispensers' of diplomas and certificates for the middle class was confirmed and accentuated.

This weakness reacted unfavourably on the Fascist drive, also starting in 1925, to make education into an instrument of ideological co-ordination, even though this aim also required modification of the reforms. The contrast between verbal ideological intransigence and a practical tendency to compromise made the process of 'fascistization' somewhat superficial. Codignola remarked that 'the most intransigent supporters of order and discipline for others are in practice the living testimony of arbitrary action and the constant violation of the law'; this was a clear reference to the interference of the party officials. Consequently, he said, 'we have been satisfied by appearances rather than by substance'.[57] What Gentile wanted was spontaneous discipline. Free culture and the totalitarian State were not, for him, incompatible : in his way he genuinely believed in both. His respect for cultural and scholarly achievement was something which obstinately resisted assimilation into his totalitarian political doctrine. Gentile's educational policy reflected these contradictions. The reform of education was to encourage at the same time individual initiative and national integration. In 1925–6 Gentile spoke of the need to make the schools Fascist in spirit ; Codignola saw the task of education as being that of internalizing the political unity which Mussolini had enforced.[58] However Gentile remained true to an ideal of culture as the free formation of the personality : he disliked direct political indoctrination and regarded it as ineffective. While impatient of the opinions of the young or the unlettered, he was sensitive to those of his own class, the high school and university people, and he knew what they would and would not stand. In subsequent years, many teachers held fast to the Gentile reforms as the best defence against the total subordination of education to propaganda.[59]

If the reforms which Gentile introduced into the content and methods of education did not directly assist political control, the same cannot be said of his administrative reforms. During the Giolittian period the teachers' associations had been successful both in improving their legal and economic status, and in obtaining the right to be consulted on educational policy. Conservatives and Nationalists reacted with marked hostility to this growth in the influence of the associations, since the latter were under Socialist or Democratic control. As for Gentile, he was determined that opposition from the teachers' associations should not be allowed to obstruct his reforms. For all its syndicalist pretensions, Fascism had no scruple about destroying those pre-existing institutions in which the representatives of a class were allowed to co-operate with the Government in preparing policy and legislation. The *gruppo di competenza* for education announced that one of the guiding principles of the reform would be the fight against 'demagogic electionism' ; in accordance with this the representatives of the teachers were eliminated from the advisory boards of the Ministry, which henceforward were composed entirely of ministerial nominees. Gentile took sanctions against leaders of the Unione Magistrale who criticized his policies, and ordered officials not to receive 'class representatives . . . who have shown themselves unworthy to speak in the name of the Italian schoolmasters'. The suppression of the elective principle did not only affect policy-making : it removed the safeguard of the teachers' independence, since they were no longer represented on the disciplinary boards. As their legal status was also modified to their disadvantage, the guarantees of teachers against arbitrary administrative action were severely reduced. Gentile himself was ready on at least one occasion to transfer a professor who was causing trouble to a local Fascist chief.[61]

The Fascist strategy, in this as in other fields, was to combine administrative pressure from above with the creation of rival organizations which, favoured by the State, would gradually attract the members of the old free associations. The Fascist Corporation of the School fulfilled this purpose : in October 1925 the Minister, Fedele, accepted its demands and refused to receive the representatives of the Catholic and democratic associations.[62] The law on the bureaucracy made it possible for the Fascists to carry out a purge of educational officials and teachers during 1926 ; the purge seems to have been on a larger scale than in other ministries.[63] In December 1925 Mussolini, speaking to the Corporation of the School, declared that 'the Government demands that the schools should be inspired by the ideals of Fascism : it demands that the schools should be, I will not say hostile, but not even foreign to Fascism or agnostic with regard to Fascism'.[64]

The Corporation of the School, headed by Acuzio Sacconi, had hoped to obtain an exclusive legal monopoly of the representation of all teachers from the elementary schools to the universities. But this ambition was incompatible with the ideas of Rocco, who did not regard it as legitimate for employees of the State to form syndicates or corporations. The Corporation was dissolved (together with the old democratic associations), and substituted by separate associations for primary and secondary schoolteachers under the control of the party. The teachers did not preserve even a nominal autonomy ; in this vital area of ideological control, the party acquired a position of hegemony even while elsewhere its prerogatives were being reduced.[65]

The regime could not, however, make all the teachers into Fascists. The primary schoolteachers had traditionally been on the left ; nevertheless the problem of 'fascistization' proved simpler in the elementary schools than in the secondary schools or universities. It was comparatively easy to find a replacement for a primary teacher, and this meant that there was greater pressure for conformity than at the higher levels of education, where there was a shortage of qualified men. Crude propaganda could be successful with children : but a certain intelligence and subtlety were needed for the indoctrination of adolescents.[66] However the regime made sure that there were reliable men at the top. 'The *provveditore* (inspector) . . . is a political official' ; this judgement could be extended also to the *presidi* (headmasters) and to the rectors of the universities. The authority of inspectors, headmasters and rectors was increased, and they were expected to exercise political surveillance over professors, teachers and even pupils. Political rather than educational merit was usually the criterion for promotion.[67]

The creation of the new Fascist man was not left to the schools. The youth organizations of the movement, which from 1922 to 1925 had lived uneasily in the shadow of the party, began in 1926 to take on a far greater importance. On 3 April 1926 they were united and given legal status under the name of the Opera Nazionale Balilla. The new institution, which comprised the *Balilla* for children aged 8–15, and the *Avanguardie* (15–18), plus the '*piccole italiane*' for girls, soon became a powerful instrument for the totalitarian regimentation of youth.[68] The ONB during 1927–8 was raised to a position of monopoly, in spite of strong resistance from the Vatican. On 12 January 1927 'additional clauses' of the law instituting the *Balilla* were published; these prohibited the creation of any new youth organization and dissolved all branches of the Catholic Boy Scouts except those in towns of more than 20,000 inhabitants. The cadres of the *Balilla* were drawn from the schoolteachers, and those of the *Avanguardie* from officers of the Militia (preferably also teachers).

In December 1927 a circular from Fedele recommended that all children should be enrolled in the *Balilla*,[69] and in April 1928 a new decree ordered the dissolution of all youth organizations except those of the ONB. In reality, however, Mussolini had to compromise with the Church, although the compromise was very favourable to Fascism. To obtain the resumption of the negotiations for the Concordat, he agreed to allow the youth circles of the Azione Cattolica 'with prevalently religious ends' to continue to exist: only the Boy Scouts, on account of their 'semi-military organization', were totally suppressed.[70]

One of the changes which Fascist writers had brought against Gentile was his neglect of physical education. The youth organizations aimed to remedy the deficiencies of the regular school system by a semi-military training based on drill, gymnastics and sport. The ONB was given exclusive control over physical education, and everything possible was done to raise the status of the PT instructor to a level with that of the other teachers. Fascist propagandists, irritated at the imperfections of indoctrination in the schools, boasted that the youth organizations embodied the true spirit of Fascist education and practised a new 'pedagogy' which was destined to exert an increasing influence.[71] It is easy to see why the disciplines of the parade ground and the gymnasium were more congenial to Fascism than those of the classroom. Besides its exclusive control over physical education, pre-military training and organized leisure, the youth movement was also supposed to carry out political and religious indoctrination. In the rallies of the ONB the cult of the Duce could be carried to greater lengths than even in the classroom. The techniques of military and political education, reinforced by rituals such as the swearing of an oath of total loyalty to the Duce, were fused to condition youth to the right attitudes of irrational submission. Future cadres were selected and given special training in the 'Dux' camps.[72]

The ONB had a tendency to expand and invade the fields of competence of other organizations. Its empire eventually embraced a wide variety of activities; it absorbed the Institutes for the Combat against Illiteracy, the Association for the Mezzogiorno, and even in 1934 took over the direct management of all rural schools with not more than twenty pupils.[73] The ONB, the bureaucracy of the Ministry of the Education, and the party were in fierce competition. In 1929 the ONB was technically placed under the Ministry of Education, but since its head, Renato Ricci, became Under-Secretary, the real effect of the measure was probably to increase its authority by removing it from party control. A serious conflict broke out in 1931 between Ricci and Scorza, who controlled the GUF for university students, and the *fasci giovanili* for youths of 18 to 21, who were not attending school or university. Ricci was formally dependent on the Ministry, Scorza on the party. In 1935 party and State bureaucracy clashed again, when the Minister of Education De Vecchi demanded control over the *Littoriali* (cultural competitions for students) and the 'courses of political culture' organized by the GUF and the party.[73] In no other field did the State bureaucracy feel so menaced by the interference of the party.

These conflicts existed also at the grassroots level, where at least in the secondary schools, tension and mutual dislike characterized the relationship between teachers and instructors of the ONB. The effects of this distrust would seem to have been rather contradictory. On the one hand, the youth organizations represented an instrument of pressure and surveillance which helped to intimidate the teachers and secure their conformity; on the other, they kept alive resentment against the party and the political ideology which it embodied. What is certain is that the morale of the teachers and the standards of education suffered. The activities of the youth movement helped to disorganize the curriculum and discourage serious study, thus adding to the effects of the emasculation of the State examination. Codignola protested in September 1928 that 'he who has the illusion that one can achieve a political education by parades . . . by distracting pupils and masters from their daily tasks, by the rhetoric of the meeting and, worse still, by police inquisition into the secrets of conscience, has nothing to do with Fascism, and is an *agent provocateur* who is digging a grave for the ideals which he claims that he wishes to diffuse'. This attack was clearly aimed at the youth movement, as was his reference in 1933 to 'imaginary political needs' which served as a pretext for the relaxation of discipline and study.[75]

The purge of the teachers was followed by a purge of texts. In 1928-9 the curricula began to be revised so as to give a much larger place to direct political indoctrination. In the elementary schools, the change was sweeping. On 24 February 1928, the Cabinet passed a decree ordering that all textbooks for history, geography, reading, economics and law used in the elementary schools and the 'supplementary courses' (aged 11 to 14) should respond to the 'requirements' of the new period inaugurated by the March on Rome.[76] This was only the prelude to a more radical measure introduced by the new Minister of Education, Belluzzo, on November 1928. A committee was set up to prepare a single State textbook whose use would be obligatory in all public elementary schools. In the new textbook every subject was used for propaganda, even music and arithmetic: the children learnt to sing Fascist hymns and their sums were illustrated by figures of the Balilla.[77]

In the secondary schools and the universities changes had to be more cautious because the regime, for the reasons mentioned, could not enforce such strict discipline on the teachers. Fascist spokesmen, however, redoubled their attacks on objectivity and impartiality. In the 1928 Congress of the Fascist Teachers' Association, Sacconi devoted part of his speech to an attack on Croce's history of Italy : 'Fascism has made an end of this culture and can no longer find any use for coldly scientific scholars, for men of erudition confined to the pedantic minutiae of their own cultural world. ...'[78] In 1929 Sacconi announced that the first priority in the 'battle' against the old school was to change the content of the curriculum. Already in 1928, 'the principles of the corporative order' had been introduced as a subject in the *licei* ; in 1930 the Fascist doctrine of the State was added. A less ambitious course in 'Fascist culture' was introduced in the technical schools.

The traditional subjects were modified more subtly so as to increase their nationalistic bias. Oriani and D'Annunzio became set texts for the study of Italian literature in 1930. The Fascist revision of the curriculum in both secondary and elementary schools accentuated the already strong emphasis on Roman history and the Risorgimento, at the expense of the study of ancient Greece and modern Europe. The teaching of history also prepared the background for the cult of the Duce ; in the new elementary school curriculum (introduced only in 1934) the first two courses dealt exclusively with heroes and great men.[79] Although history, philosophy and literature were the favourite subjects of the propagandist, even the physical sciences could be put to use : 'the teacher ... should know how to illustrate the demonstration of e.g., the theories of Galileo and Marconi with remarks designed to make evident the priority and the excellence of the Italian genius.'[80]

The effort to use education for propaganda was, however, by no means wholly successful even in the 1930s. The influence of the thoroughly 'fascistized' elementary schools on the mass of the population was limited by class solidarity, religion, and last but not least, by some inextinguishable residue of humanity and good sense. No doubt unquestioning faith in the Duce was widespread ; but many who believed in the Duce rejected the ideals of Fascism, or were simply ignorant of their existence. Fascist propaganda was far more successful among the middle classes ; it was, after all, their creation. But in the secondary schools many professors were able to maintain genuine independence of mind, and their criticism of the regime was often all the more effective for being implicit. In the universities, many students resisted 'fascistization' even though the social activities of the GUF (Gioventù Universitaria Fascista) made a great impact. Scorza in 1931 reported that while the regime had little to fear from the practically minded students of medicine and engineering, in the more intellectually ambitious faculties of law, letters and philosophy, 'the pernicious non-Fascist, and anti-Fascist action of the professors hostile to the regime' was still effective in contesting the influence of the party.[81] On the other hand, when in the same year the professors were required to take an oath of loyalty to the regime, only 11 out of 1,200 refused. If wholehearted commitment to Fascism was comparatively rare among university professors, so, clearly, was active opposition. The authoritarian structure of Italian universities and their traditional subordination to the State seem to have been effective in fostering a conformist mentality. It is true that it was possible for a professor to believe with a certain justification that it was more important to continue teaching than to make a sterile gesture of opposition, but the result of the oath was none the less an unquestionable propaganda success for the regime.

The idealists, although they might protest against the increasing attempt to apply crude political criteria to the study of history and philosophy, had themselves given a strongly nationalistic interpretation of the classical and humanist tradition. Codignola defended the pre-eminence of classical education by the argument that the knowledge of Latin and antique culture was essential to give Italians a proper sense of their own past, and thus save them from the hegemony of foreign culture and 'atomistic libertarian individualism'. Gentile's former personal secretary, F. E. Boffi, wrote that the education of teachers must be based on the classics because 'the whole of Fascism is a resurrection of *romanità*'.[82] It may be that the idealists emphasized the nationalist uses of classical education in part as a defence against their adversaries, who were demanding a more practical curriculum. Certainly Gentile never believed that the significance of classical culture could be subsumed under the concept of the Roman imperial mission, destined to be inherited by Italy; in the 1930s many teachers, including disciples of Gentile, were able to use the teaching of the classics as a means of exposing the shallowness and poverty of Fascist ideals. But it remains true that Gentile and his school have some responsibility in making the rhetoric of *romanità* intellectually respectable. Of course this rhetoric was nourished by plenty of other sources in academic life; the chief contribution came from the ancient historians and archaeologists, always ready to play up the relevance for contemporary Italian expansion of Roman monuments and conquests.[83] However the most distinguished classical historian in Italy, Gaetano De Sanctis, reacted vigorously against the trend. The advent of Fascism converted him to a committed view of history: he expressed his anti-Fascism through the defence of the values of Greek liberty and culture against the uncritical glorification of Roman imperialism. In spite of this, Gentile made him an editor of the classical section of the *Enciclopedia Italiana*, a striking example of that impartiality and tolerance which he often showed in his dealings with scholars.[84]

Even at the university level, Fascism could draw upon a well-established tradition of nationalist historiography. The 'unity of the history of Italy' from ancient Rome to Fascism: the polemic against Renaissance individualism and 'utilitarianism', held responsible for servitude to the foreigner: the denial of the European and liberal aspects of the Risorgimento, which was seen instead as the emancipation of national individuality from foreign influence, and as the preparation for a future mission of expansion: the political history of united Italy as a record of corrupt *trasformismo*, the decadence of parliamentarianism and the dissolution of the State, redeemed only by the solitary and misunderstood figure of Crispi : intervention as the new 'revolt of the ideal' against materialism, finally brought to fruition by Fascism : these were the essentials of the view of history which can be called 'national-Fascist'. Most of these clichés can be found in the works of authoritative nationalist historians such as Volpe, Solmi and Ercole, though it would be unfair to suggest that any one of these writers subscribed to all of them.[85]

On the whole, Fascism naturally frowned upon Marxist or sociological interpretations of history which minimized the role of the great man. However Volpe, the most coherent and talented of the nationalist historians, and also the officially recognized historian of Fascism, was rather exceptional in this respect. Before the war he had been one of the two leading pioneers (the other was Salvemini) of the economic interpretation of medieval history. This gave a certain force to his later claim to be the practitioner of a new political history, based, unlike the old, on an understanding of social and economic development. One can see a parallel here with Rocco's political and legal theory. Volpe's history, like Rocco's State, was to overcome the deficiencies of liberalism by comprehending the social and economic sphere within the purview of the political vision.[86]

From 1922 on, Volpe put his very considerable talents as a historian unreservedly at the service of Fascism. He edited the *Archivio storico per la Corsica*, which was created at the desire of Mussolini with the intention of furthering the idea of the island's *italianità* : he published a history of the Fascist movement : and his best known work, *Italia in Cammino*, was centred on the idea of expansion. Retrospectively, he tried to give political relevance even to his medieval studies ; in 1922 he republished his book on medieval heresies with an introduction which drew the parallel between millenarianism and modern social agitations.[87] However, except partially in his book on Fascism, Volpe never abandoned scholarly standards. Moreover, like Gentile in his field, Volpe helped to keep open the possibility of free and independent research. He interceded on behalf of Nello Rosselli, the brother of Cosimo, the founder of *Giustizia e Libertà*, and his interest in the economic interpretation of history led him even to protect historians who made little secret of their Marxist sympathies. The major rift in Italian historical writing was that between the idealist and materialist schools, and this did not at all coincide with the distinction between Fascism and anti-Fascism ; Salvemini and Croce, Volpe and Gentile were opposed in methodology but allied in politics. This helped to preserve for scholars the freedom to write as they wished.

A new Fascist interpretation of history, as distinct from the older nationalist tradition, did not emerge. There were a few attempts to fuse nationalism with populism to serve as the basis of such an interpretation : there was a new sympathy for the reactionary popular risings of the *sanfedisti* during the French domination of Italy, and in the 1930s the cult of the popular hero Garibaldi was again encouraged, at the expense of the nationalists' hero Cavour.[88] In 1934 the Quadrumvir De Vecchi took over the Institute for the History of the Risorgimento and proceeded, in peremptory barrack-room style, to lay down guidelines for the writing of history,[89] but this only served to alienate scholars from Fascism. Among younger historians, the influence of Croce's *History of Italy*, which challenged the nationalist interpretation of the post-Risorgimento, was profound.[90] Although the regime made research more difficult, there was no fundamental break in the development of Italian scholarship, as the career of a man like Chabod will demonstrate.

In the social sciences direct efforts were made to introduce the teaching of Fascist ideas into the university. The University of Rome led the way, under the 'Fascist rectorate' of G. Del Vecchio ; Forges Davanzati taught political science, the rector himself taught corporate law, and there were courses in Fascist culture.[91] The lawyers and the economists both took up the study of the corporative order ; the development of Italian economics was seriously affected by this trend. The regime also profited from one of the omissions of the liberal university system. In 1922, there were no faculties or even regular courses of political science, although a special Institute existed in Florence, intended primarily for future diplomats and colonial administrators. The regime therefore had *carte blanche* in drawing up the curriculum for the new subject, and the faculties of political science were designed exclusively for the teaching of Fascist principles. The fact that the most distinguished contributions to Italian political science had been made by the elitists Mosca and Pareto also assisted this aim and gave the courses some intellectual content. Mosca's German disciple Roberto Michels, a convert from socialism to Fascism, taught political science at Perugia, the most important centre of the new discipline.[92] However he was an exception : the new faculties were mainly staffed by party men and other mediocrities.

Several conflicting ideals of culture had existed within Fascism during the 1920s. Futurism, Gentile's actualism, the ruralism of Maccari's *Selvaggio* : all these were visions of life which could be identified with Fascism. But none of these 'won' ; nor can it be said that they were simply silenced by the demands of political propaganda. The uncertainty and fear of change which underlay the revolutionary slogans still uttered by Mussolini and his lieutenants were reflected in all cultural fields by the submission to prevailing standards of taste, by a growing intolerance of the new, the critical, or the shocking. The *arrivistes* who had crowded into the Fascist movement had now arrived ; and they did not like to be disturbed. Their preference for the safe and the known was reinforced by the growing influence of clericalism.

At the same time the Fascists, and Mussolini in person, could not altogether repudiate their original identification with the modern, and with the irrationalist faith in action. Youth was still encouraged to believe in the original mystique of Fascism, but got little encouragement for its confused and rebellious aspirations towards a 'true' Fascism from the adult world.[93] However one should not underrate the enthusiasm which Fascism could evoke in the 1930s. Nationalism, reinforced by the idea of a crusade against the corrupt democracies, could absorb a part of the dissatisfactions denied outlet at home. The 'dynamic' of Fascism was only finally broken when the hollowness of Mussolini's military pretensions was revealed.

16

THE REGIME

The Catholic Church

Mussolini was an atheist, from the most anti-clerical region in Italy. The first pamphlet he ever wrote was called 'God does not exist'. Even after he had left the Socialist party, his attacks on the Vatican and the priests continued for some years with equal vehemence.[1] Many early Fascists were also distinguished by their hatred of the Church; Marinetti in 1919 had called for the 'de-Vaticanization' of Italy, and the most notorious of Italian anti-clerical publicists, Guido Podrecca, stood on the Fascist electoral list. Nor was anti-clericalism a feature confined to the Fascism of 1919; large sectors of the patriotic petty-bourgeoisie and middle class who formed the backbone of the mass movement were still faithful in this respect to the traditions of the Risorgimento left. Extreme patriotism and anti-clericalism were, indeed, still naturally associated. The emergence of a new Catholic nationalism, apparent during the Libyan war, had been obscured by the events of 1914–18, when the Vatican again came under suspicion of favouring the enemies of the nation. Although a number of good Catholics joined the Fascist movement out of a fear of socialism, the typical Fascist enthusiast ranked the priest only a short way after the Socialist agitator in his list of enemies.

However Mussolini was too great a realist not to see the necessity of coming on terms with the Church. Religion remained utterly alien to him. But as a connoisseur of collective psychology he could not fail to appreciate the force of the Church. In his first speech to Parliament in June 1921, Mussolini declared that 'Fascism does not preach and does not practise anti-clericalism', and hinted at his interest in a settlement of the Roman question.[2] His immediate aim during the years 1921–5 was to outflank the Popolari by demonstrating that his defence of Catholic interests made their existence unnecessary. On the other side, the dignitaries of the Church were ready to respond to his overtures. They might dislike and fear the Fascists, but they disliked and

416

feared the Socialists more. In addition, the old running feud with the Liberal State, though much diminished in intensity, had not been forgotten. The authoritative *Civiltà Cattolica*, the organ of the Jesuits, underlined the continuity between Liberal and Socialist error, in perfect agreement with the Nationalist theses of Alfredo Rocco. The new Fascist accent on 'hierarchy' or authority was equally in accord with traditional Catholic thinking.[3]

The succession of Pope Pius XI to the Papal tiara in March 1922 helped the rapprochement between the Church and Fascism. The new Pope's ideas had been formed by the conservative traditions of Milanese Catholicism, which were favourable to a conciliation between Church and State and hostile to the intransigent Catholic Democrats.[4] He was prepared, therefore, to listen to the insinuations of Nationalists and Fascists who represented Don Sturzo and his party as the main obstacle to a satsifactory settlement. One should not exaggerate this point or anticipate developments which only matured slowly under the pressure of events ; when he ordered Don Sturzo to surrender in 1923, Pius XI was probably more influenced by fear of immediate Fascist violence than by calculations of future advantage. However the various initiatives taken by the Government in favour of the Church made a good impression. Mussolini proved his respect for the Church during his first eighteen months in office by the restoration of the crucifix in schools and other public places, the introduction of religious teaching in the primary schools, the raising of the stipends of the clergy and the salvage of the Bank of Rome.

During the Matteotti crisis the Church and the clerico-moderates accentuated their attitude of benevolent neutrality towards Fascism, in contrast to the Liberals. Catholics were reminded that obedience to the constituted government was the first of all political virtues and no doubts were cast on the legitimacy of Mussolini's rule.[5] After 3 January, when the Liberal ministers had resigned, the clerico-moderate Nava continued in office.

During 1925-6 the elimination of the Popolari and the consolidation of the dictatorship altered the character of the relationship between the Church and Fascism. The new slogans of the 'totalitarian state' seriously alarmed the Church. Nor was it just a matter of slogans. If Pius XI had no great sympathy for the Popolari, part of the reason was that they interfered with his plans for controlling and disciplining the social activities of the Catholic movement. The structure of Catholic Action in its modern form, as a network of youth, professional and other associations strictly subordinated to ecclesiastical authority and independent of political party, goes back to the reforms which he introduced in September 1923.[6] There had always been great practical difficulty, however, in getting the Fascists to distinguish between the 'a-political' activities of Catholic Action and the 'political' activities of the Popolari, especially since they were inevitably often carried on by the same people, both priests and laymen. The Fascist accusation that Catholic Action served to camouflage the survival of the cadres of the political party frequently had some truth. Catholic Action suffered severely at the hands of the extremists, particularly during the November 1926 'reprisals' after the attempt on Mussolini's life. The establishment of the supremacy of the state over the party diminished the incidence of this sort of violence; however this was not the only threat to Catholic Action. So long as Fascism was only concerned to suppress rival political parties, the Catholic associations were not officially menaced; but from 1925 on the 'totalitarian state' proclaimed its intention of absorbing all other associations as well.[7]

It is against this background that one must view the decision taken by the Pope to undertake serious negotiations for a settlement of the Roman question. In itself, this decision was not altogether new or surprising. The Vatican had indicated its readiness for a settlement in 1919, during the Orlando government. Only the obstinacy of Victor Emmanuel, who threatened to abdicate rather than to agree to the Holy See's demands for full sovereignty over the Vatican, prevented the conclusion of an agreement. It is ironic that it should have taken a dictator to overcome the King's loyalty to this particular aspect of the Risorgimento tradition.[8]

The real novelty was the Vatican's decision that negotiations for a treaty which would settle the dispute over the question of Papal sovereignty (the Conciliation) must be accompanied by a Concordat which would regulate the position of the Church within Italy; it does not seem as if the Vatican had posed this condition during the 1919 discussions. Even at the beginning of 1925, Pius XI and his advisers were still apparently prepared to consider the two questions separately. It was only at the end of the year that Conciliation and Concordat were explicitly linked. Rocco had appointed a commission to reform Italian ecclesiastical law, almost certainly with the approval of the Pope; but when the draft legislation was submitted to him on 26 December he flatly rejected it, on the grounds that any unilateral settlement of the Church's position by the State was unacceptable in principle. He made clear that even a bilateral agreement would be possible only if the Roman question were resolved at the same time. While the Church regarded the Treaty and the Concordat as indissolubly associated, the Italian representatives insisted, in private, that legally speaking the Treaty and the Concordat should remain separate; while the first would be 'irrevocable', the second would be subject to revision.

Vatican policy was probably dictated both by fear and hope. The proclamation of the 'totalitarian state' made it obviously more urgent than before to secure real safeguards for the freedom of the Church and the existence of the gravely menaced associations of the Catholic laity. On the other hand, Mussolini's evident interest in a deal with the Church must have given the shrewd Vatican diplomats the idea that he would be willing to surrender a great deal in return for the immense prestige which he would win if he could settle the Roman question. The dictator would be able to concede better terms than a democratic government which would have been preoccupied with the resistance of public opinion. During the crucial final phase of the negotiations, the Vatican showed itself willing to make concessions on the territorial and financial settlement in order to get its own way on the questions of education, marriage, etc., dealt with by the Concordat.[9]

The negotiations began in August 1926 and were concluded by the signature of the Lateran Pacts on 11 February 1929. The most serious obstacle which had to be surmounted was the conflict, already described, over the future of the Catholic youth movement. The Fascist reluctance to permit any limitation of their monopoly of the organization of youth was so great that the 1928 compromise marked only a temporary truce in the hostilities.

Under Article 43 the Concordat recognized the organizations of Catholic Action 'inasmuch as . . . according to the dispositions of the Holy See, they carry out their activities independently from all political parties and in immediate dependence on the hierarchy of the Church'.[10] Even this limited recognition was a great victory for the Church. Catholic Action was the only major network of associations which survived the establishment of the Fascist regime. In spite of the ban on political activity, Catholic Action was an invaluable training-ground for the future cadres of the Christian Democrat movement. Moderate Fascists like Bottai, while they did not of course foresee the supersession of Fascism by Christian Democracy, may have been willing to admit the possibility of a pluralist development of the regime, in which the Catholic elite would take its place alongside the Fascist. However the dominant attitude among Fascists in 1929 was still one of suspicion and frustration at having to permit the revival of an independent force with obvious political potential. The reports of the Prefects in the Catholic heartland of north-eastern Italy during 1929 are interesting. At first they show satisfaction with the great effect of the Lateran Pacts in rallying Catholic opinion to the regime ; but from April 1929 onwards they show increasing concern at the rapid growth of the Catholic associations, and the revival of activities often in conflict with the directives of the regime.[11] These suspicions help to explain the violent campaign of 1931 against Catholic Action, which was for a time seriously to imperil the whole settlement of 1929. The result of this conflict was further to circumscribe the independence and range of activities permitted to Catholic Action, and particularly those of the youth associations ; however, the organization survived.[12]

Mussolini's solution of the Roman Question was a personal triumph which enormously increased his prestige and popularity, both at home and abroad. After Pius XI had described Mussolini as 'the man of Providence', there was little reason in the eyes of most Catholics to object to the extravagant cult of the Duce. The conquest of Catholic opinion gave the regime a much wider social base than it had previously possessed. Catholic Action contributed to the success of the plebiscite in March 1929 by instructing its members to vote for the Government.[13] Mussolini obtained this victory, however, at the expense of the party and of ideological coherence. It is significant that the Grand Council was not consulted until after the signature of the Pacts ; this bypassing of Fascism's supreme organ of collective decision-making set an important precedent. On the ideological front, the chief objections were expressed by Gentile, who in 1927 attacked the idea of the Conciliation as an 'utopia'. Alfredo Rocco, although one of the architects of the policy of conciliation, was deeply disturbed by Mussolini's remissness over questions of jurisdiction. The ideology of the 'ethical state', and still more that of the 'totalitarian state', was incompatible with the recognition of the Church as an independent centre of doctrine and propaganda.[14] Although it was often forced to give way on practical questions, especially those relating to the activities of Catholic Action, the Church fought its ideological battles with vigour. At the end of 1926, the Vatican had drawn a clear line between orthodoxy and the doctrines of extreme nationalism by publishing the decree of the Holy Office condemning the *Action Française*. The Vatican continued to make use of the Index to combat the danger of Fascist deviations in Catholic doctrine. The condemnation of Missiroli's book *Date a Cesare* (Give to Caesar) can be interpreted as a way of officially repudiating the version of the Conciliation which Mussolini wanted to have propagated. The works of Gentile were put on the Index in 1934, and some years later the writings of Oriani, a favourite author of the regime, were also condemned.[15] The rejection of the idea of the totalitarian state was explicit. As early as 1926, in his Christmas allocution, Pius XI took a firm stand against the theory by which the rights of the individual were derived from the State. In 1929 Padre Rosa, in the *Civiltà Cattolica*, issued an authoritative rejection of the totalitarian idea, and compared Mussolini's attitude to the Church to that of Napoleon. This was not meant to be flattering. Finally, during the 1931 conflict over Catholic Action, the Pope personally condemned the totalitarian doctrine with even greater solemnity.[16]

It would be too simple, however, to regard the ideological contest between the Church and Fascism after 1929 as simply consisting in the former's defence of an 'island of separateness' against the totalitarian state. One of the first disputes in the aftermath of the Lateran agreements was caused by the Church's complaint about the excessive tolerance accorded to other religious denominations.[17] The Church claimed that the principle of 'absolute freedom of conscience' had been superseded by the recognition of Catholicism as the State religion. At the same time Catholic spokesmen made it clear that they expected education to conform with Catholic dogma. Article 36 of the Concordat laid down that the teaching of Christian doctrine was 'the foundation and crown of public education' ; this formula had already been used in 1923, but with respect only to primary education. Now, at the 1929 Philosophical Congress, the neo-scholastic Padre Gemelli denounced the 'error' of believing that youths in their teens could engage in free enquiry and rejected 'the so-called freedom of thought'. He interpreted Article 36 as signifying that no professor had the right to teach a philosophy of which the Church disapproved. Foremost amongst such inadmissible philosophies was that of Gentile: 'there is nothing less religious or less Christian than the thought of Gentile and the idealists. . . . In a Catholic nation, the schoolmaster has no right to administer philosophical poison, the poison of idealism, to the young sons of Catholic parents.'[18] The Catholic onslaught on Gentile in the short term restored him to Mussolini's favour. In his May 1929 speech to the Chamber, Mussolini made explicit reference to the doctrine of the 'ethical state',[19] and in 1932 the official Doctrine of Fascism was framed in Gentilian terms. However, after 1932, it was Gentile and the idealists who fell increasingly under suspicion, while the neo-scholastics were accepted. This was a major ideological defeat for Fascism, but hardly an unequivocal victory for liberty.

The most insidious and serious danger which Fascism posed to the Church and the Catholic religion lay in the attempt to annex their force for the purposes of secular imperialism abroad, and political conformity at home. The Fascist mystique could not supplant Catholicism, but it might pervert it. The Nationalists and Mussolini tried to identify Catholicism with the Roman imperial idea; in his June 1921 parliamentary speech Mussolini declared that 'the Latin imperial tradition of Rome is to-day represented by Catholicism'. In 1929 Mussolini gave this identification a more offensive significance. In his speech to the Chamber after the conclusion of the Lateran Pacts he remarked that 'this religion was born in Palestine, but it became Catholic at Rome. If it had remained in Palestine, very probably it would have been just one of the many sects which flourished in that turbulent atmosphere . . . and very probably it would have disappeared without trace'.[20] Of course Pius XI and the Church were quick to point out that such views were profoundly heretical. However the contamination of the Church by 'Romanism' and nationalism was none the less serious. During the period 1931–8 the forces of Catholicism went a long way in adopting the slogans of the regime, especially in the fields of demographic policy, corporativism, and imperial expansion.[21] The spread of a hybrid clerico-fascist ideology was only halted by the alliance with Hitler and the racial laws. In spite of Pius XI's solemn condemnation of the theory of the totalitarian state and the Fascist cult of violence, the defence of Christian values by the Church left much to be desired. The Fascist celebration of violence, national hatred and war was often excused, and the deep incompatibility between Fascism and Christianity thus obscured.

Foreign Policy and the Seizure of Power

There is no place here for a detailed discussion of Fascist foreign policy. However the Fascist seizure of power cannot be fully understood, either in its causes or its consequences, without some reference to foreign policy. Both the movement and Mussolini's regime constantly proclaimed national greatness, measured in terms of international prestige and expansion, to be the supreme end of their actions.

Undoubtedly during 1919–20 and even later, nationalist motifs were essential in Fascist agitation. Yet the relationship between the rise of Fascism and the primacy of foreign policy is paradoxical. The success of Fascism depended on re-directing the energy expended on the cause of Fiume and Dalmatia into the battle against the 'internal enemy' and in acknowledging this as the first priority. Until 1926, Mussolini's own chief concern remained internal policy, and he viewed foreign policy largely, if not exclusively, with an eye to the situation at home.

Even before the war democracy and the popular press had begun to involve the public in questions of foreign policy more than ever before. Fascism was the child of this involvement. The piazza had, of course, played a role in Italian foreign policy on many occasions, most spectacularly in 1915. But Fascism made the piazza into a permanent institution by a technique of continuous agitation. The Government authorities in 1919–20, at first disposed to look with sympathy on the rise of a new 'patriotic' force, soon noted with some concern that the new movement could neither be controlled nor satisfied. 'If we get Fiume, they will think of Dalmatia, if we get Dalmatia they will think of Corsica, Nice, Savoy, and Malta, some useless bit of ground can always be found to be called national and to give life to the party.'[22] The *fasci* cashed in with success on the reaction against secret diplomacy, and appealed to popular feeling, as embodied in their own demonstrations, against the closed caste of the old diplomats, accused of indifference and estrangement from the life of the nation.[23] Although, as we shall see, when in power Mussolini gave 'secret diplomacy' a new and more sinister meaning, his concern for publicity did not end in 1922. Diplomacy became closely linked to propaganda; in no other field did Mussolini seek, or receive, the applause of the crowd with such persistence as in foreign policy. He never ceased to evaluate diplomacy with the eye of a journalist.[24]

Fascism drew on many precedents. In foreign policy Fascism cannot be regarded as the true heir either of the historic right or of the historic left. It repudiated the former's realism and trust in diplomacy and the latter's belief in self-determination and the friendship of free peoples. The Nationalists had gone out of their way to emphasize their contempt for vague, sentimental 'patriotism'. Fascism thrived on vagueness and sentiment and exploited the traditions of Mazzini and Garibaldi. In Fascist propaganda, especially in the early stages, democratic motifs appear alongside those of the new imperialism. The 1921 party programme on foreign policy preserved a semblance of continuity with the Risorgimento by talking about the completion of national unity,[25] and on various occasions lip-service was paid to the idea of self-determination. But on 1 January 1919 Mussolini had already announced that 'Imperialism is the eternal and immutable law of life'.[26] The frequent later insistence on the differences between Fascist 'expansionism' and Nationalist 'imperialism' was essentially camouflage. In fact the concept of 'expansion' as embracing not only territorial conquest but 'peaceful penetration' – economic, cultural or even religious – had been particularly stressed by Corradini. However the distinction was useful. When accused of planning war and conquest, Mussolini and the Fascists could always retreat behind the excuse that all they meant to do was to increase Italy's influence in the world.

Fascism exploited the feeling that Italy had been betrayed by her allies in the peace settlement. In 1919–20 this resentment was the dominant note in Fascist propaganda. Mussolini declared his support for a policy of 'revisionism'; Italy should detach herself from the 'plutocratic nations' and force a revision of the peace treaties through a rapprochement with her former enemies (Germany, Turkey, Austria, Hungary) and with Soviet Russia. The attack on the plutocracies that had robbed Italy of her rights mirrored the social dissatisfactions of the petty-bourgeoisie and the ex-combatants, who felt that they had fought the war while others prospered. However during 1921–2 the inconsistencies of Fascist party policy became more evident. Mussolini was unable to choose between incompatible alternatives.[27] This did not reflect simply the deliberate inconsistency practised by a movement which uses foreign policy issues as a means for winning power. To be fair, the position of Italy was genuinely contradictory. As the weakest of the victor powers, she had reason both to desire and fear the revival of the defeated nations. On the one hand, the help or at least the threat of Germany and Russia was needed to restore Italy's bargaining power. But a German revival would endanger Italy's northern frontier in the Alto Adige, while the grandiose schemes, dear both to D'Annunzio and the early Fascists, for subverting the British Empire with the aid of Turkey and Arab nationalism could hardly be combined with the reassertion of control over Libya. Mussolini and the Fascists were the first to condemn the post-war governments for their weakness in handling rebels or national minorities,[28] and the October 1922 'March on Bolzano' was not calculated to win the sympathy of German nationalists.

However 'revisionism' remained popular in Fascist circles and Mussolini himself never lost sight of the aspiration to bring about a sweeping change in the power relationships determined by the peace treaties. For all the similarities between Nationalist and Fascist imperialism, there was a significant difference of emphasis. The Fascist version gave a greater place to the aim of expansion within Europe itself, in the Balkans, while the Nationalists, in common with most of the career diplomats, concentrated more on the need for expansion in Africa and the eastern Mediterranean.[29] The difference was important, for the programme of Balkan expansion was ultimately incompatible with the idea of the solidarity of the victor powers, or later of the four Locarno powers, while the traditional form of imperialism outside Europe seemed to carry no such radical implications. However the myths of the revived Roman Empire and '*mare nostrum*' were in the event (though not till the 1930s) to prove equally disruptive.

Mussolini certainly did not allow the extremists of the Fascist party to dictate his policy in any obvious sense. In his first years of power he won credit abroad for the firmness with which he treated the Dalmatian lobby and the professional Slav-haters among his own followers and those of D'Annunzio. The signature of the Pact of Rome with Yugoslavia on 27 January 1924 seemed to mark the decisive repudiation of the demands for Adriatic expansion which had been the central theme of Fascist agitations up till 1922.[30]

When Mussolini took power, two leading ambassadors, Sforza and Frassati, resigned. However the majority of the officials of the diplomatic service were ready to co-operate. Mussolini made a good impression by admitting his ignorance and submitting to tuition on deportment and other technicalities. The Secretary-General Contarini and his collaborators believed that they had a duty to moderate and educate Mussolini. They also saw the advent of Fascism in a more positive light. Guariglia, who became one of the most important permanent officials, wrote that 'I understood clearly that our then allies were profiting from our instability to delay the solution of the Mediterranean and African problems which were of the most interest to us.' Not only would the establishment of a strong government under Mussolini put an end to this situation, but the aggressive reputation of Fascism and its leader could be exploited to make Britain and France take up a more conciliatory attitude to Italian claims The advent of Fascism might therefore represent 'a substantial advantage for Italian interests'.[31] Contarini, however, had no desire to see Italy engage in dangerous adventures and he tried with apparent success to persuade Mussolini of the advantages of good relations with Yugoslavia and Czechoslovakia.

However Mussolini's acquiescence in this policy of influence through friendship was only temporary. Even during this first period the occupation of Corfu (31 August 1923) showed the latent aggressive tendencies of Fascism. The seizure of Corfu was ostensibly a reprisal for the murder of the Italian members of the Greco-Albanian boundary commission. For some time there had been tension between Italy and Greece over the Dodecanese, occupied by Italy since the war with Turkey. A month before the action, the Navy Minister, Thaon di Revel, had held a conference which discussed the formulation of a contingency plan for action by the fleet in case of a 'provocation' by the Greek Government. One of the 'provocations' foreseen as possible was an incident involving the boundary commission; so it is clear that the actual incident was only a pretext. Mussolini was unable to maintain his occupation of Corfu in the face of British disapproval; but the Greeks were compelled to pay an indemnity. This enabled him to claim a victory, and the result of the Corfu affair was highly favourable for Mussolini's prestige at home. Even newspapers like the *Corriere della Sera*, which opposed Fascism and had taken a moderate line over the Adriatic question, backed the Government's action in public.

The anti-Fascist press was afraid of being accused of lack of patriotism, and so failed to point out the dangers or to rebut the claims of Fascist propaganda. The Corfu crisis was also an ideological victory for Fascism on the international plane, inasmuch as it dealt a severe blow to the authority of the League of Nations, whose jurisdiction was successfully contested.[32] Mussolini, however, recognized that he had run serious risks and the effect of Corfu was to make him more cautious, especially in relation to Britain.

The dynamism of Mussolini's foreign policy was also held in check during 1922–5 by the requirements of internal consolidation. During this period Mussolini needed the approval both of foreign powers and of the permanent officials and elder statesmen at home. Conservatives like Salandra feared his rashness and lack of experience in foreign affairs, and he had to calm their suspicions. An orthodox conduct of foreign affairs helped to create the necessary illusion of continuity. It was necessary for Mussolini to balance the desire of his own supporters and a large part of the public for national self-assertion against these factors. During the Matteotti crisis, the moderation of Italian foreign policy was especially marked ; Mussolini's chief concern at this time appears to have been to minimize unfavourable foreign comment. He was successful in avoiding international isolation, and it was during this period, indeed, that his cordial relationship with Austen Chamberlain began.[33]

A curious kind of complicity developed between Mussolini and British statesmen and diplomats. They accepted his excuse that he ranted in public only so as to preserve his freedom to be reasonable in private, and they were willing to help him. Even Curzon, who had a strong dislike for Mussolini, thought it wise to flatter him in public.[34] From 1924 to 1929 Austen Chamberlain willingly co-operated in building up the image of Mussolini as a statesman of the first rank. He did not do so out of blind admiration (though he did admire Mussolini) but because he believed that by according the Duce the status that he demanded for himself and Italy he would remove his motive for undertaking adventures. This was a shrewd view ; Chamberlain's tactics of flattery combined with firmness helped to keep Mussolini relatively quiet. Unfortunately the price of this success was to convince a growing number of people in England and elsewhere that Mussolini really was a great statesman and to encourage unjustified optimism about his intentions. It would be unrealistic to criticize Chamberlain or the Foreign Office for trying to find a *modus vivendi* with Mussolini ; but in the process their view of his character and the regime's achievements was subtly distorted.[35] No doubt conservative sympathies for the conqueror of Bolshevism were also important in producing this result. The measure of success which Austen Chamberlain had in taming Mussolini encouraged illusions that similar tactics would work with Hitler.

Between 1926 and 1927, when the period of internal consolidation was over, Mussolini's foreign policy entered a new phase. The influence of Contarini declined rapidly once Mussolini had made sure of his power at home. He resigned on 19 March 1926 ; the immediate cause of his resignation was Mussolini's quarrel with Stresemann over the Alto Adige. But the deeper reason lay in his recognition that Mussolini had repudiated his Balkan policy, and that he was beginning to conduct a secret policy of his own outside Foreign Office channels.[36] With a degree of frankness rare among diplomats, Contarini explained to the British ambassador Graham that 'he found himself alone in endeavouring to stem the tide of violence of Fascism which would end by sweeping Mussolini off his feet'. One of the factors which contributed to his feeling of isolation was the attitude of the ex-Nationalists Federzoni and Rocco, who on this occasion sided with the extremists instead of acting as a brake on them.[37]

Italian diplomats after Contarini did not determine foreign policy, although Grandi, who had become Under-Secretary for Foreign Affairs in May 1925, proved 'malleable' to the influence of the permanent officials.[38] However the diplomats no longer dared to disagree with Mussolini on the major issues of foreign policy. They could only try to modify the details. At the beginning of 1927 further changes weakened the influence of the old group of officials associated with Contarini still further; the post of Secretary-General, held for a year by Chiaromonte Bordonaro, was in effect abolished, and the ambassadors in Paris and London resigned. The nationalist spirit reigned increasingly unchecked within the Foreign Office itself.[39]

The British ambassador wrote at the end of 1925 that 'The Fascist party is now so strong at home that, in the search for fresh fields to conquer, it is tempted to turn its attention to the domain of foreign policy.'[40] In fact Mussolini firmly repressed any ambitions the party might have had to interfere directly in foreign policy. During the first years after the March on Rome, the *fasci all' estero*, formed among Italians living abroad and directly controlled by the PNF through their general secretary Bastianini, had tried to exercise political surveillance over the career diplomats. The ambassador to the USA, Caetani, one of Mussolini's own special appointments, resigned in protest against the political activity of the *fasci all' estero*, which he was not allowed to control.[41] In 1927–8 the *fasci all' estero* were placed under the control of the ambassadors and consuls, in the same way as the *federale* was subordinated to the Prefect at home. Nevertheless the absorption of the party by the State did not have the same effect on foreign policy as on internal policy. 'In internal policy the revolutionary and subversive demands of the party were rigidly contained or dissolved; the same cannot be said as regards foreign policy.'[42] In fact one of the functions of an aggressive foreign policy was to compensate for the restraints on the party's 'dynamism' at home. Both in 1926–7 and again in 1932, when Starace took over and still more rigid discipline was established, the reduction of the party's independence coincided with a more aggressive turn in foreign policy. The occupation of Corfu in September 1923 already suggests the connection; it is probably not accidental that Mussolini's first aggressive venture abroad was taken at a time when he was particularly concerned with the problem of reducing the party to order.

The Fascist pursuit of empire was designed to direct attention and energy away from internal conflicts. Corradini, with his theory of the 'proletarian nation' and the transference of the class struggle to the international plane, had already constructed a doctrine around this aim. Although it is doubtful whether the industrial proletariat was ever taken in by the argument that they would be rewarded for loss of the right to strike by a bigger share of the imperial cake, the slogans of Fascist imperialism had greater efficacy among the impoverished middle classes (the *morti di fame*), the rural population and the *lumpenproletariat* of the Southern cities. Italian imperialism, it has been observed, was an 'imperialism of poverty', which shared with National Socialism a central concern with the problem of overpopulation.[43] In spite of the blatant inconsistency of taking measures to increase the birth rate while insisting on the absolute necessity of an outlet for surplus population, the propaganda effect of 'demographic imperialism' was successful both at home and abroad. Even the British Foreign Office was impressed by the demographic argument for Italian expansion, without asking where and how an 'outlet' for surplus population could really be found.[44]

The direct economic pressures behind Italian imperialism would seem to have been relatively unimportant compared with the political motives. Business showed little enthusiasm for risky foreign investments and, except for the armaments industry, had to be prodded and cajoled by the Government into playing its part in 'expansion'.[45] There were, of course, schemes for the settlement of Italian peasants abroad ; but these had more ideological than economic importance even at a later date. However demographic considerations contributed to form a harsh view of the relationship between colonists and subject peoples, characteristic of agrarian rather than industrial thinking. Not only in Libya, but also in Rhodes, the regime planned eventually to expropriate the native population. Guariglia endorsed the Fascist view that 'the poor Greek population . . . must accustom itself to becoming the labour force for the Italian peasants who will settle there', or else emigrate.[46]

Internal politics also at times had a more direct effect on foreign policy. Thus the repression of the German and Slav minorities, which was intensified as the dictatorship tightened its hold, was a cause of recurrent tension with Germany, Austria and Yugoslavia. More important, during 1924–9 Mussolini's basic anti-French and pro-British orientation was much influenced by the question of the political exiles. France was the main centre of exile activity and Mussolini suspected the French Freemasonry and even the Government of encouraging and aiding their efforts. In March 1927 he wrote, 'I believe that there is no difference in intention or action between the French government, French organizations and Italian organizations in France.'[47] The presence of the exiles served, in fact, to exacerbate a more general ideological hostility to the democratic Republic. It would be a dangerous oversimplification to draw a contrast between an orthodox period of diplomacy down to 1936, in which ideological factors played little part, and a later period in which they were of decisive importance. Even in the 1920s Mussolini showed a marked partiality for dictatorships and a loathing of progressive democracy as represented by men like Herriot, Briand or Benes. His relations with England were much better under Conservative than under Labour governments.[48]

During 1926 Mussolini multiplied his verbal threats.[49] These bore little correspondence to his actions, which were by comparison unadventurous. It was easy, therefore, for foreign observers to write off his aggressive speeches as mere propaganda ; in a sense this was often true. But, as Salvemini pointed out, Fascist propaganda was in itself dangerous. It encouraged 'a state of apocalyptic expectancy'.[50] Mussolini could not for years go on indefinitely whipping up enthusiasm without taking action. Moreover orators can only with difficulty avoid sharing the emotions they inspire in their audience.

If Mussolini's public speeches are not to be read as evidence of his true intentions, his secret, personal policy gives more concrete proof of his desire to disrupt the European order. Even during the early period he had made use of unofficial agents in his contacts with the German nationalists, while other overtures, though known to De Bosdari, the ambassador at Berlin, were kept secret from Contarini. A fondness for tactics of internal subversion and intrigue with foreign political movements was a marked feature of Fascist policy from the beginning. Although 'fascist' movements were at first treated with some scepticism, usually justified by their unimportance, Mussolini took an active interest in irredentist movements in Corsica and Malta. Arms were promised for the secret rearmament of Hungary and Germany.[51]

These first attempts proved abortive, but in the spring of 1927 secret policy again became important. This was at the same time as the signature of the Italo-Magyar Pact and shortly after the changes in the foreign service. Individual Italian agents and the military intelligence service (SIM), which had been created in July 1926, made contact with Macedonian terrorists, Croat separatists and other groups in the underworld of Balkan politics.[52]

In 1928 Bethlen, the Prime Minister of Hungary, persuaded Mussolini also to support the Austrian *Heimwehr* with arms and money.[53] This was the first significant example of 'international Fascism', or support given to a foreign Fascist movement on partly ideological grounds. Mussolini aimed both to extend his influence in Austria and to destroy Viennese socialism. Meanwhile there were new contacts between Government and Fascist party authorities and the German extreme right. Hitler's promise not to raise the South Tyrol question aroused interest, and some kind of understanding seems to have been reached between the Fascist and the Nazi parties ; Nazis were exempted from the harsh treatment shown to other German agitators in the South Tyrol.[54] All this added up to a programme for changing the balance of power in Central Europe by an international alliance of extreme right-wing and separatist movements, menacing Yugoslavia and Czechoslovakia. In this area, Fascist ideology and revisionist foreign policy aims became inextricably linked. Italian power and the prestige of Fascism among enemies of democracy reinforced each other. It would be foolish to see the causes of this development as lying entirely within Italy. Indigenous political tensions in Austria and Yugoslavia became even greater than before during 1927. As in Italian internal politics, Mussolini seized the opportunity to exploit a situation of growing confusion and conflict.

The general character of Fascist foreign policy towards the end of the decade shows, indeed, some analogy with the tactics Mussolini had pursued in internal politics. It was a 'zig-zag' policy which employed both orthodox and unorthodox methods and preserved a choice of ultimate options. From 1927 onwards, Mussolini's constant aim was to unsettle Europe and to produce a more fluid situation in which his freedom of action would be increased. He was opposed to those politicians who tried to reduce tensions and enmities, such as Stresemann or Briand. He was, in short, a disturber of the peace. However in 1929 it would have been impossible to predict that he would throw in his lot with a powerful Germany against England. That momentous choice determined the development and ultimate fate of his regime.

Conclusion

By 1929 Mussolini had laid the foundations for his personal supremacy over the Italian State. His agreement with the Church had helped to stabilize his power and make him independent of the party. His promises of future expansion abroad provided an outlet for the enthusiasm repressed at home. The moderate Grandi was made Foreign Secretary to leave Mussolini free to speak as he liked inside Italy. However this division of responsibilities was not likely to be a permanent solution.

At home, the institutions by whose aid Mussolini had seized and established his power were rapidly losing their autonomy and vitality. This was true of both the party and the corporations. On the other hand rival bureaucracies were proliferating everywhere.

It has been suggested that it is the need of modern dictators for mass support which condemns them to a policy of dynamism, expressed both in permanent revolution at home and in military expansion and subversion abroad. I believe that this explanation is valid but incomplete. To give a satisfactory account of the way a modern dictatorship works, it is necessary to take into account not merely the relationship between the dictator and the masses, but also the intermediate levels of power represented by (1) the governing elite and the bureaucratic apparatus which it commands, and (2) the militant following of the party. The dictator remains in power through his ability to combine control from above through his mastery of the Government and party machines with control from below, through his popularity with the mass of his subjects. He uses the governing elite to control the masses by means of the single party, the police, the unions, the youth movement, etc., but at the same time he holds the elite in check by his ability to appeal directly to the public, who have come to regard him as a father figure. In order to prevent either the public or the elite getting out of hand, it is essential for him to retain the loyalty of his militant followers. It is to occupy and satisfy them, rather than the population at large, that dynamism is essential.

The restlessness and changes of course of dictatorship have another function which has been understood since the time of Aristotle. The crystallization of power in any permanent form is a potential danger to the dictator ; it can be persuasively argued that the characteristic of one-man rule in modern societies has been to attack and destroy the structure of the party as a stable institution with its own norms.[56] However a party or some equivalent instrument is still essential to ensure a regime's permanence ; modern dictatorships are therefore all characterized by an unresolved tension between rule by one man through his personal network and a stable oligarchy, usually based on the party.

Even in Mussolini's Italy, the party could not be suppressed or too openly disparaged without weakening the regime. Indeed the non-totalitarian features of the situation, such as the survival of the monarchy and its control over the Army, made it all the more necessary to retain the party as a check and as a source of legitimacy.[57] On the other hand, Mussolini was always keenly aware of the dangers which might result from allowing his subordinates to acquire too much power in their own right. His abrupt choices and dismissals of his collaborators had little to do with their fitness for office. A good example is Mussolini's removal of Balbo from the Air Ministry in 1933. Balbo had become too popular and that was sufficient reason for ending his tenure. The development of the regime during 1929–33 showed Mussolini's determination not to allow any stable governing elite to crystallize. The power lost by the party was not gained by the Cabinet or by any other institution, but only by the Duce.[58]

The conflicting tendencies towards one-man rule and oligarchy can be illustrated by the two most important constitutional laws of the regime. The first, the 24 December 1925 law on the position of the Head of the Government ended the collective responsibility of the Cabinet to Parliament and gave formal sanction to Mussolini's hegemony. Henceforward, he was responsible only to the King and could appoint and dismiss ministers as he pleased. The Presidency of the Council (Prime Ministership) became a 'super-ministry' with direct control over a variety of institutions, from the armed forces to the Institute of Statistics.[59] But even this concentration of powers did not satisfy Mussolini, who also took over the portfolios of other ministries as well. At one time in 1929 he held no less than nine ministries.[60] This extreme nominal centralization, however, led to the dispersion of decision-making and frustrated rational planning. An under-secretary nominally at the direct orders of the Duce often enjoyed more independence than a minister, and everywhere Mussolini's suspicion of office-holders and personalities tended to throw power into the hands of the faceless bureaucrats and the backstairs cliques. The consequences were seen most clearly in the abysmal failure to co-ordinate the planning and conduct of war.[61] Theoretically the Fascist state was organized for war; yet the despised Liberal governments of 1915–18 made a better job of mobilizing and directing the energies of the nation.

On the other hand, the Grand Council Law of 9 December 1928 illustrates the need felt to secure the dictatorship against the Crown and to provide for the future by emphasizing the role of the party and the special institutions created by the revolution. The Grand Council was given the power to determine the choice of Mussolini's eventual successor, and even that of expressing an opinion on the succession to the royal throne. In the words of Gentile, the law showed a concern for the 'conservation' of the Fascist state beyond the period of Mussolini's own life-span: 'the will of a man of extraordinary gifts becomes an organic and lasting institution. What might appear to be the daily but contingent creation of an individual becomes the constitutional structure of the nation itself. The hero becomes depersonalized and is converted into the spirit of his people.'[62] However the sequel to the passing of the law shows very clearly the difficulty of resolving the tension between personality and institution. The hero, it seems, was none too anxious to be depersonalized.

The 1928 law had attempted to give the Grand Council a stable structure by increasing the number of the members with permanent or *ex officio* qualifications. In this way, the Duce's freedom of choice was somewhat restricted. The law probably reflected the ideas of Rocco, who was impressed by the success of the Sacred College and the Roman Senate in securing continuity. But Mussolini in 1929 brusquely overturned this part of the law; he declared that the Grand Council in its new shape had become 'an assembly of institutions, instead of an assembly of leaders', and 'that it should be reduced to a small general staff'. The category of permanent members was abolished, except for the 'quadrumvirs' of the March on Rome, and that of *ex officio* members was also greatly reduced. The Grand Council was also charged by the 1928 law with the task of drawing up a list of possible successors to the Duce, but Mussolini, while he did not repeal this clause, prevented it being put into effect. During the 1930s, moreover, the meetings of the Grand Council became irregular and infrequent.[63]

All this shows Mussolini's determination to preserve his own freedom of action at the cost of institutional stability. The 'deliberate fragmentation of the Fascist governing class'[64] by Mussolini reached its apex in 1932–3, with the dismissal of Rocco, Balbo, Bottai and Grandi. This coincided with the appointment of Starace as secretary of the party. The grand design of the regime's great legislator, Rocco, for an 'authoritarian mass state' in which party, corporations, youth movement, Militia, etc., would forge the whole people into an instrument for the execution of the will of the ruler, revealed its weaknesses.[65] The will of the ruler in fact disorganized and weakened the connecting links between society and the State. Mussolini continued to improvise rather than dictating new norms.

Mussolini's personal dictatorship was absolutely secure so long as his luck held and he could claim successes in foreign policy. His popularity reached its height with the conquest of Ethiopia. The regime seemed to have two paths of development open before it : one choice was what one might call the 'German solution', with a revival of the movement, the strengthening of totalitarian controls, and an attempt to end the autonomous power of the King, the Church, and the social and business elites. The other choice one could call the 'Spanish solution' : it would entail a further reduction in the power of the party, a larger share in government for Catholics, technocrats and other groups, and an evolution in the direction of a conservative authoritarianism in which the prerogatives of Throne and Altar would be respected.

The decision on which road to take was closely bound up with the course of foreign policy. When Mussolini allied with Germany, he also opted for 'dynamic Fascism'.[66] If he had instead tried to defend Austria in alliance with the Western powers, then clerical conservatism would have been strengthened. Italy might have become the leader of a bloc of clerico-Fascist and authoritarian states, with satellites in Dollfuss' Austria, Horthy's Hungary and Gil Robles' Spain. Had Mussolini practised pure *realpolitik*, he might well have opted for this second solution, which could alone preserve a certain independence for Italian foreign policy. However his ambitions pointed to the first course. Alliance with Hitler held out greater opportunities for the expansion which his propaganda had promised : and at home Mussolini, in spite of all his compromises, had never abandoned his totalitarian aspirations. Before 1933 he could pretend to himself that they had been achieved, but afterwards he was forced to recognize that his pupil, Hitler, had far surpassed him in the degree of regimentation and indoctrination he had imposed upon his people. The master, therefore, began in turn to imitate the pupil. In his boundless appetite for self-aggrandisement, Mussolini had boasted in 1932 that 'within ten years all Europe will be Fascist or Fascistized',[67] and in this sense at least he could see Hitler's triumph as his own.

The alliance with Hitler posed a threat to the position of the monarchy, the Church and the non-party elites, all of whom tried to keep Italy out of the war. The racial laws, especially, antagonized the Church and public opinion, and caused heart-searchings even among committed Fascists. The hostile reactions of Balbo and Gentile were particularly significant.[68] Even the trivialities of the 'anti-bourgeois' campaign caused deep resentment among Fascism's more conservative supporters. Without military defeat, these dissatisfactions would not have been decisive, but the strength and popularity of the regime had been considerably eroded by 1940.

It has been possible to speak of a 'Fascist era'.[69] Although only two regimes in Europe, those of Hitler and Mussolini, have claims to be considered wholly Fascist, a number of others adopted several of the features of Fascism, from corporate ideology to para-military techniques. In the 1930s Fascism rather than communism became the spectre haunting Western democracy, and the threat was not just external. If it was Hitler's success which alone gave Fascism a truly European dimension, Mussolini for a long time had more admirers outside his own country. The extent of conservative sympathy for Mussolini in Britain, France and the USA is well known : and the force of his example could attract and convert a brilliant radical like Mosley. The errors of judgement made by Mosley are, indeed, striking proof of the inter-national prestige of Fascism in the thirties. At no other time would an intelli-gent English politician have conceived the idea that dressing his supporters in black shirts and training a corps of strong-arm boys to steward his meetings would be likely to further his success. But the great slump had bred disillusion-ment with the workings of democratic government, and Fascist propaganda exploited this with success. Even non-Fascists tended to believe, on dubious grounds, that Fascist 'efficiency' had found an answer to the economic crisis ; this conviction was widespread even before it was given a measure of substance by the spectacular successes of the Nazis and Schacht in dealing with German unemployment. Mussolini's ability to appear all things to all men, the skill with which he exploited 'social' and anti-capitalist slogans, as well as those of order and the defence of property, were effective in international propaganda.

The most important effect of the Fascist seizure of power was that it showed that such things were possible. Hitler has left unequivocal testimony to the immense impression which Mussolini's success made upon him.[70] He copied both the techniques of the movement and Mussolini's tactics in first winning over and then ousting the conservatives. Of course, Hitler was no slavish imitator ; he learnt in 1923 the danger of sticking too closely to Mussolini's prescription. Hitler had to adopt the 'legality tactic' and rely on mass pro-paganda rather than the violent conquest of local power to extend the influence of his movement. This in turn made it necessary to build up a political machine which was vastly superior to that of the Fascist party. With the aid of this machine, Hitler was then able to carry through his 'revolution from above' with far greater speed and thoroughness than had proved possible for Mussolini.

The Fascist epoch is over ; yet in its country of origin the legacy and threat of Fascism are still present. Even the legacy of Fascism was not wholly nega-tive. Some institutions created by or at least under Fascism have proved useful ; the IRI is the best example. In some of the more backward areas of Italy the social welfare measures of the corporate state represented an advance on what was there before. But there is little evidence in favour of the view that Fascism was a modernizing or 'developmental' dictatorship, at least if performance rather than aspiration is the yardstick. Economic growth was slower than either before or after Fascism and the technical modernization of Italian industry was retarded by the tendency towards a closed economy. However it is political development that has been most obviously retarded.

The survival of authoritarian attitudes and practices, the inefficiency and irresponsibility of the State machine, and the failure to develop a language of communication between the political class and the people; for all these difficulties of the Republic the long silence imposed by Fascism must bear some, if not all, of the responsibility.

Ironically the way in which political development has lagged behind economic has helped to keep alive the danger of a new Fascism. Discontent with the political system has reached such serious proportions that its survival appears in doubt. In these circumstances, the old myth of Fascism as the only alternative to communism has retained credibility for some.

Nationalism is a weakened force in present-day Italy, and European integration has certainly diminished the chance of Fascism ever regaining power. The modern sector of the Italian economy cannot desire the establishment of a total dictatorship on Fascist lines, which would have disastrous results for Italy's position in Europe. Whether more moderate authoritarian solutions would be equally unacceptable is, of course, a different matter.

Recently, however, neo-Fascism has shown that it is more than just a movement of the ageing and nostalgic. The 'new' neo-Fascism at the very least seems capable of introducing a fresh complication into the already unstable and over-burdened political system. In parts of Southern Italy and Sicily many of the conditions which made for the success of Fascism fifty years ago in the North are still present. Indeed the diffusion of small property and the existence of strong regional resentments against the prosperous and progressive North are advantages which the old Fascism did not possess to the same degree.[71] Discussion of how many neo-Fascist voters are 'really' Fascist is rather beside the point; it is obvious enough that most of those who voted for Hitler or Mussolini were not Fascist in this sense either. One crucial difference between the new Fascism and the old, however, which one may reasonably hope will prove decisive, is that it has arisen in the most backward rather than the most developed areas of Italy. The power of the Communist party is certainly a major obstacle to any repetition of 1921–2; so are the traditions of the Resistance. If the democratic parties remain firm, then neo-Fascism will soon once again come to seem an anachronism. But there are disturbing signs that some politicians may be ready to make concessions, to slur over differences and to exploit the neo-Fascist phenomenon in order to resist reform or to gain political advantages. To exaggerate the threat of neo-Fascism would be to give it unintentional encouragement; as one brilliant analysis of Fascism pointed out, the classic Fascist movements were held together by their faith in the future seizure of power and would have disintegrated without it. However the neo-Fascist revival is a storm signal which democrats neglect at their peril.[72]

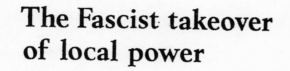

The Fascist takeover of local power

Stage 1 ■ Spring 1921. The initial expansion
Stage 2 ▤ Until July 1922
Stage 3 □ August–October 1922. After the failure of the 'legalitarian general strike'
Stage 4   1922–4. After the March on Rome. All other provinces except Cuneo and Palermo. These were taken over only in 1925–6

ABBREVIATIONS

AHR	*American Historical Review.*
JCH	*Journal of Contemporary History.*
JMH	*Journal of Modern History*
MLI	Il movimento di liberazione in Italia.
RSI	*Rivista storica italiana.*
RSS	*Rivista storica del socialismo.*
SS	*Studi storici.*

O.O.		*Opera Omnia di B. Mussolini*, 35 vols., ed. E. D. Susmel, Florence 1951–63.
T-K.		F. Turati & A. Kuliscioff, *Carteggio*, 6 vols., ed. A. Schiavi, Turin 1949.
De Felice	I	R. De Felice, *Mussolini il rivoluzionario* (1883–1920), Turin 1965.
	II	*Mussolini il fascista*, vol. 1, *La conquista del potere* (1921–25), Turin 1966.
	III	*Mussolini il fascista*, vol. 2, *L'organizzazione dello stato fascista* (1925–29), Turin 1968.
AP, C		Atti Parlamentari del Regno d'Italia, Camera dei Deputati, discussioni.
ACS		Archivio centrale dello stato.
ASB		Archivio di stato di Bologna, gabinetto della prefettura.

The following abbreviations refer to individual series of documents in the Archivio centrale dello stato:

PS	Ministero dell'interno, direzione generale pubblica sicurezza, divisione affari generali e riservati.
GF	Ministero dell'interno, gabinetto Finzi, ordine pubblico (1922–1924).
Ufficio cifra	Ministero dell' interno, gabinetto, ufficio cifra.
PC	Presidenza del Consiglio dei ministri, gabinetto, atti.
V	Consiglio dei ministri, Verbali.

SPCR	Segreteria particolare del Duce, carteggio riservato.
MRF	Mostra della rivoluzione fascista.
SPP	Partito Nazionale Fascista, direttorio nazionale, situazione politica delle provincie.
SCN	Senatori e consiglieri nazionali.
CF	Carte Farinacci

NOTES

1 Introduction

[1] G. M. Trevelyan, *The Historical Causes of the Present State of Affairs in Italy* (London 1923), pp. 7–9; G. Salvemini, *Scritti sul fascismo*, I, ed. R. Vivarelli, pp. 343–53; II, ed. N. Valeri, pp. 583–4.

[2] G. Fortunato, *Pagine e ricordi parlamentari* (Florence 1926–7), II, pp. xxxviii–xli.

[3] *La Rivoluzione Liberale: Antologia*, ed. N. Valeri (Turin 1948), pp. 239–42; for Carlo Rosselli's further development of Gobetti's themes and description of Fascism as 'the autobiography of the nation', see De Felice, *Il Fascismo* (Bari 1970), pp. 128–35. See also F. Cusin, *Antistoria d'Italia* (Turin 1948), passim.

[4] G. A. Borgese, *Goliath* (New York 1938), pp. 473–5.

[5] E.g. B. Roselli, *Italy under Fascism*, Foreign Policy Association Pamphlet No. 42 (New York 1927), p. 10 in Salvemini, *Scritti*, II, pp. 254–5.

[6] Salvemini, *Scritti*, I, p. 343.

[7] C. Casucci, 'Fascismo e Storia', in *Il Fascismo*, ed. C. Casucci (Bologna 1961), p. 425.

[8] B. Croce, *Storia d'Europa*, pp. 224–32, 278–83; *Il Fascismo*, ed. Casucci, pp. 165–74; De Felice, *Interpretazioni*, p. 401.

[9] J. A. Thayer, *Italy and the Great War, Politics and Culture 1870–1915* (Madison 1964).

[10] See A. W. Salomone, 'The *Risorgimento* between ideology and history: the political myth of "*Rivoluzione mancata*"', *AHR*, 68 (1962), pp. 38–56.

[11] G. Dorso, *La rivoluzione meridionale*, 3rd ed. (Turin 1955), pp. 5–6.

[12] Gramsci, *Il Risorgimento*, 4th ed. (Turin 1952), pp. 69–104; for criticism, see R. Romeo, *Risorgimento e capitalismo* (Bari 1959), pp. 17–51; G. Galasso, *Croce, Gramsci e altri storici* (Milan 1969), pp. 94–146.

[13] See the classic attack on 'the humanistic petty bourgeoisie' in L. Salvatorelli, *Nazionalfascismo* (Turin 1923), pp. 20–3.

[14] L. Salvatorelli, *Pensiero e azione del Risorgimento* (Turin 1960), p. 182.

[15] E. Flora, 'Lo Statuto Albertino', *Rassegna Storica del Risorgimento* 1958, pp. 27, 34–5. A. Caracciolo, *Stato e società civile*, p. 110.

[16] H. McGaw Smyth, 'Piedmont and Prussia: the influence of the campaigns of

1848–1849 on the constitutional development of Italy', *AHR*, 55 (1949–50), pp. 479–502 ; for criticism, see W. Maturi, *Interpretazioni del Risorgimento* (Turin 1962), p. 583.

[17] A. W. Salomone, 'Freedom and power in liberal Italy', in *Italy from the Risorgimento to Fascism, an Inquiry into the Origins of the Totalitarian State*, ed. A. W. Salomone (New York 1970), p. 129 ; F. Della Peruta, *Democrazia e socialismo nel Risorgimento* (Rome 1965), pp. 166, 171, 243–5.

[18] R. Grew, 'How success spoiled the Risorgimento', *JMH*, 31, n. 3 (Sept. 1962), pp. 239–53.

[19] Caracciolo, *Stato e società*, p. 14.

[20] G. De Ruggiero, *The History of European Liberalism* (Boston 1959), pp. 281, 312–13 ; G. De Ruggiero, *Il pensiero politico meridionale nei secoli XVIII e XIX* (Bari 1922), pp. 301–2 ; for other aspects of Southern influence on the state, Vivarelli, 'Italia liberale e fascismo : considerazioni su una recente storia d'Italia', *RSI*, 1970, 3, p. 693.

[21] E. Ragionieri, *Politica e amministrazione nella storia dell'Italia unìta* (Bari 1967), pp. 73–104. A different view is taken by E. Passerin D'Entrèves, *L'ultima battaglia politica del conte di Cavour* (Turin 1956), passim.

[22] C. Pavone, *Amministrazione centrale e amministrazione periferica da Rattazzi a Ricasoli* (Milan 1964), p. 194.

[23] For statistics, C. Seton-Watson, *Italy from Liberalism to Fascism* (London 1967), p. 79; Istituto Centrale di Statistica, *Compendio delle statistiche elettorali italiane* (Rome 1946–7), I, pp. 68–9. On political consequences, see D'Entrèves, *L'ultima battaglia*, p. 204; D. Mack Smith, *Cavour and Garibaldi, 1860*, p. 59.

[24] E.g. R. C. Fried, *The Italian Prefect* (Newhaven 1963), p. 158.

[25] G. Salvemini, *Il ministro della mala vita e altri scritti sull'Italia giolittiana*, ed. A. Apih (Milan 1962), p. 554. For further references see A. Lyttelton, 'Political Patronage in Giolitti's Italy', in *Caciquismo y Política de Clientelas* (Madrid 1973).

[26] A. Tasca, *Nascita e avvento del fascismo* (Bari 1965), I, pp. 9–11, 29.

[27] Salvemini, *Il ministro*, pp. 548–9.

[28] C. Morandi, *I partiti politici nella storia d'Italia* (Florence 1945), p. 37.

[29] See G. Mosca, *Sulla teorica dei governi e sul governo parlamentare* (Turin 1884) ; P Turiello, *Governo e governati in Italia* (Bologna 1882); M. Delle Piane, *G. Mosca, classe politica e liberalismo* (Naples 1952), p. 37.

[30] See M. Minghetti, *I partiti politici e la pubblica amministrazione* (Bologna 1881) ; S. Sonnino, 'Torniamo allo Statuto', in N. Valeri, *La lotta politica in Italia* (Florence 1958), pp. 251–69.

[31] A. Caracciolo, *Il parlamento nella formazione del regno d'Italia* (Milan 1960), p. 31 ; for 1860 elections see pp. 210–13.

[32] For the politics of the period, see G. Carocci, *A. Depretis e la politica interna italiana dal 1876 al 1887* (Turin 1956).

[33] G. Fortunato, *Il Mezzogiorno e lo Stato italiano*, I, *Discorsi politici 1880–1910* (Florence 1926), pp. 24–5.

[34] For the debate, see A. Gerschenkron, *Economic backwardness in historical perspective* (Cambridge, Mass. 1962), pp. 79–89; R. Romeo, *Risorgimento e capitalismo* (Bari 1959), and the essays in *La formazione dell'Italia industriale*, ed. A. Caracciolo (Bari 1969), esp. S. Fenoaltea, 'Decollo, ciclo e intervento dello Stato', pp. 95–113, and Gerschenkron, 'Romeo debate', pp. 53–81.

[35] R. Vivarelli, 'Italia liberale e fascismo', *RSI*, 3 (1970), p. 693; R. Romeo, *Breve storia della grande industria in Italia*, p. 43; E. Sereni, *Capitalismo e mercato nazionale* (Rome 1966), pp. 151–6, 249–57.

[36] For the consequences of the wheat tariff, see D. Tosi, 'Forme iniziali di sviluppo e lungo periodo: la formazione di un'economia dualistica', in *La formazione*, ed. Caracciolo, pp. 274, 280; P. Sylos Labini, *Problemi dello sviluppo economico* (Bari 1970), pp. 239–41. See also: Barrington Moore Jr, *The Social Origins of Dictatorship and Democracy: lord and peasant in the making of the modern world* (London 1967), p. 423.

[37] For production figures see Romeo, *Grande industria*, pp. 160–81; Gerschenkron, *Economic backwardness*, pp. 364–6; G. Procacci, 'Crisi dello Stato liberale e origini del fascismo', *SS*, 2 (1965), pp. 223–4.

[38] Seton-Watson, *Liberalism to Fascism*, p. 307; Vivarelli, 'Italia liberale e fascismo', p. 674. For the failure of industry to absorb the excess agricultural population (owing to the decline of the artisanate), see *La formazione*, p. 21; on the political consequences, see I. Barbadoro, 'Problemi e caratteristiche storiche del movimento sindacale italiano', *RSS*, August 1963, pp. 231–6.

[39] E. Santarelli, *La revisione del Marxismo in Italia* (Milan 1964), p. 144.

2 The Crisis of the Liberal State

[1] F. Chabod, *Storia della Politica Estera Italiana dal 1870 al 1896: Le premesse* (Bari 1965), I, p. 23.

[2] F. Chabod, *L'idea di nazione* (Bari 1962), pp. 61–79.

[3] A. Oriani, *Opere: Fino a Dogali* (Bologna 1943), pp. 293–4.

[4] See G. Papini, *Opere* (Verona 1962), 9; pp. 773–5, 843.

[5] N. Valeri, *La lotta politica*, pp. 173–91.

[6] N. Valeri, *Da Giolitti a Mussolini: momenti della crisi del liberalismo* (Florence 1956), pp. 21–3.

[7] Chabod, *Le premesse*, pp. 301, 315.

[8] G. D'Annunzio, 'L'armata d'Italia', in *Prose di Ricerca* (Milan 1956), 3, pp. 51–2; see also C. Salinari, *Miti e coscienza del decadentismo italiano* (Milan 1960), pp. 34–7.

[9] Gramsci, *Risorgimento*, p. 204.

[10] M. Praz, *The Romantic Agony* (Oxford 1951), pp. 29–105.

[11] R. Vivarelli, *Il Dopoguerra in Italia e l'avvento del fascismo* (Naples 1967), pp. 474–6. Interesting notes on D'Annunzio's loss of literary inspiration and his search for popularity through action as compensation in F. Martini, *Diario 1914–18*, ed. G. De Rosa (Verona 1966), pp. 493, 503, 1200.

[12] Chabod, *Le premesse*, p. 302.

[13] Valeri, *Da Giolitti*, p. 24.

[14] P. Melograni, *Storia politica della grande guerra* (Bari 1969), pp. 250–1; see also A. Gramsci, *Letteratura e vita nazionale* (Turin 1966), p. 122–4.

[15] G. Amendola, 'La guerra' (1911), in *La cultura italiana dell' 900 attraverso le riviste*, 3, *La Voce* (1908–1914), ed. A. Romano, p. 400.

[16] G. Gentile, 'Manifesto degli intellettuali fascisti', in E. R. Papa, *Storia di due manifesti: il fascismo e la cultura italiana* (Milan 1958), p. 61.

[17] A. Oriani, *Opere: La rivolta ideale* (Bologna 1943), p. 70; see also pp. 29–36.

[18] On the relationship of Pareto's thought to Fascism, the best summary is that

given by N.Bobbio, *Saggi sulla scienza politica* (Bari 1971), pp. 72–3, but see also R.Aron, *Main Currents in Sociological Thought* (London 1967), II, pp. 166–75. who is less inclined to believe Pareto's claim to political neutrality, and the general observations on 'value-free' political science, in A.Macintyre, *Against the Self-Images of the Age* (London 1971), pp. 277–9.

[19] Particularly significant is Pareto's judgement that 'if there is a great European war, Socialism will be put back at least half a century and the bourgeoisie will be safe for that length of time. But as the war would be so disastrous for the Socialists how is it that their opponents cannot talk of it without real terror?'; M.Isnenghi, *Il mito della grande guerra* (Bari 1970), p. 8. For the passage from the 'value-free' to the 'value-loaded' concept of the elite, see Papini in *Vecchio e nuovo nazionalismo* (Milan 1914), p. 15 – 'A society is not organic except when there is in it a minority which organizes, but this minority cannot exercise its directive function, if there is no one who knows how to execute orders . . .'

[20] *La cultura italiana attraverso le riviste*, 7, *Leonardo-Hermes-Il Regno*, ed. D. Frigessi (Turin 1960), pp. 467–71. For Pareto's favourable judgement on the *Regno* group, see V.Pareto, *Les systèmes socialistes*, 2, p. 436; *Il Regno*, pp. 479–81, 522–3.

[21] Bobbio, *Saggi*, pp. 67–8; V.Pareto, *Scritti sociologici*, ed. G.Busino, pp. 1147–52; G.Sorel, *Reflections on Violence*, tran. T.E.Hulme and G.Roth, with an introduction by E.A.Shils (Glencoe, Ill. 1950), p. 104. *Contra*, Busino, *Scritti*, introd., p. 28.

[22] Moreover two of the group of the *Idea nazionale*, Maurizio Maraviglia and Roberto Forges Davanzati, were ex-syndicalists. For the best summary of Pareto's influence on Mussolini see Santarelli, *La revisione del marxismo*, pp. 306–8; also G. Prezzolini and G. Papini, *Vecchio e nuovo nazionalismo*, p. x. – 'Revolutionary socialism has the same task among the proletarian classes as nationalism among the bourgeois.'

[23] F. Gaeta, *Nazionalismo italiano* (Naples 1965), pp. 74–5.

[24] E. Corradini, *Discorsi politici* (Florence 1923), p. 91.

[25] C. Seton-Watson, *Liberalism to Fascism*, p. 313.

[26] G. Salvemini, *Opere*, Pt III, *Scritti di politica estera*, I, *Come siamo andati in Libia e altri scritti, 1900–15*, ed. A.Torre (Milan 1963), pp. 180–2.

[27] Gaeta, *Nazionalismo italiano*, p. 142; G.Prezzolini and G.Papini, *Vecchio e nuovo nazionalismo*, pp. ix–x : 'Nationalism is at the same time the expression of a just pride at material improvement and a reaction to moral disintegration.'

[28] Ibid., p. 119; S. Bertelli, 'Gli incunaboli del nazionalismo'*Nord e Sud* (1961), p. 83; and see further below, Ch. 9.

[29] G. Sorel, *Reflections on Violence*, pp. 87–8, 99, 107.

[30] Santarelli, *La revisione*, pp. 94, 108.

[31] 'Nationalism and syndicalism are both doctrines of energy and will, opposed to the doctrines or rather the practices of compromise. Syndicalism and nationalism are therefore anti-democratic, anti-pacifist, anti-bourgeois. They are the only aristocratic schools in a basely hedonistic and mercenary society. They share in common a cult of the heroic which they wish to revive in a society of grocers and jobbers' (Isnenghi, p. 21, quoting the syndicalist Angelo Olivetti; for Corradini on syndicalism, ibid., pp. 10–11). The Libyan War received the approval of a number of syndicalists, and some, like Olivetti and Paolo Orano, went as far as to proclaim

a new theory of 'subversive nationalism' which can be seen as a direct anticipation of the positions of early Fascism. (E. Santarelli, *Origini del fascismo*, pp. 111–20).

[32] *La Voce*, pp. 303–4, 399–406.

[33] L. Cafagna, in *La formazione* cit., pp. 157–8 ; Carocci, *Giolitti*, p. 78 ; Procacci, 'Crisi', p. 227.

[34] G. Arfe, *Storia del socialismo italiano, 1892–1926* (Turin 1965), pp. 136–46 ; L. Cortesi, *Il socialismo italiano tra riforme e rivoluzione* (Bari 1969), pp. 314–19 ; F. Manzotti, *Il socialismo riformista in Italia* (Florence 1965), pp. 6–7.

[35] Arfe, *Storia del socialismo*, pp. 146–7.

[36] Carocci, *Giolitti*, pp. 139–48.

[37] *Antologia della 'Critica Sociale,'* ed. G. Pischel (Milan 1945), pp. 339–44 ; F. De Felice, 'L'eta giolittiana', *SS* (1969), 1, p. 179.

[38] For the rise of Mussolini, see De Felice, I, pp. 79–135 ; Santarelli, *Revisione*, p. 155.

[39] G. Spadolini, *Giolitti e i cattolici (1901–1914)* (Florence 1960), pp. 283–352 ; Carocci, *Giolitti*, pp. 151, 163–4 ; *Epistolario Albertini*, 1, pp. 203, 206, 229.

[40] C. Seton-Watson, *Liberalism to Fascism*, pp. 390–1.

[41] B. Croce, *Cultura e vita morale* (Bari 1926), p. 197 ff, 'Il partito come giudizio e pregiudizio'. E. Garin, *La cultura italiana tra '800 e '900* (Bari 1962), pp. 134–7.

[42] L. Lotti, *La settimana rossa* (Florence 1965), pp. 42–3 ; Arfe, *Storia del socialismo*, p. 192.

[43] B. Vigezzi, *Da Giolitti a Salandra* (Florence 1969), pp. 72–5.

[44] De Felice, I, p. 177 ff; Lotti, *Settimana Rossa*, p. 33.

[45] Between 1912 and 1914 the membership of the Socialist party rose from 30,000 to 58,330. The readership of the party newspaper *Avanti !* also rose sharply during Mussolini's editorship. L. Ambrosoli, *Nè aderire nè sabotare 1915–1918* (Milan-Rome 1961), p. 413 ; Lotti, *Settimana rossa*, pp. 38–9.

[46] *Ibid.*, p. 153; see also Santarelli, *Revisione*, pp. 152–8.

[47] Lotti, *Settimana rossa*, p. 264.

[48] B. Vigezzi, *l'Italia di fronte alla prima guerra mondiale*, 1, *l'Italia neutrale* (Naples 1966), pp. 27–39, 143–80 ; the Foreign Secretary, San Giuliano, wrote that 'in a democratic country like Italy, it is not possible to make war when the will and feeling of the nation are opposed' (V. De Caprariis, 'Partiti politici ed opinione pubblica durante la grande guerra' in *Istituto per la storia del Risorgimento, Atti del XLI Congresso* (Rome 1965), p. 83).

[49] Vigezzi, ibid., pp. 151, 167–8, 828–78 ; L. Valiani, 'La guerra del 1914 e l'intervento italiano', *RSI* (1966) 3, pp. 609–12.

[50] Arfe, *Storia del socialismo*, pp. 208–9.

[51] Ambrosoli, *Nè aderire nè sabotare*, pp. 88–9.

[52] Vigezzi, *Da Giolitti*, p. 94 ; *Epistolario Albertini*, 1, p. 316, for belief that Giolitti would take Italy into the war.

[53] See Vigezzi, *Da Giolitti*, p. 93, for Salandra's 30 September 1914, letter to Victor Emmanuel : 'a true national war would serve . . . to reinvigorate the morale of the army and to restore its popularity and prestige.'

[54] V. Castronovo, *La stampa italiana dall' unità al fascismo* (Bari 1970), pp. 222–3.

[55] See Vigezzi, *Atti XLI Congresso*, pp. 479–80, for the economic interests behind this campaign.

⁵⁶ Valeri, *Da Giolitti*, p. 26; full text of D'Annunzio's speeches in *Prose di ricerca*, 3, pp. 7–62.

⁵⁷ Vigezzi, *Da Giolitti*, pp. 103–10.

⁵⁸ A. Gramsci, *Passato e presente*, 2nd ed. (Turin 1952), pp. 42–4; Martini, *Diario*, pp. 557–9, 579–80, 620–63, 696–715.

⁵⁹ A. Caracciolo, 'La grande industria nella prima guerra mondiale', in *Formazione*, pp. 163–219; V. Castronovo, *La stampa italiana*, pp. 238–86.

⁶⁰ See comments of Martini, *Diario*, p. 758.

⁶¹ Vivarelli, *Dopoguerra*, p. 41; Salvemini, *Il ministro della mala vita*,, pp. 397–9; Martini, *Diario*, p. 657.

⁶² P. Spriano, *Storia del Partito Communista*, 1, pp. 8–9. For the general situation see R. De Felice, 'Ordine pubblico e orientamenti delle masse popolari italiane nel 1917', *RSS* (September–December 1963), p. 488 ff.

⁶³ Ambrosoli, *Nè aderire*, pp. 184, 228, 234–5.

⁶⁴ O. Malagodi, *Conversazioni della guerra*, ed. B. Vigezzi (Milan 1960), 1, pp. 140–1, 164; De Caprariis, 'Partiti', pp. 140–3.

⁶⁵ De Felice, I, p. 414.

⁶⁶ Melograni, *Storia politica*, pp. 434–42.

⁶⁷ De Caprariis, loc. cit., pp. 135–40; De Felice, I, pp. 391, 704–6, 722–4; Ambrosoli, *Nè aderire*, pp. 218–19.

⁶⁸ R. De Felice, 'Giovanni Preziosi e le origini del fascismo (1917–1931)' *RSS* (September–December 1962), pp. 502–4; Martini, *Diario*, pp. 1072, 1079–80.

⁶⁹ De Caprariis, p. 93; De Felice, I, pp. 371–2; Santarelli, *Origini del fascismo*, pp. 78–9.

⁷⁰ Melograni, *Storia politica*, pp. 503–26; see esp. p. 514: 'the myth of the revolutionary war, practically forgotten from 1915 to 1917, became for the first time a propaganda argument for the mass of the troops.'

⁷¹ See Vivarelli, *Dopoguerra*, pp. 115–218.

⁷² Ambrosoli, *Nè aderire*, pp. 173, 278–9, 296–9, 316; Arfe, *Storia del socialismo*, pp. 230–8, 264; Vivarelli, *Dopoguerra*, pp. 83–4.

⁷³ L. Sturzo, *Discorsi politici* (Rome 1951), pp. 58–9.

⁷⁴ Tasca, *Nascita e avvento del fascismo*, I, p. 18; for the question of land reform, see A. Papa, 'Guerra e terra 1915–18', *SS* (1969), 1, pp. 6, 29–39, 44–5.

⁷⁵ For D'Annunzio's invention of the slogan 'mutilated victory' see Vivarelli, *Dopoguerra*, pp. 483–5.

⁷⁶ Ibid., p. 374.

⁷⁷ Ibid., pp. 426–7.

⁷⁸ I. J. Lederer, *Yugoslavia at the Paris Peace Conference* (New Haven & London 1963), pp. 66, 71–5, 168–70.

⁷⁹ G. Salvemini, *Scritti sul fascismo*, 1, pp. 453–5.

⁸⁰ De Felice I, pp. 527–32; Tasca, *Nascita e avvento*, 1, p. 202; P. Alatri, *Nitti, D'Annunzio e la questione adriatica* (Milan 1959), p. 78. Salvemini, *Scritti*, 2, pp. 45, 128.

⁸¹ Vivarelli, *Dopoguerra*, pp. 551–2.

⁸² Ibid., pp. 326–7, 452–4; Malagodi, *Conversazioni*, 2, p. 278 (Nitti, 9 February 1918): 'I'm not particularly afraid of a descent into the piazza because this never happens when there is another faction ready to give a hand to the authorities.'

⁸³ For the effects of the introduction of proportional representation see G.

Maranini, *Storia del potere in Italia 1848–1967* (Florence 1967), pp. 283–5. (Maranini, however, in my opinion is much too partisan in his attribution of responsibility to Nitti; for a more balanced assessment, see E. Santarelli, *Storia del movimento e del regime fascista* (Rome 1967), 1, p. 164. See also A. Predieri, 'I partiti politici' in *Commentario sistematico alla costituzione italiana*, ed. P. Calamandrei and A. Levi (Florence 1950), pp. 180, 193.

[84] Tasca, *Nascita e avvento*, 1, pp. 98–9.

[85] For an interesting criticism of Nitti from the point of view of a Giolitti follower, see M. Soleri, *Memorie* (Turin 1949), pp. 83–5.

[86] For Giolitti's 'Dronero speech' (12 October 1919) in which he set out his postwar programme, see Giolitti, *Discorsi extraparlamentari* (Turin 1952), pp. 294–327.

[87] T-K, 5, p. 285.

[88] P. Ungari, L'idea del partito moderno nella politica e nella sociologia di L. Sturzo', *Rivista sociologica* I, n 2 (1963), pp. 46–7.

[89] G. de Rosa, *Storia del movimento cattolico in Italia*, 2, *Il partito popolare Italiano* (Bari 1966), pp. 97–9.

[90] For the financial backing of Giolitti and Nitti, see p. 207. Personal relations between Giolitti and Nitti remained fairly cordial until the 1921 elections: see *Carteggio Giolitti*, 3, pp. 330–1.

[91] See G. Amendola, *Una battaglia liberale, Discorsi politici, 1919–1923* (Turin 1924), pp. 91–2; speech of August 1920; Manzotti, *Il socialismo riformista*, p. 171.

[92] See pp. 155, 203.

[93] Tasca, *Nascita e avvento*, I, p. 83.

[94] For the career and character of the young Mussolini see De Felice, I, passim., and G. Megaro, *Mussolini in the Making* (London 1938); Vivarelli, *Dopoguerra*, pp. 219–23.

[95] Vivarelli, *Dopoguerra*, p. 225 ff; De Felice, I, pp. 269–81, 467–8; see also note 49 above.

[96] See P. Spriano, *L'occupazione della fabbriche* (*Settembre 1920*), (Turin 1964).

[97] Spriano, *Partito comunista*, 1, p. 96.

[98] De Felice, pp. 631–3; Spriano, *L'occupazione*, p. 72.

[99] For a good survey of the agrarian labour movement, see Barbadoro 'Problemi e caratteristiche', pp. 231–63; L. Preti, *Le lotte agrarie nella valle Padana* (Turin 1955).

[100] Tasca, *Nascita e avvento*, I, pp. 156–7, 172.

[101] Spriano, *L'occupazione*, pp. 122, 187–91.

[102] Tasca, *Nascita e avvento*, I, p. 194.

[103] R. Vivarelli, 'Bonomi e il fascismo', *RSI* (1960), pp. 147–57.

[104] G. Rochat, *L'Esercito italiano da Vittorio Veneto a Mussolini* (Bari 1967), pp. 398–9.

[105] Vivarelli, *Dopoguerra*, p. 404; Rochat, *L'Esercito italiano*, pp. 31–2.

[106] See for example P. Badoglio, *Rivelazioni su Fiume* (Rome 1946), pp. 226–30.

[107] A. Gatti, *Tre anni di vita militare italiana* (Milan-Rome 1924), pp. 222–3.

[108] See De Felice, II, pp. 35–9, for revealing figures on the numbers of arrests and prosecutions, and *ibid.*, I, pp. 603–4.

[109] Ibid., II, pp. 25–6; De Rosa, *Storia del movimento cattolico*, II pp. 174–5.

[110] See (with some reservations) A. Repaci, *La marcia su Roma*, I, pp. 186–90.

2, pp. 243–4; Maranini, *Storia del potere*, pp. 272–3; and esp. G.Neppi Modona, *Sciopero potere politico e magistratura, 1870–1922* (Bari 1969), pp. 250–80, 304–6. A good study of the magistracy in this period is lacking.

3 The Rise of the Fascist Movement

[1] The words *'fascismo'* and *'fascisti'* were already current around the end of the war as a designation for the whole range of patriotic movements connected with the *fascio di difesa parlamentare*: see E.Santarelli, *Origini del fascismo* (Urbino 1963), pp. 202–3. The word *fascio*, which literally means a 'bundle', has much the same significance as the German *Bund*; 'league', 'alliance', or 'union' would be the nearest English equivalents.

[2] Eg. C.Rossi, 'La critica alla critica del fascismo', *Gerarchia* (1922), pp. 189–90.

[3] *O.O.*, 12, p. 27 (23 November 1918); p. 309 (18 March 1919).

[4] G.A.Chiurco, *Storia della rivoluzione fascista* (4 vols.), (Florence 1929), I, p. 39, for facsimile of the membership card of the *fasci d'azione rivoluzionaria* (1914): 'The *fasci* do not constitute a party. They are free groupings of those subversives of all schools, doctrines and policies who believe that they can find in the present moment . . . a propitious field for the fertilization of revolutionary ideals and do not intend therefore to let slip the occasion for a movement in common.'

[5] See K.Mannheim, *Ideology and Utopia* (London 1966), pp. 113–30; also A. Gramsci, *Socialismo e fascismo, L'ordine nuovo 1921–1922* (Turin 1966), p. 205; E.Nolte, *Three Faces of Fascism* (London 1965), p. 165.

[6] Nolte, *Three Faces*, pp. 151–67. See also G.Megaro, *Mussolini in the Making* (London 1938), p. 321. Instead, Nolte's statement (p. 155) that 'When Mussolini says "will", we see that all he means is "dialectic"' seems at least partially misleading.

[7] *O.O.*, 4, p. 156; Y. de Begnac, *Palazzo Venezia, Storia di un regime* (Rome 1950), p. 140. Santarelli, *Origini*, p. 150–61; comment on the death of Cesare Battisti: 'No Christian, no Socialist, has gone to his death in the name of Christianity or Socialism . . .'; cf. Nolte, *Three Faces*, p. 162: 'Would intensity of faith . . . become the measure of validity?'

[8] R.De Felice, *Sindacalismo rivoluzionario e fiumanesimo nel carteggio De Ambris – D'Annunzio* (Brescia 1966), p. 36; see also De Felice, I, pp. 245–6, 293 (S. Panunzio and F. Corridoni).

[9] *O.O.*, 13, p. 310 (18 March), 'We interventionists are the only people in Italy who have the right to talk of revolution . . .'

[10] Vivarelli, *Dopoguerra*, p. 277.

[11] G.Rumi, 'Mussolini e il programma di S. Sepolcro', *MLI*, April–June 1963, n. 2, p. 7; *O.O.*, 12, pp. 27–8 (23 November 1918), 13, pp. 17, 63–4; Chiurco, *Storia della rivoluzione*, I, p. 95.

[12] G.Pini and D.Susmel, *Mussolini*, 2, p. 34; A.Canepa, *L'organizzazione del PNF* (Palermo 1939), p. 53.

[13] See *ACS, MRF*, b. 65, Carte Gioda, fasc. 9 (*relazioni* of August and October 1919). *O.O.*, 13, pp. 218–20.

[14] *O.O.*, 16, p. 212, 23 March 1921. (See Pini and Susmel, 2, p. 38: 'Fascism is . . . the refuge of all the heretics.') Cf. also De Begnac, *Palazzo Venezia*, pp. 182–3.

[15] H.Arendt, *The Origins of Totalitarianism*, p. 325; De Felice, I, p. 507.

[16] Rumi, *Mussolini e il programma*, p. 7; Vivarelli, *Dopoguerra*, pp. 297–8. For

the June programme, see De Felice, op cit., pp. 744–5, and Vivarelli, p. 498 and G. Rumi, 'Il popolo d'Italia', in *1919–1925, Dopoguerra e fascismo. Politica e stampa in Italia*, ed. B. Vigezzi (Bari 1965), p. 441n.

[17] *O.O.*, 18 April 1919 ; Santarelli, *Origini*, p. 276.

[18] *Dai fasci al PNF* (Rome 1942), p. 133 ff.

[19] PNF, *Le origini e lo sviluppo del fascismo attraverso gli scritti e la parola del Duce e le deliberazioni del PNF dall'intervento alla marcia su Roma* (Rome 1928), pp. 115–16. On the Second Congress of the *fasci* (May 1920), see De Felice ibid., pp. 595–8, 746–8.

[20] E. Ragionieri, introd. to P. Togliatti, *Lezioni sul fascismo* (Rome 1970), p. xv.

[21] De Felice, *Sindacalismo*, pp. 508–9, 569 ; Santarelli, *Origini*, p. 216 ; and see note 18 above.

[22] This study is based on the lists of *Sansepolcristi* contained in St Antony's documents, J. 160 (046466–605) ; of the sample of 66 members listed, 8 cannot be placed. The remaining 58 can be classified as follows : 6 nobles, landowners, and industrialists, 12 free professionals, 17 petty bourgeois, 11 journalists and publicists and 12 manual workers and artisans. There were 9 known syndicalists, 3 interventionist Socialists, and 6 others mentioned as active in the interventionist movement.

[23] *Il Fascio* 20 May 1920 ; also ibid., 13, 27 September 1919 (Celso Morisi).

[24] R. Vicentini, *Il movimento fascista veneto attraverso il diario di uno squadrista* (Venice 1935), p. 91.

[25] *O.O.*, 12, p. 146 (16 January 1919).

[26] *Il Fascio*, 18 October 1919.

[27] Vivarelli, *Dopoguerra*, p. 472.

[28] W. Sauer, 'National Socialism : Totalitarianism or Fascism ?' *AHR* 1967, p. 411. Rumi. 'Mussolini e il programma', pp. 8–9. For the *arditi* and Fascism, see F. Cordova, *Arditi e legionari dannunziani* (Padua 1969), pp. 1–37 ; *O.O.*, 11, pp. 241–3.

[29] De Felice, *Sindacalismo rivoluzionario*, pp. 119–26 ; Cordova, op. cit., pp. 113–17.

[30] See De Felice, I, p. 523 for the position in July 1919.

[31] E. Mecheri, 'Chi ha tradito ?', *Rivelazioni e documenti inedite di un vecchio fascista* (Milan 1947), p. 55.

[32] *Il Fascio*, 17 April, 22 May 1920.

[33] Ibid., 25 October 1919. For the ties between the Futurists and the *arditi* see Vivarelli, *Dopoguerra*, pp. 284–5. The problem of intellectual unemployment must be borne in mind here. Between 1913–14 and 1921–2, the number of students in law, science, mathematics, letters, philosophy, medicine and chemistry increased from 24,000 to 40,000 approx. ; V. Castrilli, 'L'utilizzazione del lavoro intellettuale', *La Stirpe*, Dec. 1923.

[34] Ibid., 26 June 1920 ; De Felice, I, p. 594 ; *Dai fasci al PNF*, pp. 145–6 ; Marinetti, *Futurismo e fascismo*, p. 157.

[35] Santarelli, *Origini*, pp. 115–16.

[36] *Dai fasci*, p. 146. It is significant that at the 1919 meeting of the Nationalist association more than one speaker criticized their leaders for neglecting the problems of the middle class and petty bourgeoisie: *Il nazionalismo e i problemi del lavoro e della scuola*, ed. P. L. Occhini (Rome 1919), pp. 59–60, 78–9. On the growth

of the white-collar class in the services and administration 1901–21, see P. Sylos Labini, *Problemi dello sviluppo economico*, p. 143.

[37] A. Lanzillo, *Lo stato e la crisi sociale e monetaria postbellica* (Milan 1920), p. 163 ff.

[38] Vivarelli, *Dopoguerra*, pp. 589–92 ; De Felice, p. 479.

[39] Rumi, *Mussolini e il programma*, p. 7.

[40] On Mussolini's productivism, see De Felice, pp. 494–7, with criticisms of Vivarelli, *Dopoguerra*, pp. 270–4 ; Santarelli, *Origini*, pp. 168, 216.

[41] Vivarelli, *Dopoguerra*, p. 274 ; Rumi, 'Il Popolo d'Italia', p. 443.

[42] Rumi, ibid., p. 444.

[43] Vivarelli, *Dopoguerra*, p. 275.

[44] *O.O.*, 12, p. 325.

[45] E. Santarelli, *Storia*, 1, pp. 102, 115–16.

[46] *O.O.*, 14, p. 468.

[47] M. Rocca, *Il primo fascismo* (Rome 1964), pp. 37–44.

[48] De Felice, pp. 589, 597.

[49] *Popolo d'Italia*, 6 March 1919. G. Prezzolini, *Fascism* (trans. London 1926), p. 50.

[50] Vivarelli, *Dopoguerra*, pp. 287–8, and see note 38 above.

[51] Ibid., pp. 335–8.

[52] ACS, PS, 1919, b.78, fasc. Fasci Roma, 5 July 1919 ; De Felice, op. cit., p. 533n.

[53] Ibid., 8 July.

[54] De Felice, op. cit., p. 560 ; D'Annunzio to Mussolini, 16 September 1919 : 'Where are the combatants, the volunteers, the *arditi*, the futurists ?'

[55] ACS, MRF, b. 107 fasc., Verona.

[56] Ibid., b. 102 fasc. Ferrara.

[57] Gramsci, *Socialismo e Fascismo*, p. 10.

[58] ACS, MRF, b. 101 fasc. Crema, 14 September 1920.

[59] F. Ercole, *Dal Nazionalismo al Fascismo* (Rome 1928), p. 206.

[60] ACS, MRF, fasc. Trieste, 10 September 1920 F. Giunta ; cf. also ibid., 26 August.

[61] C. Silvestri, *Dalla redenzione al fascismo (Trieste 1918–1922)* (Udine 1959), p. 50.

[62] Chiurco, *Storia della rivoluzione fascista*, 2, p. 57.

[63] Silvestri, *Dalla redenzione*, pp. 54–67.

[64] See U. Banchelli, *Memorie di uno squadrista*, pp. 11, 12 for a classic example of this mentality.

[65] D. Grandi, 5 February 1921, letter to Mario Missiroli (St Antony's documents, J. 330, 113304).

[66] Gramsci, *Socialismo e Fascismo*, pp. 297–302.

[67] A. Lanzillo, *Le rivoluzioni del dopoguerra* (Citta di Castello, 1922), pp. 222–6. See also M. Rocca, *Idee sul fascismo* (Florence 1924), pp. 31–43.

[68] Owing to the special facilities granted to officers to complete their studies, there were a large number of 'officer-students' who attended university while still technically belonging to the army.

[69] P. A. Vecchia, *Storia del fascismo bresciano* (Brescia 1929), pp. 29–31.

[70] A. M. Parmeggiani, 'I giovani nelle origini del fascismo', *Ricerche storiche* (1967) passim, esp. pp. 22, 34, 48.

[71] M. Vaini, *Le origini del fascismo a Mantova* (Rome 1961), pp. 64–5, 102–3.

[72] ACS, MRF, b. 107, fasc. Vigevano (11 October 1920 and n.d.); ACS, PS, 1925. b. 96, fasc. costituzione fasci Bergamo (18 February 1921) for other examples of student predominance in the Fascist movement. In Bergamo, while the *fascio* was still in course of formation 'the greater part of the secondary school students and of the demobilized officers have joined'. On 7 May 1921 the *Avanguardia Studentesca* numbered 350 members, the *fascio* proper only 300. See also ACS, MRF, b. 101 fasc. Cremona (9 November 1920).

[73] ACS, MRF, b. 100, fasc. Bologna (14 August 1919), 'V.G.'

[74] For the psychological atmosphere, see E. Vittorini, *Il garofano rosso* (Milan 1963); M. Bergamo, *Il fascismo e i partiti politici*, pp. 70–1. The fascist movement supported the agitation of the students in polytechnics and faculties of chemistry for higher professional status; *Dai fasci*, p. 448.

[75] De Felice, op. cit., pp. 590–2.

[76] Ibid., pp. 636–7.

[77] G. Gervasi, 'Le origini del fascismo in Arezzo e provincia', unpublished MS, p. 243; P. Cordoni, 'Le origini del fascismo a Siena' (MS), p. 167.

[78] L. Arbizzani, 'L'avvento del fascismo nel bolognese, 1920–1922', *Movimento operaio e socialista* (1964), pp. 92, 94; Parmeggiani, 'I giovani', pp. 29–30.

[79] Presidenza del Consiglio dei Ministri – Istituto Centrale di Statistica, *Censimento della popolazione del Regno d'Italia al 7 dicembre 1921* (Rome 1927), VIII (Emilia), p. 161 (19.1 per cent industrial workers and 7.1 per cent employees).

[80] ACS, PS, 1921, b. 73 fasc., Bologna Associazione combattenti (18 May 1919).

[81] ACS, MRF, b. 100, fasc. Bologna (20 October 1919). G. Pedrini to Pasella.

[82] See note 80.

[83] ACS, PS, ibid. (15 June 1919); ACS, MRF, n.d. (but August 1919), G. Pedrini; see *Il Fascio* 4 October 1919.

[84] B. Uva, 'la crisi del massimalismo e la nascita del fascismo a Bologna', *Pagine libere*, 1961, n. 2–3, p. 74.

[85] Arbizzani, pp. 83–5.

[86] ACS, MRF, b. 103, fasc. Milano (10 September 1920). Gen. Sailer; see also ibid., 30 September Bolzon and undated leaflet headed 'Ai giovani il governo del fascio Milanese di combattimento' which protests against outside (political and military) interference.

[87] ACS, MRF, b. 100, fasc. Bologna (26 April 1920).

[88] Ibid., 28 April.

[89] Uva, 'La crisi del massimalismo', p. 72.

[90] ACS, MRF, ibid. (4 May 1920).

[91] Ibid., 23, 27 August (Ghinelli), 1 September (Arpinati).

[92] ACS, PS, 1925, b. 96, fasc. Costituzione fasci Bologna (17 February 1921); see also ACS, PS, 1921, b. 77 (28 October 1920).

[93] ACS, PS, AGR, *Atti Speciali*, b. 3, f. 28, Di Tarsia report (15 July 1922).

[94] See 'le origini dello squadrismo – Il convegno agrario di Rimini', *Emilia* (July–August 1951), pp. 232–6.

[95] *La Stampa*, 10–11 May 1921.

[96] ACS, PS, 1925, b. 96 constit. fasci (17 February, 9 May 1921). For polarization of political forces and the absorption of minor 'bourgeois' parties by Fascism, see ACS, MRF b. 101 fasc. Cremona (9 November 1920).

[97] In Ferrara province 51.2 per cent of all heads of family were employed in agriculture, compared with 37.1 per cent in Bologna (Censimento, pp. 101–2).

[98] R.Forti and G.Ghedini, *L'avvento del fascismo: cronache ferraresi* (Ferrara 1922), pp. 52–4, 64–7 cf. Lucca, where the first notable act of the *fascio* was to remove the white flag of the PPI from the town hall and to substitute the tricolour. After this exploit, money began to come in from the 'citizenry' : (ACS, MRF, b. 103, fasc. Lucca 7 November 1920).

[99] Ibid., p. 55, 76 ; ACS, MRF, b. 102, fasc. Ferrara (19 November), O. Gaggioli. Significantly, the first reported contact between Fascists and agrarians was established through the 'administrator' (i.e. treasurer) of the *fascio*. See also F.Pittorru, 'Origini del fascismo ferrarese', *Emilia* (October 1951), pp. 293–8.

[100] ACS, ibid. (19 November, 8 December 1920). 6000 members took part in the assembly of the *fascio* on 16 February 1921 (ACS, ibid., 16 February).

[101] Forti and Ghedini, *L'Avvento del fascismo*, p. 123 ; I. Torsiello, *Il tramonto delle baronie rosse* (Ferrara 1921), p. 183.

[102] ACS, ibid. (29 December 1920), I. Gaggioli (the brother of O. Gaggioli, the First Secretary of the *fascio* and later leader of the dissident group in Ferrara).

[103] Torsiello, *Il tramonto*, p. 184.

[104] ACS, MRF, b. 107, fasc. Umbertide, 27 August 1920.

[105] For threat of secession, see Gaggioli letter cit. note 104.

[106] ACS, MRF, b. 102, fasc. Ferrara (2 January 1921).

[107] ACS, MRF, ibid., 8 January 1921; Pittorru, 'Origini', pp. 294–5; the *fascio*'s 'land office', run by the rich landowner Vittorio Pedriali, distributed 7000 hectares of land in February and March 1921, and about 12,000 hectares in all.

[108] M.Missiroli, *Il fascismo e il colpo di stato dell'ottobre 1922* (Rocca S. Casciano 1966), pp. 120–30.

[109] De Felice, II, pp. 55–6, 736–40. F.Catalano, *Potere economico e fascismo, la crisi del dopoguerra 1919–1921* (Milan 1964), pp. 237–9.

[110] De Felice, II, pp. 74–5 ; *Popolo d'Italia* 15 February, 1 March 1921 ; Catalano, *Potere economico*, pp. 239–40.

[111] ACS, MRF, b. 103, fasc. Modena (12 March 1921). De Felice, p. 76 mentions this report, but does not note the contrast between the two halves of the motion voted.

[112] Rocca, *Idee sul fascismo* (Florence 1924), pp. 36–41.

[113] ACS, MRF, b. 106, fasc. Monza (22 June 1921), Setti; Vicentini, op. cit, p. 104 ; ACS, ibid., b. 101, fasc. Crema (23 March, 10 April 1921). (See also Catalano, *Potere economico*, pp. 245–6.)

[114] Catalano, *Potere economico*, pp. 243–5.

[115] ACS, MRF, b. 102, fasc. Ferrara (17 February 1921). For the circumstances of Balbo's adherence to Fascism, see *Voce Repubblicana*, 29 November 1924 ; however, the evidence of Balbo's enemies as to his motives cannot be regarded as conclusive. His membership of the Republican party was not at that time inconsistent with Fascist sympathies, and he had been an ardent interventionist.

[116] ACS, Min. Interno, Gabinetto Bonomi Ordine pubblico b. 1, fasc. 3 – Fascisti e socialisti – pacificazione (14 August 1921), Prefect of Ferrara.

[117] ACS, PS, 1925 b. 96, fasc. costituzione fasci – Ferrara (5, 27 October 1921). Pittorru, 'Origini', p. 297 ff.

[118] Repaci, 2 pp. 273–5 ; see also 1, pp. 369–71.

[119] Letter cit., note 107.

[120] Loc. cit., note 117 above. Cf. ACS, PS, b. 103, fasc. Modena (n.d. but September 1921) for similar protest by urban Fascists against agrarians, including Carlo Zuccoli.

[121] Pittorru 'Origini', p. 297; St Antony's documents, J 263/1, 073792–9, report of T. Beltrani to Grand Council, July 1923.

[122] See note 120.

[123] Lanzillo, *Lo stato e la crisi*, p. 227. Cf. C. Scorza, *Brevi note sul fascismo, sui capi, sui gregari* (Florence 1930), pp. 78–9, for a typical Fascist exaltation of the mass of the petty and middle bourgeoisie as the backbone of Fascism.

[124] This was the case, for example, in Genoa, Milan (where the bloc gained only 1.8 per cent but in absolute terms increased its vote by over a third) and Florence. The same was true in provincial towns (Mantua and Brescia) and in smaller centres (Empoli and S. Miniato in Tuscany); see V. Giusti, *Le correnti politiche italiane attraverso due riforme elettorali dal 1909 al 1921* (Florence 1922).

[125] Gervasi MS. cit., p. 488ff. In larger cities, such as Milan and Florence, the elections to the *Direttori* of the *fascio* reveal a high number of petty-bourgeois candidates.

[126] *Il Fascio*, 29 November 1919.

[127] ACS, PS 1921, b. 72 fasc. Genova (6 May 1919).

[128] ACS, MRF, b. 102, fasc. Genova (20 August 1919). Dagnino to Mecheri; ibid., b. 106 fasc. Spezia 4 February, 7 April 1920, Rapuzzi to Pasella.

[129] Ibid., b. 102, fasc. Genova (July 1920).

[130] Ibid., b. 106, fasc. Spezia (3 July 1920); (see also ACS, PS, 1925, b. 97 Costituzione fasci, which reports that the Savona *fascio* was subsidized by the industrialists).

[131] ACS, MRF, b. 99, fasc. Cengio (22 December 1921), E. Mazzocchi. See also ibid., fasc. Spezia (12 March 1921), Del Santo.

[132] 'Il fascismo in Liguria', *Critica politica*, 25 May 1923. ACS, MRF, b. 102 fasc. Genova (1 April, 28 May, 18 June 1921).

[133] ACS, ibid. (5 April 1921 General A. Scotti. 9 April C. Rossi).

[134] Ibid. (16 June, 18 August 1921).

[135] *Critica politica*, loc. cit.

[136] ACS, PS, 1925 b. 96, fasc. Alessandria (20 January 1921); ibid., b. 97, fasc. Pavia (20 January, 28 February 1921); ibid., b. 96, fasc. Arezzo (4, 15 February 1921); ibid., b. 95, fasc. Grosseto (27 May 1921). ACS, MRF, b. 99, fasc. Alessandria (13 August 1920): 'Fortunately I have the support of the local newspaper of the agrarian party, *La Terra*. What do you expect, Signor Rossi? We could of course form a kind of association of *carbonari* for beginners, if need be, but what I'm after is to have a body which answers to the Fascist programme, and which will work – under cover – to prepare the ground for a more vigorous action tomorrow!

[137] Rumi, 'Il popolo d'Italia', pp. 472–3.

[138] *O.O.* 18, pp. 201–7, 'Il fascismo e i rurali' (25 May 1922); see also A. Serpieri, *La guerra e le classi rurali italiane* (Bari 1930), pp. 246–8.

[139] The data on social composition comes from the answers to the questionnaire sent out by the secretariat in preparation for the 1921 Congress. Out of the 151,644 members (about half the total) surveyed, the overall social composition was as follows: 2.8 per cent industrialists, 7.7 per cent free professions and teachers,

12 per cent agricultural proprietors and leaseholders, 13 per cent students, 9.8 per cent private employees, 4.8 per cent public employees, 9.2 per cent shopkeepers and artisans, 16.4 per cent industrial and transport workers, 24.3 per cent agricultural workers and sharecroppers. (Tasca *Nascita e avvento*, 1, p. 257.)

[140] Vaini, *Le origini del fascismo*. The participation of peasants in the *directtori* of the *fasci* was small; in Alessandria province a sample shows it as 4.7 per cent while the participation of artisans and workers was considerably greater (16 per cent in Pisa, and 27 per cent in Alessandria). ACS, PS, 1925, b. 98, fasc. Costituzione *fasci* Pisa: ibid., b. 96, Alessandria).

[141] Catalano, *Potere economico*, pp. 262–4. Chiurco, *Storia della Rivoluzione*, 3, p. 59 for unemployed Fascists in Cremona; for Piedmont, see M. Abrate, *La lotta sindacale nella industrializzazione in Italia, 1906–26* (Turin 1967), pp. 375–6; for mobilization of unemployed against unions, see *Rivoluzione Liberale*, 27 August 1922, S. Caramella (Ferrara, Polesine, Piedmont).

[142] P. Corner, 'Fascism in Ferrara 1915–25', unpublished MS, Ch. 7, passim.

[143] On the problem of the *mezzadri* and Fascism, see E. Rossi, *Popolo d'Italia*, 13 March 1921 (who advocated the encouragement of the creation of smallholdings by the *mezzadri*); *Unità*, 31 July 1924.

[144] Gervasi MS, cit., p. 271ff. *Itinerari*, 1960 'Contadini della Toscana', ed. F. C. Rossi, p. 471–3.

[145] *Il movimento delle squadre*, 2, *Italia centrale*, p. 46; the secretary of the *fascio* in February 1921 was also the secretary of the Ilva dockyards, although it seems that at first the capitalists were hesitant in their support because they were too afraid of the revolutionaries; see also ACS, MRF, b. 104, fasc. Piombino 28 February 1921; ACS, PS 1925 b. 98. fasc Pisa, 11 March 1922.

[146] A. Bernieri, 'Il fascismo a Carrara tra il 1919 e il 1931', *Movimento operaio e socialista* (1964), p. 47ff.

[147] ACS, MRF, b. 100, fasc. Carrara (October 1921); out of 1600 members 5 were industrialists, 65 white collar workers, 42 shopkeepers and traders, 220 students and 1270 workers.

[148] ACS, PS 1925, b. 96, fasc. Costituzione fasci (6 January 1921).

[149] De Felice, II, p. 98; Vicentini op. cit., p. 129; the majority of deputies in Emilia, Lombardy, the Veneto and Venezia Giulia favoured the republican tendency. In Piedmont, Liguria and all the regions of central and southern Italy the monarchist deputies were in the majority. See also A. Misuri, *Rivolta morale* (Milan 1924), pp. 24, 28.

[150] De Felice II, p. 96–7; ACS, MRF, b. 107, fasc. Venezia (14 January 1921), Lanfranchi; ibid., b. 102, fasc. Genova (16 June 1921); Colapietra, *Napoli*, p. 165.

[151] ACS, MRF, b. 106 fasc. Torino (26 May, 7, 16 June).

[152] E.g. Arezzo: see Gervasi MS cit., pp. 348–53, 479–81.

[153] M. Rocca, *Il primo fascismo*, pp. 27–54; *Idee sul fascismo*, pp. 23–30.

[154] See Rocca, *Idee sul fascismo*, pp. 34–5, for a particularly clear expression of the elite conception.

[155] *Dai fasci al PNF*, p. 170; however, the first statute of the PNF in fact established a dual system of authority. The squads were to depend 'politically' on the *direttorio* of the *fascio*, but in matters of discipline on their own commander.

[156] ACS, MRF, b. 103, fasc. Mantova passim; for Scorza and Tamburini, see below, Ch. 7.

[157] Vicentini, *Movimento fascista veneto*, p. 163.

[158] ACS, MRF, b. 101, fasc. Cremona (25 November, 26 December 1920, 6 January 1921), Farinacci; ibid., fasc. Crema (13 August 1921), G. Bianco.

[159] Vicentini, op. cit., p. 154.

[160] *Dai fasci al PNF*, p. 179.

[161] Ibid., pp. 177–8; De Felice, II, p. 187.

[162] Tasca, *Nascita e avvento*, p. 260.

[163] *Il Fascio*, 11 June 1921.

[164] Vicentini, op. cit., pp. 163–7.

[165] Ibid., pp. 195–200; De Felice, II, pp. 198–200.

[166] St Antony's documents, J. 330 113307–10. For the earlier overtures (August 1921) of Grandi, Balbo and Marsich to D'Annunzio, see De Felice, II, p. 151; for the rank and file view that Mussolini had become too much of a 'politician', see Banchelli, *Memorie*, pp. 149–52.

[167] *Gerarchia*, October 1922, p. 590. See also ibid., January 1922, pp. 1–2 and June 1922, pp. 295–300 (Mussolini); ibid., October 1922, p. 600 ('Volt'). 'Fascism once in power will presumably no longer organize punitive expeditions, but will be able to employ the bureaucracy, the magistracy, the police, the schools and the army in the same spirit as it formerly showed in manœuvring the action squads.'

[168] *O.O.*, 18, pp. 66–72.

[169] A. Aquarone, *L'organizzazione dello stato totalitario* (Turin 1965), pp. 315–29.

4 The March on Rome

[1] Tasca, *Nascita e avvento*, pp. 552–3; ibid., 1, pp. 195, 223–4.

[2] The Socialists, together with the Communists, won 139 seats, compared with 156 in 1919; the Popolari won 106, a gain of 6. The Fascists won 35 seats, and the Nationalists 10.

[3] I. Balbo, *Diario 1922* (Milan 1932), pp. 11–12; Salvemini, *Scritti*, 1, p. 564.

[4] Tasca, *Nascita e avvento*, 1, pp. 263–5.

[5] Santarelli, *Storia del movimento*, p. 277.

[6] Tasca, *Nascita e avvento*, 1, pp. 292–3.

[7] De Rosa, *Storia del movimento cattolico*, p. 218; D. Veneruso, *La vigilia del fascismo* (Bologna 1968), pp. 210–14, 330–3, 337–9.

[8] De Felice, II, p. 279; De Rosa, *Storia del movimento cattolico*, p. 237; Veneruso, *La vigilia*, pp. 287–9.

[9] S. Jacini, *Storia del partito popolare* (Milan 1951), pp. 297–9; De Rosa, *Storia del movimento cattolico*, pp. 241–2, 249; and see also C. Corradini's letter to Giolitti (18 June) in *Carteggio Giolitti*, 3, pp. 369–70.

[10] De Felice, II, pp. 268–70.

[11] Valeri, *Da Giolitti a Mussolini*, pp. 109–10; Tasca, *Nascita e avvento*, pp. 331–3, 376–84.

[12] The King intervened in person to bring the crisis to an end. He had been alarmed by rumours of an impending Fascist coup. *Il diario di Salandra*, ed. G.B. Gifuni (Milan 1969), pp. 256–7.

[13] Repaci, *Marcia su Roma*, 1, p. 210.

[14] Spriano, *Partito comunista*, p. 230.

[15] Repaci, *Marcia*, 1, pp. 135–51, 387–98; N. Valeri, *D'Annunzio davanti al fascismo* (Florence 1963), pp. 48–87.

[16] Balbo, *Diario*, pp. 178–81 ; Repaci, *Marcia*, 1, pp. 429–35 ; 2, pp. 309–10.

[17] Repaci, *Marcia*, 2, p. 60 ; Valeri, *Da Giolitti a Mussolini*, pp. 133–8, 144–63.

[18] Repaci, *Marcia*, 1, pp. 403–11 ; *Carteggio Giolitti*, 3, pp. 386–8, 392–3.

[19] Repaci, *Marcia*, 2, pp. 47, 68–9.

[20] Ibid., 1, pp. 415–24 ; 2, pp. 70–1 ; the hypothesis that Facta was playing a deliberate double game is advanced by Valeri, *Da Giolitti a Mussolini*, pp. 129–33.

[21] Repaci, *Marcia*, 1, pp. 451–5 ; *Diario Salandra*, pp. 269–70.

[22] Valeri, *Da Giolitti a Mussolini*, pp. 170–1.

[23] Repaci, *Marcia*, 1, pp. 445–8.

[24] Ibid., pp. 465–72, 481–7.

[25] C. Malaparte, *Technique du coup d'état* (Paris 1948).

[26] ACS, Uff. cifra tel. in arrivo (26 October), n. 28090 ; Balbo, *Diario*, pp. 195–8. Balbo, it must be remembered, had every motive to emphasize the heroic aspect of the March on Rome.

[27] Repaci, *Marcia*, 2, pp. 282–3.

[28] Valeri, *Da Giolitti a Mussolini*, pp. 172–3.

[29] Repaci, *Marcia*, 1, pp. 506–7.

[30] E. Ferraris, *La Marcia su Roma veduta dal Viminale* (Rome 1946), p. 95.

[31] Repaci, *Marcia*, 1, p. 497 ; 2, pp. 429, 500–1.

[32] ACS, Uff. cifra tel. in arrivo (28 October) 1 am n. 28224, Prefect of Siena.

[33] Repaci, *Marcia*, 1, pp. 498–9, 539 ; ACS, ibid. (27 October) 11.45 pm n. 28217, Prefect of Cremona.

[34] ACS, ibid., n. 28252 11.10 am (28 October).

[35] ACS, ibid., n. 28268 10 am (28 October); ibid. n. 28282, 28320.

[36] ACS, ibid., n. 28428 (29 October), Prefect of Bergamo ; Repaci, op. cit., 1, pp. 537–9.

[37] ACS, ibid., n. 28374 (29 October).

[38] Repaci, *Marcia*, 1, pp. 503–4.

[39] Vivarelli, *Dopoguerra*, p. 461n.

[40] Repaci, *Marcia*, 2, p. 51.

[41] Ibid., pp. 66–8.

[42] P. Puntoni, *Parla Vittorio Emmanuele III* (Milan 1958), pp. 40, 288.

[43] Repaci, *Marcia*, 2, p. 69.

[44] Ibid., 1, pp. 504–5.

[45] Ibid., 1, p. 501.

[46] Salvemini, *Scritti*, 2, p. 60. N.B. Also Salandra's evidence (*Diario*, p. 271): 'The King told me on his own initiative that he had twice refused to sign the decree for the *stato d'assedio*. He asked me bluntly if he had done well. I replied in the affirmative, above all because the government did not have the force to put the threat of resistance into effect. The King agreed with me in deriding the military preparations that had been made around Rome'.

[47] Repaci, *Marcia*, 2, p. 386.

[48] Ibid., p. 392 (F. Cocco Ortu).

5 Mussolini and his Allies

[1] De Felice, II, p. 372.

[2] Melograni, 'Confindustria e fascismo tra il 1919 e il 1925', *Il Nuovo Osservatore*,

1965, pp. 843–5; *Epistolario Albertini*, 3, p. 1594; ACS, Uff. cifra, tel in arrivo n. 28373, Lusignoli to Facta, 11.55 pm (28 October).

[3] Salandra, *Memorie*, p. 25; Salvatorelli and Mira, *Storia d'Italia nel periodo fascista* (Turin 1956), p. 222.

[4] E. Ferraris, *La marcia su Roma veduta dal Viminale*, pp. 122–3 (telephone conversation between Albertini and d'Atri); Repaci, *Marcia su Roma*, 2, pp. 151–2; *Corriere della Sera*, 30 October; *La Stampa*, 30–31 October.

[5] See above p. 82; Repaci, *Marcia*, 2, p. 422.

[6] Repaci, *Marcia*, 2, p. 380; De Felice, II, p. 383; Valeri, *D'Annunzio davanti al fascismo* (Florence 1963), pp. 95–6; *Corriere della Sera*, 30 October; *La Stampa*, 29–30 October (G. Bevilacqua).

[7] *Filippo Turati attraverso le lettere di corrispondenti*, A. Schiavi, (Bari 1947), pp. 201–2; A. Schiavi, *La vita e l'opera di Giacomo Matteotti* (Rome 1957), pp. 294–6; *Battaglie Sindacali*, 7 November.

[8] See Salvemini, *Scritti*, 2, pp. 77, 81–2.

[9] See note 4 above.

[10] M. Rocca, *Come il fascismo*, p. 116.

[11] See note 4 above; *Epistolario Albertini*, 4, pp. 1644–5.

[12] Oviglio (Justice), De Stefani (Finance), Giuriati (Liberated Territories), Federzoni (Colonies), De Capitani (Agriculture), Teofilo Rossi (Industry), Carnazza (Public Works), Colonna di Cesaro (Post Office), Tangorra (Treasury), Cavazzoni (Labour), Diaz (War), Thaon di Revel (Navy), and Gentile (Education).

[13] Repaci, op. cit., 2, pp. 228–9, 375–6; *Epistolario Albertini*, 4, pp. 1641–2.

[14] Melograni, *Corriere della Sera*, pp. 169–70; cf. V. Ojetti, *I Taccuini 1914–1943* (Florence 1954), pp. 103–4; and Charles-Roux, *Souvenirs Diplomatiques: Ambassade a Rome 1919–1925* (Paris 1961), p. 194.

[15] C. Rossi, *Mussolini com'era* (Rome 1947), pp. 132–3.

[16] De Rosa, *Storia del movimento cattolico*, 2, p. 306–7; Repaci, *Marcia*, 2, pp. 351–2.

[17] De Rosa, *Storia*, 2, p. 299ff.; E. Pratt Howard, *Il partito popolare italiano* (Florence 1957), pp. 385–7.

[18] De Rosa, *Storia*, p. 305.

[19] E. Ferraris, op. cit., pp. 126–7.

[20] *O.O.*, 19, pp. 347–8; *Giornale d'Italia*, 3 November; G. Rochat, op. cit., pp. 418–19.

[21] L. Ganapini, 'L'Italia', in *Dopoguerra e fascismo*, p. 576.

[22] *Giornale d'Italia* 5 November; Charles-Roux, *Souvenirs diplomatiques* pp. 195–8.

[23] *Giornale d'Italia*, 8 November.

[24] Ibid., 3 November.

[25] Rocca, *Come il fascismo*, p. 116; *Giornale d'Italia*, 23 November; Pratt Howard, *Partito popolare*, pp. 360–1.

[26] G. Matteotti, *Reliquie* (Milan 1962), pp. 55–8; Aquarone, *L'organizzazione dello stato totalitario*, pp. 6–14.

[27] *Giornale d'Italia*, 12 November; ibid., 14 November.

[28] *O.O.*, 19, pp. 15–24.

[29] AP, C, XXVI legis., 1st session, 9, pp. 8416–36; both the *Mondo* (17, 18

November) and the *Corriere della Sera* (18 November) agreed that after Mussolini's speech it would be best if there were an immediate dissolution.

[30] Valeri, *Da Giolitti a Mussolini*, p. 180.

[31] Manzotti, *Socialismo riformista*, pp. 206–7.

[32] Salvatorelli and Mira, op. cit., pp. 232–3 ; *Domani d'Italia*, 31 December 1922 ; APC, ibid., pp. 8443–5 (De Gasperi).

[33] 7 November 1922.

[34] Ibid., 16, 26 November.

[35] De Felice, II, pp. 480, 770.

[36] In general, see Valeri, *D'Annunzio*, pp. 91–103 ; De Felice, II, op. cit., pp. 602–9 ; *Carteggio D'Annunzio – Mussolini (1919–1938)* ed. R. De Felice and F. Mariano (Milan 1971), pp. xxxiii–xxxviii

[37] *l'Internazionale* (Parma) 16 December 1922 ; *La Stampa*, 12 December.

[38] 7 November 1922 ; see also Salvemini *Scritti*, 2, pp. 7–8 ; *Il Mondo*, 26 November, 30 November, 1, 2 December.

[39] Turati, *Lettere* cit., pp. 204–6 ; Arfe, op. cit., pp. 359–60.

[40] Valeri, *Da Giolitti*, p. 97.

[41] T. Zaniboni, *Testamento spirituale* (Milan 1949), pp. 14–15 ; De Felice, II, p. 605 ; *Popolo d'Italia*, 3, 5 December ; *La Stampa*, 5–6, 6–7, 7–8 December.

[42] O.O., 19, p. 383 ; *Giornale d'Italia*, 5–6 December ; *La Giustizia*, 8 December ; *La Stampa*, 8–9 December ; *Cremona Nuova*, 7, 8 December.

[43] O.O., 19, p. 66. *Il Nuovo Paese* 16 December 1922 ; *Giornale d'Italia*, 17 December. For the Lusignoli intrigue, see ACS, SPCR, H/R, Bergamini, 16 December 1922, Mussolini to B.

[44] Valeri, *Da Giolitti*, pp. 101–2 ; Cordova, op. cit., pp. 156–7.

[45] Spriano, *Partito comunista*, 1, pp. 260–72.

[46] *Il Mondo*, 17 December 1922.

[47] Salvatorelli, *Nazionalfascismo*, pp. 145–8.

[48] *Corriere della Sera*, 2 August 1923.

[49] De Felice, II, pp. 510–12.

[50] *Giornale d'Italia*, 28 January 1923 ; *Corriere della Sera, La Stampa*, 30–31 January ; *Il diario di Salandra*, pp. 279–86.

[51] ACS, PS, 1921 b-89, fasc. Bologna, Congresso liberale democratico (19, 22 November 1921). Valeri, *Da Giolitti*, pp. 105–9.

[52] *Giornale d'Italia*, 11 October 1922, gives a breakdown of the voting at the First Congress of the Liberal party at Bologna : For young Liberals, see ibid., 5 January 1923.

[53] Ibid.

[54] Ibid., 30 January 1923.

[55] See note 52 above.

[56] M. Missiroli, *Una Battaglia perduta* (Milan 1924), p. 376.

[57] *Carteggio Giolitti*, 3, p. 416, Senator Rolandi Ricci.

[58] *Corriere della Sera*, 15 June 1923. *Il nord nella storia d'Italia*, ed. L. Cafagna (Bari 1962), pp. 496–507.

[59] ACS, GF, b. 7, fasc. Napoli, report on Consiglio Nazionale of Liberal party.

[60] *Giornale d'Italia*, 17 March 1923.

[61] ACS, GF, b. 7 fasc. Novara (4, 10 July 1923), Liberal congress at Biella.

[62] See De Felice, II, pp. 508-12 for complaints of the Liberal party and the Democrazia Sociale on this score.

[63] De Rosa, *Giolitti e il fascismo*, pp. 23, 28. Giolitti's phrase about 'mistakes' echoes the interview given by Croce to the *Giornale d'Italia*, 27 October 1923 ; see B. Croce, *Pagine sparse* (Naples 1943) 2, p. 372.

[64] Valeri, *Da Giolitti*, p. 177 for Lusignoli; cf. also ACS Carte Giolitti, b. 9, fasc. 121, 12 November 1922, Garroni.

[65] See the review of Giolitti's memoirs by F. Ciarlantini, *Popolo d'Italia*, 17 December 1922.

[66] Valeri, *Da Giolitti*, p. 181.

[67] G. Giolitti, *Discorsi extraparlamentari*, p. 345.

[68] Valeri, *Da Giolitti*, p. 187.

[69] ibid., p. 180 (letter to Malagodi).

[70] M. Soleri, *Memorie*, (Turin 1949), p. 179.

[71] Giolitti, *Discorsi extraparlamentari*, pp. 342-3, 348-51; *Carteggio Giolitti*, 3, pp. 396-7, 4 February 1924, Sforza ; ACS, Carte Giolitti, b. 9 fasc. 121 (2 May 1923) C. Corradini.

[72] L. Salvatorelli, 'Giolitti', *RSI* 1950, p. 532.

[73] See Salvatorelli, ibid., p. 531.

[74] *I grandi discorsi elettorali del 1924* (Milan 1924), p. 73.

[75] A. Salandra, *Memorie politiche 1916–1925* (Milan 1951), pp. 39-40.

[76] Giolitti, *Discorsi extraparlamentari*, p. 262 ; Valeri, *Da Giolitti*, p. 183ff.

[77] A. Salandra, *La neutralità italiana (1914)*, (Verona 1928), pp. 129-98, 372-3. For the themes of 'senility' and 'rejuvenation', see A. Salandra, *La politica nazionale e il partito liberale* (Milan 1912), p. xx ; C. De Biase, 'Salandra e il fascismo', *La vita italiana* April 1923, pp. 6-8.

[78] Salandra, *La politica nazionale*, p. 223.

[79] Salandra, *Memorie*, pp. 15-16.

[80] Ibid., p. 14.

[81] *Il Mondo*, 2 November 1922.

[82] Salandra, *Memorie*, p. 46.

[83] Ibid., pp. 37-8.

[84] Ibid., p. 31.

[85] Decleva, 'Il Giornale d'Italia' in *Dopoguerra e fascismo*, p. 42.

[86] *Giornale d'Italia*, 30 March 1923.

[87] *Grandi discorsi*, p. 75.

[88] Bianchi proposed that once the government's programme had been approved it should not have to ask for future votes of confidence until the end of the legislature (M. Bianchi, *I discorsi, gli scritti*, Rome 1931, p. 92).

[89] O. Barié, 'Luigi Albertini, il "Corriere della Sera" e l'opposizione a Giolitti', pt. 1, *Clio* 1966. 1, pp. 43, 56.

[90] L. Albertini, *In difesa della libertà* (Milan 1947), p. 38, speech of 9 August 1922.

[91] *Corriere della Sera*, 26 April 1923.

[92] See Barié, *Clio* 1966, pp. 52, 61 ; ibid., pt. 2, 1967, pp. 89-90.

[93] Melograni, *Il Corriere*, pp. xxii-iii, 14-15 ; *Corriere della Sera*, 29 October 1919.

[94] Albertini, *Difesa*, p. 28.

[95] For evidence of Albertini's personal reservations about Fascism, see Ojetti, *Taccuini*, p. 47 (May 1921) ; Melograni, *Il Corriere*, pp. xxv-xxxiii ; the *Corriere's*

line became more pro-Fascist during the period from October 1921 to March 1922 when Albertini was representing Italy at the disarmament conference in Washington and left the editorship, to his brother.

96 Albertini, *Difesa*, p. 31. A. Albertini, *Vita di Luigi Albertini* (Rome 1945), p.185.

97 Valeri, *Da Giolitti*, pp. 181–9 ; Melograni, *Il Corriere*, pp. 209–24 ; P. Alatri, *Le origini del fascismo* (Bologna 1962), p. 371.

98 Melograni, *Il Corriere*, pp. xli–ii.

99 See note 91 above.

100 Ojetti, *Taccuini*, p. 145.

101 Salvemini, *Scritti sul fascismo*, 2, p. 61.

102 Gaeta, *Nazionalismo italiano*, p. 220.

103 Ibid., pp. 221–5.

104 St Antony's documents, J. 166, 048963–048969.

105 Gaeta, *Nazionalismo*, pp. 229–30 ; for communique on the merger, see *La Stampa*, 31 January – 1 February 1923.

106 De Felice, II, p. 502 ; *Il Nuovo Paese*, 17 December 1922, G. Pighetti.

107 Gaeta, *Nazionalismo*, pp. 204–5.

108 *Il Nuovo Paese*, 17 December 1922.

109 See E. Corradini, *Popolo d'Italia*, 14 June 1923 ; 'Fascism must undoubtedly remain as a political party and as a militia ; but for only one reason : because other political parties survive and the enemies of the nation... have by no means vanished.'

110 M. Missiroli, *Il fascismo e il colpo di stato dell'ottobre 1922* (Rocca S. Casciano 1966), pp. 158–62 ; *Il Mondo*, 27 February 1923.

111 Salvemini, *Scritti*, 2, p. 138.

6 Normalization

1 For the conquest of local power by the Fascists, see in general G. Matteotti, *Un anno di dominazione fascista*, (Rome n.d.), pp. 30, 34–5 ; G. Amendola, *La democrazia italiana contro il fascismo*, (Milan–Naples 1960), pp. 102–6. Particularly significant was the forced resignation of the communal council of Turin. The Liberals had hoped that the Prefect would support them against the threats of the local Fascists, but they discovered otherwise (*La Stampa*, 16–22 June 1923). See also ACS, PS, 1923 E 2, b 41, passim. For events in Milan, see *Corriere della Sera*, 8–10 June.

2 De Rosa, *Partito popolare*, pp. 325–8, 346.

3 Sturzo, *Discorsi politici*, pp. 217–60 ; De Rosa, op. cit., pp. 329–41.

4 I. Giordani, *Alcide de Gasperi, Il ricostruttore* (Rome 1955), p. 79.

5 See, e.g. ACS, GF, b. 10, f 92, Treviso (10 September 1923) Bishop of Treviso ; ibid., b. 3, f. 33, Bergamo 1923 ; ibid., b. 8, f. 78, Ravenna (16 January 1923).

6 Salvemini, *Scritti*, 2, p. 165.

7 De Rosa, *Partito popolare*, p. 349.

8 *Corriere della Sera*, 15 March 1923 ; *Cremona Nuova*, 3 April.

9 De Rosa, *Partito popolare*, pp. 350–1, 370n ; see also *Giornale di Roma*, 12 April 1923.

10 De Rosa, *Partito popolare*, pp. 352–80 ; De Felice, II, p. 500.

11 *Popolo d'Italia*, 21 April 1923 ; however, on 19 April the newspaper had stated

that the resignation of Don Sturzo was a necessary condition for the maintenance of the coalition.

[12] De Rosa, *Partito popolare*, pp. 381–2; *Corriere della Sera*, 24–5 April; *La Stampa*, 24–5 April.

[13] *Giornale di Roma*, 16 April 1923.

[14] *Corriere della Sera*, 6, 10 February 1923.

[15] Ibid., 14 February.

[16] *Corriere della Sera*, 2 April 1923.

[17] *Giornale d'Italia*, 8 April.

[18] *Il Gran Consiglio, nei primi dieci anni dell'era fascista* (Rome 1933), pp. 55–6.

[19] See below, Ch. 8, note 44.

[20] *La Stampa*, 27–8 April.

[21] A. Aquarone, *L'organizzazione dello stato totalitario*, p. 38n.

[22] *Corriere della Sera*, 22 May; *Popolo d'Italia*, 19, 20, 23 May; T–K, VI, pp. 25–6; De Rosa, *Partito popolare*, pp. 387–8.

[23] *Giornale d'Italia*, 23 May; *Il Mondo*, 25 May; *Popolo d'Italia*, 26 May.

[24] *La Stampa*, 26–7 May.

[25] See pp. 165, 179.

[26] *Il Mondo*, 25, 27, 30 May; *Popolo d'Italia*, 26 May.

[27] *Cremona Nuova*, 28 May; T–K, VI, p. 30.

[28] *La Stampa*, 26–7 May; for Fascist change of attitude, compare *Popolo d'Italia*, 27 May with 30–31 May.

[29] *Il Mondo*, 5 June; *O.O.*, 19, p. 241–63.

[30] See below, Ch. 8.

[31] The Liberal party *direzione* voted in favour of the 'fundamental principles' of the Electoral Bill (*Corriere della Sera*, 9 June 1923); for other statements accepting the bill, see *Il Mondo* 8 June (Orlando), 13 June (Democrazia Sociale); for the attitude of Giolitti, see De Rosa, *Giolitti e il fascismo*, pp. 19–20 (5 April).

[32] For the voting on the law, see AP, C, XXVI, legisl. 15 July, pp. 10681–4.

[33] E.g. 'Rastignac' (V. Morello), *Popolo d'Italia*, 6 June.

[34] *Popolo d'Italia*, 1, 16 June: the purpose of Mussolini's tour of the regions was to establish 'direct and immediate communication between the popular will and the person of the head of the Government'; see also Salvemini, *Scritti*, 2, p. 219,

[35] *Popolo d'Italia*, 19 June.

[36] C. Rossi, *Mussolini, com'era* (Rome 1947), p. 166.

[37] T–K, VI, pp. 86–7; see also pp. 63–4.

[38] A. C. Jemolo, *Chiesa e stato in Italia negli ultimi centi anni* (Turin 1948), p. 591.

[39] De Rosa, *Partito popolare*, pp. 378–9.

[40] De Felice, II, p. 199; Salvemini, *Scritti*, pp. 194–5.

[41] De Rosa, *Partito popolare*, pp. 381–9; on June 13 the *Popolo d'Italia* still hoped that an agreement could be reached with the parliamentary group. For the negotiations between the Fascists and the Popolari, see also M. Terzaghi, *Fascismo e Massoneria* (Milan 1950), pp. 84–6.

[42] De Rosa, *Partito popolare*, pp. 394–405; F. L. Ferrari, *L'azione cattolica e il regime* (Florence 1957), pp. 33–4, who contradicts Sturzo's claim to have resigned on his own initiative.

[43] De Rosa, *Partito popolare*, p. 405–6.

[44] See ACS, Ufficio Cifra tel. in arrivo (14–15 July) passim; ACS, GF, b. 8, f. 74 Pisa (14 July 1923) shows that the campaign was directly organized by the Government. For Pius XI's protest and its limitations see Ferrari, op. cit., p. 38.

[45] AP, C, XXVI legisl. discussioni, pp. 10530–8 (12 July), pp. 10612–20 (14 July).

[46] T–K, VI, pp. 63–4 (9 July). Turati reported, however, that De Nicola had a battalion of *carabinieri* within the building ready to repel an invasion.

[47] Rossi, *Mussolini*, pp. 174–5.

[48] G. Amendola, *La nuova democrazia* (Naples 1951), pp. 161–2. AP, C, ibid., pp. 10654–61, 15 July.

[49] Salvemini, *Scritti*, 2, p. 216 (Sforza's conversation with Victor Emmanuel); Rossi, op. cit., p. 166; De Felice, II, pp. 518, 523; *Giornale d'Italia*, 16 June 1923.

[50] T–K, VI, pp. 85–7.

[51] *O.O.*, 19, p. 308ff.

[52] For a criticism by a supporter of Amendola's decision to abstain in the vote on the bill, see E. Kühn Amendola – *Vita con Giovanni Amendola* (Florence 1960), p. 497 (G. Marone). It should be noted that 21 out of 35 members of the *Democrazia italiana* (the group of Nitti and Amendola) voted for the bill, only 5 abstaining. Among the former Social-Reformists, 15 out of 25 voted in favour, 5 against and 2 abstained. See n. 32 above.

[53] De Rosa *Partito popolare*, pp. 412–15.

[54] Salvemini, *Scritti*, p. 225; G. Carocci, *Giovanni Amendola nella crisi dello stato italiano* (Milan 1956), p. 106.

[55] T–K, VI, pp. 94–7; AP, C, 20–21 July; *Il Mondo*, 21 July 1923; Acerbo showed himself ready to accept a reduction in the quotient, but his concession was repudiated by Mussolini.

[56] ACS, V, 16 (27 November 1923).

[57] ACS, SPCR, 318/R De Nicola (25 November 1923), De Nicola to Mussolini. For general situation Salvatorelli and Mira, *Storia d'Italia*, pp. 280–2.

[58] T–K, VI, p. 91; see also *Corriere Italiano*, 10 December 1923, interview with Giolitti.

[59] See p. 187; T–K, VI, pp. 154–5; A. Gramsci, 'le parlementarisme et le fascisme en Italie', *RSS* (1961), p. 629ff.

[60] *Il Mezzogiorno*, 3 January 1924; *Popolo d'Italia*, 5 January; *La Tribuna*, 6 January.

[61] De Felice, II, pp. 564–8; De Rosa, *Partito popolare*, pp. 445–50.

[62] Spriano, *Partito comunista*, pp. 326–31.

[63] Salvatorelli and Mira, *Storia*, p. 290; *Antologia della rivoluzione liberale*, p. 168 (Gobetti); T–K, VI, pp. 146–8; Matteotti, *Reliquie* (Milan 1962), pp. 228–9.

[64] Salvatorelli and Mira, *Storia*, p. 283; G. Pini and D. Susmel, *Mussolini, l'uomo e L'opera*, 2: p. 349.

[65] *Corriere della Sera*, 30 January 1923; the spoken version of Mussolini's speech differed quite considerably from that printed in *O.O.*, 20, p. 161ff.

[66] P. Gobetti, *Scritti politici*, ed. P. Spriano, *Opere complete*, 1 (Turin 1960), pp. 585–90.

[67] *La Stampa*, 1–2 February 1924; *Giornale d'Italia*, 1 February; *Idea Nazionale*, 1 February.

[68] *Il Mondo*, 5 August 1923.

[69] *Corriere della Sera*, 4–5, 12, 15–8, 28 August 1923; *Cremona Nuova*, 7 February

1924. It was typical of the party's hybrid heritage that Di Cesarò claimed both Cavallotti and his great opponent Crispi as ideological forebears.

[70] *Giornale d'Italia*, 6 February ; *La Stampa*, 6 February.

[71] See *Giornale d'Italia*, 15 January, 3 February, 1924.

[72] *Giornale d'Italia*, 7 February.

[73] *La Stampa*, 5–6, 7–8, 8–9, 11–12 February ; *Corriere della Sera*, 9–11 February ; C. Rossi, *Trentatre vicende mussoliniane* (Milan 1958), pp. 190–3.

[74] *Popolo d'Italia*, 13, 14 February. N.B. also comment of *Times*, 13, 14 February. 'Adhesion to the Government leaders is unconditional except in the South, where Sign. Orlando has been strong enough to make terms in return for his acceptance of the government coupon.'

[75] *Il Mezzogiorno* 15–16, 16–17 February ; *Impero*, 15 February.

[76] *Popolo d'Italia*, 19 February.

[77] One of Orlando's chief political lieutenants was the deputy Scialabba, 'held to be an exponent of the Mafia dominant in the territory of Termini and Bagheria'. The reformist deputy Drago and Raia, one of the friends to whom Orlando addressed his open letter, were supported by the famous Mafia chief Don Ciccio Cuccia of Piana dei Greci and by 'the dangerous Bellissimo of the Petralie'. One can see that Pantaleoni's attack was not without its justification. On the other hand, the provincial secretary of the Fascist party, Cucco, was the representative of a rival Mafia coalition usually known as the 'young' Mafia. See ACS, PS, 1924, b. 81 (18 26 January) ; b. 80, (16–18 February).

[78] ACS, Ufficio Cifra, tel. in partenza, 5, n 4251 (25 February) ; ibid., tel in arrivo, 7, n. 6688, ibid.

[79] ACS, SPCR, fasc 318/R De Nicola (2 April 1924).

[80] Ibid., 1 April (record of telephone conversations between De Nicola and Comm. Montalcini), 3 April, Prefect of Naples.

[81] See ACS, PS, 1924, b. 80, fasc. lotta elettorale (27 March), 'Giudizi sul governo nazionale'. Ibid. (22 February), Orlando.

[82] *Corriere della Sera*, 3 March 1924.

[83] *O.O.*, 20, pp. 371–2.

[84] *Popolo d'Italia*, 8 April (on election results) : 'The plebiscitary consecration of the Fascist revolution . . . One should talk, rather than of an electoral victory, of a real national plebiscite'. See also *Corriere della Sera*, 26 January (statement on dissolution of Parliament) ; Amendola, *La democrazia italiana*, p. 228 ; Matteotti, *Reliquie*, p. 249 : 'the elections were invalid, because the Government had declared that it would maintain its power by force in any case. There was no free vote, since the citizen knew *a priori* that even if the majority voted against the government, the latter could amend the result.'

[85] See Melograni, *Corriere della Sera*, pp. xlvi–xlix. ACS, GF, b. 3, f. 30, Bari (13 February 1924), for a typical incident.

[86] E.g. ACS ibid., b. 13 f. 161, Potenza (9 February 1924) : Mussolini orders Finzi to 'serve notice on, suspend or suppress' the newspaper *La Basilicata* (pro-Amendola).

[87] Bottai, *Pagine di critica fascista*, ed. F. M. Pacces (Florence 1941), p. 308 ; G. Volpe, *Guerra, dopoguerra, fascismo* (Venice 1928), pp. 304–5.

[88] De Felice, II, p. 556 ; Melograni, 'Confindustria', p. 851 ; *La Giustizia*, 20 February 1924.

⁸⁹ ACS, Ufficio cifra, tel in partenza, 5, n. 4457 (28 February), Acerbo circular to Prefects; ibid., n. 4456 to Prefect of Milan; ibid., tel. in arivo, 7, n. 6835 (26 February), Prefect of Trieste to Acerbo.

⁹⁰ See *I 535 di Montecitorio* (Bologna 1924).

⁹¹ F. Guarneri, *Battaglie economiche tra le due grandi guerre*, 2 vols (Milan 1953), 1 : *1918–1935*, p. 57. E. Rossi, *Padroni del vapore e fascismo* (Bari 1966), p. 33.

⁹² See Benni's speech in *Grandi discorsi*, p. 330.

⁹³ *Corriere della Sera*, 14 March.

⁹⁴ *O.O.*, 20, p. 216 (23 March 1924).

⁹⁵ ACS, MRF, b. 69, Ufficio propaganda (21 March 1924), E. Bodrero to Maraviglia and passim. A special increase in the salaries of priests was granted twenty days before the elections. For propaganda in general, see also *Times*, 4 April 1924.

⁹⁶ De Felice, II, p. 563.

⁹⁷ ACS, PS, 1924, b. 80, fasc. Sicilia (9, 10, 23 March).

⁹⁸ 1 April, see note 80.

⁹⁹ Pareto, *Trasformazioni della democrazia*, introd. M. Missiroli, 2nd ed. (Rocca S. Casciano 1966).

¹⁰⁰ AP, C, XXVII legisl., 1st session discussioni, p. 60, Matteotti.

¹⁰¹ ACS, PS, 1924, b. 80, fasc. Affari generali (10 March) Mussolini to Prefects: *Corriere della Sera*, 13 March 1924.

¹⁰² See Colapietra, *Napoli tra dopoguerra e fascismo* (Milan 1962), p. 275. When Amendola was due to speak in Naples 1500 clients of the ex-Nationalist deputy Paolo Greco invaded Naples armed with shotguns. The owner of the theatre where Amendola was to speak withdrew his permission, alarmed by Fascist threats.

¹⁰³ See *L'Assalto*, 22 March 1924 : 'Fascists of all Emilia on guard . . . The underhand activity of the Socialist party revealed in a secret circular.'

¹⁰⁴ *La Giustizia*, 10, 12 February 1924. On this occasion the Ministry of the Interior apparently ordered that the meeting should be permitted ; but the Prefect instead followed the directives of the local fascists. (ACS, GF, b. 3, f. 30, Bari, 10, 13 February).

¹⁰⁵ For this and other incidents, see Salvatorelli and Mira, *Storia*, pp. 290–3.

¹⁰⁶ *Popolo d'Italia*, 28 February ; see also ibid., 13 March, for communiqué ordering that dissident Fascists should be treated as 'traitors'.

¹⁰⁷ De Felice, II, p. 579 ; Ferrari, *Azione cattolica*, pp. 61–2. For examples see *Il Mondo*, 13, 26 March. However some of the higher clergy intervened on behalf of the Government list (*Il Mondo*, 5 April, circular from Bishop of Potenza).

¹⁰⁸ Matteotti, *Reliquie*, pp. 227–31.

¹⁰⁹ Colapietra, *Napoli*, p. 271. For the conduct of the elections, see Matteotti's famous speech of 30 May, *Reliquie*, pp. 247–66.

¹¹⁰ See *La Giustizia*, 8 April.

¹¹¹ For results, see Ministero dell'Economia Nazionale – *Statistica delle elezioni generali politiche per la XXVII legislatura* (6 April 1924) (Rome 1924), p. xxxii–xxxiii. The Government lists obtained 64.9 per cent of the total vote. In the south and centre eight out of ten regions returned a vote for the national list above this average, while in all five of the north regions the vote was lower (highest 85.9 per cent in Abruzzi-Molise, lowest 45 per cent in Piedmont). The rate of abstention was also generally higher in the cities. In the north and centre of Italy this was unusual and suggests forced voting in the rural areas. Even in the smaller centres of

Catanzaro and Aquila the Government vote was much lower than in the rest of their respective constituencies (39.9 per cent and 41.3 per cent cf. 76.5 per cent and 85.9 per cent).

[112] See *Il Mondo*, 4 March 1924, for Fascist directives.

[113] The best evidence for the existence of this system is contained in the memorial of T. Beltrani, the former *federale* of Ferrara. (*Voce repubblicana*, 6 December 1924). See also *Corriere della Sera*, 4 April; *Giustizia*, 4 April.

[114] See *Il Mondo*, 1, 3 April 1924. (Piombino, Mantua); ACS, PS 1925 b. 89, fasc. Forli (10, 16 April), Cesena.

[115] ACS, PS 1924 b. 93, fasc. Milan s/f Monza (17 April) A. Grandi to Mussolini; G. Pastore, *A. Grandi e il movimento sindacale italiano nel primo dopoguerra* (Rome 1960), p. 81. ACS, GF, fasc. 147 Milan (10 April). In Monza district the national list obtained 12,522 votes (about 19 per cent), compared with 24,123 for the Popolari and 29,117 for the three working-class parties (PSU – PCI – PSI).

[116] ACS, PS, 1924 b. 80, fasc. affari generali, 4, 11 April.

[117] G. Dorso, *La rivoluzione meridionale* (Turin 1955), pp. 107–11. For the elections in the Abruzzi, where especially severe intimidation was employed to prevent the return of Giolitti's lieutenant, Camillo Corradini, see ACS, PS, E. 1., b. 81, fasc. Abruzzi s/f Aquila passim; De Rosa *Giolitti e il fascismo*, pp. 20–4, 89–97.

7 The Party and the State (I)

[1] C. J. Friedrich and Z. Brzezinski, *Totalitarian Dictatorship and Autocracy* (Cambridge, Mass. 1965), p. 22; for criticism, see H. Seton-Watson's review in *Government and Opposition* October 1966–January 1967, pp. 153–9, and L. Schapiro, 'The Concept of Totalitarianism', *Survey* 1969, 3, pp. 105–6. Cf. G. Lumbroso, *La crisi del fascismo* (Florence 1925), p. 69, for the comment that previous revolutions (except for the Bolshevik) 'were never supported by a party with a bureaucratic and military organization such as the Fascist.'

[2] George Kennan in *Totalitarianism*, ed. C. J. Friedrich (Cambridge, Mass. 1954), p. 20.

[3] A. Inkeles in ibid., p. 116; W. Gurian, *Bolshevism: Theory and Practice* (London 1932), p. 150.

[4] See Juan J. Linz, 'An Authoritarian Regime: Spain', in *Cleavages, Ideologies and Party Systems*, ed. E. Allardt and Y. Littunen (Transactions of the Westermarck Society, vol. X, 1964), pp. 305–6; G. Germani, 'Political Socialization of Youth in Fascist Regimes: Italy and Spain', in *Authoritarian Politics in Modern Society, the Dynamics of Established One-Party Systems*, ed. S. P. Huntington and C. H. Moore (New York 1970), p. 342.

[5] C. J. Friedrich and Z. Brzezinski, *Totalitarian Dictatorship and Autocracy*; see also the analysis of E. Fraenkel, *The Dual State* (New York 1941), especially pp. xiii–xvii: fusion of government and party apparatus in the 'prerogative state', a governmental system which exercises unlimited arbitrary power and violence unchecked by any legal guarantees, existing alongside the old normative state.

[6] A. Lyttelton, 'Fascism in Italy: the Second Wave', *JCH* 1966, p. 76. For Michele Bianchi's constitutional reform proposals and their rejection, see M. Bianchi, *I discorsi; gli scritti* (Rome 1931), p. 92; A. Solmi, 'Riforma costituzionale', *Gerarchia*, August 1923, p. 1125.

[7] *O.O.*, 19, p. 121.

[8] Ibid., pp. 195–6.

[9] V. Pareto, 'Paragoni', *Gerarchia*, January 1923, pp. 669–72.

[10] G. Bottai, *Pagine di critica fascista*, ed. F. M. Pacces (Florence 1941), p. 352; see also pp. 221–2.

[11] Ibid., p. 277.

[12] *Cremona Nuova*, 10 May.

[13] See Linz, 'Authoritarian Regime', passim.

[14] G. Gentile, in Casucci, *Il fascismo*, p. 46; U. Formentini, *Gerarchie sindacali* (Turin 1923), p. 5. (The impossibility of adapting the great masses to the needs of an elite party of moral leadership.)

[15] Bottai, *Pagine*, pp. 242–3, 263, 302, 380–1; for a reply from the side of the *ras*, see Melchiorri, *Cremona Nuova*, 22 July 1924. For Farinacci and 'mass Fascism', see Rossini, *Il delitto Matteotti tra Viminale e Aventino* (Bologna 1966), p. 65. Very relevant here is the distinction drawn by D. Lerner in his analysis of *The Nazi Elite* (Stanford 1951), between two basic types of militant, the 'propagandist' and the 'organizer'.

[16] R. De Felice, 'I fatti di Torino del dicembre 1922', *SS* January–March 1963, pp. 51–122.

[17] See pp. 65–7, 72–3.

[18] Rocca, *Come il fascismo*, pp. 93, 127, 145–57; and *Idee sul fascismo*, pp. 63–86.

[19] *Nuovo Paese*, 7 May 1924.

[20] Rocca, *Il primo fascismo*, p. 32.

[21] A. Aquarone, 'Aspirazioni tecnocratiche del primo fascismo', *Nord e Sud*, April 1964, pp. 109, 128; C. S. Maier, 'Between Taylorism and Technocracy: European Ideologies and the Vision of Industrial Productivity in the 1920s', *JCH*, 1970, 2, pp. 40–4. *Popolo d'Italia*, 18 March, 12 April 1923; *la Stirpe*, 18 April 1924.

[22] See G. Prato, *Riforma sociale*, March 1923, pp. 126–7.

[23] Lanzillo, *Le rivoluzioni*, p. 17.

[24] For Salandra's purge, see *Carteggio Giolitti*, 3, p. 137; the fascists in 1919 still identified the bureaucracy with Giolitti; see ACS, MRF, b. 65, *Carte Gioda* fasc. 9.

[25] Valeri, *Da Giolitti*, pp. 150–77.

[26] R. Bachi, *L'Italia economica, 1919* (Annuario, Turin), p. 341; see also C. Petrocchi, *Il problema della burocrazia* (Rome 1944), p. 149.

[27] Prato, loc. cit.; A. Monti, *Rivoluzione liberale*, 9 April 1922; Atti parlamentari 26th legislature documenti, 2, doc. XIV *bis*, Relazione della Corte dei Conti sul Rendiconto generale consultivo dell'amministrazione dello stato (1920–1), pp. 139–143; ibid., doc. XIV (1921–2), p. 156ff.

[28] C. Pavone, *Amministrazione centrale e amministrazione periferica* (Milan 1964), p. 738.

[29] Taylor Cole, 'Italy's Fascist Bureaucracy', in *American Political Science Review* (1938), p. 1144.

[30] Pavone, *Amministrazione*, p. 682.

[31] De Rosa, *Giolitti e il fascismo*, pp. 48–52.

[32] Monti, loc cit.

[33] Ibid.

[34] E. Lolini, *Burocrazia* (Rome 1919), especially 88–93; S. Sechi, *Dopoguerra e fascismo in Sardegna*, p. 152n.

[35] See p. 200.

[36] The *Popolo d'Italia*, 6 December 1922, attacked 'the failure of the directors of the public administrations to achieve harmony with the outlook and state of mind of the head of the government'.

[37] ACS, Uff. Cifra tel. in arrivo, 4 December 1922. See also De Felice, II, p. 458, and ACS, GF, b. 8, fasc. Pavia (6 February 1923) for local Fascist reactions to attempts to come to an agreement with co-operatives.

[38] ACS, GF, b. 5, f. 51, 4 November 1922, ibid. (25 January 1923). For control of *commissari prefettizi* by Fascists, see MRF, b. 103, fasc. Mantova 3 November 1922.

[39] ACS, Uff. cifra tel. in partenza (1 December), n. 26527, Finzi to Prefect of Modena; ACS, ibid., 11 December, n. 27313, Finzi to Prefect of Turin.

[40] ACS, GF, b. 8, f. 78 (11, 13 February 1923).

[41] ACS, GF, b. 4, f. 35.

[42] ACS, Uff. cifra tel. in arrivo (6 December), n. 33118; *Corriere della Sera*, 12 December.

[43] *Corriere della Sera*, 12 December. See also ACS, GF, ibid., (11 December 1922), Sansanelli to Fed. PNF Brescia, Minniti to Turati; (16 December 1922), Minniti to Buttafochi.

[44] ACS, uff. cifra tel. in partenza (12 December), note 27405, De Bono to Farinacci; see also ibid., n. 27410, 27437, De Bono to Forni; ACS, GF, loc. cit. (12 December 1922, 9 January 1923).

[45] ACS, GF, ibid. (9, 16 December), Corgini–Finzi and Finzi–Corgini.

[46] For demand to remove Prefect see ACS Uff., cifra tel. in arrivo, n. 33796 (12 December 1922), Forni. For sequel to Bianchi question, see ACS, PC 1923. fasc. 3/1–2 (23 August 1923); ACS, GF, b. 4, fasc. 35 (17 August), Farinacci (22 August), Turati (24 August).

[47] ACS, GF, b. 7, f. 63 (1 May 1923), Marinelli: Salvemini, *Scritti*, 2, p. 217; St Antony's documents, J. 253, n. 069142–3 (5 June 1923), Giampaoli, Mussolini.

[48] *Corriere della Sera*, 9 June 1923.

[49] ACS, GF, b. 4, fasc. 34 Bologna (13 October 1923), Prefect Aphel.

[50] Federzoni, *Italia di ieri per la storia di domani* (Milan 1967), p. 88.

[51] Misuri, *Rivolta morale* (Milan 1924), p. 119. See ACS Carte M. Bianchi, fasc. 3 (anon. memo, n.d.) for the intrigues in the personnel division of the Ministry of the Interior.

[52] For the movement of Prefects see ACS, Cons. dei ministri, *Verbali*, passim. For Farinacci's relationship with the Prefect of Cremona, Rossi, see ACS, GF, b. 3, f. 11, F. to M. Bianchi (n.d.).

[53] ACS, GF, b. 12, f. 145, Massa-Carrara (24 January 1924). The Prefect's reports (e.g. ibid., b. 6., f. 61, 23 March 1923) bear out these accusations.

[54] See *Voce Repubblicana*, Foggia, 15, 17, 25 August 1923; *Popolo d'Italia*, Pisa, 30 August 1924.

[55] *Giornale d'Italia*, 22 July 1924 (Di Scalea interview); Federzoni, *Italia di ieri*, pp. 91–2.

[56] *Nuovo Paese*, 16 December 1922; *Giornale d'Italia*, 17 December (communiqué of PNF *Direzione*).

[57] *La Stampa*, 20 December 1922 ; *Popolo d'Italia*, 24 December.

[58] G. Giuriati 'I tre tabù della Marcia su Roma', *La settimana incom illustrata*, 31 December 1955.

[59] Rocca, *Dittatura*, pp. 114–7; Rossi, *Vicende*, pp. 153–4 ; *Il Secolo*, 27 October 1922.

[60] *Gerarchia*, December 1922.

[61] *Popolo d'Italia*, 19 December 1922 ; *La Stampa*, 18–19 December.

[62] For military appointments, see Salvemini, *Scritti*, 2, pp. 137, 219.

[63] *Popolo d'Italia*, 29 December 1922.

[64] General Gandolfo, who had played an active part in Ligurian Fascism, was made Prefect of Cagliari with almost proconsular powers. See p. 201.

[65] *Corriere della Sera*, 12 January 1923.

[66] *Il Gran Consiglio nei primi 10 anni*, p. 52; see ACS, GF, b. 5, f. 50, Foggia (9 April 1923); Salvemini, *Scritti*, p. 185; *Giornale di Roma*, 25 April 1923; *Popolo d'Italia*, 27 April; *La Stampa*, 2–3 May.

[67] *Popolo d'Italia*, 1 February 1923 ; *Cremona Nuova*, 17 April.

[68] Significantly, Farinacci's *Cremona Nuova* (26 April 1923), while praising the other decisions of the Grand Council, omitted to mention the abolition of the *Alti Commissari*.

[69] *Popolo d'Italia*, 5 May 1923.

[70] ACS, GF, b. 10, f. 94 (8 August 1923).

[71] Ibid., 8, 17, 19 November.

[72] The appointment of Fascists as Prefects also aroused jealousy within the party ; see ACS, ibid., b. 10, f. 95, Venezia (1 October 1923) Colonel Barbieri.

[73] ACS, MRF, b. 103, fasc. Lucca (10 July 1921); also De Felice, 'I fatti', pp. 79–80 and see p. 73 above.

[74] For Ricci, see St Antony's documents, J. 270, 078309–10.

[75] ACS, GF, b. 6, f. 58, Maria Bianchini (n.d.).

[76] Ibid., b. 8, f. 73 (August 1923), 'Un agricoltore fascista' ; 13 November 1923, A. Marazzani.

[77] Salvemini, *The Fascist Dictatorship in Italy* (London 1928), pp. 208–9 218–27. G. Lumbroso, *la crisi del fascismo* (Florence 1925), pp. 80–2.

[78] See note 53 above.

[79] ACS, PS, 1925, b. 92, fasc. Piacenza (8 July, 6–7 October 1924).

[80] See note 76 above. *Voce Repubblicana*, 9, 25 December 1924.

[81] *Corriere della Sera*, 29 November 1924.

[82] For examples of 'self-financing,' see ACS, GF, b. 9, f. 82. Rovigo (2 April, 20 June 1923) ; ibid., b. 8., f. 80. Reggio Emilia (16 September, 8–9 October 1923) ; ACS, PC 1923, fasc. 18/9, n. 1426, (10 May 1923), E. Civelli (Milan industry).

[83] ACS, ibid., b. 6, f. 61, Massa Carrara (24 April 1923), Pocherra (mayor of Carrara).

[84] Salvemini, *Scritti*, 1, pp. 134–8; ACS, PS, 1924, b. 93, fasc. Milan s/f Monza.

[85] See note 83 above.

[86] ACS, ibid., b. 13, f. 157 (12–13 April).

[87] ACS, ibid., b. 8, f. 73, M. Cerioli (n.d.). Cf. also G. Berti, 'Note sul fascismo piacentino 1925–40', *MLI* April–June 1969, pp. 77–85.

[88] ACS, PS 1925, b. 97 (1 October 1921). A. Bernieri, 'Il fascismo a Carrara', pp. 105–9; ACS, SPCR, fasc. 242/R, R. Ricci.

[89] ACS, GF, b. 13, f. 157, fasc. Piacenza (15 April).

[90] Manzotti, *Socialismo riformista*, pp. 118, 163–4.

[91] St Antony's documents, J. 112, 030776–80, 030942–4 ; for activity of Professor Groppali see A. Zanibelli, *Le leghe bianche nel cremonese* (Rome 1961), pp. 41–2, 211.

[92] ACS, MRF, b. 101, fasc. Cremona (10 March 1920), Farinacci ; (31 March), Pasella.

[93] Ibid., 14 August 1919, 2 May 1920.

[94] Ibid., 3 February 1921 (Farinacci), 4 February 1921 (Rossi).

[95] ACS, CF, b. 1, fasc. 3, B (26 April 1924), Balestrieri ; ibid., M, (3 July 1924), Compagnia Anonima cremonese di assicurazioni e riassicurazioni.

[96] St Antony's documents, J. 111, 030699–030702. By February 1923 the capital had been increased to 642,500 lire. ACS, CF b. 2, f. 7 (13 March 1926), E. Varenna.

[97] ACS, CF, b. 1, f. 2 s/f C. (managing director Banca Italiana di Credito e Valori) ; Rossini, *Il movimento cattolico nel periodo fascista* (Rome 1966), p. 56.

[98] For finance in April 1932, see n. 96 above and ibid., 030648–9 (September 1926). The leading subscribers were Puricelli (100,000 lire), Donegani (50,000), and Borletti (30,000). The Edison firm also made a corporate subscription of 50,000 lire.

[99] St Antony's documents, J. 112, 030838–41 (February 1923), Farinacci to Mussolini ; *L'Internazionale*, 10, 17 March 1923 ; *Avanti !*, 8 March 1924 (Lusignani hostility to Ponzi).

[100] St Antony's documents, J. 330, 113307–10.

[101] ACS, SPCR, 242/R, s/4 14, F. to Mussolini (24 January 1924); ACS, CF, b. 1, fasc. 2, s/4 B (Bocchini).

[102] St Antony's documents, J. 112, 030961 (26 June 1923) ; *Cremona Nuova*, 8 May 1923 ; ACS, Uff. cifra, tel in arrivo, 21, n. 20756 (16 June 1924).

[103] St Antony's documents, J. 112, 030843–6 (13 August 1923).

[104] *Cremona Nuova*, 5–6 April 1923 ; *Il Mondo*, 6 April 1923. *Corriere della Sera*, 4 April 1923.

[105] ACS, CF, b. 1, f. 2, s/f D (5 July 1923).

[106] Ibid., fasc. 5, s/f G, (4 December 1924). Associazione fra le società italiane per azioni.

[107] *Giornale d'Italia*, 17 December 1922.

[108] *Corriere della Sera*, 12 January, 19 February 1923 ; Rossini, op. cit., pp. 69–70 for Bastianini's report of 20 April 1923.

[109] E.g. T–K. 6, pp. 16, 21, 31 (8, 15, 31 May 1923).

[110] Lumbroso, *La crisi del fascismo*, p. 69.

[111] Bottai, *Pagine*, p. 221.

[112] *Critica politica*, 25 December 1923 ; ACS, GF, b. 3, f. 25 Ancona (19–20, 25, 28 April 1923) ; *Popolo d'Italia*, 1 May.

[113] *La Stampa*, 16–17 May.

[114] ACS, ibid., b. 3, f. 25 Alessandria (7–12 May) ; Salvemini, *Scritti*, 2, p. 209.

[115] Lumbroso, *Crisi*, pp. 107–9, 118, 127–42 ; Misuri, op. cit, pp. 28, 32, 47–8, 104, 166–8 ; ACS, PC, 1924, fasc. 1/6. 3 n. 741 (4 April 1924), programme of *fasci nazionali* of Pisa.

[116] ACS, MRF, b. 106, fasc. Livorno (7 September 1922), to M. Bianchi.

[117] Lumbroso, op. cit., p. 113 ; *Times*, 17 June 1924 ; *Giornale d'Italia*, 13, 21 April 1923 ; *Cremona Nuova*, 16 December 1923.

[118] ACS, GF, b. 13, f. 146 Pesaro (copy of *Il movimento fascista*, 'settimanale di

battaglia della Associazione dei liberi fascisti Marchegiani', 16 March 1924) ; ACS, PS 1925, b. 95 fasc. Dissidenti fascisti Ascoli Piceno (20 November 1924), 'linee programmatiche'.

8 The Party and the State (II)

[1] *Il Gran Consiglio*, pp. 52–8 ; *Giornale di Roma*, 25 April 1923 ; *La Stampa*, 2–3 May.

[2] Bottai, *Pagine*, pp. 313–14.

[3] *Il Gran Consiglio*, loc. cit. ; *Popolo d'Italia*, 16 May 1923.

[4] *Il Mondo*, 30 May, 5 June ; *La Stampa*, 30–1 May.

[5] Salvemini, *Fascist Dictatorship*, p. 169.

[6] Only about half the *fiduciari* who held office in April were still in office in July ; two-thirds of those who held office in July were still there in January 1924. In particular of the 31 *fiduciari* who survived the turbulent period of April–July 1923, 27 held office in January 1924. A hard core of local leaders had won through. (*Giornale d'Italia*, 10 April 1923 ; *Il Gran Consiglio* pp. 67–83 ; *Popolo d'Italia*, 30 January 1924.)

[7] St Antony's documents, J. 53, 026223–4 (4 August 1923).

[8] De Felice, II, pp. 541–3.

[9] Ibid., pp. 547–8.

[10] *Cremona Nuova*, 18 September 1923.

[11] ASB, 1923, fasc. 7.1 (25 September 1923), Baroncini to Farinacci.

[12] *Cremona Nuova*, 22, 30 September.

[13] *Popolo d'Italia*, 21, 22 September.

[14] *Corriere italiano*, 19 September.

[15] Ibid., 22 September. On Milanese fascism, see also *Popolo d'Italia*, 11 July 1923 (A. Longoni).

[16] De Felice, II, pp. 550–2.

[17] *Giornale di Genova*, 9 October ; *Popolo d'Italia*, 11 October ; Bottai, *Pagine*, p. 288.

[18] *Il Gran Consiglio*, pp. 88–9, 102–4.

[19] St Antony's documents, J. 263/1, 073854–6 ; see also ibid., 07382–4 for Marinelli's draft.

[20] Ibid., 073845–7.

[21] *Popolo d'Italia*, 29 January 1924 ; *O.O.*, 20, pp. 172–3.

[22] See Ch. 7, note 76 (A. Marazzani).

[23] For the beginnings of the polemic between Finzi and Baroncini, see *Popolo d'Italia*, 15, 18, 28 August 1923. *O.O.*, 19, pp. 383, 393 ; ACS, GF, b. 4, fasc. 34, Bologna (13, 16 October, 1 November); AS B 1923, 7.1 (3, 5 November).

[24] ACS, GF, b. 4, fasc. 34 (21 September).

[25] *Unità*, 15 October 1924 ; AS B 1923, 7.1. (2–10 December); ibid., s/f: Congresso Federale Provinciale, 7 December 1923 ; ibid. s/f Consorzio Co-operativo Macchine Agricole, passim. It was Baroncini's attempt to found a consortium for hiring agricultural machines to the peasants at a controlled price that led to the formation of an opposition led by Regazzi and others.

[26] ACS, GF, b. 13, f. 157 passim.

[27] ACS, ibid., b. 9, fasc. 89 Torino (26 May 1923) ; ACS, PS, 1925, b. 94, fasc. Torino (29 September, 3 December 1923).

[28] *Giornale di Genova*, 1, 4 August, 23, 25, 29 September, 28 November, 11 December; *Il Secolo XIX*, 30 September, 3, 4, 21 October.

[29] ACS, Carte M. Bianchi, fasc. 43 Firenze (3, 5 October); U. Banchelli, *Fascisti di professione alla sbarra* (Florence 1924), pp. 25–45.

[30] Aquarone, *L'organizzazione dello stato totalitario*, pp. 34, 342–3; ACS, GF, b. 13, f. 153, 2, 3, 5, 7 February 1924; *Polenica fascista*, 6, 13 January 1924, which pointed out that regular elections take place only in the 'large centres'.

[31] *Il Gran Consiglio*, pp. 123–4, 132–6.

[32] *Corriere della Sera*, 30 April 1924.

[33] For Apulia, see S. Colarizi, *Dopoguerra e fascismo in Puglia 1919–26* (Bari 1971); for Syracuse see *La Stampa*, 28–9 May 1923 : 'Fascism is here no different from Fascism in the Po Valley'.

[34] See the lists of newly founded *fasci* in the *Popolo d'Italia*; e.g. on 28 December 1922, out of a list of 54 new *fasci*, 47 were in the South.

[35] ACS, GF, b. 8, fasc. 79 Reggio Calabria (1 July).

[36] ACS, Carte Bianchi, fasc. 18 Messina (April 13); A. Bianco, *Il fascismo in Sicilia* (Catania 1923), pp. 14, 45–51.

[37] *Popolo d'Italia*, 28 December 1922; cf. *Il Mondo*, 30 December; and ACS, GF, b. 8, f. 77 Potenza, 6 February 1923, on conflict between Fascists and Nationalists at Bernalda : the *fascio* contained 32 condemned criminals and the commander of the Militia had been convicted on various occasions of insulting or threatening behaviour, slander and the usurpation of public functions, and was furthermore suspected of fraud.

[38] G. Jannelli, *La crisi del fascismo in Sicilia* (Messina 1924), for the radical aspirations of the Fascist intransigents in the South; see also ACS, MRF, b. 104, fasc. Napoli, 28 August 1919, E. Mecheri to De Angelis.

[39] R. Colapietra, *Napoli tra dopoguerra e fascismo*, pp. 163–5, 185, 193–8, 204–29; *Critica politica*, 25 June 1923, 'Il fascismo a Napoli', 25 July 1926 (C. Bellieni).

[40] Colapietra, *Napoli*, pp. 203–8.

[41] Ibid., pp. 196–7, 208; *Il Mondo*, 9 September 1922.

[42] 'Il fascismo a Napoli', cit.; *Roma*, 11 January 1924 for one of Padovani's 'grandi elettori', Vito Chianese, who obtained through him a contract to exploit the Lago Fusano.

[43] Colapietra, *Napoli*, pp. 229–39; ACS, SPCR, 242/R fasc. Padovani (22 April 1, 19 May); ACS, GF, b. 7, f. 65 Napoli (20–5 May); *Popolo d'Italia*, 24 May.

[44] A series of anti-Fascist demonstrations broke out in Messina, Reggio Calabria and a few other Southern cities; the demonstrators wore a coin, showing the head of the King, pinned to their jackets, to emphasize their loyalty to the monarchy. The chief instigator of the movement, which considerably alarmed Mussolini, seems to have been a Messina deputy Lombardo Pellegrino; see *Il Lavoro* (Messina) passim; *Popolo d'Italia*, 26, 30 May 1923; abundant documentation in ACS, PS C 2 b. 37, fasc. Disposizioni di vigilanza s/f *affari generali* (12, 16 May); ibid., fasc. Movimento anti-fascista; ibid., b. 70, 1925 Reggio Calabria, Catanzaro.

[45] For the conservative viewpoint, see *Giornale di Sicilia*, 19–20, 23–4 May 1923.

[46] ACS, PS, 1923, b. 52, fasc. Catania (14 February); ibid., b. 10, f. 90 Trapani (22 August 1923).

[47] *Voce Repubblicana*, 2 October 1923; in general see comments of A. Monti, *La rivoluzione liberale*, 18 September 1923.

[48] *Giornale di Sicilia*, 10–11, 21–2 February 1923.

[49] ACS, Carte Bianchi, fasc. 19 Catania (10 May 1923). Even in regions of the South such as Apulia where the Fascist party had real strength, 1923 saw its successful penetration by the clienteles: see ACS, fasc. 15, 7 July 1923; Relazione sulla situazione delle Puglie e della Sicilia (Starace), Dorso, *La rivoluzione meridionale*, pp. 98–101.

[50] Dorso, *Rivoluzione*, pp. 91–4.

[51] See F.Vöchting, *La questione meridionale* (trans. from German, Naples 1955), pp. 326–8.

[52] For further details see the excellent study of S.Sechi, *Dopoguerra e fascismo in Sardegna*, especially pp. 351–433.

[53] ACS, GF, b. 6, f. 62, Messina (10 November 1923), Prefect Frigerio. See also Starace, *Relazione*, note 50 above.

[54] Danilo Dolci, *Waste*, trans. R.Munroe (London 1963), pp. 97–100. ACS, Carte Bianchi, fasc. 18 Messina (April 7, 13).

[55] ACS, ibid., (1 September, 10 October 1923); Jannelli, *La crisi del fascismo*, p. 36.

[56] M.Vaina, *Popolarismo e nasismo in Sicilia* (Florence 1911), pp. 78–84, 120–1; Manzotti, *Il socialismo riformista*, pp. 71–4.

[57] ACS, Uff. cifra, tel. in arrivo, n. 28364, 28640, 28666 (31 October 1922), n. 28760, 28765 (1 November).

[58] Ibid. n. 28968, 28989 (2 November).

[59] Ibid. n. 28843 (2 November), tel. in partenza, n. 24199 (3 November); ACS, GF, b. 4, fasc. 40 (3 November 1922). Giuffrida to Finzi, 4 November.

[60] *Giornale d'Italia*, 18 November 1922.

[61] ACS, GF, ibid. (20 November 1922).

[62] See note 49 above; ACS, PS, 1923, b. 52, fasc. Catania (24 February 1923).

[63] ACS, GF, ibid. (14 February 1923).

[64] Ibid., 20 November 1922, 24 February 1923; ACS, Carte Bianchi, fasc. 10, 19 March 1923.

[65] ACS, Carte Bianchi, ibid., 10, 14, 20–1, 28 April, 1 May. ACS, PS, 1923, b. 52, fasc. Catania (20 April).

[66] ACS, GF, b. 13, f. 170, (19 May 1924).

[67] Jannelli, op. cit., pp. 40–2.

[68] ACS, GF, b. 10 f. 93 Trapani (28 February 1923). For the general situation of the mafia at this time, see M.Pantaleone, *Mafia e politica* (Turin 1962), pp. 49–52.

[69] Pantaleone, *Mafia*, p. 59; ACS, PS, 1924, b. 81 fasc. Sicilia (26 January 1924). Cucco has ties with the mafia of Bagheria and Castelbuono.

[70] ACS, PS, 1924, b. 80 fasc. Sicilia (26 January 1924).

[71] ACS, PS, 1924, b. 81 fasc. Sicilia (27 March 1924).

[72] Pantaleone, *Mafia*, pp. 56–60.

[73] ACS, MRF, b. 69, 12 August 1923.

[74] See ACS, GF, b. 8, f. 79 Reggio Calabria, 1 July, 12 September 1923; the vice-Prefect complained that the retirement of Prefect Bode, who had quarrelled with the *fiduciario* Minniti, had demoralized the officials.

[75] Prefect of Messina, ACS, Carte Bianchi, loc cit., n. 36; ACS, GF, b. 3, fasc. 32 Benevento (22 December 1922, 8 August 1923).

[76] ACS, Carte Bianchi, loc. cit.

[77] ACS GF, b. 10, f. 90 Trapani (26 April, 30 May, 22 August); ibid., b. 13, f. 176 (22 March, 9 May 1924); ibid., Girgenti, b. 6, f. 53, b. 12, fasc. 137, passim; Benevento, b. 3, f. 32.

9 Employers and Unions

[1] On Fascist anti-capitalism, see Barrington Moore, *Social Origins*, p. 448.

[2] P. Ungari, *Alfredo Rocco e l'ideologia giuridica del fascismo* (Brescia 1963), p.79n.

[3] See R. Dahrendorf, *Class and Class Conflict in an Industrial Society* (London 1967), p. 259, for a general approach to the problem.

[4] A 'Confederazione dell'Industria Italiana' had been founded in 1910, but it was not fully representative: see M. Abrate, *La lotta sindacale nella industrial-izzazione in Italia 1906-1926* (Turin 1967), pp. 54-6, 206-7; R. Sarti, 'Fascism and the industrial leadership in Italy before the March on Rome', *Industrial and Labor Relations Review*, 21, n. 3 (April 1968), p. 401.

[5] *O.O.*, 13, pp. 17-18; *La Confederazione Generale del Lavoro 1906-1926*, ed. F. Catalano (Milan 1962), pp. xlviii-xlvix, 260, 263, 284.

[6] Abrate, *La lotta sindacale*, p. 203.

[7] E. Tagliacozzo, *Il Mondo*, 29 December 1951.

[8] C. Pellizzi, *Una rivoluzione mancata* (Milan 1948), pp. 41-3, see also pp. 29-31, 35; Lanzillo, *Lo stato*, pp. 163-4; Rocca, *Il primo fascismo*, p. 32.

[9] L. Einaudi, *Cronache economiche e politiche di un trentennio* (Turin 1961), 3, pp. 340-5.

[10] Ibid., 5, pp. 527-31; 6, pp. 333, 373-4.

[11] G. P. Nitti, 'Appunti bio-bibliografici su Ernesto Rossi', MLI 1967, I, pp. 94-107; see also G. Prato, 'Fascismo e sindacalismo', *Popolo d'Italia*, 4 October 1922; De Stefani, Discorsi (Milan 1923), p. 99; E. Giretti to P. Gobetti, 11 March 1923, quoted De Rosa, *Partito popolare*, pp. 434-5.

[12] ACS, Carte Giolitti, b. 9, fasc. 121, 2 May 1923; C. Corradini. S. M. Lipset, *Political Man* (London 1960), pp. 132-7, for analysis of fascism as the extremism of the 'centre'; for the concept of the 'paranoid style' in politics, see R. Hofstadter, *The Paranoid Style in American Politics* (London 1966), pp. 3-7, 38-40.

[13] Rocco, *Scritti*, 2, p. 477.

[14] Ibid., 2, pp. 631-45, 'Crisi dello stato e sindacati' (15 November 1920).

[15] S. Panunzio, *Stato fascista* (Bologna 1923), pp. 87-92, 111-12; R. Melis, *Sindacalisti italiani* (Rome 1964), pp. 304-7.

[16] Gaeta, *Nazionalismo italiano*, pp. 89, 119-20.

[17] U. Ricci, 'Il mito dell'independenza economica', *Riforma sociale*, March-April 1918.

[18] Gaeta, op. cit., p. 195.

[19] *Carteggio Giolitti*, 3, p. 286; Castronovo, *La Stampa*, pp. 246-8.

[20] E. Corbino, *Annali dell'economia italiana* (Citta di Castello 1938), 4, pp. 119-27.

[21] R. Paci, in A. Caracciolo et al., *Il trauma dell'intervento, 1914-1919* (Florence 1968), pp. 37-9.

[22] Einaudi, *Cronache*, 5, pp. 643-7; E. Conti, *Dal taccuino di un Borghese* (Milan 1946), pp. 224-6; R. Bachi, *l'Italia economica nel 1919* (Annuario, Turin), pp. 66-8.

[23] *Carteggio Giolitti*, 3, pp. 274, 278.

[24] *Carteggio Giolitti*, 3 pp. 278-9, 286-7; R. Vivarelli, 'A proposito di un recente libro su Francesco Saverio Nitti,' *RSI* 1964, pp. 177-8.

[25] For other examples, n.b. Dante Ferraris, who having financed the Nationalists was also a supporter of Nitti and *Il Mondo* (*Popolo d'Italia*, 17 September 1922); similarly the *Edison* electrical company, although its effective head, Giacinto Motta, was a friend of Albertini and supported the Liberals, also backed Farinacci; ACS, CF, fasc. 3, (10, 19 January 1924), G. Motta to F.

[26] *Resto del Carlino*, 3 April 1921.

[27] Ibid.

[28] Paci, in *Il trauma*, pp. 30, 49–50. G. Borgatta, 'L'economia bellica e postbellica e le società per azioni', *Rivista di politica economica*, March 1923, p. 254.

[29] One mouthpiece of the Commerciale's opponents was *Il Nuovo Paese*, edited by Carlo Bazzi, a close friend of Cesare Rossi : see nos of 8, 15, 17 December 1922.

[30] Conti, |*Taccuino*, p. 77; see also B. Caizzi, *Camillo e Adriano Olivetti*, (Turin 1962) pp. 93–4, 107.

[31] Abrate, *La lotta sindacale*, pp. 99–101 ; *Conflitti del lavoro e legislazione sociale. Relazione della Presidenza della Confederazione Italiana dell'Industria all'Assemblea dei delegati* (Turin, 13 February 1914), pp. 5–13.

[32] Sarti, art. cit., pp. 407–8. See also Silvestri's speech at the Confindustria meeting of 6 March 1920 (*Il Sole*, 10 March).

[33] Catalano, *Potere economico*, pp. 175–88 ; *Il Sole*, 23 February 1921. Conti, *Taccuino*, pp. 240–51. Spriano, *Occupazione*, pp. 121–3, 188–90.

[34] Catalano, op. cit., pp. 74–7. 114–15 ; Einaudi, *Cronache*, 5, pp. 424–4, 506–8.

[35] Abrate, *La lotta sindacale*, pp. 348–9.

[36] ACS, PC, 1922 fasc. 3/7, memorial presented by Conti on behalf of the Associazione fra le societa italiane per azioni, 9 August 1922 ; ibid., fasc. 1/3–4, Della Torre for Associazione bancaria, 2 August 1922 ; ibid., fasc. 9/1, 19 April, 3 May, 19 June 1922 (Lombard, Ligurian and Venetian industrial associations).

[37] Rossi, *Padroni del vapore*, p. 39 ; Repaci, *Marcia su Roma*, 1, p. 343 ; Einaudi, *Cronache*, 6, p. 531, 811–15; Sarti, art. cit., pp. 411–2.

[38] De Felice, 'Primi elementi sul finanziamento del fascismo dalle origini al 1924', *RSS* August 1964, pp. 224ff; see also Castronovo, *La stampa italiana*, pp. 265–9 for finance of *Popolo d'Italia*.

[39] For Tuscany, see above Ch. 3, notes, 144–6; on the sugar industry, see Corner MS, 'Fascism in Ferrara', pp. 149–51. The Florentine Liberal deputy Dino Philipson boasted that during early 1921 'I was the organizer . . . of a financial consortium, of which I was named President, which subsidized the principal patriotic initiatives in the province, and gave the *fasci* several hundred thousand lire' (ACS, GF, b. 5, f. 48).

[40] ACS, MRF, b. 70 fasc. Corrispondenza produttori, (10 November 1920, 4 July 1921), Veneto; (13, 17 December 1921), Liguria; (4 August, 8 November 1922), Piedmont.

[41] Ibid., 2 July 1922, General Peluso to Marinelli.

[42] Castronovo, *La stampa italiana*, pp. 265–73.

[43] E.g. D. Guérin *Fascisme et grand capital* (Paris 1945), pp. 38–41.

[44] See *Avanti!*, 12 December 1922 ; ACS, PC 1923, fasc. 3/7, 8, 26 August 1923 (Giunta, Banelli and Suvich).

[45] Abrate, *La lotta sindacale*, p. 374 (speech of Mazzini, President of the Turin Lega Industriale); P. Melograni, 'Confindustria e fascismo, p. 839.

[46] Abrate, *La lotta sindacale*, pp. 374–7, 392.

[47] Melograni, 'Confindustria', pp. 842-4, is to be preferred to earlier versions: cf. also Sarti, 'Fascism and the industrial leadership', pp. 416–21. However Melograni's assertion that the Confindustria favoured a Giolitti government with the participation of the Socialists and the Popolari appears unfounded. For one thing, Giolitti himself had ceased to believe in such a solution.

[48] Ibid.; Conti, *Taccuino*, pp. 298–300; *Carteggio Albertini*, 3, pp. 1593–4.

[49] Melograni, art. cit., p. 845; see also Sarti, art. cit., p. 417.

[50] Colapietra, *Napoli*, p. 213; *La Stampa*, 20 December 1922, and Matteotti, *Un anno*, p. 17, for examples of occupation of factories or land by Fascists.

[51] *La Stampa*, 22–3 December 1922.

[52] Abrate, *La lotta sindacale*, pp. 377, 382–3; Castronovo, *La stampa italiana*, pp. 323–9 for financial control of the Press.

[53] Abrate, *La lotta sindacale*, p. 394.

[54] *Dizionario biografico degli Italiani*, 8, p. 519, Benni; *Carteggio Albertini*, 4, p. 1789.

[55] Barbadoro, 'Problemi', p. 282.

[56] *Resoconto del Congresso agrario, 1909*, pp. 83–4; cf. *Il discorso programma del conte Cavazza agli elettori del terzo collegio* (Bologna 1913).

[57] *Resoconto* cit., p. 108. Carrara's 'phalanxes of free workers' had notoriously employed systematic violence: for this reason his reference to 'active propaganda' was greeted with appreciative laughter.

[58] Ibid., pp. 149–57.

[59] Corbino, *Annali*, 4, pp. 454–5.

[60] Serpieri, *La guerra*, pp. 331, 336–7.

[61] The *interprovinciale* comprised the associations of Bologna, Ferrara, Parma, Piacenza, Ravenna and Rovigo.

[62] G. Pesce, *La marcia dei rurali* (Rome 1929), pp. 48–9.

[63] Ibid., pp. 51, 106–7. The breakdown of the State's mediating function was more complete in agriculture even than in industry. The concentration in the hands of the Prefect of both coercive and mediating powers was a factor which probably exacerbated rather than reduced class tension: see Dahrendorf, op. cit., p. 260.

[64] *Resto del Carlino*, 17–8 February 1921.

[65] F. Cordova, 'Le origini dei sindacati fascisti', pp. 951–7, *Storia contemporanea*, 1, No. 4, December 1970 (*Momenti di storia dell'organizzazione sindacale in Italia*).

[66] Ibid., pp. 958–9, 965–9; E. Malusardi, *Elementi di storia del sindacalismo fascista* (Genoa 1932), p. 61; *PNF Origini e sviluppo*, pp. 121–2; De Felice, I, pp. 623–4.

[67] ACS, MRF, b. 107, fasc. Verona (3), Pasella to Bresciani (28 June 1921); Malusardi, p. 75.

[68] Cordova, art. cit., pp. 982–90; *L'internazionale*, 12 November 1921.

[69] *Popolo d'Italia*, 25–6 January 1922; *l'Internazionale* (Parma), 4 February 1922; Cordova, art. cit., pp. 990–2.

[70] Cordova, art. cit., pp. 933–4, 951; Salvemini, *Under the Axe of Fascism*, p. 21.

[71] *L'internazionale*, 14 May 1921.

[72] *Popolo d'Italia*, 25 January, 7 June 1922.

[73] *Battaglie sindacali*, 22 July, 18, 31 August, 23 September 1922.

[74] Einaudi, *Cronache*, 6, pp. 863–6, 897–900; Vicentini, *Movimento fascista*, pp. 224–5.

[75] De Rosa, *Storia del partito popolare*, pp. 277–8.

[76] Cordoni, MS cit., 'Le origini del fascismo a Siena', pp. 278–80; see also *Popolo d'Italia*, 22 October 1922.

[77] *Popolo d'Italia*, 6 June 1922.

[78] *O.O.*, 12, pp. 314–15.

[79] R. Bachi, *L'Italia economica nel 1921*, p. ixff; *Ordine Nuovo*, 1 September 1922; for dockworkers see St Antony's documents, J. 263/1. 073914ff. April 1925. A partial exception to the above is provided by the situation in the Naples region, where most of the textile workers' union passed over to Fascism at about the time of the March on Rome. Even there, however, the textile workers had previously joined the unions set up by D'Annunzio's legionaries and only passed to Fascism after these proved unable to protect them (*Battaglie Sindacali*, 13 September 1923).

[80] Ibid.; *Popolo d'Italia*, 3, 4 October, 12 November 1922.

[81] ACS, MRF, b. 106, fasc., Monfalcone.

[82] ACS, MRF, b. 106, fasc. Livorno, 4 (30 May 1922); ibid. (16 September, 7, 11 October).

[83] ACS, PC, 1922, fasc. 3/7, n. 1586; see also ACS 1922, fasc. 3/3, for similar efforts on behalf of the Società Mineraria del Valdarno.

[84] ACS, GF, b. 8, fasc. 71 Perugia (28 June 1923).

[85] Pesce, *La marcia dei rurali*, pp. 114–23; *Cremona Nuova*, 1 April 1923.

[86] Pesce, op. cit., pp. 131–6, 170–1.

[87] *Battaglie Sindacali*, 8 November 1923 : the agrarians were 'intolerant of every contractual tie', even those concluded by the Fascist organizations.

[88] Einaudi, *Cronache*, 8, pp. 338–9; also Pesce, op. cit., pp. 16–18.

[89] Pesce, op. cit., pp. 114–15, 131, 148–51; Cacciari, one of the two founders of the FISA, was a graduate in agrarian sciences. The Fascist unions (both of employers and workers) did much to solve the difficulties which this class formed in obtaining employment; for the Tuscan *fattori*, see Cordoni, MS cit., p. 276 (Fascists supported their demand for higher salaries from the landowners), and 'Contadini in Toscana' pp. 450–1, 469.

[90] *Popolo d'Italia*, 21 January, 5 December 1923; Pesce, op. cit., pp. 177–8; *Resto del Carlino*, 16 November 1922.

[91] *Popolo d'Italia*, 30 December 1922; *Resto del Carlino*, loc. cit.

[92] *Battaglie sindacali*, 30 August 1923.

[93] *Battaglie sindacali*, 14 December 1922.

[94] F. Vöchting, *Die Romagna* (Karlsruhe 1927), pp. 400–2; F. Luzzatto, 'Osservazioni sopra i concordati collettivi di lavoro agrario 1923–4', *Riforma sociale*, p. 395.

[95] *Popolo d'Italia*, 23 December 1922; Pesce, op. cit., pp. 135–9; E. Rossoni, *Le idee della ricostruzione* (Florence 1923), pp. 60–1, 65.

[96] *Popolo d'Italia*, 16 March 1923; ACS, PC 1923, fasc. 3/5, passim, especially Soldati to Belloni, 10 August 1923, Prefect of Forlì 18 October. From these letters it transpires that the projects were financed by an obligatory levy on existing local industries, imposed by the Fascist party. *Gran Consiglio*, p. 100.

[97] *L'Internazionale*, 16 December 1922; see also *Corriere della Sera*, 17 April 1923.

[98] *Popolo d'Italia*, 27 December 1922; *L'Internazionale*, 13 January 1923.

[99] *L'Internazionale*, 10 February 1923; see also ibid., 14, 24 January, 3 February.

[100] ACS, PC, 1923 fasc. 3/1–2 n. 106, Confederazione Generale dell'Agricoltura (28 February 1923).

[101] For Parma, ACS, PS, 1923, C. 1, b. 32 (8 November 1923); ibid., 1924, G. 1, b. 87 (28 January 1924); *Popolo d'Italia*, 3 February, 18 March, 5 December 1923, 30 January 1924.

[102] For Reggio, ACS, Carte Bianchi, fasc. 58 (7, 9 May, 30 September 1923); ACS, PC, 1923, fasc. 3/1–2, n. 1297 (1 March 1923), memo from Camera Provinciale of Agriculture.

[103] ACS, Carte Bianchi, fasc. 52 (27 August 1923); *Popolo d'Italia*, 1 March 1923, mentions Piacenza, Forlì, Ravenna and Padua as other provinces where the agrarian associations had officially adhered to the FISA.

[104] *Battaglie sindacali*, 14 December 1922, 4 January 1923; *Giornale d'Italia*, 17, 19 December 1922.

[105] See above Ch. 7, n. 82.

[106] Pesce, *La Marcia dei rurali*, pp. 185–7; S. Sechi, *Dopoguerra e fascismo*, pp. 436–43; F. Coletti, *Economia rurale e politica rurale in Italia* (Piacenza 1926), pp. 228–58; *Giornale d'Italia*, 13 April 1923.

[107] Pesce, op. cit., p. 261; ACS, Carte Bianchi, fasc. 61, Padova (10 August 1923), memo from Pezzoli.

[108] *Popolo d'Italia*, 18 February.

[109] Ibid., 12 November 1922.

[110] E.g. ACS, GF, b. 7, f. 66 Novara (3, 11 January 1923).

[111] *Popolo d'Italia*, 9 February 1923; Pastore, *A. Grandi*, pp. 85–7.

[112] ACS, Pres. Cons. 1923, fasc. 3/3, n. 2477 (20 August 1923), L. Pezzoli.

[113] *Battaglie sindacali*, 28 June, 13 September 1923; De Felice, 'Preziosi', pp. 535–8; Colapietra, *Napoli*, pp. 251–2.

[114] ACS, PC, 1924, f. 3/5, (17, 28 January 1924); ibid., fasc. 3/3, (28 July 1923); ACS, GF, b. 9, fasc. 89, (17, 30 November 1923); ibid., fasc. 81, 13 (16 June).

[115] Abrate, *La lotta sindacale*, pp. 393–4 (5 April 1923).

[116] *Il Gran Consiglio*, p. 40ff.

[117] See also *Popolo d'Italia*, 18 March 1923, article by Arnaldo Mussolini.

[118] *Corriere della Sera*, 23 March 1923.

[119] Abrate, *La lotta sindacale*, p. 394.

[120] *Il Gran Consiglio*, pp. 59–62; see also Abrate, op. cit., p. 402; *Battaglie sindacali*, 3 May 1923; *La Stampa*, 2–3 May.

[121] *Il Gran Consiglio*, pp. 91–2.

[122] Abrate, *La lotta sindacale*, pp. 384–9; ACS, GF, b. 9, f. 89 (19–20 October, 8–10, 19 November). The Prefect of Turin, always hostile to Agnelli and Olivetti, underlined the fact that they financed the local Liberal association.

[123] ACS, ibid., b. 5 fasc. 52 (22 October 1923); ACS, PS, b. 47B., G. 1, 22 (28 October).

[124] *Il Gran Consiglio*, pp. 116–17.

[125] Abrate, *La lotta sindacale*, p. 390; Rossi, *Padroni*, pp. 150–1. Rossi, however, exaggerates the importance of the agreement; *L'organizzazione industriale*, 1 January 1924; G. Olivetti, A. Gramsci, 'L'échec du syndicalisme fasciste', in 'Note sulla situazione italiana 1922–4', ed. A. Romano, *RSS* (1961), n. 13–14, pp. 133–6.

[126] It appears that the leaders of the corporations had hoped that by using the liaison machinery it would be possible to negotiate national wage agreements, but the industrialists showed little interest: *Popolo d'Italia*, 15 July 1924. L. Razza;

T. Cianetti, in De Felice, III, App. 1, pp. 487–94 (which seems to me incorrectly dated); *Il lavoro d'Italia*, 24 May 1924 (Malusardi).

[127] Pesce, op. cit., pp. 204, 226–30; ACS, PC, 1924, fasc. 3/1–1, n. 529 (20 February 1924); St Antony's documents, J. 263/1, 073875–8 (November 1923).

[128] E.g. *Battaglie sindacali*, 19 April, 26 July, 4 October 1923.

[129] See *Corriere della Sera*, 9, 21, 30 November 1922; *la Giustizia*, 15 November.

[130] ACS, PC, 1924, fasc. 3/5, n. 577 (n.d.), memo from D'Aragona on behalf of the CGL; for Catholic unions, see ibid., 20 December 1923, A. Grandi memo.

[131] *Battaglie sindacali*, 25 January 1923.

[132] For wage and price indexes, see C. Vannutelli, *Occupazione e salari dal 1861 al 1961* in *l'economia italiana dal 1861 al 1961* (Milan 1961), pp. 569–70. However, it seems probable that this index underrates the rise in the cost of living; for different estimates, see Einaudi, *Cronache*, 8, p. 39. The detailed study of E. Rossi, 'I salari degli operai milanesi 1921–6', *Riforma sociale*, November–December 1926, shows severe wage reductions in the engineering industry and among unskilled labourers in building as well as in agriculture. Certain skilled trades (e.g. printers) were less affected.

[133] *Battaglie sindacali*, 10 May, 14 June 1923; Salvemini, *Under the Axe of Fascism*, pp. 277, 303–4.

[134] G. Baldesi, *Di tante briciole fare una briciola sola*, (Florence 1923), pp. 8, 49; *Battaglie sindacali*, 8 February, 1 March, 26 July 1923.

[135] Ibid., 22 February 1923.

[136] T–K, 6, pp. 83–4, 87.

[137] De Felice, II, p. 613.

[138] T–K, 6, p. 90.

[139] *Corriere della Sera*, 26 July 1923; *Battaglie Sindacali*, 18 December 1924; B. Buozzi, *Scritti dell'esilio*, pp. 34–8.

[140] *Popolo d'Italia*, 26 July 1923; *Battaglia Sindacali*, 9 August 1923; *Corriere della Sera*, 21 August.

[141] *Il Mondo*, 31 July, 13 August.

[142] Gramsci, *L'échec du syndicalisme*, loc. cit.; ACS, PS, 1923, G. 1., b 47B. (16 January), De Bono.

[143] *Battaglie Sindacali*, 5 July; *Lavoro d'Italia*, 11 August.

[144] *La Confederazione generale del lavoro*, pp. 370–2.

[145] *Battaglie sindacali*, 30 August, 6 September 1923.

[146] Ibid., 20 September.

[147] Ibid., 11 October.

[148] *Corriere della Sera*, 12, 16 August.

[149] *Battaglie sindacali*, 8 November, 22 November 1923.

[150] Ibid., 6, 20 December.

[151] Aquarone, *Organizzazione*, pp. 117–18.

[152] See note 130.

[153] De Felice, II, pp. 616–17.

10 The Matteotti Crisis

[1] Rossini, *Delitto Matteotti*, p. 93; Pareto, *Trasformazioni della democrazia*, pp. 167–8.

[2] *Assalto*, 7 June 1924; see also ibid., 24 May, 21 June.

[3] *Il Mondo*, 23 March 1923.

[4] Rossini, op. cit., pp. 97–103.

[5] *Giornale d'Italia*, 3 June 1924 ; T–K, 6, pp. 167, 174.

[6] Lyttelton, 'Second Wave', 1, p. 78.

[7] Salvemini, *Fascist Dictatorship*, p. 289. Rossini, op. cit., pp. 260–6 (which also gives evidence for Mussolini's order, not executed, to 'teach Piero Gobetti a lesson'.

[8] On the Fascist 'Ceka', see Rossini, *Delitto*, pp. 302–4, 316, 325, 332–3, 451, 458, 461, 716–17 ; a decision to set up a unit for spying and aggression on opponents would seem to have been taken in January or February 1924. However, according to Rossi, in June the 'Ceka' still had not been constituted.

[9] For the intrigues surrounding the *Corriere italiano*, see Rossini, op. cit., pp. 95–6.

[10] Salvemini, op. cit., pp. 319–24. The gang had a sixth member, the Austrian Otto Thierschwald, who was employed to shadow Matteotti. On 1 June 1924, De Bono had personally given orders for his release from prison at the request of Marinelli. (ACS, Uff. cifra, tel in partenza, 13, n. 12104.)

[11] L. Valiani, 'La storia del fascismo nella biografia di Mussolini e nella problematica della storia contemporanea', *RSI* 1967, 2, pp. 473–9. However his argument that if Mussolini had not given direct orders for the murder he would have had Marinelli and Rossi arrested immediately is not conclusive. They were his closest aides and they had plenty on him anyway, as the Rossi memorial was to show.

[12] Salvemini, *Fascist Dictatorship*, p. 318 ; T–K, 6, p. 192.

[13] Rossini, *Delitto*, p. 229.

[14] For evidence on Mussolini's state of mind, see, e.g. A. Pirelli, *Dopoguerra 1919–1932* (Milan 1961), p. 133.

[15] E.g. *Popolo d'Italia*, 10 August 1924. See Valiani, 'La storia', p. 472.

[16] Federzoni, *Italia d'ieri*, pp. 89–90 ; St Antony's documents, J. 274,079799–800.

[17] E.g. V. Ojetti, *Taccuini*, pp. 144–5.

[18] T–K, 6, p. 208.

[19] T. Zaniboni, *Testamento spirituale*, p. 16 ; Valiani, art. cit., p. 479.

[20] See Spriano, *Partito communista*, p. 407 (Humbert-Droz).

[21] Ibid., pp. 208–9, 227–8.

[22] R. Webster, *Christian democracy in Italy 1860–1960* (London 1961), pp. 96–7 ; the Pope's judgement had been anticipated by an article of the Jesuit *Civiltà Cattolica*, 16 August 1924 (De Rosa, *Partito popolare*, pp. 492–3).

[23] Salvatorelli and Mira, op. cit., p. 315 ; *Carteggio Giolitti*, 3, pp. 420–2 ; A. Hamilton, *The Appeal of Fascism* (London 1971), pp. 50–1.

[24] Milizia Volontaria sicurezza nazionale. On the problem of the half-pay officers see ACS, SPCR 31/R, fasc. De Bono, s/f 5, 25 November 1922, Diaz to Mussolini and De Bono minute.

[25] Lumbroso, *Crisi*, p. 37.

[26] E. De Bono, 'Le origini della milizia e i suoi primi ordinamenti', in T. Sillani, *Le forze armate dell'Italia fascista* (Rome 1939), pp. 288–91 ; see *Gazzetta ufficiale*, 26 April for *Regolamento* of Militia (esp. articles 26 and 29). ASB, 1923, b. 7, 1 fasc. MVSN, 29 January 1923, Teruzzi circular.

[27] A. di Giorgio, *Scritti e discorsi vari 1899–1927* (Rome 1938), pp. 324–5, 388–9.

[28] Rochat, *Esercito*, pp. 366–72. On Militia and 'armed nation' see ACS, PC, 1922, fasc. 1, s/f 2–1 (8 November 1922), General Grazioli.

[29] See *Popolo d'Italia*, 27 December 1922; *Giornale d'Italia*, 28 December; Salvemini, *Scritti*, 2, p. 56; De Felice, II, p. 434.

[30] For Douhet's ideas, see G. Douhet, *La difesa nazionale* (Rome 1925), and *Popolo d'Italia*, 23 November, 7, 10, 21 December 1922.

[31] Salvemini, *Scritti*, pp. 57–8; see also ACS, PS, 1923, G. 1, b. 59, fasc. Perugia (16 May 1923).

[32] De Bono, 'Le origini della milizia', p. 292; Rossini, op. cit., p. 540.

[33] *Il Gran Consiglio*, pp. 88–9.

[34] *O. O.*, 20, pp. 147, 175–6.

[35] St Antony's documents, J. 53, 026224.

[36] Rochat, op. cit., p. 436; *Popolo d'Italia*, 30 September 1923; *Corriere della Sera*, 12 May 1924. At the end of May 1924, a new plan for 'gearing' the Militia to the Army, this time drawn up by Mussolini, was discussed (*Giornale d'Italia*, 23–4 May).

[37] ACS, PS, 1924, b. 87, fasc. MVSN Affari generali s/f 2, De Bono circular (1 May 1924); ibid. (10 May), De Bono to Perol. Understandably, the above circular was not included among those exhibited in De Bono's defence when he was tried by the Senate. (See Rossini, *Delitto*, pp. 540–601.)

[38] The arguments and figures of Salvemini *Fascist Dictatorship*, p. 345, cannot here be accepted; see ACS, Uff. cifra, tel, in partenza (13 June 1924), n. 12887; ibid., tel in arrivo (14 June), n. 20381, 20383, 20392, 20396, 20418, 20460; (15 June), n. 20645.

[39] ACS, PS, 1924, loc. cit. (23–4 June); Federzoni, p. 93.

[40] ACS, PS, loc. cit., passim.

[41] *O. O.*, 21, p. 14.

[42] ACS, loc. cit. (22 June); Prefect of Perugia, ibid., Uff. cifra, (22 June), tel. in arrivo, n. 21539. On the evening of 19 June rumours of an impending *coup* were current in Rome itself: T–K, 6, pp. 216–17. See also *Carteggio Giolitti*, 3, p. 422, 3 July, Sforza to Giolitti; *Il Mondo*, July 2, 5.

[43] *Il Balilla* (Ferrara), 21, 29 June. The accusation by Farinacci (see St Antony's documents, J. 53, 026236, 8 July 1926) that in June or December 1924 'others, at Bologna, tried to convince many provincial leaders to abandon you and give birth to a new movement', presumably refers to this meeting and to the attitude of Balbo.

[44] ACS, PS, 1924, b. 89, fasc. Bologna (22 June); and report of Prefect of Perugia, see note 42.

[45] *Popolo d'Italia*, 4 July.

[46] Ibid., 2, 11 July; *Corriere della Sera*, 3, 17 July.

[47] ACS, PS, 1924, b. 87, loc. cit., s/f 3, 5 July.

[48] *Il Mondo*, 22 July, 2 August.

[49] *Il Mondo*, 3 September; *Popolo d'Italia*, 6 September.

[50] *Popolo d'Italia*, 28 November 1924.

[51] ACS, Uff cifra, tel. in arrivo, 21, n. 20510 (15 June 1924), Ciano to De Bono; ibid., n. 20353, 20364, 20399–20401, 20421–2, 20427 (13–14 June) for reports on reactions in Naples, Bologna, Turin, Milan, Florence and Ferrara.

[52] *Tribuna*, 6 July, 1924.

[53] *Critica fascista*, 1, 15 July, 1 August.

[54] *La Conquista dello Stato*, 25 January 1925.

[55] Ibid., *Il Selvaggio*, 13 July 1924.

[56] *Il Selvaggio*, 23 August, 23 November.

[57] *La Conquista dello Stato*, 30 July 1924, 'Verso l'assemblea costituente'.

[58] *Idea Nazionale*, 9, 10 July.

[59] *O.O.*, 21, pp. 21–9.

[60] *O.O.*, 21, p. 459.

[61] Ibid., pp. 37–8.

[62] See comments of *Giornale d'Italia*, 5, 6 August; *Il Messaggero*, 9 August (interview with Acerbo).

[63] *Popolo d'Italia*, 5 August (speech of Pala), 8 August; *Corriere della Sera*, 15 August.

[64] *Popolo d'Italia*, 5 August.

[65] Ibid.

[66] Ibid., 7 August; *Conquista dello Stato*, 10 August.

[67] De Felice, II, pp. 670–3, 775–85.

[68] *Giornale d'Italia*, 21, 30 June.

[69] Ibid., 11 July.

[70] *Il diario di Salandra*, pp. 302, 306.

[71] A. Codignola, *La resistenza de' 'I combattenti di Assisi'* (Modena 1965), p. 109; *Popolo d'Italia*, 5 August.

[72] *Conquista dello Stato*, 20 October 1924; De Felice, II, p. 670.

[73] *l'Unita*, 2, 12 July 1924; *Il Messaggero*, 13 August 1924; *Rassegna italiana*, August 1925, 'la pace dei produttori'.

[74] T–K, 6, p. 270; St Antony's documents, J. 3, 001090–001105.

[75] *O.O.*, 21, 1, pp. 57, 59–65.

[76] St Antony's documents, J. 274, 079805–11.

[77] *O.O.*, 21, p. 28.

[78] Melograni, 'Confindustria', November–December 1965, pp. 854–5; *Epistolario Albertonini*, 4, pp. 1788–90.

[79] Abrate, *Lotta sindacale*, pp. 422–3.

[80] Ibid., pp. 423–5, 485–8. (See also comments of *L'Unità*, 18 September 1924.)

[81] Ibid., p. 426.

[82] Melograni, art. cit., pp. 864–5; *Epistolario Albertini*, 4, p. 1863; *Carteggio Giolitti*, 3, p. 427.

[83] Lyttelton, 'Second Wave', 1, p. 99. (Even the attitude of Senator Conti was ambiguous: although he was not present at the 28 December meeting of the Milanese Liberals which declared support for the Government, according to the Prefect's account he adhered to the pro-Government motion of Senator Greppi.)

[84] De Felice, II, pp. 679–80.

[85] Ibid., pp. 683–5; Salandra, *Diario*, pp. 300–1.

[86] *O.O.*, 21, p. 182.

[87] *Giornale d'Italia*, 26 November; *Popolo d'Italia*, 27, 29 November; *O.O.*, 21, p. 177 (the discussion went on into the small hours of the morning).

[88] Lyttelton, art. cit., pp. 84–5, 87–9.

[89] *Conquista dello Stato*, 7 December, G. de Luca; see also ibid., the curious article 'la tesi de "la conquista dello Stato", analizzata da un comunista'.

[90] Lyttelton, art. cit., p. 92.

[91] Ibid., p. 89.

[92] Ibid., pp. 79–80.

[93] De Felice, II, pp. 689–90.

[94] Lyttelton, art. cit., pp. 81–2.

[95] Ibid., pp. 83–5.

[96] Ibid., p. 82 ; De Felice, II, pp. 690, 717.

[97] Lyttelton, art. cit., pp. 85–7.

[98] T–K, 6, p. 314.

[99] See note 97.

[100] De Felice, II, pp. 690–4 ; Lyttelton, art. cit., p. 90.

[101] Lyttelton, art. cit., pp. 91, 99.

[102] Ibid.

[103] Ibid. ; De Felice, II, pp. 697–700.

[104] *Cremona Nuova*, 24 December 1924 ; *Giornale d'Italia*, 23–4, 28 December. (Michele Bianchi is said to have described the electoral reform as a 'miserable expedient') ; for reactions, see also ACS, Uff. cifra, tel. in arrivo (22–6 December), passim.

[105] Lyttelton, art. cit., pp. 91–2, 99.

[106] Ibid.; Salandra, *Diario*, p. 311 ; De Felice, II, pp. 702–4.

[107] Lyttelton, art. cit., pp. 92–5. *Regime Fascista*, 31 January 1926. ACS, CF, b. 2, f. 7 (5 February 1926), Negrini to F., which substantiates the story about Torre.

[108] De Felice, II, pp. 718–21.

[109] *Popolo d'Italia*, 1 January 1925 ; T–K, 6, p. 314.

[110] See P.Puntoni, *Parla Vittorio Emmanuele III* (Milan 1958), p. 352 ; I.Bonomi, *Diario di un anno* (Cernusco 1947), pp. xxvi–xxvii; T–K, 6, p. 348 ; for Salandra's scruples, see *Diario*, p. 292.

[111] *O.O.*, 21, p. 238 ff.; T–K, 6, p. 345 (Mussolini's speech was imposed on him by the Consuls)'.

[112] Salandra, *Diario*, pp. 321–2 ; L.Peano, *Ricordi della guerra dei trent'anni (1915–45)* (Citta di Castello 1948), pp. 83–7.

[113] Ibid., and see note 84 above.

[114] Salandra, *Diario*, pp. 322–3 ; De Felice, II, p. 727.

[115] Aquarone, *Organizzazione*, pp. 347–8. *Giornale d'Italia*, 1, 8 January 1925 ; ACS, SPCR, 242/R s/f 3 *Gran Consiglio*. According to official statistics, by January 6, 95 circles, 150 wineshops, etc., 25 subversive organizations and 120 groups of *Italia Libera* had been closed or dissolved, and 655 houses searched. However a report from Ancona (ACS, Uff, cifra, tel. in arrivo, 5 January n. 548) suggests that the real number of operations may have been considerably higher.

[116] T–K, 6, pp. 348–55 (6 January) ; Salandra, *Diario*, p. 323.

[117] Spriano, *Partito comunista*, 2, pp. 89–92.

11 The Defeat of the Party

[1] *O.O.*, 21, p. 362 (Mussolini's speech to Fourth Fascist Congress, 22 June 1925). L. Schapiro, 'The concept of totalitarianism', *Survey*, Autumn 1969, 95 ff. The first use of the term that I have been able to trace occurs in an article in *Il Mondo*, 12 May 1923, which refers to the 'totalitarian system' applied by Fascism in local elections, i.e., the determination not merely to win a bare majority, but an almost unanimous plebiscite. This example, even if isolated, is suggestive. One of the salient characteristics of totalitarianism is that it is based on a democratic formula or fiction.

[2] *O.O.*, 21, p. 425 (28 October 1925).

[3] M. Maraviglia, *Alle basi del regime*, p. 34 ff; G. Ambrosini, 'Il partito fascista e lo stato', *Civiltà fascista*, August–September 1934.

[4] Friedrich and Brzezinski, *Totalitarian Dictatorship*, p. 206; but see also L. Schapiro's comments in 'Reflections on the changing role of the party in the totalitarian polity', *Studies in Comparative Communism*, 1969, 2, pp. 4–7.

[5] *Conquista dello Stato*, 4 January 1925; *Il Selvaggio*, 13 January.

[6] ACS, PS, 1925, b. 88, G 1, 3–7, 13, (17–18 January, 6 February 1925).

[7] ACS, PS, 1925, b. 89, fasc. Forlì (8–9 January 1925); ibid., b. 90, fasc. Genova (4 January); ibid., b. 93, fasc. Siena (4–5 January).

[8] *Conquista dello Stato*, 25 January, 8 February.

[9] *Battaglie Fasciste*, 31 January, 7 February 1925.

[10] See *Carteggio Albertini*, 4 p. 1853 (G. Emmanuel, 19 February).

[11] 'Giovincelli Kulturizzati': this sarcastic epithet was presumably aimed at the Germanic descent of Suckert.

[12] C. Pellizzi, 'la funzione di Farinacci'; *Critica fascista*, 1 October 1925.

[13] *O.O.*, 21, p. 359; *Corriere della Sera*, 23 June 1925.

[14] *Corriere della Sera*, ibid., Farinacci, op. cit., pp. 156–8; *Corriere Padano*, 17 April 1925. (When Pala asked that the new *direttorio* should contain representatives of the regions, Turati replied that 'the Rt Hon. Pala has no need to worry since full powers have been given to Farinacci, who has always brought to Rome the voice of the provinces'.

[15] R. Farinacci, *Un periodo aureo del Partito Nazionale Fascista* (Foligno 1927), p. 294; *Carteggio Albertini*, 4, p. 1898.

[16] *Idea Nazionale*, 30 July 1924; ACS, CF, b. 3, f. 12 (9 January 1926), G. Masi. *Corriere della Sera*, 24 June 1925.

[17] Farinacci, op. cit., p. 162.

[18] ACS, PS, 1925, b. 92 (1 March, 4 April, 28 September, 26 October 1925).

[19] Ibid., b. 95, G. 1, fasc. Pavia (14 July 1925); *Corriere della Sera*, 1 November 1925, ACS, CF, b. 2, f. 6 (16 February 1926), Ces. Forni.

[20] ACS, PS, Ibid., b. 91 (29 March, 15, 21 April, 6 May).

[21] For Farinacci's opposition to Banca Commerciale and connections with Pogiliani (former managing director of the Banca di Sconto), see ACS, SPCR242/R s/f 14 (19 August 1925); ACS, CF, b. 2, f. 7 (15 December 1926), A. Pogliani; ibid. (n.d.), and b. 4, f. 14 (30 March 1927), G. L. Riatti; *Regime Fascista*, 15–20 February 1926. For Southern grievances against Volpi, see ACS, PS, 1926, b. 95 (12 August 1926).

[22] G. Masi, 'Il partito fascista nello stato fascista', *Educazione Politica*, April 1926.

[23] ACS, PS, 1925, b. 87, fasc. Bari (10 April 1925).

[24] Ibid., b. 89 (20 May 1925), G. Masi to Teruzzi; and ACS, CF, b. 2, f. 7 (30 May 1926); for Messina, ACS, PS, ibid., b. 91 (30 April, 1 June).

[25] *Il Mezzogiorno*, 1–2, 2–3, 4–5 October 1925. ACS, CF, b. 2, f. 6 (17 April 1926), G. Bellacosa to Farinacci; ibid. ACS, PC, 1926, fasc. 6. 1, n. 2180 (Bellacosa represented the Cotoniere Meridional firm, which financed Preziosi).

[26] De Felice, *Preziosi*, pp. 542–4; ACS, PS, 1925, b. 91, fasc. Napoli (12, 30 December 1925); ACS, CF, b. 2, f. 6 (7 January 1926), Gobbi.

[27] E. Apih, *Italia, fascismo e antifascismo nella Venezia Giulia, 1918–43* (Bari

1966), pp. 191–2, 259–61. For Suvich, see St Antony's documents, J. 267, 077065–6, January 1929.

28 See *Associazione fra le società italiane per azioni, Notizie statistiche* (Rome 1928).

29 Apih, op. cit., p. 219 ; ACS, PS, 1925, b. 94 (13, 24 November 1925).

30 ACS, PS, 1925, b. 94 (13 December 1925) ; ACS, CF, b. 2, f. 7 (11 February 1926) ; see also ibid., 25 April.

31 *Corriere Emiliano*, 12 March 1926 ; in the summer of 1926 Ricci attempted to take over the *Società filarmonica*, the meeting-place of the Liberal bourgeoisie, demanding that it should be handed over to the *fascio*. However after conflicts between the *squadristi* and the police on 13–4 September, Ricci had to accept a compromise solution ; see Apih, op. cit., pp. 263–4.

32 ACS, SCN, b. 27, f. 397, Spezzotti ; I. Silone, 'La società italiana e il fascismo', *Tempo Presente*, December 1962, pp. 861–2.

33 *Giornale del Friuli*, 28 February, 1, 2, 5 March 1926 ; *Popolo d'Italia*, 5 March.

34 *Regime fascista*, 17 April 1926 ; for similar conflicts in the rest of the Veneto, St Antony's documents, J. 113, 031038 ff ; P. Pedrazza, the secretary of the Treviso *fascio* wrote to Farinacci on 24 May 1926, 'of all the provinces, this is the one which perhaps feels most keenly the consequences of the passage of power from your hands to those of the new *direzione* of the PNF'. (ACS, CF, b. 2, f. 7.)

35 ACS, Uff. cifra, tel in partenza, 27, n. 26014 (2 December 1924).

36 Aquarone, *Organizzazione*, pp. 68–73.

37 *O.O.*, 21, pp. 287–8, 347–9. However the party clashed with Mussolini when Giunta and others demanded a purge of the Foreign Ministry. See below, Ch. 14.

38 *Battaglie fasciste*, 24 January 1925. See also Misuri, *Rivolta morale*, p. 105, for earlier period.

39 *Critica fascista*, 15 February 1926.

40 ACS, PC, 1925, fasc. 1/3–1, (23 October, 26 November 1925); ACS, CF, b. 4, f. 13 (4 January 1927), Bisi; ibid., b. 3, f. 12 (6 January 1926), Masi.

41 ACS, PS, 1925, b. 92, fasc. Pavia (28 August 1925), Bisi to Farinacci ; ibid., fasc. Piacenza, 28 September. See also ACS, SPCR, 242/R s/f 6 ins. A. (19 August 1925), Farinacci to Mussolini.

42 ACS, PS, 1925, b. 85, fasc. 1, Repressione violenza fascista (9 April 1925) ; *Corriere della Sera*, 17, 25 April.

43 *Corriere Padano*, 23 May 1925.

44 *Corriere della Sera*, 16 May 1925 ; Federzoni, *Italia di ieri*, pp. 100, 289.

45 ACS, PS, 1925, b. 85, fasc. 1 (25 June). From 15 February to 23 March Mussolini was incapacitated by a duodenal ulcer ; this strengthened Farinacci's position *vis-à-vis* Federzoni (De Felice, III, p. 55n.).

46 ACS, PS, 1925, b. 93, fasc. Rovigo (27 May 1925), Bishop of Adria, *Corriere della Sera*, 23 June, 28–30 July, 3–5 August; De Felice, III, pp. 103–14.

47 ACS, PS, 1925, b. 85 loc. cit. (27 June, 8 July), Bologna; (2 October), Turin; (27 September) Federzoni to Farinacci ; St Antony's documents, J. 263/1, 073965 ff, 28 September 1925, General Perol. ACS, PS, 1925, b. 90, fasc. Genova (4 December 1924, 11, 13 August, 15 October 1925).

48 E.g. ACS, PS, 1925, b. 93, fasc. Roma (27 August 1925).

49 ACS, PS, 1925, b. 85 (7 July 1925).

50 Perol report cit.

[51] Galbiati, *Il 25 luglio*, pp. 59–61 ; ACS, CF, b. 3, f. 12 (14 January 1926), Melchiorri.

[52] *Voce Repubblicana*, 18 September 1925 ; *Cremona Nuova*, ibid.

[53] A. Pavolini, *Rivoluzione fascista*, 1 May 1925.

[54] *Battaglie fasciste*, 27 June 1925.

[55] Ibid., 18 July.

[56] Ibid., 12 September.

[57] Ibid., 26 September. The 'circular' was first published in the *Idea Nazionale*. When the editor Forges-Davanzati was asked to submit proofs of the circular's authenticity to a Press tribunal, he replied (1) that the evidence offered by a secret society could have no value, and (2) that he feared 'secret Masonic solidarity' among the members of the tribunal. Masi added that it would not be fair to expose the informers who had provided the evidence to Masonic vengeance ! (*Corriere della Sera*, 15–16 October). In spite of the part played by the *Idea Nazionale*, the campaign does not seem likely to have been Government-inspired ; (Federzoni, circular ibid., 4 October ordering it to cease).

[58] Ibid., 27 September 1925.

[59] Salvemini, *The Fascist Dictatorship*, pp. 178–86 ; ACS, PS, b. 89, fasc. Firenze, 4 October ; ibid., 1926, b. 98 (7 October 1925).

[60] *Popolo d'Italia*, 6 October.

[61] St Antony's documents, J. 263/1, 074278–85.

[62] See also ACS, PS, 1925, C. 1, b. 56 (12 October).

[63] See *Corriere della Sera*, 17 October 1925.

[64] Federzoni, *Italia di ieri*, pp. 103–4 ; (though his account confuses the two different episodes of December 1924 and October 1925).

[65] Rocco, *Scritti*, 3, p. 821 ff.

[66] *Corriere della Sera*, 9 October.

[67] ACS, PS, 1925, b. 93, fasc. Roma 1, (12, 19 October); ibid., b. 87, fasc. Bari (6 October); ibid., b. 91, fasc. Modena (6 October); ibid., b. 89, fasc. Forlì (11 October); ibid., b. 90, fasc. Genova, (10 October, 5 November).

[68] ACS, ibid., b. 91, fasc. Modena (10 October) ; b. 94, fasc. Torino, (14 October).

[69] St Antony's documents, J. 112, 030830 ff (13–14 October).

[70] *Giornale d'Italia*, 14 October ; Mussolini may himself have been doubtful, as he postponed the meeting for a few days.

[71] *Popolo d'Italia*, 20 October 1925.

[72] ACS, PS, 1925, b. 89, fasc. Firenze (9 October).

[73] ACS, CF, b. 2, fasc. 5, (17, 21 October 1925).

[74] ACS, PS, 1925, b. 89, fasc. Firenze (19 October, 7, 14 November). D. Fantozzi, the head of the Information Office of Tamburini's legion, described as 'a violent individual, without scruples, of very dubious morality, capable of any illicit action, the blind instrument of the aforesaid Consul in every enterprise', was reported to have organized 'a regular police service for private ends'.

[75] Ibid. (3, 6, 13 December) ; St Antony's documents, J. 266 076679–80 (9, 12 December). Tamburini to Mussolini. ACS, CF, b. 2, f. 7 (19 January 1926).

[76] ACS, PS, 1927, b. 134, fasc. Firenze (14 March 1926). *Battaglie fasciste*, 11 June 1926.

[77] St Antony's documents, ibid., 076720 ff.

[78] ACS, PS, 1925, b. 85 ; ibid. (26 November 1925) ; ibid., 1926, b. 95 (29 May 1926) ; *Regime fascista*, 28 October 1926.

[79] For crime figures see *Ministero della Giustizia – Statistica penale, 1927–1928* (Rome 1931). For survival of squads, ACS, SPP, Padova fasc. 5 (September 1929).

[80] ACS, PS, 1925, b. 91, 12–30 December 1925 ; ACS, CF, b. 2, f. 6 (3 January 1926), Lusignani ; ibid., f. 7 (6 January, 8 February 1926), Ricci.

[81] *La Nazione*, 26 January 1926 ; *Popolo d'Italia*, 27 January.

[82] *Regime fascista*, 28 January.

[83] G. Masi, *Educazione politica*, April 1926.

[84] Farinacci, *Un periodo aureo*, p. 367, 31 January 1926.

[85] De Felice, III, p. 170. *Corriere della Sera*, 22 December 1925.

[86] ACS, CF, b. 2, f. 6 (27 January 1926). St Antony's documents, J. 111, 030786–90 (12–13 January 1926).

[87] Farinacci, *Un periodo aureo*, p. 367. On extremism and the Fascist mass base, see speech of the Communist deputy Maffi, AP, C. XXVII legisl. 6, p. 5508, 1 May 1926 ; on unemployment among Fascists see ACS, PS, 1926, b. 98, fasc. Livorno, 6 July 1926 ; *Giornale del Friuli*, 13 May 1926.

[88] *Voce Repubblicana*, 28 January, 16 March 1926. ACS, CF, b. 2, fasc. 7, 2 February 1926, for an unconvincing denial by Arnaldo Mussolini of divergence on this issue.

[89] *Popolo d'Italia*, 26 February 1926 ; *Regime fascista*, 27 February.

[90] De Felice, III, pp. 172–5.

[91] St Antony's documents, J. 113, 031034–7, 031063–4 (24 April 1926). The demonstrators were also reported to have shouted 'long live the republic with Farinacci'.

[92] ACS, CF, b. 3, f. 12 (11 November 1926) Starace. St Antony's Documents, J. 113, 031038 (22 April 1926) ; J. 277, 081506. For discontent of Farinacci's followers, see ACS ibid., b. 2, f. 6 (19 August 1926), mayor of Sestri Levante ; ibid., f. 7 (13 August), Masi : 'The situation is such that I am ashamed not yet to be in prison for disturbing the peace.'

[93] *Corriere Emiliano*, 25–7 May, 9, 26 June 1926 ; *Voce Repubblicana*, 16 January 1947 ; ACS, PS, 1926, b. 97 (24 April, 17 May, 27 June, 1926) ; ibid., b. 99, fasc. Parma (6 November 1926).

[94] St Antony's documents, J. 53, 02635–46 (8 July). J. III 030744–8 (1 July 1926) Arnaldo Mussolini to Farinacci.

[95] Letter of Turati, ACS, CF, b. 3, f. 12 (7 September 1926). Ibid., b. 2, f. 4 (8 September 1926), Barbiellini.

[96] ACS, PS, b. 99, fasc. Napoli (26 July 1926).

[97] *Il Gran Consiglio*.

[98] ACS, PS, 1926, b. 95, G. 1 (20 October 1926) ; see also ibid., 12 August 1926.

[99] *Corriere Padano*, 18 September 1926 ; ibid., 23 September.

[100] St Antony's documents, J. 116, 049002–24 (16 April 1926) ; ACS, V, 16 (5 November 1926).

[101] *Il Tevere*, 7–8 December 1926.

[102] O. O., 22, pp. 467–70. The laws of 4 February and 3 September 1926 abolished local elective councils. Their functions were to be exercized by the *podestà*, assisted by a small advisory council. The *podestà* were nominated by the Prefect. The effect

of the change was that the party, at least formally, lost control over local administration. However it is clear that the separation between party and state functions was not as sharp in practice as in theory : see ACS, SPP, Siena (13 August 1928).

[103] Aquarone, *Organizzazione*, pp. 67-8, 386-92.

[104] *Regime fascista*, 31 August 1926.

[105] *Critica fascista*, 15 September 1926. For an example of the system in action, see *Roma fascista*, 23 January 1926.

[106] *Regime fascista*, 28 November 1926.

[107] *Corriere Padano*, 17, 22-4, 28 September, 5 November 1926.

[108] *Il Gran Consiglio*, p. 236 ; ACS, PS, 1926, b. 98, fasc. Ferrara (2 November 1926).

[109] G. Leto, *OVRA Fascismo antifascismo* (Bologna 1951), pp. 13-14 ; *Popolo d'Italia*, 22 November, 28 December 1922 ; ACS, PS, 1926, b. 70, b. 5, fasc. Riforma della Pubblica amministrazione (17 September 1923).

[110] Leto, op. cit., pp. 14-15. Leto's conclusions are borne out by a reading of the reports from the political offices of the Militia which are to be found in the archives. But after November 1926 their quality undoubtedly improved.

[111] ACS, SPAD, b. 3, f. V (A), Bazan to Mussolini, 23 May 1927. Ibid., PNF, SPP, Padova.

[112] ACS, PS, 1926, b. 70, B. 5, fasc. 'Riforma della pubblica amministrazione', 5 May 1925 (Crispo Moncada) ; ibid., fasc. 'Relazioni a S. E. il Ministro', memo from 'the head of the police', n.d. but prob. by Bocchini November/December 1926.

[113] Leto, op. cit., p. 34.

[114] S. Trentin, *Les transformations récentes du droit public italien* (Paris 1929), p. 380.

[115] Ministero dell'Interno, *Bollettino ufficiale, legislazione e disposizioni*, pp. 723-4. Aquarone, op. cit., pp. 100, 422-6.

[116] Aquarone, op. cit., pp. 555-60 ; Bollettino cit., pp. 735-6. P. Barile, 'La pubblica sicurezza', in *La pubblica sicurezza*, ed. P. Barile (Milan 1967), p. 26.

[117] St Antony's documents, J. 268, n. 077487, 3, 7 June, September 1927.

[118] Aquarone, op. cit., pp. 103-5.

[119] Aquarone, op. cit., p. 99n. Barile, 'La pubblica sicurezza', pp. 14-15, 21, 26.

[120] Aquarone, op. cit., p. 49.

[121] F. L. Ferrari, *Le régime fasciste italien* (Paris 1928), pp. 219-21. In general, Vivarelli, 'Italia liberale e fascismo'.

[122] See A. L. Maraspini, *The Study of an Italian Village* (Hague 1968), p. 232.

[123] *Critica fascista*, 15 May 1926.

[124] Ibid., 15 September, 15 October, 1 December 1926 ; O. Zuccarini, *Critica politica*, October 1926.

[125] Ibid., 1 November 1926 ; C. Sgroi, 15 February 1927.

[126] *Il Tevere*, 7-8 December 1926.

[127] Fried, *Italian Prefect*, p. 183 ; in 1937 they numbered 34 out of 65 studied.

[128] ACS, SPP, Siena (3 November 1929).

[129] Ibid., fasc. Reggio Emilia, passim ; St Antony's documents, J. 252 068947-5 ; see also G. Berti, 'Note sul fascismo piacentino 1925-40', *MLI*, April-June 1969, pp. 85-7, for the similar relations between Barbiellini and the Fascist Prefect, Tiengo.

[130] ACS, SPCR, 242/R G.Bonelli (23, 28 April, 8, 12 September 1972, 16 May 1929); ibid., PNF, SPP, Genova (23 April 1928).

[131] ACS, SCN, b. 18, fasc. 169, F.Lantini.

[132] C.Scorza, *Brevi noti sul fascismo*, pp. 281–5; also ACS, SPP, *Reggio Emilia*, 17 February 1929.

[133] ACS, ibid., Piacenza, 13 January 1928.

[134] L.Paladin, 'Il problema della rappresentanza nello stato fascista', *Jus* 1968, pp. 69–87.

[135] ACS, ibid., Padova (26 July 1928, 18 January 1929). For similar complaints from a great city, see ibid., Genova, 8 March 1928, 22 November 1929.

[136] *Critica fascista*, 15 September 1928; ACS, ibid., Reggio Emilia, 17 February 1929. (For later complaints see *Critica fascista* 1, 15 May 1931, 1 December 1933.)

[137] ACS, ibid., Roma (13 November, 13 December 1928, 28 March 1929).

[138] Ragionieri, 'Il Partito fascista', pp. 23–8 of *Fascismo in Toscana*.

[139] However for conditions in Turin, see ACS, Agenzia Stefani-Manlio Morgagni, fasc. 1, n. 6A (summer 1931), 'at Turin an old Fascist has the impression that he is living in a large Italian community abroad'.

[140] St Antony's documents, J. 254 069593 ff, memorandum from Giampaoli (23 August 1930); ibid., J. 253, n. 069243 ff (20 December 1928).

[141] Silone, 'la societa italiana', p. 857 ff. Augusto Turati paid tribute to the 'attention and acumen' shown by the enquiry (18 June 1926 circular, ACS, PS, 1926, b. 95, G. 1).

[142] *Popolo d'Italia*, 18 February 1926; *Tribuna*, 8 March 1926.

[143] See above, Ch. 3 note 140.

[144] See Silvestri, *Il fascismo salernitano*.

[145] Silone loc. cit., see also *Regime Fascista*, 12 May 1926. Officials of the civil service formed a larger percentage of the party as a whole than of the *direttori rionali* (ward committees); this shows that they were mostly late and inactive members (*Roma fascista*, 13 March 1926).

[146] See note 140 above. St Antony's documents, J. 255, 070120ff. (Perugia); Ragionieri, 'Il partito fascista', pp. 69–72.

[147] Out of 64 *federali* in 1928, in 1934 3 had become members of the Government, 1 a Prefect and 1 a member of the party *direttorio*. 23 had become deputies and 6 remained *federali*. (E.Savino, *La nazione operante*, Milan 1928, 1934).

[148] St Antony's documents, J. 54 026360–1, 8 January 1933 Farinacci to Mussolini; Federzoni, *Italia di ieri*, pp. 155–65.

[149] '*L'organizzazione dello stato totalitario*' (discussion of Aquarone, op. cit.), *Il cannocchiale* 1966 1/3, p. 101 (C.Pavone).

[150] See Federzoni, op. cit., pp. 287–8 (Grandi's 1943 speech to the Grand Council).

[151] R.Michels, *Nuovi studi sulla classe politica*, pp. 136 ff.

12 The Origins of the Corporate State

[1] Rossoni, *Le idee della ricostruzione*, p. 100.

[2] *La Stirpe*, December 1923, 'Ipotesi ed eventi'. For earlier statements by Panunzio, see R.Melis, *Sindacalisti*, pp. 304–7.

[3] Within Fascism, the industrialists' point of view, favourable to the freedom of

organization, was maintained by Costamagna and the *gruppi di competenza; Battaglie sindacali*, 15 November 1923.

⁴ F.Coletti, *Economia rurale*, pp. 114–19.

⁵ St Antony's documents, J. 263/1, 673875–8, memorandum of Confederazione Generale dell'Agricoltura, Bartoli and Donini (12 November 1923).

⁶ S.Gatti, *La Stirpe*, May 1924. 'I sindacati nell'ordine giuridico'.

⁷ F.Cordova, *Arditi*, pp. 161–80.

⁸ De Felice, II, pp. 592–6; *Nuovo Paese*, 5 May 1924. While I agree with Professor De Felice's general assessment of the situation after the elections, it seems to me very doubtful that, even assuming the removal of Rossoni, an alliance with the CGL would have 're-launched' Fascist syndicalism. If Mussolini intended some sort of move to the left, he would still have had to choose between conciliating the CGL and promoting Fascist syndicalism.

⁹ *L'Assalto*, 24, 31 May 1924; ACS, GF, b. 11, f. 118, 3, 9, 11 February, 21–8 May. Baroncini tried to exploit the discontent to make a comeback; he was reported to be considering the foundation of a labour party.

¹⁰ ACS, PS, 1924, G. 1, b. 87, fasc. affari generali sindacali fascisti, Ancona (18 March 1924).

¹¹ Unemployment figures for the period 1922–4 are unfortunately almost worthless for an estimation of the trend, owing to changes in the method of their collection. But it seems fairly certain that the spring and summer of 1924 saw a substantial reduction; see E.Rossi, 'Che cosa valgono le statistiche di disoccupazione in Italia', *Riforma sociale*, September/October 1926.

¹² *O. O.*, 20, p. 277 ff.

¹³ *Unità*, 20 July 1924; see also ibid., 12, 17 July, Milan, and ACS, PS, 1924, G. 1, b. 87, fasc. affari generali sindacati fascisti, Genova (5 July 1924).

¹⁴ ACS, loc. cit., Firenze (19 July); *La Nazione*, 19–21 July. Malusardi, a Fascist from 1919, was an important figure in the corporations. He was the director-general of the Glassworkers' Corporation, the provincial secretary for Florence, and a member of the National Directorate. 16 out of 22 union secretaries in Florence resigned in sympathy. For later repercussions, see *Unità*, 26 July, 2 August; ACS, PC, 1925 fasc. 3/5 n. – 330 (10 February 1925).

¹⁵ *Unità*, 20, 24 August, 7, 10, 17, 24 September.

¹⁶ *Popolo d'Italia*, 22 July. *La Nazione*, 22 July; *La Stirpe*, July 1924, Rossoni, '*Restare nella nuova storia*'; ibid., A.Casalini, '*Esigenze immediate ed esigenze giuridiche del sindacalismo fascista*'.

¹⁷ *Cremona Nuova*, 13 July 1924.

¹⁸ ACS, loc. cit., Lucca (3 September 1924); ibid., Grosseto (18 September); *La Nazione*, 17, 19, 21 August.

¹⁹ In the first half of 1924 the Società Elettrica e Mineraria del Valdarno placed three full page advertisements and an article in *La Stirpe; Unità*, 22 July 1924.

²⁰ On Valdarno strike, see ACS, PC, 1924, fasc. 3/3, n. 1744 passim; *La Nazione*, 8, 12, 28, 31 August, 2, 3, 12 September 1924. *Lavoro d'Italia*, 6 September. The settlement provided increases (for adult workers) ranging from 2.1 to 1.9 lire. Previously the average daily wage had been 16 lire, which was below the national average, in spite of the heavy nature of the work. Real wages showed a marked deterioration during 1924 and in spite of the increase won by the strike wages still lagged behind prices during 1925 (see ACS, ibid., f. 3/1–3, n. 1192).

[21] ACS, PC, 1924, fasc. 3/3 n. 1744.

[22] ACS, PC, 1924, f. 1/6–3, n. 1838 (30 July). ACS, PS, 1924, G. 1., b. 87, fasc. MVSN s/f 5, *Rapporti sulla situazione politica* ; ACS, ibid., fasc. Sindacati fascisti, Novara (2 October, 12 November 1924).

[23] St Antony's documents, J. 104, 028096 (14 November 1924).

[24] Melograni, Confindustria, p. 865 ; St Antony's documents, J. 250, 067864 (30 December 1932) ; *La Stirpe*, December 1924.

[25] St Antony's documents, J. 104, 028114–7 ; *La Stirpe*, December 1924.

[26] N. Cilla, *Effetti economici del fascismo* (Milan 1925), pp. 15–17 ; B. Uva, 'Gli scioperi dei Metallurgici italiani del marzo 1925', *Storia contemporanea*, 1970, 4, pp. 1011–15.

[27] *Corriere della Sera*, 14 March 1925.

[28] Farinacci, *Un periodo aureo*, p. 44 ; cf. the June 1924 memorandum of Bagnasco, in Salvemini, *Under the Axe of Fascism*, p. 29.

[29] De Felice, III, p. 91 ; ACS, PS, 1925, G. 1, b. 85, fasc. affari generali sindacati.

[30] *Il Gran Consiglio*, pp. 179–80.

[31] E. Rossi, 'I salari degli operai milanesi, 1921–6', *Riforma sociale*, November to December 1926, p. 554 ff. *Inizio e sviluppo del sindacalismo fascista nella provincia di Brescia* (Brescia 1926).

[32] Uva, art. cit., pp. 1016–18.

[34] *Corriere della Sera*, 17, 19 February, 4–9 March 1925 ; Abrate, p. 417 ; Uva, art. cit., p. 1023.

[34] Uva, art. cit., p. 1028.

[35] *Popolo d'Italia*, 14 March 1925.

[36] ACS, PC, 1925, fasc. 3/3, n. 813 (14 March), Prefect of Trieste ; Uva, art. cit., pp. 1062–4.

[37] ACS, ibid., 16–8 March ; *Corriere della Sera*, 19 March ; Uva, art. cit., pp. 1053–67.

[38] *Corriere della Sera*, 17 March ; Uva, art. cit., pp. 1049–50.

[39] ACS, PC, 1925, fasc. 3/3, n. 813 (17–8 March).

[40] Aquarone, *Organizzazione*, pp. 119–20, 437–8.

[41] See articles of A. Lusignoli in *La Stirpe*, April–May 1925.

[42] *Corriere della Sera*, 28 April 1925.

[43] *La Stirpe*, December 1925.

[44] Ibid., October 1925.

[45] *Corriere della Sera*, 23 June 1925.

[46] Salvemini, *Under the Axe*, p. 30 ; between November 1924 and spring 1925, in 24 factory committee elections the Fascists obtained only about 7 per cent of the votes.

[47] ACS, PS, 1925, G. 1., b. 85 (15 July 1925); Abrate, *Lotta sindacale*, pp. 438–9.

[48] ACS, PC, 1925, fasc., 3/3 n. 813 (23, 26, 28 August 1925); ACS, PS, 1925, G. 1, b. 94, fasc. Torino (24 August).

[49] ACS, PS, loc. cit. (30, 31 August); ACS, PS, 1925, b. 87, G. 1., fasc. Alessandria (29 August) ; Abrate, op. cit., p. 440.

[50] Abrate, op. cit., pp. 442–3.

[51] De Felice, III, pp. 98–100 ; *Epistolario Albertini*, p. 1914.

[52] *Corriere della Sera*, 13 September 1925.

[53] Aquarone, op. cit., p. 122; G. Giugni, 'Esperienze corporative e post-corporative nei rapporti collettivi di lavoro in Italia', *Il Mulino*, January/February 1956, p. 5.

[54] Abrate, op. cit., p. 440 (see also p. 444); for the effectiveness of 'regulation' as opposed to 'suppression' of class conflict, see Dahrendorf, *Class and Class Conflict*, p. 259.

[55] See below, Ch. 13, n. 21.

[56] G. Arias, 'La nazione delle arti', *Cremona Nuova*, 5 August 1924; St Antony's documents, J. 263/1 074116–074150.

[57] Ibid., 074257–8; De Felice, III, pp. 94–6 and see note 45 above.

[58] AP, C, 27th legist., 5, p. 4888 (9 December 1925).

[59] *Il Gran Consiglio*, pp. 204–7.

[60] Aquarone, op. cit., p. 139; AP, C, 27th legisl., 5, p. 4793 ff (4 December 1925), Belluzzo.

[61] ACS, PC, 1925, 3/5, n. 3869 (13 November 1925).

[62] *Popolo d'Italia*, 27 November 1925; Rocco interview in *La Tribuna*, 30 June 1926.

[63] AP, C, loc. cit., pp. 4851–5 (5 December); Aquarone, op. cit., pp. 129–30, 131n, 468–9. Lanzillo and Rocco exemplified respectively what Dahrendorf has termed the 'political' and the 'judicial' concept of arbitration. Dahrendorf has suggested that the first method is likely in the long run to prove a better method for the regulation of class conflict. (Op. cit., pp. 229–30.)

[64] AP, C, loc. cit., pp. 4879–89, 10 December.

[65] *O.O.*, 22, p. 37 ff.

[66] AP, C, loc. cit., pp. 4914–19, 10 December.

[67] G. Moschini, *Scritti* (Mantua 1934), pp. 80–4.

[68] De Felice, III, pp. 397, 453–6. Ferrari, *Azione Cattolica*, p. 92 ff; G. Castagno, *Bruno Buozzi* (Milan 1955), p. 80 ff.

[69] *La Stirpe*, December 1925, 'Il bilancio delle corporazioni'.

[70] Ibid., February 1926; *Regime Fascista*, 17–18 January 1926.

[71] Moschini, op. cit., pp. 78–91.

[72] ACS, V. 16 (31 December 1925, 1 May 1926).

[73] St Antony's documents, J. 263/2, 074558–9, 074571 (Bottai report to 1928 Grand Council).

[74] ACS, PS, 1929 b. 55 (2), fasc. Firenze, 2 November 1929 (procedure). For complaints about the growth of *affarismo*, see ACS, PS, 1926, G. 1, b. 95, fasc. Fasci affari generali (conversation of Porzio on rival economic groups and their search for 'protection' in Fascist circles), and especially *Il Mezzogiorno*, 13–14 August 1926, article by Melchiorri, the vice-secretary of the party; 'Fascists . . . should be forbidden to join with such ease the boards of the most varied types of firms . . . if they do not possess the right technical qualifications.'

[75] ACS, PC, 1925, f. 3/7, n. 3614 (11 October).

[76] *L'organizzazione industriale*, 15 December 1925; ACS, PC, 1926, fasc. 3/2, n. 1206, 1740; fasc. 3–3, n. 3598; ibid., 3.7, n. 1206.

[77] Abrate, op. cit., p. 452.

[78] St Antony's documents, J. 263/2, 074296 ff, speech to 30 March 1926 Grand Council; *O.O.*, 22, pp. 102–3.

[79] Rossoni, 'Principio e metodo unitario' *La Stirpe*, March 1926; Moschini, pp. 108–11, 117–18.

[82] De Felice, III, p. 273.

[81] *Lavoro d'Italia*, 28 May 1926.

[82] Ibid., 7 May, 21 November 1926; *La Stirpe*, April–May 1926, 'l'ordine economico della Corporazione'.

[83] *La Tribuna*, 4 May 1926; *L'organizzazione industriale*, 15 May. It should be explained that Italian legislative practice allowed the details of a bill to be defined by the *regolamento*, which was an administrative measure not requiring parliamentary sanction.

[84] *La Stirpe*, June 1926, 'Il sindacalismo nello stato'.

[85] Ibid., March 1926, 'Principio e metodo unitario'.

[86] *O.O.*, 22, p. 129 (18 May).

[87] Ibid., pp. 162–4. The compromise was evidently reached after arduous and minute discussions, since it went on for two sessions and ended at 4.00 in the morning. For the text of the *regolamento* before and after the Grand Council's modifications, see *Lavoro d'Italia*, 19 May, 11 July 1926, and ACS, PC, 1927, fasc. 3/5, n. 761.

[88] Pesce, *Marcia dei rurali*, pp. 253–5, 275–8, 289; ACS, PC 1925, fasc. 1–3/3 (14 January 1926), Cacciari to Suardo.

[89] ACS, CF, b. 2, f. 6 (13 May 1926); *Lavoro d'Italia*, 19, 27 May; ACS, PS, 1927 3/5, n. 761 (22 May 1926), circular from Cacciari; *Resto del Carlino*, 25 June 1926; *Avanti!* ibid., ACS, ibid., n. 2073, 31 May, 2 June 1926 (Prefect of Modena to Suardo and reply).

[90] ACS, PC, 1927, fasc. 3/5, n. 761 (1 May 1926).

[91] L. Rosenstock-Franck, *L'économie corporative fasciste en doctrine et en fait* (Paris 1934), p. 182. R. Nenci, *Saggi ed esperienze di sindacalismo fascista e corporativismo* (Florence 1938), pp. 42, 57–61.

[92] *La Stirpe*, September 1926; Rossoni, 'Lavoro e capitale in regime totalitario'; *Lavoro d'Italia*, 30 November, 29 December 1926.

[93] *Lavoro d'Italia*, 20 October 1926; 2, 10 March 1927; Capoferri, *Vent'anni coi sindacati* (Milan 1957), p. 121. ACS, PC, 1926, fasc. 3/5, n. 4260 (12 November 1926); Nenci, *Saggi*, p. 59.

[94] *O.O.*, 22, pp. 463–4; ACS, PC, 1927, fasc. 3/5, n. 761.

[95] ACS, PC, 1927, fasc. 3/5, n. 761, Rossoni Memorandum (n.d.). *Regime fascista*, 11 January 1928; *Lavoro d'Italia*, 11 January 1928; Rosenstock-Franck, op. cit., pp. 163–7.

[96] *Lavoro d'Italia*, 1 May 1927.

[97] Ibid., 1 January 1927.

[98] ACS, SPCR, 242/R 1927, s/f 5 Ins. A (27 December 1926), Employers' Confederations; (6–7 January 1927), workers; De Felice, III, pp. 288–9.

[99] De Felice, III, pp. 292–5, 525–47; see U. Romagnoli, 'Il diritto sindacale corporativo ed i suoi interpreti', *Storia contemporanea*, 1, No. 1, March 1970, pp. 113–20; F. Catalano, 'Le corporazioni fasciste e la classe lavoratrice, *Nuova Rivista Storica* (1959), pp. 56, 58.

[100] Aquarone, *Organizzazione*, p. 143n.

[101] Rosenstock-Franck, *L'économie corporative*, pp. 179–203.

[102] Capoferri, *Vent'anni*, p. 49.

13 The Fascist Economy

[1] *O.O.*, 22, p. 37ff. On the prevalence among Fascists generally of the belief that economic problems could be solved by 'an act of will', see G. Luzzatto, Le incognite della politica economica', *Critica politica*, 25 March 1923 ; and M. Pantaleoni, 'Finanza fascista' (*Politica* June 1923, p. 175).

[2] See F. Perroux, *Contribution à l'étude de l'économie et des finances publiques de l'Italie depuis la guerre* (Paris 1929), p. 12. For an extreme view, see the article of the syndicalist A. Fioretti, *Lavoro d'Italia*, 15 December 1926 : 'Italy is today one huge Corporation : . . . the economic battle requires the civil and economic conscription of all the citizens.'

[3] De Felice, III, pp. 230–1.

[4] Ibid., p. 233 ; *O.O.*, 22, pp. 196–8.

[5] For the 'command economy', see F. Neumann, *Behemoth : The Structure and Practice of National Socialism* (New York 1966), pp. 291–361. See also T. W. Mason, 'The Primacy of Politics ; Politics and Economics in National Socialist Germany', in *The Nature of Fascism* (1968 Reading Conference), pp. 165–95.

[6] See below note 67.

[7] L. Rougier, *Les mystiques économiques : comment l'on passe des démocraties libérales aux états totalitaires* (Paris 1938), pp. 111, 127–9.

[8] Rocco, *Scritti*, 2, p. 477 ff.

[9] ACS, PC, 1924, fasc. 6/1, n. 1295.

[10] Production indices in 1921 (by amount, not value ; 1917 = 100) are Pig-Iron 28, Steel 53, Electricity 105, Sulphuric acid 76 (1915 base) : see Tables in Romeo, *Grande industria*.

[11] G. Carocci, 'L'imperialismo fascista negli anni 20', *SS*, 8, January–March 1967, p. 115.

[12] *Il Tevere*, 19–23 October 1926 ; *Corriere Padano*, 21 October.

[13] *La Tribuna*, 30 June 1926.

[14] Perroux, op. cit., pp. 136–9 ; B. Griziotti, *La politica finanziaria italiana* (Milan 1926), p. 28. A. De Stefani *Discorsi* (Milan 1923), p. 177. For discussion of the problem of over-population in general see P. Saraceno, *Lo sviluppo economico dei paesi sovrapopolati* (Rome 1952).

[15] See S. Lombardini, 'Italian Fascism and the Economy', p. 157 in *The Nature of Fascism*, ed. Woolf, for the high rate of investment achieved between 1921 and 1926.

[16] See Pantaleone, 'Finanza fascista'. On the policy of 'privatization see Rossi, *Padroni*, pp. 62–8 ; De Stefani, *Discorsi*, p. 181.

[17] Salvemini, *Under the Axe*, p. 174. M. Abrate in *Il problema storico del fascismo* (Florence 1970), pp. 87–9, whose view of De Stefani's achievements is excessively favourable, makes no direct reference to this fact.

[18] Romeo, *Grande industria*, p. 99.

[19] Pantaleone, art. cit., p. 177 ; E. Rossi, 'La questione doganale dopo la guerra, in A. De Viti De Marco, *Un trentennio di lotte politiche (1894–1922)* (Rome 1929), pp. 461–3.

[20] The tariffs on cotton goods and woollen cloth were not lowered. The index of share prices shows that the textile industries made greater gains than any other sector. Vice versa during 1925–6 the fall was greatest in the consumer goods industries.

[21] ACS, PC, 1926, fasc. 3/8, n. 1121 (24 April 1924), reply to memorial from D.Civita, the director of the Associazione Esercenti Imprese Elettriche.

[22] De Stefani, *Baraonda bancaria*, passim; (n.b. p. 273 his threat to resign in April 1923); *Critica politica*, G.Luzzatto 'Le incognite'.

[23] G.Prato, 'I disfattisti della lira', *Riforma sociale*, January–February 1925, pp. 1–5.

[24] De Stefani, op. cit., pp. 37–8, 54–5.

[25] Whether this is true or not, the Commerciale was certainly opposed to a policy of resolute deflation of the kind adopted by Mussolini in August 1926 (Banca Commerciale, Relazione, in *Rassegna Italiana*, April 1925).

[26] De Felice, III, pp. 86–9; ACS, PC, fasc. 9/9, n. 872, 6 April, Benni for Giunta Esecutiva of Confindustria; ibid., 9, 17, 18, 20 April; memorial of bankers' confederation cit. note 20 above.

[27] Einaudi, *Cronache*, 8, pp. 62, 78–9, 87–9; Rossi, 'Questione doganale,' pp. 463–4, 470–5.

[28] ACS, PC, 1924, fasc. 3/8, n. 2660; ibid., 1925, fasc. 3/8, n. 2282 (24 September 1924), Barbiellini (15 November 1924), Prefect of Rovigo.

[29] ACS, PC, 1925, fasc. 3/8, n. 2282; *Corriere Padano* (9, 12 April 1925).

[30] F.A.Repaci, 'La redazione della commissione per il regime doganale delle bietole e dello zucchero in Italia', *Riforma sociale*, November–December 1925, pp. 552–3; Einaudi, op. cit., pp. 484–5. (For attitude of corporations, see Rossoni, 'Il sindacalismo e la protezione delle industrie', *La Stirpe*, August 1925.)

[31] V.Calderoni, *I cento anni della politica doganale italiana* (Padova 1961), p. 149. De Stefani in 1923 described the idea of a tariff which would increase the price of bread as 'diabolic' (op. cit., p. 209).

[32] A.Serpieri, *La politica agraria in Italia* (Piacenza 1925), p. 206.

[33] Benni, 'La politica doganale italiana' (text of lecture 22 February 1925, in ACS, SPCR, 173/R, A. S. Benni).

[34] C.T.Schmidt, *The Plough and the Sword* (New York 1938), p. 46; *O.O.*, 22, p. 178.

[35] The best analysis is in F.Vöchting, *La questione meridionale*, pp. 329–30, 534–44; see also G.Mortara, *Prospettive economiche 1929*, pp. 33–4; E.Rossi, loc. cit., pp. 463–4, 470–5; 'La politica agraria del regime e le esportazioni', L.Nina, *Critica fascista*, 1 June 1929 (1926–8 food imports rose from 23.6 to 27.5 per cent of total imports, while food exports declined from 25.8 to 22.8 per cent).

[36] ACS, PC, 1925, fasc. 3/16, n. 240.

[37] Rossi, 'Questione doganale', p. 464 ff.

[38] On rivalry between the Commerciale and its enemies and Volpi's role, see *Rassegna italiana*, August 1925, 'La pace dei produttori'.

[39] De Felice, III, pp. 227–34. See also G.Migone, *Problemi di storia nei rapporti tra Italia e Stati Uniti* (Turin 1971), pp. 46–7; revaluation was not (as De Felice suggests) merely a 'political imposition', but a measure designed to consolidate the social basis of Fascism by protecting the petty and middle bourgeoisie.

[40] *Regime Fascista*, 20 August 1926; for preceding campaign against the Banca Commerciale, ibid., 27 July, 7. 8, 12 August; St Antony's documents, J. 53, (9 August 1926); ibid., J. 111 030645 ff (15 November 1926), Mussolini to Farinacci. ACS, CF, b. 2, f. 7 (21 September 1926), D. Sacerdoti to F.

[41] B.Griziotti et al., op. cit. (Milan 1926), pp. 25–30, 37–9, 79–91, 130–2.

For influence on Mussolini, De Begnac, *Palazzo Venezia : storia di un regime* (Rome 1950), p. 381, confirmed by ACS, Carte Volpi b. 6 (19 June 1927), Mussolini to Volpi (though this refers to a different book). See also Perroux, *Contribution*, p. 270.

[42] However the electrical industry also applied pressure for an alternative solution; they demanded a system such that electricity prices should be automatically adjusted in accordance with the rise or fall in the real value of the lira: Scalfari, *Storia segreta dell'industria elettrica* (Bari 1963), pp. 64–5, and ACS, Pres. Cons. 1926, fasc. 3/8, n. 1121 (9 October 1926). Since this memorial dates from after the Pesaro speech, it would seem that the electricity industry lacked confidence in the Government's ability to carry out a successful stabilization.

[43] For the general interpretation of the 'Battle of the lira', see R. De Felice, 'I lineamenti politici della "quota 90" attraverso i documenti di Mussolini e di Volpi', *Il Nuovo Osservatore*, May 1966, pp. 370–95, and R. Sarti, 'Mussolini and the industrial leadership in the battle of the lira 1925–1927', *Past* and *Present* May 1970 pp. 97–112.

[44] Romeo, op. cit., Table 13; P. Grifone, *Il capitale finanziario in Italia* (Turin 1971), p. 70.

[45] *O.O.*, 22, p. 234.

[46] *Lavoro d'Italia*, 22 October 1926; ibid., 3, 7 October, *Regime Fascista*, 20 November.

[47] G. Belluzzo, *Economia fascista* (Rome 1928), pp. 182–3.

[48] C. Toesca di Castellazzo and G. Binello, *Il partito nella vita economica. La politica fascista degli approvigionamenti e dei prezzi* (Turin 1938), p. 70; ACS, SPCR, 242/R s/f 5 ins. C., 10 October 1927.

[49] *O.O.*, 22, pp. 463–4, 19 November 1926.

[50] De Felice, III, pp. 287–8.

[51] *Lavoro d'Italia*, 16 January 1927.

[52] Ibid., 29 January, A. Fioretti.

[53] Salvemini, *Under the Axe*, p. 207; *Lavoro d'Italia*, 8 May 1927. ACS, PC, 1927, fasc. 3/5, n. 761.

[54] Salvemini, op. cit., pp. 210–11. On the propaganda drive to reduce wages and prices, see the comments in *The Economist*, 11 June 1927: 'It is doubtful whether such a unified drive towards a lower level of costs and prices as is proceeding in Italy today has ever been organized anywhere.'

[55] St Antony's documents, J. 104, 028104 (20 September 1927). The government and industry collaborated in manipulating the cost of living index. *L'organizzazione industriale*, 1 August 1926. (Benni points out that cost of living index will be calculated on basis of prices in special shops): Salvemini, op. cit., p. 256. *Lavoro d'Italia*, 30 December 1927.

[56] ACS, V, 16 (31 December 1925). See also comments in ACS, PS, 1926, G. 1, b. 95 (12 August 1926). *Critica fascista*, 1 August 1926; *Popolo d'Italia*, 3, 19 August.

[57] *Battaglie fasciste*, 24 July 1926.

[58] *Regime fascista*, 16 November 1926. Many Fascists believed that the party and the unions should be merged: (see report of 12 August 1926, cit., note 56 above).

[59] *Lavoro d'Italia*, 3, 6, 8 July; De Felice, III, pp. 282–4.

[60] Toesca and Binello, op. cit., pp. 80–1; see Aquarone, *Organizzazione*, p. 531 for Turati's claims for the advantages of party control.

[61] Toesca and Binello, op. cit., pp. 83–8, 94, 156. Rosenstock-Franck, op. cit., pp. 359, 394.

[62] *Lavoro d'Italia*, 11 August 1927.

[63] *Corriere Padano*, 2 March, 20 November 1926. (The party was, however, also asked to assist the Government in seeing that the agreement not to raise steel prices during 1926 was observed – ACS, PC, 1926, fasc. 1/3–5 [16 July 1926].)

[64] *Corriere della Sera*, 2–3 November 1927; *Lavoro d'Italia*, 5 November; St Antony's documents, J. 104, 028139 (14 July 1927).

[65] St Antony's documents, J. 263/2, 074573.

[66] *Critica fascista*, 1 January 1928, 1 February, 15 May 1929.

[67] Aquarone, op. cit., pp. 214–15; Turati, in spite of his earlier alliance with Bottai against Rossoni, criticized this development. See also Giugni, 'Esperienze corporative', p. 6.

[68] St Antony's documents, J. 263/2, 074574 ff.

[69] 'Sindacalismo fascista', *La Stirpe*, December 1928. For reactions to 'unblocking', see St Antony's documents, J. 104, 028112–3, 028149–52.

[70] De Felice, III, pp. 337–41; Aquarone, op. cit., pp. 148–9.

[71] Pesce, *Marcia dei rurali*, p. 206.

[72] Acerbo to M., St Antony's documents, J. 267, 077328 (9 November 1931).

[73] A. Serpieri, *La politica agraria in Italia e i recenti provvedimenti legislative* (Piacenza 1925), pp. 51–3; Serpieri, *La guerra*, p. 248; for Pareto see *Gerarchia*, January 1923, 'Paragoni', p. 672.

[74] Serpieri, *Politica agraria*, p. 128.

[75] Vöchting, *Questione meridionale*, pp. 435–9.

[76] *Il sud nella storia d'Italia*, ed. R.Villari (Bari 1961), pp. 595–600; ACS, PC, 1925, f. 3/18, n. 633.

[77] *O. O.*, 22, pp. 361–90; ibid., 23, p. 296, 5 August 1927; ACS, Carte Volpi, b. 6, Mussolini to Volpi, 21 March 1927.

[78] *O. O.*, 23, pp. 256–8, 263; ACS, PC, 1928–30, fasc. 3–2/10, n. 9261 (20 June 1928); E.Rossi, *Il Malgoverno*, (Bari 1954), p. 49.

[79] ACS, SPCR, fasc. 242/R, Farinacci, s/f 20 (1 September 1927); De Felice, III, p. 261n.

[80] E.Campese, *Il fascismo contro la disoccupazione* (Rome 1929), p. 317; G. Tassinari, *La distribuzione del reddito nell'agricoltura italiana* (Piacenza 1931) shows that the only capitalist farms to maintain and even increase their profits during 1927 were those in which the workers were paid in kind (pp. 56–8).

[81] G.Lorenzoni, in *Studi in memoria di Giovanni Dettori* (Florence 1941), pp. 383, 398–9; E. Sereni, *La questione agraria nella rinascita nazionale italiana*, pp. 130–5, 150, 238–9, 244; F.Vöchting, op. cit., p. 331; M.Rossi-Doria, 'L'agricoltura italiana, il dopoguerra e il fascismo', in Casucci, *Il fascismo*, p. 310.

[82] See *Cremona Nuova*, 16 December 1923. 'Urbanism must cease: all those young peasants who came to the cities after the war must be sent back to the land.'

[83] G.Manzoni, *L'assalto*, 5 June 1926.

[84] *Stato operaio*, November–December 1928; however this factor cannot account for the beginnings of the new policy.

[85] The 'principles' of Fascist emigration policy were explained by Grandi in a speech to the Chamber on 1 April 1927: 'Why should our mothers continue to make sons who will be soldiers of nations other than Italy?' (Campese, op. cit.,

p. 251); see also Carocci, 'L'imperialismo fascista', pp. 123–4, and *Lavoro d'Italia*, 23 August 1927.

[86] Schmidt, *The Plough and the Sword*, p. 42n.

[87] *O.O.*, 23, pp. 231–7, 14 October 1928. Campese, op. cit., pp. 314–15.

[88] *Stato operaio*, September 1927, 'La crisi agraria nel ferrarese', pp. 825–7.

[89] ACS, SPCR, 7/R fasc. Gentile (October 1928); Lorenzoni, art. cit., *Studi*, pp. 255–7.

[90] *O.O.*, 22, p. 367; *Critica fascista*, 15 January 1929.

[91] Vöchting, op. cit., pp. 329–33; Togliatti, *Lezioni*, pp. 131–3; G. Lumbroso, *Critica fascista*, 15 February 1929.

[92] L. Radi, *I mezzadri: le lotte contadine nell'Italia centrale* (Rome 1962), pp. 274–7.

[93] Ibid., pp. 278, 288; Bandini, *Cento anni di storia agraria italiana* (Rome 1963), pp. 169–72.

[94] Radi, op. cit., p. 335 ff.; L. Faenza, *Communismo e cattolicesimo in una parrocchia di campagna* (Bologna 1959), p. 37 ff. However, in Tuscany, where their economic position declined sharply, the *mezzadri* were more hostile to the regime; although Fascist propaganda made some impact. See L. Guerrini and G. Bertolo, 'Le campagne toscane e marchigiane durante il fascismo. Note sulla situazione economica e sociale dei ceti contadini', *MLI*, 1970, 4, pp. 123 ff, 128–9.

[95] See Sereni, *La questione agraria*, pp. 260–72.

[96] G. Hildebrand, *Growth and Structure in the Economy of Modern Italy* (Cambridge, Mass. 1956), pp. 350–5.

[97] See his election speech, 2 April 1924. 'Industria italiana e il governo nazionale' (ACS Segr. part. del Duce, carteggio ordinario n. 549, 130); Carocci, 'L'imperialismo fascista', p. 119n.; Perroux, *Contribution*, p. 152; *Dizionario biografico degli italiani* (Rome 1960), 8, pp. 14–16.

[98] ACS, PC, 1924, fasc. 3/7 (4 June 1924) and passim.

[99] Rochat, *L'esercito*, pp. 495–6, 499–501; ACS, PC, 1925, fasc. 1/3–4, n. 2882 (24 November 1924).

[100] I am in partial disagreement here with Carocci, loc. cit., For Belluzzo's criticisms of steel and sugar protection, see *Popolo d'Italia*, 28 April 1923; ACS V, 17 (30 March 1928). But it is significant that F. Perroux, op. cit., pp. 140–2, 149–50, uses the term 'Autarchy' to describe the trend of Belluzzo's policy, some years before the term became officially current.

[101] Perroux, op. cit., pp. 143–4.

[102] Belluzzo, *Economia fascista* (Rome 1928), pp. 54, 103. One of the reasons for Belluzzo's hostility to the steel manufacturers was their failure to develop the national supplies of combustible fuel. He considered it their duty to help the Government increase the exploitation of Italian coal and lignite deposits; ACS, PC, 1926, fasc. 3/7, n. 3521 (9 October 1926) exchange of letters between Belluzzo and Falck. One very useful reform carried out by Belluzzo was the unification of Italian mining law: see Perroux, op. cit., pp. 158–9.

[103] ACS, PC, 1926, fasc. 3/7, n. 4230 (November 1926).

[104] Caracciolo in *La formazione*, p. 173; *Popolo d'Italia*, 17 March 1923, A. Lanzillo 'Nuove forme economiche'.

[105] De Felice, III, p. 231; in 1925 the deficit in cereals was 3151 million lire, in iron and steel and other metals 2110 millions, coal and other minerals, 1530, oil

958 millions, on timber 881 million. Silk and agricultural produce were the leading exports. *O. O.*, 22, pp. 176–82). 8 July 1926 speech inaugurating Istituto Nazionale Esportazioni : 'We must realize that there is iron in Italy too.'

[106] ACS, V, 16, 2 June 1926.

[107] See Ernesto Belloni's speech, AP, C, 27th legis., 6, p. 5980 ff. Carocci, art. cit., pp. 118–19.

[108] Carocci, *La politica estera*, p. 37; Caracciolo, in *Il trauma*, p. 183 (Caucasus); ACS, PC, fasc. 3/7 (20 May 1924), L. Parodi Delfino for Soc. Italiana Petroli e Bitumi.

[109] ACS, V, 16 (1 March, 14 May 1926); an added complication arose from the fact that the Ministry of Communications controlled the Italian oil concession in Albania. Volpi attempted to eliminate Belluzzo from the project by making the AGIP dependent on Ciano, who was notoriously pliable where the interests of private capital were concerned. ACS, PC, fasc. 3/1–3, n. 2096; Carte Volpi, b. 6, (7 December), Petretti; (29 December), AGIP Presidenza; (30 December), Volpi.

[110] This development only took place under the Republic; during the 1930s *IRI* failed to have a programme of its own or to exercise a guiding function in the economy : see *Ministero per la costituente, Rapporto della commissione economica*, Pt 2 'Industria', 2, pp. 185, 189–90. See also A. Shonfield, *Modern Capitalism* (Oxford 1965), p. 178.

[111] G. Scagnetti, *Gli enti di privilegio nell'economia corporativa italiana* (Padua 1942), pp. 34, 45 and passim.

[112] Ibid., p. 25, and ACS, V, 14 May 1926: 40 per cent of the capital for the creation of AGIP came from the Istituto Nazionale di Assicurazione and the Cassa Assicurazione Sociali.

[113] Carocci, loc. cit.

[114] Belluzzo, op. cit., pp. 173, 218 ff, 240–3; Perroux, op. cit., pp. 144–6; *Lavoro d'Italia*, 15 March 1927. On the other hand Belluzzo's policy of course signified the deliberate creation of unemployment.

[115] See note 105.

[116] *Ministero per la Costituente, Rapporto*, 2, pp. 60–1.

[117] *Popolo d'Italia*, 29 September 1926; ibid., 26, 27 September; see also Shonfield, *Modern Capitalism*, p. 178, n. 6, for comment on another statement by Arnaldo, 'Fascism clearly and resolutely denies the individualism of the nineteenth century.' He points out that in less pretentious language this signifies 'a refusal to accept the decisions of the market-place as a necessary guide to action and the abandonment of the model of the perfectly competitive market' which still dominated orthodox economics.

[118] Perroux, op. cit., pp. 281–2.

[119] *Stato operaio*, September 1927, A. Tasca, 'L'analisi dell'imperialismo e l'economia italiana': one should note that the high price of electricity and of fertilizers was a major obstacle to an effective policy of rural development; see Rosenstock-Franck, op. cit., pp. 354–7. *Popolo d'Italia*, 13 July 1927 (G. Arias).

[120] S. Cassese, 'La politica industriale fascista', in *Studi politici* 1957, p. 692. *Min. per la Costituente, Rapporto*, 2, Ch. 6, passim.

[121] F. Vito, *I sindacati industriali Cartelli e gruppi* (Milan 1930), pp. 288–93. *N.B.* also the foundation by the Confindustria in July 1928 of the Ente Nazionale per l'unificazione nell' industria (*La confederazione generale fascista dell' industria-relazione all'assemblea dei delegati*, Milan 1930, p. 52). ACS, PC, 1929, fasc. 3/10, n. 8331 (30 August 1929), A. Bagnari to F. Guarneri.

122 See note 65 above.

123 Salvemini, op. cit., p. 421n. See also R. Romeo, 'Aspetti teorici dello sviluppo della grande impresa in Italia', *Storia contemporanea*, March 1970, pp. 19–21.

124 Aquarone, *Organizzazione*, pp. 190–3, 455–63 ; Salvemini, op. cit., pp. 120–6.

125 G. Luzzatto, *Critica politica*, 25 February 1924 ; of the 25 principal firms in which the Commerciale had a large holding, 21 were in electricity, mining and steel, engineering and shipping. The 25 firms owned 10 per cent of the share capital of all Italian joint stock companies ; and since a number were in fact holdings which in turn controlled many other companies, their real importance was considerably greater.

126 Grifone, *Capitale finanziario*, p. 65 ; *The Economist*, 6 February 1926. ACS, Carte Volpi, b. 3 (25 January 1927), Toeplitz to Stringher (complaints of Government policy).

127 ACS, Carte Volpi, b. 3 (12 December 1927), Direzione Centrale of Credito Italiano.

128 Grifone, op. cit., p. 66. Scalfari, *Industria elettrica*, pp. 64–9. For the holding company, ACS, Carte Volpi, b. 6, 5 December 1927, 16 January 1928 ; b. 3, 1 May 1928, Stringher to Azzolini ; 31 May. Direz. centrale BCI to Volpi.

129 ACS, V., 17 (22 February 1928).

130 *Dizionario biografico*, 8, pp. 455–66, *Alberto Beneduce ;* De Stefani, *Baraonda*, p. 517 ; for ICIPU and electrical industry, see ACS, PC 1926, fasc. 3/8 n. 4032.

131 S. B. Clough, *The Economic History of Modern Italy* (New York 1964), p. 229. Migone, *Problemi di storia*, pp. 64–5 shows, however, that the proposal to unify the banks of issue did not originate with Volpi, but with J. P. Morgan and Co.

132 Carte Volpi, b. 3, f. 140 (4 February 1928), Volpi to Mussolini ; ACS, 1927, fasc. 6/1, n. 1907, 2075.

133 ACS, SPCR, 64/R Bottai, s/f 1 ; Carte Volpi b. 6, 26 May 1928 (Boncompagni Ludovisi).

134 G. Rossini, *Il movimento cattolico nel periodo fascista* (Rome 1966), 1, 5–62 ; M. Rossi-Doria, 'L'agricoltura italiana, il dopoguerra e il fascismo', in Casucci ; *Fascismo*, p. 310.

135 Calderoni, *Politica doganale*, pp. 157, 161.

136 A. De Stefani, *La resa del liberalismo economico* (Milan 1932), pp. 64–5.

137 See S. J. Woolf, 'Did a Fascist Economic System Exist ? in *The Nature of Fascism*, pp. 119–51.

14   Ideology and Culture

1 A. J. Gregor, *The Ideology of Fascism* (Toronto 1969), p. 3, gives this as his working definition of the 'doctrinal' component of ideology ; however his criteria for assessing whether a political movement has a 'doctrine' or not do not seem clear. I do not believe that Fascism possessed a 'doctrine' in this sense, at least at the outset. The distinction between 'mentality' and 'doctrine' (or theory) which I have drawn corresponds to the distinction between a system of ideas which has an unconscious unity, and one which is deliberately structured. For this distinction, see F. L. Schurmann, *Ideology and Organisation in Communist China* (Berkeley 1968), p. 18, who points out the importance which conscious 'theory' has for the maintenance of Communist organization. Fascism, on the other hand, had a set of

'myths' designed to evoke a corresponding set of emotional responses, but no comprehensive rational theory. See further, Mannheim, *Ideology and Utopia* (London 1966), pp. 119–30 (still the best general approach to the problem of Fascist ideology) ; Z.Barbu, *Democracy and Dictatorship* (London 1956), pp. 131–43 ; also P.Drieu la Rochelle, *Notes pour comprendre le siècle* (Paris 1941), p. 160 ; the Fascist is 'un homme qui ne croit que dans les actes et qui enchaîne ses actes selon un mythe très sommaire'.

[2] De Felice, III, pp. 367–9 ; G.L.Mosse. 'The Genesis of Fascism', *JCH* 1966, 1, pp. 15–16 ; P.Melograni, 'Mussolini e la società di massa', *Il Nuovo Osservatore*, October–November 1967 ; Mussolini, *My Autobiography*, trans. R.W.Child (London 1928), pp. 25, 36.

[3] V.Pareto, *Scritti sociologici*, pp. 1097–103.

[4] *Popolo d'Italia*, 7 November 1922 ; A.Soffici, *Una battaglia fra due vittorie* (Florence 1923), p. 206.

[5] Talcott Parsons, 'Sociological aspects of the Fascist movements', in *Essays in Sociological Theory*, 3rd ed. (Glencoe 1963), pp. 125–34. See also I.Horowitz, *Radicalism and the revolt against reason ; the social theories of Georges Sorel* (London 1961), pp. 1–11, 172.

[6] G.Mosse, 'Fascism and the Intellectuals' in *The Nature of Fascism*, p. 207.

[7] *History of Europe in the 19th Century*, trans. H.Furst (London, 1939), p. 258. (I have, however, altered the translation) ; also pp. 339–46.

[8] A. Tilgher, *Relativisti contemporanei* (Rome 1923), p. 33. See also, Drieu la Rochelle, op. cit., pp. 150–2 : the 'new man' – 'se trouvait nihiliste devant une table rase où étaient abolies toutes les catégories et les restrictions vétustes de la raison tournée en rationalisme et de la morale tournée en hypocrisie'.

[9] 22 November 1921, review of A.Tilgher's book, *O.O.*, 17, pp. 267–9 ; Salvatorelli, *Nazionalfascismo*, pp' 93–4.

[10] For the revolt against positivism see in general H. Stuart Hughes, *Consciousness and Society* (London 1959), pp. 37–42.

[11] For their influence on Mussolini, see G.Prezzolini, *L'Italiano inutile* (Florence 1964), p. 241.

[12] *Leonardo-Hermes–Il Regno*, pp. 41–3 ; G.Papini 'Pragmatismo' in *Opere ;* 2, pp. 331–468; ibid., 9, pp. 907–8.

[13] A.Lovejoy, 'The Practical Tendencies of Bergsonism', *International Journal of Ethics* (1912–13), pp. 423–9. Sorel, *Reflections on Violence*, p. 140 ; see also, pp. 57–8, 144–5 ; Horowitz, *Radicalism*, pp. 39–56.

[14] Mannheim, *Ideology*, pp. 122–4. For Mussolini and the new intellectual trends, B.Croce, *History of Italy, 1871–1915*, trans. C.M.Ady (Oxford 1929), pp. 266–7.

[15] See Ch. 5, note 29.

[16] M.Missiroli, introduction to Tilgher, *Relativisti*, p. 11.

[17] Volpe, *Guerra, dopoguerra, fascismo*, p. 309. M.Missiroli, introduction to Tilgher, op. cit., p. 11 ; for the psychological significance of this idea as a rationalization for aggression, see T.W.Adorno *et al.*, *The Authoritarian Personality* (New York, 1964), p. 246.

[18] Pareto, *Les systèmes socialistes*, 2, p. 450.

[19] Sorel, *Reflections on Violence*, pp. 102–4.

[20] M.Isnenghi, *Il mito della Grande Guerra* (Bari 1970), p. 11.

[21] F.T.Marinetti, *Futurismo e Fascismo* (Foligno 1924), pp. 13, 16. See also the

first Futurist Manifesto in J. Joll, *Intellectuals in Politics* (London 1960), p. 181 ; and in general L. De Maria, introd. to Vol. 2 of F. T. Marinetti, *Opere* pp. xxviii–xlv (Milan 1968).

[22] Marinetti, *Futurismo e Fascismo*, pp. 113–14, 56–7, 154–5. See also comments of L. Trotsky, *Literature and Revolution* (Michigan 1966), pp. 128–9.

[23] For this 'programme' see S. J. Woolf, 'Italy', in *European Fascism*, ed. S. J. Woolf (London 1968), p. 44.

[24] Marinetti, *Futurismo*, p. 39.

[25] *L'Assalto*, 18 December 1926.

[26] G. Masi, *Educazione politica* (1926), pp. 23–5.

[27] C. Pellizzi, *Problemi e realtà del fascismo* (Florence 1924), pp. 163–4 ; for reference to Gentile, p. 181.

[28] C. Pellizzi, *Fascismo-aristocrazia* (Milan 1925), p. 46. On Pellizzi, see further M. Isenghi and S. Lanaro, Fascismo esorcizzato. Cinque schede sulla 'Rivolta Piccolo Borghese' (*Belfagor 1970*), 1, pp. 226–7.

[29] R. Poggioli, *Teoria dell'arte d'avanguardia* (Bologna 1962), pp. 91 ff.

[30] See Pareto, *Systèmes socialistes*, pp. 11–12, and Sorel, *Reflections*, p. 62.

[31] Soffici, *Battaglia fra due vittorie*, p. 106.

[32] Marinetti, *Futurismo*, pp. 131, 142.

[33] M. Bontempelli, *L'Avventura novecentista* (Florence 1938), pp. 148–9.

[34] On Marinetti's legacy to Mussolini, see Joll, *Intellectuals*, p. 172. For sport and Fascism, see Drieu la Rochelle, *Notes*, p. 153, on 'La Restauration du Corps'. See also Maier, 'Taylorism', JCH 1970, pp. 39–45.

[35] C. Malaparte, *L'Europa vivente ed altri saggi politici* (Florence 1961), pp. 125, 342.

[36] *Popolo d'Italia*, 7 November 1922.

[37] E. Codignola, *Battaglie fasciste*, 28 March 1925 ; G. Saitta, *Vita Nova*, August 1925 ; U. D'Andrea, *Critica Fascista*, January 1926.

[38] See R. Stéphane, *Portrait de l'aventurier* (Paris 1950), for an analysis of the type.

[39] Isenghi, Fascismo Esorcizzato, p. 365 ; G. Grana, *Malaparte* (Florence 1968), pp. 7–8.

[40] Malaparte, *L'Europa vivente*, p. 97 ; Isenghi, op. cit., pp. 338–42 ; ACS, MRF, b. 106, Fasc. Livorno, Perrone Compagni to M. Bianchi (11 October 1922).

[41] Malaparte, op. cit., pp. 335–6, 429–42.

[42] Malaparte, 'Ragguaglio sulla stato degli intellecttuali rispetto al fascismo', Introd. to Soffici, *Battaglia*, pp. xxii–xxix.

[43] C. Gini, *I fattori demografici dell'evoluzione delle nazioni* (Turin 1912), pp. 2, 30–62, 83, 93. For correspondence between Mussolini and Gini, see ACS (Segreteria particolare del Duce) Autografi del Duce b. 3, f. V (A).

[44] *O.O.*, 23, pp. 209–16 (September 1928) ; R. Korherr, *Regresso delle nascite : morte dei popoli* (Rome 1928).

[45] De Felice, III, p. 571 for Mussolini's speeches and directives on the issue; for an example of the provincial response, see A. Pavolini in *Il Bargello* (Florence), 9 June 1929.

[46] For this trend see particularly the periodical *Antieuropa* founded in 1929 by the former youth leader Asvero Gravelli ; e.g. 25 August 1929, I. Cattani : 'It is possible to change the Italian physically'. 'The athletic type must become dominant

... as willed by the Duce, that is to say solidly structured, with finely developed firm muscles, a face with a strong bone structure, a strongly developed chin, long neck, broad shoulders and majestic thorax.' Whatever the effect on the 'race' this vision of the new Italian, all chin and muscles, can be seen in the work of countless Fascist artists. The same article advocated the sterilization of those suffering from grave nervous disorders, and discussed whether manic depressives should be allowed to marry. See also R. Suster, 'La differenza delle razze' in *Antieuropa*, December 1929.

[47] *Inchiesta sulla Massoneria*, ed. E. Bodrero (Milan 1925). Answers of G. A. Borgese (p. 36), V. Cian (p. 67); see also Gentile (p. 128).

[48] G. Prezzolini, *Fascism* (London 1926), p. 86.

[49] See Ch. 5, n. 100.

[50] Gaeta, *Nazionalismo*, pp. 19-21, 38-44, 237-45; G. Gentile, *Guerra e fede* (Naples 1919) pp. 202-12, 221; Gaeta, *Fascismo e cultura*, p. 50 ff; N. Bobbio, *Politica e cultura* (Turin 1955), p. 221 ff; Volpe, *Guerra, dopoguerra fascismo*, p. VIII.

[51] Volpe, *Guerra*, pp. 4-5; Gentile, *Guerra e fede*, pp. 258-62; Gentile 'La crisi morale', *Politica*, 3.1, 24 November 1919; H. D. Harris, *The Social Philosophy of Giovanni Gentile* (Urbana 1960), p. 152. See also Gentile's comments in the Manifesto of the Fascist Intellectuals; on the advent of Fascism in 1922, 'it suddenly appeared that the Italian people had recovered the enthusiastic unanimity which it had had on the eve of war'. Valeri, *Lotta politica*, p. 585, and E. Codignola, *Critica fascista*, 15 January 1933; 'the historical *raison d'être* of Fascism consists in its having revived the wartime policy of forced unification.'

[52] Gentile, *Guerra e fede*, pp. ix-x.

[53] Harris, *Social Philosophy of Gentile*, p. 139.

[54] Gentile, *Profeti del Risorgimento italiano* (Florence 1923), p. 41.

[55] Gentile, *L'eredità di V. Alfieri* (Venice 1926), pp. 1-2; *Fascismo e cultura* (Milan 1928), p. 12, where he describes Renaissance individualism as 'the germ of the age-old malady of the Italian people'; F. De Sanctis, *History of Italian literature*, trans. Joan Redfern (London 1932), pp. 587-93.

[56] Gentile, *Profeti*, Chs. 1-10, passim. esp. pp. 52-63, 73-82. This work, a collection of articles originally published in *Politica* during 1919, was dedicated to 'Benito Mussolini, a true-bred Italian, worthy to hear the voice of the prophets of the new Italy'. The other 'prophet' recognized by Gentile is Gioberti; his implicit message is that Mazzini's ideals should be complemented by Gioberti's 'realism' typified by his acceptance of the monarchy. Gentile's earler view of Mazzini had been much less favourable: see his review of Bolton King's biography in *La Critica*, 1904.

[57] Gentile, *Profeti*, p. 90; the invocation of Mazzini by the Democrats during the controversy over the Adriatic question and the rights of nationalities was probably the prime motive which led Gentile to undertake a study of Mazzini; see *Guerra e fede*, pp. 330-5.

[58] E. Garin, *Cronache di filosofia italiana* (Bari, 1959), pp. 309-10, 393-5; Gentile's preface to C. Licitra, *Dal liberalismo al fascismo* (Rome 1925), p. xvi. For an example of Gentile's influence, see the biography of the historian Delio Cantimori, G. Miccoli, *Delio Cantimori, la ricerca di una nuova critica storiografica* (Turin 1970), pp. 12, 22-3.

[59] ACS, SPCR, fasc. 7/R., Gentile, 4 January 1925.

[60] See Harris, *Social Philosophy of Gentile*, pp. 111–27, 172, 224–30; Bobbio, *Politica e cultura*, p. 213 ff; A. Del Noce, 'Idee per l'interpretazione del fascismo', in Casucci, *Fascismo*, pp. 370–83.

[61] Harris, *Social Philosophy of Gentile* p. 191.

[62] Comments of Gobetti in *La Rivoluzione liberale*, 18 January 1923, on Gentile's 'complete lack of contact with reality'; H. Marcuse, *Reason and Revolution* (London 1955), pp. 404–9.

[63] Del Noce, 'Idee' p. 377.

[64] Gentile, *Fascismo e cultura*, pp. 48–9.

[65] See Harris, op. cit., pp. 203–9, 295 ff.

[66] E.g. Gentile, *Che cosa è il fascismo* (Florence 1925), p. 38.

[67] See E. Papa, *Storia di due Manifesti* (Milan 1958), p. 57. 'Fascist culture can for the most part be held to be either just culture, or just Fascism'; this, I think, is a good example of how to eliminate a real problem by means of a definition. The problem has instead been well posed by Casucci in *Il fascismo*, pp. 431–2; see also discussion between Casucci and V. Stella in *Il Mulino* (1960), and G. Veronesi, *Le difficoltà politiche dell'architettura in Italia, 1920–40* (Milan 1953), pp. 50, 54.

[68] F. Volpe, *Guerra*, pp. 304–5, for comments on limitations of Fascist propaganda. According to C. Rossi (*L'Elefante*, 1949, n. 25) nearly all the characteristic rituals were created by the local *ras*; this is an interesting suggestion, but needs confirmation. Obviously the role of D'Annunzio cannot be overlooked.

[69] *Cremona Nuova*, 3 November 1923; for later evolution, see *Popolo d'Italia*, 28–31 October 1926.

[70] See note 40. above.

[71] *Popolo d'Italia*, 9 December 1923.

[72] G. Gentile, *Origini e dottrina del fascismo*, pp. 35–6; also Forges-Davanzati, *Fascismo e cultura*, p. 40.

[73] For this important literary review, which published among other writers Montale, Gadda, and Vittorini, see G. Luti, *Cronache letterarie tra le due guerre* (Bari 1966), pp. 77–142, and *Antologia di 'Solaria'*, ed E. Siciliano (Milan 1958).

[74] Salvatorelli and Mira, *Storia*, pp. 496–7.

[75] E.g., as late as 1933, 'the State cannot create its own literature' (*Dizionario della dottrina fascista*, p. 19); A. Turati, *Il partito e i suoi compiti* (Rome 1928), p. 90.

[76] Garin, *Cronache*, pp. 424, 487–8; *Il Tevere*, 1–2 April 1926; Gentile, *Fascismo e Cultura*, p. 103 ff.

[77] R. Forges-Davanzati, *Gerarchia*, April 1925, pp. 226–31. (Resumé of speech to Bologna meeting of Fascist intellectuals.)

[78] A. Carocci, Introd. to *Antologia di 'Solaria'*, p. 10; *La Critica* (1925), pp. 380–1, on F. Ciarlantini's 'spiritual imperialism'. One contradiction which Forges-Davanzati and the other Nationalists were unable to resolve was that of their attitude to German culture. On the one hand, they attacked Croce as the agent of cultural enslavement to Germany, but at the same time they held up German intellectuals as a model for their readiness to harness culture to national ends.

[79] J. Benda, *La trahison des clercs* (Paris 1928), pp. 29–30, 112–13. For Gentile's position, see *L'eredità di V. Alfieri*, pp. 127, 135, and *La riforma dell' educazione* (Bari 1920), Ch. 1.

[80] The lowest depths of absurdity were attained by O. Dinale, 'Il dominatore della filosofia'; *Gerarchia*, July 1930, pp. 581–7; 'He was named Benito Mussolini,

but he was instead Alexander the Great and Caesar. Socrates and Plato, Virgil and Lucretius, Horace and Tacitus, Kant and Nietzsche, Marx and Sorel, Machiavelli and Napoleon, Garibaldi and the Unknown Soldier.'

[81] Papa, *Storia di due manifesti*, pp. 42–5.

[82] *Arte fascista* (Turin 1928), p. 27.

[83] For lists of participants and speeches see Papa, op. cit. A list of the more distinguished participants would have included Gentile, Pirandello, Marinetti, Soffici, Agnoletti, the historians Cian, Volpe, Solmi, and Lionello Venturi (who in 1931 was to refuse the oath of loyalty to the regime), the painter Prampolini, the novelist Panzini, the composer Pizzetti, the critic Ugo Ojetti, and a few others.

[84] *O.O.*, 21, p. 358.

[85] Hamilton, *The Appeal of Fascism*, p. 65.

[86] Gentile, *Fascismo e cultura*, pp. 45–6.

[87] The successive changes in the title of Gentile's review are revealing. Founded in 1923 under the name of *La Nuova Politica Liberale*, it became successively *Educazione Politica*, *Educazione Fascista*, and *Civiltà Fascista*.

[88] Gentile, *Fascismo e cultura*, pp. 67–9, 81, 84. The Council of the Institute included Turati, Bottai, Rocco and Rossoni and Arpinati.

[89] ACS, SPCR, 242/R, Gran Consiglio s/f 6 (23 September 1928). However the Bologna Institute, under the protection of Arpinati, was Gentilian in tendency.

[90] ACS, Carte Orlando, b. 6, fasc. 254 (22 August 1923).

[91] G. Levi Della Vida, *Fantasmi ritrovati*; (Venice 1966) pp. 227 ff, 241–3) St Antony's documents, J. 151, 044355–58, 044387; *Il Tevere*, 24–5, 28–9 April 1926; G. Fanelli, *Contra Gentiles* (Rome 1923), pp. 94–5.

[92] *La critica* (1926), p. 126; for Gentile's defence, see *Fascismo e cultura*, pp. 110–11.

[93] Levi Della Vida, *Fantasmi*, pp. 234 ff. 'G. Volpe, G. Gentile, e l'Enciclopedia Italiana', in G. Gentile, *La vita e il pensiero* (Florence 1948), 1, pp. 344–5, 360.

[94] E.g. the composer A. Casella, in *Italia d'oggi*, p. 104.

[95] Prezzolini, *Fascism*, p. 63.

[96] *Arte fascista*, pp. 88–92.

[97] L. Alloway, *The Venice Biennale – 1895–1968. From salon to goldfish bowl* (London 1969), p. 107.

[98] *Arte fascista*, pp. 20–1; Prezzolini, *Fascism*, pp. 84–9; on the origins of the 'international style', see Rayner Banham, *Theory and Design in the first machine age* (London 1960), pp. 274–5.

[99] *Arte fascista*, p. 82.

[100] See Alloway, *Venice Biennale*, p. 113: 'There has yet to be an obscure public art.'

[101] C. Sanguineti Lazagna, 'La concezione delle arti figurative nella politica culturale del fascismo', *MLI*, October–December 1967, pp. 9–10.

[102] Ibid., pp. 10–13; *Gerarchia*, December 1922, 1, p. 9 ff. See also *Lo Spettatore Italiano*, 1 May 1924.

[103] Sanguineti Lazagna, art. cit., pp. 13–15; *O.O.*, 22, pp. 82–4; Ojetti, *Taccuini*, p. 204 ff.

[104] For the *Novecento* style in general, see Sanguineti Lazagna, art. cit.; C. Maltese, *Storia dell'arte in Italia 1785–1943* (Turin 1960), pp. 332–5; Alloway, *Venice Biennale*, pp. 96–102. R. De Grada, 'Le arti figurative all'origine del fascismo', in *Il 45* (Milan 1956), p. 13.

[105] *O. O.*, 22, p. 230.

[106] Cannistraro, 'Burocrazia e politica culturale nello stato fascista: il ministero della cultura popolare', *Storia Contemporanea*, June 1970, 1, n. 2, p. 285n.; *Critica fascista*, October 1926–January 1927. Maltese, *Storia dell'arte*, p. 336.

[107] *Critica fascista*, 15 October 1926.

[108] M.Sarfatti, 'L'arte e il fascismo', in *La civiltà fascista illustrata nelle dottrine e nelle opere*, ed. G. L. Pomba (Turin 1928), pp. 218–19.

[109] Salvatorelli and Mira, *Storia*, p. 532; for the demolitions and their extremely grave social effects, see I. Insolera, *Roma moderna* (Turin 1971, 2nd ed.), pp. 127–51.

[110] *Popolo d'Italia*, 19 March 1926.

[111] Sanguineti Lazagna, 'La concezione delle arti figurative', p. 19 ff; *Il Raduno*, 31 December 1927, 28 January, 17 March 1928; Maltese, *Storia dell'arte*, p. 411. For the structure of the Confederation of Professional Men and Artists, see *Annuario della Stampa Fascista 1931–2*, p. 490 ff.

[112] *Il Selvaggio*, 3 March 1927, 'Ufficio e fini della Corporazione delle arti'.

[113] Alloway, *Venice Biennale*, pp. 96, 103–6; Sanguineti Lazagna, art. cit., Maltese, op. cit., pp. 361–5.

[114] Alloway, op. cit., p. 109; Maltese op. cit., p. 368; see also *Aeropittura futurista*, ed. Galleria Blu (Milan 1970).

[115] E.Rogers, 'L'esperienza degli architetti', in *Fascismo e antifascismo, Lezioni e testimonianze* (Milan 1963, 2nd ed.), p. 335.

[116] Veronesi, *Difficoltà politiche*, p. 87. This seems to me one of the most illuminating essays so far written on culture under Fascism.

[117] Veronesi, op. cit., pp. 62, 64, 70; Alloway, op. cit., p. 106.

[118] *Critica Fascista*, 15 April 1931, 'La tessera e l'ingegno'; ibid., 15 May 1933; A.Livingston, 'Homemade literature under Fascism', *American Scholar*, 8, No. 4 (Autumn 1939), pp. 416–20.

[119] A.Moravia, 'Ricordi di censura', *Rassegna d'Italia*, December 1946, p. 96; for another characteristic condemnation, see *Antieuropa*, 15 November 1929. 'Always obscene nudity, obscene desires, perverse squalor, abject aridity'; Moravia writes of someone as 'a cursed figure of our corrupt time'. 'Of what time is Moravia speaking? Our time is . . . luminous.'

[120] For a sample, see *Antologia degli scrittori fascisti* ed. M.Carli and G.Fanelli (Florence 1931).

[121] *Il Raduno*, No. 1, 31 December 1927; for reaction, *Il Selvaggio*, 15, 30 January 1928.

[122] *Antologia Scrittori Fascisti*, pp. 77–8.

[123] Luti, *Cronache litterarie*, pp. 146–70; *Il Selvaggio di Mino Maccari*, ed. C. L. Ragghianti (Venice 1955).

[124] Bontempelli, *L'avventura novecentista*, pp. 23–5.

[125] Bontempelli, *L'Avventura*, pp. 121, 135–6; Luti, op. cit., pp. 146–52.

[126] Luti, op. cit., p. 148; Bontempelli, op. cit., pp. 20, 135, 245, 497–505.

[127] For defence of literary freedom, see Bontempelli, op. cit., pp. 200, 310–11, 324–5; for his Fascist 'credo', see *Annuario della Stampa 1931–2*, p. 63.

[128] *Il Selvaggio*, ed. Ragghianti, p. 10 ff. 73.

[129] A.Soffici, *Lemmonio Boreo* (Florence 1912); P.Vita-Finzi, *Le delusioni della libertà* (Florence 1961), pp. 93–100.

[130] *Il Selvaggio*, ed. Ragghianti, p. 12.

[131] Ibid., p. 20 ff; the *Selvaggio* identified their antagonists with Jewish international plutocracy. (*Il Selvaggio*, 15 October 1927.)

[132] A. Asor Rosa, *Scrittori e popolo* (Rome 1966), 1, p. 104, and in general, pp. 101–52.

[133] For Blasetti, see G. Aristarco, 'Le cinéma italien pendant le régime fasciste' in *Fascisme et résistance dans le cinéma italien*, Paris 1970, p. 27.

[134] Cannistraro, 'Burocrazia e politica culturale' pp. 288–94, 298; Moravia, 'Ricordi di censura', pp. 95–6, 101–5.

15 Propaganda and Education

[1] See Castronovo, *La stampa italiana*, pp. 323–4; T.K., 6, pp. 15, 19–20, 38–40.

[2] Castronovo, op. cit., pp. 323–4.

[3] Thus *Il Lavoro*, the important Reformist Socialist paper of Genoa, was closed 28 October–9 November 1922, and was forced to dismiss two of its journalists, the deputy Canepa and Ansaldo, before it could appear again. On 10 November it published a 'safe-conduct' from the secretary of the *fascio*, Pala.

[4] For the view of Bergamini, editor of the *Giornale d'Italia*, in December 1922 that his kind of journalism was 'no longer possible', see St Antony's documents, J. 290, 089188–90, Bergamini to Mussolini (15 December 1922). Castronovo, op. cit., p. 332; Rocca, *Come il fascismo*, p. 151.

[5] Castronovo, op. cit., p. 348.

[6] Text in ibid., pp. 435–6. Before the decree came into force, it had been the usual practice of Italian newspapers to appoint a 'straw man' as their responsible editor so that the real editor would escape the danger of prosecution. When possible, these editors were senators or deputies, because of their parliamentary immunity. Both these loopholes were closed by the decree of 8 July 1924.

[7] E. Decleva, 'Il Giornale d'Italia', in *Dopoguerra e fascismo*, p. 54.

[8] ACS, PS, 1924, C. 1. (Agitation against censorship decree.)

[9] Castronovo, op. cit., 344, 351; *Popolo d'Italia*, 16 July 1929. *Avanti!* suffered 36 confiscations between July and December 1924. For an example of Mussolini's personal intervention to silence an opposition paper, ACS, Uff. cifra, tel. partenza (9 December), n. 26944.

[10] See pp. 263–4.

[11] *O.O.*, 23, p. 231, 10 October 1928.

[12] *Corriere della Sera 1919–43*, ed. P. Melograni., pp. lv–lvi; *Popolo d'Italia*, 13 January 1925; Castronovo, op. cit., p. 338.

[13] Castronovo, op. cit., pp. 336–7.

[14] Ibid., pp. 443–5; *Annuario della stampa 1926*, pp. 60–1.

[15] ACS, SPCR, 242/R, *Gran Consiglio*, S/F 5 ins, C (16 November 1927), Memo of E. Amicucci. Castronovo, op. cit., pp. 397–8.

[16] E. Amicucci, *Il giornalismo nel regime fascista* (Rome 1930), p. 155; *Annuario della Stampa 1931*, pp. 417 ff, 425–6.

[17] Amicucci, *Il giornalismo*, p. 61.

[18] ACS, loc. cit., note 15.

[19] M. Carli to Mussolini, 14 June 1928 (Castronovo, op. cit., app. 1, p. 410).

[20] See *Annuario della Stampa 1931–2*. The total number of periodicals in Italy was reduced from 763 in 1919 to 633 in 1926 and 401 in 1968. The figures for daily

newspapers are respectively 120, 85 and 71. For examples of takeovers of periodical press by the Fascist party, ibid., pp. 129, 131, 133, 191, 251, 259.

[21] Castronovo, op. cit., p. 366.

[22] See R. Bilenchi, 'La funzione della stampa provinciale', in *Critica Fascista*, 1 May 1933.

[23] Castronovo, op. cit., pp. 381–93.

[24] Ibid., pp. 403–7; see p. 395 for Arnaldo Mussolini's opinion (November 1925) that 'to fascistize the *Stampa* in an absolute sense would be an absurdity'.

[25] Melograni, *Corriere*, pp. lxviii–lxxiii.

[26] *Annuario della Stampa 1931*, p. 158.

[27] Mussolini, 10 October 1928 (see note 11).

[28] Cannistraro, 'Burocrazia e politica culturale', pp. 276–84.

[29] ACS, loc. cit., note 15.

[30] De Felice, III, p. 554. On the 'moralization' of the press, see Forges-Davanzati to Mussolini, ACS, loc. cit. (15 November 1927); and for related climate of opinion, Moravia, 'Ricordi di censura', p. 97.

[31] Moravia, art. cit., p. 100; for general position of *Il Tevere*, see G. Carocci, *La politica estera dell Italia fascista, 1925–8* (Bari 1969), pp. 30–1, 262.

[32] The best study of radio under Fascism remains A. Galante Garrone, 'L'aedo senza fili', *Il Ponte*, October 1952, pp. 1401–24. See also EIAR, *Dieci anni di radio in Italia*, and for importance attached by regime to radio, PNF, *Dizionario di politica* (Rome 1940), 4, p. 8.

[33] PNF *Foglio d'ordini*, 11 September 1926; *Annurio della Stampa 1931*, p. 375.

[34] *Nuovo digesto italiano* (Turin 1938), pp. 50, 128; L. Freddi, *Il Cinema* (Rome 1949), p. 71. *Il Raduno*, 7 January–28 February passim (articles of M. Gallian demanding State film industry).

[35] On the *fasci femminili*, see ACS SPCR – Gran Consiglio S/F 4, 7 October 1926; E. Ragionieri, 'Il Partito Fascista', in *La Toscana nel regime fascista*, 1, p. 83.

[36] P. Togliatti, *Lezioni sul fascismo*, ed. E. Ragionieri; pp. 97–116; see also Albertina Baldi, 'Il dopolavoro, strumento di propaganda del fascismo', in *La Toscana nel regime fascista*, 2, pp. 635–54; G. di Nardo, 'Il Dopolavoro', in *La civiltà fascista*, p. 393 ff.

[37] On sport as the cornerstone of the new Fascist education, Bontempelli, op. cit., pp. 158–9. See also pp. 370, 409.

[38] Cannistraro, 'Burocrazia e politica culturale', p. 280; A. Ghirelli, *Storia del calcio italiano* (2nd ed. Turin 1967), pp. 131–2, 154 ff.

[39] The elementary teachers were organized in the Unione Nazionale Insegnanti; the secondary school teachers in the Federazione Nazionale Insegnanti Scuole Medie (FNISM).

[40] T. Tomasi, *Idealismo e fascismo nella scuola Italiana* (Florence 1969), pp. 4–6; L. Borghi, *Educazione e autorita nell'Italia moderna* (Florence 1969, 2nd ed.), p. 99.

[41] Borghi, op. cit., pp. 143–5, p. 208.

[42] Tomasi, op. cit., pp. 16–25; Allied Commission in Italy, *La politica e la legislazione scolastica in Italia dal 1922 al 1943* (Milan 1947), pp. 148 ff, 167 ff.

[43] Borghi, op. cit., pp. 182–5, Gentile, *Sommario di pedagogia come scienza filosofica* (Bari 1920–2)

[44] L. Ambrosoli, *La federazione nazionale insegnanti scuole medie* (Florence 1967) pp. 178–83, Tomasi, op. cit., p. 23.

[45] See the analysis of Gramsci, *Gli intellettuali e l'organizzazione della cultura* (Turin 1966), pp. 106–14. Tomasi, op. cit., 25, 53–4, 83 ; Borghi, op. cit., pp. 187, 191, 194 (see also pp. 63–7 for derivation of Gentile's views from De Meis) ; *La politica e la legislazione*, p. 74.

[46] D.Bertoni Jovine, *La scuola Italiana dal 1870 ai giorni nostri* (Cassino 1958), pp. 208–14, 215–17 ; see *La scuola nazionale*, ed. Cento (Milan 1918), pp. 24–9. For the criticisms of the Nationalists, see *Il nazionalismo e i problemi del lavoro e della scuola*, ed. P.L.Occhini (Rome 1919) (pp. 91, 116–17, 125–34).

[47] Bertoni Jovine, *La Scuola Italiana*, pp. 198–9, 220–1 ; Volpe, *Guerra, dopoguerra, fascismo*, p. 6.

[48] Ambrosoli, op. cit., pp. 291–5.

[49] Bertoni Jovine, op. cit., pp. 220–1.

[50] *Vita Nuova*, August 1925, 'Scuola Fascista'; *Critica Fascista*, 15 January 1933, 'Dieci Anni di Educazione Fascista'; Tomasi, op. cit., p. 6.

[51] Borghi, *Educazione e autorità*, p. 238n.

[52] Tomasi, op. cit., pp. 77–8; Bertoni Jovine, op. cit., pp. 259–60.

[53] *Rivoluzione Liberale*, 1 January 1923.
The most significant points in Gentile's reforms were :
1. The introduction of religious teaching in the elementary schools.
2. The State examination.
3. The abolition of the Ginnasio Moderno (ages 11–14), instituted in 1911, with a modified curriculum giving more time to science and modern languages.
4. The abolition of the old 'Scuola Tecnica' (ages 11–14) ; it was replaced by two alternatives, the Istituto Tecnico Inferiore and the Scuola Complementare. Of these only the first qualified its pupils for further education, in the Istituto Tecnico Superiore.
5. The abolition of mathematics and physics in the Istituto Tecnico Superiore. This meant that the pupils of the technical institutes could no longer gain admission to the university science faculties.
For further information, see Tomasi, *La politica e la legislazione scolastica* pp. 74–85 ; see also Bertoni Jovine, op. cit., pp. 270–3 and for comment, G.Preti in *Il Politecnico, Antologia critica*, ed. M.Forti and S.Pautasso (Milan 1960), pp. 787–94.

[54] Marinetti, *Futurismo e Fascismo*, p. 150 ; B.Corra, *Gli intellettuali creatori e la mentalità fascista* (Milan 1923), pp. 57–62. Garin, *Cronache*, pp. 366–7; Croce, *La critica* 1924, p. 192 ; for other Fascist and Nationalist criticism, M.Govi, *Popolo d'Italia*, 16 June 1923 ; Bertoni Jovine, pp. 263–5.

[55] *La politica e la legislazione scolastica*, pp. 254–62.

[56] Bertoni Jovine, op. cit., pp. 274–5.

[57] *Critica fascista*, art. cit. ; for party support for easier examinations, Tomasi, op. cit., pp. 84–5.

[58] Papa, op. cit., p. 155n ; Codignola, art cit.

[59] See Borghi, p. 263–14 for large degree of continuity between the pre-1914 proposals for reform and Gentile's measures.

[61] Bertoni Jovine, op. cit., pp. 282–4; *La politica e la legislazione scolastica*. pp. 64–6; ACS, PS, 1923, b. 5 f. 47 (1 June 1923).

[62] Bertoni Jovine, op. cit., pp. 291–3.

[63] St Antony's documents, J. 252. The purge of teachers seems to have begun to take effect only in November 1926. (*Il Tevere* 18–19 November.) The purge of officials presumably began earlier.

[64] Bertoni Jovine, op. cit., p. 294. *O.O.*, 8 December 1925.

[65] *O.O.*, p. 294; Dante Germino, *The Italian Fascist Party in Power; a study in totalitarian rule* (Minneapolis 1959), pp. 90–1 : Tomasi, op. cit., p. 93.

[66] *O.O.*, 23, p. 61. In October 1927, 72,000/95,000 elementary schoolteachers belonged to the Fascist Association (ANIF) (Bertoni Jovine, op. cit., p. 306); see also A. Sacconi, *Cultura Fascista*, 22 December 1927.

[67] V. Renda, *Scuola e fascismo* in *La civiltà fascista illustrata*, p. 469; Germino, op. cit., p. 90.

[68] See analysis of Togliatti, op. cit., pp. 66–9.

[69] Borghi, op. cit., p. 273. This circular it should be noted, applied only to the *Balilla* and the elementary schools, not to the *Avanguardie* and the secondary schools, where membership remained voluntary.

[70] On conflict with the Vatican, see De Felice, III, pp. 399–402, 412–13, D. A. Binchy, *Church and State in Fascist Italy* (2nd ed., Oxford 1970), pp. 407–33. The numbers enrolled in the ONB rose from 480,000 in October 1926 to 1,236,000 in July 1927; before the creation of the ONB, in September 1925, the numbers of Balilla and Avanguardie had been 100,000. See Germino, op. cit., p. 72. table 4; 1927–37, membership of the *Balilla* multiplied ten times, while that of the *Avanguardie* only doubled.

[71] Cammarata, *Pedagogia di Mussolini, La Scuola dell'ONB* passim. (Palermo 1932).

[72] On religion in the ONB, Borghi, pp. 273–80. There is no consensus on the question of how effective the youth movement's indoctrination proved; a careful study is needed. However, reminiscences such as R. Zangrandi, *Il lungo viaggio attraverso il fascismo* (1st ed., Milan 1962) and L. Preti's 'Giovinezza, Giovinezza !' (in novel form) indicate that it was at least partially successful. For an excellent analysis of the problem, see G. Germani (loc cit. ch. 7, n. 4.)

It seems likely that while the youth movement in general succeeded in producing a feeling of identification with Fascism, it was unsuccessful in its other more ambitious aim of selecting and training a future elite. The special schools or camps designed for the purpose were a failure.

[73] Tomasi, op. cit., pp. 141–2.

[74] St Antony's documents, J. 131, 036344 ff (1935). Starace replied to De Vecchi that if it were deprived of control over initiatives relating to youth, 'the party would be unquestionably robbed of its most substantial tasks'. Aquarone, op. cit., p. 180, also pp. 143–4.

[75] Tomasi, op. cit., pp. 90, 143–7; Bertoni Jovine, op. cit., p. 310. *Critica Fascista* 1 March 1933.

[76] *Scuola fascista* – 26 February 1928.

[77] Bertoni Jovine, op. cit., p. 311; *Politica e legislazione*, cit., pp. 73, 154–5. The obligatory State text was prepared in 1929 and first came into use in 1930.

[78] *Scuola fascista*, 10 May 1928.

[79] *Politica e La Legislazione*, pp. 153, 163 ff; Tomasi, op. cit., pp. 112–15. See G. Vidali, *Cultura fascista*, 1 July 1928, for an attempt to draft a curriculum for Fascist political education.

[80] Renda, loc. cit., p. 467.

[81] Tomasi, op. cit., p. 151n.

[82] *Critica fascista*, 15 January 1933 ; F.E.Boffi, *La scuola media fascista* (Rome 1929), pp. 53–5.

[83] E.g. R.Paribeni in *Italia d'oggi* (Rome 1941), pp. 39–45.

[84] B.Croce, *Storia della storiografia italiana nel secolo decimonono* (Bari 1964), pp. 241–6.

[85] A.Solmi, *Discorsi sulla storia d'Italia* (Florence 1933), pp. xxv–xxix. On the Nationalist interpretation of history, see also M.Ciliberto, *Studi storici* 4,1969, 'Appunti per una storia della fortuna di Machiavelli in Italia', pp. 801–28. F.D'Amoia, *La politica estera dell'impero* (Padua 1967), pp. 3–17.

[86] G.Volpe, *Storici e maestri* (Florence 1967), p. 244.

[87] Ibid., p. 238.

[88] See C.Morandi, 'Rinnovamento di metodo e rivalutazioni storiche del fascismo', *Italia d'oggi*, pp. 14–19.

[89] For De Vecchi's programme, *Rassegna Storica del Risorgimento*, 1933, p. i. 'We wish to prove, through scholarly inquiry, the relationship of father and son which all the periods of Italian history, the Risorgimento included, from Rome to Fascism, have to each other.' De Vecchi's demand that the history of the Risorgimento should aim at the education of 'character' not merely erudition had already been anticipated by C.Di Marzio at the eighteenth Congress for the history of the Risorgimento in 1930 ; see *RSI* (June 1930), pp. 225–6. The *Rivista Storica Italiana* from March 1930 onwards appeared under the auspices of the Turin Istituto Fascista di Coltura, with the Fasces on its title page. This was presumably the price for the maintenance of scholarly freedom.

[90] *Critica fascista*, 15 March 1927.

[91] See Germani, 'Political Socialization of Youth', pp. 355–69. For the cult of youth and the 'New Man' in the 1930s, see M.Ledeen, 'Italian Fascism and Youth', *Journal of Contemporary History* (1969), n. 3, pp. 137–52.

16   The Regime

[1] D.A.Binchy, *Church and State in Fascist Italy* (2nd ed, Oxford 1970), p. 105 ; F.Margiotta Broglio, *Italia e Santa Sede dalla grande guerra alla conciliazione : aspetti politici e giuridici* (Bari 1966), pp. 73–4.

[2] Binchy, op. cit., p. 108 ; *O.O.*, 16, p. 431 ff.

[3] A.C.Jemolo, *Chiesa e stato in Italia negli ultimi cento anni* (Turin 1948), pp. 625–7.

[4] P.Scoppola, *La chiesa e il fascismo : documenti e interpretazioni* (Bari 1971), p. 65.

[5] Ibid., pp. 64–7, 81–7 ; Webster, *Christian Democracy*, pp. 95–7 ; De Felice, II, pp. 656–7.

[6] Binchy, op. cit., pp. 500–1.

[7] Ibid., p. 165 ; Scoppola, op. cit., pp. 106–7.

[8] Margiotta Broglio, op. cit., pp. 49–57 ; however, see De Felice, III, pp. 393–4, for the difficulties raised by Victor Emmanuel during the negotiations of 1926–8.

[9] Scoppola, op. cit., pp. 122–44 ; Binchy, op. cit., pp. 242–53 ; Margiotta Broglio, op. cit., pp. 193–4.

[10] Scoppola, op. cit., p. 189.

[11] Ibid., pp. 239–52.

[12] For this conflict, see Binchy, op. cit., pp. 506–31.

[13] Ibid., p. 504.

[14] De Felice, III, p. 404 ff; Gentile, *Fascismo e cultura*, pp. 182–95; Aquarone, *Organizzazione*, pp. 293–4; P. Ungari in *Il cannoccchiale* (1966), n. 3, p. 96.

[15] St Antony's documents, J. 104,028374; Binchy, op. cit., pp. 180–1, 322.

[16] Scoppola, op. cit., pp. 129, 264–70; Binchy op. cit., p. 351; Webster, *Christian Democracy*, p. 127.

[17] De Felice, III, p. 428; Friedrich and Brzezinski, *Totalitarian Dictatorship*, pp. 279, 299–315 for churches as 'islands of separateness'.

[18] Garin, *Cronache*, pp. 489–90; G. Calogero, 'Mussolini, la conciliazione e il congresso filosofico del 1929', *La cultura*, October 1966, pp. 433–68.

[19] De Felice, III, p. 430.

[20] Scoppola *La chiesa e il fascismo*, pp. 53, 209; De Felice, III, pp. 417–18.

[21] Binchy, *Church and State*, pp. 672–80; Jemolo, *Chiesa e stato*, pp. 677–85.

[22] G. Rumi, *Alle origini della politica estera fascista (1918–23)* (Bari 1968), p. 85; see also pp. 52–4.

[23] Ibid., pp. 69, 116–17.

[24] G. Craig, *War, politics and diplomacy: selected essays* (London 1966), pp. 221–2; G. Rumi, 'I documenti diplomatici italiani e la recente storiografia', *Rassegna degli archivi di stato*, May–August 1969, pp. 407–8.

[25] De Felice, II, p. 758.

[26] Rumi, *Origini*, p. 24.

[27] Ibid., p. 159.

[28] Ibid., pp. 138–41, 202–4; D. Rusinow, *Italy's Austrian Heritage*, pp. 168–76.

[29] Carocci, *La politica estera*, pp. 25–6.

[30] A. Cassels, *Mussolini's Early Diplomacy* (Princeton 1970), pp. 139–45; see also contemporary comments of R. Michels, *Sozialismus und Faschismus als politische Strömungen in Italien* (Munich 1925), pp. 292–4.

[31] R. Guariglia, *La diplomatie difficile*, trans. L. Bonalumi (Paris 1955), pp. 3–5; see also H. S. Hughes, 'Early diplomacy of Italian Fascism, 1922–32', in *The Diplomats, 1919–39*, ed. G. Craig and F. Gilbert, pp. 211–16; Cassels, op. cit., pp. 3–9; R. Moscati, 'Gli esordi della politica estera fascista: il periodo Contarini–Corfu' in *La politica estera italiana dal 1914 al 1943* (Rome 1963), p. 78.

[32] J. Barros, *The Corfu incident of 1923. Mussolini and the League of Nations.* (Princeton 1965), passim. Also Cassels, op. cit., pp. 98–126; Seton-Watson, *Italy*, pp. 672–3. For the English reactions, see the documents published by Rumi, *Origini*, pp. 300–4: King George V compared Mussolini's ultimatum to Greece to the Austrian ultimatum after Sarajevo.

[33] Cassels, op. cit., pp. 233–41, 248–55; P. G. Edwards, *Anglo-Italian relations 1924–29* (unpublished MS), pp. 41 ff.

[34] See the report of the British ambassador, Sir Ronald Graham, on his first meeting with Mussolini in Rumi, *Origini*, pp. 268–73. Seton-Watson, *Italy*, p. 670, for Curzon's views.

[35] P. G. Edwards, 'The Foreign Office and Fascism 1924–1929', *JCH* (1970), n. 2, pp. 153–61.

[36] Seton-Watson, *Italy*, pp. 695–7.

[37] Carocci, *La politica estera*, p. 56.

[38] Cassels, *Mussolini's Early Diplomacy*, p. 261.

[39] Hughes, *Early diplomacy*, p. 226 ; Cassels, op. cit., p. 388.

[40] Cassels, op. cit., p. 490.

[41] Rumi, *Origini*, pp. 241–5.

[42] Carocci, op. cit., pp. 28–9.

[43] Ibid., pp. 3, 10–11.

[44] *Documents on British Foreign Policy 1919–39*, Series Ia, ed. W. N. Medlicott, D. Dakin and M. E. Lambert (London 1966), I, p. 608 (Chamberlain to Graham) and pp. 700–2 (Graham to Lampson).

[45] Carocci, 'L'imperialismo fascista' passim.

[46] Carocci, *La politica estera*, pp. 15, 255.

[47] Ibid., p. 109.

[48] Cassels, op. cit., p. 396. In the case of France, however, it seems to me that Cassels exaggerates the 'gulf' between Mussolini and his advisers (p. 376), Carocci shows (pp. 111–2) that in 1928–9 it was Guariglia and not Mussolini who torpedoed the Italian-French conversations.

[49] Seton-Watson, *Italy*, p. 697.

[50] Salvemini, *Scritti*, 2, p. 281 (originally published in *Century Magazine*, May 1927).

[51] Cassels, op. cit., pp. 152–66 ; Rumi, *Origini*, pp. 238–41.

[52] Carocci, op. cit., pp. 84–9, 292–7.

[53] Ibid., p. 194.

[54] Ibid., pp. 195–7 ; M. Michaelis, *I rapporti tra fascismo e nazismo prima dell' avvento di Hitler al potere* (MS).

[55] E.g., C. J. H. Hayes, 'Totalitarianism in Western Civilization' in *Symposium on the Totalitarian State* (Philadelphia 1941), pp. 98–9.

[56] Schapiro, 'The Party in the Totalitarian Polity', pp. 4–7.

[57] R. De Felice in *Il cannocchiale*, pp. 98–9.

[58] Ungari, *Rocco*, p. 79 ; Ungari in *Il problema storico del fascismo*, p. 74.

[59] Aquarone, *L'organizzazione*, pp. 75–7.

[60] De Felice, III, App. II, table 5.

[61] See Deakin, *Brutal Friendship*, p. 444 (criticisms of Bottai) ; G. Rochat, 'L'esercito nel ventennio,' MLI, 1969, 2, pp. 9–10, 17–18.

[62] Aquarone, op. cit., pp. 159–62, 496–500.

[63] Ibid., pp. 169–72, 611.

[64] Deakin, op. cit., p. 45.

[65] Ungari, *Rocco*, pp. 105–6, 115–16.

[66] See H. Trevor-Roper, 'The phenomenon of Fascism,' in Woolf, *European Fascism*, pp. 25–8.

[67] *O.O.*, 25, p. 148 (25 October 1932).

[68] De Felice, *Storia degli Ebrei italiani sotto il fascismo* (Turin 1961), pp. 282–4, 443.

[69] See Nolte, *Three Faces of Fascism*, pp. 3–9.

[70] Nolte, 'Nazionalsocialismo e fascismo nel giudizio di Hitler e di Mussolini' in *Faschismus –Nationalsozialismus* (Brunswick 1964), pp. 163–5.

[71] See D. Singer, *New Statesman*, 24 September 1971 ; 'Tecnica e sociologia del colpo di stato in Italia', *Tempi moderni* (1971), ns. 3–6 ; R. De Felice, *Il giorno*, 19 March 1971.

[72] R. Löwenthal, 'Il fascismo', in De Felice, *Il fascismo* (1970), p. 321.

BIBLIOGRAPHY

BIBLIOGRAPHY

Archive Sources

The major part of the documents I have consulted come from the Archivio Centrale dello Stato in Rome. For the individual files consulted, see under abbreviations. In addition I have been able to consult the Italian collection in St Antony's College, which in the main consists of photocopies of the files of the Segreteria Particolare del Duce. As, however, not all the documents were copied, I have also consulted the originals in Rome. The Italian collection is cited in the text as 'St Antony's documents'. For a brief further account of their nature and provenance, see Deakin, *The Brutal Friendship*, pp. 819–20.

Published Sources

M. Abrate, *La lotta sindacale nella industrializzazione in Italia 1906–26*, Turin 1967.
T. W. Adorno et al., *The Authoritarian Personality*, 2 vols., New York 1964.
Aeropittura Futurista, ed. Galleria Blu, Milan 1970.
P. Alatri, *Le origini del fascismo*, Bologna 1962.
    Nitti, D'Annunzio e la questione adriatica, Milan 1959.
L. Albertini, *Epistolario*, ed. O. Barié, 4 vols. Verona 1968.
    In difesa della libertà, Milan 1947.
Allied Commission in Italy, *La politica e la legislazione scolastica in Italia dal 1922 al 1943*, Milan 1947.
L. Alloway, *The Venice Biennale : from Salon to Goldfish Bowl*, London 1969.
L. Ambrosoli, *La FNISM dalle origini al 1925*, Florence 1967.
    Ne aderire ne sabotare, 1915–1918, Milan and Rome 1961.
G. Amendola, *Una battaglia liberale : discorsi politici, 1919–1923*, Turin 1924.
    La democrazia italiana contro il fascismo, Milan and Naples 1960.
    La nuova democrazia, Naples 1951.
E. Amicucci, *Il giornalismo nel regime fascista*, Rome 1930.
Antologia degli scrittori fascisti, ed. M. Carli and G. Fanelli.
    Antologia di "Solaria", ed. E. Siciliano, Milan 1958.
E. Apih, *Italia, fascismo e antifascismo nella Venezia Giulia, 1918–1943*, Bari 1966.
A. Aquarone, *L'organizzazione dello stato totalitario*, Turin 1965.
H. Arendt, *The Origins of Totalitarianism*, London 1967.

515

G. Arfé, *Storia del socialismo italiano, 1892–1926*, Turin 1965.

Arte Fascista, Turin 1928.

A. Asor Rosa, *Scrittori e popolo : il populismo nella letteratura italiana contemporanea*, 2 vols., 2nd ed., Rome 1966.

Associazione fra le società italiane per azioni, *Notizie statistiche*, Rome 1928.

R. Bachi, *L'Italia economica : Annuario*, Turin 1919–22.

I. Balbo, *Diario 1922*, Milan 1932.

G. Baldesi, *Di tante briciole fare una briciola sola*, Florence 1923.

U. Banchelli, *Memorie di uno squadrista*, Florence 1922.

M. Bandini, *Cento anni di storia agraria italiana*, Rome 1963.

Reyner Banham, *Theory and Design in the First Machine Age*, London 1960.

Z. Barbu, *Democracy and Dictatorship*, London 1956.

J. Barros, *The Corfu Incident and the League of Nations*, Princeton 1965.

G. Belluzzo, *Economia fascista*, Rome 1928.

J. Benda, *La trahison des clercs*, Paris 1928.

A. S. Benni, *La politica doganale italiana*, Milan 1925.

D. Bertoni Jovine, *La scuola italiana dal 1870 ai giorni nostri*, Cassino 1958.

M. Bianchi, *I discorsi ; gli scritti*, Rome 1931.

A. Bianco, *Il fascismo in Sicilia*, Catania 1923.

D. A. Binchy, *Church and State in Fascist Italy*, 2nd ed., Oxford 1970.

N. Bobbio, *Politica e cultura*, Turin 1955.
> *Saggi sulla scienza politica in Italia*, Bari 1971.

E. F. Boffi, *La scuola media fascista*, Rome 1929.

I. Bonomi, *Diario di un anno, 2 giugno 1943 – 10 giugno 1944*, Cernusco 1947.
> *Dal socialismo al fascismo*, 2nd ed., Milan 1946.

M. Bontempelli, *L'avventura novecentista*, Florence 1938.

G. A. Borgese, *Goliath*, New York 1938.

L. Borghi, *Educazione e autorità nell'Italia moderna*, 2nd ed., Florence 1969.

G. Bottai, *Pagine di 'Critica Fascista'*, ed. F. M. Pacces, Florence 1941.
> *Scritti*, ed. R. Bartolozzi and R. Del Giudice, Bologna 1965.
> *Vent'anni e un giorno*, Milan 1949.

B. Buozzi, *Scritti dell'esilio*.
> *Pagine polemiche*, Milan 1950.

B. Caizzi, *Camillo e Adriano Olivetti*, Turin 1962.

U. Calderoni, *La politica doganale italiana*, Padua 1961.

A. Cammarata, *Pedagogia di Mussolini : la scuola dell'ONB*, Palermo 1932.

E. Campese, *Il fascismo contro la disoccupazione*, Rome 1929.

A. Canepa, *L'organizzazione del PNF*, Palermo 1939.

P. Capoferri, *Vent'anni coi sindacati*, Milan 1957.

A. Caracciolo, *Il parlamento nella formazione del regno d'Italia*, Milan 1960.
> *Stato e società civile, Problemi dell'unificazione italiana*, Turin 1960.
> et al., *Il trauma dell'intervento 1914–1919*, Florence 1968.

G. Carocci, *Agostino Depretis e la politica interna italiana dal 1876 al 1887*, Turin 1956.
> *Giovanni Amendola nella crisi dello stato italiano, 1911–1925*, Milan 1956.
> *Giolitti e l'età giolittiana*, 2nd ed., Turin 1961.
> *La politica estera dell'Italia fascista, 1925–1928*, Bari 1969.

A. Cassels, *Fascist Italy*, London 1969.
    Mussolini's Early Diplomacy, Princeton 1970.

G. Castagno, *Bruno Buozzi*, Milan 1955.

V. Castronovo, *La stampa italiana dall'unità al fascismo*, Bari 1970.

F. Catalano, *Potere economico e fascismo : La crisi del dopoguerra 1919–1921*, Milan 1964.

F. Cavazza, *Il discorso programma del Conte Cavazza agli elettori del terzo collegio*, Bologna 1913.

F. Chabod, *A History of Italian Fascism*, tran. M. Grindrod, London 1963.
    L'idea di nazione, Bari 1962.
    Storia della politica estera italiana dal 1870 al 1896 : le premesse, 2 vols., Bari 1965.

F. Charles-Roux, *Souvenirs diplomatiques : une grande ambassade à Rome 1919–1925*, Paris 1961.

G. A. Chiurco, *Storia della rivoluzione fascista*, 4 vols., Florence 1929.

N. Cilla, *Effetti economici del Fascismo*, Milan 1925.

I 535 di Montecitorio, Bologna 1924.

La civiltà fascista illustrata nelle dottrine e nelle opere, ed. G. L. Pomba, Turin 1928.

Cleavages, Ideologies and Party Systems. Contributions to Comparative Political Sociology, ed. E. Allardt and Y. Littunen (Transactions of the Westermarck Society, Vol. X), Helsinki 1964.

S. B. Clough, *The Economic History of Modern Italy*, New York 1964.

A. Codignola, *La Resistenza de'i combattenti di Assisi*, Modena 1965.

R. Colapietra, *Napoli tra dopoguerra e fascismo*, Milan 1962.

S. Colarizi, *Dopoguerra e fascismo in Puglia (1919–1926)*, Bari 1971.

F. Coletti, *Economia rurale e politica rurale in Italia*, Piacenza 1926.

La Confederazione generale del lavoro 1906–1926, ed. F. Catalano, Milan 1962.

La Confederazione generale fascista dell'industria – relazione all'assemblea dei delegati, Milan 1930.

Conflitti del lavoro e legislazione sociale. Relazione della presidenza della confederazione italiana dell'industria all'assemblea dei delegati, Turin 1914.

E. Conti, *Dal taccuino di un borghese*, Milan 1946.

E. Corbino, *Annali dell'economia italiana*, 4 vols., Citta di Castello 1938.

F. Cordova, *Arditi e legionari dannunziani*, Padua 1969.

B. Corra, *Gli intellettuali creatori e la mentalità fascista*, Milan 1923.

E. Corradini, *Discorsi politici*, Florence 1923.
    La marcia dei produttori, Rome 1916.

L. Cortesi, *Il socialismo italiano tra riforme e rivoluzione*, Bari 1969.

B. Croce, *Cultura e vita morale*, Bari 1926.
    Epistolario, vol. 1, Naples 1967.
    History of Europe in the 19th Century, tran. H. Furst, London 1939.
    History of Italy 1871–1915, tran. C. M. Ady, Oxford 1929.
    Pagine sparse, 2 vols., Naples 1943.
    Pagine sulla guerra, 4th ed., Bari 1964.
    Storia della storiografia italiana, 2 vols., 4th ed., Bari 1964.

La cultura italiana del'900 attraverso le riviste, vol. 1, 'Leonardo', 'Hermes', 'Il Regno', ed. D. Frigessi, Turin 1960.

vol. 3, "La Voce" (1908–1914), ed. A.Romano, Turin 1960.

vol. 4, 'Lacerba', 'La Voce' (1914–1916), ed. G.Scalia, Turin 1961.

F. Cusin, *Antistoria d'Italia*, Turin 1948.

R. Dahrendorf, *Class and Class Conflict in an Industrial Society*, London 1967.

Dai fasci al PNF, Rome 1942.

F. D'Amoja, *La politica estera dell'impero*, Padua 1967.

G. D'Annunzio, *Carteggio D'Annunzio-Mussolini 1919–1938*, ed. R. De Felice and F.Mariano, Milan 1971.

 Opere : Prose di ricerca, 2 vols., Verona 1947–.

F. W. Deakin, *The Brutal Friendship: Mussolini, Hitler and the Fall of Italian Fascism*, London 1962.

Y. De Begnac, *Palazzo Venezia : Storia di un regime*, Rome 1950.

R. De Felice, *Il fascismo : le interpretazioni dei contemporanei e degli storici*, Bari 1970.

 Le interpretazioni del fascismo, Bari 1969.

 Sindacalismo rivoluzionario e Fiumanesimo nel carteggio De Ambris-D'Annunzio, Brescia 1966.

F. Della Peruta, *Democrazia e socialismo nel Risorgimento*, Rome 1965.

M. Delle Piane, *Gaetano Mosca, classe politica e liberalismo*, Naples 1952.

G. De Rosa, *Giolitti e il fascismo in alcune sue lettere inedite* (with app., 'Venti anni di politica nelle carte di Camillo Corradini'), Rome 1957.

 Storia del movimento cattolico in Italia, 2 vols., Bari 1966.

G. De Ruggiero, *The History of European Liberalism*, tran. R.G.Collingwood, Boston 1959.

 Il pensiero politico meridionale, nei secoli xviii e xix, Bari 1922.

F. De Sanctis, *History of Italian Literature*, tran. Joan Redfern, London 1932.

A. De Stefani, *Baraonda bancaria*, Milan 1960.

 Discorsi, Milan 1923.

 La resa del liberalismo economico, Milan 1932.

A De Viti De Marco, *Un trentennio di lotte politiche (1894–1922)*, with introd. by E.Rossi, Rome 1929.

A. Di Giorgio, *Scritti e discorsi vari 1899–1927*, Rome 1938.

The Diplomats, ed. G.A.Craig and F.Gilbert, 2 vols., New York 1965.

Dizionario biografico degli Italiani, Rome 1960–.

D. Dolci, *Waste*, tran. R.Munroe, London 1963.

1919–1925, Dopoguerra e fascismo. Politica e stampa in Italia, ed. B.Vigezzi, Bari 1965.

G. Dorso, *La rivoluzione meridionale*, Turin 1955.

G. Douhet, *La difesa nazionale*, Rome 1925.

P. Drieu La Rochelle, *Notes pour comprendre le siècle*, Paris 1941.

L'Economia italiana dal 1861 al 1961, Milan 1961.

EIAR, *Dieci anni di radio in Italia*, Rome 1935.

L. Einaudi, *Cronache economiche e politiche di un trentennio*, Turin 1961.

F. Ercole, *Dal nazionalismo al fascismo*, Rome 1928.

European Fascism, ed. S.J.Woolf, London 1968.

The European Right, ed. H.Rogger and E.Weber, London 1965.

L. Faenza, *Comunismo e cattolicesimo in una parrocchia di campagna*, Bologna 1959.

G. Fanelli, *Contra gentiles*, Rome 1933.

BIBLIOGRAPHY

R. Farinacci, *Andante mosso*.
     Un periodo aureo del Partito Nazionale Fascista, Foligno 1927.
Il fascismo, Antologia di scritti critici, ed. C. Casucci, Bologna 1961.
Fascismo e antifascismo : Lezioni e testimonianze, 2nd ed., Milan 1963.
Il fascismo e i partiti politici italiani : testimonianze del 1921–1923, ed. R. De Felice,
     Rocca S. Casciano, 1966.
Federazione nazionale dei lavoratori della terra. – lotte agrarie in Italia, ed.
     R. Zangheri, Milan 1960.
L. Federzoni, *Italia di ieri per la storia di domani*, Milan 1967.
F. L. Ferrari, *L'azione cattolica e il regime*, Florence 1957.
     Le régime fasciste italien, Paris 1928.
E. Ferraris, *La marcia su Roma veduta dal Viminale*, Rome 1946.
H. Finer, *Mussolini's Italy*, 2nd ed., London 1964.
R. Forges Davanzati, *Fascismo e cultura*, Florence 1926.
La formazione dell'Italia industriale, ed. A. Caracciolo, Bari 1969.
U. Formentini, *Gerarchie sindacali*, Turin 1923.
R. Forti and G. Ghedini, *L'avvento del fascismo : cronache*, Ferrara 1922.
G. Fortunato, *Pagine e ricordi parlamentari*, 2 vols., Florence 1926–7.
E. Fraenkel, *The Dual State : A Contribution to the Theory of Dictatorship*, New
     York 1941.
L. Freddi, *Il cinema*, 2 vols., Rome 1949.
R. C. Fried, *The Italian Prefect*, New Haven 1963.
C. J. Friedrich and Z. Brzezinski, *Totalitarian Dictatorship and Autocracy*, 2nd ed.,
     Cambridge, Mass. 1965.
F. Gaeta, *Nazionalismo italiano*, Naples 1965.
G. Galasso, *Croce, Gramsci e altri storici*, Milan 1969.
E. Galbiati, *Il 25 luglio e la MVSN*, Milan 1950.
E. Garin, *Cronache di filosofia italiana*, Bari 1959.
     La cultura italiana tra '800 e '900, Bari 1962.
G. Gentile, *Che cosa è il fascismo*, Florence 1925.
     Dopo la vittoria, nuovi frammenti politici, Rome 1920.
     L'eredità di V. Alfieri, Venice 1926.
     Fascismo e cultura, Milan 1928.
     Guerra e fede, Naples 1919.
     Origini e dottrina del fascismo, 3rd ed., Rome 1934.
     I profeti del Risorgimento italiano, Florence 1923.
     La riforma dell'educazione, Bari 1920.
     Sommario di pedagogia, come scienza filosofica, 2 vols., 2nd ed., Bari
     1920–2.
     La vita e il pensiero, ed. Fondazione G. Gentile per gli studi filosofici,
     Florence 1948.
D. Germino, *The Italian Fascist Party in Power : a Study in Totalitarian Rule*,
     Minneapolis 1959.
A. Gerschenkron, *Continuity in History and Other Essays*, Cambridge, Mass. 1968.
     Economic Backwardness in Historical Perspective, Cambridge,
     Mass. 1962.
A. Ghirelli, *Storia del calcio italiano*, 2nd ed., Turin 1967.
C. Gini, *I fattori demografici dell'evoluzione delle nazioni*, Turin 1912.

G. Giolitti, *Discorsi extraparlamentari*, ed. N. Valeri, Turin 1952.
I. Giordani, *Alcide De Gasperi, il ricostruttore*, Rome 1955.
U. Giusti, *Le correnti politiche italiane attraverso due riforme elettorali dal 1909 al 1921*, Florence 1922.
P. Gobetti, *Scritti politici*, ed. P. Spriano, Turin 1960.
A. Gramsci, *Gli intellettuali e l'organizzazione della cultura*, 8th ed., Turin 1966.
    Letteratura e vita nazionale, 6th ed., Turin 1966.
    Passato e presente, 2nd ed., Turin 1952.
    Socialismo e Fascismo, L'Ordine Nuovo 1921–1922, Turin 1966.
Il Gran Consiglio nei primi dieci anni dell'era fascista, Rome 1933.
G. Grana, *Malaparte*, Florence 1968.
I Grandi discorsi elettorali del 1924, Milan 1924.
A. J. Gregor, *The Ideology of Fascism*, Toronto 1969.
P. Grifone, *Il capitale finanziario in Italia*, Turin 1971.
B. Griziotti et al., *La politica finanziaria italiana*, Milan 1926.
R. Guariglia, *La diplomatie difficile, mémoires 1922–1946*, tran. L. Bonalumi, Paris 1955.
F. Guarneri, *Battaglie economiche tra le due grandi guerre*, 2 vols., Milan 1953.
W. Gurian, *The Future of Bolshevism*, tran. E. I. Watkin, London 1936.
A. Hamilton, *The Appeal of Fascism*, London 1971.
H. S. Harris, *The Social Philosophy of Giovanni Gentile*, Urbana 1960.
G. Hildebrand, *Growth and Structure in the Economy of Modern Italy*, Cambridge, Mass. 1965.
R. Hofstadter, *The Paranoid Style in American Politics and Other Essays*, London 1966.
I. Horowitz, *Radicalism and the Revolt against Reason : the Social Theories of Georges Sorel*, London 1961.
Inchiesta sulla Massoneria, ed. E. Bodrero, Milan 1925.
Inizio e sviluppo del sindacalismo fascista nella provincia di Brescia, Brescia 1926.
I. Insolera, *Roma moderna*, 2nd ed., Turin 1971.
M. Isnenghi, *Il mito della grande guerra*, Bari 1970.
Istituto Centrale di Statistica, *Compendio delle statistiche elettorali italiane dal 1848 al 1934*, 2 vols., Rome 1946–7.
Istituto per la storia del Risorgimento italiano, *Atti del XLI Congresso*, Rome 1965.
Italia d'oggi, Rome 1941.
S. Jacini, *Storia del partito popolare*, Milan 1951.
G. Jannelli, *La crisi del fascismo in Sicilia*, Messina 1924.
A. C. Jemolo, *Chiesa e stato in Italia negli ultimi cento anni*, Turin 1948. (Tran. [partially] D. Moore, as *Church and State in Italy 1850–1960*, Oxford 1960.)
J. Joll, *Intellectuals in politics*, London 1960.
R. Korherr, *Regresso delle nascite : morte dei popoli*, Rome 1928.
E. Kühn Amendola, *Vita con Giovanni Amendola, Epistolario 1903–1926*, Florence 1960.
A. Lanzillo, *La disfatta del socialismo*, 2nd ed., Rome 1918.
    Le rivoluzioni del dopoguerra, Città di Castello 1922.
    Lo stato e la crisi sociale e monetaria postbellica, Milan 1920.
I. J. Lederer, *Yugoslavia at the Paris Peace Conference*, London 1963.
M. Lerner, *The Nazi Elite*, Stanford 1951.

G. Leto, *OVRA fascismo, antifascismo*, Bologna 1951.

G. Levi Della Vida, *Fantasmi ritrovati*, Venice 1966.

C. Licitra, *Dal liberalismo al fascismo*, Rome 1925.

S. M. Lipset, *Political Man*, London 1960.

E. Lolini, *Burocrazia*, Rome 1919.

    Per l'attuazione dello stato fascista, with pref. by G. Gentile, Florence 1928.

L. Lotti, *La settimana rossa*, Florence 1965.

G. Lumbroso, *La crisi del fascismo*, Florence 1925.

G. Luti, *Cronache letterarie tra le due guerre*, Bari 1966.

D. Mack Smith, *Cavour and Garibaldi, 1860*, Cambridge 1954.

    Italy, A Modern History, Ann Arbor and London 1959.

    Victor Emmanuel, Cavour and the Risorgimento, London – New York – Toronto 1971.

O. Malagodi, *Conversazioni della guerra*, ed. B. Vigezzi, 2 vols., Milan 1960.

C. Malaparte, *L'Europa vivente ed altri saggi politici*, Florence 1961.

    Technique du coup d'état, Paris 1948.

C. Maltese, *Storia dell'arte in Italia 1785–1943*, Turin 1960.

E. Malusardi, *Elementi di storia del sindacalismo fascista*, Genoa 1932.

K. Mannheim, *Ideology and Utopia*, London 1966.

F. Manzotti, *Il Socialismo riformista in Italia*, Florence 1965.

A. L. Maraspini, *The Study of an Italian Village*, Hague 1968.

M. Maraviglia, *Alle basi del regime*, Rome 1929.

H. Marcuse, *Reason and Revolution, Hegel and the Rise of Social Theory*, 2nd ed., London 1955.

F. Margiotta Broglio, *Italia e Santa Sede dalla grande guerra alla conciliazione: aspetti politici e giuridici*, Bari 1966.

F. T. Marinetti, *Futurismo e Fascismo*, Foligno 1924.

    Opere; vol. 2, *Teoria e invenzione Futurista*, ed. L. De Maria, Milan 1968.

F. Martini, *Diario 1914–1918*, ed. G. De Rosa, Verona 1966.

G. Matteotti, *Un anno di dominazione fascista*, Rome n.d.

    Reliquie, Milan 1962.

W. Maturi, *Interpretazioni del Risorgimento*, Turin 1962.

E. Mecheri, *Chi ha tradito?*, Milan 1947.

G. Megaro, *Mussolini in the Making*, London 1938.

R. Melis, *Sindacalisti italiani*, Rome 1964.

P. Melograni, *Storia politica della grande guerra*, Bari 1969.

G. Miccoli, *Delio Cantimori: la ricerca di una nuova critica storiografica*, Turin 1970.

R. Michels, *Nuovi studi sulla classe politica*, Rome 1936.

    Sozialismus und Faschismus als politische Strömungen in Italien, 2 vols., Munich 1925.

Ministero dell'Economia Nazionale, Direzione Generale della Statistica, *Statistica delle elezioni generali politiche per la XXVII legislatura*, Rome 1924.

Ministero della Giustizia. *Statistica giudiziaria penale per gli anni 1927 e 1928*, Rome 1931.

Ministero per la Costituente, *Rapporto della commissione economica*.

M. Missiroli, *Una battaglia perduta*, Milan 1924.

    Il fascismo e il colpo di stato dell'ottobre 1922, Rocca S. Casciano 1966.

A. Misuri, *Rivolta morale*, Milan 1924.

R. Molinelli, *Per una storia del nazionalismo italiano*, Urbino 1966.

Barrington Moore Jr., *The Social Origins of Dictatorship and Democracy : Lord and Peasant in the Making of the Modern World*, London 1967.

C. Morandi, *I partiti politici nella storia d'Italia*, Florence 1945.

G. Mortara, *Prospettive economiche*, Città di Castello 1921–.

G. Mosca, *Sulla teorica dei governi e sul governo parlamentare*, Turin 1884.

G. Moschini, *Scritti*, Mantua 1934.

Il Movimento delle Squadre.

B. Mussolini, *My Autobiography*, tran. R. W. Child, London 1928.

The Nature of Fascism, ed. S. J. Woolf (proceedings of 1968 Reading Conference).

Il Nazionalismo e i problemi del lavoro e della scuola, ed. P. L. Occhini, Rome 1919.

R. Nenci, *Saggi ed esperienze di sindacalismo fascista e corporativismo*, Florence 1938.

G. Neppi Modona, *Sciopero, potere politico e magistratura, 1870–1922*, Bari 1969.

E. Nolte, *Three Faces of Fascism*, London 1965.

Il Nord nella storia d'Italia, ed. L Cafagna, Bari 1962.

Nuovo Digesto italiano, Turin 1938.

U. Ojetti, *I Taccuini 1914–1943*, Florence 1954.

A. Oriani, *Opere : Fino a Dogali*, Bologna 1943.

> *Opere : La rivolta ideale*, Bologna 1943.

M. Pantaleone, *Mafia e politica*, Turin 1962.

S. Panunzio, *Stato fascista*, Bologna 1923.

E. R. Papa, *Storia di due manifesti : il fascismo e la cultura italiana*, Milan 1958.

G. Papini, *Opere : vol. 2, Filosofia e letteratura*, Verona 1961.

> *Opere : vol. 9, Autoritratti e ritratti*, Verona 1962.

> *Vecchio e nuovo nazionalismo*, Florence 1914.

V. Pareto, *Scritti sociologici*, ed. G. Busino, Turin 1966.

> *Les systèmes socialistes*, 2 vols., Paris 1902–3.

> *Trasformazioni della democrazia*, introd. M. Missiroli, 2nd ed., Rocca S. Casciano 1966.

Talcott Parsons, *Essays in Sociological Theory*, 3rd ed., Glencoe 1963.

Partito Nazionale Fascista, *Dizionario di Politica*, Rome 1940.

> *Fogli d'ordini, dal 31 luglio IV al 28 ottobre XIII*, Rome 1935.

Partito Nazionale Fascista, *Le origini e lo sviluppo del fascismo attraverso gli scritti e la parola del Duce e le deliberazioni del PNF dall'intervento alla Marcia su Roma*, Rome 1928.

E. Passerin D'Entreves, *L'ultima battaglia politica del Conte di Cavour*, Turin 1956.

G. Pastore, *A. Grandi e il movimento sindacale italiano nel primo dopoguerra*, Rome 1960.

C. Pavone, *Amministrazione centrale e amministrazione periferica da Rattazzi a Ricasoli (1859–1866)*, Milan 1964.

L. Peano, *Ricordi della guerra dei trent'anni (1915–1945)*, Città di Castello 1948.

C. Pellizzi, *Fascismo-aristocrazia*, Milan 1925.

> *Problemi e realtà del fascismo*, Florence 1924.

> *Una rivoluzione mancata*, Milan 1948.

F. Perroux, *Contribution à l'étude de l'économie et des finances publiques de l'Italie depuis la guerre*, Paris 1929.

G. Pesce, *La marcia dei rurali*, Rome 1929.

C. Petrocchi, *Il problema della burocrazia*, Rome 1944.

D. Petroccia, *Il fascismo nel Sannio*.

G. Pini and D. Susmel, *Mussolini, l'uomo e l'opera*, 4 vols., Florence 1953–5.

A. Pirelli, *Dopoguerra 1919–1932*, Milan 1961.

R. Poggioli, *Teoria dell'arte d'avanguardia*, Bologna 1962.

Il Politecnico, antologia critica, ed. M. Forti and S. Pautasso, Milan 1960.

La politica estera italiana dal 1914 al 1943, Rome 1963.

M. Praz, *The Romantic Agony*, Oxford 1951.

Presidenza del Consiglio dei Ministri, Istituto Centrale di Statistica, *Censimento della popolazione del regno d'Italia al 1 dicembre 1921*, Rome 1927.

L. Preti, *Giovinezza! Giovinezza!*, Milan 1964.

Le lotte agrarie nella valle padana, Turin 1955.

G. Prezzolini, *Fascism*, tran. K. Macmillan, London 1926.

L'Italiano inutile, Florence 1964.

La pubblica sicurezza, ed. P. Barile (Atti del Congresso celebrativo del centennio delle leggi amministrative di unificazione, vol. 2), Vicenza 1967.

P. Puntoni, *Parla Vittorio Emmanuele III*, Milan 1958.

Quarant'anni di politica, Dalle carte di Giovanni Giolitti, 3 vols., Milan 1962.

L. Radi, *I Mezzadri: le lotte contadine nell'Italia centrale*, Rome 1962.

E. Ragionieri, *Politica e amministrazione nella storia dell'Italia unita*, Bari 1967.

A. Repaci, *La marcia su Roma*, 2 vols., Rome 1963.

Resoconto del Congresso Agrario (1909).

M. Rocca, *Come il fascismo divenne una dittatura*, Milan 1952.

Idee sul fascismo, Florence 1924.

Il primo fascismo, Rome 1964.

A. Rocco, *Scritti e discorsi politici*, 3 vols., Milan 1938.

G. Rochat, *L'esercito italiano da Vittorio Veneto a Mussolini*, Bari 1967.

R. Romeo, *Breve storia della grande industria in Italia*, Rocca S. Casciano 1961.

Risorgimento e capitalismo, Bari 1959.

L. Rosenstock-Franck, *L'économie corporative fasciste en doctrine et en fait*, Paris 1934.

C. Rossi, *Mussolini com'era*, Rome 1947.

Trentatre vicende mussoliniane, Milan 1958.

E. Rossi, *Il malgoverno*, Bari 1954.

Padroni del vapore e fascismo, Bari 1966.

G. Rossini, *Il delitto Matteotti tra Viminale e Aventino*, Bologna 1966.

Il movimento cattolico nel periodo fascista, Rome 1966.

E. Rossoni, *Le idee della ricostruzione*, Florence 1923.

L. Rougier, *Les mystiques économiques: comment l'on passe des democraties liberales aux états totalitaires*, Paris 1938.

G. Rumi, *Alle origini della politica estera fascista (1918–1923)*, Bari 1968.

D. I. Rusinow, *Italy's Austrian Heritage, 1919–1946*, Oxford 1969.

A. Salandra, *Il diario di Salandra*, ed. G. B. Gifuni, Milan 1969.

Memorie politiche 1916–1925, Milan 1951.

La neutralità italiana (1914), Ricordi e pensieri, Verona 1928.

La politica nazionale e il partito liberale, Milan 1912.

C. Salinari, *Miti e coscienza del decadentismo italiano*, Milan 1960.

A. W. Salomone, *Italian Democracy in the Making*, Philadelphia 1945.
  Italy from the Risorgimento to Fascism, an inquiry into the origins of the totalitarian state, New York, 1970.

L. Salvatorelli, *Nazionalfascismo*, Turin 1923.
  Pensiero e azione del Risorgimento, Turin 1960.
  and G. Mira, *Storia d'Italia nel periodo fascista*, Turin 1956.

G. Salvemini, *The Fascist Dictatorship in Italy*, London 1928.
  Opere: Il mezzogiorno e la democrazia italiana: il ministro della malavita e altri scritti sull'Italia giolittiana, ed. E. Apih, Milan 1962.
  Opere: Scritti di politica estera, vol. 1; *Come siamo andati in Libia e altri scritti, 1900–1915*, ed. A. Torre, Milan 1963.
  Opere: Scritti sul fascismo, 2 vols. (vol. 1 ed. R. Vivarelli, Milan 1961; vol. 2 ed. N. Valeri and A. Merola, Milan 1966).
  Under the Axe of Fascism, London 1936.

E. Santarelli, *Origini del fascismo*, Urbino 1963.
  La revisione del marxismo in Italia, Milan 1964.
  Storia del movimento e del regime fascista, 2 vols., Rome 1967.

P. Saraceno, *Lo sviluppo economico dei paesi sovrapopolati*, Rome 1952.

E. Savino, *La nazione operante*, Milan 1928, 1934.

G. Scagnetti, *Gli enti di privilegio nell'economia corporativa italiana*, Padua 1942.

E. Scalfari, *Storia segreta dell'industria elettrica*, Bari 1963.

A. Schiavi, *La vita e l'opera di Giacomo Matteotti*, Rome 1957.

C. T. Schmidt, *The Plough and the Sword; Labor, Land and Property in Fascist Italy*, New York 1938.

P. Scoppola, *La chiesa e il fascismo: documenti e interpretazioni*, Bari 1971.

C. Scorza, *Brevi note sul fascismo, sui capi, sui gregari*, Florence 1930.
  La scuola nazionale, ed. V. Cento, Milan 1918.

S. Sechi, *Dopoguerra e fascismo in Sardegna*, Turin 1971.

'*Il Selvaggio*' di Mino Maccari, ed. C. L. Ragghianti, Venice 1955.

E. Sereni, *Capitalismo e mercato nazionale in Italia*, Rome 1966.
  Il capitalismo nelle campagne, 1860–1900, 2nd ed., Turin 1971.
  La questione agraria nella rinascita nazionale italiana, Rome 1946.

A. Serpieri, *La guerra e le classi rurali italiane*, Bari 1930.
  La politica agraria in Italia e i recenti provvedimenti legislativi, Piacenza 1925.

C. Seton-Watson, *Italy from Liberalism to Fascism*, London 1967.

A. Shonfield, *Modern Capitalism: the Changing Balance of Public and Private Power*, Oxford–London–New York–Toronto 1965.

C. Silvestri, *Dalla redenzione al Fascismo (Trieste 1918–1922)* Udine 1959.

Silvestri, *Il fascismo salernitano*.

A. Soffici, *Una battaglia fra due vittorie*, Florence 1923.
  Lemmonio Boreo.

M. Soleri, *Memorie* Turin, 1949.

G. Sorel, *Reflections on violence*, tran. T. R. Hulme and J. Roth, with introd. E. A. Shils, Glencoe 1950.
  Scritti politici, ed. R. Vivarelli, Turin 1963.

G. Spadolini, *Giolitti e i cattolici (1901–1914)*, Florence 1960.

P. Spriano, *L'occupazione delle fabbriche (sett. 1920)*, Turin 1964.
   Storia del partito comunista, 3 vols., Turin 1967.
La stampa nazionalista, ed. F. Gaeta, Rocca S. Casciano 1965.
R. Stéphane, *Portrait de l'aventurier : T. E. Lawrence, Malraux, Von Salomon*, (pref. by J. P. Sartre), Paris 1950.
H. Stuart Hughes, *Consciousness and Society*, London 1959.
Studi in memoria di Giovanni Dettori, Florence 1941.
L. Sturzo, *I discorsi politici*, Rome 1951.
   Opera Omnia, Bologna 1954–.
Il Sud nella storia d'Italia, antologia ed. R. Villari, Bari 1961.
P. Sylos Labini, *Problemi dello sviluppo economico*, Bari 1970.
A. Tasca, *Nascita e avvento del fascismo*, Bari 1965 (English edition under the pseudonym of A. Rossi, *The Rise of Italian Fascism*, London 1938).
G. Tassinari, *La distribuzione del reddito nell'agricoltura italiana*, Piacenza 1931.
M. Terzaghi, *Fascismo e Massoneria*, Milan 1950.
J. A. Thayer, *Italy and the Great War. Politics and Culture, 1870–1915*, Madison 1964.
A. Tilgher, *Relativisti contemporanei*, 4th edn., Rome 1923.
C. Toesca, di Castellazzo and G. Binello, *Il partito nella vita economica : la politica fascista degli approvigionamenti e dei prezzi*, Turin 1938.
P. Togliatti, *Lezioni sul fascismo*, introd. E. Ragionieri, Rome 1970.
T. Tomasi, *Idealismo e fascismo nella scuola italiana*, Florence 1969.
I. Torsiello, *Il tramonto delle baronie rosse*, Ferrara 1921.
La Toscana nel regime fascista (1922–1939), Florence 1971. (Atti del Convegno di studi promosso dall'Unione regionale delle province toscane et al., May 1969.)
Totalitarianism, ed. C. J. Friedrich, Cambridge, Mass. 1954.
S. Trentin, *Les transformations récentes du droit public italien*, Paris 1929.
G. M. Trevelyan, *The Historical Causes of the Present State of Affairs in Italy*, London 1923.
L. Trotsky, *Literature and Revolution*, Michigan 1966.
A. Turati, *Il partito e i suoi compiti*, Rome 1928.
Filippo Turati attraverso le lettere di corrispondenti, ed. A. Schiavi, Bari 1947.
P. Turiello, *Governo e governati in Italia*, Bologna 1882.
P. Ungari, *Alfredo Rocco e l'ideologia giuridica del fascismo*, Brescia 1963.
M. Vaina, *Popolarismo e nasismo in Sicilia*, Florence 1911.
M. Vaini, *Le origini del fascismo a Mantova*, Rome 1961.
N. Valeri, *Da Giolitti a Mussolini : momenti della crisi del liberalismo*, Florence 1956.
   La lotta politica in Italia. Dall'unita al 1925, idee e documenti, Florence 1958.
   D'Annunzio davanti al fascismo, Florence 1963.
P. A. Vecchia, *Storia del fascismo bresciano*, Brescia 1929.
D. Veneruso, *La vigilia del fascismo : il primo ministero Facta nella crisi dello stato liberale in Italia*, Bologna 1968.
G. Veronesi, *Le difficoltà politiche dell'architettura in Italia, 1920–1940*, Milan 1953.
R. Vicentini, *Il movimento fascista veneto attraverso il diario di uno squadrista*, Venice 1935.
B. Vigezzi, *Da Giolitti a Salandra*, Florence 1969.
   L'Italia di fronte alla prima guerra mondiale, vol. 1, *L'Italia neutrale*, Naples 1966.

P. Vita-Finzi, *Le delusioni della libertà*, Florence 1961.

F. Vito, *I sindacati industriali. Cartelli e gruppi*, Milan 1930.

E. Vittorini, *Il garofano rosso*, Milan 1963.

R. Vivarelli, *Il dopoguerra in Italia e l'avvento del fascismo (1918–1922)*, vol 1:
        Dalla fine della guerra all'impresa di Fiume, Naples 1967.

F. Vöchting, *La questione meridionale*, tran. from German, Naples 1955.
        Die Romagna, Karlsruhe 1927.

G. Volpe, *Guerra, dopoguerra, fascismo*, Venice 1928.
        L'Italia in cammino, 3rd ed., Milan 1931.
        Storici e maestri, 2nd ed., Florence 1967.

R. A. Webster, *Christian Democracy in Italy 1860–1960*, London 1961.

R. Zangrandi, *Il lungo viaggio attraverso il fascismo*, Milan 1962.

A. Zanibelli, *Le leghe bianche nel Cremonese*, Rome 1961.

T. Zaniboni, *Testamento spirituale*, Milan 1949.

Newspapers and Journals

Annuario della Stampa
Antieuropa
L'Assalto
Avanti!
Il Balilla (Ferrara)
Il Bargello
Battaglie Fasciste
Battaglie Sindacali
Civiltà Cattolica
La Conquista dello Stato
Corriere della Sera
Corriere Emiliano
Corriere Italiano
Corriere Padano
Cremona Nuova (From 1 January 1926, Regime Fascista)
La Critica
Critica Fascista
Critica Politica
Cultura Fascista
Domani d'Italia
Educazione Politica (Later Educazione Fascista)
Il Fascio (Milan)
Gazzetta Ufficiale
Gerarchia
Giornale del Friuli
Giornale di Genova
Giornale d'Italia
Giornale di Roma
Giornale di Sicilia
La Giustizia
Idea Nazionale
L'Impero

L'Internazionale (Parma)
Il Lavoro (Genoa)
Il Lavoro (Messina)
Lavoro d'Italia
Il Messaggero
Il Mezzogiorno
Il Mondo
La Nazione
Il Nuovo Paese
Ordine Nuovo
L'Organizzazione Industriale
Politica
Popolo d'Italia
Il Raduno
Rassegna Italiana
Resto del Carlino
Riforma Sociale
Rivoluzione Fascista
Rivoluzione Liberale
Roma (Naples)
Roma Fascista
Scuola Fascista
Il Secolo
Il Secolo XIX
Il Selvaggio
Il Sole
La Stampa
Stato Operaio
La Stirpe
Il Tevere
La Tribuna
L'Unità
Vita Nova
Voce Repubblicana

Periodicals

Clio
Emilia
Itinerari
Movimento Operaio e Socialista
Il Mulino
Nord e Sud
Il Nuovo Osservatore
Nuova Rivista Storica

Pagine Libere
Passato e Presente
Il Ponte
Rassegna Storica del Risorgimento
Ricerche Storiche
Storia Contemporanea
Studi Politici
Tempo Presente

INDEX